One-Stop Internet Resources

Log on to ett.glencoe.com

ONLINE STUDY TOOLS

- Chapter Overviews
- Interactive Tutor
- Self-Check Quizzes
- E-Flashcards

ONLINE RESEARCH

- Student Web Activities
- Web Resources
- Current Events
- State Resources
- Beyond the Textbook Features

ONLINE STUDENT EDITION

- Complete Interactive Student Edition
- Textbook Updates

FOR TEACHERS

- Teacher Forum
- Web Activity Lesson Plans
- Literature Connections

Honoring America

For Americans, the flag has always had a special meaning. It is a symbol of our nation's freedom and democracy.

Flag Etiquette

Over the years, Americans have developed rules and customs concerning the use and display of the flag. One of the most important things every American should remember is to treat the flag with respect.

- The flag should be raised and lowered by hand and displayed only from sunrise to sunset. On special occasions, the flag may be displayed at night, but it should be illuminated.
- The flag may be displayed on all days, weather permitting, particularly on national and state holidays and on historic and special occasions.
- No flag may be flown above the American flag or to the right of it at the same height.
- The flag should never touch the ground or floor beneath it.

- The flag may be flown at half-staff by order of the president, usually to mourn the death of a public official.
- The flag may be flown upside down only to signal distress.
- The flag should never be carried flat or horizontally, but always carried aloft and free.
- When the flag becomes old and tattered, it should be destroyed by burning. According to an approved custom, the Union (stars on blue field) is first cut from the flag; then the two pieces, which no longer form a flag, are burned.

★ ★ ★ ★ ★ ★ ★ ★

The American's Creed

I believe in the United States of America as a Government of the people, by the people, for the people, whose just powers are derived from the consent of the governed; a democracy in a republic; a sovereign Nation of many sovereign States; a perfect union, one and inseparable; established upon those principles of freedom, equality, justice, and humanity for which American patriots sacrificed their lives and fortunes.

I therefore believe it is my duty to my Country to love it; to support its Constitution; to obey its laws; to respect its flag, and to defend it against all enemies.

The Pledge of Allegiance

I pledge allegiance to the Flag of the United States of America and to the Republic for which it stands, one Nation under God, indivisible, with liberty and justice for all.

Glencoe

Economics

Today and Tomorrow

Roger LeRoy Miller, Ph.D.

With Features From

BusinessWeek STANDARD & POOR'S

New York, New York Columbus, Ohio Chicago, Illinois Peoria, Illinois Woodland Hills, California

About the Author

Roger Leroy Miller graduated Phi Beta Kappa from the University of California at Berkeley, where he also won the Department Prize in Economics. He was a Woodrow Wilson Honor Fellow, National Science Foundation Fellow, and Lilly Honor Fellow at the University of Chicago, where he received his Ph.D. in economics in 1968. Now at the Institute for University Studies in Arlington, Texas, Dr. Miller has taught at the University of Washington, the University of Miami, Clemson University, and the University of Texas. He has also taught methodology to teachers of high school economics for the National Council on Economic Education. Among the more than 200 books he has written or co-authored are works on economics, statistics, law, consumer finance, and government. Dr. Miller also has operated several retail and Internet businesses and served as a consultant to government agencies, private corporations, and law firms.

Contributors

BusinessWeek

Business Week is the most widely read business publication in the world and is the only weekly business news publication in existence. *Business Week* provides incisive and comprehensive interpretation of events by evaluating the news and its implications for the United States, regional, and world economies.

STANDARD & POOR'S

Standard & Poor's is a leading source of data, news, and analyses on regional, national, and global economic developments. Standard & Poor's information is used by industrial firms, financial institutions, and government agencies for setting policy, managing financial positions, planning production, formulating marketing strategies, and a range of similar activities. Standard & Poor's data services represent the single most sophisticated source of information for organizations that need to understand the impact of the path of economic growth and of government fiscal and monetary policies on their activities.

Mc Graw Hill Glencoe

The McGraw·Hill Companies

Send all inquiries to:
Glencoe/McGraw-Hill
8787 Orion Place
Columbus, OH 43240

ISBN: 0-07-860696-9

5 6 7 8 071/055 08 07 06 05

REVIEWERS

Academic Consultants

Candace Allen
Economics Education Consultant
Tucson, Arizona

Ryan C. Amacher
Professor of Economics
University of Texas
Arlington, Texas

David M. Blitzer, Ph.D.
Managing Director & Chief Investment Strategist
Standard & Poor's
New York, New York

Roger E. Meiners
Professor of Economics
University of Texas
Arlington, Texas

Joe Mullin
Professor of Economics
Columbus State Community College
Columbus, Ohio

Harold S. Stovall
Senior Investment Strategist
Standard & Poor's
New York, New York

Educational Reviewers

Joanna Ackley
John F. Kennedy High School
Taylor, Michigan

Eleanor Allen
Foothill High School
Sacramento, California

Lourdes Rayneri Barrenechea
LaSalle High School
Miami, Florida

Charles E. Cleveland
Belen Jesuit Preparatory School
Miami, Florida

Charles Erlandson
All Saints Episcopal School
Tyler, Texas

Jeff Harris
Dinuba High School
Dinuba, California

Denny C. Jackson
Switzerland County High School
Vevay, Indiana

Rick Johnson
New Harmony Public School
New Harmony, Indiana

Richard P. Joyce
Wilmington High School
Wilmington, Illinois

Hal Kraynek
Valley High School
Santa Ana, California

Roger C. Lyder
Pelham High School
Pelham, New Hampshire

Howard D. Merrick, Jr.
Pottsville Area High School
Pottsville, Pennsylvania

Bill Nichols
The Lovett School
Atlanta, Georgia

Greg Parsley
Roncalli High School
Indianapolis, Indiana

Nancy Peterson
Gilbert Junior–Senior High School
Gilbert, Iowa

Brian M. Sage
Niagara Falls High School
Niagara Falls, New York

Ann Tapp
Southern Baptist Educational Center
Olive Branch, Mississippi

Douglas J. Woods
Washington High School
Cherokee, Iowa

Christopher S. Ziller
Tecumseh Junior–Senior High School
Lynnville, Indiana

CONTENTS

Economic Handbook . . . . **xiv**
Reading for Information . . . . **xxiv**
NCEE's Basic Economic Concepts . . . . . . **xxvi**

Unit 1 An Introduction to Economics **1**

Chapter 1 What Is Economics? **2**
1 The Basic Problem in Economics 3
2 Trade-Offs 12
3 What Do Economists Do? 18

Chapter 2 Economic Systems and the American Economy **30**
1 Economic Systems 31
2 Characteristics of the American Economy 40
3 The Goals of the Nation 46

Unit 2 Practical Economics: How Theory Works for You **56**

Chapter 3 Your Role as a Consumer **58**
1 Consumption, Income, and Decision Making 59
2 Buying Principles or Strategies 66
3 Consumerism 72

Chapter 4 Going Into Debt **82**
1 Americans and Credit 83
2 Sources of Loans and Credit 88
3 Applying for Credit 96
4 Government Regulation of Credit 101

Chapter 5 Buying the Necessities **110**
1 Shopping for Food 111
2 Clothing Choices 117
3 To Rent or to Buy 121
4 Buying and Operating a Vehicle 129

Chapter 6 Saving and Investing **140**
1 Why Save? 141
2 Investing: Taking Risks With Your Savings 146
3 Special Savings Plans and Goals 155

Unit 3 Microeconomics: Markets, Prices, and Business Competition **166**

Chapter 7 Demand and Supply **168**
1 Demand 169
2 The Demand Curve and Elasticity of Demand 177
3 The Law of Supply and the Supply Curve 186
4 Putting Supply and Demand Together 194

Chapter 8 Business Organizations **206**
1 Starting a Business 207
2 Sole Proprietorships and Partnerships 213
3 The Corporate World and Franchises 219

Chapter 9 Competition and Monopolies . . **232**
1 Perfect Competition 233
2 Monopoly, Oligopoly, Monopolistic Competition 239
3 Government Policies Toward Competition 248

Unit 4 Microeconomics: American Business In Action **260**

Chapter 10 Financing and Producing Goods **262**
1 Investing in the Free Enterprise System 263
2 Types of Financing for Business Operations 270
3 The Production Process 277

Chapter 11 Marketing and Distribution . . **288**
1 The Changing Role of Marketing 289
2 The Marketing Mix 296
3 Distribution Channels 302

Chapter 12 The American Labor Force . . . 312
1 Americans at Work 313
2 Organized Labor 321
3 Collective Bargaining 328

Unit 5 Macroeconomics: The Nation's Economy 340

Chapter 13 Measuring the Economy's Performance 342
1 National Income Accounting 343
2 Correcting Statistics for Inflation 350
3 Aggregate Demand and Supply 356
4 Business Fluctuations 360
5 Causes and Indicators of Business Fluctuations 364

Chapter 14 Money and Banking 374
1 The Functions and Characteristics of Money 375
2 History of American Money and Banking 381
3 Types of Money in the United States 387

Chapter 15 The Federal Reserve System and Monetary Policy 398
1 Organization and Functions of the Federal Reserve System 399
2 Money Supply and the Economy 407
3 Regulating the Money Supply 412

Chapter 16 Government Spends, Collects, and Owes 422
1 Growth in the Size of Government 423
2 The Functions of Government 429
3 The Federal Budget and the National Debt 435
4 Taxation 440

Chapter 17 Stabilizing the National Economy 450
1 Unemployment and Inflation 451
2 The Fiscal Policy Approach to Stabilization 457
3 Monetarism and the Economy 462

Unit 6 The International Scene 470

Chapter 18 Trading With Other Nations . . . 472
1 The Benefits of World Trade 473
2 Financing World Trade 479
3 Restrictions on World Trade 486

Chapter 19 Converging Economic Systems 496
1 Comparing Capitalism and Socialism 497
2 Changing Authoritarian Socialism—The Case of China 503
3 Nations Move Toward the Market System 508

Chapter 20 Economic Growth in Developing Nations 516
1 Characteristics of Developing Nations 517
2 The Process of Economic Development 523
3 Obstacles to Growth in Developing Nations 529
4 Industrialization and the Future 534

Chapter 21 The Global Economy 542
1 Reasons for and Results of Global Integration 543
2 Direct Foreign Investment—Should We Be Worried? 548
3 Multinationals and Economic Competition 553

Chapter 22 Cybernomics 564
1 The Growth of E-Commerce 565
2 A New Economy? 571
3 Issues in Cybernomics 576

Reference Handbook 586
NATIONAL GEOGRAPHIC Reference Atlas A1
STANDARD &POOR'S Databank A14
Glossary A30
Spanish Glossary A42
Spanish Chapter Summaries A55
Index A77
Acknowledgments A89

FEATURES

You can visit ett.glencoe.com— the Web site companion to **Economics Today and Tomorrow**. This innovative integration of electronic and print media offers a wealth of opportunities. The student text directs students to the Web site for the following options:

- **Chapter Overviews**
- **Student Web Activities**
- **Self-Check Quizzes**
- **Textbook Updates**

Use the Glencoe Web site for additional resources. All essential content is covered in the Student Edition.

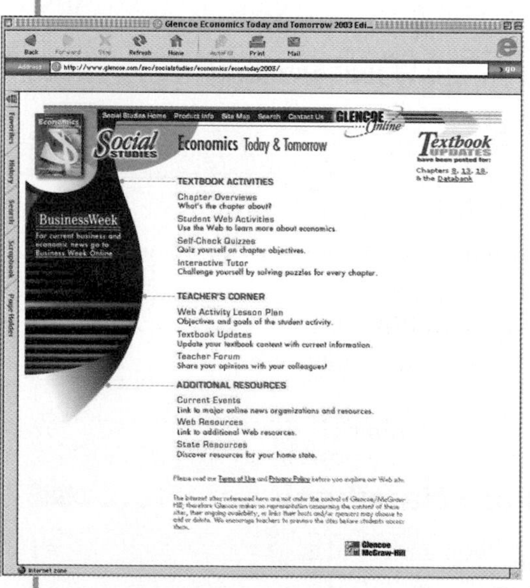

BusinessWeek

SPOTLIGHT ON THE ECONOMY

Coasters Find a Whole New Way to Roll 17
Save the Species–but Add Incentives 50
Grab Some Cash, Check Out a Flick 71
A Hard Lesson on Credit Cards 100
Backseat Driver on the Dash 134
Intro to Haggling 160
How to Make a Mint 176
Hate to Eat and Fly, but 226
Celebrity Can Really Be a Gas 247
Going All Out to Pick Up a Gig 282
Generation Y 295
Pink Slips with a Silver Lining 320
Unveiling the Secrets of the CPI 355
How Higher Fees Hurt Banks 386
Why the Fed's Open-Mouth Policy Works 411
Social Security Is Aptly Named 434
Your Next Job 456
Mexican Makeover 490
China's Transformation to a Market Economy 507
Indonesia–A Pariah State? 533
Does Globalization Get a Bad Rap? 547
Chips That Mimic the Human Senses 570

Focus on Free Enterprise

Amazon.com....................................28
Dell Computer Corporation.............80
The Home Depot 258
eBay, Inc. 338
The Trek Bicycle Corporation.........448
Industrial Light & Magic 584

Economics Lab

Testing Consumer Products.............54
Making a Budget 164
Setting Up a Business......................230
Analyzing and Creating
Advertisements 310
Constructing a Market Basket 372
Buying a New Car 562

Global Economy

Pencils–An International Product...........10
Rain Forest Trade-Offs 13
The Cybermarket......................................48
Consumers in Canada 62
Loans for the Poor...................................99
Housing in Japan 127
A Day on the Town 138
Comparing Saving Rates........................143
Demand for American TV Shows 180
Demand for Oil 204
Big Business!..220
Reducing Postal Monopolies.................243
It Started With the Dutch......................265
Worldwide Advertising..........................286
Kmart Shoppers 305
Improving Working
Conditions Worldwide.......................324
Per Capita GDP 347
Russia's Barter Economy.......................377
A Brief History of Money.......................396
Worldwide Influence 414
Working in Britain.................................433
Unemployment......................................454
The Big Mac Index 482
The European Union 494
Learning About Capitalism 510
Leading Suppliers of Foreign Aid 527
Leading Foreign Investors.....................549
Web Site Challenges 572

FEATURES

People & Perspectives

Robert L. Heilbroner 24
Adam Smith 45
Oprah Winfrey............................76
Kenneth Chenault 106
Lloyd Ward 116
John W. Rogers, Jr. 154
Alfred Marshall.........................200
John H. Johnson 218
William Gates 254
Thomas Sowell..........................276
Margaret Whitman 301
Walter Reuther 327
Janet Yellen 368
Hector Barreto 392
Alan Greenspan 418
John Maynard Keynes..............428
Milton Friedman 466
James Tobin 485
Karl Marx.................................502
Thomas Malthus 522
Alice Rivlin...............................558
Steven Spielberg 580

CAREERS

Economist...19
Environmental Scientist 41
Advertising Manager.........................69
Consumer Loan Officer 90
Real Estate Agent 125
Stockbroker 151
Buyer 172
Restaurant Manager........................215
Graphic Designer............................245
Financial Manager 274
Market Research Analyst................294
Labor Relations Specialist..............329
Statistician......................................365
Bank Teller 389
Accountant......................................417
City Manager..................................427
Social Worker..................................463
Customs Inspector..........................487
Foreign Correspondent..................504
Peace Corps Worker.......................526
Computer Programmer 546
Systems Analyst 568

SKILLS

ECONOMIC HANDBOOK

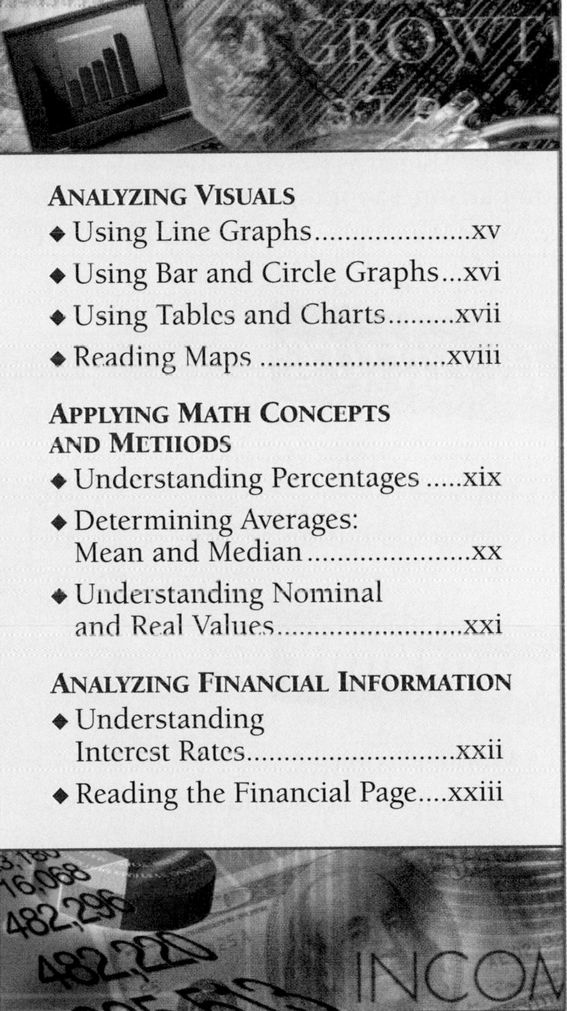

ANALYZING VISUALS
- Using Line Graphs....................xv
- Using Bar and Circle Graphs...xvi
- Using Tables and Charts.........xvii
- Reading Maps xviii

APPLYING MATH CONCEPTS AND METHODS
- Understanding Percentages xix
- Determining Averages: Mean and Median xx
- Understanding Nominal and Real Values........................xxi

ANALYZING FINANCIAL INFORMATION
- Understanding Interest Rates...........................xxii
- Reading the Financial Page....xxiii

CRITICAL THINKING SKILLS

- Sequencing and Categorizing Information 9
- Making Comparisons..............................39
- Distinguishing Fact From Opinion.........65
- Finding the Main Idea 128
- Understanding Cause and Effect 193
- Drawing Inferences and Conclusions....238
- Making Generalizations........................269
- Synthesizing Information......................380
- Summarizing Information.....................461
- Making Predictions 512
- Recognizing Bias 552
- Evaluating Primary and Secondary Sources...............................575

Technology Skills

- Using a Database....................................95
- Using a Spreadsheet..............................145
- Using the Internet 212
- Developing Multimedia Presentations ...306
- Using E-Mail 444

Study & Writing Skills

- Using Library Resources 334
- Taking Notes..349
- Outlining...406
- Applying the Writing Process 478
- Taking a Test..538

FEATURES

Economic Connection to...

History

- The Soviet Union's Quota System 36
- The First Credit Card 92
- The Dow Jones and S&P 152
- Franchises, Franchises, Everywhere! ...223
- A Chocolate Lover's Dream 379
- The First Central Bank 401
- Jobs Programs 460
- Socialist Party of America 500
- Ancient Multinationals 554

MATH

- Do Coupons Add Up to Savings? 115
- Advertising-to-Sales Ratio 298
- Compiling the CPI 351
- Tax Freedom Day 442
- Comparative Advantage 475

Technology

- Technology Saves You a Trip to the Store 8
- Comparison Shopping on the Web 69
- No More Waiting? 281

Literature

- Tom Sawyer Creates Demand 173
- Muckrakers 249
- Shakespeare as Business Guru? 317

Geography

- The World's People 530
- Learning Knows No Boundaries 577

Graphs, Charts, & Tables

Graphs

- ◆ Production Possibilities for Jewelry 15
- ◆ Production Possibilities–The Classic Example.......................................16
- ◆ Economic Models...21
- ◆ Consumer Spending.......................................60
- ◆ Consumer Installment Debt 84
- ◆ Graphing the Demand Curve 178
- ◆ Determinants of Demand............................182
- ◆ Elastic Versus Inelastic Demand 184
- ◆ Graphing the Supply Curve.........................188
- ◆ Determinants of Supply 191
- ◆ Graphing the Equilibrium Price..................195
- ◆ Changes in Equilibrium Price 196
- ◆ Price Ceilings and Price Floors 198
- ◆ Comparing Corporations, Partnerships, and Proprietorships....................................221
- ◆ Selected Oligopolies 244
- ◆ Employment Status of U.S. Population.......314
- ◆ Labor Strikes Involving 1,000 Workers......331
- ◆ Union Membership 332
- ◆ GDP and Its Components...........................344
- ◆ Current and Real GDP 354
- ◆ Aggregate Demand Curve 357
- ◆ Aggregate Supply Curve.............................358
- ◆ Equilibrium Price Level 359
- ◆ Business Activity in the United States 362

Credit Card Charge of $200 at 10% Interest

Amount Charged	$200.00	$200.00
Interest at 10%	$20.00	$20.00
Annual Membership Fee	none	$5.00
APR	10%	12.5%

- ◆ Growth in the Money Supply 390
- ◆ Government Purchases 426
- ◆ Government Spending as a Percentage of GDP 426
- ◆ Spending by the Federal Government 436
- ◆ Spending by State Governments 436
- ◆ United States Net National Debt 438
- ◆ The Unemployment Rate 452
- ◆ Changing Monetary Policies of the Fed 464
- ◆ Current U.S. Exports and Imports 476
- ◆ United States Balance of Trade....................483
- ◆ Tax Levels in Sweden and the United States 510
- ◆ Per Capita GDP Around the World.............519
- ◆ The Falling Cost of Computing Power 544
- ◆ Foreign Ownership of the United States Public Debt..550
- ◆ The Spread of Products Into American Households 567

Charts and Tables

- ◆ Using a Hypothesis 20
- ◆ Circular Flow of Economic Activity 37
- ◆ How Education Affects Income 61
- ◆ Federal Agencies and Consumerism.............74
- ◆ Loan Payments...85
- ◆ Different Methods of Computing Finance Charges...93
- ◆ Computing APR 94
- ◆ Major Federal Laws Regulating Consumer Credit 103
- ◆ Advantages and Disadvantages of Owning and Renting 122
- ◆ Lender's Rules...123
- ◆ Types of Mortgages......................................124
- ◆ Factors Affecting Automobile Insurance Rates..132
- ◆ Savings Institutions' Services and Insurers 144

GRAPHS, CHARTS, & TABLES

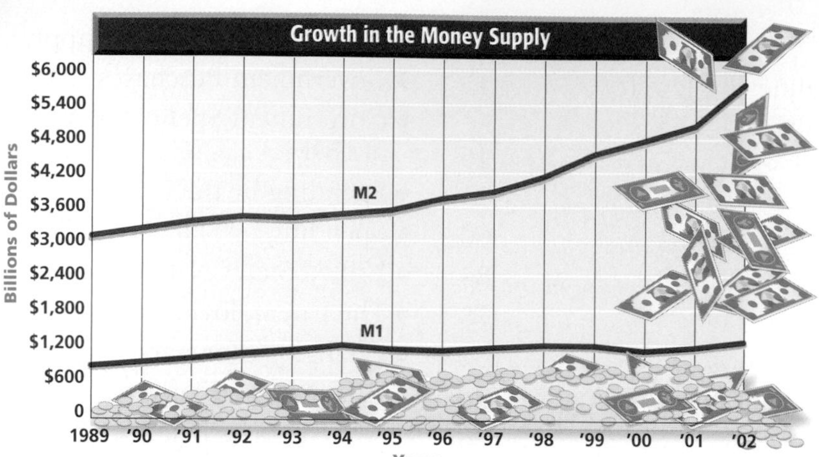

Source: Board of Governors of the Federal Reserve System

- Differences Between Stocks and Bonds......148
- Selected Investments Ranked by Risk and Potential Return 158
- Advantages and Disadvantages of Sole Proprietorships 214
- Advantages and Disadvantages of Partnerships 216
- Advantages and Disadvantages of Corporations 222
- Structure of a Typical Corporation 224
- Comparing Four Market Structures 234
- Antitrust Legislation 250
- Types of Mergers 251
- Federal Regulatory Agencies 252
- Financing Business Expansion 264
- Short-Term Financing 271
- Intermediate-Term Financing 272
- Long-Term Financing 273
- Channels of Distribution 303
- Labor-Management Legislation 323
- Union Contract Issues 330
- Four Categories of GDP 346
- Consumer Price Index of Selected Categories 352
- A Model of the Business Cycle 361
- Major Economic Indicators 366
- Characteristics of Money 378
- Time Line of American Money and Banking 382
- Keeping a Checking Account 388
- Organization of the Federal Reserve System 400
- How a Check Clears 403
- Functions of the Federal Reserve 404
- Balancing Monetary Policy 408
- Expanding the Money Supply 409
- Raising and Lowering Reserve Requirements 413
- Major Functions of Government Regulations 432
- Steps in the Budget Process 437
- Major Taxes 441
- Types of Unemployment 453
- The Circular Flow of Income 458
- Foreign Exchange Rate Listing 480
- Effects of Official Devaluation of Japanese Yen 481
- Characteristics of Pure Capitalism 498
- Characteristics of Pure Socialism 498
- The Change From Capitalism to Socialism According to Marx 499
- Two Developing Nations 518

◆ Economic and Social Statistics for Selected Nations 520
◆ Nations in the Agricultural Stage of Development 524
◆ Indonesia's Economy Under Sukarno and Suharto 531
◆ The Largest American Multinationals 555
◆ Schumpeter's Waves 574

Maps

◆ Labor's Early Struggle for Recognition 322
◆ States With Right-to-Work Laws 325
◆ The Twelve Districts of the Federal Reserve System 402

Checklists

◆ Checklist for Consumer Decision Making ...63
◆ Checklist for Analyzing Ads 68
◆ Checklist for Buying on Credit 87
◆ Checklist for Food Shopping 112
◆ Checklist for Determining Clothing Wants 120
◆ Checklist for Clauses in Housing Leases ...126
◆ Checklist for Buying an Automobile 131

NATIONAL GEOGRAPHIC Reference Atlas

World Political A2
United States Political A4
World Land Use A6
United States Land Use A8
World GDP Cartogram A10
World Population Cartogram A12

STANDARD & POOR'S DATABANK

The American People

U.S. Population Projections A15
Civilian Labor Force A15
Hours and Earnings in Private Industries A16

The U.S. Economy

Gross Domestic Product A17
A Look at Market History (S&P 500) A17
Personal Consumption Expenditures A18
Personal Consumption Expenditures, Nondurable Goods A18
Average Prices of Selected Goods A19
Annual Changes in Consumer Price Indexes A20
Inflation in Consumer Prices A20

The Government Sector

Federal Government Expenditures A21
Total Government Expenditures A21
Federal Government Total Receipts and Total Outlays A22
Federal Debt Held by the Public A22
Financial Debt Held by the Public Per Capita A22
Federal Budget Receipts A23

The Financial Sector

Interest Rates A24
Consumer Credit Outstanding A24
Personal Saving A25
Money Stock A25

The Global Economy

Economic Groups: Population, Exports, and GDP A26
Growth Rates in Real GDP Per Capita A26
World Population by Age A27
Countries Ranked by Population A27
Aging Index in Selected Nations of the Americas A28
Median Age, World A28
U.S. Exports and Imports A29
Inflation and Unemployment, Selected Economies A29

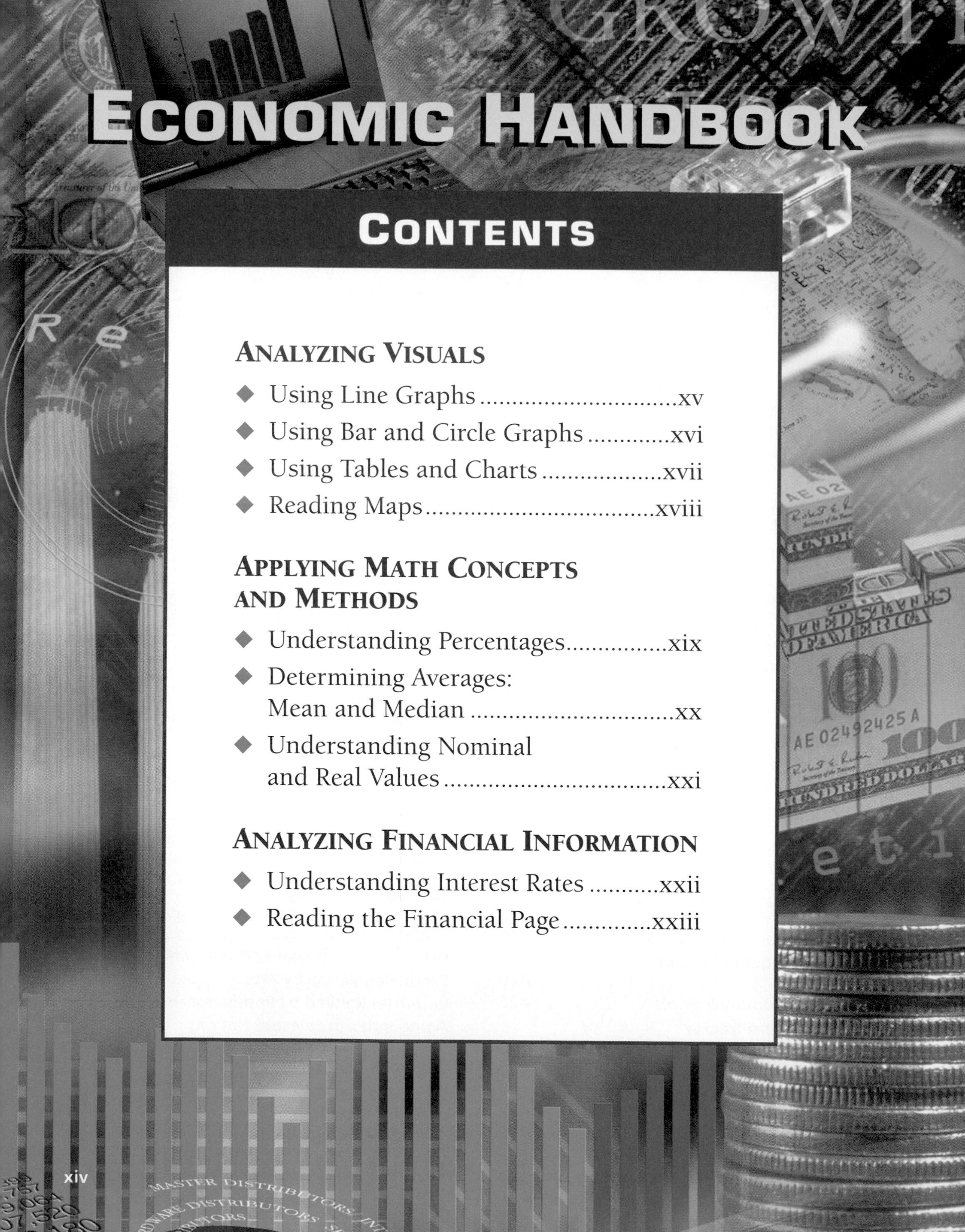

Economic Handbook

Contents

Analyzing Visuals

- Using Line Graphs xv
- Using Bar and Circle Graphs xvi
- Using Tables and Charts xvii
- Reading Maps xviii

Applying Math Concepts and Methods

- Understanding Percentages................xix
- Determining Averages: Mean and Median xx
- Understanding Nominal and Real Values xxi

Analyzing Financial Information

- Understanding Interest Rates xxii
- Reading the Financial Page xxiii

Using Line Graphs

A graph, like a picture, may present information in a more concise way than words. Line graphs are drawings that compare numerical values. They often are used to compare changes over time or differences between places, groups of items, or other related events.

Learning the Skill

Follow these steps to learn how to understand and use line graphs. Then answer the questions below.

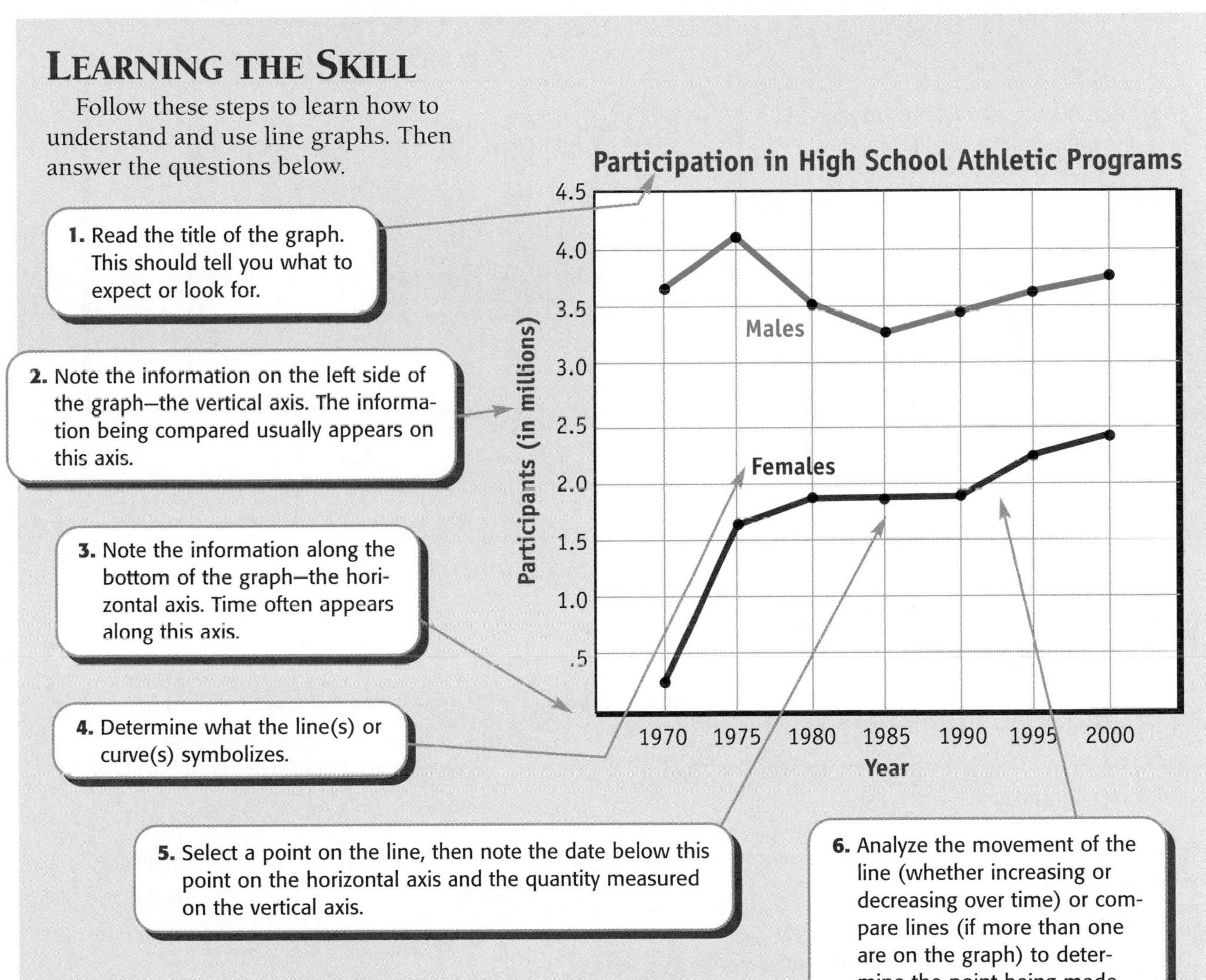
Participation in High School Athletic Programs
Participants (in millions)
4.5
4.0
3.5
3.0
2.5
2.0
1.5
1.0
.5
Males
Females
1970 1975 1980 1985 1990 1995 2000
Year
1. Read the title of the graph. This should tell you what to expect or look for.
2. Note the information on the left side of the graph—the vertical axis. The information being compared usually appears on this axis.
3. Note the information along the bottom of the graph—the horizontal axis. Time often appears along this axis.
4. Determine what the line(s) or curve(s) symbolizes.
5. Select a point on the line, then note the date below this point on the horizontal axis and the quantity measured on the vertical axis.
6. Analyze the movement of the line (whether increasing or decreasing over time) or compare lines (if more than one are on the graph) to determine the point being made.

Practicing the Skill

1. About how many males participated in high school athletic programs in 1970? In 1997?
2. About how many females participated in high school athletic programs in 1970? In 1997?

Applying the Skill to Economics

1. What trends are shown on the graph?
2. How do you think these trends affected the manufacture and sale of sports-related products from the early to late 1990s?

Using Bar Graphs

Learning the Skill

Follow these steps to learn how to understand and use bar graphs.

1. Read the title and labels. They tell you the topic, what is being compared, and how it is counted or measured.

2. Examine a bar on the graph. Note the date below the bar on the horizontal axis and the quantity measured on the vertical axis.

3. Analyze the change over time or compare bars to determine the point being made.

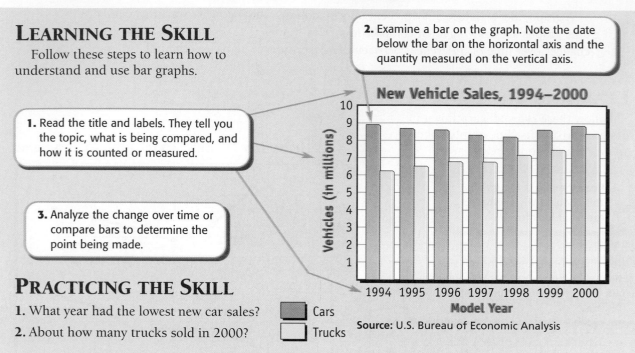

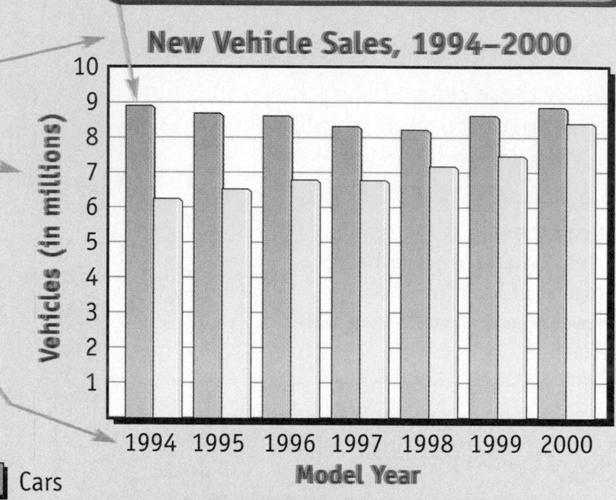

Source: U.S. Bureau of Economic Analysis

Practicing the Skill

1. What year had the lowest new car sales?
2. About how many trucks sold in 2000?

Using Circle Graphs

Learning the Skill

Follow these steps to learn how to understand and use circle graphs.

1. Examine the title to determine the subject.

2. Read the legend to see what each segment represents.

3. Compare the relative sizes of the circle segments, thus analyzing the relationship of the parts to the whole.

High School Student Foreign Language Enrollment

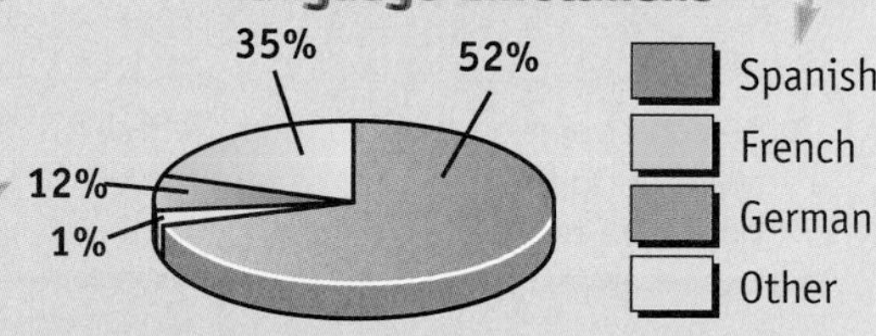

Source: *Statistical Abstract of the United States,* 2002

Practicing the Skill

1. What percent of foreign language students are studying German?
2. What foreign language has the greatest student enrollment?

Applying the Skill to Economics

1. Using the bar graph, what projection could you make about the future of new car sales?
2. Based on the circle graph, which foreign language textbooks probably have the greatest sales volume?

Using Tables and Charts

Tables and charts are often used to show comparisons between similar categories of information. Tables usually compare statistical or numerical data. Tabular data are presented in columns and rows. Charts often show a wider variety of information than tables.

Learning the Skill

Follow these steps to learn how to understand and use tables. Then answer the questions below.

Average Earnings of Full-Time Workers by Age and Education

Age and Sex	All Workers	Some High School	High School Graduate	Four-Year College Degree
Male	**$51,590**	**$28,890**	**$37,362**	**$77,963**
18–24	24,315	20,109	23,416	40,726
25–34	40,895	25,705	32,130	59,482
35–44	56,265	32,348	39,535	81,528
45–54	69,337	32,240	42,064	84,175
55–64	60,682	35,951	41,961	93,523
Female	**$35,348**	**$24,318**	**$26,660**	**$47,224**
18–24	23,642	28,807	19,092	28,109
25–34	34,273	33,131	25,353	42,330
35–44	36,395	20,421	27,248	53,594
45–54	38,493	21,586	29,238	49,305
55–64	36,189	20,160	27,806	50,137

Source: CPS Annual Demographic Survey (Bureau of Labor Statistics and Bureau of the Census); *Statistical Abstract of the United States, 2002*

1. Read the title of the table to learn what content is being presented.

2. Read the headings in the top row. They define the groups or categories of information to be compared.

3. Examine the labels in the left-hand column. They describe ranges or subgroups, and are often organized chronologically or alphabetically.

4. Note the source of the data. It may tell you about the reliability of the table.

5. Compare the data presented in the other columns. This is the body of the table.

Practicing the Skill

1. What are the average earnings for 25- to 34-year-old women with college degrees?
2. What are the average earnings for 18- to 24-year-old males without high school diplomas?

Applying the Skill to Economics

1. What age-related trends do you notice?
2. What conclusions could you draw from this data about the economic effect of education on earnings?

Reading Maps

Maps are visual tools that show to scale the relative size and location of specific geographic areas. There are political maps, which show human-made boundaries. There are physical maps, which show physical features of an area. There are also special purpose maps that can show historical change, cultural features, population, climate, land use, or resources. Regardless of type, all maps use symbols to convey information.

LEARNING THE SKILL

Follow these steps to learn how to understand and use maps. Then answer the questions below.

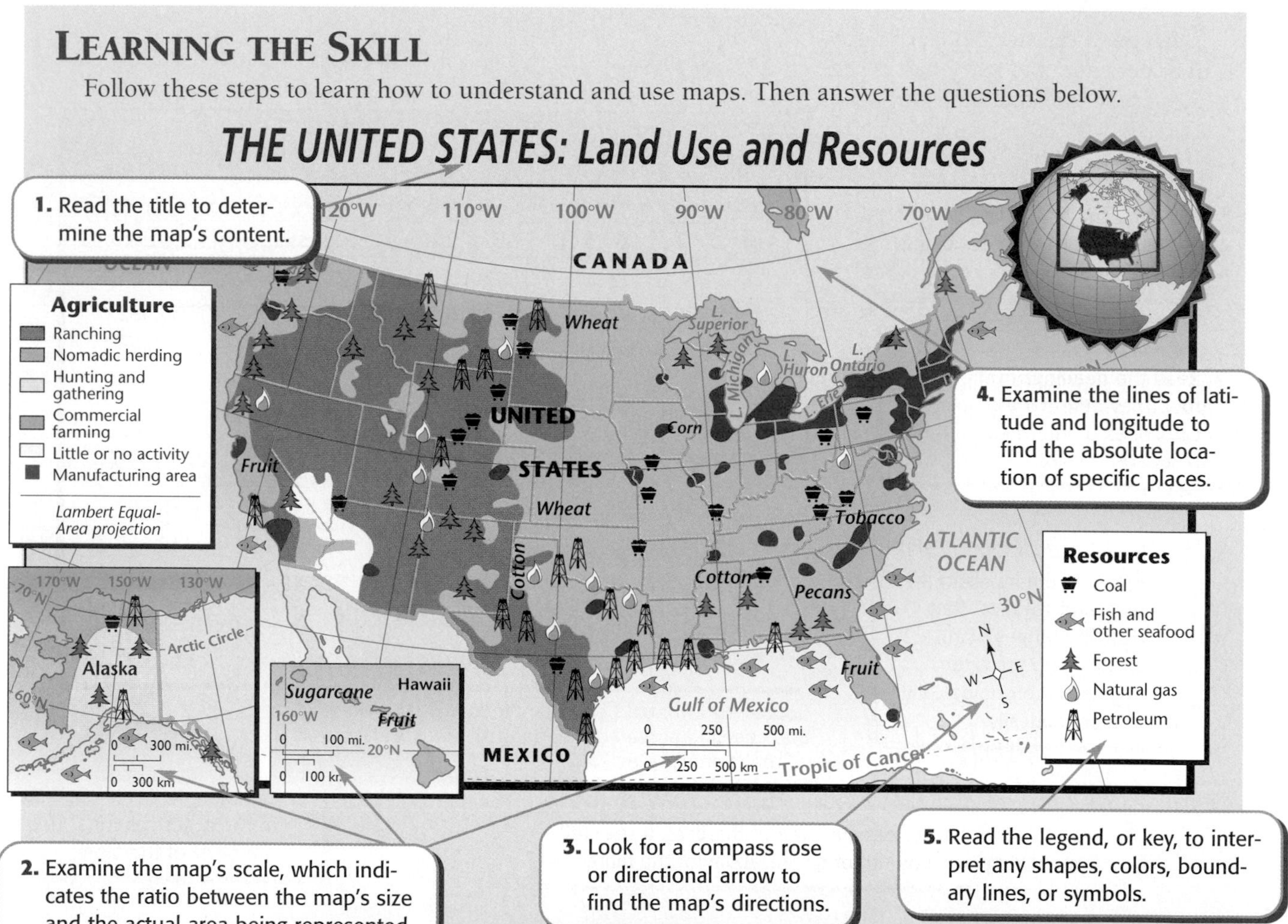

PRACTICING THE SKILL

1. What is the primary content shown on this map?
2. Which region of the United States has the heaviest concentration of manufacturing areas?

Applying the Skill to Economics

1. How could this map be a helpful reference if you were planning to buy ranch land to raise cattle?
2. What generalizations could you draw from this map about energy resources in the United States?

Understanding Percentages

If you shop, you probably like seeing the word *percent.* Stores often advertise sale prices as a percent of regular price. *Percent* means "parts per hundred." So, 30 percent means the same thing as 30/100 or 0.30. Expressing change as a percentage allows you to analyze the relative size of the change.

Learning the Skill

Follow these steps to learn how to calculate and use percentages. Then answer the questions below.

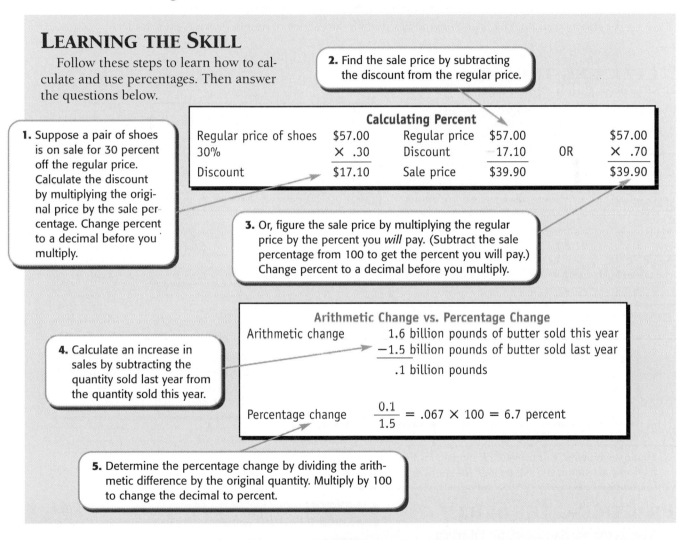

1. Suppose a pair of shoes is on sale for 30 percent off the regular price. Calculate the discount by multiplying the original price by the sale percentage. Change percent to a decimal before you multiply.

2. Find the sale price by subtracting the discount from the regular price.

3. Or, figure the sale price by multiplying the regular price by the percent you *will* pay. (Subtract the sale percentage from 100 to get the percent you will pay.) Change percent to a decimal before you multiply.

Calculating Percent

Regular price of shoes	$57.00	Regular price	$57.00		$57.00
30%	× .30	Discount	−17.10	OR	× .70
Discount	$17.10	Sale price	$39.90		$39.90

4. Calculate an increase in sales by subtracting the quantity sold last year from the quantity sold this year.

5. Determine the percentage change by dividing the arithmetic difference by the original quantity. Multiply by 100 to change the decimal to percent.

Arithmetic Change vs. Percentage Change

Arithmetic change	1.6 billion pounds of butter sold this year
	−1.5 billion pounds of butter sold last year
	.1 billion pounds
Percentage change	$\frac{0.1}{1.5} = .067 \times 100 = 6.7$ percent

Practicing the Skill

1. A store advertises a shirt at 25 percent off the original price of $44. What is the sale price?
2. What is the percentage increase in high school enrollment from 1,165 students to 1,320?

Applying the Skill to Economics

In 1997 about 32 percent of all music recordings sold were classified as rock music. That year about $12 billion was spent on all recordings. How much was spent on rock music?

Determining Averages: Mean and Median

The most commonly used summary statistic is the average. There are two ways to compute the average: by using the mean or the median. The *mean* is the average of a series of items. When your teacher computes the class average, he or she is really computing the mean. Sometimes using the mean to interpret statistics is misleading, however. This is especially true if one or two numbers in the series are much higher or lower than the others. The median can be more accurate. The *median* is the midpoint in any series of numbers arranged in order.

Learning the Skill

Follow these steps to learn how to determine and use averages. Then answer the questions below.

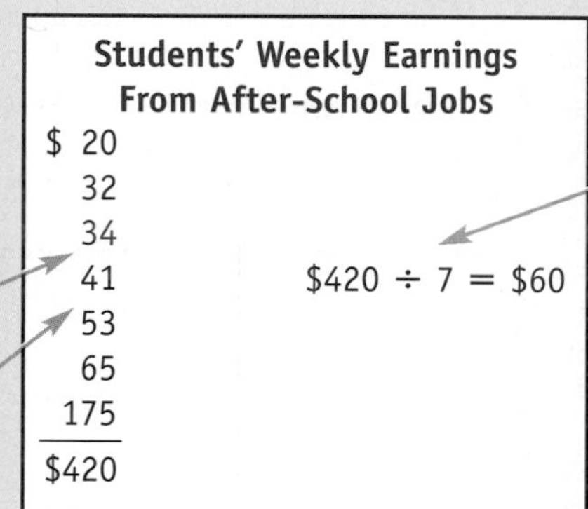

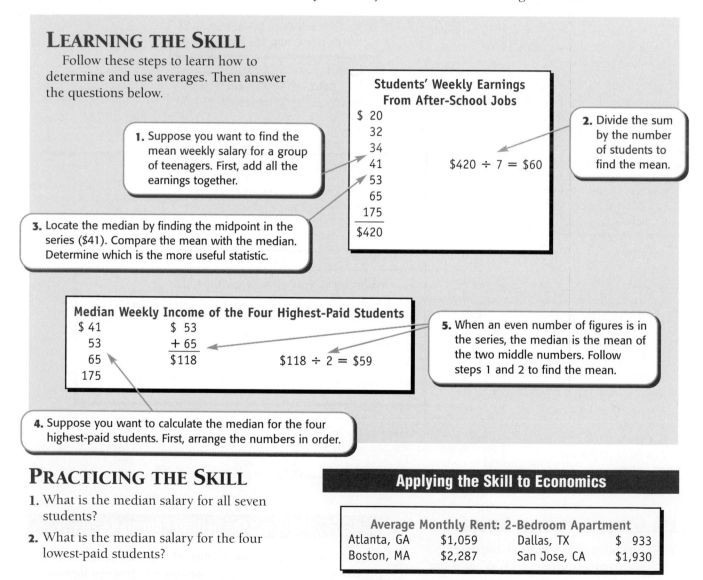

Students' Weekly Earnings From After-School Jobs

$ 20
32
34
41
53
65
175
$420

$420 ÷ 7 = $60

1. Suppose you want to find the mean weekly salary for a group of teenagers. First, add all the earnings together.

2. Divide the sum by the number of students to find the mean.

3. Locate the median by finding the midpoint in the series ($41). Compare the mean with the median. Determine which is the more useful statistic.

Median Weekly Income of the Four Highest-Paid Students

$ 41
53
65
175

$ 53
+ 65
$118

$118 ÷ 2 = $59

4. Suppose you want to calculate the median for the four highest-paid students. First, arrange the numbers in order.

5. When an even number of figures is in the series, the median is the mean of the two middle numbers. Follow steps 1 and 2 to find the mean.

Practicing the Skill

1. What is the median salary for all seven students?
2. What is the median salary for the four lowest-paid students?

Applying the Skill to Economics

Average Monthly Rent: 2-Bedroom Apartment

City	Rent	City	Rent
Atlanta, GA	$1,059	Dallas, TX	$ 933
Boston, MA	$2,287	San Jose, CA	$1,930

1. What is the mean monthly rent for these four cities?
2. What is the median monthly rent?

Understanding Nominal and Real Values

The rise in the economy's average price level is called inflation. To make comparisons between the prices of things in the past and those of today, you have to make the distinction between *nominal,* or current, and *real,* or adjusted for inflation, values. You can use the consumer price index (CPI), an index of average prices for consumer goods, to calculate real values. Then you can *accurately* compare changes in income and prices over time.

LEARNING THE SKILL

Follow these steps to learn how to understand and calculate nominal and real values. Then answer the questions below.

1. Suppose a family sells a house after living there for 10 years. To calculate whether they made any profit from the sale, they need to know the real sale price of their house. First, find the nominal price increase.

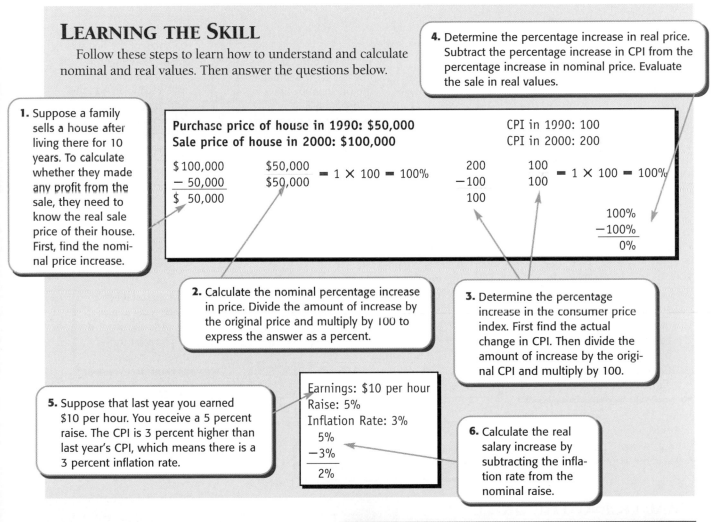

Purchase price of house in 1990: $50,000
Sale price of house in 2000: $100,000

CPI in 1990: 100
CPI in 2000: 200

$100,000 − 50,000 = $ 50,000

$\frac{\$50,000}{\$50,000} = 1 \times 100 = 100\%$

200 − 100 = 100

$\frac{100}{100} = 1 \times 100 = 100\%$

100% − 100% = 0%

2. Calculate the nominal percentage increase in price. Divide the amount of increase by the original price and multiply by 100 to express the answer as a percent.

3. Determine the percentage increase in the consumer price index. First find the actual change in CPI. Then divide the amount of increase by the original CPI and multiply by 100.

4. Determine the percentage increase in real price. Subtract the percentage increase in CPI from the percentage increase in nominal price. Evaluate the sale in real values.

5. Suppose that last year you earned $10 per hour. You receive a 5 percent raise. The CPI is 3 percent higher than last year's CPI, which means there is a 3 percent inflation rate.

Earnings: $10 per hour
Raise: 5%
Inflation Rate: 3%

5% − 3% = 2%

6. Calculate the real salary increase by subtracting the inflation rate from the nominal raise.

PRACTICING THE SKILL

1. What was the nominal price increase on the sale of the house?
2. How much money, in real dollars, was made on the house?
3. How much was the real value of the raise?

Applying the Skill to Economics

Between 1980 and 1997, the amount spent on advertising in the United States increased by 240 percent. How could you adjust this figure for inflation?

Understanding Interest Rates

When you deposit money in a savings account, the bank pays you interest for the use of your money. The amount of interest is expressed as a percent, such as 6 percent, for a time period, such as per year. Two types of interest exist: simple and compound. *Simple interest* is figured only on the principal, or original deposit, not on any interest earned. *Compound interest* is paid on the principal plus any interest that has been earned. Over time, there is a significant difference in earnings between simple and compound interest.

Learning the Skill

Follow these steps to learn how to understand and calculate interest rates. Then answer the questions below.

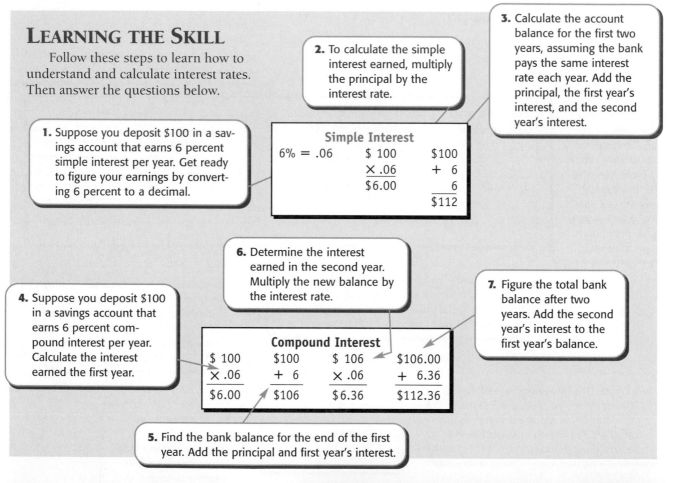

1. Suppose you deposit $100 in a savings account that earns 6 percent simple interest per year. Get ready to figure your earnings by converting 6 percent to a decimal.

2. To calculate the simple interest earned, multiply the principal by the interest rate.

3. Calculate the account balance for the first two years, assuming the bank pays the same interest rate each year. Add the principal, the first year's interest, and the second year's interest.

Simple Interest

6% = .06	$ 100	$100
	× .06	+ 6
	$6.00	6
		$112

4. Suppose you deposit $100 in a savings account that earns 6 percent compound interest per year. Calculate the interest earned the first year.

5. Find the bank balance for the end of the first year. Add the principal and first year's interest.

6. Determine the interest earned in the second year. Multiply the new balance by the interest rate.

7. Figure the total bank balance after two years. Add the second year's interest to the first year's balance.

Compound Interest

$ 100	$100	$ 106	$106.00
× .06	+ 6	× .06	+ 6.36
$6.00	$106	$6.36	$112.36

Practicing the Skill

1. What would be the difference in earnings between simple and compound interest if your initial balance was $1,000 rather than $100?
2. What would be the difference in earnings between simple and compound interest on your $100 savings after five years?

Applying the Skill to Economics

1. What would be the impact of compounding interest on a daily basis rather than an annual basis?
2. Banks often pay higher rates of interest on money you agree to keep in the bank for longer periods of time. Explain why this might be.

Reading the Financial Page

A stock market report alphabetically lists stocks and provides information about stock prices and trades. Every business day, shares of stock are bought and sold. At the beginning of each trading day, stocks open at the same prices they closed at the day before. Prices generally go up and down throughout the day as the conditions of supply and demand change. At the end of the day, each stock's closing price is recorded.

Learning the Skill

Follow these steps to learn how to understand and use the financial page. Then answer the questions below.

1. Locate the stock in the alphabetical list. Names are abbreviated.
2. Examine the stock's history over the last 52 weeks. The high and low prices for one share of stock appear.
3. Note the ticker symbol, or computer code, for the stock.
4. Evaluate the annual dividend. Stockholders receive this dividend, or payment, for each share of stock they own.
5. Review the yield. The yield is the return on investment per share of stock. It is calculated by dividing the dividend by the closing price.
6. Read the price/earnings ratio. Lower price/earnings ratios generally mean more earnings per share.
7. Note the volume, or number of shares of stock, traded that day. The number given represents hundreds of shares.
8. Examine the day's high, low, and closing stock price.
9. Examine how the day's closing stock price compares with the prior business day's closing price. Positive numbers indicate a price increase. Negative numbers mean a price drop.

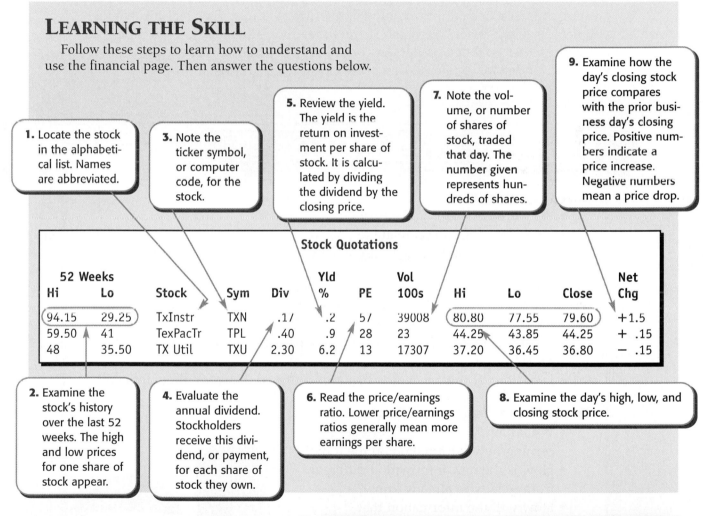

Stock Quotations

52 Weeks					Yld		Vol				Net
Hi	Lo	Stock	Sym	Div	%	PE	100s	Hi	Lo	Close	Chg
94.15	29.25	TxInstr	TXN	.17	.2	57	39008	80.80	77.55	79.60	+1.5
59.50	41	TexPacTr	TPL	.40	.9	28	23	44.25	43.85	44.25	+ .15
48	35.50	TX Util	TXU	2.30	6.2	13	17307	37.20	36.45	36.80	− .15

Practicing the Skill

1. How many shares of Texas Instruments stock were traded on the day shown?
2. What was the day's highest price for a share of Texas Utilities stock?
3. Which stock had the greatest increase in closing price from the previous day?

Applying the Skill to Economics

If you had purchased 100 shares of Texas Instruments stock at its lowest 52-week price and sold it at this day's closing price, how much money would you earn?

Reading for Information

Think about your textbook as a tool that helps you learn more about the world around you. It is an example of nonfiction writing—it describes real-life events, people, ideas, and places. Here is a menu of reading strategies that will help you become a better textbook reader. As you come to passages in your textbook that you don't understand, refer to these reading strategies for help.

✓ BEFORE YOU READ

Set a Purpose

- Why are you reading the textbook?
- How does the subject relate to your life?
- How might you be able to use what you learn in your own life?

Preview

- Read the chapter title to find what the topic will be.
- Read the subtitles to see what you will learn about the topic.
- Skim the photos, charts, graphs, or maps. How do they support the topic?
- Look for vocabulary words that are boldfaced. How are they defined?

Draw From Your Own Background

- What have you read or heard about concerning new information on the topic?
- How is the new information different from what you already know?
- How will the information that you already know help you understand the new information?

AS YOU READ

Question

- What is the main idea?
- How do the photos, charts, graphs, and maps support the main idea?

Connect

- Think about people, places, and events in your own life. Are there any similarities with those in your textbook?
- Can you relate the textbook information to other areas of your life?

Predict

- Predict events or outcomes by using clues and information that you already know.
- Change your predictions as you read and gather new information.

Visualize

- Pay careful attention to details and descriptions.
- Create graphic organizers to show relationships that you find in the information.

LOOK FOR CLUES AS YOU READ

- **Comparison-and-Contrast Sentences:**

  Look for clue words and phrases that signal comparison, such as *similarly, just as, both, in common, also,* and *too.*

  Look for clue words and phrases that signal contrast, such as *on the other hand, in contrast to, however, different, instead of, rather than, but,* and *unlike.*

- **Cause-and-Effect Sentences:**

  Look for clue words and phrases such as *because, as a result, therefore, that is why, since, so, for this reason,* and *consequently.*

- **Chronological Sentences:**

  Look for clue words and phrases such as *after, before, first, next, last, during, finally, earlier, later, since,* and *then.*

AFTER YOU READ

Summarize

- Describe the main idea and how the details support it.
- Use your own words to explain what you have read.

Assess

- What was the main idea?
- Did the text clearly support the main idea?
- Did you learn anything new from the material?
- Can you use this new information in other school subjects or at home?
- What other sources could you use to find more information about the topic?

Basic Concepts in Economics

Economics Today and Tomorrow incorporates the 21 basic concepts established in *A Framework for Teaching Basic Economic Concepts,* published by the National Council on Economic Education.

FUNDAMENTAL ECONOMIC CONCEPTS

1. **Scarcity and Choice** *Scarcity* is the universal problem that faces all societies because there are not enough resources to produce everything people want. Scarcity requires people to make *choices* about the goods and services they use.

2. **Opportunity Cost and Trade-Offs** *Opportunity cost* is the foregone benefit of the next best alternative when scarce resources are used for one purpose rather than another. *Trade-offs* involve choosing less of one thing to get more of something else.

3. **Productivity** *Productivity* is a measure of the amount of output (goods and services) produced per unit of input (productive resources) used.

4. **Economic Systems** *Economic systems* are the ways in which people organize economic life to deal with the basic economic problem of scarcity.

5. **Economic Institutions and Incentives** *Economic institutions* include households and families and formal organizations such as corporations, government agencies, banks, labor unions, and cooperatives. *Incentives* are factors that motivate and influence human behavior.

6. **Exchange, Money, and Interdependence** *Exchange* is a voluntary transaction between buyers and sellers. It is the trading of a good or service for another good or service, or for money. *Money* is anything that is generally accepted as final payment for goods and services, and thus serves as a medium of exchange. *Interdependence* means that decisions or events in one part of the world or in one sector of the economy affect decisions and events in other parts of the world or sectors of the economy.

MICROECONOMIC CONCEPTS

7. **Markets and Prices** *Markets* are arrangements that enable buyers and sellers to exchange goods and services. *Prices* are the amounts of money that people pay for a unit of a particular good or service.

8. **Supply and Demand** *Supply* is defined as the different quantities of a resource, good, or service that will be offered for sale at various possible prices during a specific time period. *Demand* is defined as the different quantities of a resource, good, or service that will be purchased at various possible prices during a specific time period.

9. **Competition and Market Structure** *Competition* is the struggle between businesses that strive for the same customer or market. Competition depends on *market structure*–the number of buyers and sellers, the extent to which firms can control price, the nature of the product, the accuracy and timeliness of information, and the ease with which firms can enter and exit the market.

10. **Income Distribution** *Income distribution* refers to the way the nation's income is distributed by function–to those who provide productive resources–and by recipient, primarily individuals and families.

11. Market Failures *Market failures* occur when there is inadequate competition, lack of access to reliable information, resource immobility, externalities, and the need for public goods.

12. The Role of Government *The role of government* includes establishing a framework of law and order in which a market economy functions. The government plays a direct and an indirect role in the economy as both a producer and a consumer of goods and services.

MACROECONOMIC CONCEPTS

13. Gross Domestic Product *Gross Domestic Product (GDP)* is defined as the market value of the total output of all final goods and services produced within a country's boundaries during one year.

14. Aggregate Supply and Aggregate Demand *Aggregate supply* is the total amount of goods and services produced by the economy during a period of time. *Aggregate demand* is the total amount of spending on goods and services in the economy during a period of time.

15. Unemployment *Unemployment* is defined as the number of people without jobs who are actively seeking work. This is also expressed as a rate when the number of unemployed is divided by the number of people in the labor force.

16. Inflation and Deflation *Inflation* is a sustained increase in the average price level of the entire economy. *Deflation* is a sustained decrease in the average price level of an entire economy.

17. Monetary Policy *Monetary policy* consists of actions initiated by a nation's central bank that affect the amount of money available in the economy and its cost (interest rates).

18. Fiscal Policy *Fiscal policy* consists of changes in taxes, in government expenditures on goods and services, and in transfer payments that are designed to affect the level of aggregate demand in the economy.

INTERNATIONAL ECONOMIC CONCEPTS

19. Absolute and Comparative Advantage and Barriers to Trade *Absolute advantage* and *comparative advantage* are concepts that are used to explain why trade takes place. *Barriers to trade* include tariffs, quotas, import licenses, and cartels.

20. Exchange Rates and the Balance of Payments An *exchange rate* is the price of one nation's currency in terms of another nation's currency. The *balance of payments* of a country is a statistical accounting that records, for a given period, all payments that the residents, businesses, and governments of one country make to the rest of the world as well as the receipts that they receive from the rest of the world.

21. International Aspects of Growth and Stability *International aspects of growth and stability* are more important today than in the past because all nations are much more interdependent.

UNIT 1

An Introduction to Economics

Chapter 1
What Is Economics?

Chapter 2
Economic Systems and the American Economy

In this unit, read to FIND OUT . . .

- what role economics plays in your life.
- what role you play in the economic system of the United States.
- the various kinds of economic systems in the world.

You—and every consumer around the world—face trade-offs among your economic choices.

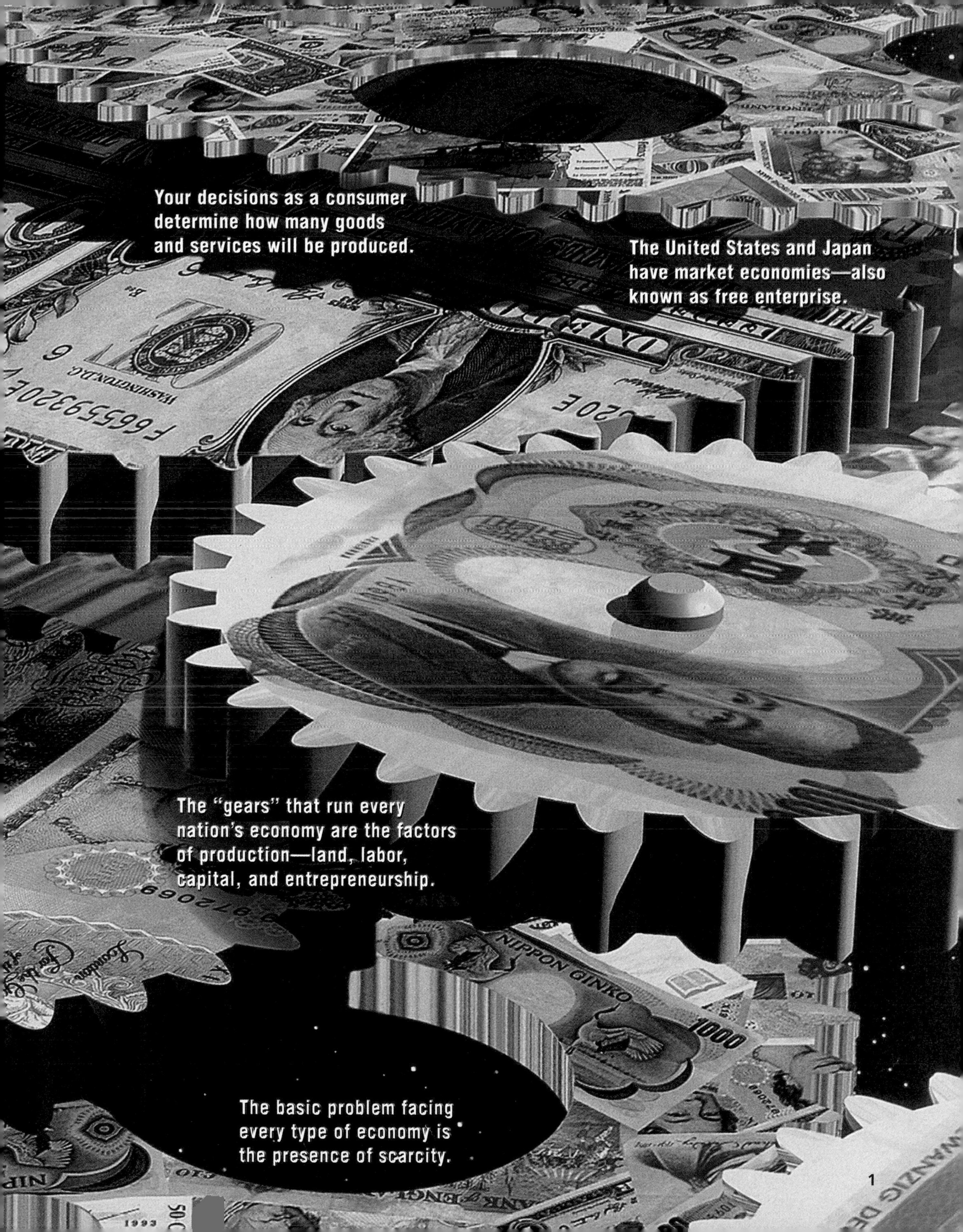
Your decisions as a consumer determine how many goods and services will be produced.
The United States and Japan have market economies—also known as free enterprise.
The "gears" that run every nation's economy are the factors of production—land, labor, capital, and entrepreneurship.
The basic problem facing every type of economy is the presence of scarcity.
NIPPON GINKO
1000

CHAPTER 1

What Is Economics?

Why It's Important

How do scarce resources—including time—affect you and everyone around you? How do economists simplify the world to help us better understand it? This chapter will explain what economics is, and how it is part of your daily life.

To learn more about scarcity and how it forces you to make choices, view the **Economics & You** *Chapter 2 video lesson:* **What Is Economics?**

Chapter Overview Visit the *Economics Today and Tomorrow* Web site at ett.glencoe.com and click on ***Chapter 1—Chapter Overviews*** to preview chapter information.

SECTION 1

The Basic Problem in Economics

Cover Story

THE COLUMBUS DISPATCH, DECEMBER 7, 2002

Although kids know better than anyone what should be on Santa's list, this year they can't seem to agree on which toy should be at the top.

Many trendy toys are expected to do well, too. They include Bratz merchandise, *Dora the Explorer*, Hot Wheels, anything Spiderman, Harry Potter toys and PlayStation2 items, according to the National Retail Federation.

Reader's Guide

Terms to Know

- economics
- scarcity
- factors of production
- land
- labor
- goods
- services
- capital
- productivity
- entrepreneurship
- technology

Reading Objectives

1. How do wants and needs differ?
2. Why does scarcity face all people at all times?
3. What are the four factors of production?

Starting at a very young age, many Americans use the words *want* and *need* interchangeably. How often do you think about what you "want"? How many times have you said that you "need" something? When you say, "I need some new clothes," are you stating a want, or a real need? As you read this section, you'll find that economics deals with questions such as these.

What, exactly, is economics? **Economics** is the study of how individuals, families, businesses, and societies use limited resources to fulfill their unlimited wants.

economics: *the study of how individuals and societies make choices about ways to use scarce resources to fulfill their wants*

ZITS

FIGURE 1.1

Wants Versus Needs
Luxuries such as concert tickets often become necessities in the eyes of consumers. ***How do consumers satisfy their seemingly unlimited wants?***

Wants Versus Needs

Typically the term *need* is used very casually. When most people use the word, as shown in **Figure 1.1,** they really mean that they want something they do not have. Obviously, everyone needs certain things to survive–food, clothing, and shelter. Americans also consider education and health care as needs.

To economists, however, everything other than basic survival needs is considered a *want*. People want such items as new cars and personal computers. What begins as a luxury, or want, becomes to many people a necessity.

So how do individuals satisfy their unlimited wants in a world of limited resources? They must do this by making choices.

FIGURE 1.2

Economic Choices
Everyone, including governments, must make choices in a world of limited resources. If the government allocates funds to build Stealth bombers, then funds for higher education could be limited. ***What is the basic economic problem that makes choices necessary?***

Choices

As a student, you probably have a small income from an allowance or a part-time job. As a result, you have to make choices about its use. Whenever you make such a spending decision, each available choice competes with every other available choice. Suppose you have $20.00 to spend. When you decide whether to spend your money on lunch or clothes or a new CD, you are making an economic choice.

Like individuals, businesses must also make choices. Businesspeople make decisions daily about what to produce now, what to produce later, and what to stop producing. These decisions in turn affect workers' incomes and people's ability to buy. Societies, too, face choices about how to utilize their resources in the production of goods and services. As shown in **Figure 1.2,** elected government representatives in the United States must decide how much to spend on defense (Stealth bombers) versus higher education, for example. How people and societies make these choices is the focus of economics.

The Problem of Scarcity

The need to make choices arises because everything that exists is limited, although some items (such as trees in a large forest) may appear to be in abundant supply. At any single moment, a fixed amount of resources is available. At the same time, people have competing uses for these resources. This situation results in scarcity–the basic problem of economics.

Scarcity means that people do not have and cannot have enough income, time, and other resources to satisfy their every want. What you buy as a student is limited by the amount of income you have. In this case, your income is the scarce resource. Even if everyone in the world were rich, however, scarcity would continue to exist–at least with respect to time. Even the richest person does not have unlimited time.

scarcity: *condition of not being able to have all of the goods and services one wants, because wants exceed what can be made from all available resources at any given time*

It is important not to confuse scarcity with *shortages.* Scarcity always exists because of competing alternative uses for resources, whereas shortages are temporary. Shortages often occur, for example, after hurricanes or floods destroy goods and property.

Factors of Production

When economists talk about scarce resources, they are referring to the **factors of production,** or resources needed to produce goods and services. Traditionally, economists have classified

factors of production: *resources of land, labor, capital, and entrepreneurship used to produce goods and services* these productive resources as land, labor, capital, and entrepreneurship. **Figure 1.3** shows you the four factors of production.

land: *natural resources and surface land and water*

Land As an economic term, **land** refers to natural resources present without human intervention. "Land" includes actual surface land and water, as well as fish, animals, forests, mineral deposits, and other "gifts of nature."

labor: *human effort directed toward producing goods and services*

goods: *tangible objects that can satisfy people's wants or needs*

services: *actions that can satisfy people's wants or needs*

capital: *previously manufactured goods used to make other goods and services*

Labor The work people do is **labor**—which is often called a human resource. Labor includes anyone who works to produce goods and services. As you know, economic **goods** are tangible items that people buy, such as pharmaceuticals, shampoo, or computers. **Services** are activities done for others for a fee. Doctors, hair stylists, and Web-page designers all sell their services.

Capital Another factor of production is **capital**—the manufactured goods used to make other goods and services. The machines, buildings, and tools used to assemble automobiles, for example, are *capital goods.* The newly assembled goods are not considered capital unless they, in turn, produce other goods and services, such as an automobile performing services as a taxicab.

The Four Factors of Production The four general categories of resources needed in the production of all goods and services include land, labor, capital, and entrepreneurship.

A Land
Natural resources, such as timber, are all the things found in nature—on or in water and the earth.

B Labor
This child-care worker falls under the category of labor*—she is performing a service for a fee.*

When capital is combined with land and labor, the value of all three factors of production increases. Think about the following situation. If you combine an uncut diamond (land), a diamond cutter (labor), and a diamond-cutting machine (capital), you end up with a highly valued gem.

Capital also increases **productivity**—the ability to produce greater quantities of goods and services in better and faster ways. Consider how much faster a mechanical reaper—a capital good—can harvest grain than a person clearing the field with a scythe.

productivity: *the amount of output (goods and services) that results from a given level of inputs (land, labor, capital, entrepreneurship)*

Entrepreneurship The fourth factor of production is **entrepreneurship.** This refers to the ability of individuals to start new businesses, to introduce new products and processes, and to improve management techniques. Entrepreneurship involves initiative and willingness to take risks in order to reap profits.

entrepreneurship: *ability of risk-taking individuals to develop new products and start new businesses in order to make profits*

Entrepreneurs must also incur the costs of failed efforts. About 30 percent of new business enterprises fail. Of the 70 percent that do survive, only a few become wildly successful businesses such as Microsoft, The Limited, or Blockbuster Video.

Technology Some economists add technology to the list of factors of production. In the past, **technology** included any use of land, labor, and capital that produced goods and services more efficiently. For example, computerized word processing was a technological advance over the typewriter.

technology: *advance in knowledge leading to new and improved goods and services and better ways of producing them*

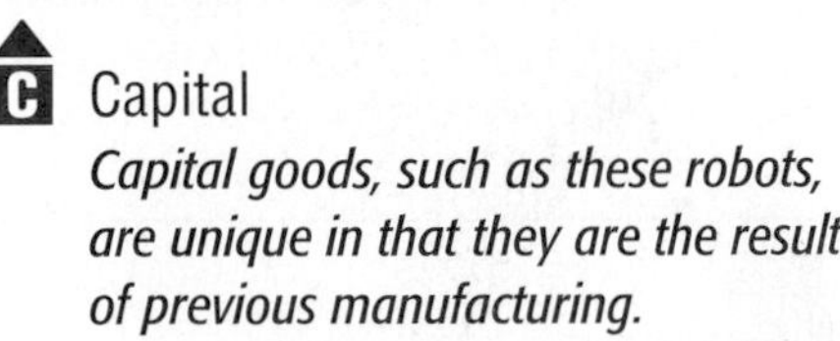

C Capital

Capital goods, such as these robots, are unique in that they are the result of previous manufacturing.

D Entrepreneurship

These entrepreneurs are taking a financial risk to make a profit for themselves and to bring innovative products and services to consumers.

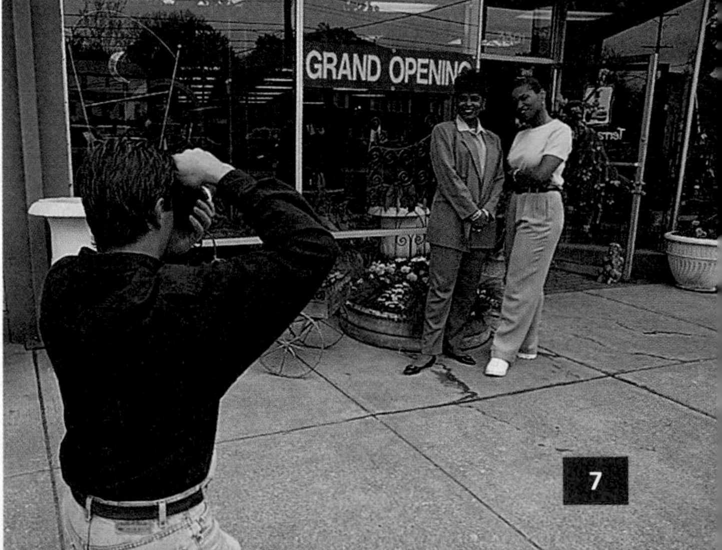

Economic Connection to... 

Technology Saves You a Trip to the Store

Only a few years ago, computers were as big as refrigerators. Now, Frigidaire Home Products has unveiled a fridge that contains a computer. The computer has a touch-screen monitor and a bar code scanner mounted on the freezer door. There's even a jack for an Internet connection. After emptying a carton of milk, you could swipe the carton past the bar code scanner, tap a couple of buttons on the screen, and the fridge would order replacements from an online grocery store. ■

How much of each of the factors of production you have determines an individual's wealth. The more land and capital you have, the richer you will be. The greater your entrepreneurial skills, the more income you might earn. In other words, the distribution of factors of production affects a nation's income distribution—what percentage of Americans are rich and what percentage are poor.

Practice and **assess** key skills with ***Skillbuilder Interactive Workbook, Level 2.***

SECTION 1 Assessment

Understanding Key Terms

1. **Define** economics, scarcity, factors of production, land, labor, goods, services, capital, productivity, entrepreneurship, technology.

Reviewing Objectives

2. What is the difference between wants and needs?
3. Explain why scarcity and choice are basic problems of economics.
4. **Graphic Organizer** Create a chart like the one shown in the next column, then list the four factors of production and provide two examples of each.

Factor of Production	Example 1	Example 2

Applying Economic Concepts

5. **Factors of Production** Describe a situation in which a capital good has improved your personal productivity.

Critical Thinking Activity

6. **Summarizing Information** Use a search engine to research an entrepreneur from the past or present, such as Andrew Carnegie, Mary Kay Ash, or Bill Gates. Explain what benefits were brought to society by his or her risk-taking entrepreneurship.

CRITICAL THINKING SKILLS

Sequencing and Categorizing Information

Sequencing *involves placing facts in the order in which they occurred.* Categorizing *entails organizing information into groups of related facts and ideas. Both actions help you deal with large quantities of information in an understandable way.*

- Look for dates or clue words that provide you with a chronological order: *in 2004, the late 1990s, first, then, finally, after the Great Depression,* and so on.
- If the information you're studying did not happen in a sequential order, you may categorize it instead. To do so, look for information with similar characteristics.
- List these characteristics, or categories, as the headings on a chart.
- As you read, fill in details under the proper category on the chart.

LEARNING THE SKILL

To learn sequencing and categorizing skills, follow the steps listed on the left.

PRACTICING THE SKILL

Read the passage below, then answer the questions that follow.

> *"Twinkies were invented in 1930 by James A. Dewar, a plant manager for Continental Baking Company. Faced with economic hardship, it didn't make sense to Dewar that the bakery had lots of expensive pans dedicated to a product called Little Short Cake Fingers that was baked only six weeks a year—during strawberry season. Dewar thought the little cakes could sell year-round if the company came up with something to replace the strawberry cream placed inside. He mixed up a banana-flavored 'crème' and figured out a way to inject it into the shortcake using three syringe-like injection tubes."*
>
> —Adapted from Jack Mingo's *How the Cadillac Got Its Fins,* HarperCollins, ©1994

1. How can the facts here be organized sequentially?
2. Now organize the facts under the categories of *Land, Labor, Capital,* and *Entrepreneurship.*

Practice and **assess** key skills with ***Skillbuilder Interactive Workbook, Level 2.***

APPLICATION ACTIVITY

Find a newspaper or magazine article about a local business. Sequence or categorize the information in a chart.

Global Economy

Pencils—*An International Product* As you've learned, the "land" factor of production includes natural resources. The natural resources that make up a pencil come from all over the world. So a pencil—yes, the simple writing tool you hold in your hand—is an international product.

Manufacturers

The Eberhard Faber Division makes its pencils in Lewisburg, Tennessee. The company produces almost a billion pencils every year. The J.R. Moon Pencil Company is also located in Lewisburg.

The Lead

The lead in a pencil is not really lead at all. It's a mixture of graphite and clay. The best graphite comes from Sri Lanka, Madagascar, and Mexico. Many pencil makers prefer the graphite from Mexico because it makes the blackest marks. Clay comes from Germany and Georgia.

The Casing

The casing (material around the lead) of most wooden pencils is made from incense cedar. Most of this cedar comes from the High Sierras in California, but some of it comes from Oregon and Washington.

Wax

Wax from Brazil coats the lead and soaks into the wood. The wax on the lead helps the pencil write more smoothly. Wax in the wood makes the wood easier to run through the machines at the factory and also makes the finished pencil easier for you to sharpen.

Yellow Pencils

Pencils were first painted yellow to honor China, where the best graphite came from. In China, yellow is a color of royalty and respect.

The Eraser

Rubber and pumice are the traditional ingredients of erasers. Pumice is the part that actually erases—the rubber just holds it together. The pumice comes from Italy, and the rubber comes from Malaysia. Modern erasers mix pumice with either vinyl or synthetic rubber.

Thinking Globally

1. List all the locations that supply resources for making pencils.

2. What are the specific resources supplied by the locations you listed in question 1?

SECTION 2 Trade-Offs

READER'S GUIDE

Terms to Know
- trade-off
- opportunity cost
- production possibilities curve

Reading Objectives
1. How are trade-offs and opportunity costs related?
2. How can society's trade-offs be shown on a production possibilities curve?

COVER STORY

BUSINESS WEEK, MAY 19, 2003

Job prospects for fresh grads haven't been this bleak in a decade. In 2002, companies hired one-third fewer college grads than in the previous year, according to the National Association of Colleges. . . .

Of course, not everyone is hurting: Prospects remain relatively strong in accounting, health care, and education.

As you learned in Section 1, scarcity forces people to make choices about how they will use their resources. In this section you'll learn that the effects of these choices may be long-lasting. For example, you may go to college or work full-time after graduating from high school. This decision affects not only your life now, but also what you'll earn in the future.

Trade-Offs

The economic choices people make involve exchanging one good or service for another. If you choose to buy a DVD player, you are exchanging your money for the right to own the player. Exchanging one thing for the use of another is called a **trade-off**.

trade-off: *sacrificing one good or service to purchase or produce another*

Individuals, families, businesses, and societies are forced to make trade-offs every time they use their resources in one way and not another. **Figure 1.4** shows a trade-off common to growing communities.

The Cost of Trade-Offs The result of a trade-off is what you give up in order to get or do something else. Time, for example, is

FIGURE 

Trade-Offs The trade-off of maintaining a historical community is the convenience that modern roads would provide. ***How can a trade-off you make today affect your future?***

a scarce resource—there are only so many hours in a day—so you must choose how to use it. When you decide to study economics for an hour, you are giving up any other activities you could have chosen to do during that time.

In other words, there is a cost involved in time spent studying this book. Economists call it an **opportunity cost**—the value of the next best alternative that had to be given up to do the action that *was* chosen. You may have many trade-offs when you study—connecting to your favorite Web site, going to the mall, or practicing the guitar, for example. But whatever you consider the *single next best alternative* is the opportunity cost of your studying economics for one hour.

A good way to think about opportunity cost is to realize that when you make a trade-off (and you *always* make trade-offs), you lose. What do you lose? You lose the ability to engage in your next highest valued alternative, as shown in **Figure 1.5** on page 14. In economics, therefore, opportunity cost is always an opportunity that is given up.

Considering Opportunity Costs

Being aware of trade-offs and their resulting opportunity costs is vital in

opportunity cost: *value of the next best alternative given up for the alternative that was chosen*

 **Global** *Economy*

Rain Forest Trade-Offs

How do trade-offs of resources affect our future? The Amazon River Basin in Brazil is the world's largest tropical rain forest and river system. But within the Basin an area equal to 5,000 soccer fields is being destroyed every day. Farmers burn the forests to gain farmland for other profitable crops. Loggers cut and export the fine hardwoods for a profit. And people have penetrated the forests to strip the Amazon of its curative and medicinal plants.

What are the trade-offs for the future? Many scientists believe the destruction of the forest will speed up global warming. Rain forests supply one-fifth of the world's oxygen supply, as well as trap poisonous carbon compounds. If the area is destroyed, its untold medicinal secrets also will be lost forever. ■

FIGURE 1.5

Opportunity Cost Any time you pay money to purchase a good or service, you lose the opportunity to purchase your next best alternative. ***How do trade-offs and opportunity costs differ?***

making economic decisions at all levels. Businesses must consider trade-offs and opportunity costs when they choose to invest money or hire workers to produce one good rather than another.

Consider an example at the national level. Suppose Congress votes $220 billion to finance needed highways. Congress could have voted for increased spending on new schools. The opportunity cost of building new highways, then, is fewer new schools.

Production Possibilities Curve

Obviously, many businesses produce more than one type of product. An automobile company, for example, may manufacture several makes of cars per plant in a given year. Does this mean that the company makes no trade-offs? No, what this means is that the company produces combinations of goods–which still results in an opportunity cost.

production possibilities curve: *graph showing the maximum combinations of goods and services that can be produced from a fixed amount of resources in a given period of time*

Economists use a model called the **production possibilities curve** to show the maximum combinations of goods and services that can be produced from a fixed amount of resources in a given period of time. This curve can help people and businesses determine how much of each item to produce, thus revealing the trade-offs and opportunity costs involved in each decision.

Imagine that you run a jewelry-making business. Working 20 hours a week, you have enough resources to make either 10 bracelets or 5 pairs of earrings. If you want to make some of both, **Figure 1.6** shows your production possibilities.

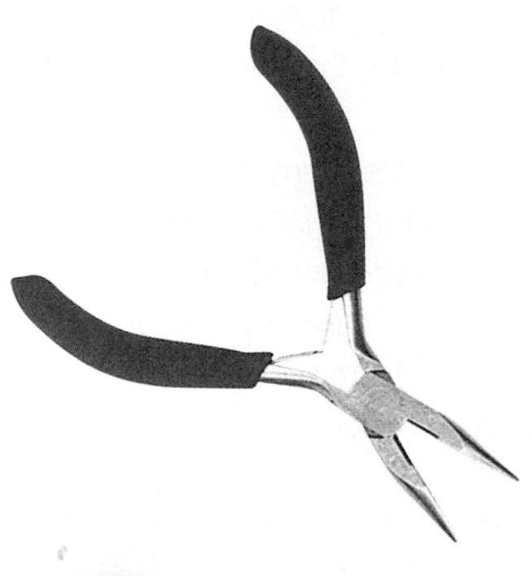

The Classic Example The classic example for explaining production possibilities in economics is the trade-off between military defense and civilian goods, sometimes referred to as *guns* versus *butter*. The extremes for a nation would be using all its resources to produce only one or the other.

Look at **Figure 1.7** on page 16. Point A on the graph represents all resources being used to produce only guns (military defense). Point E represents the other extreme—all resources being used to produce only butter (civilian goods). The amount of military goods given up in the year is the opportunity cost for increasing civilian goods production. Members of the federal government determine where on the curve the nation will be.

The real world and our graphs are not always quite the same, however. In the real world, it takes time to move from point A to point B. The important point is that by using a production possibilities curve, a nation, business, or individual can decide how best to use its resources.

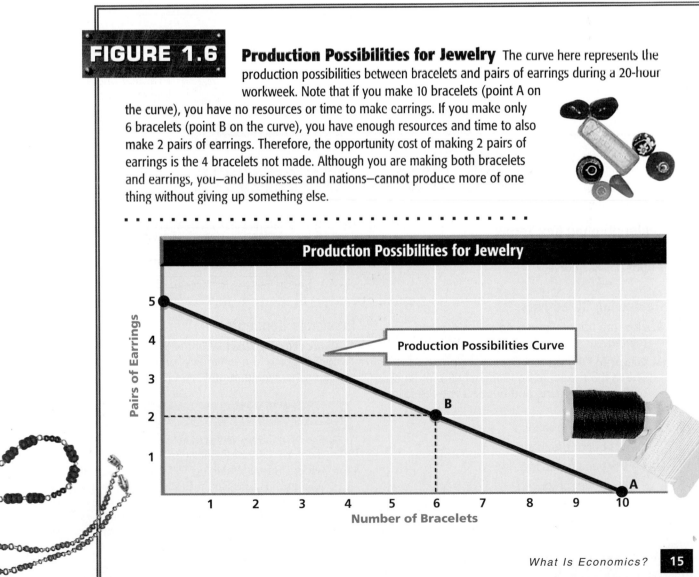

FIGURE 1.6 **Production Possibilities for Jewelry** The curve here represents the production possibilities between bracelets and pairs of earrings during a 20-hour workweek. Note that if you make 10 bracelets (point A on the curve), you have no resources or time to make earrings. If you make only 6 bracelets (point B on the curve), you have enough resources and time to also make 2 pairs of earrings. Therefore, the opportunity cost of making 2 pairs of earrings is the 4 bracelets not made. Although you are making both bracelets and earrings, you—and businesses and nations—cannot produce more of one thing without giving up something else.

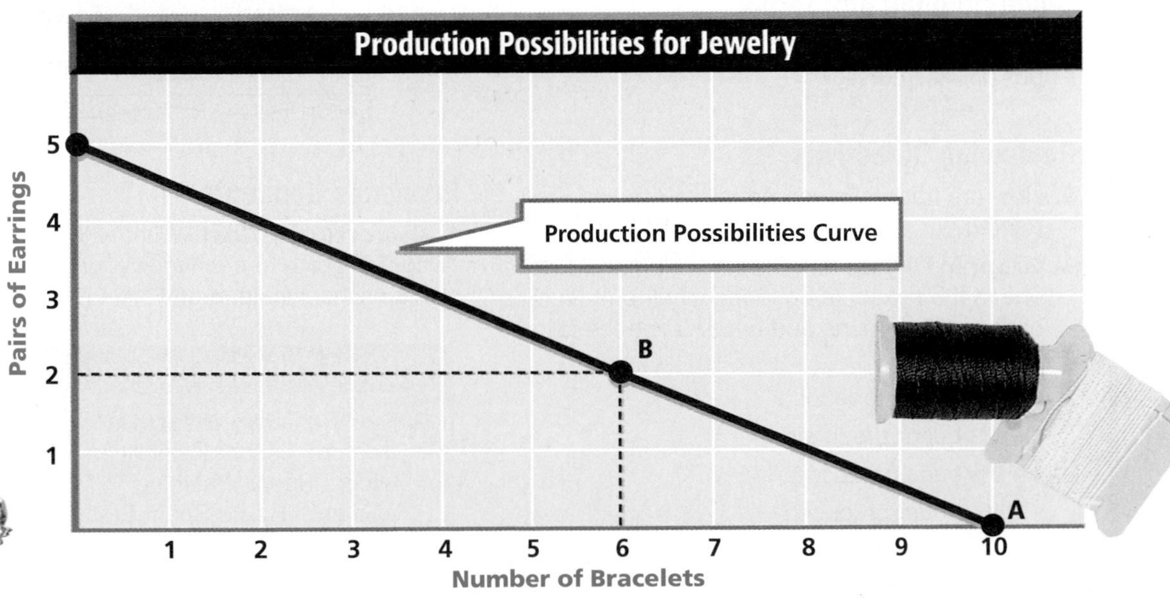

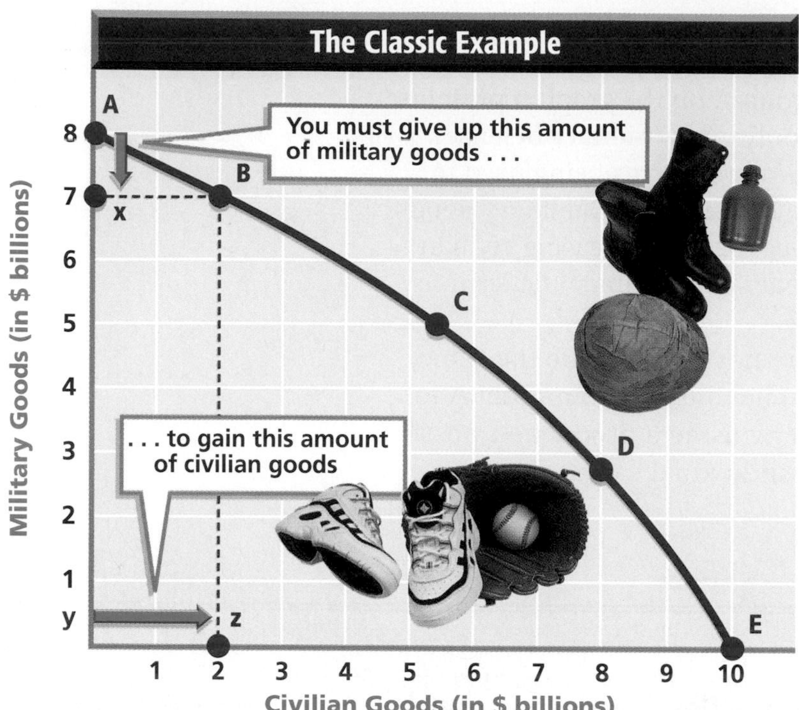

FIGURE 1.7

Production Possibilities–Military Goods Versus Civilian Goods Nations produce combinations, or mixes, of goods. If the nation starts with all gun production and no butter production (point A), it can only get to some butter production (point B) by giving up some gun production. In other words, the cost of having some civilian goods (represented by the horizontal distance from y to point z) is giving up some military goods (represented by the vertical distance from point A to point x).

Practice and **assess** key skills with ***Skillbuilder Interactive Workbook, Level 2.***

SECTION 2 Assessment

Understanding Key Terms

1. **Define** trade-off, opportunity cost, production possibilities curve.

Reviewing Objectives

2. How are trade-offs and opportunity costs related?
3. **Graphic Organizer** Create a diagram like the one in the next column to identify the production possibilities of guns and butter using the following actions:
   - 100% guns produced
   - 70% butter produced
   - 40% guns produced
   - 25% butter produced

Action	⟶	Result
1.	⟶	
2.	⟶	

Economic Concepts

4. **Opportunity Cost** What is the opportunity cost of going to a university for four years after high school instead of working?

Critical Thinking Activity

5. **Synthesizing Information** Build your own production possibilities curve with "Hours Spent Watching TV" on the horizontal axis and "Hours Spent Studying Economics" on the vertical axis. Write a caption explaining the opportunity cost of each activity.

Coasters Find a Whole New Way to Roll

Check It Out! In this chapter you learned about the factors of production—land, labor, capital, and entrepreneurship. In the following article, read to learn how traditional roller coasters are being modernized, keeping in mind the factors of production needed to perform this modernization.

Hold on tight. The Joker's Jinx, a new roller coaster at the Six Flags America theme park in Largo, Maryland, will make its debut this coming May. And its trick piece of technology, the linear induction motor (LIM), is helping redefine the way roller coasters roll. The new beasts are faster, smoother, and scarier than their wooden predecessors.

So far, Premier Rides of Maryland, the roller coaster manufacturer that helped develop the technology, has launched seven LIM coasters. Three more, including The Joker's Jinx, will follow this year. Conventional roller coasters are dragged by chains or cables–clank, clank, clank–to the top of the first hill. Then gravity causes the cars to accelerate. In contrast, Premier Rides' coasters slingshot passengers out of the loading station, accelerating from zero to 70 miles per hour in less than four seconds. The secret is the high-tech motors, about 200 of which are used in each coaster. When juiced with an alternating current, the motors create an electromagnetic force that accelerates the coaster over the first 200 feet of the ride.

Think About It

1. **Provide two examples of each factor of production that went into developing the new coasters.**
2. **What is the opportunity cost of spending a day at an amusement park?**

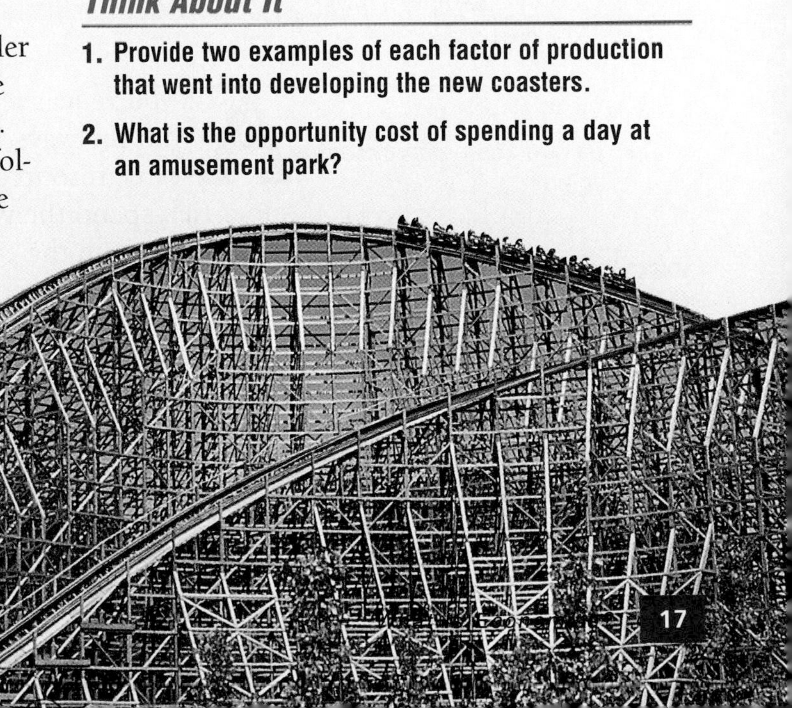

SECTION 3

What Do Economists Do?

READER'S GUIDE

Terms to Know
- microeconomics
- macroeconomics
- economy
- economic model
- hypothesis

Reading Objectives
1. How do economists use models to study the real world?
2. Why are there different schools of economic thought?

COVER STORY

THE COLUMBUS DISPATCH, JUNE 3, 2003

Teenagers going through the high-school rite of passage . . . found welcome mats out across the city at fine-dining establishments.

Prom season usually means added restaurant business on most weekend evenings during the spring. . . .

[N]ational numbers published by the Conde Nast magazine *Your Prom* said the average 17-year-old spent $638, or more than $1,200 per couple.

Proms are big business, estimated to bring in $2.7 billion nationally.

As you've learned, economics is a social science concerned with the ways individuals and nations choose to use their scarce resources. Economists might analyze how the super-rich spend their income, for example, and the effect this spending has on the economy. As you read this section, you'll find that something economists *don't* do, however, is judge whether there *should be* a social strata of the super-rich. They leave value judgments up to other social scientists.

Another thing to keep in mind as you read this textbook is that economics is divided into two parts. **Microeconomics** is the branch of economic theory that deals with behavior and decision making by small units such as individuals and firms. **Macroeconomics** is that branch of economic theory dealing

microeconomics: *the branch of economic theory that deals with behavior and decision making by small units such as individuals and firms*

macroeconomics: *the branch of economic theory dealing with the economy as a whole and decision making by large units such as governments* with the economy as a whole and decision making by large units such as governments.

Economic Models

To economists, the word ***economy*** means all the activity in a nation that together affects the production, distribution, and use of goods and services. When studying a specific part of the economy—rising teenage unemployment, for example—economists often formulate theories and gather data. See **Figure 1.8.** The theories that economists use in their work are called **economic models,** which are simplified representations of the real world. Solutions that emerge from testing economic models often become the basis for actual decisions by private businesses or government agencies.

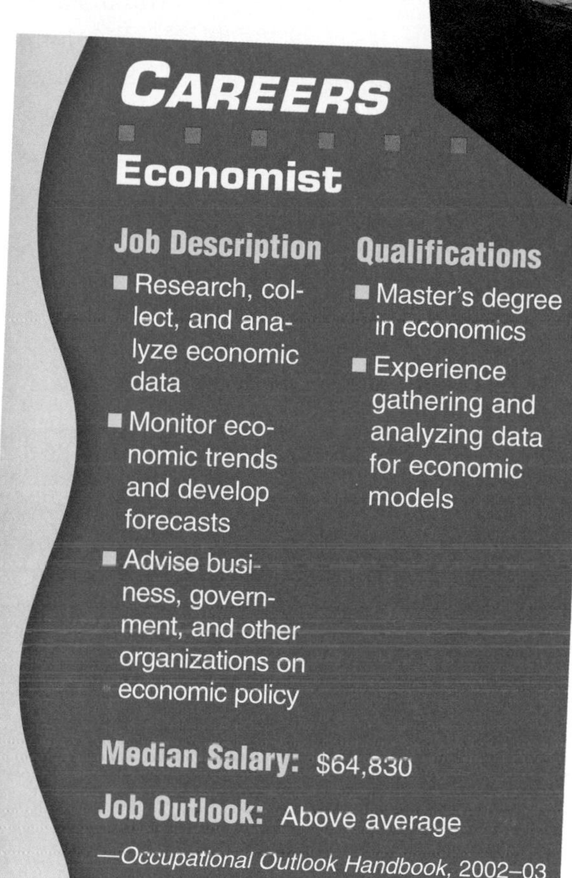

CAREERS
Economist
Job Description
■ Research, collect, and analyze economic data
■ Monitor economic trends and develop forecasts
■ Advise business, government, and other organizations on economic policy
Qualifications
■ Master's degree in economics
■ Experience gathering and analyzing data for economic models
Median Salary: $64,830
Job Outlook: Above average
—Occupational Outlook Handbook, 2002–03

What Models Show Physicists, chemists, biologists, and other scientists use models to understand in simple terms the complex workings of the world. Similarly, one purpose of economic models is to show visual representations of consumer, business, or other economic behavior. The production possibilities curve that you learned about in Section 2 is an economic model that reveals opportunity cost. The most common economic model is a line graph explaining how

economy: *the production and distribution of goods and services in a society*

economic model: *a theory or simplified representation that helps explain and predict economic behavior in the real world*

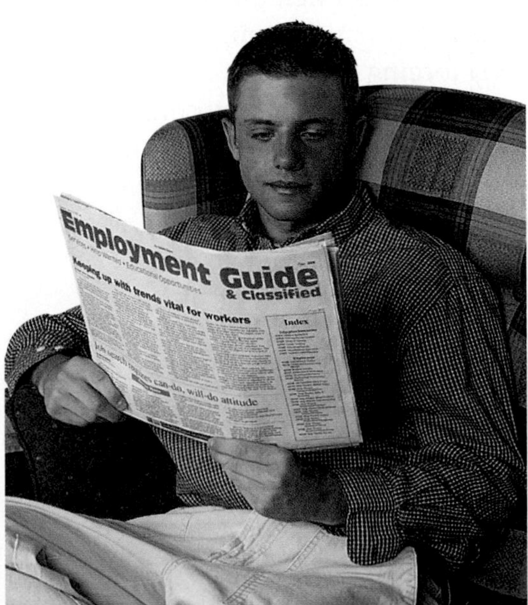

FIGURE 1.8

Help Wanted Economic models are developed to help solve problems such as teenage unemployment. ***What is the purpose of economic models?***

consumers react to changes in the prices of goods and services. You'll learn about this model in Chapter 7.

hypothesis: *an assumption involving two or more variables that must be tested for validity*

Economic models assume that some factors remain constant. In studying the production possibilities curve for making jewelry in Section 2, for example, we assumed that the price of inputs (beads, wire, and so on) would not increase. We also assumed that inclement weather would not close schools for a day, which would have enabled you to work more than 20 hours a week on jewelry.

Why are these constant-factor assumptions important? Economists realize that, in the real world, several things may be changing at once. Using a model holds everything steady except the variables assumed to be related. In the same way that a map does not show every alley and building in a given location, economic models do not record every detail and relationship that exists about a problem to be studied. A model will show only the basic factors needed to analyze the problem at hand.

FIGURE 1.9

Using a Hypothesis

The list below reviews the steps involved in making and testing hypotheses. In working with models, economists use these same steps.

1. Define the problem.
2. From the possible alternatives, state a hypothesis that appears to offer the best solution to a problem or explanation of an event.
3. Gather data to test the hypothesis. Besides using facts from the real world, an economist must identify economic principles involved.
4. Evaluate the data and discard any that are not relevant, or related to the immediate situation, or that are not based on fact.
5. Make sure there are enough data to test the hypothesis thoroughly.
6. Develop a conclusion based on the data. To do this, an economist evaluates whether the alternative is the best, in view of its consequences and trade-offs.
7. If the hypothesis appears to be valid, retest it with new data to see if the same results can be obtained again.
8. If the hypothesis still appears to be valid, form a generalization that can be applied to other cases. A *generalization* pulls together common ideas among facts and is true in most cases. For an economist, this step involves developing an economic policy based on the best alternative.

Creating a Model Models are useful if they help us analyze the way the real world works. An economist begins with some idea about the way things work, then collects facts and discards those that are not relevant. Let's assume that an economist wants to find out why teenage unemployment rises periodically. Perhaps this unemployment occurs when the federal minimum wage goes up, thereby forcing employers to pay their teenage workers more or to lay some workers off. The economist can test this theory, or model, in the same way that other scientists test a **hypothesis**—an educated guess or prediction. **Figure 1.9** explains how hypotheses are used as the starting point for investigations.

Testing a Model Testing a model, or hypothesis, allows economists to see if the model represents reality under certain conditions. Suppose an economist has developed the model shown in *Graph A* of **Figure 1.10.** The economist would collect data on the amount of teenage unemployment every year for the last 30 years. He or she would also gather 30 years of information on federal legislation that increased the legal minimum wage paid to teenagers.

The economist can be fairly satisfied with the model if teenage unemployment rose every time the minimum wage rate increased. But suppose that the data instead resulted in *Graph B* of **Figure 1.10,** which does not show a relationship between teenage unemployment and increases in the legal minimum wage. The economist then will have to develop another model to explain changes in teenage unemployment.

Applying Models to Real Life Much of the work of economists involves predicting how people will react in a particular situation. Individual human behavior is not always predictable, though. As a result, an economist's predictive model may not apply under different conditions.

FIGURE 1.10

Economic Models The purpose of economic models is to show visual representations of consumer, business, or other economic behavior. Economic models, however, must be tested to see if they represent reality. Graph A supports the theory that a direct relationship exists between increases in the minimum wage rate and increases in teenage unemployment. Graph B does not support that theory.

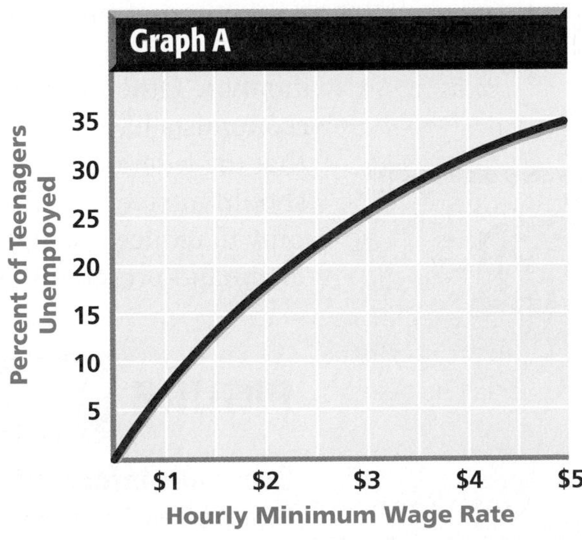

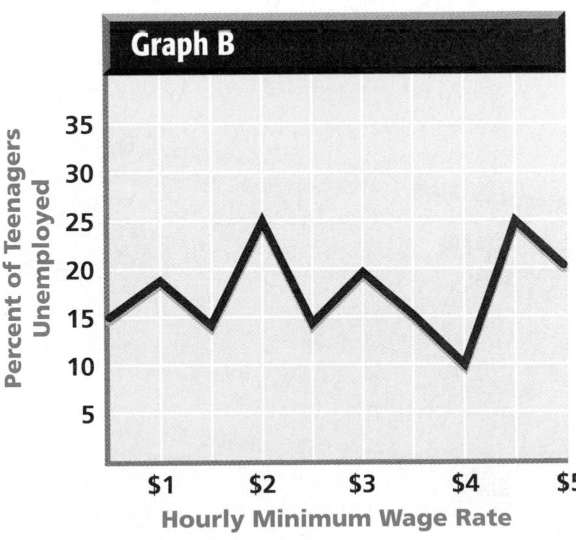

Student Web Activity Visit the *Economics Today and Tomorrow* Web site at ett.glencoe.com and click on ***Chapter 1—Student Web Activities*** to learn about famous economists and their contributions.

For example, some economists believe that to stimulate the economy, taxes should be cut and government spending increased. Cutting taxes, these economists believe, may put more income into consumers' pockets, which will increase personal spending and increase total production. However, some people's fears concerning possible higher taxes in the future might cause them to save the extra income rather than spend it. As this example illustrates, economists cannot take into account all of the factors that may influence people's behavior.

Schools of Economic Thought

Economists deal with facts. Their personal opinions and beliefs may nonetheless influence how they view those facts and fit them to theories. The government under which an economist lives also shapes how he or she views the world. As a result, all economists will not agree that a particular theory offers the best solution to a problem. Often, economists from competing schools of thought claim that their theories are better in predicting a certain result than are others' theories. See **Figure 1.11.**

During a given period of time, a nation's political leaders may agree with one school of economic thought and develop policies based on it. Later, leaders may agree with another group of economists. Throughout American history, many economists have stressed the importance of government maintaining "hands off" in business and consumer affairs as a method of preventing increased unemployment and inflation. Other influential economists have proposed that the federal government should intervene in the economy to reduce unemployment and prevent inflation.

FIGURE 1.11

Economic Information
Economists analyze events and their effects on the economy.

Values and Economics Learning about economics will help you predict what may happen if certain events occur or certain policies are followed. But economics will *not* tell you whether the results will be good or bad. Judgments about results depend on a person's values.

Values are the beliefs or characteristics that a person or group considers important, such as religious freedom, equal opportunity, individual initiative, freedom from want, and so on. Even having the same values does not mean that people will agree about solutions to problems, strategies, or interpretation of data, however.

For example, those in favor of decreasing teenage unemployment in order to bring about economic opportunity may disagree about the best way to solve this problem. If you were a legislator, you might show your commitment to this value by introducing a bill to decrease teenage unemployment. The economists who help you research the causes of teenage unemployment will tell you, based on their expertise, whether the proposed solution will actually reduce teenage unemployment.

Remember, however, that the science of economics is not used to judge whether a certain policy is good or bad. Economists only inform us as to likely short-term and long-term outcomes of these policies.

Practice and **assess** key skills with ***Skillbuilder Interactive Workbook, Level 2.***

SECTION 3 Assessment

Understanding Key Terms

1. **Define** microeconomics, macroeconomics, economy, economic model, hypothesis.

Reviewing Objectives

2. **Graphic Organizer** Create a diagram like the one below to show how economists use models to study the real world.

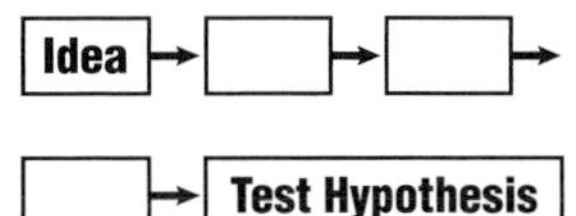

3. Why are there different schools of economic thought?

Applying Economic Concepts

4. **Economic Models** If you were to make a model showing the effect of hiring senior citizens into previously held teenage job markets, what factors would you analyze?

Critical Thinking Activity

5. **Distinguishing Fact From Opinion** Write three "headlines" about the economy that reveal a value judgment. Then rewrite the headlines to omit the value judgment.

People & Perspectives

Robert L. Heilbroner

ECONOMIST (1919–)

- **Attended Harvard University and the New School for Social Research in New York City**
- **Has taught at the New School for Social Research since 1971**
- **Published *The Worldly Philosophers* (1953), *The Future as History* (1960), *Visions of the Future* (1995), and *The Crisis of Vision in Modern Economic Thought* (1996)**

Robert L. Heilbroner's book *The Worldly Philosophers* gives a unique and insightful look into the lives and works of the great economists of the past. In his introduction, Heilbroner explains the importance of these great economists to history:

> "*By all rules of schoolboy history books, they were nonentities: they commanded no armies, sent no men to their deaths, ruled no empires, took little part in history-making decisions. . . . Yet what they did was more decisive for history than many acts of statesmen who basked in brighter glory, often more profoundly disturbing than the shuttling of armies back and forth across frontiers, more powerful for good and bad than the edicts of kings and legislatures. It was this: they shaped and swayed men's minds.*"

Heilbroner expresses his belief that economists have a major impact on the world. He disagrees with the perception that the work of economists is dull and boring:

> "*A man who thinks that economics is only a matter for professors forgets that this is the science that has sent men to the barricades. . . . No, the great economists pursued an inquiry as exciting–and dangerous–as any the world has ever known. . . . The notions of the great economists were world-shaking, and their mistakes nothing short of calamitous.*"

Checking for Understanding

1. **Why is it important to study the great economists of the past?**
2. **What impact have economists made in the world? Explain your answer.**

CHAPTER 1 Summary

Chapter Overview Visit the *Economics Today and Tomorrow* Web site at ett.glencoe.com and click on ***Chapter 1—Chapter Overviews*** to review chapter information.

SECTION 1 The Basic Problem in Economics

- **Economics** is the study of how individuals, families, businesses, and societies use limited resources to fulfill their unlimited wants.
- Individuals satisfy their unlimited wants in a world of limited resources by making choices.
- The need to make choices arises because of **scarcity,** the basic problem of economics.
- The resources needed to make goods and services are known as the **factors of production.**
- The four factors of production include **land,** or natural resources; **labor,** also known as human resources; **capital,** the manufactured goods used to make other goods and services; and **entrepreneurship,** the ability of risk-taking individuals to start new businesses and introduce new products and processes.
- Some economists add **technology** to the list of factors of production.

SECTION 2 Trade-Offs

- People are forced to make **trade-offs** every time they use their resources in one way and not another.
- The cost of making a trade-off is known as **opportunity cost**—the value of the next best alternative that had to be given up to do the action that was chosen.
- A **production possibilities curve** is a graph that shows the maximum combinations of goods and services that can be produced from a fixed amount of resources in a given period of time.
- The classic example for explaining production possibilities in economics is the trade-off between guns (military defense) and butter (civilian goods).

SECTION 3 What Do Economists Do?

- Economists study the **economy**—all the activity in a nation that together affects the production, distribution, and use of goods and services.
- Economists also formulate theories called **economic models,** which are simplified representations of the real world.
- Economists test their models in the same way that other scientists test **hypotheses,** or educated guesses.
- Economists deal with facts, although their personal opinions may sway their theories.
- Economists offer solutions to economic problems, but they do not put value judgments on those solutions.

CHAPTER 1

Assessment and Activities

Self-Check Quiz Visit the *Economics Today and Tomorrow* Web site at ett.glencoe.com and click on ***Chapter 1—Self-Check Quizzes*** to prepare for the Chapter Test.

Identifying Key Terms

Write a short paragraph about the factors of production in the United States using all of the following terms.

- scarcity
- factors of production
- entrepreneurship
- technology
- trade-off
- land
- labor
- capital
- goods
- services

Recalling Facts and Ideas

Section 1

1. What is the condition that results because wants are unlimited?
2. What is the difference between scarcity and shortages?
3. Your friend says, "I need some new clothes." Under what conditions would this be expressing a need? A want?
4. What are the four factors of production?

Section 2

5. What does making a trade-off require you to do?
6. What do economists call the next best alternative that had to be given up for the one chosen?
7. In economics, what is cost?
8. What does a production possibilities curve show?

Section 3

9. For what purposes do economists use real-world data in building models?
10. An economic theory is another name for what?
11. When does an economist consider an economic model useful?

Thinking Critically

1. **Drawing Inferences and Conclusions** Some people argue that air is not an economic good. Explain why you agree or disagree with this statement.
2. **Categorizing Information** Create three diagrams like the one below and label the center oval with one of the following services: providing financial advice, teaching economics, producing a movie. Fill in examples of each factor of production that went into developing these services.

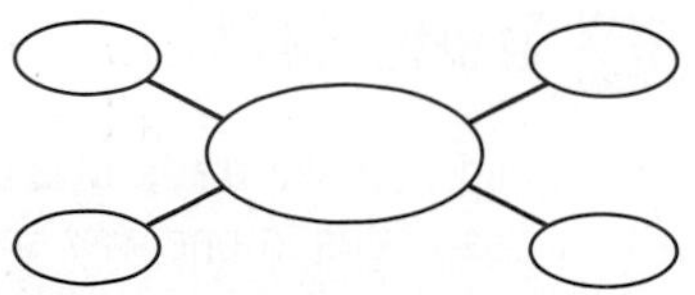

3. **Summarizing Information** Why will studying economics not tell you whether a possible solution to a problem is either good or bad?

Applying Economic Concepts

Trade-Offs and Opportunity Costs Because your time is scarce, you are constantly facing trade-offs. Make a list of the trade-offs you have made in choosing how you used your time during a one-week period. What activities did you choose to do? What were the opportunity costs involved in your choices?

Cooperative Learning Project

Working in groups of four, choose a consumer product such as a DVD player, a pair of sunglasses, or an automobile. Determine and list the elements of each of the four factors of production that went into making that consumer product. Discuss your lists with the rest of the class.

Technology Activity

Using the Internet Each time you access the Internet you see advertising–banners, buttons, keywords, click-on ads, and other promotions. Home pages of popular Web search engines like Yahoo! face an opportunity cost: any screen space that a site uses to promote its own services cannot be sold to advertisers.

Design a home page for your own Web site. Assume that you can sell some screen space to advertisers, but be aware that too many ads will cause users to switch to a less cluttered site. Consider every square inch on your home page as having an opportunity cost.

Reviewing Skills

Sequencing and Categorizing Information In this chapter you learned that some economists add technology as a fifth factor of production. *Technology,* as you recall, is an advance in knowledge leading to new and improved goods and services and better ways of producing them. This includes any use of land, labor, capital, and entrepreneurship that produces goods and services more efficiently.

Choose a product or service, and then research the technology that went into developing it. Construct a diagram like the one below that displays in sequential order the technology involved in preparing the factors of production that ultimately create your good or service. Share your diagram with the rest of the class.

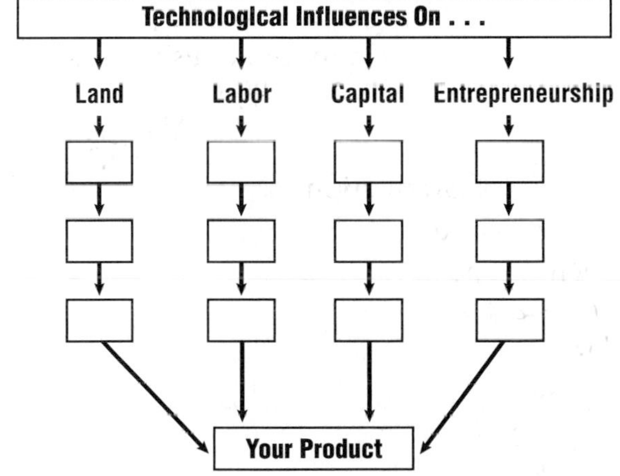

Analyzing the Global *Economy*

Watch television news reports and read newspapers and/or news magazines every day for one week. Make a list of proposed actions on the part of international governments that involve trade-offs and opportunity costs. Report your findings to the class.

Focus on Free Enterprise

Amazon.com

In 1994 30-year-old Jeff Bezos, a Princeton summa cum laude graduate, noticed that this newfangled thing called the World Wide Web was growing by 2,300 percent a year. He wanted in by the smartest available route. Methodically, he drew up a list of products that could be sold on the Internet, including computers, software, music, videos, and clothing.

Jeff Bezos

Curling Up With a Good Book

He finally decided on books because of the variety of product (more than a million titles in print), because no single merchandisers dominated the market, and because computer search engines could be very useful in helping customers find hazily remembered volumes.

Jeff Bezos, founder of Amazon.com, wasn't the first to see that the Internet offered a useful way to match up people and books, but he has pushed the concept harder and faster. Three years after making its first sale, Amazon.com was the third-largest bookseller in the country, selling about $400 million worth of books, music, and videos.

Click and Buy

The central concept of online bookselling is breathtakingly simple: Instead of people going in search of books, make it so the books can come to them. For the first time, nearly any book is only a mouse click and a few days away from any reader in the country.

In a business using the most sophisticated technology, Bezos's whole purpose is to retrieve something that thrived in the past. "I want to transport online bookselling," he says, "back to the days of the small bookseller who got to know you very well."

Once the customer has made his choice, a premium is put on speed. Customer service workers at Amazon.com take the orders and pass them along to a wholesale book company, which ships the books immediately. Most books arrive at the customer's front door only a few days after the order is sent–so quickly, so painlessly that the buyer is supposed to lose interest in going to the library or superstore. "I abide by the theory that says in the late 20th century, the scarcest resource is time," Bezos says. "If you can save people money and time, they'll like that."

Virtual Overhead

Since Amazon.com is virtual, it doesn't have many of the fixed costs for real estate and employees that real-world bookstores do. As a company, Amazon initially owned little–no buildings, no factories, nothing that qualifies as equity in the traditional sense. It also takes advantage of its medium to allow its customers to post their own book reviews online–which costs nothing, yet bonds its readers into a community.

Another advantage is that it doesn't have to order most books from publishers or wholesalers until a customer actually wants them. A bookstore in the real world has to do things the opposite way: It orders a stack of books and hopes customers will want them.

Cyber Irony

Only a few years ago, futurists were predicting that the digital age would be the death of conventional publishing. Instead, the hottest business on the burgeoning Internet is selling old-fashioned books.

–Adapted from *The Washington Post National Weekly Edition*, July 20–27, 1998.

> ***Free Enterprise in Action***
>
> **1. What is the basic concept of online bookselling?**
>
> **2. Why does Amazon.com have lower fixed costs than regular bookstores?**

CHAPTER 2

Economic Systems and the American Economy

Why It's Important

Why do we, as American consumers, have so many choices? How is our economy different from the economies of other countries? This chapter will explain the different kinds of economic systems.

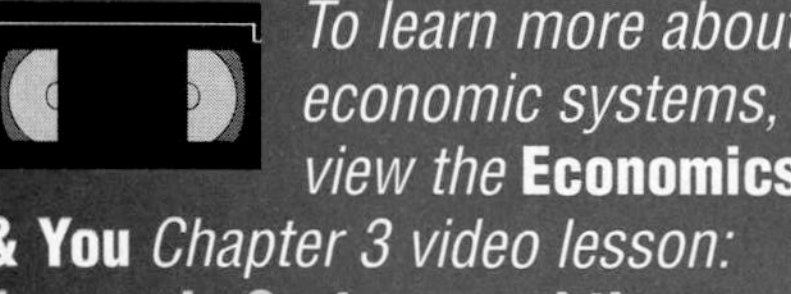

To learn more about economic systems, view the **Economics & You** *Chapter 3 video lesson:* **Economic Systems and the American Economy**

ECONOMICS Online

Chapter Overview Visit the *Economics Today and Tomorrow* Web site at ett.glencoe.com and click on ***Chapter 2—Chapter Overviews*** to preview chapter information.

SECTION 1

Economic Systems

COVER STORY

WE LIVE IN ARGENTINA, BY ALEX HUBER

Diaguita Indians have lived in this region for generations. . . . We grow beans, corn and potatoes on the mountain slopes. To irrigate these crops, we still use the channels built centuries ago by our ancestors. We also breed llamas. . . . In our community, the more llamas you own, the richer you are. . . . You can tell to which community someone belongs by the way they dress, the color of their clothes, and the hairstyle of the women.

READER'S GUIDE

Terms to Know

- economic system
- traditional economy
- command economy
- market economy
- market
- circular flow of economic activity
- mixed economy

Reading Objectives

1. What three questions must all economic systems answer?
2. What are the major types of economic systems and their differences?

You probably have set some goals for your life, such as going to college, learning a trade, or opening a business. If you were to compare your personal goals to the goals of a Diaguita living in Argentina or to a North Korean teenager, the lists might vary widely. One of the reasons for this variance is that each of these persons lives in a community or nation with a different **economic system,** or way of determining how to use resources to satisfy people's wants and needs. In this section, you'll learn about the different kinds of economic systems in the world.

economic system: *way in which a nation uses its resources to satisfy its people's needs and wants*

Three Basic Questions

Although nations will have different economic systems, each system is faced with answering the same three basic questions:

What goods and services should be produced? How should they be produced? Who should share in what is produced?

What Should Be Produced? As you've learned, we live in a world of scarcity and trade-offs. If more of one particular item is produced, then less of something else will be produced. If the government decides to use resources to build new roads, then fewer resources are available to maintain national parks. If a city decides to hire more police officers, fewer funds are available to add teachers to classrooms. Similarly, as shown in **Figure 2.1,** an automobile manufacturer must decide whether to produce pickup trucks, minivans, sports utility vehicles, or luxury cars—and how much of each.

FIGURE 2.1

What to Produce? An automobile manufacturer must decide which types of cars to produce with its limited supplies of labor, steel, rubber, and so on. ***Why can't businesses or nations produce as much as they want?***

How Should It Be Produced? After deciding what to produce, an economic system must then decide *how* those goods and services will be produced. Will more laborers be hired? Will skilled laborers or unskilled laborers do the work? Will capital goods be used to manufacture the products, thereby reducing the number of laborers needed? As shown in **Figure 2.2,** a decision must be made as to how the combination of available inputs will get the job done for the least cost.

FIGURE 2.2

How to Produce? Trade-offs exist among the available factors of production. A farmer could use a horse-drawn plow to prepare a field for planting, or instead use modern equipment. ***What factors must be considered when deciding how to produce a good or service?***

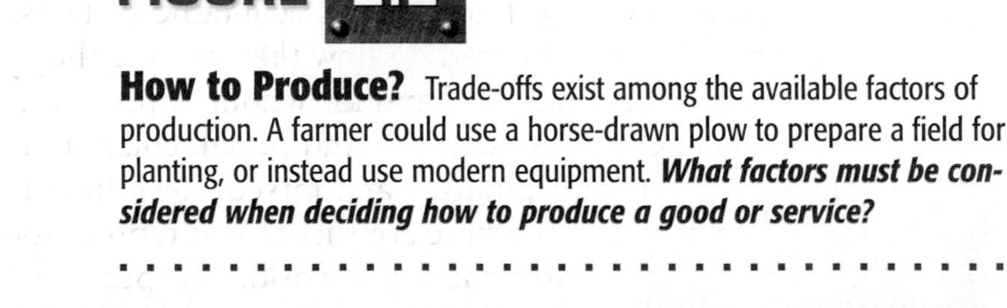

HAGAR THE HORRIBLE

For Whom Should It Be Produced? After goods or services are produced, the type of economic system under which people live determines how the goods and services will be distributed among its members. See **Figure 2.3.** Who receives the new cars? Who benefits from a new city school? Who lives in new apartment buildings? As you will read, most goods and services in the United States are distributed to individuals and businesses through a price system. Other economies may distribute products through majority rule, a lottery, on a first-come-first-served basis, by sharing equally, by military force, and in a variety of other ways.

FIGURE 

For Whom to Produce?
In the United States economy, people's career choices determine their level of income, which in turn affects their ability to purchase produced items. ***How do you think people's educational choices play in the career choices that they have later in life?***

Types of Economic Systems

Economists have identified four types of economic systems. They differ from one another based on how they answer the three basic questions of what, how, and for whom to produce. The four types of economic systems are traditional, command (or controlled), market (or capitalist), and mixed. Keep in mind that the four systems described here are theoretical representations of economies found throughout the world. No "pure" systems really exist–they are all mixed economies to some degree.

Traditional System A pure **traditional economy** answers the three basic questions according to tradition. In such a system, things are done "the way they have always been done." Economic decisions are based on customs and beliefs–often religious–handed down from generation to generation.

traditional economy: *system in which economic decisions are based on customs and beliefs that have been handed down from generation to generation*

If you lived in a traditional economic system, your parents would teach you to perform the same tasks that they learned from their parents. As a male, for example, if your father was a fisherman, you would become a fisherman. You would learn to make fishing nets the same way he was taught. And you would distribute your catch in the manner that it had always been done.

An advantage of living in a traditional economy is that you know what is expected of you. In addition, family and community ties are usually very strong. Disadvantages include an economy in which change is discouraged and perhaps even punished, and one in which the methods of production are often inefficient. Consequently, choices among consumer goods are rare.

As *Part C* of **Figure 2.4** shows, traditional economies exist to some extent in very limited parts of the world today. The Inuit of North America, the San of the Kalahari in Africa, and the Aborigines of Australia are organized into traditional economic systems.

command economy: *system in which the government controls the factors of production and makes all decisions about their use*

Command System The pure **command economy** is somewhat similar to the traditional economy in that the individual has little, if any, influence over how the basic economic questions are answered. In a command or controlled system, however, government leaders–not tradition–control the factors of production and, therefore, make all decisions about their use.

Decisions in government may be made by one person, a small group of leaders, or a group of central planners in an agency. These people choose what is to be produced and how resources are to be used at each stage in production. They also decide how goods and services will be distributed. If you lived in a command economy, you would be paid according to what the central planners decide, and you might even lose your ability to make a career choice. Through a series of regulations about the kinds and amounts of available education, the government guides people into certain jobs.

An advantage of a controlled economy is the speed with which resources can be rerouted. If war is likely, the central planning agency can halt all manufacturing of civilian goods and channel the factors of production into making strictly military goods. Disadvantages include a lack of incentives to work hard or to show inventiveness, as well as a lack of consumer choices. Because the government sets workers' salaries, there is no reason to work efficiently or smartly.

Only a few countries in the world today still have much of a command economy. North Korea and the People's Republic of China are the two main examples because so much economic activity there is government-planned. See *Part B* of **Figure 2.4.**

FIGURE 2.4

Types of Economic Systems The types of economic systems differ from one another based on how they answer the three basic questions of what, how, and for whom to produce.

A Market Economy

In a market economy, prices are an efficient means of providing information for voluntary exchange. ***Why do you suppose that prices are considered "neutral"?***

B Command Economy

Command economies were common throughout history. China's economy is still considered to be government-controlled, although that is changing rapidly. ***Who makes economic decisions in a command economy?***

C Traditional Economy

Nomadic herders in the Andes retain many elements of a traditional economy, in which economic decisions are based on customs. ***How are the basic economic questions answered in a traditional economy?***

Economic Connection to... History

The Soviet Union's Quota System

In the former Soviet Union, workers often used resources inefficiently or completely wasted them when trying to fill government production quotas. For example, after the central planning committee ordered a quota for glass based on the number of panes, workers made *many* panes of glass—each extremely thin and shattering easily! When the production quota was changed to be based on the weight of the panes, workers made the glass panes so thick that they were useless. ■

market economy: *system in which individuals own the factors of production and make economic decisions through free interaction while looking out for their own and their families' best interests*

market: *freely chosen activity between buyers and sellers of goods and services*

Market System The opposite of a pure command economy is a pure **market economy**–also called capitalism. In a market system, economic decisions are not made by government, but by individuals looking out for their own and their families' best interests. A limited government makes it possible for individuals to decide for themselves the answers to the three basic questions. Individuals own the factors of production, and therefore choose what to produce and how to produce it. Individuals also choose what to buy with the income received from selling their labor and other resources. All of these choices are guided not by tradition or a central planning agency, but by information in the form of market prices.

A **market** is not necessarily a place. Rather, it is the *voluntary exchange* of goods and services between buyers and sellers. This exchange may take place in a worldwide market for a good such as crude oil. It may also take place in a neighborhood market for services such as paper delivery, snow shoveling, and baby-sitting.

Student Web Activity Visit the *Economics Today and Tomorrow* Web site at ett.glencoe.com and click on ***Chapter 2—Student Web Activities*** to learn more about the command economy of the former Soviet Union.

As shown in *Part A* of **Figure 2.4** on page 35, prices in a market coordinate the interaction between buyers and sellers. As prices change, they act as signals to everyone within the system as to what should be bought and what should be produced. A high price for a good generally means that it is relatively scarce. A low price suggests that it is relatively abundant. The freedom of prices to rise and fall results in a neutral, self-organizing, incentive-driven system.

The flow of resources, goods and services, and money in a market system is actually circular, as shown in **Figure 2.5.** Economists use this model, called a **circular flow of economic activity,** to illustrate how the market system works. Note how dollars flow from businesses to individuals and back to businesses again. The factors of production flow from individuals to businesses, which use them to produce goods and services that flow back to individuals. The circular flow works because the information needed for its operation is scattered among all participants in the economy.

circular flow of economic activity: *economic model that pictures income as flowing continuously between businesses and consumers*

The advantages of a pure market system are many. People have freedoms–to choose a career, to spend or not spend their income how they wish, to own private property, to take risks and earn profits. In addition, the existence of competition provides consumers in a market economy with a wide array of goods and services from which to choose, as well as an efficient system of determining how much they cost. One disadvantage of a pure market system involves concern about those too young, too old,

FIGURE 2.5

Circular Flow The inside arrows on the graph show individuals selling the factors of production to businesses, who use them to produce goods and services. The outside of the graph shows the flow of money income from businesses to individuals in the form of rents, wages, interest, and profits; and the return of money to businesses as consumer spending. ***What underlying factor makes this circular flow work?***

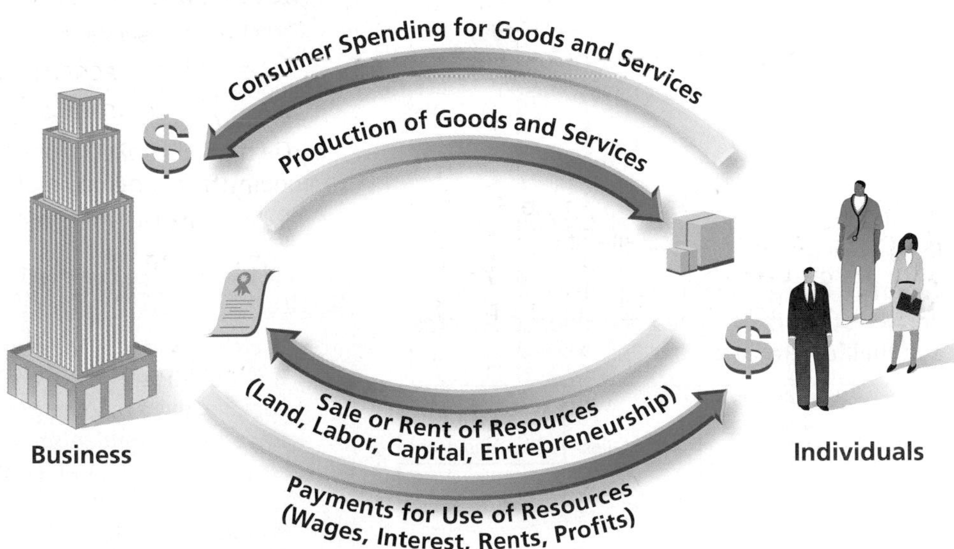

or too sick to work. Many fear that survival for these people would be difficult unless the government, churches, family members, or other organizations stepped in to provide goods and services.

mixed economy: *system combining characteristics of more than one type of economy*

Mixed System A **mixed economy** combines basic elements of a pure market economy and a command economy. Most countries of the world have a mixed economy in which private ownership of property and individual decision making are combined with government intervention and regulations. In the United States, most decisions are made by individuals reacting as participants within the market. However, federal, state, and local governments make laws protecting private property and regulating certain areas of business. In Section 2, you'll learn more about the United States's mixed economy, and the role of government in it.

To summarize, consider why a society has one type of economic system and not another. The goals that individuals set for their society help determine their economic system. The amount of government involvement in allocating scarce resources also determines a society's economic system.

Practice and **assess** key skills with ***Skillbuilder Interactive Workbook, Level 2.***

SECTION 1 Assessment

Understanding Key Terms

1. **Define** economic system, traditional economy, command economy, market economy, market, circular flow of economic activity, mixed economy.

Reviewing Objectives

2. What three questions must all economic systems answer?
3. **Graphic Organizer** In a chart like the one below, list the major types of economic systems and their differences.

Type of System	Who Answers 3 Basic Questions?	Advantages	Disadvantages

Applying Economic Concepts

4. **Economic Systems** A society's values determine how it allocates its resources. Identify and describe a societal value (for example, stability, certainty, quality, or personal freedom) that influences a traditional economy and a command economy. Then identify and describe a time in American history when each system was used.

Critical Thinking Activity

5. **Synthesizing Information** Using **Figure 2.5** as a base, make a circular flow of economic activity reflecting your own life. Replace the general information shown on **Figure 2.5** with detailed specifics about your income, items you purchase, and so on. *For help in using graphs, see page xvi in the Economic Handbook.*

Critical Thinking Skills

Making Comparisons

When you make comparisons, you determine similarities and differences among ideas, objects, or events. Making comparisons is an important skill because it helps you choose among alternatives.

- Identify or decide what will be compared.
- Determine a common area or areas in which comparisons can be drawn.
- Look for similarities and differences within these areas.

Learning the Skill

To learn how to make comparisons, follow the steps listed on the left.

Practicing the Skill

Read the passages below, then answer the questions.

> *"So long as mankind lived by raising crops and herding animals, there was not much need for measuring small units of time. The seasons were all important–to know when to expect the rain, the snow, the sun, the cold. Why bother with hours and minutes? Daylight was the only important time, the only time when men could work."*
>
> –From Daniel J. Boorstin's *The Discoverers: A History of Man's Search to Know His World and Himself*, 1985

> *"Getting workers to work at the appointed clock hours was a recurring problem. In industrial cities, a steam whistle would blow at five in the morning to wrest people from their sleep. If that proved insufficient, employers would hire 'knockers,' men who went from flat to flat 'rapping on bedroom windows with long poles.' Sometimes the knockers even pulled on strings 'dangling from a window and attached to a worker's toe.'"*
>
> –From Jeremy Rifkin's *Time Wars: The Primary Conflict in Human History*, 1987

1. What is the topic of these passages?
2. How are the passages similar? Different?

Application Activity

Survey your classmates about an issue in the news. Summarize the opinions and write a paragraph comparing the different opinions.

Practice and **assess** key skills with ***Skillbuilder Interactive Workbook, Level 2.***

SECTION 2

Characteristics of the American Economy

READER'S GUIDE

Terms to Know

- capitalism
- laissez-faire
- free enterprise system
- profit
- profit incentive
- private property
- competition

Reading Objectives

1. What is the role of government in our free enterprise economy?
2. How do freedom of enterprise and freedom of choice apply to the American economy?
3. What roles do private property, the profit incentive, and competition play in the American economy?

COVER STORY

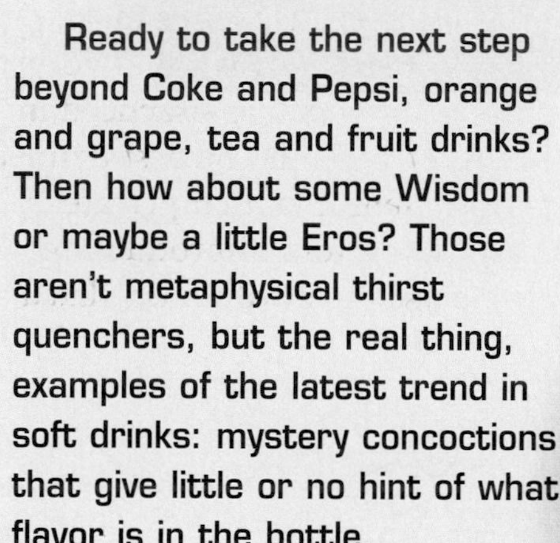

BUSINESS WEEK, MARCH 22, 1999

Ready to take the next step beyond Coke and Pepsi, orange and grape, tea and fruit drinks? Then how about some Wisdom or maybe a little Eros? Those aren't metaphysical thirst quenchers, but the real thing, examples of the latest trend in soft drinks: mystery concoctions that give little or no hint of what flavor is in the bottle.

Perhaps you wouldn't buy a soft drink called "Wisdom," but someone will. That's one of the characteristics of a market economy—freedom of choice. A seller can choose to make or not make a product, and you can choose to buy it or not.

In this section you'll learn that a pure market economic system has six major characteristics: (1) little or no government control, (2) freedom of enterprise, (3) freedom of choice, (4) private property, (5) the profit incentive, and (6) competition. These characteristics are interrelated, and all are present in the American economy to varying degrees.

Limited Role of Government

In his book *An Inquiry into the Nature and Causes of the Wealth of Nations,* economist Adam Smith in 1776 described a system in which government has little to do with a nation's economic activity. He said that individuals left on their own would work for their own self-interest. In doing so, they would be guided as if by an "invisible hand" to use resources efficiently and thus achieve the maximum good for society.

Smith's version of the ideal economic system is called **capitalism,** another name for the market system. Pure capitalism has also been called a **laissez-faire** system. The French term means "let [people] do [as they choose]." A pure capitalist system is one in which the government lets people and businesses make their own economic decisions without government constraints. Capitalism as practiced in the United States today would be best defined as an economic system in which private individuals own the factors of production, but decide how to use them within legislated limits. See **Figure 2.6.**

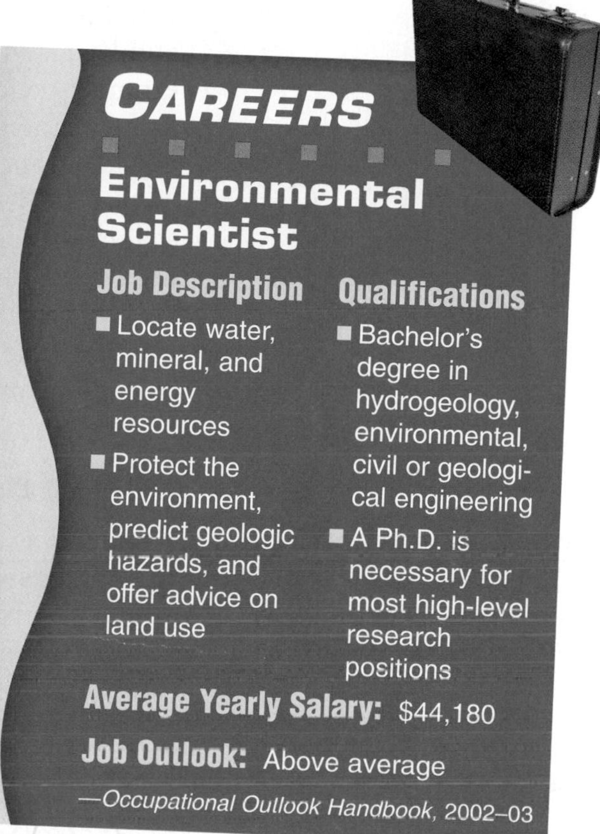

CAREERS

Environmental Scientist

Job Description

- Locate water, mineral, and energy resources
- Protect the environment, predict geologic hazards, and offer advice on land use

Qualifications

- Bachelor's degree in hydrogeology, environmental, civil or geological engineering
- A Ph.D. is necessary for most high-level research positions

Average Yearly Salary: $44,180

Job Outlook: Above average

—Occupational Outlook Handbook, 2002–03

capitalism: *economic system in which private individuals own the factors of production*

laissez-faire: *economic system in which the government minimizes its interference with the economy*

FIGURE 2.6

Role of Government The government acts as a provider of public services, such as maintaining our national parks. It also acts as protector in the form of food and drug inspection. ***List three more examples of how the government is involved in our economy.***

Smith's ideas influenced the Founders of the United States, who limited the role of government mainly to national defense and keeping the peace. Since the 1880s, however, the role of government–federal, state, and local–has increased significantly. Among other things, federal agencies regulate the quality of various foods and drugs, watch over the nation's money and banking system, inspect workplaces for hazardous conditions, and guard against damage to the environment. The federal government also uses tax revenues to provide social programs such as Social Security and Medicare. State and local governments have expanded their roles in such areas as education, job training, recreation, and care for the elderly.

Freedom of Enterprise

free enterprise system: *economic system in which individuals own the factors of production and decide how to use them within legal limits; same as* capitalism

As well as *capitalist,* the American economy is also called a **free enterprise system.** This term emphasizes that individuals are free to own and control the factors of production. If you go into business for yourself, you may become rich selling your product. However, you may instead lose money, because you–or any entrepreneur–have no guarantee of success.

The government places certain legal restrictions on freedom of enterprise. For instance, just because you know how to fix cars does not mean that you can set up an automobile-repair business in your backyard. Zoning regulations, child-labor laws, hazardous waste disposal rules, and other regulations limit free enterprise to protect you *and* your neighbors.

Freedom of Choice

Freedom of choice is the other side of freedom of enterprise. It means that buyers, not sellers, make the decisions about what should be produced. The success or failure of a good or service in the marketplace depends on individuals freely choosing what they want to buy. If a music company releases a new CD, but few people buy it, the music company most likely will not sign that particular group again. Buyers have signaled that they do not like that group.

Although buyers are free to make choices, the marketplace has become increasingly complex. The government has intervened in various areas of the economy to protect buyers. As shown in **Figure 2.7,** laws set safety standards for such things as toys, electric appliances, and automobiles. In industries dominated by just a few companies–such as public utilities selling natural gas or electricity–the government regulates the prices they may charge.

FIGURE 2.7

Freedom of Choice Consumers in a market economy have the advantage of being able to choose among products. Laws require producers to make sure that the products consumers choose are safe ones. ***How do consumers' choices determine what will be produced?***

Profit Incentive

When a person invests time, know-how, money, and other capital resources in a business, that investment is made with the idea of making a profit. **Profit** is the money left after all the costs of production have been paid, including wages, rents, interest, and taxes. The desire to make a profit is called the **profit incentive**, or profit motive. This desire motivates entrepreneurs to establish new businesses and produce new kinds of goods and services.

The risk of failing is also part of the free enterprise system. What happens when profits are *not* realized–when businesses fail? Losses are a signal to move resources elsewhere. Thus, the interaction of both profits and losses leads to an economy that is more efficient, adaptable to change, and continuously growing.

profit: *money left after all the costs of production—wages, rents, interest, and taxes—have been paid*

profit incentive: *desire to make money that motivates people to produce and sell goods and services*

Private Property

One of the most important characteristics of capitalism is the existence of **private property**, or property that is held by individuals or groups rather than by the federal, state, or local governments. You as an individual are free to buy whatever you can afford, whether it is land, a business, an automobile, or baseball cards. You can also control how, when, and by whom your property is used. What are called the rights of property, however, are actually the rights of humans to risk investment, own productive assets, learn new ways of producing, and then to enjoy the benefits if these choices result in profits.

private property: *whatever is owned by individuals rather than by government*

The Founders of the United States recognized that such rights must not be violated, because these rights are the invisible engine for creating wealth and prosperity for all. The Constitution guarantees an owner's right to private property and its use. Thus, in principle, no level of government in the United States can seize or use private property, at least not without paying the owners.

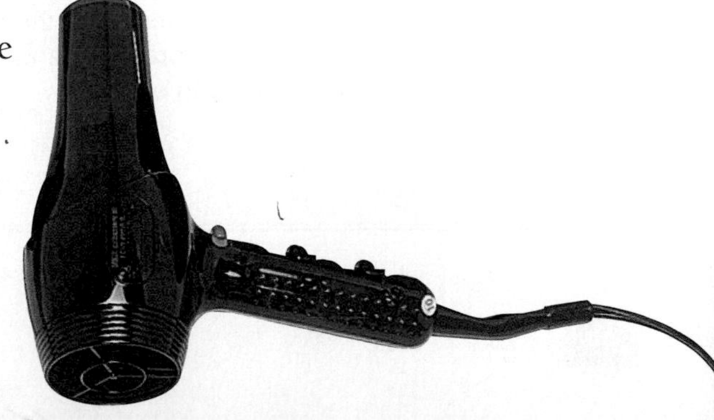

Competition

competition: *rivalry among producers or sellers of similar goods and services to win more business*

In a free enterprise system, the lure of profits encourages **competition**–the rivalry among producers of similar products to win more business by offering lower prices or better quality. Effective competition requires a large number of independent sellers, which means that no single company can noticeably affect the price of a particular product or service. If one company raises its prices, potential customers can simply go to other sellers.

Competition leads to an efficient use of resources. How so? Businesses have to keep prices low enough to attract buyers, yet high enough to make a profit. This forces businesses to keep their costs of production as low as possible.

For competition to exist, barriers to enter and exit from industries must be weak. Businesses must be free to expand into other industries. For the most part, the United States has weak barriers to entry and exit. Yet some industries have tougher barriers to entry. For example, a person cannot become a physician until he or she has received a license from a state government.

Practice and **assess** key skills with ***Skillbuilder Interactive Workbook, Level 2.***

SECTION 2 Assessment

Understanding Key Terms

1. **Define** capitalism, laissez-faire, free enterprise system, profit, profit incentive, private property, competition.

Reviewing Objectives

2. What is the role of government in our free enterprise economy?
3. How do freedom of enterprise and freedom of choice apply to the American economy?
4. **Graphic Organizer** Create a chart like the one in the next column to summarize the roles that profit incentive, private property, and competition play in the American economy.

Characteristic	Definition	Role in Capitalism

Applying Economic Concepts

5. **Competition** Describe a situation in which a lack of competition caused you to pay more for a good or service.

Critical Thinking Activity

6. **Synthesizing Information** Shoe Store A offers a pair of high-top sneakers for $48, whereas a competitor—Shoe Store B—offers the same shoe at 25 percent off their regular price of $62. From which store should you buy the shoes? *For help in understanding percentages, see page xix in the Economic Handbook.*

People & Perspectives

- Born in Kirkaldy, County Fife, Scotland
- Called the founder of classical economics
- Teacher at the University of Glasgow
- Lectured and wrote on moral philosophy
- Wrote *An Inquiry into the Nature and Causes of the Wealth of Nations* (1776)

Adam Smith

ECONOMIST (1723–1790)

In *An Inquiry into the Nature and Causes of the Wealth of Nations,* Adam Smith argues against government interference in the marketplace. He believed that individuals, seeking profit, end up benefiting society as a whole.

"[E]very individual, therefore, endeavours as much as he can [to direct his resources toward his own business] so that its produce may be of the greatest value; every individual . . . neither intends to promote the public interest, nor knows how much he is promoting it. . . . He intends only his own gain, and he is in this, as in many other cases, led by an invisible hand to promote an end which was no part of his intention. . . . By pursuing his own interest he frequently promotes that of the society more effectually than when he really intends to promote it."

Smith criticized government officials who had "the folly" to attempt to direct people in what they should produce. He believed that no single person could direct resources more efficiently than individuals watching out for their own self-interest.

"It is the maxim of every prudent master of a family, never to attempt to make at home what it will cost him more to make than to buy. The ta[i]lor does not attempt to make his own shoes, but buys them of the shoemaker. The shoemaker does not attempt to make his own clothes, but employs a ta[i]lor. The farmer attempts to make neither the one nor the other, but employs those different [craftsmen]. All of them find it [in their best interests] to employ their whole industry in a way in which they have some advantage over their neighbours, and to purchase . . . whatever else they have occasion for."

Checking for Understanding

1. **How does an "invisible hand" directing an individual's economic choices benefit society as a whole?**
2. **In Smith's opinion, why should people not attempt to "employ their resources" in many industries?**

SECTION 3

The Goals of the Nation

READER'S GUIDE

Terms to Know
- economic efficiency
- economic equity
- standard of living
- economic growth

Reading Objectives
1. What are the major goals of a market economy?
2. How can people balance economic rights with economic responsibilities?

COVER STORY

PREAMBLE TO THE CONSTITUTION OF THE UNITED STATES

We, the people of the United States, in Order to form a more perfect Union, establish Justice, insure domestic Tranquility, provide for the common defense, promote the general Welfare, and secure the Blessings of Liberty to ourselves and our Posterity, do ordain and establish this Constitution for the United States.

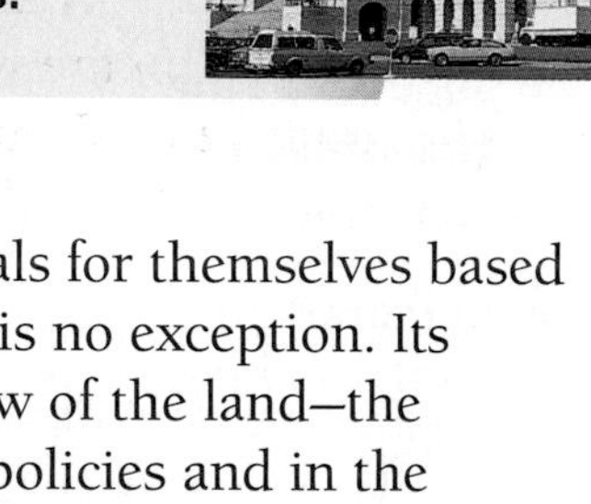

Nations have values, and they set goals for themselves based on those values. The United States is no exception. Its goals are evident in the supreme law of the land—the Constitution—as well as in its government policies and in the actions of people like you. In this section you'll learn how the American economy strives to "promote the general Welfare."

Goals of Free Enterprise

The United States has a free enterprise, or capitalist, system. Therefore, the major characteristics of a market economy should be evident in its goals. Among the national goals of Americans are freedom, efficiency, equity, security, stability, and growth. Although these goals have ethical, social, and religious elements, let's focus on their economic implications instead.

Economic Freedom The goal of economic freedom is to allow each member of society to make choices. Americans have the highest degree of freedom in the world to start their own businesses, to own private property, to make decisions in the marketplace,

Economic Freedom Along with the freedom to strive for profit comes the freedom to fail. ***What economic choices will you be free to make upon graduating from high school?***

and to pursue other economic choices. People may choose to work nights or part-time, to have several jobs, and to move from place to place in search of work.

Along with this freedom come certain costs as shown in **Figure 2.8.** In particular, individuals must normally accept the consequences of their decisions in our free enterprise system. If an entrepreneur starts a business that fails, for example, the government usually won't help out.

Economic Efficiency Using our limited resources wisely is the goal of **economic efficiency.** Because of scarcity, if the factors of production are wasted, fewer goods and services overall will be produced. We must always be watchful that the costs of our economic actions do not exceed the benefits.

economic efficiency: *wise use of available resources so that costs do not exceed benefits*

Economic Equity The issue of fairness underscores the goal of **economic equity.** Americans want their economic system to be fair and just. That's why we encourage our policy makers to pass laws such as those dealing with equal pay for equal work, fairness in hiring practices, and help for disabled workers. See **Figure 2.9.**

economic equity: *the attempt to balance an economic policy so that everyone benefits fairly*

Economic Equity Laws requiring employers to hire disabled persons and minorities aim to promote economic equity. ***What laws do you think should be passed to make our economy more fair? Explain.***

Global *Economy* 

The Cybermarket

Markets exist for just about everything—computers, natural gas, shoes, labor services, and so on. Many markets used to be confined to specific geographical areas. Today the Internet has created a virtual worldwide marketplace for many goods and services. Just consider recorded music. Since the introduction of a secure music standard, those connected to the Internet anywhere in the world can buy and download songs. Information about jobs available anywhere on the earth is also easily found via the Internet. You may answer a job announcement, interview, and be hired without ever leaving your desk! ■

Economic Security Americans understand that making profits often means taking risks. Yet we also want protection against risks beyond our control—accidents on the job, natural disasters, business and bank failures, poverty in old age. Our economic system provides such security through a number of government social programs.

Economic Stability The goal of economic stability seeks to reduce extreme ups and downs in the **standard of living**—the material well-being of an individual, group, or nation. The standard of living is measured by the average value of goods and services used by the average citizen during a given period of time. The United States has more individuals enjoying a high standard of living than almost anywhere in the world.

__standard of living:__ *the material well-being of an individual, group, or nation measured by how well their necessities and luxuries are satisfied*

__economic growth:__ *expansion of the economy to produce more goods, jobs, and wealth*

Economic Growth **Economic growth** means producing increasing amounts of goods and services over the long term. As the population increases, the economy must also expand in order to provide for additional needs and wants. All nations have economic growth as a goal because it helps meet other goals.

Trade-Offs Among Goals In a world of scarcity, achieving national goals requires trade-offs. For example, any program that provides economic security—Medicare, Social Security, or unemployment compensation—uses resources that could have been directed elsewhere.

A plan of action must be developed in order to accomplish the nation's goals. Such a plan often involves economic policy-making by elected or appointed officials who must face the reality of scarcity. Understanding this will help you realize that not all political desires can be turned into economic reality.

Rights and Responsibilities

The American free enterprise system bestows numerous economic rights and protections on individuals like you. You have

FIGURE 2.10

Economic Responsibility "There is no such thing as a free lunch." This quote, often used in economics, means that nothing is free–including your education. Tax dollars pay for you to learn how to become a productive citizen. ***What other economic responsibilities do you have?***

the right to enter into just about any profession or business you want. You have the right to work very little or to become a "workaholic." You have the right to buy those products and brands that you like and to reject all others.

A well-functioning free enterprise system will not continue, however, if individuals do not take on certain economic responsibilities. The first, of course, is to be able to support yourself and your family. As shown in **Figure 2.10,** you have a responsibility to use your education in a reasonable manner that helps you become a productive member of the free enterprise system.

Finally, because government has become such an important part of our economy, individuals in our system have the responsibility of electing responsible government officials. This responsibility requires both the knowledge of possible government policies and the ability to analyze the consequences of those policies.

Practice and **assess** key skills with ***Skillbuilder Interactive Workbook, Level 2.***

SECTION 3 Assessment

Understanding Key Terms

1. **Define** economic efficiency, economic equity, standard of living, economic growth.

Reviewing Objectives

2. **Graphic Organizer** Create a diagram like the one below to list and describe the major goals of a market economy.

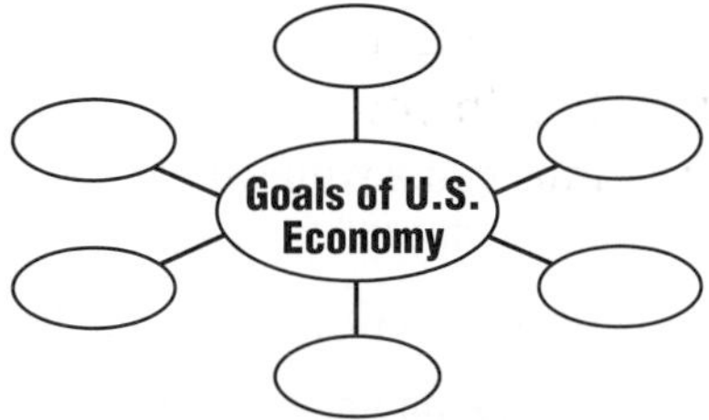

3. How can people balance economic rights with economic responsibilities?

Applying Economic Concepts

4. **Economic Goals** How can the goal of economic equity conflict with the goal of economic freedom? Provide an example for your explanation.

Critical Thinking Activity

5. **Summarizing Information** Summarize the goals of the American economy in a photo essay or through song lyrics. Share your presentation with the rest of the class. Ask class members to identify the goals evident in your presentation.

BusinessWeek

Spotlight on the Economy

Save the Species—but Add Incentives

Check It Out! In this chapter you learned about six economic goals our nation strives to meet. The following article points out how the actions of people and the government may cause some economic goals to conflict.

In 1782, when the bald eagle became the American symbol, it ruled the skies–25,000 to 75,000 patrolled what would become the lower 48 states. By the early 1960s, however, fewer than 450 nesting pairs remained. Defenseless against human predators, the bald eagle was approaching extinction.

. . . [O]n December 28, 1973, President Richard M. Nixon took decisive action to prevent that. He signed the Endangered Species Act. Despite the overwhelming support for the new law, it quickly became the most reviled piece of environmental legislation ever enacted.

With his signature, Nixon had protected not only the bald eagle but also scores of other weird animals and plants. . . .

Spotted owl

Environmentalists seized on the Act as a powerful weapon to protect sensitive habitats; meanwhile developers, loggers, and cattle ranchers, to name a few, howled in pain. . . . [C]ontroversy over protecting the spotted owl threatened to close down logging on millions of acres of forest in the Pacific Northwest. . . .

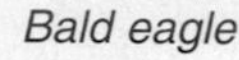

Bald eagle

Conservative critics have denounced the Act, arguing that it gives Fish & Wildlife Service biologists unlimited power to block development–without paying for it. They say that if the government cuts land values by blocking development, it should compensate the owners.

. . . Flexible interpretation of the Act now allows landowners and developers to destroy some endangered-species habitat if they agree to preserve or restore habitat for the species somewhere else. Adding more incentives, such as tax breaks, could also ease critics' concerns.

For all its shortcomings, the Act has slowed the decline of imperiled species. A few have been saved, including the bald eagle. . . .

Think About It

1. What argument do environmentalists make in support of the Endangered Species Act?
2. What argument do critics make against the Act?
3. What two economic goals are in conflict in this situation?

CHAPTER 2 Summary

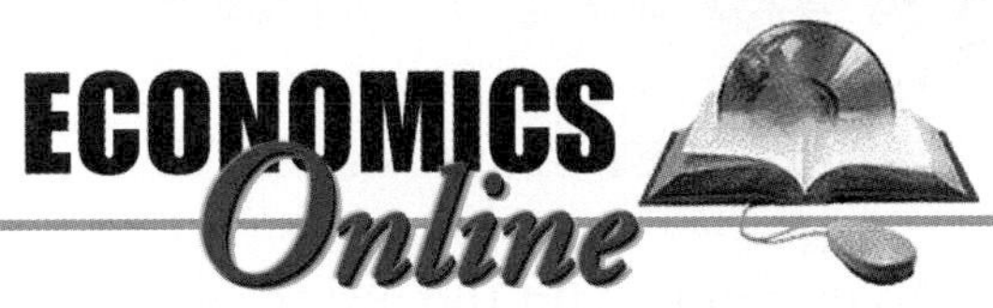

Chapter Overview Visit the *Economics Today and Tomorrow* Web site at ett.glencoe.com and click on ***Chapter 2—Chapter Overviews*** to review chapter information.

SECTION 1 Economic Systems

- Every type of **economic system** must answer three basic questions: What goods and services should be produced? How should they be produced? Who should share in what is produced?
- There are four types of economic systems: traditional, command, market, and mixed.
- In a **traditional economy,** economic decisions are based on customs and beliefs handed down from generation to generation.
- In a **command economy,** government leaders control the factors of production and, therefore, make all decisions about their use.
- In a **market economy,** individuals looking out for their own and their families' best interests make the economic decisions.
- Most countries of the world have a **mixed economy** in which private ownership of property and individual decision making are combined with government regulations.

SECTION 2 Characteristics of the American Economy

- A pure market economic system has six major characteristics: little or no government control, freedom of enterprise, freedom of choice, private property, the profit incentive, and competition.
- **Capitalism,** as practiced in the United States, has private individuals owning the factors of production but using them within the limits of the law.
- The **profit incentive** is the desire that motivates entrepreneurs to establish new businesses, expand existing ones, and change the kinds of goods and services produced.
- One of the most important characteristics of capitalism is the existence of **private property.**
- **Competition** leads to an efficient use of resources, better goods and services, and low prices for consumers.

SECTION 3 The Goals of the Nation

- The United States has a **free enterprise,** or capitalist, economic system.
- Among the economic goals of Americans are economic freedom, **economic efficiency, economic equity,** economic security, economic stability, and **economic growth.**
- A well-functioning free enterprise system requires individuals to take on certain economic responsibilities, including becoming productive members of society and electing responsible government officials.

CHAPTER 2

Assessment and Activities

Self-Check Quiz Visit the *Economics Today and Tomorrow* Web site at ett.glencoe.com and click on ***Chapter 2—Self-Check Quizzes*** to prepare for the Chapter Test.

Identifying Key Terms

Use terms from the following list to complete the sentences below.

- traditional economy
- command economy
- mixed economy
- entrepreneur
- capitalism
- free enterprise system
- private property
- profit
- invisible hand
- competition
- economic growth
- economic equity
- standard of living

1. Other terms for the market economic system are _____ and _____ .
2. Many Americans believe that their economic system accounts for the high _____ in the United States.
3. The concept of _____ allows people to buy and own land, a home, or their own business.
4. The _____ can make profits or incur great losses.
5. A person may keep the _____ they earn from selling.
6. Most people live in countries that have a _____ .
7. Adam Smith said the economy is directed by an _____ .
8. Our government promotes _____ , or fair and just economic policies.
9. The existence of _____ keeps prices low for consumers.

Recalling Facts and Ideas

Section 1

1. What basic economic question helps determine the career path of individuals?
2. What economic question is being answered if an industry replaces some workers with machines?
3. How does a traditional economy answer the basic question, "How should it be produced?"
4. Who answers the three basic economic questions in a command system?
5. Who owns the factors of production in a market economy?

Section 2

6. What are six important characteristics of free enterprise?
7. What is government's limited role in pure capitalism?
8. Why is private property important in the American economic system?

Section 3

9. What are three goals of the free enterprise system?
10. What does the United States do to promote economic security for individuals?

Thinking Critically

1. **Making Comparisons** Create a diagram like the one below to list the advantages and disadvantages of competition to buyers and sellers.

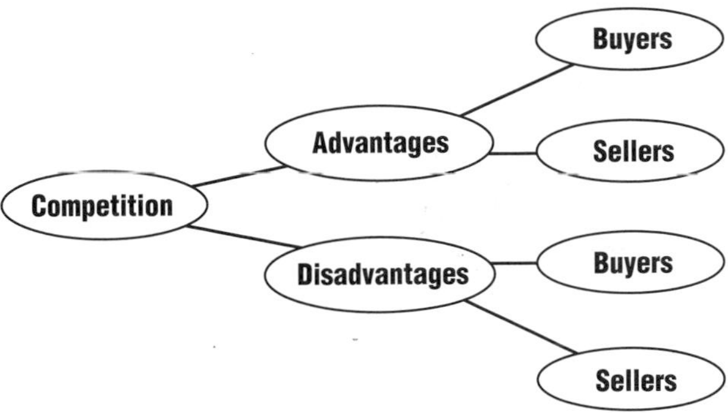

2. **Categorizing Information** Explain what U.S. economic goal is being met by the following actions: (a) The government regulates the amount that an electric company can charge you for energy. (b) Juan moves to Seattle to work for a Web page designer. (c) Your savings account is insured up to $100,000.

Applying Economic Concepts

Economic Systems An economic system within your school determines the answer to the basic question, "For whom should it be produced?" Make a list of the goods and services available to students within the school. After each item, write whether the distribution of this good or service is determined according to the principles of a market, command, or traditional economy.

Reviewing Skills

Making Comparisons Research Russia's economy today and when it was a command economy under the Soviet Union. Prepare a chart listing the similarities and differences in how the three basic economic questions were and are answered under both economies.

Cooperative Learning Project

In small groups, submit plans for a national education system in a command economy. Provide answers to such questions as: What level of education should be available without cost to everyone? Should academic achievement or testing qualify students for higher levels of education?

Technology Activity

Using a Spreadsheet Create a spreadsheet like the one below highlighting your weekly spending habits.

	A	B	C	D	E	F
1		Food	Clothing	Entertainment	Other	TOTAL
2	Monday					
3	Tuesday					
4	Wednesday					
5	Thursday					
6	Friday					
7	Saturday					
8	Sunday					
9	TOTAL					
10						

1. In cell F2, use a formula such as *=SUM(B2:E2)* to calculate total expenditures on Monday. Click and drag this formula to cells F3 through F8 to find the other weekday sums.
2. Using the above summation method, compute total expenditures for cells B9–F9.
3. Print your results.

Analyzing the Global *Economy*

Review world economic news from magazines or Web sites. List the economic decisions of several nations and make a table that classifies the decisions as supporting free market or command systems.

Economics Lab

Testing Consumer Products

From the classroom of Mitzie B. Tabor, West Carter High School, Olive Hill, Kentucky

In Chapter 2 you learned that the free enterprise system allows individuals to take risks and go into business for themselves. In this lab, you'll become a business owner and select a product to make. After shopping for the resources needed to make that product, you'll perform tests on the items to see if they are quality, yet cost-effective, goods.

STEP A Tools Needed

- ✔ copies of *Consumer Reports* magazine
- ✔ supplies pertaining to your product (see procedure #3 in the next column)
- ✔ pencil
- ✔ writing paper
- ✔ graph paper and poster board

STEP B Procedures to Follow

1. Organize into groups of three.
2. Decide upon a small business operation to run. Choose one of the product ideas that follow, or develop your own product.
   - Sell "cookie-wiches" consisting of icing between two sugar cookies.
   - Sell hot chocolate with marshmallows.
   - Sell portraits sketched with markers on drawing paper.
   - Sell orange juice-banana fruit "smoothies."
3. Gather three samples of the items (resources) you'll need to make your products. For example:
   - To make the sandwich cookies, you need three different types of sugar cookies and icing.
   - For the hot chocolate, you need three different samples of cocoa and marshmallows.
   - For the portraits, gather three different types of markers and drawing paper.
   - To make the smoothies, gather three different brand names of orange juice and bananas.

4. Now you'll devise a product-comparison test to use on the three versions of each item. Scan copies of *Consumer Reports* tests to get an idea of what categories to use in your tests—cost per unit, durability, flavor, aftertaste, ease of use, reliability, overall score, and so on.

5. Within your group, perform the product comparison tests. You may want to include the rest of the class in a blind test to get a larger response.

STEP C Creating an Economic Model

Use the results of your tests to draw a graph (bar, circle, or line) visually showing which item came out ahead of the others. Draw your graph(s) on poster board to use in a presentation to the rest of the class.

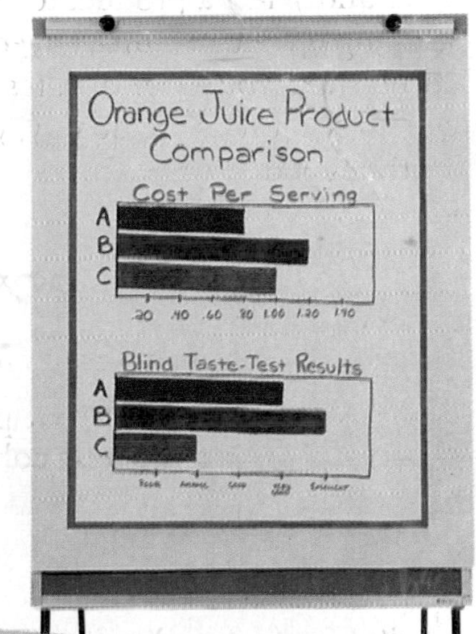

STEP D Lab Report Analysis

Study the graph that you created in step C, then answer the questions below.

1. How wide was the price difference among competing brands of resources?
2. What other factors influenced your choice of items to use in your product?
3. Were you surprised by the results of your tests? Explain.

UNIT 2

Practical Economics: How Theory Works for You

The average American owns eight credit cards.

Chapter 3
Your Role as a Consumer

Chapter 4
Going Into Debt

Chapter 5
Buying the Necessities

Chapter 6
Saving and Investing

In this unit, read to FIND OUT . . .

- how basic economic principles can help you in your daily life.
- what pitfalls to avoid when going into debt.
- what you should be aware of before buying a vehicle or house.
- why saving and investing are sound economic habits to learn.

Americans save less than 5 percent of their income.
You will spend about 14 percent of your income on food.
The median sales price of a new home is $175,200.
Americans own the most vehicles—over 200 million.
RESIDENTIAL
MORTGAGE LOANS
SAVINGS BANK
Money Market Account
FDIC
CORNER REINFORCING
HOR BOLT DETAIL
ELSIMATE EL-334A
10 Digit
0129

CHAPTER 3

Your Role as a Consumer

Why It's Important

If you are thinking about buying a computer, should you visit every computer store in the area? What should you do if your purchase is defective? This chapter will help you learn to make rational consumer choices.

To learn more about consumer choices, view the **Economics & You** *Chapter 9 video lesson:* **Your Role as a Consumer**

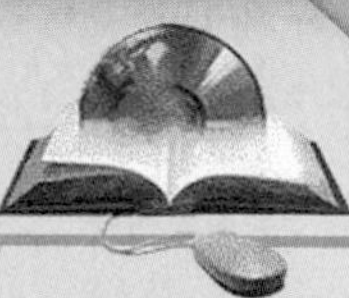

ECONOMICS *Online*

Chapter Overview Visit the *Economics Today and Tomorrow* Web site at ett.glencoe.com and click on ***Chapter 3—Chapter Overviews*** to preview chapter information.

SECTION 1

Consumption, Income, and Decision Making

COVER STORY

THE BUFFALO NEWS, JULY 1, 2003

That dog or cat may look so irresistable, but owning a pet can quickly get expensive.

Dogs don't have health insurance cards and $10 co-pays like other family members. Actually, there is such a thing as pet insurance. . . . But the insurance can be expensive, a couple hundred dollars a year, which presents another financial decision.

Frank and Nancy Mellan of Buffalo estimate they spent $3,000 to $4,000 in vet bills for their three [dogs] in the last five years.

There are trade-offs with everything when it comes to a pet.

READER'S GUIDE

Terms to Know

- consumer
- disposable income
- discretionary income
- rational choice

Reading Objectives

1. What is the difference between disposable and discretionary income?
2. What three considerations should govern your decision making as a consumer?

You and everyone around you are consumers and, as such, play an important role in the economic system. A **consumer** is any person or group that buys or uses goods and services to satisfy personal needs and wants. Consumers buy a wide variety of things—food, clothing, automobiles, movie tickets, and, as noted in the *Cover Story* above, veterinary care. In this section you'll learn how to spend—or *not* spend—your income wisely.

<u>consumer:</u> any person or group that buys or uses goods and services to satisfy personal needs and wants

Disposable and Discretionary Income

A person's role as a consumer depends on his or her ability to consume. This ability to consume, in turn, depends on available income and how much of it a person chooses to spend now or save for future spending. **Figure 3.1** shows how typical American consumers spend their money income.

disposable income: *income remaining for a person to spend or save after all taxes have been paid*

Income can be both disposable and discretionary. **Disposable income** is the money income a person has left after all taxes have been paid. People spend their disposable income on many kinds of goods and services. First, they buy the necessities: food, clothing, and housing. Any leftover income, which can be saved or spent on extras such as luxury items or entertainment, is called **discretionary income.** See **Figure 3.2.**

discretionary income: *money income a person has left to spend on extras after necessities have been bought*

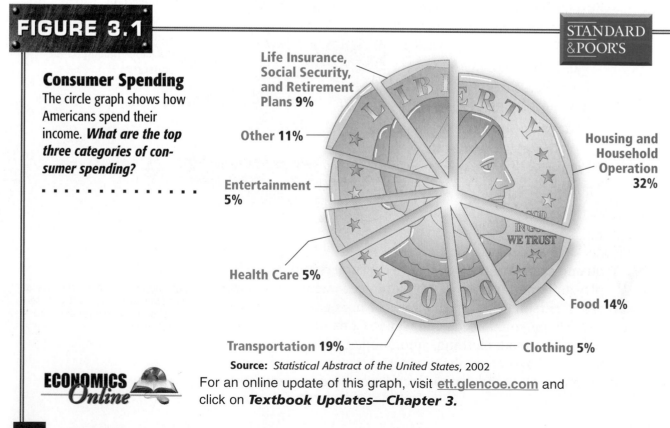

Education, occupation, experience, and health can all make differences in a person's earning power and thus in his or her ability to consume. **Figure 3.3** shows how much more you could earn with a four-year college degree. Where a person lives can also influence how much he or she earns. City dwellers tend to earn more than those who live in rural areas. Wages in some regions of the country tend to be higher than in other regions.

FIGURE 3.1

STANDARD & POOR'S

Consumer Spending

The circle graph shows how Americans spend their income. ***What are the top three categories of consumer spending?***

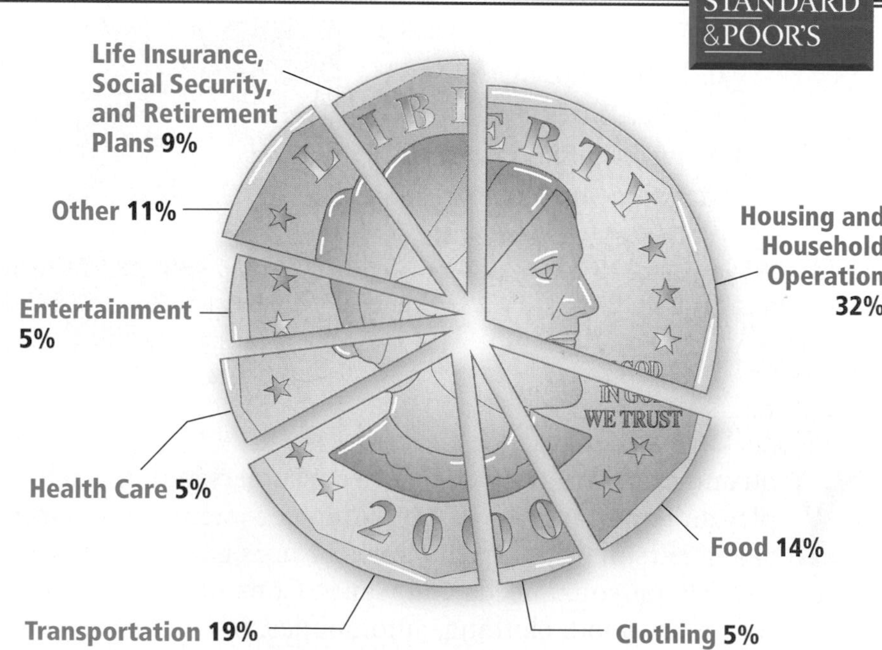

Source: *Statistical Abstract of the United States*, 2002

ECONOMICS Online

For an online update of this graph, visit ett.glencoe.com and click on ***Textbook Updates—Chapter 3.***

Discretionary Income The consumer's wants serve as a guide in spending income. Some people have more disposable and discretionary income and can therefore spend more than others on entertainment. ***What is discretionary income?***

How much a person has to spend can also be influenced by inheriting money or property.

Regardless of the size of a person's income, spending that income requires constant decision making. As a consumer, each person has a series of choices to make.

Decision Making as a Consumer

The first decision a consumer must make is whether to buy an item or not. This may sound so basic as to be unnecessary to mention, but how many times do you actually think about the reasons for the purchase you are about to make? Do you think about whether you really need the item? Do you consider the trade-offs involved?

FIGURE 3.3

Earning Power The number of years you are educated has a direct effect on your income. ***How much can you expect to make per year if you do not graduate from high school? If you graduate from college with a bachelor's degree?***

How Education Affects Income

Amount of Education	Median Income for Males	Median Income for Females
Not a High School Graduate	$18,952	$9,995
High School Graduate	$27,669	$15,120
Some College	$33,035	$20,181
Bachelor's Degree	$49,180	$30,489
Professional Degree	$81,606	$45,999

Source: *Statistical Abstract of the United States,* 2002

For an online update of this graph, visit ett.glencoe.com and click on ***Textbook Updates—Chapter 3.***

Making consumer decisions involves three parts, each including several steps. **Figure 3.4** can help guide you through the entire process. The steps in *Part A* of **Figure 3.4** will help you analyze the first consumer decision—whether to buy an item in the first place.

Global Economy

Consumers in Canada

How do our neighbors to the north spend their money? According to Statistics Canada—the Canadian equivalent of the U.S. Bureau of the Census—Canadian consumers spend each dollar as follows:

• Housing and Household Operation	$.26
• Personal Income Taxes	.21
• Transportation	.12
• Food	.11
• Insurance Payments and Pension Contributions	.05
• Recreation	.06
• Clothing	.04
• Health and Personal Care	.03
• Other	.12

Scarce Resources After you have decided to make a purchase, at least two scarce resources are involved—income and time. Before you spend your money income, you need to invest time in obtaining information about the product you wish to buy. Suppose you decide to buy a mountain bike. The time spent visiting stores checking models and prices is a cost to you. This time cannot be used for anything else.

Opportunity Cost Virtually all of the steps in consumer decision making involve an opportunity cost. Remember that opportunity cost is the value of your highest alternative choice that you did not make. In step 1 of *Part B* of **Figure 3.4,** for example, your choice between a low-, medium-, or high-quality product involves an opportunity cost.

In general, a high-quality product costs more than a low-quality product. For example, suppose that you are trying to decide between new cross-training shoes. One model has a pump system that allows you to get a closer fit on your ankle. The other model does not. The pump system model costs $80 more than the other model. If you choose the higher-priced pump system shoe, you will sacrifice $80. The opportunity cost of the pump model over the lesser-quality model shoe is therefore $80, or what you could have bought with that $80. See **Figure 3.5** on page 64.

Rational Choice When you make consumer decisions based on opportunity cost, you are engaging in **rational choice.** Economists define rational choice as the alternative that has the greatest perceived value.

<u>rational choice:</u> *choosing the alternative that has the greatest value from among comparable-quality products*

Rational choice involves choosing the best-quality item that is the least expensive from among comparable-quality products. As a consumer, you will make rational choices when you purchase the goods and services you believe can best satisfy your wants.

FIGURE 3.4 Checklist for Consumer Decision Making

Part A. Deciding to Spend Your Money
Before you buy anything, you should ask yourself:

1. Do I really require this item? Why? Real needs are few, but wants are unlimited.
2. Is this good or service worth the time I spent earning the income to pay for it?
3. Is there any better use for my income now? Should I save instead for future needs?

Part B. Deciding on the Right Purchase
After you have made up your mind to buy a good or service, you are faced with more questions:

1. Do I want high, medium, or low quality? *Quality* refers to appearance, materials used, and the length of time a product will last. For a higher price, you can usually get higher quality. For a lower price, you can usually expect a product that may not be so attractive or as long lasting. At times, such a purchase may suit your needs very well, however.
2. If I am buying an appliance or a car, do I want one that will be the most efficient to operate each year? The answer will probably involve a trade-off. A small automobile, for example, may use less gasoline than a larger one, but it provides less protection in an accident.
3. Does this particular item–a Brand Y laptop, for example–require more service than Brands A, B, and C? If so, do I want this additional problem and expense?
4. Should I wait until there is a sale on the item I want? Sales of certain items are seasonal. For example, winter clothes are on sale after Christmas and summer clothes in August.
5. If I am looking for an expensive item, should I buy it new or used? What things are better to buy new than used? How can I protect myself if I buy a used item?
6. Should I choose a product with a well-known brand name even though it costs more than a similar product without a brand name? Are there any benefits to buying a brand-name product? What are they?
7. Does anyone I know own this product so that I can get a firsthand opinion?
8. Is the warranty on this particular product comparable to warranties on similar items?
9. Is the return or exchange policy of the store where I am thinking of buying a product comparable to the policies of other stores selling similar items?
10. What do consumer magazines say about the product?

Part C. Deciding How to Use Your Purchase
Once you own something–whether it is clothing, a DVD player, or an automobile–you must decide:

1. How much time and effort should I spend personally repairing and maintaining the product?
2. How much should I spend on repairs and maintenance?
3. At what point should I replace this item? Why? (This brings you back to Part A.)

Do not get the impression that wise consumers will all make the same choices. Remember the definition: A rational choice is one that generates the greatest perceived value for any given expenditure. Rational choices that are based on careful consumer decision making will still lead to billions of different consumer choices yearly.

FIGURE 3.5

Buying Decisions If you choose the higher-priced product, you must believe that the opportunity cost for the higher quality is worth the higher price–that nothing else at that instant will give you as much value. ***What two scarce resources are involved in every consumer purchase you make?***

Practice and **assess** key skills with ***Skillbuilder Interactive Workbook, Level 2.***

SECTION 1 Assessment

Understanding Key Terms

1. **Define** consumer, disposable income, discretionary income, rational choice.

Reviewing Objectives

2. What kinds of products are purchased with discretionary income?
3. **Graphic Organizer** Create a diagram like the one below to describe three things a consumer should consider before deciding to make a purchase.

Decision to Spend Your $
1. ______
2. ______
3. ______

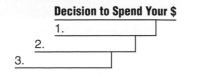

Applying Economic Concepts

4. **Rational Choice** List three major purchases you've made in the past month. Explain why you think you did or did not apply rational choice when making the purchases.

Critical Thinking Activity

5. **Categorizing Information** Draw a circle graph like **Figure 3.1**—Consumer Spending—on page 60. Develop categories that reflect how you spend your income. Then calculate and analyze the amount you spend in each category. Transpose this amount into a percentage to show your personal consumer spending as a circle graph. *For help in using circle graphs, see page xvi in the Economic Handbook.*

CRITICAL THINKING SKILLS

Distinguishing Fact From Opinion

Distinguishing fact from opinion can help you make reasonable judgments about what others say and write. Facts can be proved by evidence such as records, documents, or historical sources. Opinions are based on people's differing values and beliefs.

- Read or listen to the information carefully. Identify the facts. Ask: Can these statements be proved? Where would I find information to verify them?
- If a statement can be proved, it is factual. Check the sources for the facts. Often statistics sound impressive, but they may come from an unreliable source.
- Identify opinions by looking for statements of feelings or beliefs. The statements may contain words like *should, would, could, best, greatest, all, every,* or *always.*

LEARNING THE SKILL

To learn how to identify facts and opinions, follow the steps listed on the left.

PRACTICING THE SKILL

Read the excerpt below, then answer the questions.

"Sony's Digital Creatures Laboratory [has] introduced what is almost certainly the world's most sophisticated entertainment robot. Priced at $2,000, it's called AIBO, a Japanese word for 'companion' that's also short for Artificial Intelligence Robot. And yes, AIBO is a robotic dog. This puppy is not ready to bring you your slippers, but in sheer brain power, he puts your basic Furby to shame.

Sony hopes AIBO is just the first in a whole menagerie of artificial dogs, cats, monkeys, and creatures yet to be imagined. . . . Indeed, AIBO is just smart enough not to fall off the edge of a table. But within a few years, such companions could be running errands, helping with household chores, and assisting the handicapped."

–*Business Week,* May 24, 1999

1. What are three factual statements in the passage?
2. Which statements are opinions? Explain.

APPLICATION ACTIVITY

Record a television interview. List three facts and three opinions that were stated.

Practice and **assess** key skills with ***Skillbuilder Interactive Workbook, Level 2.***

SECTION 2

Buying Principles or Strategies

READER'S GUIDE

Terms to Know

- competitive advertising
- informative advertising
- bait and switch
- comparison shopping
- warranty
- brand name
- generic brand

Reading Objectives

1. What trade-offs occur when you are gathering information?
2. What forms of advertising exist?
3. How can you learn to practice comparison shopping?

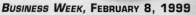

COVER STORY

BUSINESS WEEK, FEBRUARY 8, 1999

You know it's Super Bowl season in Hollywood. Top talent is switching focus from movies to 30- and 60-second ads that dazzle, that wow, and that keep millions of sports fans glued to their sets during the commercial breaks.

Companies that advertise on the championship telecast pay dearly for it—$1.6 million for one half-minute—but are rewarded with a domestic audience that is expected to exceed 140 million.

The goal of advertisements is to win your consumer dollars, and advertisers are willing to spend millions of dollars to attract your attention to their products. Because of the problems of scarce income and time, however, *your* goal should be to obtain the most satisfaction from your limited income and time. In this section, you'll learn about three basic buying principles that can help you and all consumers achieve this goal. They are: (1) gathering information; (2) using advertising wisely; and (3) comparison shopping.

Gathering Information

Suppose that you want to buy a mountain bike. After you have made this decision, you must select a brand and a model. How should you go about doing this? First, you have to obtain information about mountain bikes. You can spend time testing out friends' mountain bikes. As **Figure 3.6** shows, you could also go to different stores and discuss the good and bad points of various brands and models with salespeople. Actually, as a wise consumer, you would do both.

How Much Information Do You Need? Information is costly because obtaining it involves your time. You are faced with the problem of deciding how much information to obtain. In the case of the mountain bike, the buying principle to follow is: Obtain only as much information as is worthwhile. What, however, does *worthwhile* mean? The value of your time and effort spent gathering information should not be greater than the value you receive from making the best choice of product for yourself.

Developing a Consumer Knowledge Base As you shop for different products, you will begin to develop a consumer knowledge base. Information you obtain looking for a mountain bike might help you someday to make decisions about choosing a car or a computer. Simply getting salespeople to give you accurate information is a skill that you can acquire and sharpen over time while you shop for other products.

One relatively easy way to obtain much information in a short amount of time is to go to the Internet. Use a standard search engine to look up information on a product you wish to buy. Also, visit the numerous sites that offer such products for sale.

FIGURE 3.6

Gathering Information When shopping for a product, obtain only as much information as is worthwhile. You would not, for example, want to go to every bike store in your town or city and spend two hours with every salesperson discussing every model. In contrast, you would probably want to spend more than two minutes reading one advertisement about one model.

FIGURE 3.7 Checklist for Analyzing Ads

As you read advertisements, ask yourself:

1. Does the ad only appeal to my emotions or does it provide facts?
2. What are the special features of the product? Do I need any of these features?
3. Does the ad tell me anything about operating costs?
4. Does the ad tell me anything about a product's durability, or ability to last?
5. Does the advertised price compare favorably with the price of similar products?
6. Is the advertised price the entire price, or are there extra costs in small print?

Using Advertising Wisely

Advertising is all around you. Whenever you turn on the radio or television or log on to the Internet, you will more than likely hear or see a commercial. You also read advertising on billboards, on posters, on buses, and so on. **Figure 3.7** gives you some tips for reading these ads, which can generally be classified as competitive or informative.

Competitive Advertising Advertising that attempts to persuade consumers that a product is different from and superior to any other is **competitive advertising.** Its purpose may be to take customers away from competitors or to keep competitors from taking away customers. Ads for well-established brand names and products, such as Dell computers and Nike shoes, are often of this type. As shown in *Part A* of **Figure 3.8,** competitive ads also appeal to people's emotions.

competitive advertising: *advertising that attempts to persuade consumers that a product is different from and superior to any other*

informative advertising: *advertising that benefits consumers by giving information about a product*

Informative Advertising **Informative advertising** benefits consumers by giving information about a product. From such ads, you can learn about the existence, price, quality, and special features of products without spending much time or effort. See *Part B* of **Figure 3.8.** Informative advertising may also be competitive in nature.

FIGURE 3.8

Advertising Competitive ads often strive to evoke an emotional attachment to a product, whereas the purpose of informative ads is to provide data on a product.

A Competitive Advertisement

B Informative Advertisement

What to Look For
Some stock seats are crotch-killers, but any good shop will swap saddles; some women prefer a wider seat. The main thing is to minimize friction and pressure while pedaling.
Nine sprockets back here add up to 27 speeds on top-end bikes. Why? Closer gear ratios mean smoother shifting.
Rear suspension: heavy, pricey, so smooth.
Clipless pedals: You'll want them soon enough, so you might as well look for a bike that has them.
CANNONDALE F500 $900

Bait and Switch Some advertisers use deceptive, or false, advertising. Sellers may misrepresent the quality, features, or the true price of goods.

One of the most widely used methods of deceptive advertising is **bait and switch.** The bait is an advertised item at an unrealistically low price. When the consumer gets to the store, the item is no longer available, or the salesperson points out all the bad features of the advertised item. The salesperson then shows the customer higher-priced models and points out all their good features–the switch. This practice is both deceptive and illegal.

Careers

Advertising Manager

Job Description

- Oversees the development of advertisements
- Manages the creative services and media services departments

Qualifications

- Bachelor's degree in liberal arts, advertising, or journalism
- Knowledge of marketing and consumer behavior

Median Salary: $53,360

Job Outlook: Excellent

—*Occupational Outlook Handbook,* 2002–03

Comparison Shopping

After you have gathered the information about the make and model of the product you want, you must decide *where* to buy it. It is generally worthwhile to get information on the types and prices of products available from different stores or companies. This process is known as **comparison shopping.**

To efficiently comparison shop, read newspaper advertisements, make telephone calls, browse the Web, and visit different stores. Armed with prices that you obtain from the Web, negotiate with local merchants to get them to match (or come close to) the lowest price.

bait and switch: *ad that attracts consumers with a low-priced product, then tries to sell them a higher-priced product*

comparison shopping: *getting information on the types and prices of products available from different stores and companies*

Economic Connection to... Technology

Comparison Shopping on the Web

The Internet makes price comparisons easy. Type *comparison shopping* into your search engine. You will come up with dozens of Web sites that allow you to easily comparison shop when you know a specific brand and model of an item you wish to buy. You can also use an intelligent shopping agent, a program that continually searches the Web to find the best price for the item you wish to buy. ■

Warranties When you comparison shop, the most obvious influence on your decision will be the price you have to pay for the product. However, don't forget to find out which store offers the best **warranty**, or the promise made by a manufacturer or seller to repair or replace a product if it is found to be faulty within a certain period of time.

warranty: *promise made by a manufacturer or a seller to repair or replace a product within a certain time period if it is found to be faulty*

Brand-Name or Generic Products Another consumer choice is between buying brand-name and generic products. A **brand name** is a word, picture, or logo on a product that helps consumers distinguish it from similar products. Brand-name products are usually sold nationwide and are backed by major companies.

brand name: *word, picture, or logo on a product that helps consumers distinguish it from similar products*

Some companies produce and sell **generic brands**, which means there is no brand name at all. The word *generic* means "pertaining to a general class." It is difficult to know who produced the product. Brand-name products versus generic products will be further discussed in Chapter 5.

generic brand: *general name for a product rather than a specific brand name given by the manufacturer*

Practice and **assess** key skills with ***Skillbuilder Interactive Workbook, Level 2.***

SECTION 2 Assessment

Understanding Key Terms

1. **Define** competitive advertising, informative advertising, bait and switch, comparison shopping, warranty, brand name, generic brand.

Reviewing Objectives

2. What trade-offs occur when you are gathering information?
3. **Graphic Organizer** Create a chart like the one below to analyze and label at least 10 advertisements as to whether they are competitive or informative.

Ad Description	Type	Explain
1.		

4. How can you learn to practice comparison shopping?

Applying Economic Concepts

5. **Advertising** Think of an advertisement you've seen in the past week. Analyze the ad by applying it to the six points in **Figure 3.7** on page 68. Was the ad successful in influencing your consumer behavior? Why or why not?

Critical Thinking Activity

6. **Making Comparisons** Select a product that you use every day: a hair dryer or television, for example. Do some comparison shopping by finding at least five separate locations that sell this product. What were the differences in price for the product?

BusinessWeek

Spotlight on the Economy

Grab Some Cash, Check Out a Flick

Check It Out! In this chapter you have learned about various forms of advertising. In the following article, read to learn how advertising is popping up in some unusual places.

Is it advertising run amok? Movie trailers have come to your ATM. And more may be on the way. Full-motion video ads are now running on the screens of automated teller machines at some 7-Eleven stores in New York, Chicago, San Diego, and, naturally, Los Angeles. Customers have already seen coming attractions for some films at the convenience store, and who knows, you may yet see that *Star Wars* trailer at your local S&L.

Trailers are a natural choice for showing off the video capabilities of new, sophisticated ATMs, says Cassie Metzger, a marketing manager at Diebold, a big ATM maker. And since people often stop to pick up cash before seeing a flick, she says, a 15- or 30-second trailer, with sound, could influence what they see. The ads don't lengthen transaction time. They play while the ATM is already processing.

Banks, such as Union Federal Savings in Indiana, are still conservative. So far, they've run only bank ads. But other advertisers are expected. After all, it's a marketer's dream: Customers can't change channels and they can't walk away—at least not without leaving their cash.

Think About It

1. **Where has advertising now appeared?**
2. **Do you think this type of advertising would have an effect on your consumer decisions? Why or why not?**

SECTION 3 Consumerism

Reader's Guide

Terms to Know

- consumerism
- ethical behavior

Reading Objectives

1. What are your rights as a consumer?
2. What private and federal help can you receive as a consumer?
3. What are your responsibilities as a consumer?

Cover Story

Ohio News Network, July 7, 2003

Beginnning today, you can use a phone call to stop telemarketers.

The new national Do Not Call registry's toll-free phone line opens today. For the past two weeks, about 17 million phone numbers have been registered over the Internet. . . .

The Do Not Call Registry is the government's first list of consumers who want to block unsolicited sales calls. Phone calls from charitable organizations, political groups and companies you do business with are not covered. . . .

Most Americans are concerned with the reliability of the products and services they use. Many private groups and government actions, like the Do Not Call Registry in the *Cover Story* above, work to ensure the well-being of consumers. Consumers themselves, however, must be proactive in their buying habits. In this section, you'll learn how **consumerism**, a movement to educate buyers about the purchases they make and to demand better and safer products from manufacturers, affects you personally.

consumerism: *movement to educate buyers about the purchases they make and to demand better and safer products from manufacturers*

Consumer Rights

Since the early 1960s, consumerism has grown steadily. Businesses can no longer assume it is the buyer's responsibility to know whether a product is safe, food is healthful, or advertising is accurate. See **Figure 3.9.**

In 1962 President John F. Kennedy sent the first consumer protection message to Congress. He stated four consumer rights:

- the right to safety—protection against goods that are dangerous to life or health.
- the right to be informed—information for use not only as protection against fraud but also as the basis for reasoned choices.
- the right to choose—the need for markets to be competitive (have many firms) and for government to protect consumers in markets where competition does not exist, such as electric service.
- the right to be heard—the guarantee that consumer interests will be listened to when laws are being written.

President Richard Nixon later added a fifth right:

- the right to redress—the ability to obtain from the manufacturers adequate payment in money or goods for financial or physical damages caused by their products.

Consumer Protection
Government laws require the inspection of many products in order to protect consumers' health and safety and to raise quality standards. ***What four consumer rights did President Kennedy believe in?***

Help for Consumers

Using President Kennedy's list, Congress passed consumer-protection legislation. Today, consumers dissatisfied with a specific product can complain to the store manager or write to the manufacturer. They also may take the case to small claims court or hire a lawyer. In addition, many private and government agencies are available to help consumers.

Among the private groups that aid consumers are local citizens' action groups and local chapters of the Better Business Bureau. Many major cities and some smaller ones have Better Business Bureaus. The bureaus give consumers information on products and selling practices and help settle disagreements between buyers and sellers.

Numerous federal agencies also have programs to aid consumers. **Figure 3.10** on page 74 lists these agencies and what they do. States also have consumer affairs councils or agencies.

Consumer Responsibilities

You have consumer responsibilities as well as rights. If a product or service is faulty, it is the consumer's responsibility to initiate the problem-solving process. The Bureau of Consumer Protection suggests that you do the following:

(1) Report the problem immediately. Do not try to fix a product yourself, because doing so may cancel the warranty.

FIGURE 3.10 **Federal Agencies and Consumerism**

Agency	How It Helps the Consumer
Consumer Information Center Program	Provides free catalog of government publications on consumer topics.
Federal Trade Commission	Promotes competition by enforcing laws against monopolies, price fixing, false advertising, and other illegal business practices; regulates labeling of products and protects the public against violations of consumer credit laws.
Consumer Product Safety Commission	Protects the public against unreasonable risk of injury from consumer products; sets product safety requirements, forbids the production and sale of dangerous consumer products, and conducts research and education programs on safety concerns for industry and the public.
Government Printing Office	Sells more than 15,000 government publications on a wide variety of topics; lists those of interest to consumers in a free booklet, *Consumer Information Subject Bibliography.*
U.S. Postal Service	Through its Inspection Services, protects public from mail fraud and other violations of postal laws; through Consumer Advocate's office, acts on complaints and provides information on schemes used to cheat the public.
U.S. Department of Agriculture	Inspects and grades meat, fish, poultry, dairy products, and fruits and vegetables through the department's Food Safety and Quality Service; ensures that food production is sanitary and that products are labeled truthfully.
Bureau of Consumer Protection	Protects consumers against unfair, deceptive, or fraudulent practices; enforces a variety of consumer protection laws, as well as trade regulations; informs Congress and other government entities of the impact that proposed actions could have on consumers.
Food and Drug Administration (Department of Health and Human Services)	Protects the public against impure and unsafe foods, drugs, and cosmetics; researches and tests new products in these areas and ensures accurate labeling; publishes *FDA Consumer* magazine and maintains regional consumer affairs offices.
National Highway Traffic Safety Administration (Department of Transportation)	Sets requirements for automobile safety, maintenance, and fuel economy; tests products for compliance; researches ways to save fuel and make highways safer; investigates complaints from consumers about vehicle safety.

(2) State the problem and suggest a fair and just solution–replacement, refund, etc.

(3) Include important details and copies of receipts, guarantees, and contracts to support your case.

(4) Describe any action you have taken to try to correct the problem.

(5) Keep an accurate record of your efforts to get the problem solved. Include the names of people you speak or write to and the dates on which you communicated.

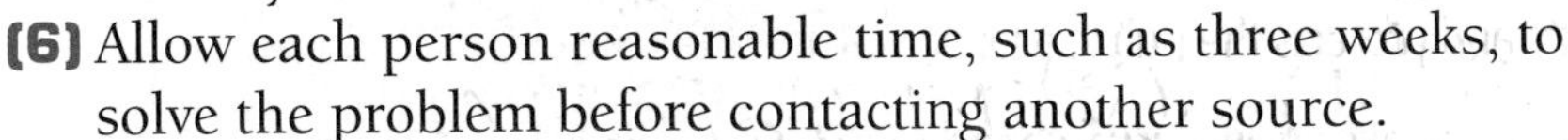

(6) Allow each person reasonable time, such as three weeks, to solve the problem before contacting another source.

(7) If you need to contact the manufacturer in writing, type your letter or send an E-mail directly. Keep a copy.

(8) Keep cool. The person who will help you solve your problem is probably not responsible for the problem.

Another responsibility of consumers is to exhibit **ethical behavior** by respecting the rights of producers and sellers. For example, a responsible consumer will not try to return a used item because it has been advertised elsewhere for a lower price.

Student Web Activity Visit the *Economics Today and Tomorrow* Web site at ett.glencoe.com and click on ***Chapter 3—Student Web Activities*** to learn more about the Office of Consumer Affairs.

ethical behavior: *acting in accordance with moral and ethical convictions about right and wrong*

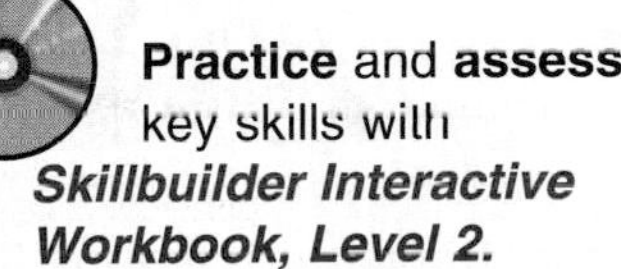

Practice and **assess** key skills with ***Skillbuilder Interactive Workbook, Level 2.***

SECTION 3 Assessment

Understanding Key Terms

1. **Define** consumerism, ethical behavior.

Reviewing Objectives

2. **Graphic Organizer** Create a diagram like the one below to list your rights as a consumer.

3. What private and federal help can you receive as a consumer?
4. What are your consumer responsibilities?

Applying Economic Concepts

5. **Consumerism** Describe two examples of how you educated yourself about a product before buying it.

Critical Thinking Activity

6. **Summarizing Information** Prepare a video or multimedia presentation for middle school students that demonstrates ethical and unethical consumer behavior. Conclude the presentation with an analysis of consumer rights and responsibilities. Share the presentation with the other members of your class.

People & Perspectives

Oprah Winfrey

ENTREPRENEUR (1954–)

- **Chairperson of HARPO Entertainment Group, a media empire**
- **Recipient of the 1996 George Foster Peabody Individual Achievement Award and the 1998 National Academy of Television Arts & Sciences' Lifetime Achievement Award**
- **One of the 100 most influential people of the 20th century (*Time,* 1998)**
- **First African American woman to become a billionaire (*Forbes,* 2003)**

Oprah Winfrey emerged from an underprivileged and abusive childhood in rural Mississippi to become one of the wealthiest and most powerful women in the United States. Today, she heads the HARPO Entertainment Group–a movie, television, and video production company headquartered in Chicago. Winfrey also hosts the widely acclaimed *The Oprah Winfrey Show,* the number-one television talk show in the world for more than 14 years. It is seen by over 15 million viewers a day in the United States and is broadcast in 132 countries.

Oprah believes that her success can be attributed, in part, to her philosophy of helping others:

> "*As a rule, we are a society that has based our lives and importance in our lives on how much we can accomplish through material goods. In the end what matters is how were you able to serve and who were you able to love.*"

She fulfills this ideal through generous donations to charities. For example, she has given millions of dollars to universities, such as Morehouse College, Spelman College, and Tennessee State University. She uses her show to encourage her viewers to "practice random acts of kindness" to make the world a better place:

> "*This show's still the thing for me. It gives me the platform to try to figure out how do you get people to lead better lives? How do you get fathers to spend more time with their children?*"

Checking for Understanding

1. **What corporation does Oprah head?**
2. **Identify ways that Oprah contributes to others.**

CHAPTER  Summary

Chapter Overview Visit the *Economics Today and Tomorrow* Web site at ett.glencoe.com and click on ***Chapter 3—Chapter Overviews*** to review chapter information.

SECTION 1 Consumption, Income, and Decision Making

- A **consumer** is any person or group that buys or uses goods and services to satisfy personal wants.
- Income can be both **disposable** and **discretionary.**
- Education, occupation, experience, and health can all make differences in a person's earning power and thus in his or her ability to consume.
- Making consumer decisions involves three parts: (1) deciding to spend your money; (2) deciding on the right purchase; and (3) deciding how to use your purchase.
- When you make consumer decisions based on opportunity cost, you are engaging in **rational choice.**

SECTION 2 Buying Principles or Strategies

- Three basic buying principles that can help you obtain the most satisfaction from your limited income and time are gathering information, using advertising wisely, and comparison shopping.
- The value of your time and effort spent gathering information should not be greater than the value you receive from making the best choice of product.
- Most advertising falls under one of two types: **competitive advertising** or **informative advertising.** Be aware of deceptive advertising, which includes **bait and switch.**
- To efficiently **comparison shop,** read newspaper advertisements, make telephone calls, surf the Internet, and visit different stores. Also consider the product's **warranty,** and **brand-name** versus **generic** manufacturers.

SECTION 3 Consumerism

- **Consumerism** is a movement to educate buyers about the purchases they make and to demand better and safer products from manufacturers.
- Consumer advocates promote the following consumer rights: the right to safety, to be informed, to choose, to be heard, and to redress.
- Private groups that aid consumers include local citizens' action groups and the Better Business Bureau.
- Numerous federal agencies have programs to aid consumers, including the Consumer Product Safety Commission and the Food and Drug Administration.
- Consumers' responsibilities include reading contracts and warranties, following directions for proper use of the product, initiating the problem-solving process, and exhibiting **ethical behavior.**

CHAPTER 3

Assessment and Activities

Self-Check Quiz Visit the *Economics Today and Tomorrow* Web site at ett.glencoe.com and click on ***Chapter 3—Self-Check Quizzes*** to prepare for the Chapter Test.

Identifying Key Terms

Write the letter of the definition in Column B that correctly defines each term in Column A.

Column A

1. disposable income
2. warranty
3. bait and switch
4. comparison shopping
5. competitive advertising
6. informative advertising
7. generic brand
8. consumer
9. discretionary income
10. brand name

Column B

a. deceptive advertising
b. getting information about similar types of products and prices
c. "pertaining to a general class"
d. money income left after paying taxes
e. attempts to persuade consumers that certain products are superior to others
f. written guarantee of a product
g. income left after buying necessities
h. provides information about the price, quality, and features of products
i. logo on a product
j. person or group that buys or uses goods and services to satisfy personal wants

Recalling Facts and Ideas

Section 1

1. Before you buy anything, what three questions should you ask yourself?
2. Do all rational consumers think alike? Why or why not?

Section 2

3. What are three important buying principles?
4. What are two types of advertising?
5. How much information should you obtain before you make a purchase?

Section 3

6. What are the four consumer rights that President John F. Kennedy stated?
7. What are two consumer responsibilities?

Thinking Critically

1. **Understanding Cause and Effect** Create a diagram like the one below to explain how education, occupation, and location make a difference in a person's earning power.

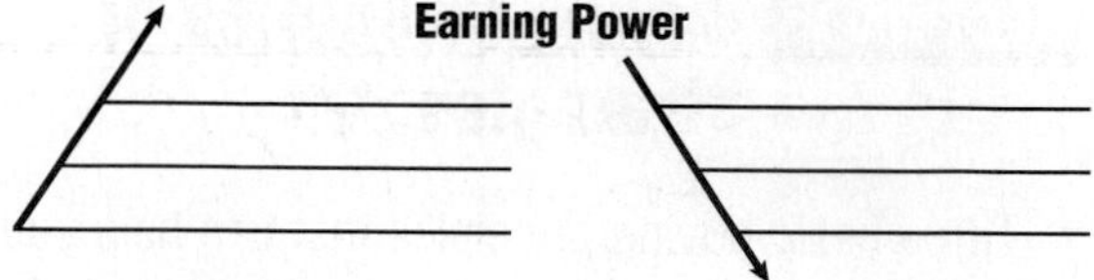

2. **Making Generalizations** Why do some people buy brand-name products and other people buy generic products? What are the trade-offs involved in this decision?

Applying Economic Concepts

Competition and Market Structure Design a print advertisement for a product of your choosing. After you complete the ad, use the checklist on page 68 to analyze it. Write a sentence to answer each of the questions on the checklist. Do you think it is a competitive ad, an informative ad, or both? Explain.

Cooperative Learning Project

Working in groups of four, take a copy of the checklist on page 63 and shop for one of the following: DVD player, portable CD player, or personal computer. Each of you should keep a record of the steps you take and the information you gather using a table like the one below. Compare your information with what others in the class found.

Checklist Number	Step	Information
1.		
2.		
3.		

Reviewing Skills

Distinguishing Fact From Opinion Analyze the advertisement below, then answer the questions that follow.

1. Which of the statements in the ad are based on facts? Explain.
2. Which of the statements are based on opinion? Explain.

WE DELIVER!

Air freight. Ocean services. Less-than-truckload. Full truckload. Nationally. Globally.

We're a group of market-leading businesses that deliver in a "need-it-now" world.

We're a $5 billion company, with 33,000 people, 25,000 pieces of equipment, up to 100 jet freighters, and the industry's most advanced information systems.

Technology Activity

Using E-Mail Many consumers will complain about a defective product or lousy service to friends and family members. Learn to address a problem purchase with someone who can solve it—the manufacturer. Think of a product or service you were dissatisfied with after purchasing it. Practice writing an E-mail to the manufacturer using the outline below.

Your Address
City, State, ZIP Code
Phone
Date

Customer Service Department
Company Name
Street Address
City, State, ZIP Code

Dear Customer Service Representative:

I bought a (product name, serial no., model no.) at (location and date of purchase). Unfortunately, (state problem, history of problem, and efforts to solve it).

I would appreciate your (state specific actions to be taken). Enclosed are copies of the following records: (list and enclose all documents connected with the problem).

I am looking forward to your reply and resolution of my problem and will wait (state reasonable time period) before seeking third party assistance. Please contact me at the above address or by phone.

Sincerely,

Analyzing the Global Economy

Research how consumers in other countries resolve unsatisfactory purchases. Use the Internet to find government agencies in foreign nations that have duties similar to the United States Department of Commerce.

Focus on Free Enterprise

Dell Computer Corporation

Michael Dell loved to tinker with computers. By the time he reached high school, he could break down and reassemble an Apple computer with ease. Also, he knew exactly what he wanted to do when he finished school—run his own business. His parents, however, had other ambitions for him. They wanted him to be a doctor. Bowing to their wishes, Dell enrolled as a premed student at the University of Texas in Austin in 1983.

Student Entrepreneur

Many students take on part-time jobs to help pay their college expenses. Dell was no exception, although the job he took was rather exceptional. He ran his own computer company! Dell bought outdated PCs from local computer stores and upgraded them with the latest technology. At first, he sold the refurbished PCs to university students. Then he started selling them by mail order.

As the business became more successful, Dell's dorm room started to look like a warehouse. PCs and computer parts occupied every free inch of space. He even used the bathtub as a storage area! Of course, running the business left him little time for his studies. When his parents discovered this, they were furious. They told him to focus on his schoolwork. Dell reluctantly agreed, promising to limit his business activities to the summer vacation.

Dell's business boomed that summer. In the last month of the vacation, he recorded $180,000 in sales. He never returned for his

sophomore year at the University of Texas. Instead, he went into the computer business full time, setting up Dell Computer Corporation in Austin. Rather than upgrade old computers, Dell Computer built new ones from scratch. The results were the same. The company consistently racked up impressive sales figures.

Dell Direct

Dell Computer Corporation's success is a result of its business approach–the direct business model. Rather than sell computers through dealers, Dell sells directly to consumers. Instead of having huge warehouses stacked with ready-made computers, Dell makes computers to customer specifications. Fast delivery–within two weeks of ordering–and excellent technical service are also part of Dell's direct business model. This approach results in cheaper, more up-to-date computers for consumers.

At first, customers ordered computers from Dell by mail or telephone. After the introduction of the Internet, Dell also offered an online ordering service. Michael Dell immediately saw the potential of the Internet: "[Y]ou could order anything [online]–including a computer. And the great thing was, you needed a computer to do this! I couldn't imagine a more powerful creation for extending our business."

Dell's view proved correct. Today, the Dell Computer Corporation Web site logs about 1 billion visitors per quarter. It generates over $50 million in sales per day, making Dell one of the leading companies in Internet commerce.

An Industry Leader

From its beginnings as a one-person, dorm-room operation in 1983, Dell Computer has grown into a multinational corporation. It maintains manufacturing centers and sales offices in several countries, and employs more than 40,000 people. With yearly revenues in the billions of dollars, Dell is the world's second-largest–only Compaq is bigger–and fastest-growing major computer manufacturer.

Future Plans

Michael Dell's immediate plans for his company involve continuing growth through increased Internet sales. To this end, Dell launched a new Web site–Gigabuys.com–in 1999. The Dell Computer Corporation's original Web site sells only Dell computers and various accessories needed to run them. Gigabuys, however, sells an array of products–everything from computers to printer paper. Introducing consumers to his services, Dell hopes, will help achieve his long-term goal–for everyone to own a Dell computer!

Free Enterprise in Action

1. **What is the Dell direct business model?**
2. **Why did Michael Dell feel that the development of the Internet was important for his company?**

Going Into Debt

Why It's Important

How do credit cards work? What happens if you can't pay back the amount of credit you've borrowed? This chapter will explain what you need to know before applying for credit and going into debt, and how to use credit wisely.

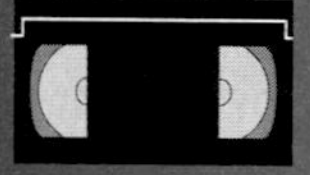

To learn more about using credit, view the **Economics & You** *Chapter 10 video lesson:* **Going Into Debt**

ECONOMICS *Online*

Chapter Overview Visit the *Economics Today and Tomorrow* Web site at ett.glencoe.com and click on ***Chapter 4—Chapter Overviews*** to preview chapter information.

SECTION 1

Americans and Credit

Cover Story

The Washington Post, May 10, 1999

Debt is not itself a bad thing. Used properly, credit allows young families to buy their own homes and acquire other trappings of middle-class life without waiting until middle age. Homeownership, in turn, gives these families a stake in their communities and encourages them to take an active role in keeping it a good place to live.

But easy credit—and plainly credit is very easy today—creates a temptation to push the envelope, to live at a higher level than the borrower can safely afford.

Reader's Guide

Terms to Know

- credit
- principal
- interest
- installment debt
- durable goods
- mortgage

Reading Objectives

1. What are the advantages of repaying installment debt over a long period?
2. Why do people go into debt?
3. What factors should you consider when deciding whether or not to use credit?

Americans use credit to make many purchases. The total amount of funds borrowed and lent each year is enormous. In addition to individuals borrowing funds, the federal, state, and local governments all borrow funds, too. The nation's economy, in fact, depends on individuals and groups being able to buy and borrow on credit. In this section, you'll learn what credit is and why people use it.

What Is Credit?

Credit is the receiving of funds either directly or indirectly to buy goods and services today with the promise to pay for them in the future. The amount owed–the debt–is equal to the principal

credit: *receipt of money either directly or indirectly to buy goods and services in the present with the promise to pay for them in the future*

principal: *amount of money originally borrowed in a loan*

interest: *amount of money the borrower must pay for the use of someone else's money*

plus interest. The **principal** is the amount originally borrowed. The **interest** is the amount the borrower must pay for the use of someone else's money. That "someone else" may be a bank, a credit card company, or a store.

Any time you receive credit, you are borrowing funds and going into debt. Taking out a loan is the same as buying an item on credit. In both cases, you must pay interest for the use of someone else's purchasing power.

installment debt: *type of loan repaid with equal payments, or installments, over a specific period of time*

durable goods: *manufactured items that have a life span longer than three years*

Installment Debt

One of the most common types of debt is **installment debt.** Consumers repay this type of loan with equal payments, or installments, over a period of time; for example, 36 equal payments over 36 months. Many people buy **durable goods,** or manufactured items that last longer than three years, on an installment plan. Automobiles, refrigerators, washers, and other appliances are

FIGURE 4.1

Increase in Borrowing More and more Americans are choosing to buy durable goods on credit. ***By how much did consumer debt increase between 1993 and 2003?***

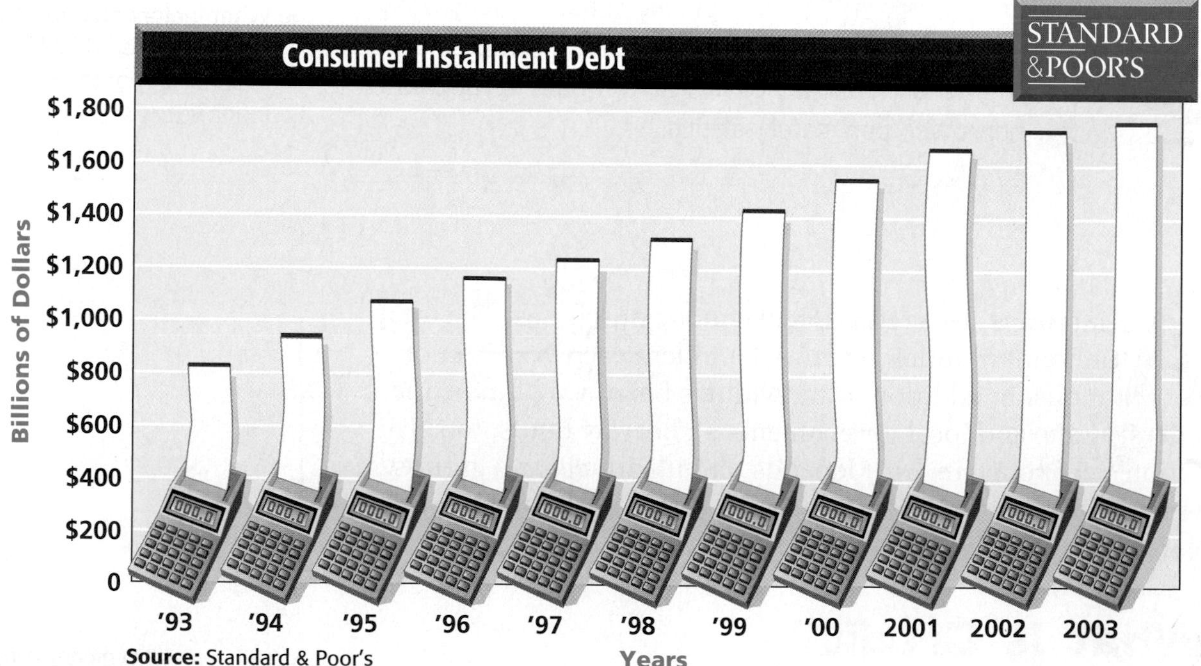

Source: Standard & Poor's

For an online update of this graph, visit ett.glencoe.com and click on ***Textbook Updates—Chapter 4.***

considered durable goods. People can also borrow cash and pay it back in installments. **Figure 4.1** shows how consumer installment debt owed each year in the United States has steadily increased.

The length of the installment period is important in determining the size of the borrower's monthly payments and the total amount of interest he or she must pay. A longer repayment period results in a smaller monthly payment. For example, **Figure 4.2** shows that if the repayment of a loan is spread over three years, the monthly payments will be smaller than if the loan were repaid in two years. There is a trade-off, however. The longer it takes to repay an installment loan, the greater the total interest the lender charges.

The largest form of installment debt in this country is the money people owe on mortgages. A **mortgage** is an installment debt owed on real property—houses, buildings, or land. See **Figure 4.3.** Interestingly, most people who owe a mortgage on their home do not consider themselves deeply in debt. Because people must have housing, they think of a mortgage as being a necessary monthly payment not similar to other kinds of debt. A mortgage is a debt, however, because somebody has provided the owner with funds to purchase property. In return, the owner must repay the loan with interest in installments over a number of years.

FIGURE 4.3

Installment Debt Mortgages make up the largest form of installment debt in the country. Most mortgages are repaid in monthly installments for 15 to 30 years.

mortgage: *installment debt owed on houses, buildings, or land*

FIGURE 4.2

Pay Now or Pay Later? Your monthly payment is lower if you choose the 36-month loan. ***How much more interest will you pay, however, if you spread the loan payment over 36 months rather than 24 months?***

$1,000 Installment Loan at 9% Interest

Term of Loan	24 Months	36 Months
Monthly Payments	$45.69	$31.80
Total Interest	$96.56	$144.80
Total Payments	$1,096.56	$1,144.80

Why People Use Credit

In a sense, people feel forced to buy items on credit because they believe they require these items immediately. They do not want to wait. Of course, consumers are not really "forced" to buy most goods and services on credit. They could decide instead to save the funds needed to make their purchases.

Some might say that you would be better off saving and waiting to buy a pickup truck. During the years you are saving for the truck, however, you forgo the pleasure of driving it. Many people do not want to postpone purchasing an important durable good. They would rather buy on credit and enjoy the use of the item now rather than later. See **Figure 4.4.**

FIGURE 4.4

Spreading Payments

Suppose you want to buy a pickup truck that costs $15,000. You have a choice. You could borrow $15,000 right now and buy the truck, but you would have to make interest payments on the borrowed funds for three to five years. However, you can also enjoy using it at the same time you are paying for it. Alternatively, you could start saving now, earn interest on your savings, and pay cash for the truck in several years.

Another reason for going into debt is to spread the payments over the life of the item being purchased. For example, people do not buy a truck or car to have it sit in the garage. What they buy is the availability of the vehicle each day, week, month, and year that they own it.

Suppose you buy the pickup truck for $15,000 and plan to keep it for five years. At the end of that time, it will be worth only $5,000. Over that five-year period, however, you will get approximately $2,000 worth of use per year, or $166 per month. By buying on the installment plan, a person makes monthly payments that more or less correspond to the value of the use he or she receives from the product.

Deciding to Use Credit

The decision to borrow or use credit involves whether the satisfaction the borrower gets from the purchases is greater than the interest payments. It is basically a question of comparing costs and benefits. The benefit of borrowing is being able to buy and enjoy the good or service now rather than later. The cost is whatever the borrower must pay in interest or lost opportunities to buy other items.

The benefit of borrowing is something only you can decide for yourself. You and every other borrower, however, should be aware of the costs involved. **Figure 4.5** can help you decide when to use credit. It can also help you avoid the improper use of credit by overspending.

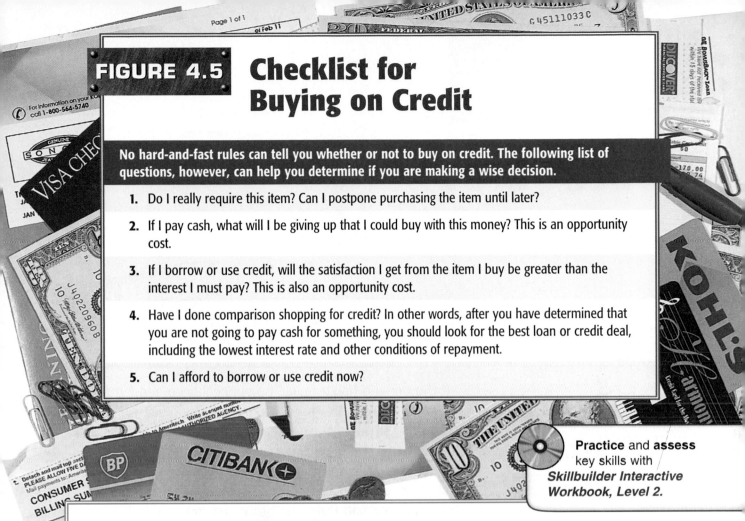

FIGURE 4.5 Checklist for Buying on Credit

No hard-and-fast rules can tell you whether or not to buy on credit. The following list of questions, however, can help you determine if you are making a wise decision.

1. Do I really require this item? Can I postpone purchasing the item until later?
2. If I pay cash, what will I be giving up that I could buy with this money? This is an opportunity cost.
3. If I borrow or use credit, will the satisfaction I get from the item I buy be greater than the interest I must pay? This is also an opportunity cost.
4. Have I done comparison shopping for credit? In other words, after you have determined that you are not going to pay cash for something, you should look for the best loan or credit deal, including the lowest interest rate and other conditions of repayment.
5. Can I afford to borrow or use credit now?

Practice and **assess** key skills with ***Skillbuilder Interactive Workbook, Level 2.***

SECTION 1 Assessment

Understanding Key Terms

1. **Define** credit, principal, interest, installment debt, durable goods, mortgage.

Reviewing Objectives

2. What are the advantages of repaying installment debt over a long period?
3. Why do people go into debt?
4. **Graphic Organizer** Create a diagram like the one below to list the factors you should consider when deciding whether to use credit.

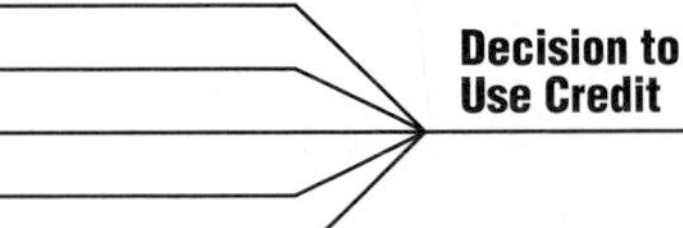

Applying Economic Concepts

5. **Opportunity Cost** Think of an item that you have been saving for. How long will it take you to save the funds needed to purchase this item? What are you giving up buying in the meantime? Explain why you are giving up buying that particular item.

Critical Thinking Activity

6. **Synthesizing Information** Imagine that you are shopping for a used car. If you borrow $10,000 to buy a used car, and the simple interest rate on the loan is 11 percent, what will your total payment be at the end of 24 months? At the end of 36 months? *For help in understanding interest rates, see page xxii in the Economic Handbook.*

SECTION 2

Sources of Loans and Credit

READER'S GUIDE

Terms to Know

- commercial bank
- savings and loan association
- savings bank
- credit union
- finance company
- charge account
- credit card
- finance charge
- annual percentage rate (APR)

Reading Objectives

1. What are six types of financial institutions?
2. What three kinds of charge accounts are available from stores?
3. How are credit cards used?
4. How do a finance charge and an annual percentage rate differ?

COVER STORY

KIPLINGER'S PERSONAL FINANCE MAGAZINE, NOVEMBER 2000

If the coming holidays will be supercharge season for your credit cards, it's more important than ever to know when payments are due. Card issuers have hair triggers when it comes to assessing late fees, so if your check arrives even one day late, you'll probably be slapped with a $29 penalty....

Fortunately, you may now get some breathing room. When Citibank recently acquired 13 million Universal card accounts, it declared that payments would never be due on holidays or weekends.

There are two major types of credit—using credit cards and borrowing money directly from a financial institution. Although lending institutions differ in their services, they all charge interest on the funds they lend. In this section, you'll learn what those financial institutions are. You'll also learn about charge accounts and credit cards—and why you should be aware of the high interest rates they charge.

Types of Financial Institutions

You should comparison shop when you have decided to apply for a loan. See **Figure 4.6.** To gather information, check various lending agencies in person, over the phone, or at their Web sites.

Commercial Banks The first place you might think to go for a loan is a **commercial bank.** Commercial banks today control the largest amount of money and offer the widest range of services. These services include offering checking and savings accounts and loans to individuals. They also transfer funds among banks, individuals, and businesses.

Savings and Loan Associations A **savings and loan association (S&L),** like a commercial bank, accepts deposits and lends funds. S&Ls make many single-family and multi-family dwelling mortgage loans. They also finance commercial mortgages and auto loans. Their interest rates for loans are often slightly less than those for commercial banks.

Savings Banks **Savings banks** were first set up to serve the small savers who were overlooked by the large commercial banks. Most savings banks, like S&Ls, lend funds for home mortgages, although they do make personal and auto loans. Since 1980, savings banks, like commercial banks, have also been able to offer services similar to checking accounts.

Credit Unions Union members and employees of many companies often have a credit union. A **credit union** is owned and operated by its members to provide savings accounts and low-interest loans only to its members. Credit unions primarily make personal, auto, and home improvement loans, although larger

<u>**commercial bank:**</u> *bank whose main functions are to accept deposits, lend money, and transfer funds among banks, individuals, and businesses*

<u>**savings and loan association (S&L):**</u> *depository institution that accepts deposits and lends money*

<u>**savings bank:**</u> *depository institution originally set up to serve small savers overlooked by commercial banks*

<u>**credit union:**</u> *depository institution owned and operated by its members to provide savings accounts and low-interest loans only to its members*

A Savings Bank

B Finance Company

C Commercial Bank

FIGURE 4.6

Financial Institutions Financial institutions differ in several factors, including differences in interest rates and loan repayment terms.

credit unions offer home mortgages as well. In general, credit unions offer higher interest rates on savings and charge lower interest rates on loans than other financial institutions.

finance company: *company that takes over contracts for installment debts from stores and adds a fee for collecting the debt; a consumer finance company makes loans directly to consumers at high rates of interest*

Finance Companies A **finance company** takes over contracts for installment debts from stores and adds a fee for collecting the debt. The consumer pays the fee in the form of slightly higher interest than he or she would pay to the retailer. Retailers use this method to avoid the risks involved in lending money to consumers.

A *consumer finance company* makes loans directly to consumers at relatively high rates of interest—often more than 20 percent a year. The people who use consumer finance companies are usually unable to borrow from other sources with lower rates because they have not repaid loans in the past or have an uneven employment record.

CAREERS

Consumer Loan Officer

Job Description
- Analyze loan applications
- Make decisions regarding the extension of credit

Qualifications
- Bachelor's degree in finance, economics, or a related field

Salary: $41,420

Job Outlook: Above average

—*Occupational Outlook Handbook, 2002–03*

Charge Accounts

A second major type of credit is extended directly to an individual, without that person having to borrow money first. This credit may be in the form of a charge account or a credit card. As shown in **Figure 4.7,** a **charge account** allows a customer to buy goods or services from a particular company and pay for them later. Department stores, for example, offer three types of charge accounts: regular, revolving, or installment.

charge account: *credit extended to a consumer allowing the consumer to buy goods or services from a particular company and to pay for them later*

Regular Charge Accounts A *regular charge account,* also known as a 30-day charge, has a credit limit such as $500 or $1,000. A *credit limit* is the maximum amount of goods or services a person or business can buy on the promise to pay in the future. At the end of every 30-day period, the store sends a bill for the entire amount. No interest is charged, but the entire bill must be paid at that time. If it is not, interest is charged on the unpaid amount.

Revolving Charge Accounts A *revolving charge account* allows you to make additional purchases from the same store even if you have not paid the previous month's bill in full. Usually you must pay a certain portion of your balance each

FIGURE 4.7

Charge Accounts Many stores issue their own charge cards, which consumers may use to purchase goods in their stores. ***What is a credit limit?***

month–one-fifth of the amount due, for example. Interest is charged on the amount you do not pay. Of course, if you pay everything you owe each month, no interest is charged. This type of account also has a credit limit.

Installment Charge Accounts Major items such as sofas, televisions, and refrigerators are often purchased through an *installment charge account*. The items are purchased and paid for through equal payments spread over a period of time. Part of the amount paid each month is applied to the interest, and part is applied to the principal. At the end of the payment period, the borrower owns the item he or she has made payments on.

credit card: *credit device that allows a person to make purchases at many kinds of stores, restaurants, and other businesses without paying cash*

Credit Cards

A **credit card,** like a charge account, allows a person to make purchases without paying cash. The difference is that credit cards can be used at many kinds of stores, restaurants, hotels, and other businesses throughout the United States and even foreign countries. As shown in **Figure 4.8,** Visa, MasterCard, and others issue cards through banks. These cards can be used to purchase items in stores that accept them, or they may be used to borrow funds up to a certain limit. This gives consumers access to loans at all times without having to apply for them.

FIGURE 4.8

Credit Card Trade-Off
Although using credit cards is convenient, it is also costly. Stores must pay a certain percentage of credit purchases to the company that issued the card. The stores include this cost in the prices they charge customers, making prices higher for everyone. ***What is the difference between a credit card and a charge account?***

Finance Charges and Annual Percentage Rates

The terms *finance charge* and *annual percentage rate* tell the consumer the same thing–the cost of credit. Each, however, is expressed in a different way.

finance charge: *cost of credit expressed monthly in dollars and cents*

Finance Charges

The **finance charge** is the cost of credit expressed in dollars and cents. It must take into account interest costs plus any other charges connected with credit. For example, yearly membership fees for the use of a credit card are included in the finance charge.

The way finance charges are computed is an important factor in determining the cost of credit. Store charge accounts and credit cards use one of four methods to determine how much people will pay for credit: previous balance, average daily balance, adjusted balance, or past due balance. Each method applies the interest rate to an account's balance at a different point during the month. The different methods can result in widely varying finance charges. See **Figure 4.9.**

annual percentage rate (APR): *cost of credit expressed as a yearly percentage*

Annual Percentage Rates

The **annual percentage rate (APR)** is the cost of credit expressed as a yearly percentage. Like the finance charge, the APR must take into account any noninterest costs of credit such as a membership fee. **Figure 4.10** on page 94 shows how a sample APR affects the cost of credit.

Knowing which creditor is charging the most for credit would be very difficult without some guide for comparison. The APR provides that guide by allowing consumers to compare costs regardless of the dollar amount of those costs or the length of the credit agreement. Suppose creditor A is charging an APR of 16 percent, while creditor B is charging 17 percent, and creditor C is charging $18\frac{1}{2}$ percent. On a yearly basis, creditor C is charging the most for credit and creditor A the least.

Economic Connection to... History

The First Credit Card

In 1958 the Bank of America mailed 60,000 BankAmericards to customers in Fresno, California. Each card had a credit line of $300 to $500 and could be used at 300 stores in the area. The next year, the bank mailed out 2 million cards and persuaded 20,000 stores to accept them.

Initially, BankAmericard proved a financial disaster. Unpaid accounts ran above 20 percent, and credit-card fraud was rampant. By early 1960, the losses on BankAmericard approached $9 million. The bank quickly addressed these problems, and within a year BankAmericard was turning a profit. ■

FIGURE 4.9 Different Methods of Computing Finance Charges

Type of Method	How Finance Charge Is Computed	Example (Based on opening balance of \$300, \$150 paid halfway through month, monthly interest rate = 1.5%)
Previous Balance	Charge is computed on the month's opening balance, even if the bill has been paid in full by the time the finance charge is figured. There is no benefit in paying off a debt early with this method.	• Amount on which interest is due: \$300, despite payment • Calculation: \$300 × .015 = \$4.50 • Finance charge: \$4.50 • Balance due: \$154.50
Adjusted Balance	Payments made during the month are deducted from the opening balance. Charge is then computed on the balance due the last day of the month. With this method you can save the most money if you pay your bill as soon as possible.	• Amount on which interest is due: \$150, balance on last day of billing period • Calculation: \$150 × .015 = \$2.25 • Finance charge: \$2.25 • Balance due: \$152.25
Average Daily Balance	Charge is applied to the sum of the actual amounts owed each day during the billing period, divided by the number of days in that period. Payments and credits–return of goods–are subtracted on the exact date of payment. With this method you can save the most money if you pay your bill as soon as possible.	• Amount on which interest is due: \$225 • Calculation: 15 days × \$300 = \$4,500 15 days × \$150 = \$2,250 30 days total = \$6,750 \$6750 ÷ 30 = \$225 \$225 × .015 = \$3.38 • Finance charge: \$3.38 • Balance due: \$153.38
Past Due Balance	No finance charge is applied if full payment is received within a certain period, usually within 25 days after the date of the last billing statement. If full payment is not received, then a finance charge for the unpaid amount is added to the next month's bill.	• Amount on which interest is due: \$0 • Calculation: \$150 × 0 = 0 • Finance charge: \$0 • Balance due: \$150.00 (Finance charge of \$2.25 (.015 × \$150) will be added to next month's bill)

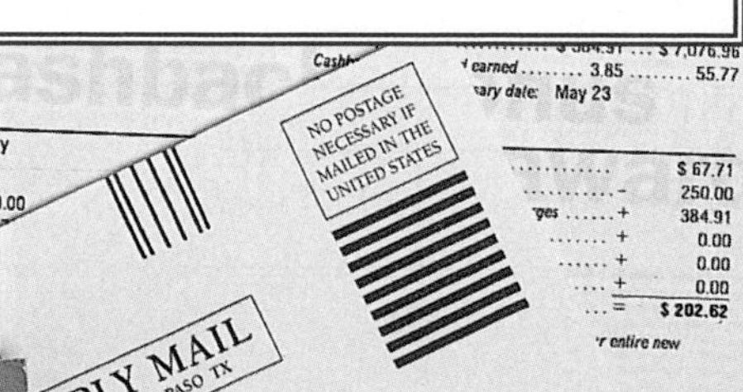

Computing APR Assume you charge $200 for clothes in a year. The interest rate charged to you, let's say, is 10 percent, but the annual fee for the credit card is $5. Your APR will be $20 of interest plus the $5 fee, or 12½ percent. The APR is normally larger than the interest rate because it includes the noninterest cost of extending credit.

Credit Card Charge of $200 at 10% Interest

Amount Charged	$200.00	$200.00
Interest at 10%	$20.00	$20.00
Annual Membership Fee	none	$5.00
APR	10%	12.5%

Debit Cards

There is another method of payment, known as a debit card. A *debit card* does not provide a loan. Instead, it makes cashless purchases easier by enabling customers to transfer funds electronically from their bank accounts directly to the store or restaurant where they purchased goods. Debit cards were first available in the 1970s but did not catch on with the public until the 1990s. At that time, banks combined credit cards with their debit cards.

Practice and **assess** key skills with ***Skillbuilder Interactive Workbook, Level 2.***

SECTION 2 Assessment

Understanding Key Terms

1. **Define** commercial bank, savings and loan association, savings bank, credit union, finance company, charge account, credit card, finance charge, annual percentage rate (APR).

Reviewing Objectives

2. **Graphic Organizer** Create a diagram like the one below to list the six types of financial institutions and describe their main functions.

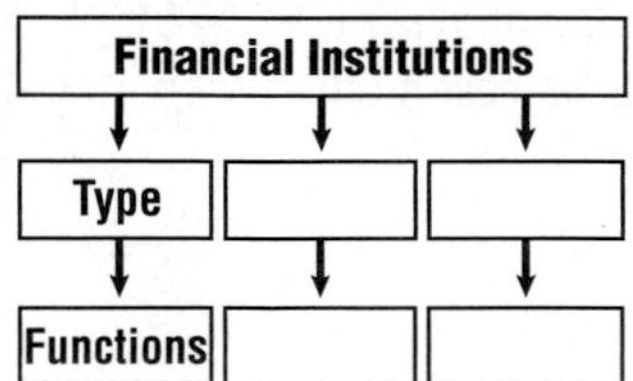

3. What three kinds of charge accounts are available from stores?
4. How are credit cards used?
5. How do a finance charge and an annual percentage rate differ?

Applying Economic Concepts

6. **Annual Percentage Rates** What would be the APR if you charged $1,000 on a credit card whose interest rate was 20 percent with an annual fee of $30?

Critical Thinking Activity

7. **Making Generalizations** Poll five adult family members. Ask: (1) Do you own a credit card? (2) Have you used an installment charge account? (3) Do you own a debit card? Tally your results, then write a generalization about the use of credit.

reveal your income, any current debts, details about your personal life, and how well you have repaid debts in the past.

The Credit Rating

The information supplied by the credit bureau provides the creditor with a **credit rating** for you. This is a rating of the risk–good, average, or poor–involved in lending funds to a specific person or business. If you have a history of poor credit use–usually late in paying debts–you will receive a poor credit rating. The creditor reviewing the credit check will be less willing to lend you money.

credit rating: *rating of the risk involved in lending money to a specific person or business*

Though past history of credit use is important in deciding a person's creditworthiness, the creditor also looks at three other factors that a credit check reveals. These are your capacity to pay, your character, and any collateral you may have. See **Figure 4.11.**

Capacity to Pay *Capacity to pay* is related to income and debt. If your employment has been spotty, your capacity to pay will be considered questionable. The amount of debt that you are already carrying is also a factor. If your debts are large, creditors will be reluctant to loan you more.

FIGURE 4.11

Creditworthiness When a creditor looks at your creditworthiness, three factors are considered: your ability to hold a steady job, your character, and any collateral you have that may secure a loan.

FIGURE 4.12

Cosigning a Loan

If someone you know asks you to cosign a loan, think carefully. If he or she does not make payments, you are responsible for the debt. ***When is a cosigner needed?***

Character *Character* refers to a person's reputation as a reliable and trustworthy person. The creditor may look at your educational background, whether or not you have had any problems with the law, and any other factors that might indicate your strength of character.

Collateral Lenders also consider **collateral,** or the size of your capital or personal wealth. Collateral is important because it indicates your past ability to save and accumulate. It also indicates your present ability to pay off a loan, even if you lose your job, because you could sell some of your belongings in order to make the payments.

Secured Loans Usually when a financial institution makes a loan, it will ask for collateral from the borrower. The collateral may be the item purchased with the loan money, such as a house or car. It may be something of value the borrower already owns. The borrower then signs a legal agreement allowing the lender to claim the collateral if the loan is not repaid. A loan that is backed up with collateral in this way is called a **secured loan.**

Unsecured Loans Usually a young adult will have little to offer as collateral. When dealing with a trusted customer, financial institutions will sometimes lend funds on the person's reputation alone. Such a loan is called an **unsecured loan.** It is not guaranteed by anything other than a promise to repay it.

A bank will sometimes lend funds to a person without a financial reputation if he or she has a cosigner. As shown in **Figure 4.12,** a *cosigner* is a person who signs a loan contract along with the borrower and promises to repay the loan if the borrower does not.

collateral: *something of value that a borrower lets the lender claim if a loan is not repaid*

secured loan: *loan that is backed up by collateral*

unsecured loan: *loan guaranteed only by a promise to repay it*

Responsibilities as a Borrower

After you have applied for credit and obtained it, you have taken on certain responsibilities. After all, the businesses that gave you credit expect to earn a profit.

If you do not pay your debts on time, the business that lends you funds may have to hire a collection agency to help get back the money loaned to you. If you never pay off your debt, the lending institution has to write it off and take a loss. These costs are passed on to all consumers in the form of higher interest rates charged.

Another negative thing happens when you do not pay your debts: you get a bad credit history. You may then have a difficult or impossible time when you really need credit for something else—to purchase a house, for example.

Another responsibility as a borrower is to keep a complete record of all the charges you have made. You also must notify the credit-card issuer immediately if your card is lost or stolen.

What if you've lost control of your debt? Financial planners advise you to make a list of everything you owe, what the interest rate is, and what the payments are. Concentrate on paying the high-interest credit cards first, and pay more than the minimum payment, or it will take you years to reduce the debt.

Global Economy

Loans for the Poor

In the mid-1970s, Muhammad Yunus, an economics professor, took a trip through Bangladesh. He saw a woman weaving bamboo chairs but earning only a few pennies a day, most of which went to pay the high interest rates on loans she took out to buy raw materials.

Yunus realized that if the woman could get loans at reasonable interest rates, she could make a living wage. So, Yunus started his own bank, the Grameen—or "Village"—Bank. Today, with more than 1,000 branch offices throughout Bangladesh, it has lent money to 2.6 million people, most of whom are women. Each loan averages $160, and over 98 percent of these loans have been repaid on time. ■

Practice and **assess** key skills with ***Skillbuilder Interactive Workbook, Level 2.***

SECTION 3 Assessment

Understanding Key Terms

1. **Define** credit bureau, credit check, credit rating, collateral, secured loan, unsecured loan.

Reviewing Objectives

2. **Graphic Organizer** Create a diagram like the one below to describe the four factors that determine a person's credit rating.

3. What are your responsibilities as a borrower?

Applying Economic Concepts

4. **Creditworthiness** Which of the four factors determining a person's credit rating do you think is most important in deciding whether a person is creditworthy? Explain.

Critical Thinking Activity

5. **Finding the Main Idea** What is the main idea of the following excerpt?

   Banks now assign point values to each item on a credit application, such as how much debt you owe, how much credit you have available, your repayment history, and your age. Your total score will determine whether you're approved.

BusinessWeek

Spotlight on the Economy

A Hard Lesson on Credit Cards

Check It Out! In this chapter you've learned about your responsibilities as a borrower. In this article, read to learn what pitfalls to avoid when applying for credit cards.

The moment college students step on campus, they become highly sought-after credit-card customers. To establish relationships card marketers hope will extend well beyond the college years, they are offering students everything from free T-shirts to chances to win airline tickets as enticements to sign up. As a result, college students now have heavy card debts.

As long as they are over 18, students can get a card without asking mom or dad to co-sign. Since card issuers' pitches may be confusing, experts dish out this advice:

- *Beware of teaser rates.* Credit-card marketers may advertise a low annual percentage rate (APR), but it often jumps substantially after three to nine months.
- *Pay on time.* Because students move often and may not get their mail forwarded quickly, bills can get lost. Then the students fall prey to late-payment fees. If one or two payments are overdue, many cards bump interest rates up as well.
- *Shun cash advances.* Students are often unaware that rates on cash advances are much higher than those on card balances.
- *Don't ask for extra credit.* Instead, find a card that has a restrictive credit line. Another option: Get a secured credit card. Its credit limit depends on your savings at the issuing bank.

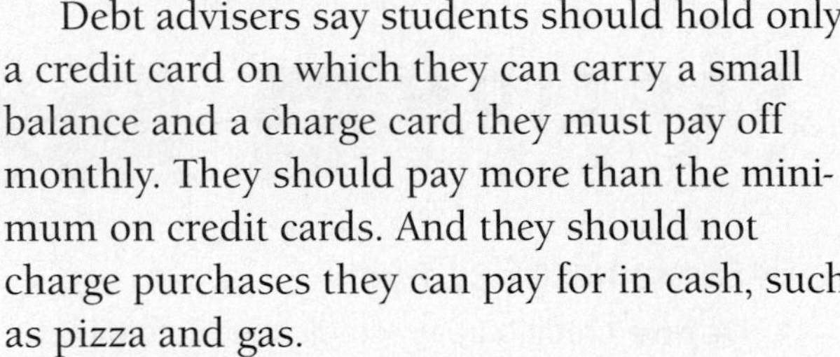

Debt advisers say students should hold only a credit card on which they can carry a small balance and a charge card they must pay off monthly. They should pay more than the minimum on credit cards. And they should not charge purchases they can pay for in cash, such as pizza and gas.

Think About It

1. **How are students enticed to get credit cards?**
2. **Describe six ways to avoid credit card debt.**

SECTION 4

Government Regulation of Credit

Cover Story

San Diego Union-Tribune, June 23, 2003

California consumers will learn next month whether their favorite shopping sites are steeled against computer fraud—or haunts of hackers and identity thieves. When a retailer discovers its credit card numbers have been stolen, it must e-mail customers, essentially saying, "We've been hacked, and the hacker may have your credit card number."

Although the FBI and Federal Trade Commission have hunted down Web site operators involved in fraudulent sales and auctions, proponents of the laissez-faire approach worry that regulations would hamper innovation in a fledgling industry.

Reader's Guide

Terms to Know

- usury law
- bankruptcy

Reading Objectives

1. How has the Equal Credit Opportunity Act affected consumer credit?
2. What are state usury laws?
3. Why might a person declare personal bankruptcy?

To protect consumers, the federal and state governments regulate the credit industry. Some states have set a maximum on the interest rates charged for certain types of credit. The federal government has also passed laws designed to increase the flow of credit information to consumers. In this section, you'll learn about these laws and how they protect consumers from unfair credit practices.

The Truth in Lending Act

The Truth in Lending Act of 1968 was the first of a series of major federal laws that greatly expanded the government's role in protecting users of consumer credit. An important aspect of the government regulation of credit is to make sure that everyone has equal access. **Figure 4.13** presents the important points about this act and other major federal government laws to regulate credit.

The Equal Credit Opportunity Act

In 1974 Congress enacted the Equal Credit Opportunity Act (ECOA) as an addition to the Truth in Lending Act of 1968. Among other things, those who provide credit cannot deny you such credit solely on the basis of your race, religion, national origin, gender, marital status, or age. In addition, no one is allowed to discriminate against you in offering credit simply because your income might come from public assistance benefits.

Historically, credit discrimination against married women has been the norm. The 1974 act made it illegal for a creditor to require the signature of an applicant's spouse unless an application for credit was made jointly by husband and wife. If a married woman qualifies on her own for the amount and terms of credit requested, she does not have to get her husband to sign the credit application. See **Figure 4.14** on page 104.

State Usury Laws

usury law: *law restricting the amount of interest that can be charged for credit*

A law restricting the amount of interest that can be charged for credit is called a **usury law.** Some states set up different maximum rates for different types of consumer credit. Maximum rates on charge accounts and credit cards, for example, are often about 18 percent a year, or $1\frac{1}{2}$ percent per month. Consumer finance agencies, in contrast, are often allowed to charge higher rates because their loans involve higher risks.

The maximum rates from usury laws were controversial in past years when interest restrictions in many states were as low as 6 or 10 percent. When interest rates in general began to rise in the early 1970s, many lenders complained that they could not keep within such restrictions and still make a profit. In states that were slow to raise interest restrictions, some lenders cut back

Student Web Activity Visit the *Economics Today and Tomorrow* Web site at ett.glencoe.com and click on ***Chapter 4—Student Web Activities*** to learn more about the Fair Debt Collection Practices Act.

FIGURE 4.13 Major Federal Laws Regulating Consumer Credit

Name of Law	Main Purpose	Major Provisions
Truth in Lending Act (1968)	Ensures that consumers are fully informed about the costs and conditions of borrowing.	• Creditors must keep borrowers informed of a credit agreement's annual percentage rate, the way charges and fees are calculated, and the payment schedule. • Consumers have a 3-day cooling-off period in which to cancel certain contracts. • Consumers are liable for only the first $50 in unauthorized purchases made on a credit card before it is reported lost or stolen.
Fair Credit Reporting Act (1970)	Protects the privacy and accuracy of information in a credit check.	• If refused credit, a consumer can request from the lender the name and address of the credit bureau issuing the report. • The credit bureau, if requested, must provide at least a summary of a consumer's credit file. • If the consumer claims part of the file is in error, the bureau must correct the record or explain it.
Equal Credit Opportunity Act (1974)	Prohibits discrimination in giving credit on the basis of sex, race, religion, marital status, age, or receipt of public assistance.	• Questions about age, sex, and marital status can be asked only if those questions relate directly to a person's ability to repay a loan. • Loan applicants must receive notice of a decision within 30 days. If the loan is denied, the lender must give the reasons.
Fair Credit Billing Act (1974)	Sets up a procedure for the quick correction of mistakes that appear on consumer credit accounts.	• Consumers have 60 days to notify a creditor of a disputed item on a billing statement. The creditor must correct the mistake or explain the charge. • While the mistake is checked, the consumer can withhold payment of the disputed sum. • Under certain circumstances, a consumer can withhold payment for defective merchandise.
Fair Debt Collection Practices Act (1977)	Prevents abuse by professional debt collectors; does not apply to banks or other businesses that collect their own accounts.	• Collectors can contact a person other than the debtor only to discover the debtor's location. • The debtor cannot be contacted at an inconvenient time or place. • All harassing behavior is prohibited, including the threat of violence, annoying phone calls, etc.

on the amount of credit they offered. Others stopped lending completely. Many consumers, particularly those who were poor credit risks, found it hard to obtain credit.

People opposed to raising interest restrictions claimed that people with lower incomes would not be able to afford credit. Supporters of higher rate restrictions claimed that low rates made credit less available because it was less profitable for lenders. Low rates actually hurt those they were supposed to help.

Personal Bankruptcy

Every day in the United States, thousands of families get into financial trouble because they have ignored the total costs of all their borrowing. They have too many credit cards, too many charge accounts, and own a home that has too large a mortgage. Just because someone offers you credit or allows you to borrow does not mean that you should accept. Buying on credit is a serious consumer activity. See **Figure 4.15.**

If debtors take out too many loans, use too many credit cards, and pile up debts that they cannot pay off, they may have to file personal **bankruptcy.** When a bankruptcy is approved through a bankruptcy court, debtors must give up most of what they own, which is then distributed to their creditors. The Constitution authorizes Congress to establish bankruptcy laws. Certain debts, such as taxes, must continue to be paid, however.

bankruptcy: *the inability to pay debts based on the income received*

If you declare personal bankruptcy, be aware that the bankruptcy proceedings remain on your credit record for 10 years. During this period, it is very difficult to reestablish credit and borrow funds for items such as a new car or home. That is why

FIGURE 4.14

Women and Credit Changes in laws regarding credit have improved a woman's opportunities to borrow money. ***What law made it illegal for creditors to deny credit on the basis of marital status?***

choosing bankruptcy to get out of your credit "mess" should be a last resort. Also, when you declare bankruptcy, you are making sure that your creditors will never be paid off (at least not in full) for what they loaned out.

FIGURE 4.15

Using Credit Just because credit card companies make it easy to obtain credit does not mean that you should accept their offers. ***What are some questions you should ask yourself before buying on credit?***

Practice and **assess** key skills with ***Skillbuilder Interactive Workbook, Level 2.***

SECTION 4 Assessment

Understanding Key Terms

1. **Define** usury law, bankruptcy.

Reviewing Objectives

2. **Graphic Organizer** Create a chart like the one below to describe how the Truth in Lending Act, the Fair Credit Reporting Act, the Equal Credit Opportunity Act, and the Fair Credit Billing Act have affected consumer credit.

Legislation	Effect on Consumer Credit

3. What are state usury laws?

4. Why might a person declare personal bankruptcy?

Applying Economic Concepts

5. **State Usury Laws** The effect of a usury law is often a shortage of available loans. What circumstances might create a *surplus* of available loans?

Critical Thinking Activity

6. **Making Comparisons** Research the two types of bankruptcy known as Chapter 7 and Chapter 13. Which requires debtors to set up a repayment plan? Which deletes the debt completely? What are the long-term effects of each type on one's future?

People & Perspectives

Kenneth Chenault

ENTREPRENEUR (1951–)

- **Chairman and chief executive officer of the American Express Company**
- **Board member of several companies, including IBM and Quaker Oats**
- **Board member of several educational, sports, and charitable organizations**
- **Recipient of many awards recognizing business achievements and charity work**

After working as a lawyer and a business consultant, Kenneth Chenault accepted a position at the American Express Company in 1981. An energetic worker and imaginative problem solver, Chenault rose steadily through company ranks. In 1997 he was named president and chief operating officer, and in 2001 he became chairman and chief executive officer.

Chenault believes that it is not so much *what* or *who* you know, but what you *do:*

> “*Having a solid track record, building relationships with the people that you work with, and then impressing them with your abilities will make people in a position to help your career take note. As a result, you will earn the respect of the people who know your work well....*”

As an African American, Chenault has faced obstacles in his career. Taking a practical approach to the situation, he believes, helps people to confront and overcome such obstacles:

> “*Everyone, regardless of their ethnic, religious, age, gender, . . . or other differences has to contend with obstacles. So you have to isolate what you can control, from what you can't. You can't control people's biases. You can control your own performance, your own behavior and the values you choose to uphold.*
>
> *I also think it's important to cultivate a measure of resilience. And, perhaps unfortunately, the best teacher of resilience is failure. There is nothing quite like overcoming failure with your character and values intact, to reinforce the fact that learning from your mistakes can be one of life's most important lessons.*”

Checking for Understanding

1. **What, according to Kenneth Chenault, is the key to success?**
2. **What advice does Chenault give people for confronting and overcoming obstacles?**

CHAPTER  Summary

Chapter Overview Visit the *Economics Today and Tomorrow* Web site at ett.glencoe.com and click on ***Chapter 4—Chapter Overviews*** to review chapter information.

SECTION 1 Americans and Credit

- **Credit** is the receiving of funds either directly or indirectly to buy goods and services today with the promise to pay for them in the future.
- The amount owed—the debt—is equal to the **principal** plus **interest.**
- Many people buy **durable goods** and obtain **mortgages** using **installment debt.**
- People go into debt because they do not want to wait to purchase an item with cash, and they want to spread the debt payments over the life of the item being purchased.

SECTION 2 Sources of Loans and Credit

- The major financial institutions that lend consumers funds include **commercial banks, savings and loan associations, credit unions,** and **finance companies.**
- A **charge account** allows a customer to buy goods or services from a particular company and pay for them later.
- A **credit card,** often charging high interest, may be used at stores, restaurants, or other businesses.
- **Finance charges** tell you the monthly cost of credit in dollars and cents.
- The **annual percentage rate** tells you the annual cost of credit in percentages.

SECTION 3 Applying for Credit

- After you have filled out a credit application, a **credit bureau** will perform a **credit check** and determine your **credit rating.**
- Before granting you credit, a creditor looks at your capacity to pay, your character, and any **collateral** you may have.
- Your responsibilities as a borrower include paying on time, keeping records of your debt, and not spending more than you can repay.

SECTION 4 Government Regulation of Credit

- Legislation states that those who provide credit cannot deny you such credit solely on the basis of your race, religion, national origin, gender, marital status, or age.
- A **usury law** restricts the amount of interest that can be charged for credit, but can lead to a shortage of available credit if interest rates rise.
- People who cannot repay their debts may have to file personal **bankruptcy.**

CHAPTER 4

Assessment and Activities

Self-Check Quiz Visit the *Economics Today and Tomorrow* Web site at ett.glencoe.com and click on ***Chapter 4—Self-Check Quizzes*** to prepare for the Chapter Test.

Identifying Key Terms

Write the letter of the definition in Column B that correctly defines each term in Column A.

Column A

1. principal
2. usury law
3. collateral
4. annual percentage rate
5. unsecured loan

Column B

a. restricts the amount of interest that can be charged for credit
b. requires only a promise to repay
c. amount of money borrowed in a loan
d. something of value that a borrower uses as a promise of loan repayment
e. cost of credit expressed as a yearly percentage

Recalling Facts and Ideas

Section 1

1. What do you have to pay when you borrow?
2. How is taking out a loan similar to buying an item on credit?
3. What type of goods do people typically use installment debt to buy?
4. Why do people use credit?

Section 2

5. What are the six types of basic lending institutions in our economy?
6. What are some of the most common types of credit cards used today?
7. When you take out a loan, what do you call the total cost of credit expressed in dollars and cents?

Section 3

8. When you make an application for a loan, what are four factors that a creditor analyzes to determine whether you are creditworthy?
9. What is the difference between a secured and an unsecured loan?
10. What are your responsibilities as a borrower?

Section 4

11. What does the Equal Credit Opportunity Act of 1974 prohibit?
12. What are three important federal laws regulating consumer credit?
13. How can usury laws be harmful to the people they are trying to help?

Thinking Critically

1. **Making Comparisons** In deciding whether to pay cash or use credit for a purchase, what are the costs involved and the benefits of each choice?

2. **Synthesizing Information** Imagine that you need both a car loan and a home mortgage. Use a chart like the one below to help decide which of the six types of lending institutions discussed in this chapter would be most appropriate for each loan.

Financial Institution	Services	Car or Home Loan?

3. **Drawing Conclusions** If you declare personal bankruptcy, your creditors clearly lose. What ethical concerns should you have before ever taking this action?

Applying Economic Concepts

The Role of Government Sometimes credit cards are lost or stolen. The owner must take steps to keep his or her card from being used by an unauthorized person. Research the Truth in Lending Act to find out what a credit card holder must do when his or her card is lost or stolen.

Cooperative Learning Project

Work in small groups to create a loan application that is appropriate for high school students, and circulate it in class. After going over the application, analyze why it is or is not difficult to decide who should receive loans. Is it difficult to decide who should *not* receive loans?

Reviewing Skills

Using a Database Call various retail stores and gas stations and ask them to send you a credit card application. Analyze the applications, then prepare a database that organizes the answers to the following questions.

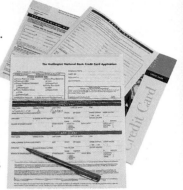

1. What questions asked on each application are virtually the same?
2. What questions asked on the gas station applications are different than those asked on the retail store applications?
3. Were any questions asked that you think violate the Equal Credit Opportunity Act? Explain.

Technology Activity

Using the Internet If you ever wish to borrow money, your credit rating will be important. You can determine what your credit rating is by going to the Internet.

Enter the words *credit rating* in your search engine. You will find numerous sites that will give you a credit check on yourself. A wealth of online credit reporting services are available, and some of these reporting services are free.

Analyzing the Global Economy

The first banks arose in Europe during the Middle Ages. Indeed, the word *bank* comes from the *banca,* or bench, that moneychangers set up at medieval fairs to exchange currencies, transfer funds, receive deposits, and arrange loans. Research these early financial institutions and the interest rates they charged their customers.

CHAPTER 5

Buying the Necessities

Why It's Important

What are the costs of owning a car? How much should you budget for clothes and food? Should you rent or buy a house? This chapter will help you learn to shop wisely for the necessities.

To learn more about buying a home or car, view the **Economics & You** *Chapter 11 video lesson:* **Buying the Necessities**

ECONOMICS *Online*

Chapter Overview Visit the *Economics Today and Tomorrow* Web site at ett.glencoe.com and click on ***Chapter 5—Chapter Overviews*** to preview chapter information.

SECTION 1

Shopping for Food

Cover Story

The Columbus Dispatch, May 26, 1999

Here's a new idea from Yoder's: sour cream in a squeeze top bottle. It's a good idea if you use sour cream mostly for topping baked potatoes, nachos, and fajitas. It's probably not a good idea if you use it primarily as an ingredient. The 16-ounce plastic bottles sell for $1.99. That compares with $1.39 for Yoder's regular 16-ounce cartons of sour cream.

Reader's Guide

Terms to Know

- club warehouse store
- convenience store
- private-labeled products

Reading Objectives

1. What are the advantages of comparison food shopping?
2. What are the advantages and disadvantages of shopping at club warehouse stores?

Americans consume a great variety of foods. They can choose from thousands of different food products and buy them at thousands of stores. Hundreds of brands offer numerous choices: for example, sour cream in a 16-ounce container, sour cream in a squeeze-top bottle, sour cream mixed with chives in an 8-ounce container, and so on. In all, American consumers spend hundreds of billions of dollars a year on food. In this section, you'll learn how to get the most from your food dollars.

Comparison Shopping

Because American families spend so much for food, comparison shopping is important. It involves making comparisons among brands and sizes before you buy. You need to decide not only what to shop for but where to shop as well.

FIGURE 5.1 Checklist for Food Shopping

The following are helpful tips for getting the most from your money when you shop for food:

1. Read the newspapers ahead of time for sales and cents-off coupons.
2. Go with a shopping list and coupons. Plan a week's worth of meals so that you will buy only what you need. A list will also help you avoid additional trips to the store.
3. Avoid impulsive buying, or buying without thinking about the purchase beforehand. Be careful in the checkout line because nonessential items are placed by the cash register.
4. Buy nutritional items first. Check labels on canned and frozen goods for nutritional value.
5. Check freshness dates on dairy and bakery items.
6. Compare prices on private-labeled, generic, and national brands.
7. Check unit prices. Buy large sizes if you can use the items immediately or can store them.
8. Do not shop when you are hungry or thirsty. You will be tempted to buy more than you need.

A consumer should do only as much comparison shopping as is worthwhile, however. It does not pay a shopper to go far out of his or her way to shop at a store that has only a few needed items at low prices. Such savings would be outweighed by the additional costs of time and transportation.

Remember, your time has an opportunity cost. The more time you spend comparison shopping for food, the less time you have to do anything else. Reading advertisements is a timesaving, inexpensive way to comparison shop. Food store ads describe sales and often contain cents-off coupons. **Figure 5.1** lists this tip as well as other suggestions to follow in your food shopping.

Trade-Offs in Food Stores

Americans typically do their food shopping in either supermarkets or **club warehouse stores**, such as Costco. These stores usually sell a limited number of brands and items, but they often sell them by the case or other large quantities. Warehouse stores typically charge the lowest prices for food.

club warehouse store: *store that carries a limited number of brands and items in large quantities and is less expensive than supermarkets*

Occasionally, you may want to use a **convenience store,** such as 7-Eleven, for just that reason—because it's convenient. They are usually open 16 to 24 hours a day, but carry a limited selection of items. The trade-off here is that you may be saving time to buy a few items you need, but you will pay a relatively higher price than you would elsewhere.

convenience store: *store open 16 to 24 hours a day, carrying a limited selection of relatively higher-priced items*

Although club warehouse stores offer the largest potential savings for your food dollars, there is a trade-off. Most food items come only in relatively large-quantity containers. So you may end up buying a "value-pack" of soups that has 24 cans, for example. Unless your family is large and eats canned soup regularly, you will have unused cans of soup in your cupboard. Therein lies an opportunity cost. You have tied up your funds in an inventory of food. Although the lost interest on those funds may not be great in any single week, it can add up to a significant amount over a several-year period.

In contrast, a large inventory can be a benefit. When you have a relatively well-stocked cupboard of food items, you do not have to return to the store to buy food so often. Thus, you save in time and the costs of transportation.

private-labeled products: *lower-priced store-brand products carried by some supermarket chains and club warehouse chains*

Brand-Name Products Versus Private-Labeled Products

When you go shopping in virtually any food store, many of the food items have well-known brand names. Some food stores also carry regional brands that are found only in certain areas of the country.

As an alternative to expensive national brands, some big supermarket chains, as well as club warehouse chains, carry their own store-brand products. These are also called **private-labeled products.** According to some consumer surveys, it is possible to save as much as 40 percent by buying store-brand (private-labeled) products. As shown in **Figure 5.2,** you can save even more when you buy generic or bulk items.

FIGURE 5.2

Generic and Bulk Foods
Some food products are available in brand-name, store-label, generic, or bulk form. Generally, price decreases in that order. ***What is the difference between private-labeled products and generic products?***

The Trade-Off Between Quality, Price, and Quantity

There is often a trade-off between quality and price in the products you buy. A lower-priced generic dishwasher soap might leave a slight film on your drinking glasses, for example, compared to a more expensive national-brand alternative.

Often you will find that the larger the quantity of any item you buy in a supermarket, the lower the per-unit price. Most states require stores to provide unit pricing for food and other products. See **Figure 5.3.** This practice makes it easy to compare prices not only for different brands, but for different sizes of the same brand. For example, the price of milk might be expressed in terms of cents per ounce. You can then tell how much you save per ounce if you buy milk in larger containers.

Cents-Off Coupons Many manufacturers give cents-off coupons. To take advantage of them, a consumer has to buy the brand, size, and quantity named on the coupon. The store then reduces the price paid by the amount printed on the coupon. The manufacturer, in turn, pays that amount to the store.

If you make a habit of using coupons, you can reduce your food bill by more than 10 percent over a one-year period. The use of cents-off coupons, however, requires time—the time to collect and match them to items when shopping. Because time is a scarce resource, you have to decide if the money you save using coupons is worth the time you spend. In addition, coupons tempt you to buy brand-name products you might not otherwise buy—thus *not* saving you money at all.

FIGURE 5.3

Unit Pricing Trying to compare the prices of different amounts of a product—one gallon of Product A versus one half-gallon of Product B—can be confusing. Unit pricing allows you to compare like amounts: ounces to ounces, pounds to pounds, and so on.

Economic Connection to... MATH

Do Coupons Add Up to Savings?

You have a problem. Spread out on the table in front of you are half a dozen discount coupons for breakfast cereal. The discounts offered range from $.75 to $1.50. Which discount coupon will you choose?

The majority of studies of consumer behavior suggest that the answer is simple. The larger the discount, the more likely consumers are to clip and use the coupon. A recent study, however, suggests that the answer may not be so straightforward.

Most subjects in this study seemed to think that the size of the discount was an indication of price. The products featured on coupons offering greater discounts, study subjects felt, probably were very expensive. Consumers, therefore, may *not* clip and use a coupon offering a large discount because they feel it might not result in real savings. ■

Practice and **assess** key skills with ***Skillbuilder Interactive Workbook, Level 2.***

SECTION 1 Assessment

Understanding Key Terms

1. **Define** club warehouse store, convenience store, private-labeled products.

Reviewing Objectives

2. What are the advantages of comparison food shopping?
3. **Graphic Organizer** Use a diagram like the one below to describe the advantages and disadvantages of shopping at a club warehouse store.

Applying Economic Concepts

4. **Trade-Offs** Do you think using cents-off coupons is worth the time spent clipping and matching them to products that you might buy? Why or why not?

Critical Thinking Activity

5. **Making Comparisons** List your five favorite foods. Then visit five different food stores, or scan food advertisements in newspapers or on television commercials, and compare the prices of your listed items at each store. Explain why you think the stores had similar or different prices for each item.

People & Perspectives

- **President and chief executive officer of Maytag Corporation, one of North America's leading producers of premium brand home appliances**
- **Named "Executive of the Year" in 1995 by *Black Enterprise Magazine***
- **Ranked among the top 25 business executives of 1998 by *Business Week***

Lloyd Ward

ENTREPRENEUR (1949–)

In the 1969–1970 season, Lloyd Ward captained the Michigan State University men's basketball team. His ability to motivate his teammates quickly became apparent. Ward continued to exhibit leadership qualities as he rose through the ranks of the business world. During his time at Maytag, Ward has become known as a team builder. He believes that motivated workers can help to get customers excited about the company's products:

> *"The focus [at Maytag] before was never disappoint the consumer, satisfy the consumer, be out there with a reliable, dependable product. Now we think of 'wowing' the customer, exceeding their expectations, and providing them with fundamental new benefits they are willing to pay for."*

Such a drastic change in approach involves giving up old and familiar ways of doing business. Persuading workers to adopt new ways, Ward believes, must be undertaken in a positive fashion:

> *"The challenge within our company is not so much people accepting new ideas as having them forget old ideas. A compelling vision provides a context to let go of tradition and the way things were done before so they can look at new things.*
>
> *You need to celebrate your failures as much as your successes. Said another way, you need to redefine failure as a learning experience. Everything you do is an opportunity to deepen focus and get better understanding, so you can do significantly better in your next try."*

Checking for Understanding

1. What does Ward mean by "wowing" the customer?
2. Why does Ward think that people should celebrate their failures as much as their successes?

SECTION 2

Clothing Choices

Cover Story

Business Week, May 7, 2001

Planet Earth now has some 3,750 Gap, Old Navy, and Banana Republic stores. That number grows daily, and by year's end Gap expects over 4,200 stores—a doubling in four years....

[At the Gap,] you'll see teenagers, alone and in groups, spending their parents' money freely. You'll see young women, alone or pushing infants in strollers. You'll see aging baby boomers buying outfits that forgive them their paunches.... Look, and you'll see Gap is now the No. 1 cradle-to-grave clothier.

Reader's Guide

Terms to Know

- durability
- service flow

Reading Objectives

1. What three factors determine clothing value?
2. When should you take advantage of clothing sales?

Americans spend about $400 billion annually on clothing and other personal products. Most people could save considerable income by purchasing only a few very durable pieces of clothing. The clothes, however, would not serve another purpose–variety. In this section, you'll learn that variety, for Americans, is typically the motivating factor involved in clothing choice.

Comparing Clothing Value

Comparison shopping is an important part of buying wisely. Comparing value in clothing means more than simply purchasing an item from the store that offers the best price. Clothing value depends on at least three other factors: style, cost of care, and durability. See **Figure 5.4** on page 118.

A Style

We often buy clothing styles that preserve our self-image. Clothing conveys a message to others about what you do, what you believe, and who you are.

FIGURE 5.4

Clothing Value When making clothing purchases, many people want to have different looks for different occasions. Also, people in different climates need different wardrobes for summer and winter.

B Cost of Care

Dry-cleaning costs can vary widely, from $3 per shirt to $10 for a skirt or sweater.

C Durability

When comparison shopping for clothing, you should try to determine how long an item will last and how long you will need it. Then you should compare prices. Suppose you think Coat A will last twice as long as Coat B, and Coat A costs only 20 percent more. Coat A, then, is a better buy.

Style You may be able to buy the minimum amount of clothing you need at a very low cost. You will, however, generally give up style to do it. You are faced with a trade-off. Should you buy stylish clothes each year to keep up with fashion, but then have less money to spend on other items? Or should you buy less stylish clothes, which results in more money to do other things?

Durability The ability of an item to last is known as **durability.** The longer a piece of clothing–or any item–lasts, the more durable it is. When you purchase an item of clothing, you are purchasing it for the service flow that it yields. **Service flow** is the amount of time you get to use a product and the value you place on this use. If you buy a jacket that will last three years and costs $300, the cost per annual service flow is $100.

durability: *ability of an item to last a long time*

service flow: *amount of use a person gets from an item over time and the value a person places on this use*

Cost of Care The cost of care is another factor in assessing value. Two shirts or blouses may cost the same, but one may require dry cleaning, which is more expensive than hand or machine washing. When deciding on the best choice in a clothing purchase, you must consider maintenance costs.

More for Less

By value shopping, consumers can help themselves in budgeting clothing allowances. It is worth noting, however, that the cost of clothing has decreased significantly over the years. Seventy years ago, a good suit cost about $40. It took an average consumer almost 80 hours to earn enough income to buy that suit. Today a comparable suit sells for just over $500, but costs the average worker the equivalent of 40 hours of work. Over the past 100 years, a pair of name-brand jeans has fallen in *work-time cost* by more than half. This means that clothing basics cost much less than they did in the early 1900s. See **Figure 5.5.**

Clothing Sales Although a smaller percentage of one's budget goes to clothing purchases now than in the past, it is still the wise consumer who buys clothing on sale. Because clothing sales are so numerous throughout the year, however, it is easy to become a bargain fanatic—buying sale items just because they are on sale. Before going shopping, make a list of the clothing you require. Having this list along may help you keep your spending within limits. It is wise to determine your wants as well as your realistic needs before shopping at any sale. **Figure 5.6** on page 120 can help you evaluate these wants.

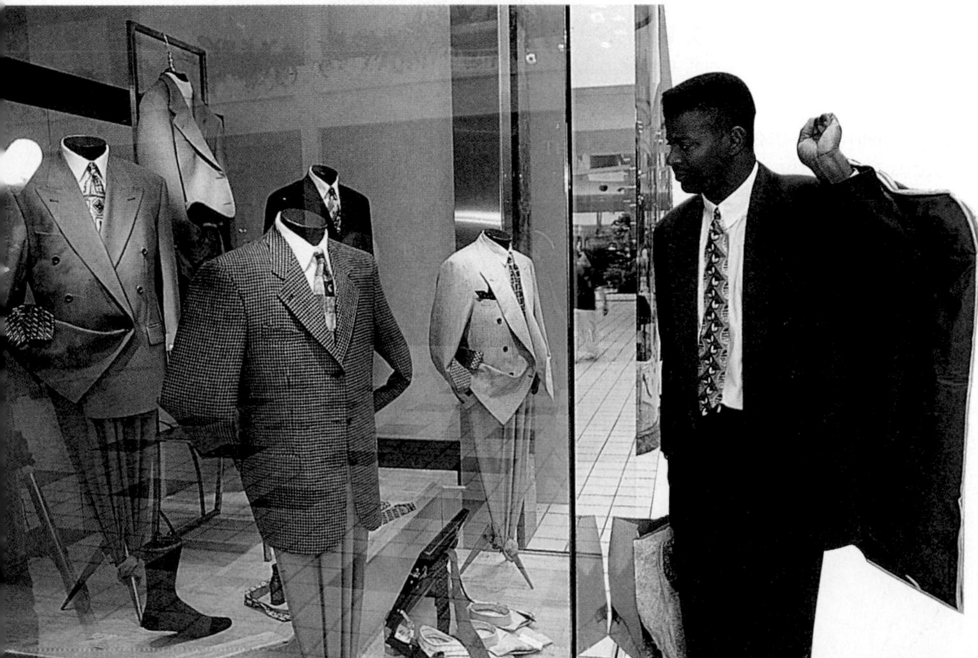

FIGURE 5.5

Work-Time Cost As a percentage of their budget, Americans spend far less on clothing today than in the past—4.8 percent today as compared to 8.4 percent in 1972–73, and 14.1 percent in 1901. A higher proportion of a family's income can be spent on other things such as education or family vacations.

FIGURE 5.6 Checklist for Determining Clothing Wants

In deciding on clothing purchases, ask yourself the following questions:

1. What do I already have? Check the condition of the clothes you have, and see what you want to replace.
2. What clothes do I wish to have for school? For my job? For my social life? For recreational activities?
3. How many changes of clothes do I require to meet my minimum standards for cleanliness, variety, and social status?
4. How do my answers to questions 1 through 3 compare with the amount of income I have to spend?
5. Should I pay cash or charge my purchases? Consider the trade-offs involved in paying cash or using credit.

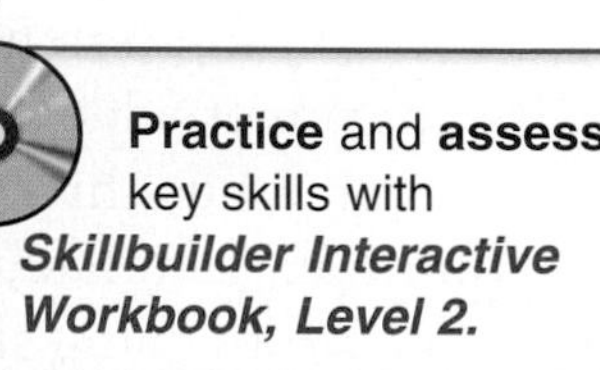

Practice and **assess** key skills with ***Skillbuilder Interactive Workbook, Level 2.***

SECTION 2 Assessment

Understanding Key Terms

1. **Define** durability, service flow.

Reviewing Objectives

2. **Graphic Organizer** Create a diagram like the one below to describe three factors that determine clothing value.

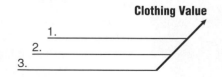

3. When should you take advantage of clothing sales?

Applying Economic Concepts

4. **Work-Time Cost** Ask your parents or other older adults to remember the cost of a pair of jeans, a jacket, and a pair of tennis shoes when they were teenagers. Then ask them to remember the amount they were paid (by the hour) for any jobs they held as teenagers. Calculate their work-time cost of buying those items.

Critical Thinking Activity

5. **Synthesizing Information** A store advertises jeans at 33 percent off the original price of $37. What is the sale price? *For help in understanding percentages, see page xix in the Economic Handbook.*

SECTION 3

To Rent or to Buy

Cover Story

The Columbus Dispatch, December 28, 2002

Motivated by some of the lowest mortgage rates seen in decades, home shoppers turned into buyers and propelled *new-home sales* in November to the highest monthly level on record. *New-home sales* for 2002 are on track for their best year.

Sales of new single-family homes clocked in at a seasonally adjusted annual rate of 1.07 million in November, representing a 5.7 percent jump from October's level, the Commerce Department reported yesterday.

Reader's Guide

Terms to Know

- closing costs
- points
- lease
- security deposit

Reading Objectives

1. What three rules should determine how much you spend for a house?
2. What are the rights and responsibilities of renters?

Some people will save for years in order to buy a small house. Others take out huge mortgages to purchase large homes. Still others are content to rent a house, condo, or apartment most of their lives. In this section, you'll learn about renting versus buying.

Figure 5.7 on page 122 compares the advantages and disadvantages of owning and renting. Wise consumers should consider both when deciding whether to buy or to rent housing.

How Much Should You Spend?

When you decide to buy a house, it is important that you do not take on financial obligations that are beyond your budget. As **Figure 5.8** on page 123 shows, lenders use certain rules to help you determine how much you can afford.

FIGURE 5.7

Advantages and Disadvantages of Owning and Renting

Home Ownership Advantages	Home Ownership Disadvantages
• Freedom of use; owners can remodel whenever or however they choose • Pride of ownership; people tend to take better care of things they own • Greater privacy • Usually a good investment that in the past has risen in value as much as, or more than, the general rise in prices • Significant income tax benefits • Creation of *equity,* the market value of the property minus the mortgage payments still owed • Good credit rating if mortgage payments are made on time • Property to use as collateral for other loans	• Less mobility, especially in years when interest rates on mortgages are high and housing is difficult to sell • Moving to another property because the present one is too small, too big, and so on is time-consuming • Necessity of a large outlay of money for a down payment • Maintenance costs, real estate taxes, and possible depreciation • Less money for other purchases because of high monthly mortgage payments • Possibility of overextending a family's debt load to make home improvements or repairs

Renting Advantages	Renting Disadvantages
• Greater mobility; a renter does not have to worry about trying to sell property • Feeling of freedom to choose another place to live if dissatisfied with current rental unit • Paying only a small security deposit rather than a large down payment • No direct maintenance costs, real estate taxes, or depreciation • Good credit rating if rent is paid on time • More money for other purchases because monthly rental payments are often less than monthly mortgage payments • No temptation to overspend on home improvements	• No freedom of use; renters may not remodel or even paint without the owner's permission • No return on rental money; a renter will never own the property regardless of how much rent he or she pays, regardless of the length of this period of time • Few or no tax benefits • Less privacy • Little feeling of responsibility for seeing that the property is well taken care of • No property for use as collateral • Need to wait for maintenance work at the convenience of the owner

FIGURE 5.8 **Lender's Rules** It would be unwise for both you and the lender if you spent more than a third of your income on the mortgage. ***Why?***

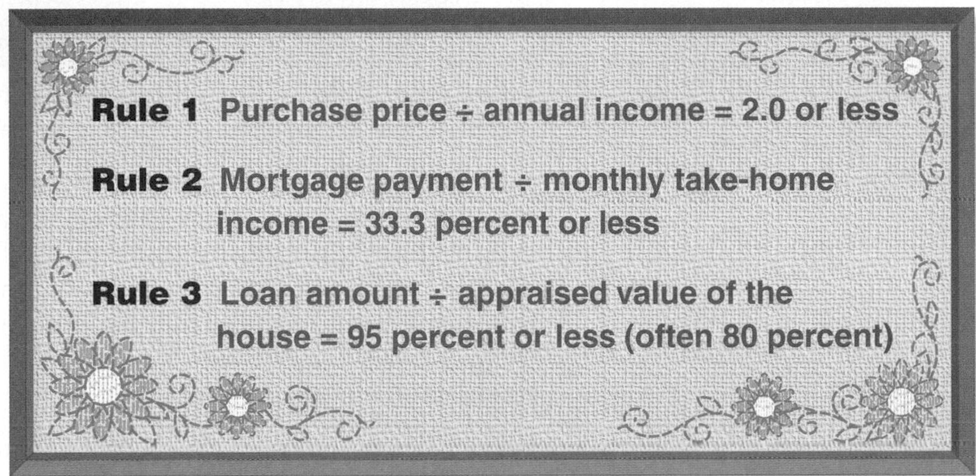

Rule 1 Purchase price ÷ annual income = 2.0 or less
Rule 2 Mortgage payment ÷ monthly take-home income = 33.3 percent or less
Rule 3 Loan amount ÷ appraised value of the house = 95 percent or less (often 80 percent)

In addition to the cash down payment, you will need money for **closing costs.** These are costs involved in arranging for a mortgage or in transferring ownership of the property. Closing costs can include fees for such items as the title search, legal costs, loan application, credit report, house inspections, and taxes. Although the person buying the house usually pays these fees, the seller may agree to pay part or all of them if this will make it easier to sell the house.

closing costs: *fees involved in arranging for a mortgage or in transferring ownership of property*

In arranging for a mortgage, it is also important to know about points, which are included in closing costs. **Points** are the fees paid to the lender and computed as a percentage of the loan. Each point the lender charges equals 1 percent of the amount borrowed. Lenders charge points–usually one to four–when they believe that the current interest rate is not high enough to pay the expenses involved in handling the mortgage and still make a profit.

points: *fees paid to a lender and computed as a percentage of a loan*

Purchasing a House

One of the major problems facing today's home buyer is obtaining a mortgage. **Figure 5.9** on page 124 shows several kinds of mortgages that are available.

Student Web Activity Visit the *Economics Today and Tomorrow* Web site at ett.glencoe.com and click on ***Chapter 5—Student Web Activities*** to compare home prices in your area and around the country.

FIGURE 5.9 Types of Mortgages

Type of Mortgage	Interest Rate Changes	Monthly Payment Changes	Description
Standard Fixed-Rate Mortgage	No	No	Interest rate and monthly payments remain the same over the term of the mortgage–usually 15 to 30 years.
Flexible Rate Mortgage	Yes	Yes	Interest rate and monthly payments float up or down along with interest rates in general. Rates can increase by no more than a few percentage points over the life of a mortgage, whereas there is often no limit on the amount of decrease. Three such plans are variable rate mortgage (VRM), adjustable rate mortgage (ARM), and renegotiable rate mortgage (RRM).
Federal Housing Administration (FHA) Mortgage	No	No	The FHA will insure the entire amount of its mortgages. This added security makes it possible for borrowers to obtain a larger loan than they would with an uninsured mortgage.
Graduated Payment Mortgage (GPM)	No	Yes	Interest rate is usually fixed for the life of the mortgage. Monthly payments are small at the beginning and increase gradually over the years. GPMs are used by people who expect their incomes to increase steadily from year to year.
Veterans Administration (VA) Mortgage	No	No	These loans can be obtained only by qualified veterans or their surviving spouses. The interest rate is generally lower than for other mortgages. The VA guarantees a large percentage of the loan. Loans with no down payment are possible under the VA program.

A mortgage usually involves a down payment and interest. If you buy a house for $100,000 and make a $20,000 down payment, you will need to obtain a mortgage for the remaining $80,000. The mortgage will then be repaid in monthly installments that include interest on the loan. Property taxes, homeowners insurance, and mortgage insurance are often included on your mortgage payment as well.

Renter Rights and Responsibilities

lease: *long-term agreement describing the terms under which property is rented*

Most renters sign a **lease,** or contract, that contains several clauses. A prospective tenant should read the lease carefully. Most leases are for one to three years, although sometimes you may pay extra to get a six-month or nine-month lease.

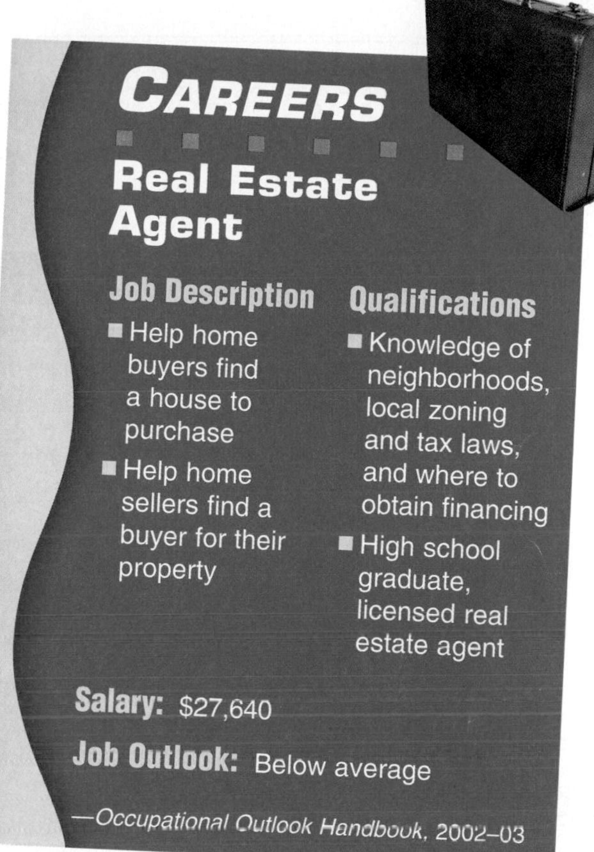

Tenant Rights Among the rights of tenants is the use of the property for the purpose stated in the lease. Tenants also have the right to a certain amount of privacy. A landlord usually cannot enter an apartment anytime he or she chooses. A landlord may enter only to make necessary repairs or to show the apartment to a potential renter.

Tenant Responsibilities In turn, the tenant's responsibilities include paying the rent on time and taking reasonable care of the property. If major repairs, such as replacing a leaky roof, are needed, the tenant is responsible for notifying the landlord.

Often a lease will limit how an apartment can be used. The lease may forbid pets, for example, or forbid anyone other than the person named on the lease from living there. In signing a lease, the tenant is usually required to give the owner a **security deposit,** or money for the owner to hold in case the rent is not paid or the apartment is damaged. The security deposit, usually equal to one month's rent, is returned after the tenant has moved. The amount returned depends on the condition of the apartment, as determined by the landlord. See **Figure 5.10.**

security deposit: *money a renter lets an owner hold in case the rent is not paid or an apartment is damaged*

Security Deposit To make sure you get your apartment security deposit returned, do an initial "walk through" with the landlord to record any damage that already exists. In addition, take dated photos when you move in and when you leave. ***How much are renters usually required to pay as a security deposit?***

FIGURE 5.11 Checklist for Clauses in Housing Leases

Avoid these types of clauses in leases:

1. **Confession-of-judgment clause:** The lawyer for the rental owner has the right to plead guilty for you in court if the owner thinks his or her rights have been violated. With a confession-of-judgment clause—illegal in some states—you are admitting guilt before committing any act.
2. **Inability-to-sue clause:** You give up your right to sue the owner if you suffer injury or damage through some fault of the owner, such as neglected repair work.
3. ***Arbitrary clauses,* or those based on one's wishes rather than a rule or law:** The owner has the right to cancel the lease because he or she is dissatisfied with your behavior. An arbitrary clause may
   - forbid hanging pictures.
   - forbid overnight guests (to make sure the apartment is occupied only by the renter).
   - forbid subleasing, or the leasing of the apartment by the tenant to someone else.
   - allow the owner or a representative, such as a plumber, to enter your apartment when you are not home.
   - make you legally responsible for all repairs.
   - make you obey rules that have not yet been written.

If possible, add these clauses to your lease:

1. The appliances that come with the apartment—dishwasher, garbage disposal, and air conditioner, for example.
2. The apartment community facilities you have been promised—recreation room, parking space, swimming pool—and whether you must pay extra for their use.
3. Any other promises made by the owner, such as painting the apartment (and what color).
4. The right to cancel your lease if you are transferred to a job in another city. Usually you must agree to pay a certain amount to do this, which should be stated in the lease.
5. The right to put in lighting fixtures, shelves, and so on, and have them remain your property when you move. Otherwise, they become part of the apartment and you may not take them with you.

The tenant is also required to give *notice,* or a formal warning, if he or she plans to move before the term of the lease is up. In this event, the landlord may ask for several months' rent to pay for any time the apartment is empty before a new tenant moves in.

Landlord Responsibilities In many states, landlords must make sure that their apartments have certain minimum services, such as heat, and that they are fit to live in. Landlords may also have to obey building safety laws. For example, fire escapes and smoke detectors may be required. Leases usually call for the landlord to make repairs within a reasonable amount of time. In many states, a tenant has the right to pay for the repairs and withhold that amount of rent if the landlord does not make the repairs. **Figure 5.11** details important items that should not be in your lease or that you should have added to your lease.

Global *Economy*

Housing in Japan

Land prices in Tokyo and other large cities in Japan are so high that most people feel they cannot buy a home. High land prices also mean that Japanese houses are quite small. On average, a house in Japan has 5 rooms and covers a floor space of about 110 square yards. In comparison, the average American home has 5.5 rooms and some 191 square yards of floor space. Average floor space is even smaller in Japan's cities–only 74 square yards in Tokyo. ■

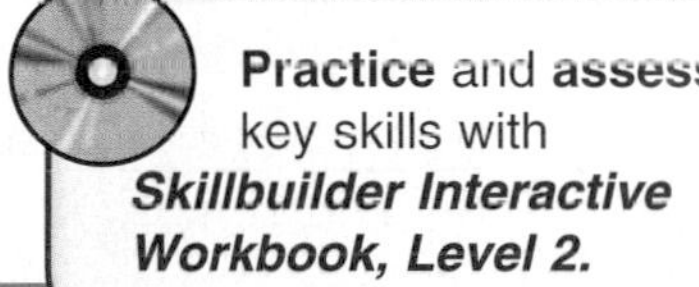

Practice and assess key skills with ***Skillbuilder Interactive Workbook, Level 2.***

SECTION 3 Assessment

Understanding Key Terms

1. **Define** closing costs, points, lease, security deposit.

Reviewing Objectives

2. What three rules should determine how much you spend on a house?
3. **Graphic Organizer** Use a chart like the one below to analyze the rights and responsibilities of renters.

Renter Rights	Renter Responsibilities

Applying Economic Concepts

4. **Demand** Based on the advantages and disadvantages listed in **Figure 5.7** on page 122, do you think you would like to rent or buy a house when you live independently? Explain your choice.

Critical Thinking Activity

5. **Synthesizing Information** Imagine you are applying for a mortgage. The monthly payment will be $800, whereas your monthly take-home income is $1,800. According to **Figure 5.8** on page 123, should the lender grant you the mortgage? Why or why not? *For help in understanding percentages, see page xix in the Economic Handbook.*

Critical Thinking Skills

Finding the Main Idea

Finding the main idea will help you see the "big picture" by organizing information and assessing the most important concepts to remember.

- Find out the setting of the article.
- As you read the material, ask: What is the purpose of this article?
- Skim the material to identify its general subject. Look at headings and subheadings.
- Identify any details that support a larger idea or issue.
- Identify the central issue. Ask: What part of the selection conveys the main idea?

Learning the Skill

To learn how to find the main idea, follow the steps listed on the left.

Practicing the Skill

Read the excerpt below, then answer the questions that follow.

"*Car shoppers who rely on the Web have traditionally bought models fresh from the factory. But Internet sales of used cars are on the rise. The Net can help you choose a model, search available inventory, and evaluate specific cars. . . . What's more, you can find low-mileage luxury cars that have just come off lease–with time remaining on their warranties. And once you've settled on your pick, you can apply for financing online.*"

–*Business Week*, August 9, 1999

1. Where did this article appear?
2. When was it written?
3. What was the purpose of this article?
4. What is the main idea of this article?
5. What additional details support the main idea?

Application Activity

Bring to class an article that you have found in a newspaper, magazine, or real estate buying guide that deals with home buying or apartment rental hints. Identify the main idea and explain why it is important.

Practice and **assess** key skills with ***Skillbuilder Interactive Workbook, Level 2.***

SECTION 4

Buying and Operating a Vehicle

Cover Story

The Columbus Dispatch, May 27, 1999

With cars and trucks driving off dealer lots at a fast clip, automakers have decided now is the time to build factories and expand others.

Even with excess capacity at factories that make passenger cars, demand is so great for their highly profitable sport-utility vehicles and pickup trucks that carmakers are willing to risk adding plants to cash in on the good times.

Reader's Guide

Terms to Know

- registration fee
- liability insurance

Reading Objectives

1. What are the trade-offs when buying a vehicle?
2. What costs are involved in operating a vehicle?

As with every decision in life, when you decide to buy a particular type of car, you are going to make a trade-off that involves an opportunity cost. Three of the major trade-offs include the following:

(1) Usually, the smaller the engine, the less gas an automobile burns. This makes a car with a smaller engine less costly to operate, but the car will accelerate less quickly. See **Figure 5.12** on page 130.

(2) Newer automobiles cost more, but they require fewer repairs than older ones. See **Figure 5.13** on page 131 for tips on choosing a new or used car.

FIGURE 5.12

Trade-Offs Some of the trade-offs you'll make when purchasing an automobile include small car versus large car, new versus used, and powerful engine versus having to buy less gasoline. ***What is an advantage of owning a small car?***

(3) The smaller the automobile, the more energy efficient it is. In an accident, however, larger automobiles usually protect passengers better.

Buying and Operating a Vehicle

Buying a car involves opportunity costs. One is the amount of money and time spent shopping for the car. Another is the amount of money and time spent in actually purchasing the car. Because of limited resources, most people have to borrow funds to buy a car. The costs of the loan are the down payment, the monthly payments on the principal, and the interest on the loan.

registration fee: *licensing fee, usually annual, paid to a state for the right to use a car*

Registration Fee The owner of an automobile must pay a state licensing fee, or a **registration fee,** to use the car. Usually the fee must be paid annually. In many states, the amount of the fee varies depending on the car's age, weight, type, and value.

Normal Maintenance and Major Repairs The amount of normal maintenance—oil and filter changes and minor tune-ups—depends on the amount the car is driven and how carefully the owner maintains the car. Major repairs are those that are normally unexpected and expensive. They include rebuilding the transmission and replacing the exhaust system. No one can guarantee that an automobile will not require major repairs while you own it, but you can follow certain steps to reduce the probability.

You should check the repair records of different cars before deciding on a particular make and model. If you are considering a used car, you should also take it to a diagnostic center, or have a mechanic check it. Sometimes dealers offer warranties on used cars for a limited time period, such as 30 days, or you can purchase a warranty covering a longer period of time.

FIGURE 5.13 Checklist for Buying an Automobile

These tips will help you in making a good choice of a new car or used car:

1. Ask friends and relatives about their satisfaction or dissatisfaction with their cars.
2. Read articles about different makes and models in car magazines such as *Car and Driver* and *Road & Track.*
3. Read *Consumer Reports* and *Consumers' Research Magazine* for reviews of new automobiles. Carefully read their reports on repair records of different models.
4. Visit dealers and read brochures about their vehicles, keeping in mind that these pamphlets promote the best features.
5. Personally inspect various makes and models in automobile showrooms.
6. Check what is covered by the service warranty. A used car may still be covered under the original manufacturer's warranty. Also, some dealers offer their own limited warranties for used cars.
7. After you decide on a particular make and model, compare the prices offered by several dealers.
8. If you are buying a vehicle off the lot rather than ordering one, check the options—air conditioning, a CD player, special paint, and so on—and their prices. If you do not want any options, the dealer may lower the price.
9. If you are buying a used car, have an automobile diagnostic center or a mechanic not connected with the dealer check it. Add the cost of needed repairs to the dealer's price. This is the real cost of the automobile to you.
10. Make sure the listed price includes federal excise taxes and dealer preparation charges. An *excise tax* is a tax on the manufacture, sale, or use of specific products, such as liquor, gasoline, and automobiles. Dealer preparation charges can include the costs of cleaning, installing certain options, and checking the car's engine before you drive it away. State and local sales taxes will be added to the total cost later.
11. Check various dealers for the reputation of their service departments. Your warranty usually allows you to take your car to any dealer selling that make of car.
12. Do not put a deposit on a car unless you are sure you are going to buy it. You may have a problem getting your deposit back if you change your mind.

FIGURE 5.14 Factors Affecting Automobile Insurance Rates

When you buy automobile insurance, the rate you are charged is determined not only by your age and sex, but also by the following:

1. **The type of car you drive.** Insurance companies consider the safety record of a car and the costs to repair it if it is involved in an accident.
2. **Where you drive.** If the rate of thefts and accidents is high in an area, the risk to the insurance company is greater. A city, for example, would have more thefts and accidents than would a rural area. Therefore, the rate the insurance company charges in a city will be higher.
3. **What you use the car for.** If you drive your car for business on a daily basis, the rate will be higher than if you use it only for errands and occasional trips.
4. **Marital status.** In general, married men and women have lower accident rates than single men and women and, therefore, pay lower insurance rates.
5. **Safety record.** If you have a history of accidents and traffic tickets, then you will be charged a high rate. Whether a new driver has had driver education is often considered in determining a rate.
6. **Number of drivers.** The number of drivers using a car increases the insurance rate.

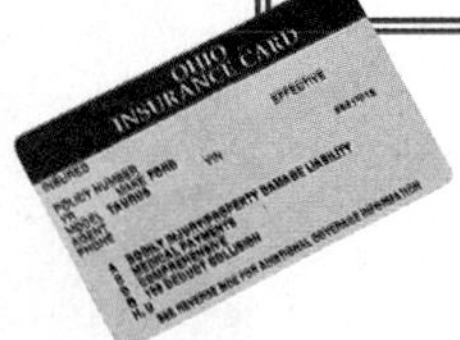

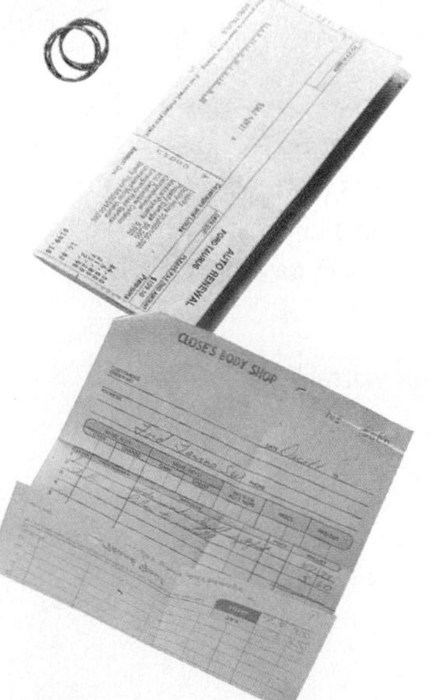

Extended Warranty One way to guard against having to pay for major repairs is to buy extended warranty coverage. New-car warranties generally protect owners for all major repairs except tune-ups and damage resulting from improper use of the automobile. New-car warranties usually last only a few years, or up to a certain limit of miles or kilometers. These warranties, however, can often be extended for another one, two, or three years by paying additional money when the car is purchased.

Depreciation *Depreciation*—a decline in value over time—takes place as an item wears out or becomes outdated. Age is the major factor. A car loses value every year even if it is not driven because an automobile is a durable good. All durable goods deteriorate, or become worse over time.

Another cause of depreciation is the technology and features of new makes and models. These changes make older models obsolete—out of date and out of style.

The amount of depreciation caused by physical wear and tear varies. It depends on how hard a car is driven, how many miles or kilometers it is driven, and how well it is maintained. Generally, cars depreciate about 20 percent each year.

Insurance A major cost of owning an automobile, especially for someone under age 25, is insurance. Many states require that liability insurance be purchased before an automobile can be licensed. **Liability insurance** pays for bodily injury as well as property damage if you are in an accident.

liability insurance: *insurance that pays for bodily injury and property damage*

Insurance companies classify drivers in various ways, usually according to age, gender, and marital status. Rates depend on the category into which a person fits. The categories, in turn, are based on statistics showing that different types of drivers have different accident rates.

Young people almost always have to pay higher insurance rates. For example, single males in the 16–25 age group have the highest accident rate of all drivers. Not surprisingly, most insurance companies charge these drivers the highest insurance rates. Married women ages 25–45 have the fewest accidents and the lowest rates.

Figure 5.14 shows factors in addition to age and sex that affect insurance rates. Rates cannot vary too widely, however, because states set limits on the rates that companies can charge within state borders.

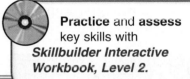

Practice and **assess** key skills with ***Skillbuilder Interactive Workbook, Level 2.***

SECTION 4 Assessment

Understanding Key Terms

1. **Define** registration fee, liability insurance.

Reviewing Objectives

2. What are the trade-offs when buying a vehicle?
3. **Graphic Organizer** Use a chart like the one below to identify the costs of operating a vehicle.

Applying Economic Concepts

4. **Insurance Risk** Apply the six factors in **Figure 5.14** to your personal driving situation. Are you a risk for insurance companies? Why or why not?

Critical Thinking Activity

5. **Making Comparisons** Search the Internet for information on car insurance in your area. Write an article about the companies that sell insurance and analyze the factors they use in determining what to charge for drivers in your age group.

BusinessWeek

SPOTLIGHT ON THE ECONOMY

Backseat Driver on the Dash

Check It Out! In this chapter you learned about the costs of owning and operating an automobile. In this article, read to learn about a new option available on some current makes and models.

The most striking thing about Alpine Electronics' computer navigation system for cars is its dead-on accuracy. Using a global-positioning system keyed to satellites and combined with gyroscopic motion sensors, the car knows its position within, at worst, half a city block. This is combined with a map database from Navigation Technologies (NavTech) that knows about details as small as right-turn cutouts at intersections.

When driving, the five-inch LCD display, which is bright enough to be seen even in strong sunlight, offers a choice between a map view, which can zoom from block-level detail to a city overview, and a diagram of driving instructions. A synthesized female voice warns you of turns, usually with ample time to maneuver safely. The display and controls are laid out to be informative without being distracting.

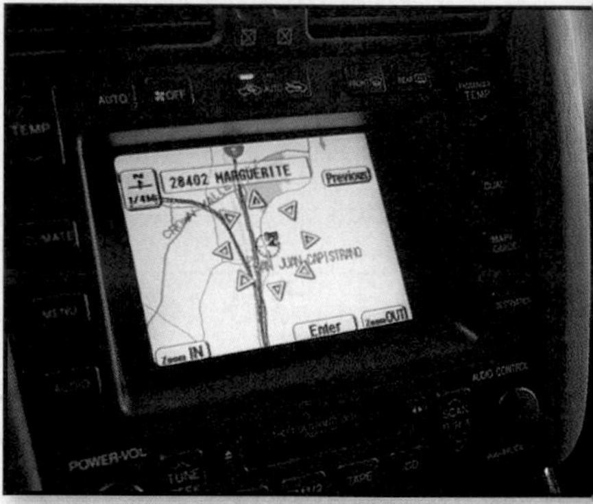

NavTech's database divides the U.S. into nine regions. You get one with the unit, and additional ones cost $150. Major metropolitan areas have block-by-block detail for all streets. Rural areas and smaller cities offer only major roads.

The only really serious flaw . . . is the cost. The price [$2,000], whether as an option in a few luxury models or as an aftermarket add-on, is way too steep for most consumers.

Of course, it wasn't long ago that auto CD players–and even antilock brakes–were luxury options, too. With prices likely to slide down the technology cost curve quickly, it's not hard to imagine the day when in-car navigation systems become standard features.

Think About It

1. **Analyze how the computer navigation system for automobiles works.**
2. **What is the main flaw of this system, and why may that change in the near future?**

CHAPTER  Summary

Chapter Overview Visit the *Economics Today and Tomorrow* Web site at ett.glencoe.com and click on ***Chapter 5—Chapter Overviews*** to review chapter information.

SECTION 1 Shopping for Food

- Comparison shopping for food involves making comparisons among brands, sizes, and stores.
- Reading advertisements and collecting cents-off coupons is a timesaving, inexpensive way to comparison shop.
- Supermarkets or **club warehouse stores** usually charge the lowest prices for food, whereas **convenience stores** charge more, but may save you time.
- Per-unit pricing of goods makes it easy to compare prices.
- If you make a habit of using coupons, you can reduce your food bill by more than 10 percent over a one-year period.

SECTION 2 Clothing Choices

- Americans spend about $400 billion annually on clothing and other personal products.
- Clothing value depends on price, style, **durability,** and cost of care.
- When you purchase an item of clothing, you are purchasing it for the **service flow** that it yields.
- The work-time cost of clothing has decreased over the past 100 years, but it is still the wise consumer who buys clothing on sale.

SECTION 3 To Rent or to Buy

- There are economic and psychological advantages and disadvantages to both owning your own home and renting.
- If you choose to buy a house, you will probably need to obtain a mortgage, which involves a cash down payment, monthly installments, and interest, plus money for **closing costs** and **points.**
- Most renters pay a **security deposit** and sign a **lease** that protects their rights as well as lists their responsibilities.
- Tenant responsibilities include paying the rent on time and taking reasonable care of the property.

SECTION 4 Buying and Operating a Vehicle

- Some of the trade-offs you'll make when purchasing an automobile include small car versus large car, new versus used, and powerful engine versus having to buy less gasoline.
- The costs of operating an automobile include the **registration fee,** normal maintenance, major repairs, depreciation, and **liability insurance.**
- One way to guard against having to pay for major repairs is to buy extended warranty coverage.

CHAPTER 5

Assessment and Activities

Self-Check Quiz Visit the *Economics Today and Tomorrow* Web site at ett.glencoe.com and click on ***Chapter 5—Self-Check Quizzes*** to prepare for the Chapter Test.

Identifying Key Terms

Write the letter of the definition in Column B that correctly defines each term in Column A.

Column A

1. service flow
2. durability
3. security deposit
4. registration fee
5. liability insurance
6. club warehouse store
7. private-labeled products
8. lease
9. closing costs
10. points

Column B

a. pays for injury or property damage
b. stream of benefits from using a good
c. usually one month's rent left on deposit
d. how long something lasts
e. fee charged by lender for paperwork, taxes, and other activities
f. goods with the store's label on them
g. large stores requiring a membership
h. money paid to license a vehicle
i. agreement describing rental terms
j. fees paid to a lender, normally when interest rates are low

Recalling Facts and Ideas

Section 1

1. What is one of the best ways to engage in comparison shopping for food products?
2. What is the trade-off involved when you buy a generic brand rather than a brand-name product?

Section 2

3. What four factors influence the kind of clothing choices people make?
4. What is the normal relationship between how long an article of clothing will last and its price?

Section 3

5. What are some of the disadvantages of owning a house?
6. What are some of the disadvantages of renting a house or an apartment?
7. State three responsibilities of landlords.

Section 4

8. If you do not pay cash for a car, what expense must be included in the cost of buying the car?
9. What is included in the cost of operating an automobile?

Thinking Critically

1. **Understanding Cause and Effect** Analyze why automobile insurance companies charge more for unmarried males between the ages of 16 and 25 than they do for married males between these ages.

2. **Making Comparisons** The two basic types of mortgages used today are flexible rate and fixed rate. Create a chart like the one below to explain the advantages and disadvantages of each.

Type of mortgage	Advantages	Disadvantages

Applying Economic Concepts

Competition and Market Structure Examine the food ads in your local newspaper for one week. List those food items that are common to each ad. Compare the prices from the different food stores for the common items. What is the largest percentage difference between the highest and lowest prices?

Reviewing Skills

Finding the Main Idea In *The Theory of the Leisure Class* (1899), economist Thorstein Veblen criticized the leisure class, or the rich, and its spending habits. He talked about "conspicuous consumption," which is buying goods and services to impress others.

List examples of conspicuous consumption that you notice throughout the day—whether on television or in real life. Write a paragraph explaining what kinds of products are typically consumed in this way.

Technology Activity

Using the Internet On the Census Bureau Web site, look up the section of the most recent Census of Housing entitled *Selected Housing Characteristics by States and Counties.* Make a table listing the following statistics for your county: (1) number of total housing units; (2) number of units occupied by owners; and (3) number occupied by renters.

Cooperative Learning Project

Organize into six groups. Call separate automobile insurance agents and ask for a rate quote by giving the following facts:

- ☐ Age: 21
- ☐ Gender: at least 3 males and 3 females should make the calls
- ☐ Automobile type: 2000 Chevy Malibu
- ☐ Use: Drive to college and part-time job (80 miles a week)
- ☐ Coverage desired: 100/300/50, which means up to $100,000 for one person injured in an accident, up to a total of $300,000 for all personal injuries suffered in the accident, and up to $50,000 for damages to private or public property caused by the accident
- ☐ Collision and comprehensive deductible: $500; no medical or towing

After each group receives its quotes, compare your information:

1. Which agent/insurance company gave the highest quote? The lowest?
2. Was there a substantial difference between the insurance rates for females and males?
3. What was the average percentage difference between the rates quoted for females and males?

Analyzing the Global Economy

Use the Internet to find automobile dealerships in major cities around the world. Compare the prices of new and used cars in various cities.

Global Economy

A Day on the Town First, you go downtown to meet a friend for lunch. Later, a friend invites you to a movie. On the way to the theater, you stop and buy gasoline for your car. Check the map below to see what your day might cost in various cities around the world.*

Vancouver, Canada	
Trolley fare, one way	$ 1.90
Lunch, per person	7.05
Gasoline, one gallon	1.70
Movie ticket	6.47

Chicago, U.S.A.	
Subway fare, one way	$ 1.50
Lunch, per person	8.74
Gasoline, one gallon	1.36
Movie ticket	6.29

Rio de Janeiro, Brazil	
Subway fare, one way	$ 0.28
Lunch, per person	13.58
Gasoline, one gallon	2.08
Movie ticket	8.11

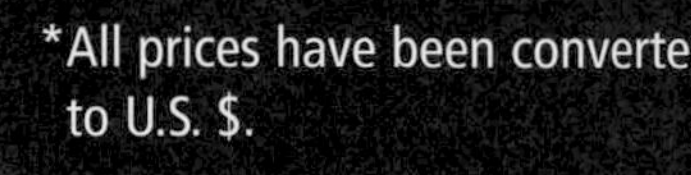
*All prices have been converted to U.S. $.

Berlin, Germany

Subway fare, one way	$ 2.60
Lunch, per person	11.76
Gasoline, one gallon	3.86
Movie ticket	6.35

Moscow, Russia

Subway fare, one way	$ 0.22
Lunch, per person	22.70
Gasoline, one gallon	1.59
Movie ticket	7.63

Mumbai, India

Subway fare, one way	$ 0.10
Lunch, per person	7.53
Gasoline, one gallon	2.16
Movie ticket	1.07

Tokyo, Japan

Subway fare, one way	$ 1.60
Lunch, per person	20.16
Gasoline, one gallon	4.58
Movie ticket	20.00

Johannesburg, South Africa

Subway fare, one way	$ 0.85
Lunch, per person	10.14
Gasoline, one gallon	1.93
Movie ticket	7.78

Sydney, Australia

Subway fare, one way	$ 1.79
Lunch, per person	9.88
Gasoline, one gallon	2.16
Movie ticket	8.23

Thinking Globally

1. In which city would your day on the town cost the most? The least?

2. Look at the prices for Mumbai. How do you think most people get around the city—by car or by public transportation? Why?

CHAPTER 6

Saving and Investing

Why It's Important

Why should you save? What is the difference between saving and investing? This chapter will explain reasons for saving, as well as the various institutions and investments in which to put your money.

To learn more about investment strategies, view the **Economics & You** *Chapter 13 video lesson:* **Saving and Investing**

ECONOMICS *Online*

Chapter Overview Visit the *Economics Today and Tomorrow* Web site at ett.glencoe.com and click on ***Chapter 6—Chapter Overviews*** to preview chapter information.

SECTION  Why Save?

Cover Story

The Columbus Dispatch, May 29, 1999

Money is burning a hole in consumers' pockets. Again last month, U.S. wage earners spent nearly as much as they made, contributing to record low savings.

But consumers have good reason to be out there spending. They've got jobs, their incomes are rising, confidence is high, and the stock market is booming.

This trend dragged down the savings rate—savings as a percentage of after-tax income—to a record low.

Reader's Guide

Terms to Know

- saving
- interest
- passbook savings account
- statement savings account
- money market deposit account
- time deposits
- maturity
- certificates of deposit

Reading Objectives

1. When should you save?
2. How do passbook, statement, and money market accounts differ?
3. What are the advantages of time deposits?

Economists define ***saving*** as the setting aside of income for a period of time so that it can be used later. You may already be saving some of your income for a future use, such as buying a DVD system or continuing your education. See **Figure 6.1** on page 142. As you read this section, you'll learn why saving is important to you and the economy as a whole.

saving: *setting aside income for a period of time so that it can be used later*

Deciding to Save

Any saving that you do now may be only for purchases that require more funds than you usually have at one time. When you are self-supporting and have more responsibilities, you will probably save for other reasons, such as having funds in case of emergencies and for your retirement.

Results of Saving When an individual saves, the economy as a whole benefits. Saving provides money for others to invest or spend. Saving also allows businesses to expand, which provides increased income for consumers and raises the standard of living.

FIGURE 6.1

Saving Goals Your saving goals will change as you move through life. Today you may be saving for a stereo, whereas in the future you may save for a college education. ***How does saving affect your future spending habits?***

Where to Save Generally, when people think of saving, they think of putting their funds in a savings bank or a similar financial institution where it will earn interest. **Interest** is the payment people receive when they lend money, or allow someone else to use their money. A person receives interest on his or her savings plan for as long as funds are in the account.

You actually have many options regarding places in which to put your savings. As you learned in Chapter 4, the most common places are commercial banks, savings and loan associations, savings banks, and credit unions. Investigate the financial institutions in your area and the services they offer.

interest: *payment people receive when they lend money or allow someone else to use their money*

In comparison shopping for the best savings plan, you need to consider the trade-offs. Some savings plans allow immediate access to your money but pay a low rate of interest. Others pay higher interest and allow immediate use of your money, but require a large minimum balance.

Savings Accounts

Passbook savings accounts are also called regular savings accounts. With a **passbook savings account,** the depositor receives a booklet in which deposits, withdrawals, and interest are recorded. A customer must present the passbook each time one of these *transactions,* or business operations, takes place.

passbook savings account: *account for which a depositor receives a booklet in which deposits, withdrawals, and interest are recorded*

A **statement savings account** is basically the same type of account. Instead of a passbook that must be presented for each transaction, however, the depositor receives a monthly statement showing all transactions. The chief appeal of these accounts is that they offer easy availability of funds. The depositor can usually withdraw funds at any time without paying a *penalty*—forfeiting any money—but there is a trade-off. The interest paid on passbook and statement accounts is low compared to the interest on other savings plans.

statement savings account: *account similar to a passbook savings account except that the depositor receives a monthly statement showing all transactions*

A **money market deposit account** (MMDA) is another type of account that pays relatively high rates of interest and allows immediate access to money through checks. The trade-off is that these accounts have a $1,000 to $2,500 minimum balance requirement. Customers can usually make withdrawals from a money market account in person at any time, but they are allowed to write only a few checks a month against the account.

Comparing Saving Rates

The percent of income that Americans save fell steadily in the 1990s. Today, the saving rate–the percentage of disposable personal income saved–stands well below 4 percent. How does this compare to the saving rates of other countries? Below are some recent statistics on saving rates for several industrialized nations. ■

Country	Saving rate
Canada	4.6%
France	12.5%
Germany	12.4%
Great Britain	11.6%
Italy	13.4%
Japan	13.2%

Time Deposits

The term ***time deposits*** refers to a wide variety of savings plans that require a saver to deposit his or her funds for a certain period of time. The period of time is called the **maturity,** and may vary from seven days to eight years or more. Time deposits are often called **certificates of deposit** (CDs), or savings certificates. CDs state the amount of the deposit, the maturity, and the rate of interest being paid.

Time deposits offer higher interest rates than passbook or statement savings accounts. The longer the maturity, the higher the interest rate that is paid. For example, a CD with a short-term maturity of 90 days pays less interest than a CD with a two-year maturity. Savers who cash a time deposit before maturity pay a penalty.

Insuring Deposits When the stock market collapsed in 1929, the resulting crisis wiped out peopleês entire savings. Congress passed, and President Franklin Roosevelt signed, legislation to protect deposits. This legislation created the Federal Deposit Insurance Corporation (FDIC).

Today there are several federal agencies that insure most banks and savings institutions. See **Figure 6.2** on page 144. Each depositorês money in a particular savings institution is insured up to $100,000. If an insured institution fails, each depositor will be paid the full amount of his or her savings up to $100,000 for each legally separate account.

money market deposit account: *account that pays relatively high rates of interest, requires a minimum balance, and allows immediate access to money*

time deposits: *savings plans that require savers to leave their money on deposit for certain periods of time*

maturity: *period of time at the end of which time deposits will pay a stated rate of interest*

certificates of deposit: *time deposits that state the amount of the deposit, maturity, and rate of interest being paid*

FIGURE 6.2 Savings Institutions' Services and Insurers

Institution	Savings Services Offered	Insured by	Number of Institutions*
Commercial banks	Passbook and statement savings accounts, certificates of deposit, money market accounts	Federal Deposit Insurance Corporation (FDIC)	8,080
Savings and loan associations (S&Ls)/savings banks	Passbook and statement savings accounts, certificates of deposit, money market accounts	S&Ls: Savings Association Insurance Fund (SAIF)/FDIC	1,533
Credit unions	Share drafts**, share accounts, share certificates	National Credit Union Share Insurance Fund	9,984

*Number of savings institutions changes often
**Interest-earning account similar to checking account

Practice and **assess** key skills with ***Skillbuilder Interactive Workbook, Level 2.***

SECTION 1 Assessment

Understanding Key Terms

1. **Define** saving, interest, passbook savings account, statement savings account, money market deposit account, time deposits, maturity, certificates of deposit.

Reviewing Objectives

2. What are three reasons that people save?
3. **Graphic Organizer** Use a chart like the one below to explain the differences among passbook, statement, and money market savings accounts.

Type of account	Similarities	Differences

4. What are the advantages of time deposits?

Applying Economic Concepts

5. **Saving** Why is it more difficult for the beginning saver to open a money market deposit account than a passbook savings account?

Critical Thinking Activity

6. **Synthesizing Information** If your bank pays 5.5 percent interest on savings deposits, what is the simple interest paid in the third year on an initial $100 deposit? What is the total amount in the account after three years? What is the amount after three years if the interest was compounded annually? *For help in understanding interest rates, see page xxii in the Economic Handbook.*

Technology Skills

Using a Spreadsheet

People use electronic spreadsheets to manage numbers quickly and easily. Formulas may be used to add, subtract, multiply, and divide the numbers in the spreadsheet. If you make a change to one number, the totals are recalculated automatically for you.

- Vertical columns are assigned letters—A, B, C, AA, BB, CC, and so on.
- Horizontal rows are assigned numbers—1, 2, 3, and so on.
- The point where a column and row intersect is called a cell—C6, for example.
- The computer highlights the cell you are in. The contents of the cell also appear on a status line at the top of the screen.
- Spreadsheets use standard formulas to calculate numbers. To create a formula, highlight the cell you want the results in. Type an equal sign (=) and then build the formula, step by step. If you type the formula =B4+B5+B6 in cell B7, the values in these cells are added together and the sum shows up in cell B7.
- To use division, the formula would look like this: =A5/C2. This divides A5 by C2. An asterisk (*) signifies multiplication: =(B2*C3)+D1 means you want to multiply B2 times C3, then add D1.

Learning the Skill

All spreadsheets follow a basic design of rows and columns. To understand how to use a spreadsheet, follow the steps on the left.

Practicing the Skill

Study the spreadsheet on this page.

1. Which cell is highlighted? What information is found in the cell?
2. What formula would you type in which cell to calculate the average life expectancy of both males and females in Sri Lanka?
3. What formula would you type in which cell to find the GNP per capita of the South Asian countries listed?

Workbook1

	A	B	C	D	E
1	Nation	GNP Per	Population	Life	Life
2		Capita	mid-1998	Expectancy	Expectancy
3		(U.S.$)	(millions)	Male	Female
4	Bangladesh	260	123.4	59	58
5	Bhutan	390	0.8	NA	NA
6	India	380	988.7	59	59
7	Nepal	210	23.7	55	54
8	Pakistan	480	141.9	58	59
9	Sri Lanka	740	18.9	70	74
10	U.S.	28,020	270.2	73	79
11					

Application Activity

Use a spreadsheet to enter your test scores and your homework grades. At the end of the grading period, input the correct formula and the spreadsheet will calculate your average grade.

SECTION 2

Investing: Taking Risks With Your Savings

Reader's Guide

Terms to Know

- stockholders
- capital gain
- capital loss
- tax-exempt bonds
- savings bonds
- Treasury bills
- Treasury notes
- Treasury bonds
- broker
- over-the-counter market
- mutual fund
- money market fund

Reading Objectives

1. How do stocks and bonds differ?
2. What investment funds are available in stock and bond markets?

Cover Story

The Economist, January 30, 1999

"Some day we'll all invest this way," runs the slogan, while the screen shows a relaxed man on a yacht tickling his laptop computer. Hardly the traditional picture of how shares are bought and sold: on a crowded floor, full of jostling, shouting traders in lurid polyester jackets. But the soaring share prices of electronic brokers suggest that investors, at least, believe online trading is the way of the future.

People have savings plans because they want a safe rate of interest. If people are willing to take a chance on earning a higher rate of return, however, they can invest their savings in others ways, such as in stocks and bonds. Stocks and bonds offer investors greater returns, but with more risk. As you read this section, you'll learn what stocks and bonds are, and why they carry a risk.

Stocks and Bonds

Corporations are formed by selling shares of stock (also called securities). By issuing stock for sale, a company obtains funds for use in expanding its business and, it hopes, in making a large profit. Shares of stock entitle the buyer to a certain part of the future profits

and assets of the corporation selling the stock. The person buying stock, therefore, becomes a part owner of the corporation. As proof of ownership, the corporation issues stock certificates. See **Figure 6.3.**

Stock Returns **Stockholders,** or owners of stock, make money from stock in two ways. One is through *dividends,* the money return a stockholder receives on the amount he or she originally invested in the company. The corporation may declare a dividend at one or more times during a year. Dividends typically are paid only when the company makes a profit.

stockholders: *people who have invested in a corporation and own some of its stock*

The other way people make money on stock is by selling it for more than they paid for it. Some people buy stock just to *speculate,* hoping that the price will increase greatly so they can sell it at a profit. They do not buy it for the dividends.

Capital Gains and Losses Suppose a person buys stock at $20 a share and sells it for $30. The profit of $10 per share is called a **capital gain.** The person has had an increase in his or her capital, or wealth, of $10 a share. Of course, the value of stock may also fall. If a person decides to sell stock at a lower price than he or she paid for it, that person suffers a **capital loss.** Money may be made or lost on bonds in much the same way.

capital gain: *increase in value of an asset from the time it was bought to the time it was sold*

capital loss: *decrease in value of an asset or bond from the time it was bought to the time it was sold*

Bonds Instead of buying stock, people with money to invest can buy bonds. A *bond* is a certificate issued by a company or the government in exchange for borrowed money. It promises to pay a stated rate of interest over a stated period of time, and then to repay the borrowed amount in full at the end of that time. A bondholder lends money for a period of time to a company or government and is paid interest on that money. At the end of the period, the full amount of borrowed money is repaid. The period of time is called the bond's maturity.

Unlike buying stock, buying a bond does not make a bondholder part owner of the company or government that issued the bond. The bond becomes part of the debt of the corporation or

FIGURE 6.3

Stock Certificates Stock certificates like these are issued to people who have invested in a corporation.

government, and the bondholder becomes a creditor. **Figure 6.4** lists these and some other differences between stocks and bonds.

tax-exempt bonds: *bonds sold by local and state governments; interest paid on the bond is not taxed by the federal government*

Tax-Exempt Bonds Local and state governments also sell **tax-exempt bonds.** The interest on these types of bonds, unlike bonds issued by companies, is not taxed by the federal government. Interest that you earn on bonds your own city or state issues is also exempt from city and state income taxes. Tax-exempt bonds are good investments for wealthier people who would otherwise pay high taxes on interest earned from investments.

FIGURE 6.4 Differences Between Stocks and Bonds

Stocks	Bonds
1. All corporations issue or offer to sell stock. That act is what makes them corporations.	**1.** Corporations are not required to issue bonds.
2. Stocks represent ownership.	**2.** Bonds represent debt.
3. Stocks do not have a fixed dividend rate (except preferred stocks).	**3.** Bonds pay a fixed rate of interest.
4. Dividends on stock are paid only if the corporation makes a profit.	**4.** Interest on bonds normally must always be paid, whether or not the corporation earns a profit.
5. Stocks do not have a maturity date. The corporation issuing the stock does not repay the stockholder.	**5.** Bonds have a maturity date. The bondholder is to be repaid the value of the bond, although if the corporation goes out of business, it does not normally repay the bondholders in full.
6. Stockholders (except those with preferred stock) can elect a board of directors who control the corporation.	**6.** Bondholders usually have no voice in or control over how the corporation is run.
7. Stockholders have a claim against the property and income of a corporation only after the claims of all creditors (including bondholders and holders of preferred stock) have been met.	**7.** Bondholders have a claim against the property and income of a corporation that must be met before the claims of any stockholders, including those holding preferred stock.

Savings Bonds The United States government issues **savings bonds** as one of its ways of borrowing money. They range in face value from $50 up to $10,000. The purchase of a U.S. savings bond is similar to buying a bank's certificate of deposit. A very safe form of investment, savings bonds are attractive to people with limited money to invest. Another attraction is that the interest earned is not taxed until the bond is turned in for cash.

A person buying a savings bond pays half the bond's face value. You could purchase a $50 bond, then, for only $25. The bond increases in value every 6 months until its full face value is reached. (The *Rule of 72* tells you how long it takes for the bond to mature: Divide the number 72 by the interest rate.) If you choose to redeem a U.S. savings bond before it matures, you are guaranteed a certain rate of interest, which changes depending on rates of interest in the economy.

savings bonds: *bonds issued by the federal government as a way of borrowing money; they are purchased at half the face value and increase every 6 months until full face value is reached*

T-Bills, T-Notes, and T-Bonds The Treasury Department of the federal government also sells several types of larger investments. **Treasury bills** mature in 3 months to 1 year. The minimum amount of investment for Treasury bills is $1,000. **Treasury notes** have maturity dates of 1 to 10 years, and **Treasury bonds** mature in 10 or more years. Notes and bonds are sold in minimums of $1,000. The interest on all three of these government securities is exempt from state and local income taxes, but not from federal income tax.

Treasury bills: *certificates issued by the U.S. Treasury in exchange for a minimum amount of $1,000 and maturing in 3 months to 1 year*

Treasury notes: *certificates issued by the U.S. Treasury in exchange for minimum amounts of $1,000 and maturing in 1 to 10 years*

Treasury bonds: *certificates issued by the U.S. Treasury in exchange for minimum amounts of $1,000 and maturing in 10 or more years*

Stock and Bond Markets

Stocks are bought and sold through brokers or on the Internet. A **broker** is a person who acts as a go-between for buyers and sellers. If an investor is interested in buying or trading corporate shares, he or she can contact a brokerage firm, which will perform the service for a fee.

broker: *person who acts as a go-between for buyers and sellers of stocks and bonds*

Thousands of full-service brokerage firms throughout the country buy and sell stocks daily for ordinary investors. The fees they charge to perform the trades–up to $500–depend on the dollar amounts invested or traded. Today, however, if an investor has an account with an Internet brokerage firm, the cost for the same trade may be as low as $7.

Savings Bond

There are well over 100 online brokerage firms, with more springing up on the Web every day. It is estimated that 20 million American investors use the Internet to make trades every year.

Stock Exchanges Brokerage houses communicate with the busy floors of the stock exchanges. See **Figure 6.5.** The largest stock exchange, or stock market, is the New York Stock Exchange (NYSE) in New York City. There are also supplemental stock exchanges and regional exchanges–such as the Midwest Stock Exchange in Chicago–and exchanges in other countries–such as the London and Tokyo stock exchanges.

To be listed on these exchanges, a corporation offering stock must prove to the exchange that it is in good financial condition. Most of the companies traded on stock exchanges are among the largest, most profitable corporations in the country.

Over-the-Counter Markets Stocks can also be sold on the **over-the-counter market**, an electronic marketplace for stocks not listed on the organized exchanges. The largest volume of over-the-counter stocks are quoted on the National Association of Securities Dealers Automated Quotations (NASDAQ) national market system, which merged with the American Stock Exchange in 1998.

over-the-counter market: *electronic purchase and sale of stocks and bonds, often of smaller companies, which takes place outside the organized stock exchanges*

Buying Stocks or Bonds If you decide to buy stocks or bonds, you may wish to contact a broker (by phone or through the Internet). You pay the broker a fee to purchase the stock at one of the stock exchanges. The stock exchanges act as a market between buyers and sellers of securities, or stocks.

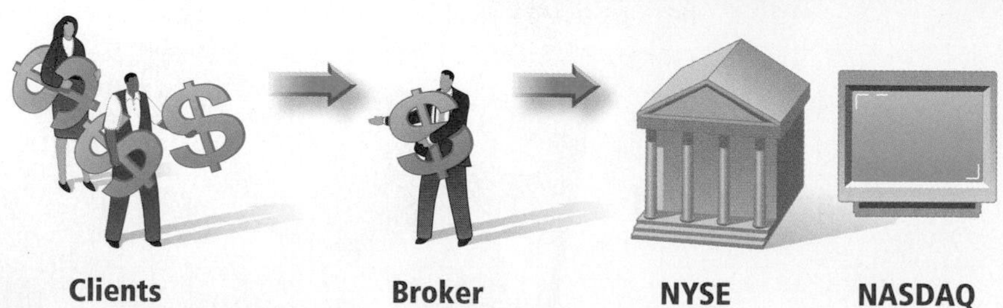

Unlike organized stock exchanges, over-the-counter stocks are not traded in any specific place. Brokerage firms hold shares of stocks that they buy and sell for investors. For example, assume that XYZ Corporation is a company that sells computers. If an investor wanted to buy stock in it, he or she would check the NASDAQ listings in the local newspaper or on the Internet. This table of over-the-counter stocks would list XYZ Corporation, the number of shares of stock sold the day before, and the price at which shares were bought and sold that day. The investor would then call a broker or use the Internet to buy a certain number of shares. Usually stocks are sold in amounts of 100 shares, but some brokers will handle smaller amounts.

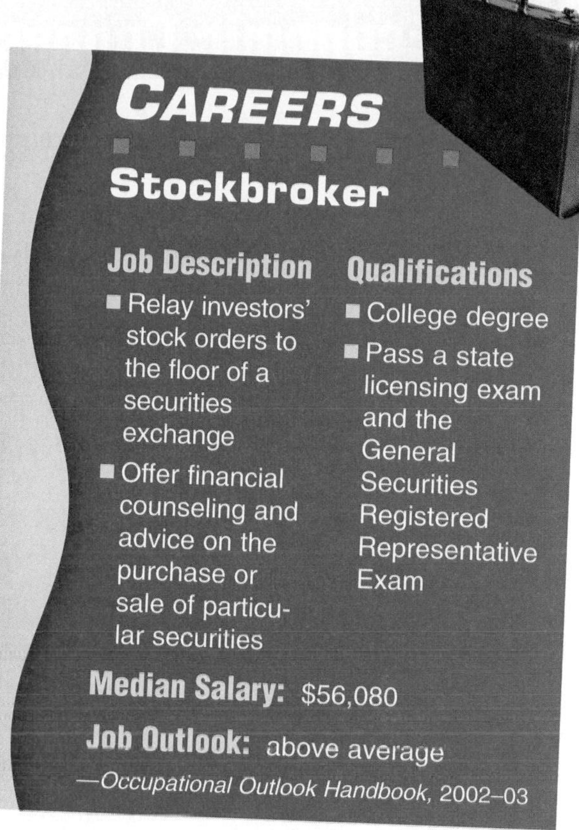

CAREERS
Stockbroker
Job Description
■ Relay investors' stock orders to the floor of a securities exchange
■ Offer financial counseling and advice on the purchase or sale of particular securities
Qualifications
■ College degree
■ Pass a state licensing exam and the General Securities Registered Representative Exam
Median Salary: $56,080
Job Outlook: above average
—Occupational Outlook Handbook, 2002–03

Bond Markets The New York Exchange Bond Market and the American Exchange Bond Market are the two largest bond exchanges. Bonds, including U.S. government bonds, are sold over-the-counter and on the Internet.

Mutual Funds Many people invest in the stock market by placing some of their savings in a **mutual fund**, an investment company that pools the money of many individuals to buy stocks, bonds, or other investments. See **Figure 6.6.** Most mutual funds hold a variety of stocks or bonds. Losses in one area are likely to be made up by gains in another.

<u>mutual fund:</u> *investment company that pools the money of many individuals to buy stocks, bonds, or other investments*

One popular mutual fund invests in stocks used in an index. An *index* is a measuring system that tracks stock prices over the long run. The Dow Jones Industrial Average (DJIA) and Standard & Poor's (S&P) are the two most common indexes. The DJIA tracks

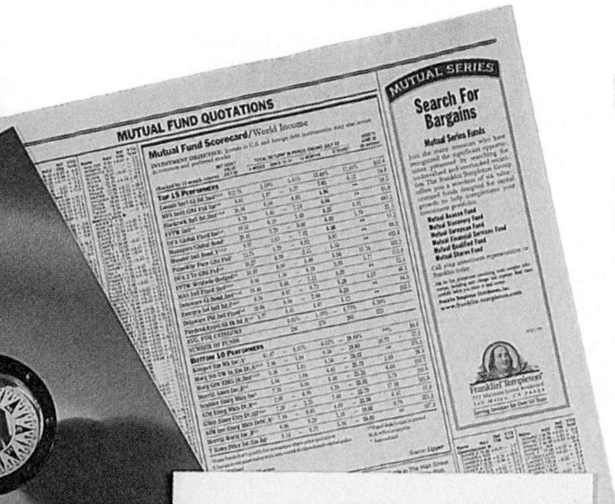

FIGURE 6.6

Mutual Funds The small investor should find out how the mutual fund he or she may choose has performed compared to index funds over a period of several years. ***Why are index funds watched so closely?***

Economic Connection to... History

The Dow Jones and S&P

The Dow was created in 1896 by Charles Dow, cofounder of Dow Jones & Co. It soon became a permanent feature in the company's newspaper, *The Wall Street Journal,* which is one of the world's most influential business publications. The Dow index grew from its original 12 stocks to 30 by 1928.

It wasn't until 1926 that Standard & Poor's introduced a broader stock index, which tracked the nation's 90 biggest companies. The now-familiar S&P 500 stock index expanded in 1957 to include the 500 biggest companies.

Although it may seem odd that the Dow uses only 30 companies to measure a market with more than 10,000 stocks, those 30 companies have a combined market value of over $2.5 trillion. The S&P's 500 companies have a combined market value of $10.5 trillion—more than three-fourths of the nation's publicly owned stocks. ■

the stocks of 30 of the largest American companies to measure the well-being of the stock market as a whole; the S&P 500 index tracks 500 companies.

Most mutual funds use the S&P 500 as the yardstick against which they compare their returns on stocks. The long-run return from index funds is higher than can be expected from almost any other investment. By investing in a broad-based index fund, investors will almost surely do better over the long run than by investing in individual stocks or in a managed mutual fund. A *managed mutual fund* is one in which the managers adjust the mix of stocks and move often in and out of the market to try to generate the highest yield.

money market fund: *type of mutual fund that uses investors' money to make short-term loans to businesses and banks*

Money Market Funds

One type of mutual fund, called a **money market fund,** normally uses investorsê money b buy the short-term debt of businesses and banks. Most money market funds allow investors to write checks against their money in the fund. Any check, however, must be above some minimum amount, usually $500. The investor then earns money only on the amount left in the account.

Banks, savings and loan associations, and savings banks now offer a similar service, called *money market deposit accounts* (MMDA). A major advantage of MMDAs is that the federal government insures them against loss. Mutual funds and money market funds are not insured by the federal government.

Government Regulations

The stock market is heavily regulated today, both at the state and federal levels. The Securities and Exchange Commission (SEC), created by the Securities Exchange Act of 1934, is responsible for administering all federal securities laws. It has regulatory authority over brokerage firms, stock exchanges, and most businesses that issue stock. It also investigates any dealings among corporations, such as mergers, that affect the value of stocks.

Congress passed the Securities Act in an attempt to avoid another stock market crash like that of 1929. The act requires that all essential information concerning the issuing of stocks or bonds be made available to investors. To accomplish this, a registration statement must be filed with the federal government. A briefer description, called a *prospectus*, must be given to each potential buyer of stocks or bonds. It lists the amount offered, the price, and the company's projected use for the money raised by the stocks or bonds. Mutual funds must also distribute a prospectus describing the fund and the way in which the money will be invested.

States also have securities laws. These are designed mostly to prevent schemes that would take advantage of small investors.

Practice and **assess** key skills with ***Skillbuilder Interactive Workbook, Level 2.***

SECTION 2 Assessment

Understanding Key Terms

1. **Define** stockholders, capital gain, capital loss, tax-exempt bonds, savings bonds, Treasury bills, Treasury notes, Treasury bonds, broker, over-the-counter market, mutual fund, money market fund.

Reviewing Objectives

2. How do stocks and bonds differ?
3. **Graphic Organizer** Use a diagram like the one below to list at least three investment funds available in stock and bond markets.

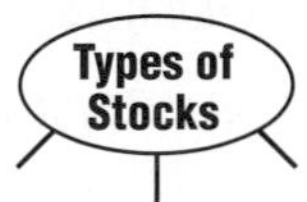

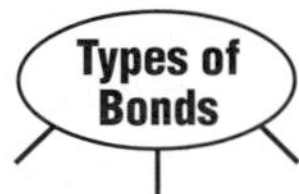

Applying Economic Concepts

4. **Financial Markets** List five possible investments you could make if you had $10,000 in available funds. Rank them from highest return to lowest return.

Critical Thinking Activity

5. **Synthesizing Information** Analyze the stocks on the New York Stock Exchange and over-the-counter market by checking the NYSE and NASDAQ quotes listed in the newspaper. Find a stock from each listing that had a net change of more than 2 percent. What corporations were they? *For help in reading the financial page, see page xxiii in the Economic Handbook.*

People & Perspectives

John W. Rogers, Jr.

ENTREPRENEUR (1958–)

- **Founder and president of Ariel Capital Management, Inc., a Chicago-based money management firm**
- **Manages over $10 billion in assets**
- **His mutual funds are ranked among the best investments by *Fortune Magazine***

John W. Rogers, Jr., is one of the country's best managers of stocks of small and medium-sized companies. Beginning in 1983 with money from associates and his parents, Rogers founded Ariel Capital Management, Inc.

Rogers explains what researchers look for in an ideal stock for the Ariel Fund, the first of their three mutual funds:

> *"Our ideal stock-investment characteristics are really four things. The most important is that the company is in the kind of industry where they have barriers to entry to stop the competition from coming in, and the kind of strong brand-name and customer awareness that brings back customers time and time again. . . .*
>
> *The second thing is the quality of the product and the quality of the management. . . .*
>
> *And the third thing is valuation, and how many other people understand the stock as well as we do. If a stock is cheap, we want to understand why its future is going to be better. . . .*
>
> *The final thing is size. We are always looking at smaller companies with new ideas, $1.5 billion or less."*

Ariel Capital Management, Inc., fund portfolios contain a wide array of companies—from drugstores to book publishers. Ariel has favored newspaper stocks. Rogers explains why:

> *"These are wonderful businesses to have, because they are basically little monopolies. . . . You have a lot of pricing power because you're the only game in town, both with how much it costs to buy the newspaper, and also what your advertisers have to pay to put their ads inside the newspaper."*

Checking for Understanding

1. **What characteristics does Rogers look for in an ideal stock?**
2. **Why does Rogers favor newspaper stocks?**

SECTION 3

Special Savings Plans and Goals

COVER STORY

KIPLINGER'S PERSONAL FINANCE MAGAZINE, AUGUST 2000

With two medical degrees in the family— and lots of education debt—Paul and Heidi Geis know how expensive college can be. No wonder their 18-month-old, Aiden, already has a college fund. But what may be surprising is that his tuition kitty resides 2,000 miles away from the Geises' home in Pittsburgh—in Utah's college-savings plan....

Utah is among several states that have dramatically improved their college-savings plans over the past year.

READER'S GUIDE

Terms to Know

- pension plans
- Keogh Plan
- individual retirement account (IRA)
- Roth IRA
- diversification

Reading Objectives

1. What kinds of retirement investments are available?
2. How much should you save and invest?

One of the reasons that people save is to send their children to college. Another reason is to have income to spend when they retire. In addition to their savings, most Americans will need additional sources of income for the years after they stop working. As you read this section, you'll learn what those additional sources of income are, and the amount of risk involved in these investments.

Investing for Retirement

Many individuals have company retirement plans called **pension plans** that provide retirement income. One of the most common types is a 401(k) plan, in which you allow a certain portion of

pension plans: *company plans that provide retirement income for their workers* your paycheck to be withheld, and the company matches that amount. Also, most people are eligible for Social Security payments when they reach retirement. Social Security by itself, however, will not provide enough income to live comfortably. It is important, therefore, for a person to provide for his or her own retirement by saving and investing in private retirement plans.

ECONOMICS Online

Student Web Activity Visit the *Economics Today and Tomorrow* Web site at ett.glencoe.com and click on ***Chapter 6—Student Web Activities*** to learn more about Roth IRAs.

A major benefit of a private or personal pension plan is the tax savings. You do not have to pay federal income tax *immediately* on the earned income that you invest in one of these retirement plans, or on the interest that the plan earns if it does not exceed a certain amount. Should you need to take money out of the plan early, however, you have to pay a tax penalty. Otherwise, you pay income tax only as you withdraw money from the plan at retirement. Because your yearly income will likely be less then, your tax rate will be lower.

Individual Pension Plans The Keogh Act of 1962 was passed to help self-employed people set up their own pension plans. The **Keogh Plan** allows those people who are self-employed to set aside a maximum of 15 percent of their income up to a specified amount each year, and then deduct that amount from their yearly taxable income.

Keogh Plan: *retirement plan that allows self-employed individuals to save a maximum of 15 percent of their income up to a specified amount each year, and to deduct that amount from their yearly taxable income*

Another form of retirement plan is the **individual retirement account (IRA).** A single person earning less than $30,000 can contribute up to $3,000 a year and deduct those contributions from taxable income. There are other income limits for married couples and those covered by employer pension plans, however. The benefit of an IRA is that the income you contribute to the IRA is not taxed in the year it is contributed. In addition, the interest you earn on that income is not taxed either. You pay the tax only when you take out funds from your IRA account, usually after age 59½.

individual retirement account (IRA): *private retirement plan that allows individuals or married couples to save a certain amount of untaxed earnings per year with the interest being tax-deferred*

A new form of IRA is called the **Roth IRA.** Again, you are allowed to put up to $3,000 a year in a Roth IRA. You do not get to deduct your contributions from your taxable income, however. The benefit is that all of the interest you earn on your contributions to a Roth IRA is tax-free forever. Thus, when you take out funds from your Roth IRA account while you are retired, you pay no additional taxes.

Roth IRA: *private retirement plan that taxes income before it is saved, but which does not tax interest on that income when funds are used upon retirement*

Real Estate as an Investment Buying real estate, such as land and buildings, is another form of investing. For the past

50 years or so, buying a home, condominium, or co-op has proven to be a wise investment in many parts of the country. Resale values have soared at times, especially during the late 1970s. In the early 1980s and again in the early 1990s, however, the growth in the price of housing slowed in some areas, particularly in California and parts of the Northeast. By the end of the 1990s, values everywhere were once again on the upswing.

Buying raw, or undeveloped, land is a much riskier investment. No one can guarantee that there will be a demand in the future for a particular piece of land. The same is true for housing, but most people do not buy housing for the purpose of reselling it.

Real estate, either as raw land or developed land, is not very easy to turn into cash on short notice. As shown in **Figure 6.7**, sometimes real property for sale stays on the market for long periods of time. This difficulty in getting cash for your investment is one of the trade-offs involved when investing in real estate. You cannot get your funds as quickly as you could if you had invested in stocks, bonds, a bank CD, or some other savings plan.

How Much to Save and Invest?

Saving involves a trade-off like every other activity. The more you save today, the more you can buy and consume a year from now, 10 years from now, or 30 years from now. You will, however, have less to spend today. Deciding what percentage of income to save depends on the following factors:

- How much do you spend on your fixed expenses?
- What are your reasons for saving?
- How much interest can you earn on your savings and, therefore, how fast will your savings grow?
- How much income do you think you will be earning in the future?

If you expect to make a much higher income tomorrow, you have less reason to save a large percentage of today's income. It is a good idea, however, to have *some* sort of savings plan. There are several questions to answer before you decide on this plan:

Real Estate as an Investment Buying real estate—whether as developed or undeveloped land—is risky. Variations in supply and demand produce different prices for houses and commercial land in different parts of the country.

- What degree of risk are you willing to take?
- How important is it that your savings be readily available in case you need immediate cash?
- Will your standard of living at retirement depend largely on your accumulated savings?

Amount of Risk Such questions are difficult to answer because there are so many ways to save and invest. Perhaps the most important factor to consider is the amount of risk that you are willing to take with your savings.

If you put a lesser amount in the more risky types of investments, you will have some security with your savings and have some funds readily available should you need cash in a hurry. You may also have a chance of making high returns, as risk and return are directly related. **Figure 6.8** ranks various investments according to risk.

Spreading Out Your Investments Investing your savings in several different types of accounts lowers the overall risk. If one investment turns sour, the others may do better. Financial planners call spreading out your investments **diversification.** See **Figure 6.9.** Mutual funds, for example, help you diversify.

diversification: *spreading of investments among several different types of accounts to lower overall risk*

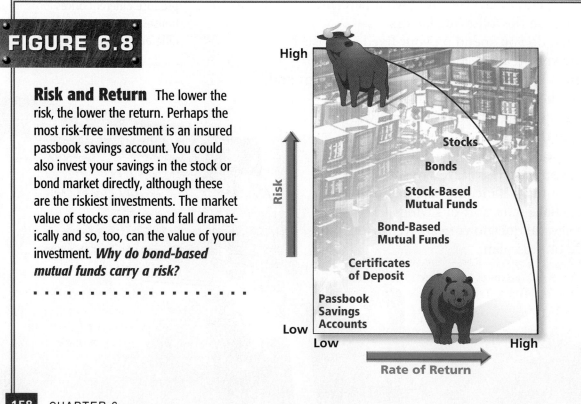

FIGURE 6.8

Risk and Return The lower the risk, the lower the return. Perhaps the most risk-free investment is an insured passbook savings account. You could also invest your savings in the stock or bond market directly, although these are the riskiest investments. The market value of stocks can rise and fall dramatically and so, too, can the value of your investment. ***Why do bond-based mutual funds carry a risk?***

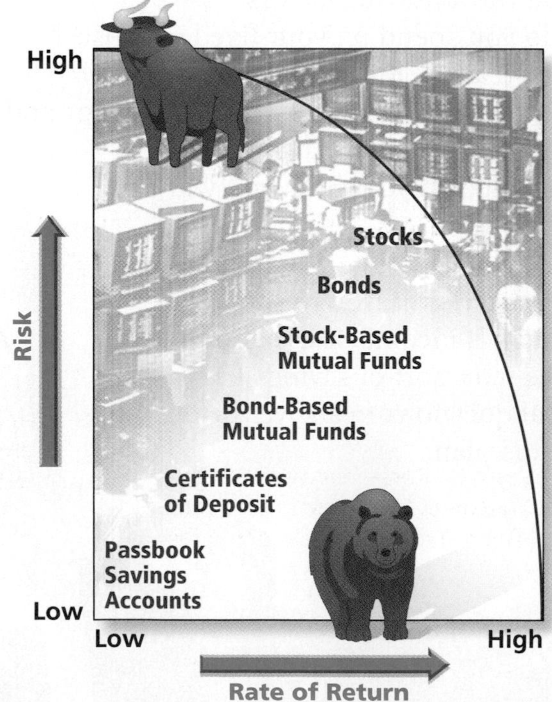

FIGURE 6.9

Lowering Risk "Don't put all your eggs in one basket" is a phrase you have certainly heard before. The theory behind it can be applied to how a person chooses to invest. ***What is the most risk-free investment?***

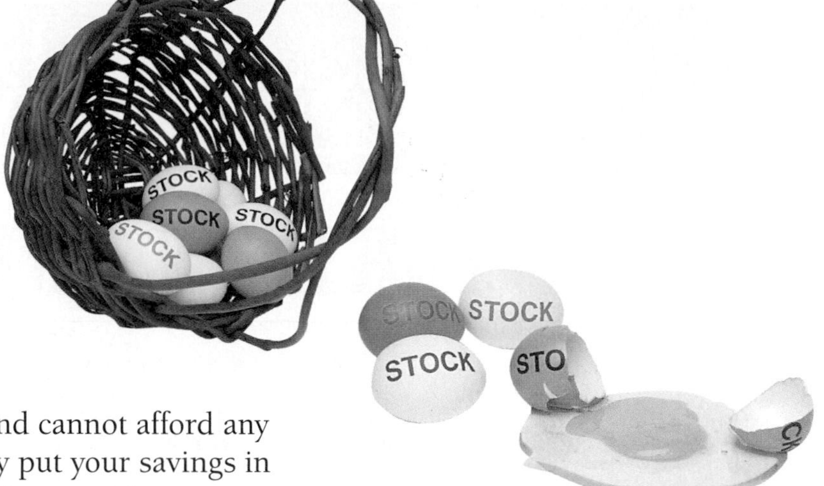

When you have very little income and cannot afford any investment losses, you should probably put your savings in insured accounts in a local bank or savings and loan, or you should buy U.S. government savings bonds. The greater your income and the more savings you have, the more you can diversify into stocks, corporate bonds, and so on.

Values Your values may also determine where you invest your savings. If you believe that your community needs more development, you might choose to put your savings in a local savings and loan that guarantees that a large percentage of its investments are made in community loans. You may also choose to invest in stocks issued by environmentally responsible companies or companies that have aggressive equal opportunity programs.

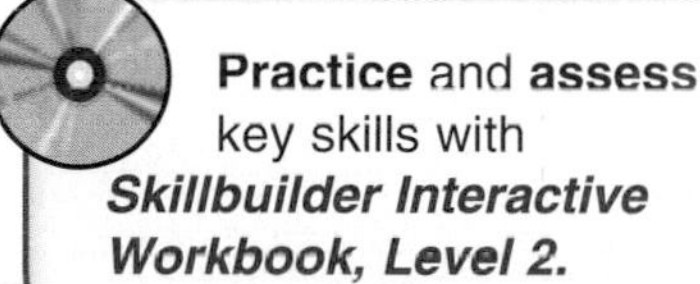

Practice and **assess** key skills with ***Skillbuilder Interactive Workbook, Level 2.***

SECTION 3 Assessment

Understanding Key Terms

1. **Define** pension plans, Keogh Plan, individual retirement account (IRA), Roth IRA, diversification.

Reviewing Objectives

2. What are three ways of investing for retirement?
3. **Graphic Organizer** Use a diagram like the one in the next column to explain how a person should determine the amount to save and the amount to invest.

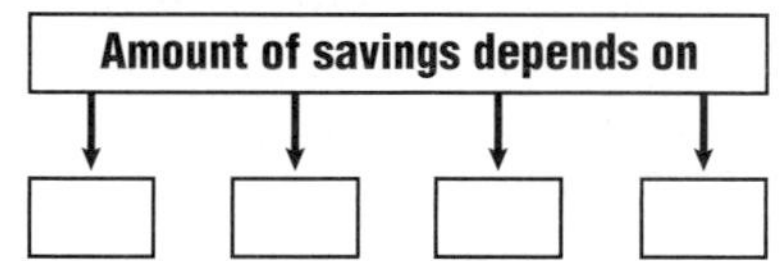

Applying Economic Concepts

4. **Risk-Return Relationship** If you had money to invest, in which type of account would you invest? Why?

Critical Thinking Activity

5. **Drawing Conclusions** Bonds yield a more certain return than stocks. Why do individuals, nonetheless, invest in stocks?

BusinessWeek

SPOTLIGHT ON THE ECONOMY

Intro to Haggling

Check It Out! **In this chapter you learned about saving and investing for the future, including paying for college. In this article, read to learn how your savings can go even further by lowering the cost of college tuition.**

It pays to be astute. Tuition and fees have risen 94% since 1989, nearly triple the 32.5% increase in inflation. The sticker price—tuition, fees, and room and board—for a year of undergraduate education ranges from $33,000 at Ivy League schools down to $10,500 at state universities.

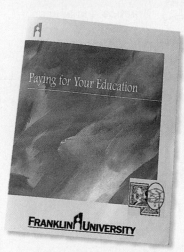

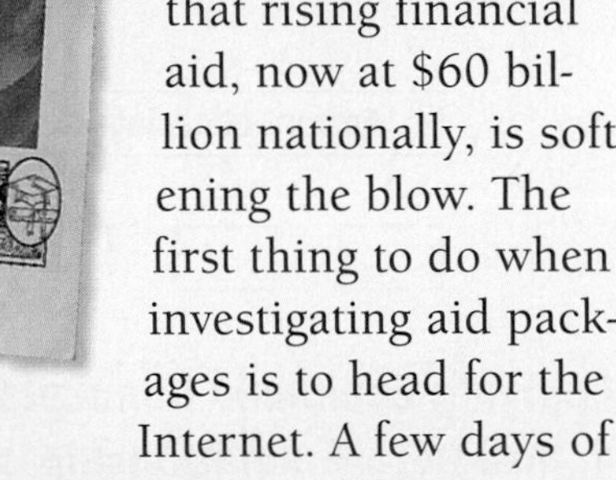

The good news is that rising financial aid, now at $60 billion nationally, is softening the blow. The first thing to do when investigating aid packages is to head for the Internet. A few days of pointing and clicking can have a lifelong payoff. You'll learn such tips as:

- Don't go the early-admission route if you want aid. Your commitment means they know they've got you.
- If you have stock set aside for college, sell it before January 1 of your child's junior year in high school. After that date, any capital gains will reduce aid eligibility.
- Apply to at least six colleges, from dreams to sure bets. Then, with offers in hand, negotiate.

If you are set on a specific college, it helps to have strong offers from direct competitors. Negotiations can be done face-to-face, by phone, or by faxing other offers with a polite cover letter. A well-spoken student may get better results than a pushy parent.

Cash-strapped students are also saving thousands by enrolling at a public college and later transferring to a private school or starting at a junior college (average tuition of $1,500 a year) and moving on to a state university.

Think About It

1. **What three actions should you follow when applying for college aid?**
2. **What is another alternative for cash-strapped students?**

CHAPTER  Summary

Chapter Overview Visit the *Economics Today and Tomorrow* Web site at ett.glencoe.com and click on ***Chapter 6—Chapter Overviews*** to review chapter information.

SECTION 1 Why Save?

- Economists define ***saving*** as the nonuse of income for a period of time so that it can be used later.
- Saving done by an individual provides money for others to invest or spend and allows businesses to expand.
- Individuals have many places to invest their savings, including **savings accounts** and **time deposits.**
- With a **passbook savings account,** the depositor receives a booklet in which deposits, withdrawals, and interest are recorded.
- A **money market deposit account (MMDA)** is another type of account that pays relatively high rates of interest and allows immediate access to money through checks. The trade-off is that these accounts have a $1,000 to $2,500 minimum balance requirement.
- Time deposits, such as **certificates of deposit (CDs),** offer higher rates of **interest,** but you must leave your funds on deposit for longer periods of time.
- The FDIC insures deposits up to $100,000 in commercial banks and savings banks.

SECTION 2 Investing: Taking Risks With Your Savings

- Shares of stock entitle the buyer to a certain part of the future profits and assets of the corporation selling the stock.
- **Stockholders** make money from stock through dividends and by selling their stock for more than they paid for it.
- Companies and all three levels of government sell bonds to borrow money. These include **tax-exempt bonds; savings bonds;** and **Treasury bills, notes,** and **bonds.**
- Stocks are bought and sold through **brokers** or on the Internet.
- Stocks of large corporations are usually traded on the organized stock exchanges, whereas stocks of smaller, new corporations usually are sold on the **over-the-counter market.**
- Many people invest in the stock market by placing some of their savings in a **mutual fund,** an investment company that pools the money of many individuals to buy stocks, bonds, or other investments.

SECTION 3 Special Savings Plans and Goals

- When they retire, most Americans will need additional sources of income besides their savings.
- **Pension plans,** the **Keogh Plan,** and **individual retirement accounts (IRAs)** are ways to increase your retirement dollars.
- Buying real estate is another form of investing for your retirement, but it carries a much higher risk.
- When deciding how much and what to invest in, consider **diversification** in order to spread out your investment risk.

CHAPTER 6

Assessment and Activities

Self-Check Quiz Visit the *Economics Today and Tomorrow* Web site at ett.glencoe.com and click on ***Chapter 6—Self-Check Quizzes*** to prepare for the Chapter Test.

Identifying Key Terms

Write the letter of the definition in Column B that correctly defines each term in Column A.

Column A

1. mutual fund
2. savings bond
3. capital gain
4. statement savings account
5. time deposit
6. diversification
7. pension plan

Column B

a. an increase in wealth realized when a person sells an asset
b. a less risky way to invest in stocks and bonds
c. a government security attractive to small investors
d. savings plan that issues a monthly summary of your transactions
e. retirement plan organized by a company
f. savings plan that requires savers to leave their funds in a financial institution for a specified length of time
g. spreading of investments among several different types of accounts to lower overall risk

Recalling Facts and Ideas

Section 1

1. What is the main advantage of passbook and statement savings accounts?
2. Why is a bank certificate of deposit called a time deposit?
3. Why are deposits of up to $100,000 in banks and savings institutions often considered very safe?

Section 2

4. What is the basic difference between a stock and a bond?
5. What are two advantages of United States savings bonds?
6. What terms describe the difference between the purchase price of a stock and the sale price of a stock?
7. What kind of investment company hires professionals to manage the investments of a pool of investors?
8. What government agency regulates stock and bond markets?

Section 3

9. What are three common types of pension plans for individuals?
10. What are some of the ways you can decide how much you should save?
11. "Don't put all your eggs in one basket." This quote is an example of what principle of investing?

Thinking Critically

1. **Identifying Alternatives** Suppose you have $300,000 that you want to save. The FDIC only insures up to $100,000. What can you do to make sure all your funds are insured by the FDIC?
2. **Understanding Cause and Effect** How does buying a U.S. savings bond increase the United States government's debt?
3. **Categorizing Information** Assume that you have $100,000 in savings. Create a chart like the one below to list the investments you might make and what percentage of the $100,000 you would invest in each. In the last column, explain how your choices will achieve investment diversification.

Investment Type	% of Funds	Diversification

Applying Economic Concepts

Scarcity and Choice List your short-term savings goals, such as saving to buy a new portable DVD player. Explain the typical ways in which you can save for such a purchase. Then list your long-term savings goals, such as saving for a house or retirement. Explain how you can achieve these goals. What is the major difference between the two ways of saving?

Cooperative Learning Project

Working in groups of four, research what $100,000 placed in each one of the following investments 10 years ago would be worth today. Rank and compare the rates of return. Obtain your information in the library, on the Internet, or through a securities brokerage firm.

- One particular stock
- A mutual stock fund
- U.S. Treasury bonds
- Residential real estate
- Commercial real estate
- Gold
- Diamonds

Reviewing Skills

Using a Spreadsheet Contact at least five financial institutions in your area. Ask them for the interest rate they offer for a passbook savings account, a certificate of deposit, and a money market deposit account with a minimum balance of $1,000 and a maturity of 16 months. Use the information you obtain as the basis for a spreadsheet showing interest rates in your community. Then prepare a bar graph of the interest rates available and present your information to the class.

Technology Activity

Using the Internet Choose two stocks on the New York Stock Exchange, and follow their prices for two weeks in the financial pages of a newspaper or on the Internet. You will need to read only the last column of figures. Note the daily closing prices for each stock, and then make a line graph showing the stocks' performance over the two-week period.

Analyzing the Global Economy

Use the Internet or business magazines to research what stocks are in demand in Italy, Finland, Israel, and Japan. Present the results of your research to the rest of the class.

Economics Lab

Making a Budget

From the classroom of Joanna Ackley, John F. Kennedy High School, Taylor, Michigan

In Unit 2 you learned how trade-offs shape consumer decisions regarding credit, food products, clothing, automobiles, housing, and saving. In this lab, you will design a strategy for earning, spending, saving, and investing your resources.

STEP A Tools Needed

- ✔ Copies of Tables 1 and 2
- ✔ Newspapers with advertisements for apartment rentals and auto sales
- ✔ Ads from local grocery stores
- ✔ Magazines with photos of apartments, automobiles, and furniture
- ✔ Pencil
- ✔ Calculator

STEP B Procedures to Follow

1. You will be sharing living quarters with another person. Annually you make $16,640, of which $1,800 goes to pay taxes. Monthly you earn $1,236.66. Your total expenditures will include the items listed in Table 1.
2. Analyze the newspaper ads to select an apartment to rent. List the rental fee in Table 1.
3. Plan your weekly menus in Table 2, then multiply these by 4 to budget your food expenses for 1 month. Use the ads from grocery stores to select and price the food products needed for your menus.
4. Decide on a type of car to buy. Analyze the newspaper ads to obtain the monthly payment for an automobile.
5. From the magazines, select items of furniture to furnish your apartment.
6. Visit or call the following places to obtain prices or monthly fees for other necessities: phone company, electric company, gas company, auto insurance, furniture store, and medical insurance. Optional costs include IRA deductions and purchases of stocks and bonds.
7. Fill in your costs in Table 1.

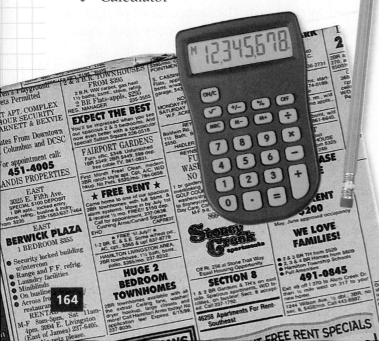

Table 1	
CATEGORIES OF EXPENDITURES	MONTHLY COST
Rent	
Rental insurance	
Telephone	
Electricity	
Gas heat	
Car payment	
Car insurance	
Car expenses (gas and repairs)	
Furniture expenses	
Clothing expenses	
Food (Eating in)	
Eating out	
Medical insurance	
Medical expenses	
Credit card bill	
Savings account	
Checking account	
Stocks and bonds	
IRA or Roth IRA	
Entertainment	
Laundry and Toiletries	
Other	
TOTAL OF EXPENSES	

Table 2	
MENUS	PRICES OF ITEMS
Monday	
Tuesday	
Wednesday	
Thursday	
Friday	
Saturday	
Sunday	
	TOTAL

STEP C Creating an Economic Model

Use the results of your cost analyses in Table 1 to draw a bar graph visually showing how your income compares to your expenditures. Draw your graph on poster board to use in a presentation to the rest of the class. In your presentation you should also include visuals of the type of apartment you chose to rent, the furniture you selected, the type of automobile you bought, evidence of car and medical insurance costs, and your calculations for credit card interest fees.

STEP D Lab Report Analysis

1. What was your largest monthly expense?
2. How much money did you have left over at the end of the month?
3. What expense(s) surprised you the most? Why?
4. What expenditures did you have to reduce in order to meet your other monthly expenses?

UNIT 3

Microeconomics: Markets, Prices, and Business Competition

Chapter 7
Demand and Supply

Chapter 8
Business Organizations

Chapter 9
Competition and Monopolies

In this unit, read to FIND OUT . . .

- how your consumer decisions affect prices.
- what risks and expectations you'll have when starting a business.
- why competition among businesses is vital to the price you pay for goods and services.

A federal government agency regulates the radio station over which you listen to the ball game.

Rawlings® currently holds a monopoly on manufacturing all baseballs for major league and minor league teams.
Some major league owners form partnerships to buy their teams.
A winning team often results in a shortage of game tickets.
The price of these tickets was determined by the interaction of demand and supply.
NEW YORK YANKEES

CHAPTER 7

Demand and Supply

Why It's Important

Why do some CDs cost more than others? Why does the price of video rentals go down when another video store opens in the neighborhood? This chapter will explain the relationship between demand and supply—and how this relationship determines the prices you pay.

To learn more about how demand and supply affect price, view the **Economics & You** *Chapter 7 video lesson:* **Demand and Supply**

Chapter Overview Visit the *Economics Today and Tomorrow* Web site at ett.glencoe.com and click on ***Chapter 7—Chapter Overviews*** to preview chapter information.

SECTION  Demand

COVER STORY

BUSINESS WEEK, FEBRUARY 15, 1999

The morning after the *Delia's* catalog arrives, the halls of Paxon High School in Jacksonville, Florida, are buzzing. That's when all the girls bring in their copies from home and compare notes.

"Everyone loves *Delia's*," says Emily Garfinkle, 15. "It's the big excitement."

If you've never heard of *Delia's*, chances are you don't know a girl between 12 and 17. The New York cataloger, with a database of 4 million names, has become one of the hottest names in retailing by selling downtown fashion to girls everywhere.

READER'S GUIDE

Terms to Know

- demand
- supply
- market
- voluntary exchange
- law of demand
- quantity demanded
- real income effect
- substitution effect
- utility
- marginal utility
- law of diminishing marginal utility

Reading Objectives

1. How does the principle of voluntary exchange operate in a market economy?
2. What does the law of demand state?
3. How do the real income effect, the substitution effect, and diminishing marginal utility relate to the law of demand?

The word *demand* has a special meaning in economics. *Delia's* catalog may be sent to 4 million people, but that doesn't mean 4 million people demand clothes from the retailer. Many girls may *want* to order items from the catalog. As you read this section, however, you'll learn that demand includes only those people who are willing *and* able to pay for a product or service.

The "Marketplace"

When you buy something, do you ever wonder why it sells at that particular price? Few individual consumers feel they have any influence over the price of an item. In a market economy,

A Local Market
A candy store located in your town or city is an example of a local market for buyers and sellers.

B National Market
Catalogs bring buyers and sellers together on a national scale—you can order chocolate from this catalog and have it shipped to you overnight.

FIGURE 7.1

Markets A market is any place where buyers and sellers come together. ***What is the basis of activity in a market economy?***

demand: *the amount of a good or service that consumers are able and willing to buy at various possible prices during a specified time period*

supply: *the amount of a good or service that producers are able and willing to sell at various prices during a specified time period*

market: *the process of freely exchanging goods and services between buyers and sellers*

voluntary exchange: *a transaction in which a buyer and a seller exercise their economic freedom by working out their own terms of exchange*

however, all consumers individually and collectively have a great influence on the price of all goods and services. To understand this, let's look first at how people in the marketplace decide what to buy and at what price. This is **demand.** Then we'll examine how the people who want to sell those things decide how much to sell and at what price. This is **supply.**

What is the marketplace? A **market** represents the freely chosen actions between buyers and sellers of goods and services. As **Figure 7.1** shows, a market for a particular item can be local, national, international, or a combination of these. In a market economy, individuals—whether as buyers or sellers—decide for themselves the answers to the WHAT?, HOW?, and FOR WHOM? economic questions you studied in Chapter 2.

Voluntary Exchange

The basis of activity in a market economy is the principle of **voluntary exchange.** A buyer and a

C International Market *The World Wide Web has helped create a massive international market. Chocolate lovers anywhere in the world can order chocolate in seconds from this Swiss manufacturer.*

seller exercise their economic freedom by working toward satisfactory terms of an exchange. For example, the seller of an automobile sets a price based on his or her view of market conditions, and the buyer, through the act of buying, agrees to the product and the price. In order to make the exchange, both the buyer and the seller must believe they will be better off–richer or happier–after the exchange than before.

The supplier's problem of what to charge and the buyer's problem of how much to pay is solved voluntarily in the market exchange. Supply and demand analysis is a model of how buyers and sellers operate in the marketplace. Such analysis is a way of explaining cause and effect in relation to price.

The Law of Demand

Demand, in economic terms, represents all of the different quantities of a good or service that consumers will purchase at various prices. It includes both the willingness and the ability to pay. A person may say he or she wants a new CD. Until that person is both willing *and able* to buy it, however, no demand for CDs has been created by that individual.

The law of demand explains how people react to changing prices in terms of the quantities demanded of a good or service. There is an *inverse,* or opposite, relationship between quantity demanded and price. The **law of demand** states:

As price goes up, quantity demanded goes down.
As price goes down, quantity demanded goes up.

law of demand: *economic rule stating that the quantity demanded and price move in opposite directions*

quantity demanded: *the amount of a good or service that a consumer is willing and able to purchase at a specific price*

Several factors explain the inverse relation between price and **quantity demanded,** or how much people will buy of any item at a particular price. These factors include real income, possible substitutes, and diminishing marginal utility.

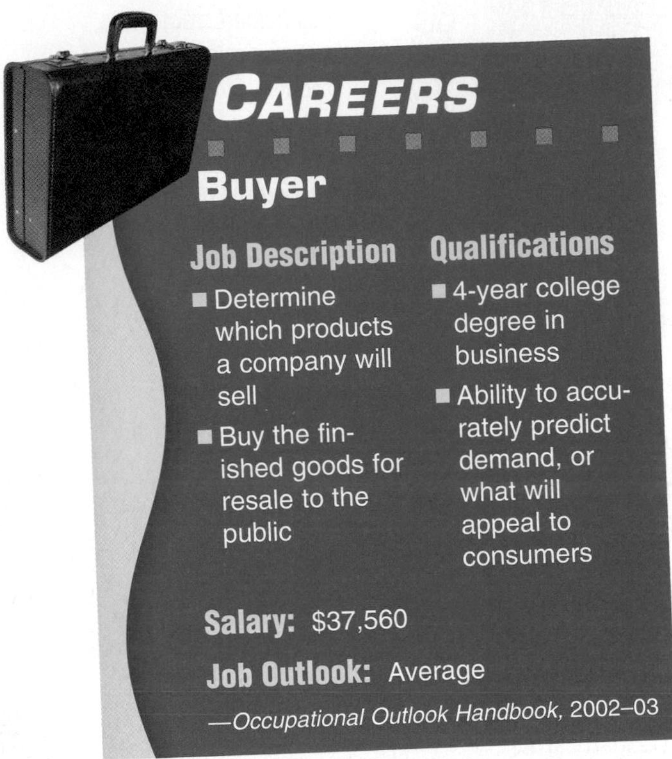

Careers

Buyer

Job Description

- Determine which products a company will sell
- Buy the finished goods for resale to the public

Qualifications

- 4-year college degree in business
- Ability to accurately predict demand, or what will appeal to consumers

Salary: $37,560

Job Outlook: Average

—Occupational Outlook Handbook, 2002–03

Real Income Effect No one—not even the wealthiest person in the world—will ever be able to buy everything he or she might possibly want. People's incomes limit the amount they are able to spend. Individuals cannot keep buying the same quantity of a good if its price rises while their income stays the same. This concept is known as the **real income effect** on demand.

Suppose that you normally fill your car's gas tank twice a month, spending $15 each time. This means you spend $30 per month on gasoline. If the price of gasoline rises, you may have to spend $40 per month. If the price continues to rise while your income does not, eventually you will not be able to fill the gas tank twice per month because your *real income,* or purchasing power, has been reduced. In order to keep buying the same amount of gasoline, you would need to cut back on buying other things. The real income effect forces you to make a trade-off in your gasoline purchases. The same is true for every item you buy, particularly those you buy on a regular basis. See **Figure 7.2.**

real income effect: *economic rule stating that individuals cannot keep buying the same quantity of a product if its price rises while their income stays the same*

Substitution Effect Suppose there are two items that are not exactly the same but which satisfy basically the same need. Their cost is about the same. If the price of one falls, people will most likely buy it instead of the other, now higher-priced, good. If the price of one rises in relation to the price of the other, people will buy the now lower-priced good. This principle is called the **substitution effect.**

substitution effect: *economic rule stating that if two items satisfy the same need and the price of one rises, people will buy the other*

Suppose, for example, that you listen to both CDs and audiocassettes. If the price of audiocassettes drops dramatically, you will probably buy more cassettes and fewer CDs. Alternately, if the price of audiocassettes doubles, you will probably increase the number of CDs you buy in relation to cassettes. If the price of both CDs *and* audiocassettes increases, you may decide to purchase other music substitutes such as concert tickets or music videos.

Economic Connection to... *Literature*

Tom Sawyer Creates Demand

Author Mark Twain introduced a different twist on the meaning of *demand* in his story "The Glorious Whitewasher." Tom Sawyer is forced to whitewash his aunt's fence. To convince other boys to do the work, Tom pretends to find it enjoyable and to consider it a special privilege. The other boys end up paying Tom to let them whitewash the fence:

Tom said to himself that it was not such a hollow world, after all. He had discovered a great law of human action, without knowing it—namely, that in order to make a man or a boy covet [demand] *a thing, it is only necessary to make the thing difficult to attain.* ■

—From *The Adventures of Tom Sawyer,* 1876

Diminishing Marginal Utility Almost everything that people like, desire, use, or think they would like to use, gives satisfaction. The term that economists use for satisfaction is *utility*. **Utility** is defined as the power that a good or service has to satisfy a want. Based on utility, people decide what to buy and how much they are willing and able to pay. In deciding to make a purchase, they decide the amount of satisfaction, or use, they think they will get from a good or service.

utility: *the ability of any good or service to satisfy consumer wants*

Consider the utility that can be derived from buying a cold soft drink at a baseball game on a hot day. At $3 per cup, how many will you buy? Assuming that you have some

FIGURE 7.2

Real Income Effect If the price of gasoline rises but your income does not, you obviously cannot continue buying the same amount of gas AND everything else you normally purchase. The real income effect can work in the opposite direction, too. If you are already buying two fill-ups a month and the price of gasoline drops in half, your real income then increases. You will have more purchasing power and will probably increase your spending.

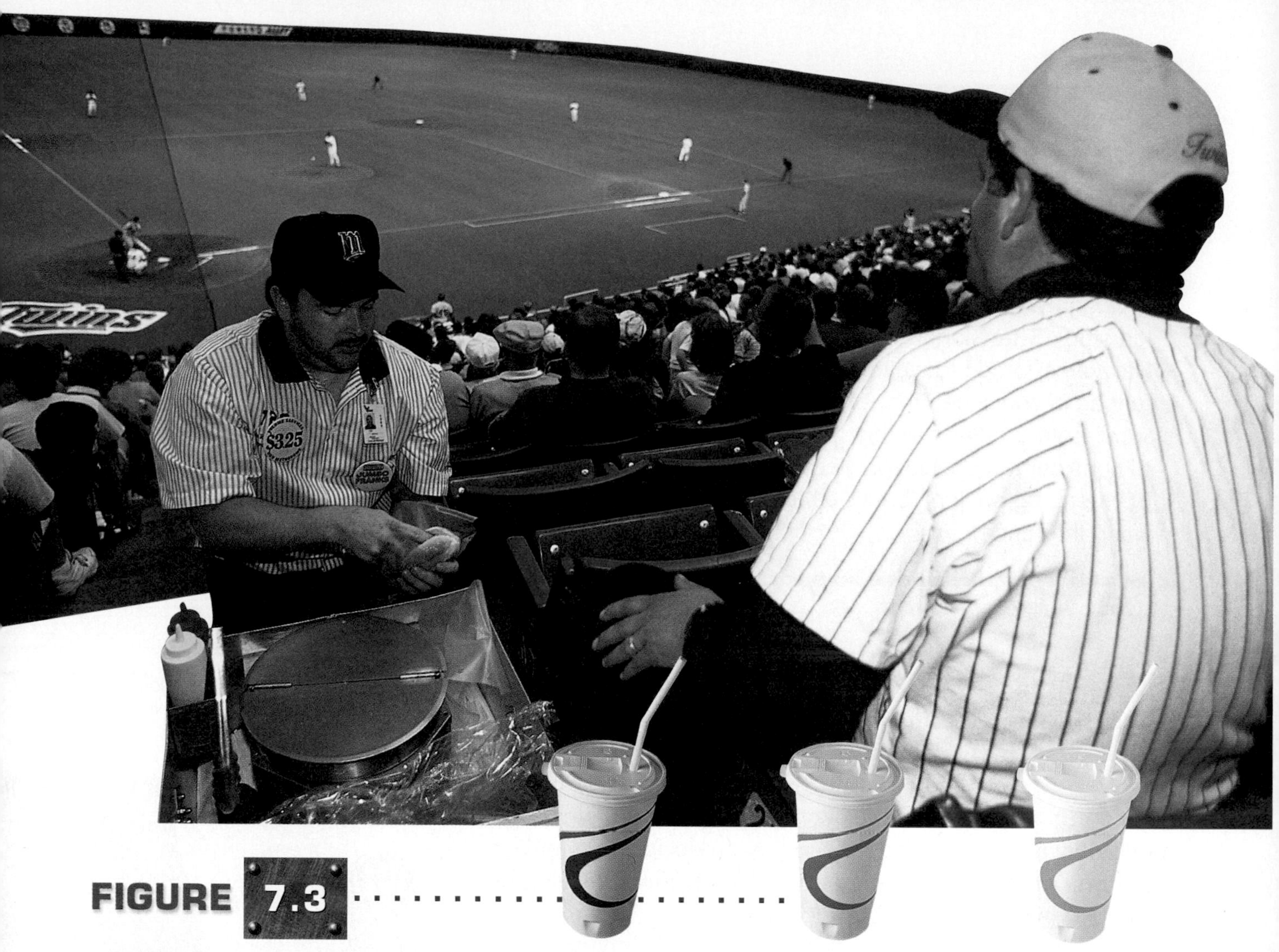

FIGURE 7.3

Diminishing Marginal Utility Regardless of how satisfying the first taste of an item is, satisfaction declines with additional consumption. Assume, for example, that at a price of $3.25 per hot dog, you have enough after buying three. Thus, the value you place on additional satisfaction from a fourth hot dog would be less than $3.25. According to what will give you the most satisfaction, you will save or spend the $3.25 on something else. Eventually you would receive no additional satisfaction, even if a vendor offered the product at zero price.

marginal utility: *an additional amount of satisfaction*

law of diminishing marginal utility: *rule stating that the additional satisfaction a consumer gets from purchasing one more unit of a product will lessen with each additional unit purchased*

money, you will buy at least one. Will you buy a second one? A third one? A fifth one? That decision depends on the additional utility, or satisfaction, you expect to receive from each additional soft drink. Your *total* satisfaction will rise with each one bought. The amount of *additional* satisfaction, or **marginal utility,** will diminish, or lessen, with each additional cup, however. This example illustrates the **law of diminishing marginal utility.**

At some point, you will stop buying soft drinks. Perhaps you don't want to wait in the concession line anymore. Perhaps your stomach cannot handle another soft drink. Just the thought of another cola makes you nauseated. At that point, the satisfaction that you receive from the soft drink is less than the value you place on the $3 that you must pay. As **Figure 7.3** shows, people stop buying an item when one event occurs–when the satisfaction from the next unit of the same item becomes less than the price they must pay for it.

What if the price drops? Suppose the owner of the ballpark decided to sell soft drinks for $2 each after the fifth inning. You might buy at least one additional soft drink. Why? If you look at the law of diminishing marginal utility again, the reason becomes clear. People will buy an item to the point at which the satisfaction from the last unit bought is equal to the price. At that point, people will stop buying. This concept explains part of the law of demand. As the price of an item decreases, people will generally buy more.

Practice and **assess** key skills with ***Skillbuilder Interactive Workbook, Level 2.***

SECTION 1 Assessment

Understanding Key Terms

1. **Define** demand, supply, market, voluntary exchange, law of demand, quantity demanded, real income effect, substitution effect, utility, marginal utility, law of diminishing marginal utility.

Reviewing Objectives

2. How does the principle of voluntary exchange operate in a market economy?
3. What is the law of demand?
4. **Graphic Organizer** Create a chart like the one in the next column to show how an increase and decrease in real income, the price of substitutes, and utility influence the quantity demanded for a given product or service.

Cause	Effect on Quantity Demanded

Applying Economic Concepts

5. **Diminishing Marginal Utility** Describe an instance in your own life when diminishing marginal utility caused you to decrease your quantity demanded of a product or service.

Critical Thinking Activity

6. **Making Predictions** Imagine that you sell popcorn at the local football stadium. Knowing about diminishing marginal utility, how would you price your popcorn after half-time?

BusinessWeek

SPOTLIGHT ON THE ECONOMY

How to Make a Mint

Check It Out! In this chapter you learned how demand can increase as tastes and preferences change. In the following article, read to learn how one entrepreneur created a demand for mints as a "fashion accessory."

Harley Cross broke pretty much every rule in the book that, if it were written, would be called *How Not to Start a Business*. He had very little business experience and no formal business education. When he needed help, he brought in a longtime friend who also had little experience in business. He ignored research that showed the market for his product was saturated. As a teenager, maybe he was too young to know better.

Today, 18 months after shipping his first order of smooth round peppermints encased in arty tins, Cross [now 20] says Hint Mint has racked up sales of more than $2.5 million....

When he came up with Hint Mint, he never intended to sell mints–just the name.... Cross found out names can't be trademarked if there's no product to go with them. So he decided to go ahead and create the product–"mint as fashion accessory." As someone who grew up in show business, he knew that "if it looks cool, you want it."

He had the name, he had the concept, but what about product development and, ahem, all the cold calling it would take to put the product in front of potential customers? Enter longtime friend Cooper Bates, a screenwriter and short-film director....

Which brings us ... to the chapter titled "Now Who Will Buy the Mints?"

Gina Casella, for one. Casella is product-development manager for Barnes & Noble cafes, where the $2.39 tin of Hint Mints can be found next to treats made by the likes of Godiva and Starbucks. "When we tested it, everyone liked the product," Casella says, adding, "It's very unique packaging ... it makes a statement when you pull out the tin."

Cross, who ended up putting everything he had saved from his 15-year acting career–roughly half a million dollars–into Hint Mint, says the company is profitable. He expects to recoup his money by the end of the year. He figures he'll sell the company for $15 million to $20 million in about two years, when he expects to have annual revenue of $6 million.

Think About It

1. **What makes Hint Mint different from other mints?**
2. **Based on the article, what elements must be considered when developing a new product?**

SECTION 2

The Demand Curve and Elasticity of Demand

Cover Story

The Economist, May 29, 2003

As demand goes up, [Mr. Stelios Haji-Ioannou] argues, so should prices. So people who buy early . . . get better deals. For example, charges at his Internet cafés rise as seats fill up. . . . Mr. Haji-Ioannou's model . . . milks the demand curve for every penny he can get. He can pocket the extra [from people] willing to pay to have just what they want when they want it.

Reader's Guide

Terms to Know

- demand schedule
- demand curve
- complementary good
- elasticity
- price elasticity of demand
- elastic demand
- inelastic demand

Reading Objectives

1. What does a demand curve show?
2. What are the determinants of demand?
3. How does the elasticity of demand affect the price of a given product?

In Section 1 you learned that quantity demanded is based on price. The case of the Internet café supports this. When demand is low, Mr. Haji-Ioannou lowers prices. Then, as more people come into the café to take advantage of the offer (increased demand), the owner can raise prices.

Graphing the Demand Curve

How can you learn to distinguish between quantity demanded and demand? And how do economists show these relationships in a visual way? It is said that a picture is worth a thousand words. For much of economic analysis, the "picture" is a graph that shows the relationship between two statistics or concepts.

The law of demand can be graphed. As you learned in Section 1, the relationship between the quantity demanded and price is inverse—as the price goes up, the quantity demanded goes down. As the price goes down, the quantity demanded goes up.

demand schedule: *table showing quantities demanded at different possible prices*

Take a look at *Parts A, B,* and *C* of **Figure 7.4.** The series of three parts shows how the price of goods and services affects the quantity demanded at each price. *Part A* is a **demand schedule**—a table of prices and quantity demanded. The numbers show that as the price per CD decreases, the quantity demanded increases. For example, at a cost of $20 each, 100 million CDs will be demanded. When the cost decreases to $12 each, 900 million CDs will be demanded.

FIGURE 7.4 Graphing the Demand Curve

Demand Can Be Shown Visually Note how the three parts use a different format to show the same thing. Each shows the law of demand—as price falls, quantity demanded increases.

Also, note that in Parts B and C we refer to the quantity of CDs demanded *per year.* We could have said one day, one week, one month, or two years. The longer the time period, the more likely that factors *other than price* will affect the demand for a given product.

A Demand Schedule

Price per CD	Quantity demanded (in millions)	Points in Part B
$20	100	A
$19	200	B
$18	300	C
$17	400	D
$16	500	E
$15	600	F
$14	700	G
$13	800	H
$12	900	I
$11	1,000	J
$10	1,100	K

Part A Demand Schedule The numbers in the demand schedule above show that as the price per CD decreases, the quantity demanded increases. Note that at $16 each, a quantity of 500 million CDs will be demanded.

In *Part B,* the numbers from the schedule in *Part A* have been plotted onto a graph. The bottom (or horizontal) axis shows the quantity demanded. The side (or vertical) axis shows the price per CD. Each pair of price and quantity demanded numbers represents a point on the graph. These points are labeled A through K.

Now look at *Part C* of **Figure 7.4.** When the points from *Part B* are connected with a line, we end up with the **demand curve.** A demand curve shows the quantity demanded of a good or service at each possible price. Demand curves slope downward (fall from left to right). In *Part C* you can see the inverse relationship between price and quantity demanded.

Student Web Activity Visit the *Economics Today and Tomorrow* Web site at ett.glencoe.com and click on ***Chapter 7—Student Web Activities*** to see how changes in population affect demand.

demand curve: *downward-sloping line that shows in graph form the quantities demanded at each possible price*

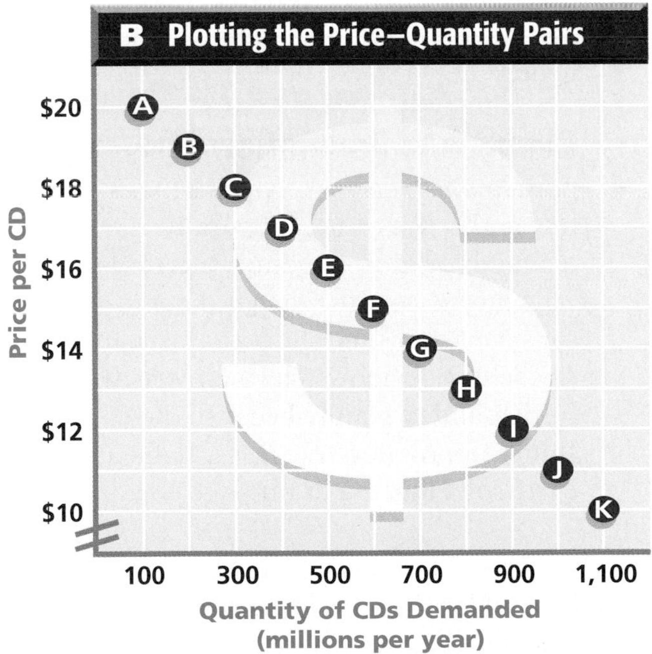

Part B Plotting Quantity Demanded Note how the price and quantity demanded numbers in the demand schedule (Part A) have been transferred to a graph in Part B above. Find letter E. It represents a number of CDs demanded (500 million) at a specific price ($16).

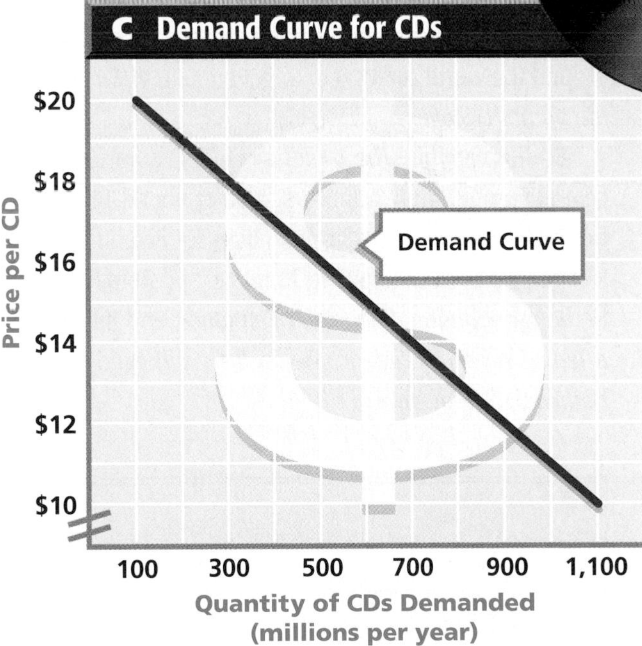

Part C Demand Curve The points in Part B have been connected with a line in Part C above. This line is the demand curve, which always falls from left to right. How many CDs will be demanded at a price of $12 each?

Quantity Demanded vs. Demand

Remember that quantity demanded is a specific point along the demand curve. A *change in quantity demanded* is caused by a change in the price of the good, and is shown as a movement along the demand curve. Sometimes, however, something other than price causes demand as a whole to increase or decrease. This is known as a *change in demand* and is shown as a *shift* of the entire demand curve to the left (decrease in demand) or right (increase in demand). If demand increases, people will buy more per year at all prices. If demand decreases, people will buy less per year at all prices. What causes a change in demand as a whole?

Global Economy

Demand for American TV Shows

Every year, hundreds of television-program buyers from around the world visit major studios in Los Angeles. What do they buy? *ER, Chicago Hope,* and *NYPD Blue* are hits in western European countries such as England, the Netherlands, and Germany. And people around the world can't seem to get enough of *Buffy the Vampire Slayer.*

Sci-fi is very big. *The X-Files* airs in 60 countries. In central Europe, "they want cars to be exploded 14 stories high," says Klaus Hallig, who buys for Poland, Hungary, the Czech Republic, Bulgaria, and Romania. He bought *Cannon, Bonanza, Miami Vice,* and the *A-Team,* as well as *Little House on the Prairie* and *Highway to Heaven.* ■

Determinants of Demand

Many factors can affect demand for a specific product. Among these factors are changes in population, changes in income, changes in people's tastes and preferences, the existence of substitutes, and the existence of complementary goods.

Changes in Population When population increases, opportunities to buy and sell increase. Naturally, the demand for most products increases. This means that the demand curve for, say, television sets, shifts to the right. At each price, more television sets will be demanded simply because the consumer population increases. Look at *Part A* of **Figure 7.5** on page 182.

Changes in Income The demand for most goods and services depends on income. Your demand for CDs would certainly decrease if your income dropped in half and you expected it to stay there. You would buy fewer CDs at all possible prices. The demand curve for CDs would shift to the left as shown in *Part B* of **Figure 7.5** on page 182. If your income went up, however, you might buy more CDs even if the price of CDs doubled. Buying more CDs at all possible prices would shift the demand curve to the right.

Changes in Tastes and Preferences One of the key factors that determine demand is people's tastes and preferences. *Tastes and preferences* refer to what people like and prefer to choose. When an item becomes a fad, more are sold at every possible price. The demand curve shifts to the right as shown in *Part C* of **Figure 7.5** on page 183.

Substitutes The existence of substitutes also affects demand. People often think of butter and margarine as substitutes. Suppose that the price of butter remains the same and the price of margarine falls. People will buy more margarine and less butter at all prices of butter. See *Part D* of **Figure 7.5** on page 183.

Complementary Goods When two goods are complementary products, the decrease in the price of one will increase the demand for it as well as its complementary good. Cameras and film are complementary goods. Suppose the price of film remains the same. If the price of cameras drops, people will probably buy more of them. They will also probably buy more film to use with the cameras. Therefore, a decrease in the price of cameras leads to an increase in the demand for its **complementary good,** film. As a result, the demand curve for film will shift to the right as shown in *Part E* of **Figure 7.5** on page 183.

complementary good: *a product often used with another product*

The Price Elasticity of Demand

The law of demand is straightforward: The higher the price charged, the lower the quantity demanded—and vice versa. If you sold DVDs, how could you use this information? You know that if you lower prices, consumers will buy more DVDs. By how much should you lower the cost, however? You cannot really answer this question unless you know how responsive consumers will be to a decrease in the price of DVDs. Economists call this price responsiveness **elasticity.** The measure of the **price elasticity of demand** is *how much* consumers respond to a given change in price.

elasticity: *economic concept dealing with consumers' responsiveness to an increase or decrease in price of a product*

price elasticity of demand: *economic concept that deals with how much demand varies according to changes in price*

Elastic Demand For some goods, a rise or fall in price greatly affects the amount people are willing to buy. The demand for these goods is considered elastic—consumers can be flexible when buying or not buying these items. For example, one particular brand of coffee probably has a very

FIGURE 7.5 Determinants of Demand

Changes in Demand Many factors can affect demand for a specific product. When demand changes, the entire demand curve shifts to the left or the right.

Part A Change in Demand if Population Increases When population increases, opportunities to buy and sell increase. The demand curve labeled D1 represents demand for television sets before the population increased. The demand curve labeled D2 represents demand after the population increased.

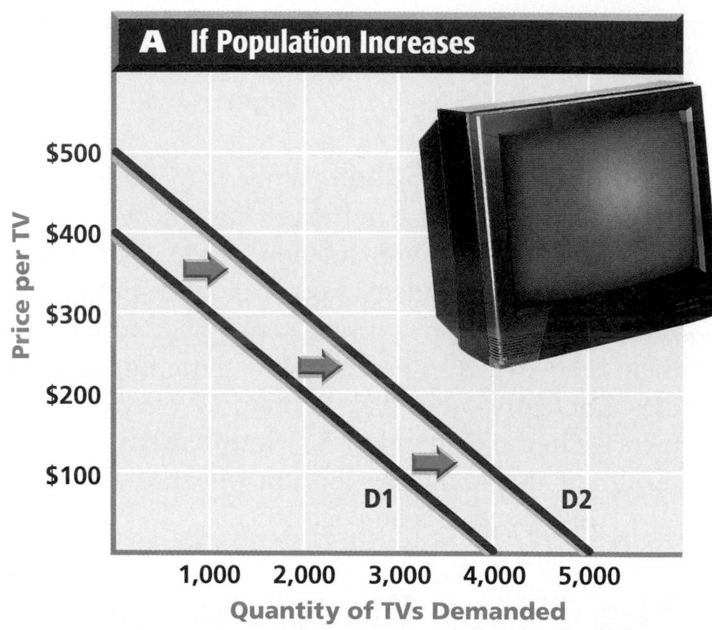

Part B Change in Demand if Your Income Decreases The demand curve D1 represents CD demand before income decreased. The demand curve D2 represents CD demand after income decreased. If your income goes up, however, you may buy more CDs at all possible prices, which would shift the demand curve to the right.

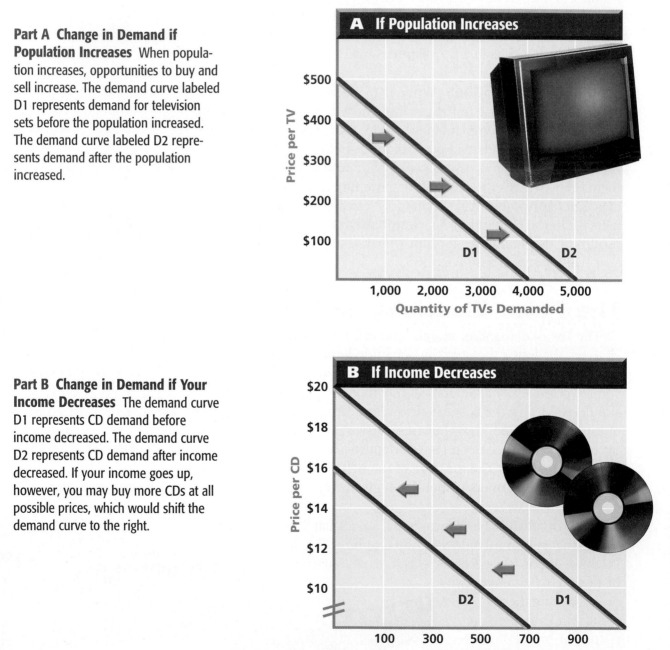

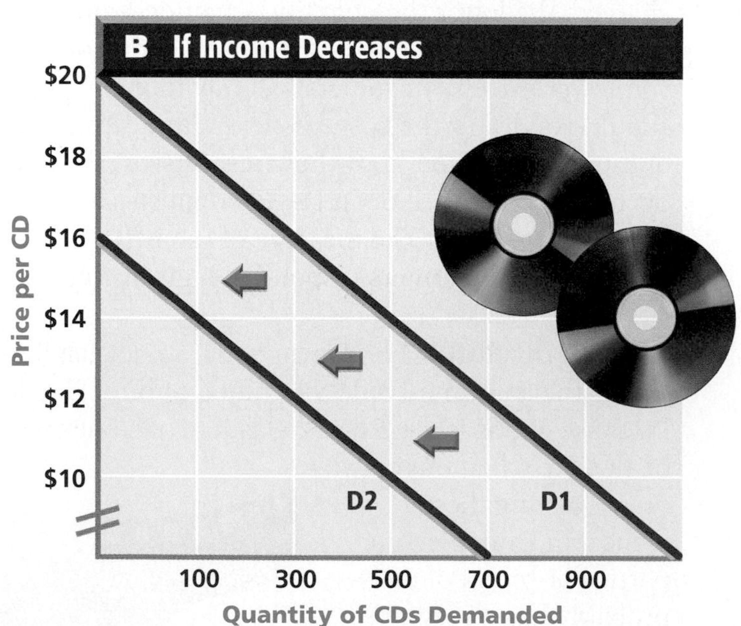

Part C Change in Demand if an Item Becomes a Fad When a product becomes a fad, more of it is demanded at all prices, and the entire demand curve shifts to the right. Notice how D1–representing demand for Beanie Babies™ before they became popular–becomes D2–demand after they became a fad.

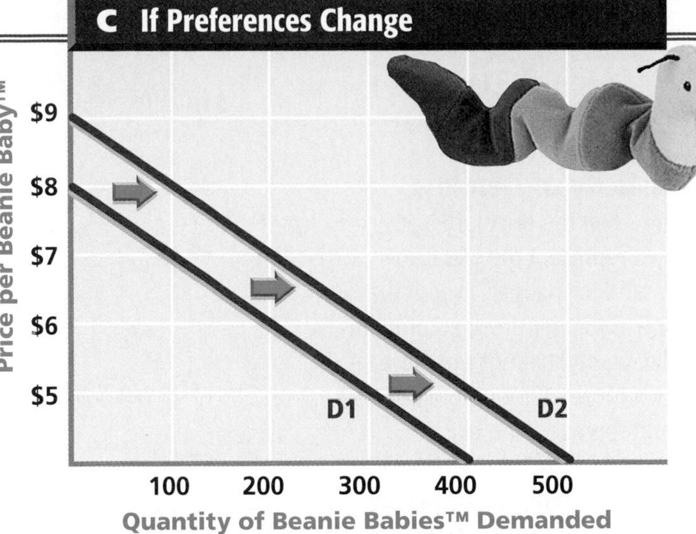

Part D Change in Demand for Substitutes As the price of the substitute (margarine) decreases, the demand for the item under study (butter) also decreases. If, in contrast, the price of the substitute (margarine) increases, the demand for the item under study (butter) also increases.

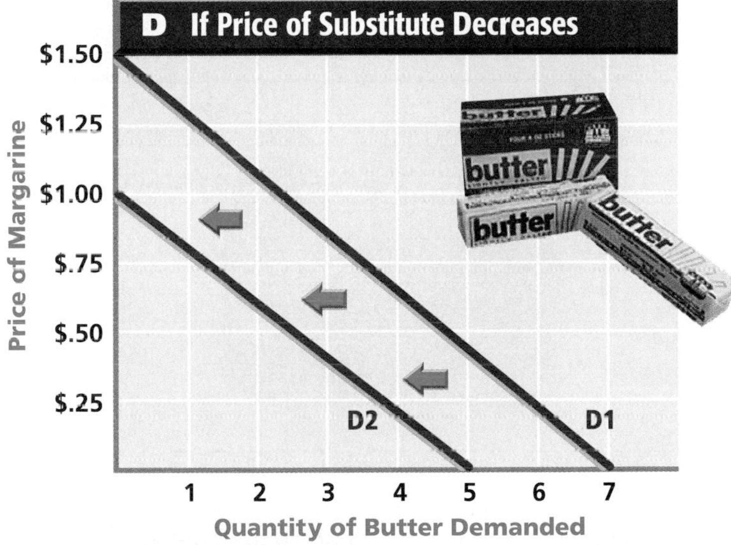

Part E Change in Demand for Complementary Goods
A decrease in the price of cameras leads to an increase in the demand for film, its complementary good. As a result, the demand curve for film will shift to the right. The opposite would happen if the price of cameras increased, thereby decreasing the demand for the complementary good, film.

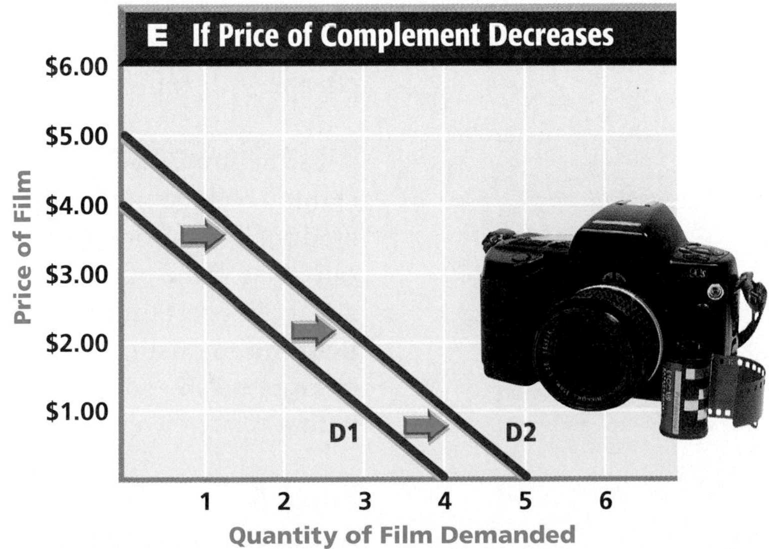

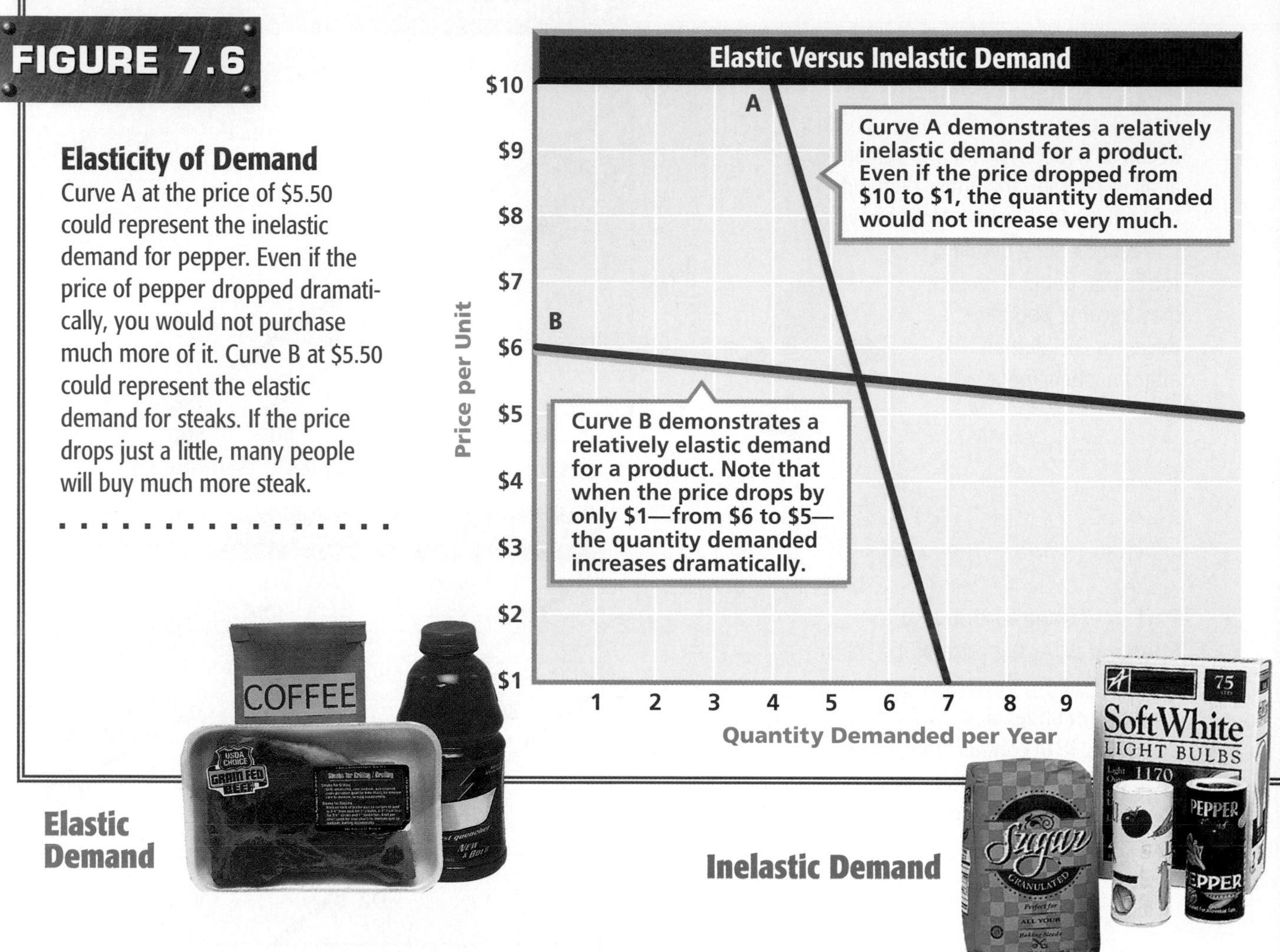
FIGURE 7.6
Elastic Versus Inelastic Demand
Elasticity of Demand
Curve A at the price of $5.50 could represent the inelastic demand for pepper. Even if the price of pepper dropped dramatically, you would not purchase much more of it. Curve B at $5.50 could represent the elastic demand for steaks. If the price drops just a little, many people will buy much more steak.
Curve A demonstrates a relatively inelastic demand for a product. Even if the price dropped from $10 to $1, the quantity demanded would not increase very much.
Curve B demonstrates a relatively elastic demand for a product. Note that when the price drops by only $1—from $6 to $5—the quantity demanded increases dramatically.
A
B
$10
$9
$8
$7
$6
$5
$4
$3
$2
$1
Price per Unit
1 2 3 4 5 6 7 8 9
Quantity Demanded per Year
COFFEE
SoftWhite
LIGHT BULBS
PEPPER
Elastic Demand
Inelastic Demand

elastic demand: *situation in which the rise or fall in a product's price greatly affects the amount that people are willing to buy*

elastic demand. Consumers consider the many competing brands of coffee to be almost the same. A small rise in the price of one brand will probably cause many consumers to purchase the cheaper substitute brands.

inelastic demand: *situation in which a product's price change has little impact on the quantity demanded by consumers*

Inelastic Demand

If a price change does not result in a substantial change in the quantity demanded, that demand is considered inelastic–consumers are usually not flexible and will purchase some of the item no matter what it costs. Salt, pepper, sugar, and certain types of medicine normally have **inelastic demand.** By using two demand curves in one diagram–as shown in **Figure 7.6**–you can compare a relatively inelastic demand with a relatively elastic demand at a particular price.

What Determines Price Elasticity of Demand?

Why do some goods have elastic demand and others have inelastic demand?

At least three factors determine the price elasticity of demand for a particular item: the existence of substitutes; the percentage of a person's total budget devoted to the purchase of that good; and the time consumers are given to adjust to a change in price.

Clearly, the more substitutes that exist for a product, the more responsive consumers will be to a change in the price of that good. A diabetic needs insulin, which has virtually no substitutes. The price elasticity of demand for insulin, therefore, is very low–it is inelastic. The opposite is true for soft drinks. If the price of one goes up by very much, many consumers may switch to another.

The percentage of your total budget spent on an item will also determine whether its demand is elastic or inelastic. For example, the portion of a family's budget devoted to pepper is very small. Even if the price of pepper doubles, most people will keep buying about the same amount. The demand for pepper, then, is relatively inelastic. Housing demand, in contrast, is relatively elastic because it represents such a large proportion of a household's yearly budget.

Finally, people take time to adjust to price changes. If the price of electricity goes up tomorrow, your demand will be inelastic. The longer the time allowed to reduce the amount of electricity you use, however, the greater the price elasticity of demand.

Practice and **assess** key skills with ***Skillbuilder Interactive Workbook, Level 2.***

SECTION 2 Assessment

Understanding Key Terms

1. **Define** demand schedule, demand curve, complementary good, elasticity, price elasticity of demand, elastic demand, inelastic demand.

Reviewing Objectives

2. What does a demand curve show?
3. **Graphic Organizer** Create a diagram like the one below to show the determinants of demand.

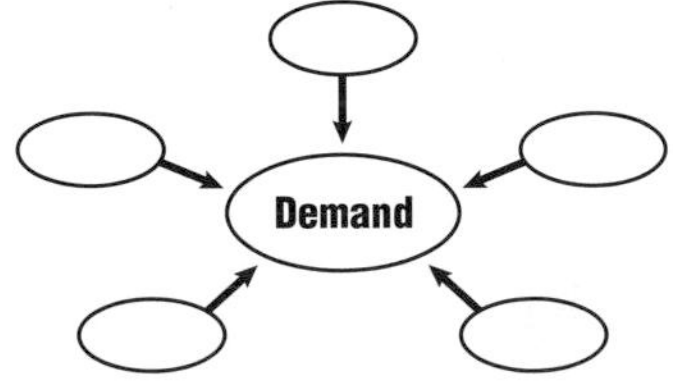

4. How does the elasticity of demand affect the price for a given product?

Applying Economic Concepts

5. **Demand Elasticity** Provide an example of two products or services for which you have elastic demand and inelastic demand. Explain your choices.

Critical Thinking Activity

6. **Making Comparisons** Write a paragraph describing how demand and quantity demanded are similar, and how they are different. Use the examples you provided in question 5 to help make the comparison in your paragraph.

SECTION 3

The Law of Supply and the Supply Curve

Reader's Guide

Terms to Know

- law of supply
- quantity supplied
- supply schedule
- supply curve
- technology
- law of diminishing returns

Reading Objectives

1. What is the law of supply?
2. How does the incentive of greater profits affect quantity supplied?
3. What do a supply schedule and supply curve show?
4. What are the four determinants of supply?

Cover Story

Business Week, May 14, 2003

Jeff Bezos got Amazon.com going from the garage of a house . . . Bill Hewitt and Dave Packard started Hewlett-Packard in a garage . . . [In contrast] many Internet companies spent large amounts of their seed money on beautiful offices . . . [w]hich was fine until [they] needed money for something important, like keeping the business running.

As you've learned, consumers demand products and services at the lowest possible prices. In contrast, suppliers—like Amazon.com and Hewlett-Packard—exist to make a profit—hopefully, a big profit. As you read this section, you'll learn about the law of supply and how it is geared toward making profits.

The Law of Supply

To understand how prices are determined, you have to look at both demand and *supply*—the willingness and ability of producers to provide goods and services at different prices in the marketplace. The **law of supply** states:

As the price rises for a good, the quantity supplied generally rises. As the price falls, the quantity supplied also falls.

law of supply: *economic rule stating that price and quantity supplied move in the same direction*

You may recall that with demand, price and quantity demanded move in opposite directions. With supply, a direct relationship exists between the price and **quantity supplied.** A direct relationship means that when prices rise, quantity supplied will rise, too. When prices fall, quantity supplied by sellers will also fall. Thus, a larger quantity will generally be supplied at higher prices than at lower prices. A smaller quantity will generally be supplied at lower prices than at higher prices.

quantity supplied: *the amount of a good or service that a producer is willing and able to supply at a specific price*

The Incentive of Greater Profits

The profit incentive is one of the factors that motivates people in a market economy. In the case of supply, the higher the price of a good, the greater the incentive is for a producer to produce more. The higher price not only returns higher profits, but it also must cover additional costs of producing more.

Suppose you own a company that produces and sells skateboards. **Figure 7.7** shows some of your costs of production. Imagine that the price you charge for your skateboards covers all of these costs and gives you a small profit. Under what circumstances would you be willing to produce more skateboards?

To take on the expense of expanding production, you would have to be able to charge a higher price for your skateboards. At a higher price per skateboard, you would be willing to supply—that is,

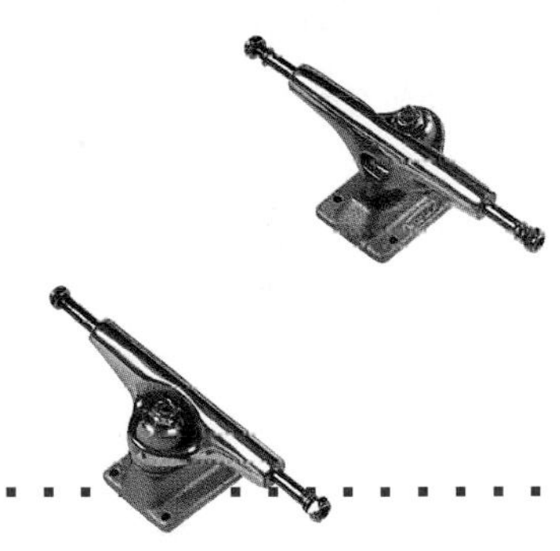

FIGURE 7.7

Production Costs As a skateboard manufacturer, you would have to consider all your costs of production, including the price of materials: decks, trucks, wheels, risers, bolts, and bearings. Don't forget to include the costs of the rent payments for the buildings in which the skateboards are produced. You also have employees to whom you must pay wages, as well as taxes and insurance. ***What motivates suppliers to take risks and go into business in the first place?***

produce and sell—more than you would at the current lower price. Even though each skateboard will cost more to produce—because of overtime payments to workers, additional machines, more repairs on machines, and so on—you could afford to pay the additional cost of increasing the quantity sold. This fact is the basis of the law of supply.

The Supply Curve

As with the law of demand, special tables and graphs can show the law of supply. Using the example of CD producers, we show a visual relationship between the price and the quantity supplied in **Figure 7.8.**

supply schedule: *table showing quantities supplied at different possible prices*

Part A is the **supply schedule**, or table, showing that as the price per CD increases, the quantity supplied increases. *Part B* of

FIGURE 7.8 Graphing the Supply Curve

Supply Can Be Shown Visually Note how the three parts use a different format to show the same thing. Each shows the law of supply—as price rises, quantity supplied increases.

A Supply Schedule for CDs

Price per CD	Quantity supplied (in millions)	Points in Part B
$10	100	L
$11	200	M
$12	300	N
$13	400	O
$14	500	P
$15	600	Q
$16	700	R
$17	800	S
$18	900	T
$19	1,000	U
$20	1,100	V

Part A Supply Schedule The numbers in the supply schedule above show that as the price per CD increases, the quantity supplied increases. At $16 each, a quantity of 700 million CDs will be supplied.

Figure 7.8 is a graph plotting the price and quantity supplied pairs from the supply schedule. Note that the bottom axis shows the quantity supplied. The side axis shows the price per CD. Each intersection of price and quantity supplied represents a point on the graph. We label these points L through V.

When we connect the points from *Part B* with a line, we end up with the **supply curve,** as shown in *Part C.* A supply curve shows the quantities supplied at each possible price. It slopes upward from left to right. You can see that the relationship between price and quantity supplied is direct—or moving in the same direction.

supply curve: *upward-sloping line that shows in graph form the quantities supplied at each possible price*

Quantity Supplied vs. Supply

Each point on a supply curve signifies that a producer will supply a certain quantity at each particular price. If the price increases

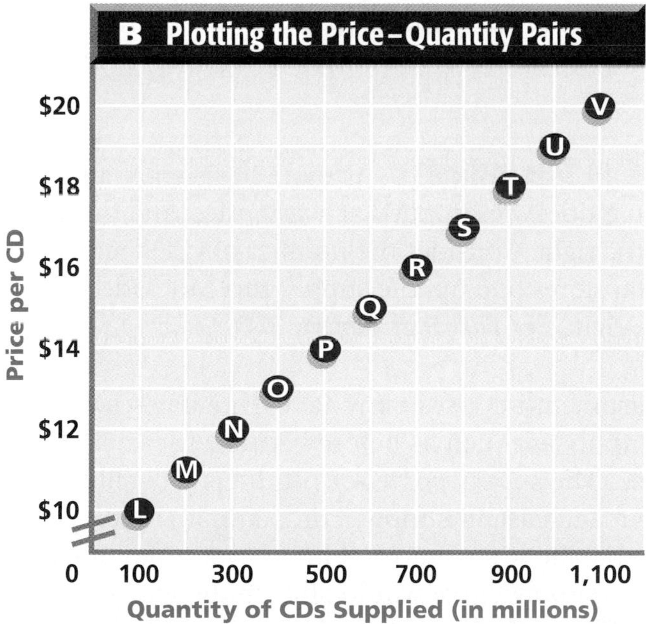

Part B Plotting Quantity Supplied Note how the price and quantity supplied numbers in the supply schedule (Part A) have been transferred to a graph in Part B above. Find letter R. It represents a number of CDs supplied (700 million) at a specific price ($16).

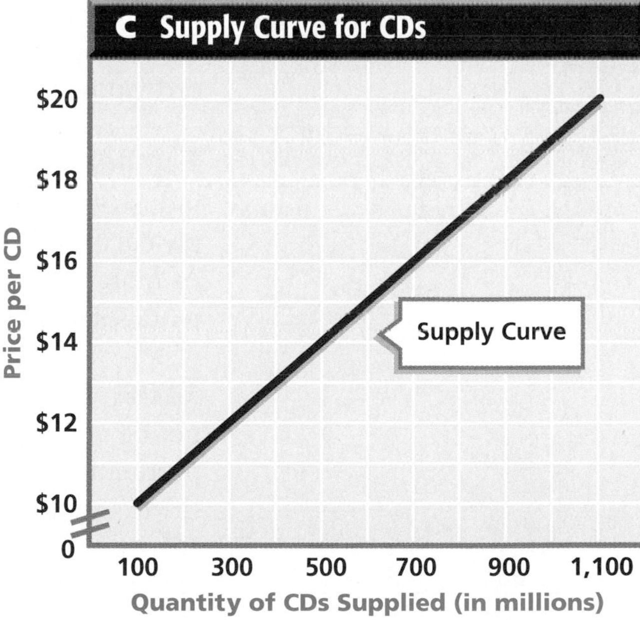

Part C Supply Curve The points in Part B have been connected with a line in Part C above. This line is the supply curve, which always rises from left to right. How many CDs will be supplied at a price of $14 each?

or decreases, the quantity supplied also increases or decreases. A *change in quantity supplied* is caused by a change in price and is shown as a movement along the supply curve.

Sometimes, however, producers will supply more goods or fewer goods at *every* possible price. This is shown as a movement of the entire supply curve and is known as a *change in supply.* A change in price does *not* cause this movement. What does cause the entire supply curve to shift to the right (increase in supply) or the left (decrease in supply)?

The Determinants of Supply

Four of the major determinants of *supply* (not *quantity supplied*) are the price of inputs, the number of firms in the industry, taxes, and technology.

Price of Inputs If the price of inputs–raw materials, wages, and so on–drops, a producer can supply more at a lower production cost. This causes the supply curve to shift to the right. This situation occurred, for example, when the price of memory chips fell during the 1980s and 1990s. More computers were supplied at any given price than before. See *Part A* of **Figure 7.9.** In contrast, if the cost of inputs increases, suppliers will offer fewer goods for sale at every possible price.

Number of Firms in the Industry As more firms enter an industry, greater quantities are supplied at every price, and the supply curve shifts to the right. Consider the number of video rentals. As more video rental stores pop up, the supply curve for video rentals shifts to the right. See *Part B* of **Figure 7.9.**

Taxes If the government imposes more taxes, businesses will not be willing to supply as much as before because the cost of production will rise. The supply curve for products will shift to the left, indicating a decrease in supply. For example, if taxes on silk increased, silk businesses would sell fewer quantities at each and every price. The supply curve would shift to the left, as shown in *Part C* of **Figure 7.9.**

Technology The use of science to develop new products and new methods for producing and distributing goods and services is called **technology.** Any improvement in technology will increase supply, as shown in *Part D.* Why? New technology usually reduces the cost of production. See **Figure 7.10** on page 192.

technology: *any use of land, labor, and capital that produces goods and services more efficiently*

FIGURE 7.9 Determinants of Supply

Changes in Supply Four major factors affect the supply for a specific product. When supply changes, the entire supply curve shifts to the left or the right.

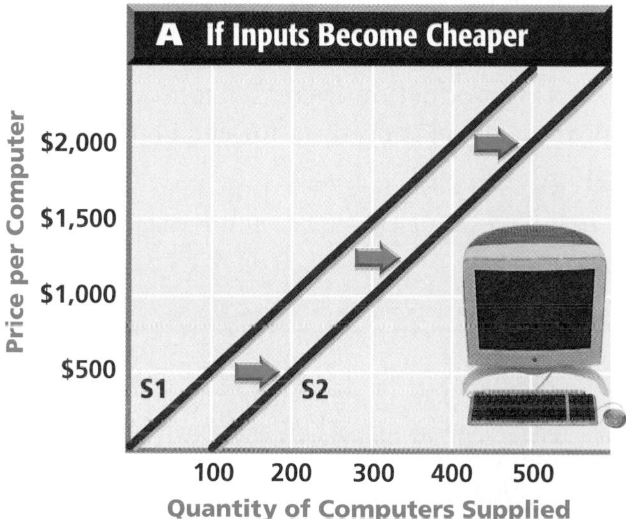

Part A Change in Supply if Price of Inputs Drops Line S1 shows the supply of computers *before* the price of memory chips fell. Line S2 shows the increased supply of computers *after* the price of memory chips fell.

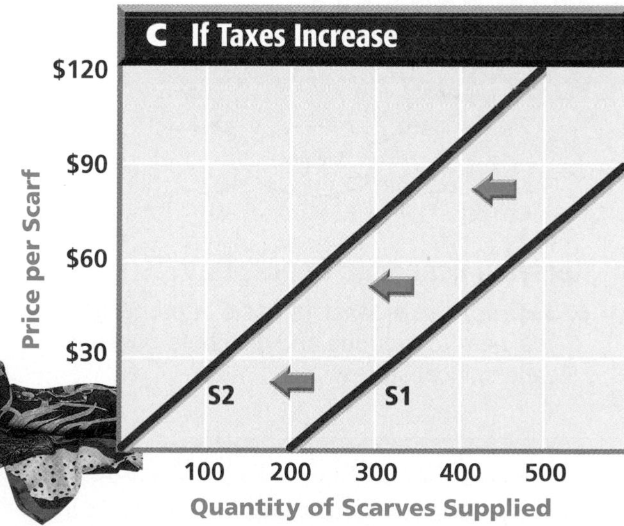

Part C Change in Supply if Taxes Increase Line S1 indicates the supply of silk scarves *before* the government raised taxes on this business. Line S2 equals the supply *after* the government raised taxes.

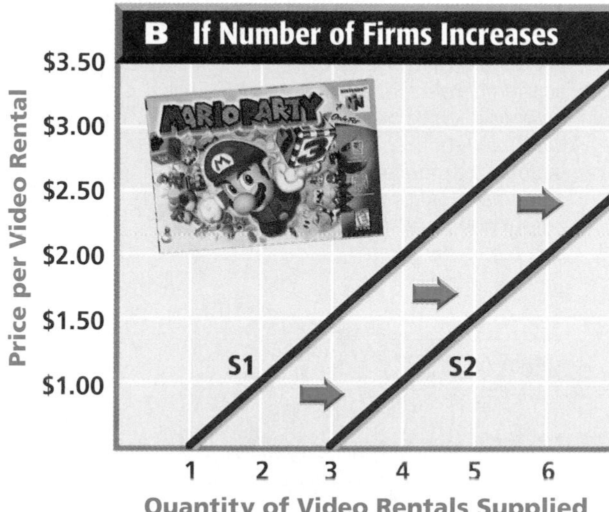

Part B Change in Supply if Number of Firms Increases Overall supply will increase if the number of firms in an industry grows. As profits from movie and game rentals increased, for example, the number of video stores supplying these items increased. With more video stores, the supply curve for video rentals increased from S1 to S2.

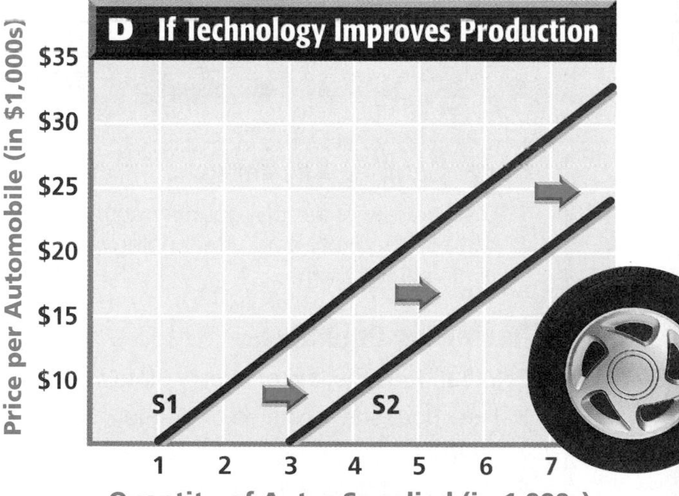

Part D Change in Supply if Technology Reduces Costs of Production Any improvement in technology will increase supply—or move the supply curve to the right from S1 to S2. Technology reduces the costs of production, allowing suppliers to make more goods for a lower cost.

The Law of Diminishing Returns

law of diminishing returns: *economic rule that says as more units of a factor of production (such as labor) are added to other factors of production (such as equipment), after some point total output continues to increase but at a diminishing rate*

You want to expand production. Assume you have 10 machines and employ 10 workers. You hire an eleventh worker. CD production increases by 1,000 per week. When you hire the twelfth worker, CD production might increase by only 900 per week. There are not enough machines to go around, and perhaps workers are getting in each other's way.

This example illustrates the **law of diminishing returns.** According to this law, adding units of one factor of production to all the other factors of production increases total output. After a certain point, however, the extra output for each *additional* unit hired will begin to decrease.

FIGURE 7.10

Technology In the early 1900s, improved technology for making automobiles drastically reduced the amount of time and other resources it took to make many new automobiles. Therefore, a larger supply of autos was offered for sale at every price.

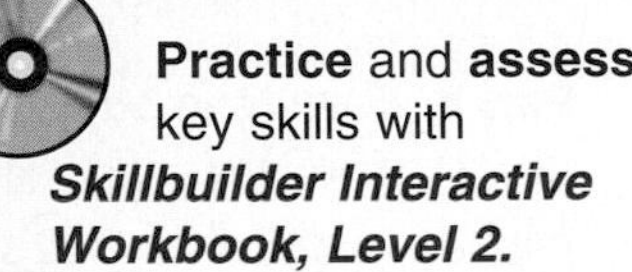

Practice and **assess** key skills with ***Skillbuilder Interactive Workbook, Level 2.***

SECTION 3 Assessment

Understanding Key Terms

1. **Define** law of supply, quantity supplied, supply schedule, supply curve, technology, law of diminishing returns.

Reviewing Objectives

2. What does the law of supply state?
3. How does the incentive of greater profits affect supply?
4. What do a supply schedule and a supply curve show?
5. **Graphic Organizer** Create a diagram like the one in the next column to explain the four determinants of supply.

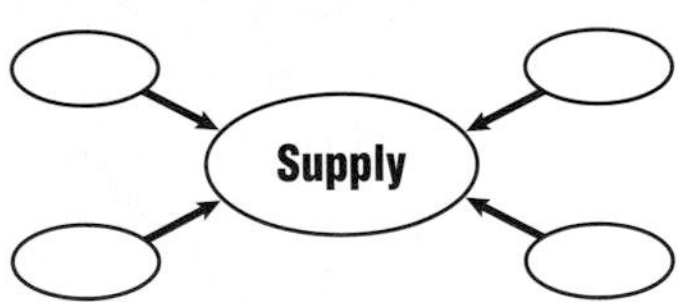

Applying Economic Concepts

6. **Supply** List at least 10 costs of production if you were to produce and distribute baseball caps to local stores.

Critical Thinking Activity

7. **Synthesizing Information** Assume that you are a successful baseball cap maker. Draw a graph that shows the various prices and quantities supplied for your caps.

CRITICAL THINKING SKILLS

Understanding Cause and Effect

Understanding cause and effect involves considering why *an event occurred. A* cause *is the action or situation that produces an event. What happens as a result of a cause is an* effect.

- Identify two or more events or developments.
- Decide whether one event caused the other. Look for "clue words" such as *because, led to, brought about, produced, as a result of, so that, since,* and *therefore.*
- Look for logical relationships between events, such as "She overslept, and then she missed her bus."
- Identify the outcomes of events. Remember that some effects have more than one cause, and some causes lead to more than one effect. Also, an effect can become the cause of yet another effect.

LEARNING THE SKILL

To identify cause-and-effect relationships, follow the steps listed on the left.

PRACTICING THE SKILL

The classic cause-and-effect relationship in economics is between price and quantity demanded/quantity supplied. As the price for a good rises, the quantity demanded goes down and the quantity supplied rises.

1. Look at **Figure A.** What caused the big sale? What is the effect on consumers?
2. Look at the demand curve for DVD systems in **Figure B.** If the price is $5,000, how many will be demanded per year? If the price drops to $1,000, how many will be demanded per year?

Figure A

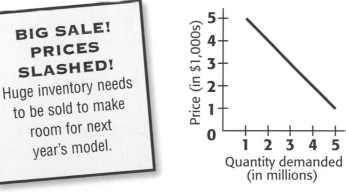

BIG SALE!
PRICES SLASHED!
Huge inventory needs to be sold to make room for next year's model.

Figure B

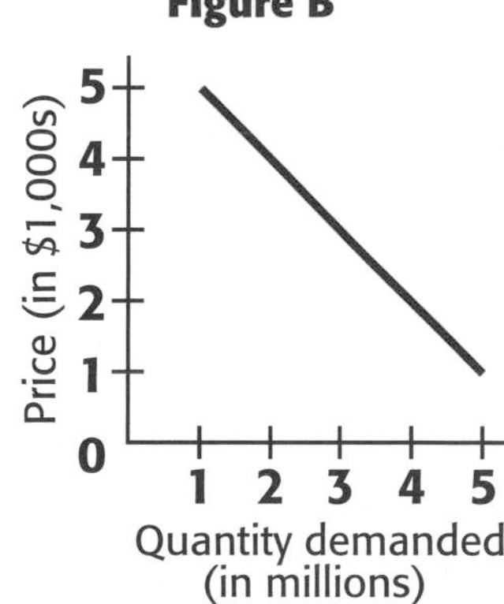

APPLICATION ACTIVITY

In your local newspaper, read an article describing a current event. Determine at least one cause and one effect of that event.

Practice and **assess** key skills with ***Skillbuilder Interactive Workbook, Level 2.***

SECTION 4

Putting Supply and Demand Together

READER'S GUIDE

Terms to Know

- equilibrium price
- shortage
- surplus
- price ceiling
- rationing
- black market
- price floor

Reading Objectives

1. How is the equilibrium price determined?
2. How do shifts in equilibrium price occur?
3. How do shortages and surpluses affect price?
4. How do price ceilings and price floors restrict the free exchange of prices?

COVER STORY

KIPLINGER'S PERSONAL FINANCE MAGAZINE, NOVEMBER 2000

Whatever toy becomes this season's Furby will probably be in skimpy supply, thanks to an industrywide shortage of the electronic guts so vital to today's playthings. So if you think your kids will be clamoring for any of the potential hot toys . . . , be sure to shop now (and find a sneaky hiding place until December). . . .

What do Furbys™, Beanie Babies™, Tickle Me Elmo™, and Cabbage Patch Kids™ all have in common? At one point in time, they all were in short supply—and usually right before the Christmas holiday season. As you will read, shortages occur when the quantity demanded is larger than the quantity supplied at the current price.

Equilibrium Price

In the real world, demand and supply operate together. As the price of a good goes down, the quantity demanded rises and the quantity supplied falls. As the price goes up, the quantity demanded falls and the quantity supplied rises.

Is there a price at which the quantity demanded and the quantity supplied meet? Yes. This level is called the **equilibrium price.** At this price, the quantity supplied by sellers is the same as the

equilibrium price: *the price at which the amount producers are willing to supply is equal to the amount consumers are willing to buy*

FIGURE 7.11

Equilibrium Price In our example, how does the market reach an equilibrium price? We start on Day 1 with sellers thinking that the price for CDs will be $20. If you examine the supply schedule and curve, you see that suppliers will produce 1,100 units. However, buyers will purchase only 100 CDs. The 1,000 unit surplus is shown in column four of the demand and supply schedule as the difference between the quantity supplied and the quantity demanded at $20. To get rid of the surplus, sellers will lower the price. Say suppliers lower the price to $10. At that price, they are willing to supply 100 CDs. However, as the schedule shows, this price turns out to be too low because 100 are supplied and 1,100 are demanded–leaving a shortage of 1,000 CDs. The price tends to go up and down until it reaches equilibrium price. ***According to the schedule and the graph, what is the equilibrium price and quantity demanded?***

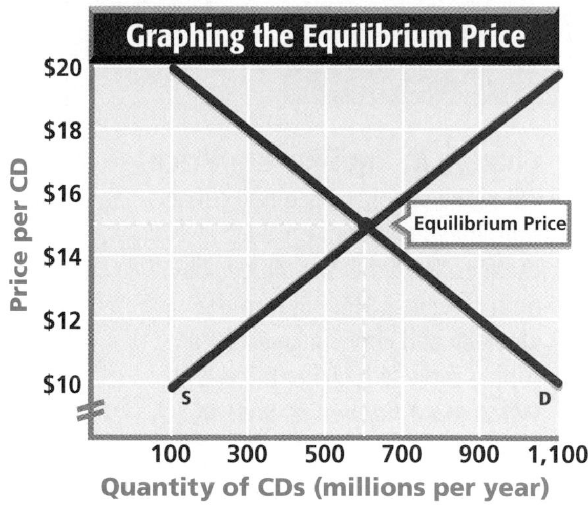

Market Demand and Supply Schedules

Quantity Demanded	Price	Quantity Supplied	Surplus/ Shortage
100	$20	1,100	1,000
200	$19	1,000	800
300	$18	900	600
400	$17	800	400
500	$16	700	200
600	$15	600	0
700	$14	500	−200
800	$13	400	−400
900	$12	300	−600
1,000	$11	200	−800
1,100	$10	100	−1,000

quantity demanded by buyers. One way to visualize equilibrium price is to put supply and demand curves on one graph, as shown in **Figure 7.11.** Where the two curves intersect is the equilibrium price.

Shifts in Equilibrium Price

What happens when there is an increase in the demand for CDs? Assume that scientists prove that listening to more music increases life span. This discovery will cause the entire demand curve to shift outward to the right, as shown in **Figure 7.12** on page 196.

What about changes in supply? You can show these in a similar fashion. Assume that there is a major breakthrough in the technology of producing CDs. The supply curve shifts outward to the right. The new equilibrium price will fall, and both the *quantity supplied* and the *quantity demanded* will increase.

FIGURE 7.12

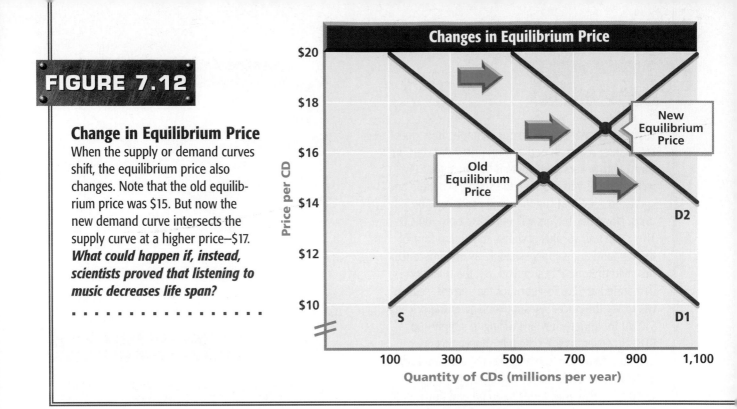

Change in Equilibrium Price
When the supply or demand curves shift, the equilibrium price also changes. Note that the old equilibrium price was $15. But now the new demand curve intersects the supply curve at a higher price–$17. ***What could happen if, instead, scientists proved that listening to music decreases life span?***

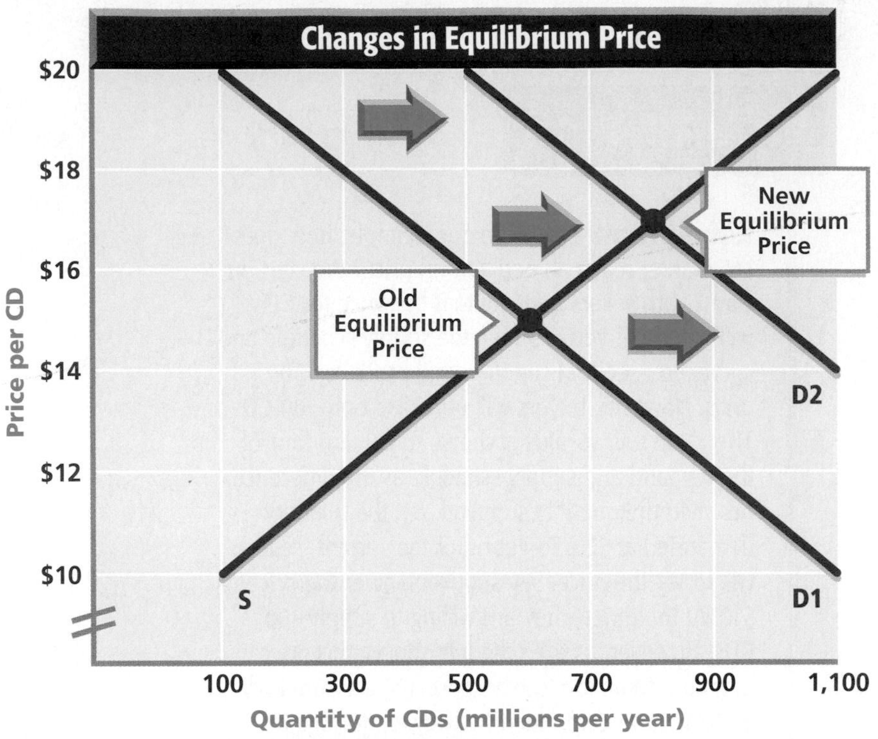

Prices Serve as Signals

In the United States and other countries with mainly free enterprise systems, prices serve as signals to producers and consumers. Rising prices signal producers to produce more and consumers to purchase less. Falling prices signal producers to produce less and consumers to purchase more.

shortage: *situation in which the quantity demanded is greater than the quantity supplied at the current price*

Shortages A **shortage** occurs when, at the current price, the quantity demanded is greater than the quantity supplied. If the market is left alone–without government regulations or other restrictions–shortages put pressure on prices to rise. At a higher price, consumers reduce their purchases, whereas suppliers increase the quantity they supply.

surplus: *situation in which quantity supplied is greater than quantity demanded at the current price*

Surpluses At prices above the equilibrium price, suppliers produce more than consumers want to purchase in the marketplace. Suppliers end up with **surpluses**–large inventories of goods–and this and other forces put pressure on the price to drop to the equilibrium price. If the price falls, suppliers have less incentive to supply as much as before, whereas consumers begin to purchase a greater quantity. The decrease in price toward the equilibrium price, therefore, eliminates the surplus.

Shortage of Games

Market Forces One of the benefits of the market economy is that when it operates without restriction, it eliminates shortages and surpluses. Whenever shortages occur, the market ends up taking care of itself–the price goes up to eliminate the shortage. Whenever surpluses occur, the market again ends up taking care of itself–the price falls to eliminate the surplus. Let's take a look at what happens to the availability of goods and services when the government–not market forces–becomes involved in setting prices.

Price Controls

Why would the government get involved in setting prices? One reason is that in some instances it believes the market forces of supply and demand are unfair, and it is trying to protect consumers and suppliers. Another reason is that special interest groups use pressure on elected officials to protect certain industries.

Price Ceilings A **price ceiling** is a government-set maximum price that can be charged for goods and services. Imagine trying to bring a 12-foot tree into your house that has 8-foot ceilings. The ceiling prevents the top of the tree from going up. Similarly, a *price ceiling* prevents prices from going above a specified amount. For example, city officials might set a price ceiling on what landlords can charge for rent. As *Part A* of **Figure 7.13** on page 198 shows, when a price ceiling is set below the equilibrium price, a shortage occurs.

price ceiling: *a legal maximum price that may be charged for a particular good or service*

Effective price ceilings–and resulting shortages–often lead to nonmarket ways of distributing goods and services. The government may resort to **rationing,** or limiting, items that are in short supply. A policy of rationing is expensive, however. Taxpayers must pay the cost of printing ration coupons, setting up offices to distribute the coupons, and maintaining the bureaucracy involved in enforcing who gets how much of the rationed goods.

rationing: *the distribution of goods and services based on something other than price*

black market: *"underground" or illegal market in which goods are traded at prices above their legal maximum prices or in which illegal goods are sold*

Shortages also may lead to a **black market,** in which illegally high prices are charged for items that are in short supply. As **Figure 7.14** on page 199 shows, items often sold on the black market include tickets to sporting events.

Surplus Cheese

Ration Coupons

price floor: *a legal minimum price below which a good or service may not be sold*

Price Floors A **price floor,** in contrast, is a government-set *minimum* price that can be charged for goods and services. Price floors–more common than price ceilings–prevent prices from dropping too low. When are low prices a problem? Assume that about 30 of your classmates all want jobs after school. The local fast-food restaurant can hire 30 students at $4.15 an hour, but the government has set a minimum wage–a price floor–of $5.15 an hour. Some of you will get hired, and you'll happily earn $5.15 an hour. Not all of you will get hired at that wage, however, which leads to a surplus of unemployed workers as shown in *Part B* of **Figure 7.13.** If the market were left on its own, the equilibrium price of $4.15 per hour would have all of you employed.

Besides affecting the minimum wage, price floors have been used to support agricultural prices. If the nation's farmers have a bumper crop of wheat, for example, the country has a huge surplus of wheat. The market, if left alone, would take care of the

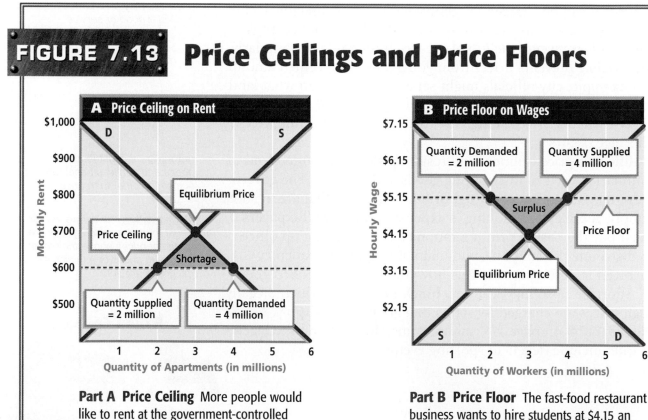

FIGURE 7.13 Price Ceilings and Price Floors

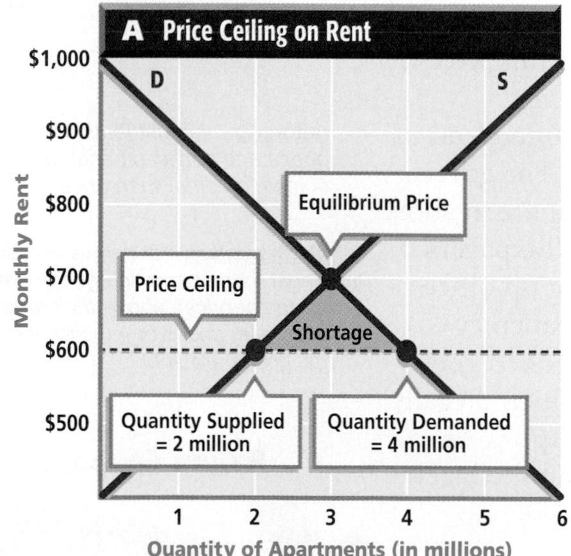

Part A Price Ceiling More people would like to rent at the government-controlled price, but apartment owners are unwilling to build more rental units if they cannot charge higher rent. This results in a shortage of apartments to rent.

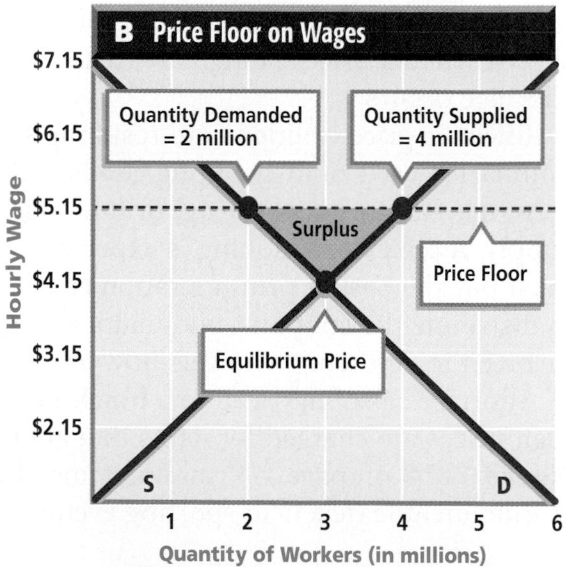

Part B Price Floor The fast-food restaurant business wants to hire students at $4.15 an hour, but the government has set a minimum wage–a price floor–of $5.15 an hour. ***What is the surplus of workers with a price floor of $5.15 per hourly wage?***

FIGURE 7.14

Black Market Scalpers selling high-priced, limited tickets—such as these tickets to a World Cup Soccer match—are part of the black market. ***How do price ceilings on tickets to sporting events lead to shortages?***

surplus by having the price drop. As prices decrease, remember, quantity supplied decreases and quantity demanded increases. But the nation's farmers might not earn enough to make a profit or even pay their bills if the price drops too much. So the government sometimes sets a price floor for wheat, which stops the price per bushel from dropping below a certain level. The farmers know this, so instead of reducing their acreage of wheat—which would reduce the surplus—they keep producing more wheat.

Practice and **assess** key skills with ***Skillbuilder Interactive Workbook, Level 2.***

SECTION 4 Assessment

Understanding Key Terms

1. **Define** equilibrium price, shortage, surplus, price ceiling, rationing, black market, price floor.

Reviewing Objectives

2. How is the equilibrium price determined?
3. How do shifts in equilibrium price occur?
4. **Graphic Organizer** Create a diagram like the one below to show how shortages and surpluses affect prices.

5. How do price ceilings and price floors restrict the free exchange of prices?

Applying Economic Concepts

6. **Shortages** Explain how a shortage of professional sports tickets determines the general price of those tickets.

Critical Thinking Activity

7. **Understanding Cause and Effect** Draw a series of three graphs.
   - The first graph should show an equilibrium price for sunglasses.
   - The second graph should show the shift that would occur if research proved wearing sunglasses increased I.Q.
   - The third graph should show the shift that would occur if research proved that wearing sunglasses caused acne. *For help in using graphs, see page xv in the Economic Handbook.*

People & Perspectives

Alfred Marshall

ECONOMIST (1842–1924)

- **Began career as a mathematician**
- **Chaired political economy at Cambridge University, England**
- **Developed supply and demand analysis**
- **Published *Principles of Economics* (1890) and *Elements of Economics* (1892)**

Alfred Marshall is known for introducing the concept of supply and demand analysis to economics. The following excerpt from *Elements of Economics* explains the concept of equilibrium:

"*The simplest case of balance, or equilibrium, between desire and effort is found when a person satisfies one of his wants by his own direct work. When a boy picks blackberries for his own eating, the action of picking may itself be pleasurable for a while. . . .*

Equilibrium is reached, when at last his eagerness to play and his disinclination for the work of picking counterbalance the desire for eating. The satisfaction which he can get from picking fruit has arrived at its maximum. . . ."

Marshall also explained how equilibrium is established in a local market. Buyers and sellers, having perfect knowledge of the market, freely compete for their own best interests. In so doing they arrive at a price that exactly equates supply and demand.

"*. . . [A price may be] called the true equilibrium price: because if it were fixed on at the beginning, and adhered to throughout, it would exactly equate demand and supply. (i.e. the amount which buyers were willing to purchase at that price would be just equal to that for which sellers were willing to take that price). . . .*

In our typical market then we assume that the forces of demand and supply have free play; that there is no combination among dealers on either side; but each acts for himself, and there is much free competition; that is, buyers generally compete freely with buyers, and sellers compete freely with sellers."

Checking for Understanding

1. **What does Marshall mean by "equilibrium between desire and effort"?**
2. **What is an equilibrium price?**

CHAPTER 7 Summary

Chapter Overview Visit the *Economics Today and Tomorrow* Web site at ett.glencoe.com and click on ***Chapter 7—Chapter Overviews*** to review chapter information.

SECTION 1 Demand

- **Demand** represents a consumer's willingness and ability to pay.
- The **law of demand** states as price goes up, **quantity demanded** goes down. As price goes down, quantity demanded goes up.
- Factors explaining the inverse relationship between quantity demanded and price include the **real income effect,** the **substitution effect,** and **diminishing marginal utility**—or how one's additional satisfaction for a product lessens with each additional purchase of it.

SECTION 2 The Demand Curve and Elasticity of Demand

- The downward-sloping **demand curve** signifies that as the price falls, the quantity demanded increases.
- Changes in population, income, tastes and preferences, and the existence of substitutes, or **complementary goods,** affect demand.
- The **price elasticity of demand** is a measure of *how much* consumers respond to a price change.
- If a small change in price causes a large change in quantity demanded, the demand for that good is said to be **elastic.**
- If a price change does not result in much of a change in the quantity demanded, that demand is considered **inelastic.**

SECTION 3 The Law of Supply and the Supply Curve

- The **law of supply** states as the price rises for a good, the **quantity supplied** also rises. As the price falls, the quantity supplied falls.
- The upward-sloping **supply curve** shows this direct relationship between quantity supplied and price.
- Four factors determine supply in a market economy. These include the price of inputs, the number of firms in the industry, taxes, and **technology.**

SECTION 4 Putting Supply and Demand Together

- In free enterprise systems, prices serve as signals to producers and consumers.
- The point at which the quantity demanded and the quantity supplied meet is called the **equilibrium price.**
- A **shortage** causes prices to rise, signaling producers to produce more and consumers to purchase less.
- A **surplus** causes prices to drop, signaling producers to produce less and consumers to purchase more.
- A **price ceiling,** which prevents prices from going above a specified amount, often leads to shortages and **black market** activities.
- A **price floor** prevents prices such as a minimum wage from dropping too low.

CHAPTER 7

Assessment and Activities

Self-Check Quiz Visit the *Economics Today and Tomorrow* Web site at ett.glencoe.com and click on ***Chapter 7—Self-Check Quizzes*** to prepare for the Chapter Test.

Identifying Key Terms

Write a short paragraph about demand using all of the following terms.

- law of demand
- quantity demanded
- law of diminishing marginal utility
- real income effect
- substitution effect
- demand curve
- price elasticity of demand

Write a short paragraph about supply using all of the following terms.

- law of supply
- law of diminishing returns
- supply curve
- shortage
- equilibrium price
- surplus

Recalling Facts and Ideas

Section 1

1. What is the basis of most activity in a market economy?
2. What generally happens to quantity demanded when the price of a good goes up (and other prices stay the same)?
3. When the price of a good changes, what effects tend to create the law of demand?

Section 2

4. How do we show in a graph an increase in the demand for a good?
5. What is the distinction between elastic and inelastic demand?
6. If income and population increase, what tends to happen to demand curves?

Section 3

7. Do suppliers tend to produce less or more when the price goes up? Why?
8. What would an increase in taxes do to the position of the supply curve?

Section 4

9. If the price of a product is above its equilibrium price, what is the result?
10. If the price of a product is below its equilibrium price, what is the result?

Thinking Critically

1. **Making Generalizations** To what extent do you think the law of demand applies in the world around you? Are there any goods or services that you think do not follow the law of demand? Explain.
2. **Making Comparisons** If you had to guess the relative price elasticities of demand for CDs compared to that of insulin needed by diabetics, what would you state?

3. **Making Predictions** Technology has decreased the cost of producing goods and services. Create a chart like the one below and list four goods or services that you think will be changed by technology in your lifetime. Explain how you think each change will affect your life.

Technological Change	Effect on My Life
1.	
2.	
3.	
4.	

Applying Economic Concepts

Supply and Demand Some prices change in our economy very seldom, whereas others change all the time, even daily. Make a list of products whose prices change slowly, if at all. Make another list of products whose prices you think change quickly.

Cooperative Learning Project

Working in groups of four, each group will interview a local merchant. Ask the following questions and others you think are relevant: What determines the prices you charge? What determines when you change prices? Are there any costs to you of changing prices (such as reprinting price lists)? One person in each group should write a summary of the interview. Then compare these summaries.

Technology Activity

Using a Spreadsheet Interview 10 students in the school, asking the following questions: (a) What three purchases have you made recently? (b) Do any of these purchases represent a change in your buying habits? (c) Was the change caused by a change in income, a change in tastes and preferences, or a change in the price of substitutes or complements? Summarize the information you obtained by placing it in a spreadsheet.

Reviewing Skills

Understanding Cause and Effect Look at the graph below, then answer the questions that follow.

1. How many pounds of beef are supplied at $1.89 per pound?
2. How many pounds are supplied at $2.69 per pound?
3. What can you infer as the cause-and-effect relationship here?

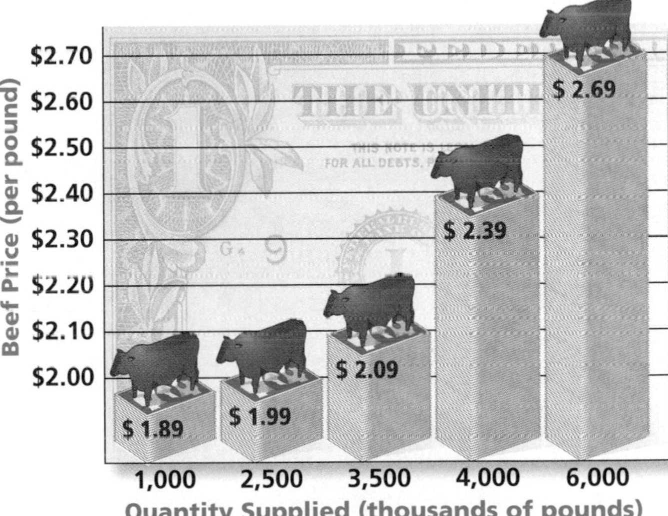

Analyzing the Global *Economy*

Clip articles from newspapers or magazines that show the laws of supply and/or demand operating in other parts of the world. Possibilities would be weather damages to crops and economic conditions affecting housing starts, and so on.

Global *Economy*

Demand for Oil Americans demand oil for many purposes, but mostly as a fuel for their automobiles. According to the Department of Energy, as of 2002 about 193 million vehicles were burning an estimated 122 billion gallons of gasoline a year. Domestic supplies meet about half of the demand for oil. The map below shows where we get the rest.

Canada supplies 13 percent

Mexico supplies 11 percent

Caribbean Nations supply 4 percent
(Leading Sources: Virgin Islands, Trinidad and Tobago, Netherlands Antilles)

South America supplies 24 percent
(Leading Sources: Venezuela, Colombia, Argentina)

On average, a barrel holding 42 gallons of crude oil produces 21 gallons of gasoline.

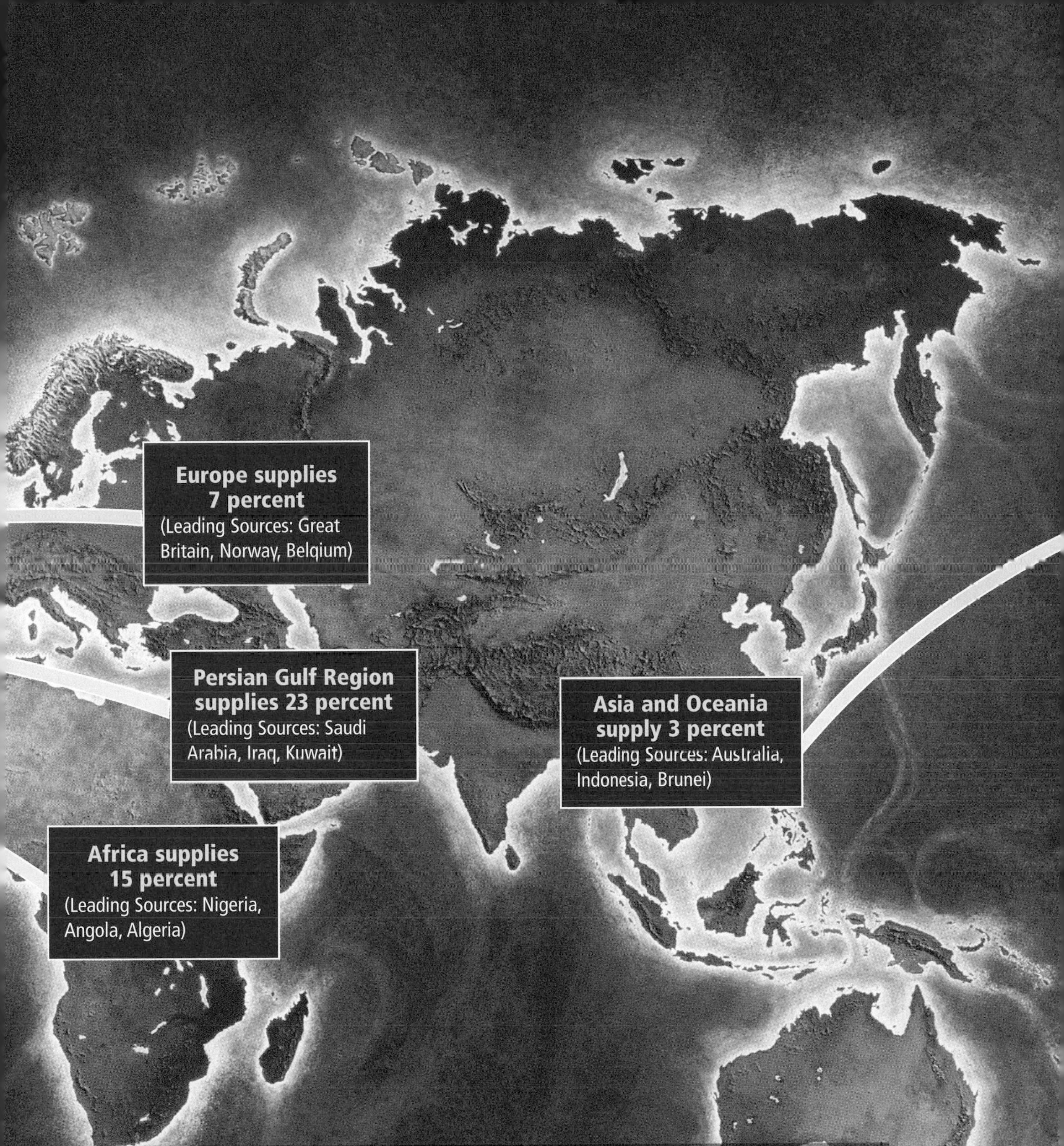

Europe supplies 7 percent
(Leading Sources: Great Britain, Norway, Belgium)

Persian Gulf Region supplies 23 percent
(Leading Sources: Saudi Arabia, Iraq, Kuwait)

Asia and Oceania supply 3 percent
(Leading Sources: Australia, Indonesia, Brunei)

Africa supplies 15 percent
(Leading Sources: Nigeria, Angola, Algeria)

Thinking Globally

1. Which region of the world is the largest source for American oil imports?
2. What percentage of American oil imports do Canada and Mexico provide?

CHAPTER 8

Business Organizations

Why It's Important

How could you start a business and operate it successfully? Which has more advantages—sole ownership of a business or a partnership? This chapter will explain how you can start a business as well as the different ways that businesses are organized.

To learn more about sole proprietorships, partnerships, and corporations, view the **Economics & You** *Chapter 4 video lesson:* **Business Organizations**

Chapter Overview Visit the *Economics Today and Tomorrow* Web site at ett.glencoe.com and click on ***Chapter 8—Chapter Overviews*** to preview chapter information.

Susan Smith/Partner

Charles Johnson/Partner

SECTION 1

Starting a Business

Cover Story

Kiplinger's Personal Finance Magazine, December 1998

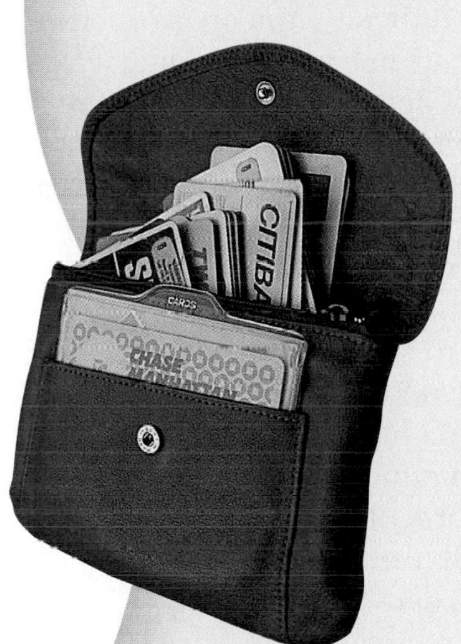

The perfect place for your credit cards is in a Beeping Wallet—a billfold with a microchip that beeps every 20 seconds when a credit card has been removed. It's both a last-gasp warning [to not spend money] and a reminder to replace the card, says David Kopel, the wallet's inventor, who says he came up with the idea after his wife lost a credit card.

Reader's Guide

Terms to Know

- entrepreneur
- startup
- small business incubator
- inventory
- receipts

Reading Objectives

1. What things must be done before starting a business?
2. What four elements are involved in every business?

How many times have you seen a product for sale and said, "That was *my* idea"? Or you see an item, nod your head, and think, "That's a good idea. I wonder how they thought of that"? Many new products and services arise from personal experience–as in the case of David Kopel's Beeping Wallet. In this section, you'll learn how to take your idea and start a business.

Getting Started

Suppose that you have been tinkering with electronic equipment since you were a child. By now you can take apart and reassemble cassette and CD players, VCRs, most computers, and

FIGURE 8.1

Entrepreneurship Starting any business, such as electronics repair, is risky. ***Why do people take the risk of becoming entrepreneurs?***

other electronic equipment without difficulty. You are so good at repairing this kind of equipment that you have been doing it for friends and relatives for some time. Then an idea occurs to you: Why not charge people for your services? Why not go into business for yourself? By starting your own business, you will become an entrepreneur.

entrepreneur: *person who organizes, manages, and assumes the risks of a business in order to gain profits*

A person who makes the decision to start a business is an **entrepreneur** because he or she is willing to take a risk. See **Figure 8.1.** People usually decide to start a business to gain profits, to "do something on their own," or to be their own boss.

After making the decision to start a business, entrepreneurs must gather the relevant factors of production to produce their good or service and decide on the form of business organization that best suits their purposes. (You'll learn about the types of business organizations in Sections 2 and 3.)

Anyone hoping to become an entrepreneur must also learn as much as possible about the business he or she plans to start. This process includes learning about the laws, regulations, and tax codes that will apply to the business.

startup: *a beginning business enterprise*

Student Web Activity Visit the *Economics Today and Tomorrow* Web site at ett.glencoe.com and click on ***Chapter 8—Student Web Activities*** to learn more about the Small Business Administration.

Help From Government For a person who wants to start a small business, help is available. The federal government's Small Business Administration often helps finance **startups,** or new small businesses. State departments of commerce and community affairs also offer assistance. Many community college and university campuses have small business development centers that are federally funded to help a small business get started.

A **small business incubator** might also aid businesses in your area. Just as incubators help hatch chicks, there are business incubators that help "hatch" small businesses. They are often operated with state and federal funds. A small business incubator might provide a low-rent building, management advice, and computers. The incubator's goal is to generate job creation and economic growth, particularly in economically depressed areas.

small business incubator: *private- or government-funded agency that assists new businesses by providing advice or low-rent buildings and supplies*

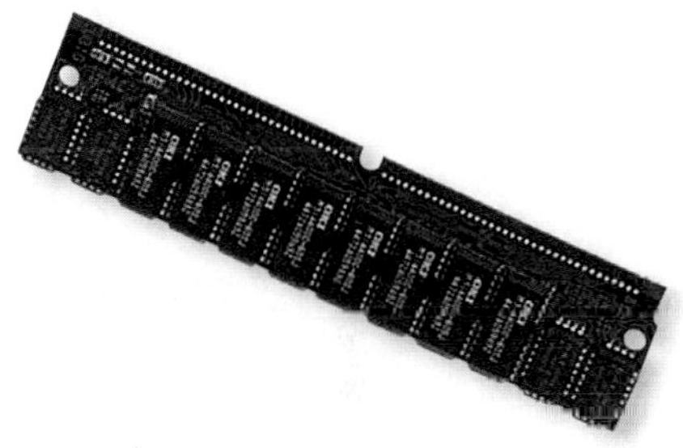

Help From the Internet Although new entrepreneurs can get help from government agencies, the Internet also provides a huge amount of information on how to start a business. By using search engines, you can find Web sites that explain everything from putting together a business plan to learning the "secrets to success."

Elements of Business Operation

Every business must consider four basic elements: expenses, advertising, record keeping, and risk.

Expenses You've probably heard the saying, "You have to spend money to make money." This is true when considering business expenses: new equipment, wages, insurance, taxes, electricity, telephone service, and so on. And depending on the kind of job you do, you may need replacement parts. At first, you might buy parts only as you need them for a particular job. In time, you will find it easier to have an **inventory,** or supply of items that are used in your business. See *Part A* of **Figure 8.2** on page 210.

inventory: *extra supply of the items used in a business, such as raw materials or goods for sale*

Wages are an expense. Because you could be working for someone else and earning an income, you should pay yourself a wage equal to what you could earn elsewhere. It's important not to forget this *opportunity cost* when you figure out the profits and losses your new business is making.

Will your business make a profit? Add your wages to your other expenses, including taxes. Then subtract your total expenses from your **receipts,** or the money income you've received from customers, and you will have your profit. Keep records of how much you owe and to whom, and of how much your business is taking in. You will need this information to do your taxes.

receipts: *income received from the sale of goods and/or services; also, slips of paper documenting a purchase*

FIGURE 8.2

Elements of Business Operation

A ▶ Expenses

The supplies you need to do your job are included under expenses. Let's imagine that you want to start a painting business. As part of your expenses, you will need to purchase brushes, paint, and ladders. As your business grows, you might invest in paint sprayers or electric sanders so you can complete jobs more quickly. This new equipment will eventually add to your income, but will probably require more money than you have on hand at the startup phase of your business.

◀ B Advertising

The cost of advertising often reduces profits substantially in the startup phase of a business. After you have several satisfied customers, however, information about your business may spread by word of mouth.

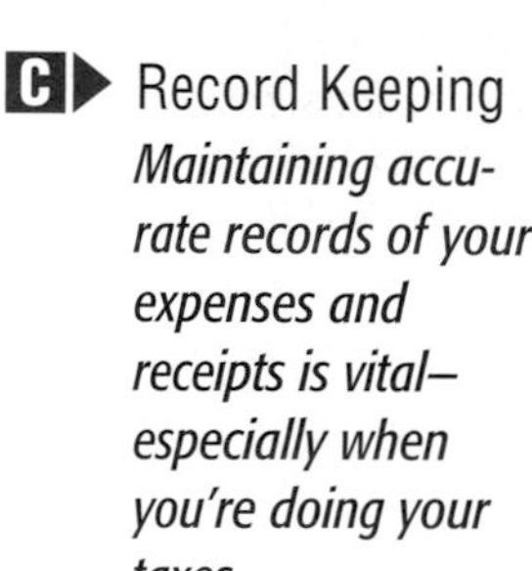

C ▶ Record Keeping

Maintaining accurate records of your expenses and receipts is vital—especially when you're doing your taxes.

D ▶ Risk

Many startups fail. If you work for a boss, your overall risks are usually small. As your own boss, your risks are greater, but so are the potential rewards. The profits you expect to make are your incentive for taking those risks.

Advertising To start a business, you must make potential customers aware that your goods or services are available for a price. You could have flyers printed and distributed to advertise your business, as shown in *Part B* of **Figure 8.2.** You could also buy advertising space in newspapers or on various Web sites.

Record Keeping No matter how small your business, having a system to track your expenses and income is key to your success. Probably one of the first things you'll need is a computer. See *Part C* of **Figure 8.2.** You should also purchase or download from the Internet the programs that will allow you to track your expenses and receipts. These programs write checks, calculate your monthly profits and losses, tell you the difference between what you own and what you owe (called *net worth*), and so on.

The slips of paper that document your purchases of supplies—also known as *receipts*—must be filed in a safe place. Business purchases can be deducted from the amount of taxes you owe.

Risk Every business involves risks. You must balance the risks against the advantages of being in business for yourself. See *Part D* of **Figure 8.2.** For example, if you spend part of your savings to pay for advertising and equipment, you are taking a risk. You may not get enough business to cover these costs.

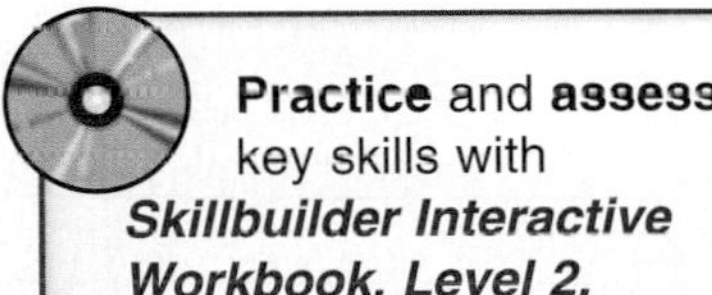

Practice and **assess** key skills with ***Skillbuilder Interactive Workbook, Level 2.***

SECTION 1 Assessment

Understanding Key Terms

1. **Define** entrepreneur, startup, small business incubator, inventory, receipts.

Reviewing Objectives

2. What are at least three things you must do before starting a business?
3. **Graphic Organizer** Create a diagram like the one below to explain the four elements common to all businesses.

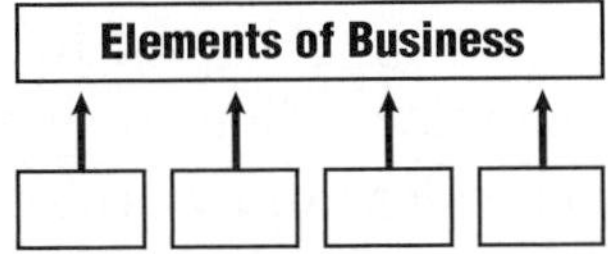

Applying Economic Concepts

4. **Entrepreneurship** Think of a product or service that you would like to produce. Be sure to consider a business that you know something about or could easily find information about. Also research if there is a demand for that product or service. What initial expenses would you have as a startup?

Critical Thinking Activity

5. **Synthesizing Information** Using your answer to question 4, compile a table listing all expenses for your startup for one month. *For help in using tables, see page xvii in the Economic Handbook.*

Technology Skills

Using the Internet

To learn more about almost any topic imaginable, use the Internet–a global network of computers. Many features, such as E-mail, interactive educational classes, and shopping services, are offered on the Net. To get on the Internet, you need three things: (a) a personal computer or WebTV, (b) a modem–or device that connects your computer to a telephone line or cable, and (c) an account with an Internet service provider (ISP). An ISP is a company that enables you to log on to the Internet, usually for a fee.

1. Log on to the Internet and access a search engine.
2. Search by typing *small business incubator* in the search engine.
3. Scroll the list of Web pages that appears when the search is complete. Select a page to bring up and read or print.
4. If you get "lost" on the Internet, click on the "back arrow" key at the top of the screen until you find a site that looks familiar.
5. Continue selecting sites until you have enough information to write a short report on the help available to startups from small business incubators.

Learning the Skill

After you are connected, the easiest way to access Internet sites is to use a "Web browser," a program that lets you view and explore information on the World Wide Web. The Web consists of many documents called "Web sites," each of which has its own address, or Uniform Resource Locator (URL). Many URLs start with the keystrokes *http://*

If you don't know the exact URL of a site, commercial "search engines" such as Yahoo! or Google can help you find information. Type a subject or name into the "search" box, then press Enter. The search engine lists available sites that may have the information you are looking for.

Practicing the Skill

To learn how the Internet can help business startups, follow the steps listed on the left.

Application Activity

Follow the above procedures to locate information about the number of women-owned businesses. Use the information you gather to create a chart or bar graph depicting the number, sales, and workforces of women-owned businesses.

SECTION 2

Sole Proprietorships and Partnerships

Cover Story

Newsweek, April 5, 1999

In the movie *The Net,* Sandra Bullock played a victimized computer hacker who, in one scene, orders a pizza on her computer. The moment flashed by most moviegoers . . . , but it gave Tim Glass an idea—not for a better movie but an Internet company. With three longtime friends and colleagues, [Glass] set about recruiting restaurants to post their menus online. The goal: point-and-click ordering. They called the company Cyberslice. . . .

Reader's Guide

Terms to Know

- sole proprietorship
- proprietor
- unlimited liability
- assets
- partnership
- limited partnership
- joint venture

Reading Objectives

1. What are the advantages and disadvantages of a sole proprietorship?
2. What are the advantages and disadvantages of a partnership?

Businesses can be organized in a number of ways. Some have one owner. Others, like Tim Glass's Cyberslice company, have multiple owners or partners. In this section, you'll learn that the two most common ways of organizing business in the United States are sole proprietorships and partnerships.

Sole Proprietorships

The most basic type of business organization is the **sole proprietorship**, a business owned by one person. It is the oldest

sole proprietorship: *business owned and operated by one person*

FIGURE 8.3

Advantages and Disadvantages of Sole Proprietorships

	Advantages	Disadvantages
Profits and Losses	• Proprietor receives all the profits because he or she takes all the risks.	• Losses are not shared.
Liability		• The proprietor has unlimited liability. • If the firm is unable to pay its bills, the proprietor can be forced to sell personal assets as well as the business to pay debts.
Management	• Decisions on starting and running the business can be made quickly. • Business operations are less complicated than other types of businesses. • There are generally fewer government regulations.	• A proprietor must handle all decision making, even for unfamiliar areas of the business. This is a severe problem for many sole proprietorships.
Taxes	• Taxes are usually low because a proprietor pays only personal income taxes on profits.	
Personal Satisfaction	• The proprietor has high satisfaction in being his or her own boss. • The owner can make the business into whatever he or she wants it to be.	• Running a sole proprietorship is demanding and time-consuming. • If the proprietor does not enjoy responsibility, he or she will find ownership a burden.
Financing Growth	• Proprietors can obtain credit relatively easily. Lenders know they can take over the assets of the business as well as personal assets of the proprietor if the loan is not paid back.	• A sole proprietor must rely on his or her own funds plus funds that can be borrowed. • Borrowing large amounts can be difficult.
Life of the Business		• If the proprietor dies, goes bankrupt, or is unwilling or unable to work, the business will probably fail. • Uncertainty about the future increases the risk both to employees and creditors.

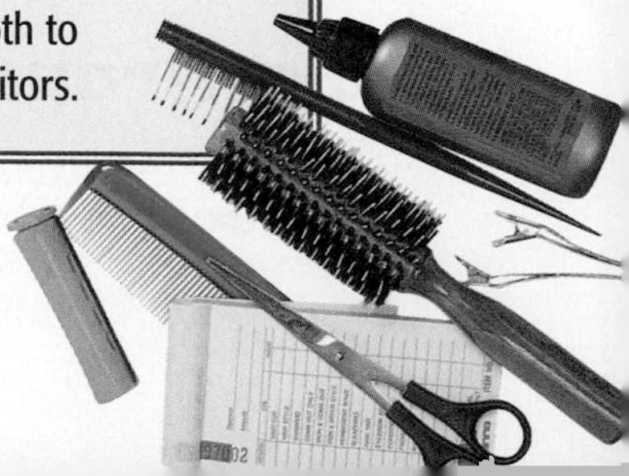

form of business organization and also the most common. The colonies of Maryland and Pennsylvania were founded as sole proprietorships.

When we speak of a **proprietor,** we are referring to the owner of a business. The word *proprietor* comes from the Latin word *proprietas,* meaning "property." A business is a kind of property.

The United States has more than 17 million such businesses, and many of them are small. For that reason, they usually are easier and less expensive to start and run. You probably have contact with many sole proprietorships every day without realizing it.

The biggest advantages of sole proprietorships are that the proprietor has full pride in owning the business and receives all the profits. The biggest disadvantage is that the proprietor has **unlimited liability,** or complete legal responsibility for all debts and damages arising from doing business. Personal **assets,** or items of value such as houses, cars, jewelry, and so on, may be seized to pay off business debts. **Figure 8.3** lists these and other advantages and disadvantages of operating a sole proprietorship.

proprietor: *owner of a business*

unlimited liability: *requirement that an owner is personally and fully responsible for all losses and debts of a business*

assets: *all items to which a business or household holds legal claim*

partnership: *business that two or more individuals own and operate*

Partnerships

Earlier in this chapter, we imagined that you had started an electronics repair business. Suppose your business is doing so well that your workload leaves you little time to do anything else. You could expand your business by hiring an employee. However, you also need financial capital to buy new equipment, and you would rather not take out a loan. You decide to take on a partner.

The best solution is to look for someone who can keep books, order supplies, handle customers, and invest in the business. You offer to form a **partnership,** a business that two or more individuals own and operate. You sign a partnership agreement that is legally binding. It describes the duties of each partner, the division of profits, and the distribution of assets should the partners end the agreement.

Much like sole proprietorships, an advantage of partnerships is the pride of sharing ownership in a business–and contributing to it in a specialized way that benefits all the partners. A disadvantage is that, like the sole proprietor, the partners have unlimited liability. **Figure 8.4** on page 216 shows other advantages and disadvantages of partnerships.

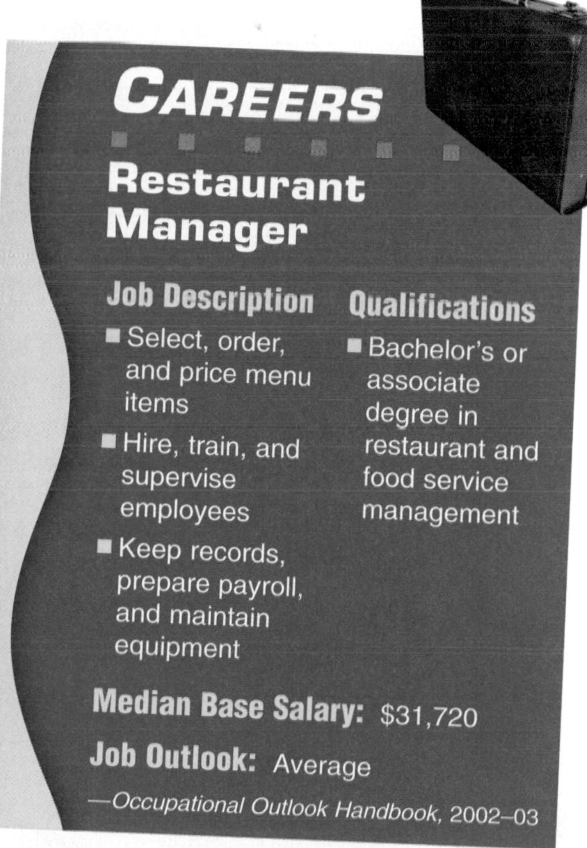

CAREERS
Restaurant Manager
Job Description
Select, order, and price menu items
Hire, train, and supervise employees
Keep records, prepare payroll, and maintain equipment
Qualifications
Bachelor's or associate degree in restaurant and food service management
Median Base Salary: $31,720
Job Outlook: Average
—Occupational Outlook Handbook, 2002–03

FIGURE 8.4

Advantages and Disadvantages of Partnerships

	Advantages	Disadvantages
Profits and Losses	• Losses are shared. • Partners may survive a loss that might bankrupt a sole proprietor.	• Because partners share the risks, they also share the profits.
Liability		• Partners have unlimited liability for debts incurred in business. • If a partner is unable to pay his or her share of a debt, the others must make up the difference.
Management	• Partnerships are usually more efficient than proprietorships. • Each partner works in areas of the business that he or she knows most about or is best at doing. • There are generally fewer government regulations.	• Decision making is often slow because of the need to reach agreement among several people. • Disagreements can lead to problems in running the business.
Taxes	• Taxes are usually low because partners pay only personal income taxes on their share of profits.	
Personal Satisfaction	• Partners feel pride in owning and operating their own company.	• Arguments may result if partners do not get along with each other.
Financing Growth	• Partnerships combine capital, making more funds available to operate a larger, more profitable business. • Creditors are often willing to lend more money to partnerships than to sole proprietorships.	• Partnerships can have trouble borrowing large amounts of capital. • The amount borrowed is usually limited by the combined value of the business assets and the personal assets of the partners.
Life of the Business		• If one partner dies or leaves, the partnership must be ended and reorganized. • The other partners may be unable or unwilling to continue operating, and the business may close—an uncertainty that is a risk to employees and creditors.

Limited Partnerships A **limited partnership** is a special form of partnership in which the partners are not equal. One partner is called the *general partner.* This person (or persons) assumes all of the management duties and has full responsibility for the debts of the limited partnership. The other partners are "limited" because all they do is contribute money or property. They have no voice in the partnership's management.

limited partnership: *special form of partnership in which one or more partners have limited liability but no voice in management*

The advantage to the limited partners is that they have no liability for the losses beyond what they initially invest. The disadvantage, of course, is that they have no say in how the business is run.

Joint Ventures Sometimes individuals or companies want to do a special project together. They do not have any desire to work together after the project is done. What they might do is form a **joint venture**—a temporary partnership set up for a specific purpose just for a short period of time.

joint venture: *partnership set up for a specific purpose just for a short period of time*

Suppose investors want to purchase real estate as a short-term investment. They may later plan to resell the property for profit. At that point, the joint venture ends.

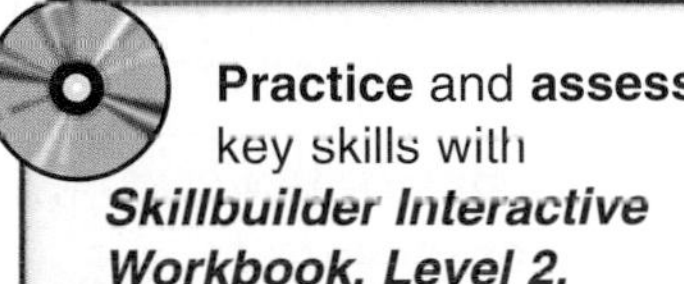
Practice and **assess** key skills with ***Skillbuilder Interactive Workbook, Level 2.***

SECTION 2 Assessment

Understanding Key Terms

1. **Define** sole proprietorship, proprietor, unlimited liability, assets, partnership, limited partnership, joint venture.

Reviewing Objectives

2. Analyze the advantages and disadvantages of a sole proprietorship.
3. Analyze the advantages and disadvantages of a partnership.
4. **Graphic Organizer** Create a diagram like the one in the next column, then analyze the similarities and differences between partnerships and sole proprietorships. In your diagram, explain the characteristics that are unique to partnerships and sole proprietorships in the outer part of each oval. Where the ovals overlap, write the characteristics shared by both.

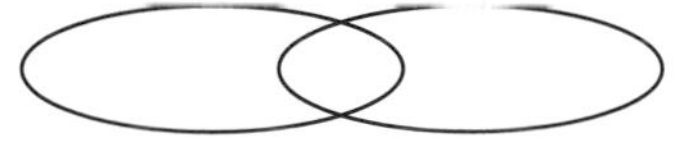

Applying Economic Concepts

5. **Partnership** Make a list describing at least five character traits that you would want a business partner to possess in order to have a successful partnership with him or her.

Critical Thinking Activity

6. **Categorizing Information** Imagine you are sole owner of an ice cream parlor. Make a spreadsheet listing all the daily and weekly duties you have to perform *in addition to* making ice cream.

People & Perspectives

John H. Johnson

ENTREPRENEUR (1918–)

- **Began publishing *Negro Digest* in 1942**
- **Published first issue of *Ebony* in 1945**
- **Was one of the first entrepreneurs to recognize and take advantage of the tremendous business opportunities in the African American community**
- **Produces American Black Achievement Awards for television, first aired in 1978**
- **Launched *Ebony South Africa* in 1995**

John Johnson began his career in 1942 at the age of 24. He used a $500 loan on his mother's furniture to start *Negro Digest*, a magazine devoted to the accomplishments of African Americans. Today Johnson Publishing Company, Inc., is the world's largest African American-owned publishing company. This media empire includes *Ebony*, *Jet*, *Ebony Man*, and *Ebony South Africa* magazines and Johnson Publishing Company Book Division. Also part of the company are Fashion Fair Cosmetics and Supreme Beauty Products.

Like many minority-owned companies, Johnson faced many setbacks:

> *"The first 25 years were difficult, trying to get circulation and to break through in advertising to get large companies to recognize that black consumers had money and would respond to advertising directed to them. The first 20 years or so in business, we couldn't get a bank loan."*

Although the second 25 years have been easier, Johnson says African American startups will face many of the same hurdles he did:

> *"But if you have the staying power and wherewithal, that is assuming you have a good product and market to sell to, you'll be successful. Never say never about new things."*

Johnson has no plans to sell his company or take it public for the following reason:

> *"If you go public, the stockholders, the board of directors, the SEC [Securities and Exchange Commission] are all your bosses and you've got to listen to them. We only have three board members: [daughter] Linda, her mother [Eunice Johnson], and I."*

Checking for Understanding

1. **What products does Johnson provide?**
2. **Why does Johnson refuse to turn his business into a corporation?**

SECTION 3

The Corporate World and Franchises

Cover Story

Business Week, August 27, 2001

John Bond runs the world's second most profitable bank. But no one will ever accuse the chairman of Britain's HSBC Holdings PLC of living it up at shareholders' expense....

HSBC's conservative strategy is paying off....[T]he 136-year-old bank [recently announced that] group pretax profit was $5.4 billion, up 4% from the same period in 2000....

Reader's Guide

Terms to Know

- corporation
- stock
- limited liability
- articles of incorporation
- corporate charter
- common stock
- dividend
- preferred stock
- franchise

Reading Objectives

1. What are the advantages and disadvantages of corporations?
2. How are corporations typically structured?
3. What types of businesses are involved in franchises?

Profits are a good thing. As a sole proprietor, you keep all the profits. In a partnership, you share the profits with one or several partners. In a corporation, such as HSBC, the profits are dispersed among thousands of shareholders. So why do entrepreneurs incorporate? In this section, read to learn why and how corporations are formed.

Why Form a Corporation?

Suppose your electronics repair business has grown. You now have several partners and have turned your garage into a

corporation: *type of business organization owned by many people but treated by law as though it were a person; it can own property, pay taxes, make contracts, and so on*

shop. You would like to expand and rent a store so that your business is more visible. You would also like to buy the latest equipment, charge a little less than your competitors, and capture a larger share of the market for electronics repair work. You need financial capital, however.

You have decided that you do not want any more partners. You would have to consult with them about every detail of the business as you do now with your present partners. What you want are financial backers who will let you use their funds while letting you run the business. What you are proposing is a corporation.

Global Economy

Big Business!

Many modern corporations are huge. A study conducted in the mid-1990s found that some of these corporations have bigger economies than the countries in which they operate! More than half of the world's 100 largest economies, the study revealed, were corporations, not nations. General Motors, the United States's largest corporation, had the 26th largest economy. This placed it above 167 nations, including Denmark, South Africa, Turkey, and Saudi Arabia. ■

What Is a Corporation?

A **corporation** is an organization owned by many people but treated by law as though it were a person. A corporation can own property, pay taxes, make contracts, sue and be sued, and so on. It has a separate and distinct existence from the stockholders who own the corporation's stock. **Stock** represents ownership rights to a certain portion of the future profits and assets of the company that issues the stock.

stock: *share of ownership in a corporation that entitles the buyer to a certain part of the future profits and assets of the corporation*

In terms of the amount of business done (measured in dollars), the corporation is the most significant type of business organization in the United States today. **Figure 8.5** on page 221 compares corporations to other forms of businesses in terms of numbers and proportion of total business revenue. You can see that although corporations make up only about 20 percent of all businesses, they earn about 90 percent of all business revenues.

Like sole proprietorships and partnerships, corporations have advantages as well as disadvantages. One of the major advantages of a corporation is **limited liability.** If a corporation goes bankrupt or is sued, only the business loses money and assets, not the stockholders. A major disadvantage of corporations is that they are taxed more heavily than other forms of business organizations. Look at **Figure 8.6** on page 222 to read about other advantages and disadvantages of corporations.

limited liability: *requirement in which an owner's responsibility for a company's debts is limited to the size of the owner's investment in the firm*

Corporate Structure

In order to form a corporation, its founders must do three things. First, they must register their company with the government of the state in which it will be headquartered. Second, they must sell stock. Third, along with the other shareholders, they must elect a board of directors.

Registering the Corporation Every state has laws governing the formation of corporations, but most state laws are similar. Suppose that you and your partners decide to form a corporation. You will have to file the **articles of incorporation** with the state in which you will run your corporation. In general, these articles include four items:

(1) Name, address, and purpose of the corporation;
(2) Names and addresses of the initial board of directors (these men and women will serve until the first stockholders' meeting, when a new board may be elected);
(3) Number of shares of stock to be issued;
(4) Amount of money capital to be raised through issuing stock.

If the articles are in agreement with state law, the state will grant you a **corporate charter**—a license to operate from that state.

articles of incorporation: *document listing basic information about a corporation that is filed with the state where the corporation will be headquartered*

corporate charter: *license to operate granted to a corporation by the state where it is established*

FIGURE 8.5

Business Organizations
Although proprietorships make up about 73 percent of American businesses, they generate only about 5 percent of total business revenues. ***What percentage of American businesses are partnerships?***

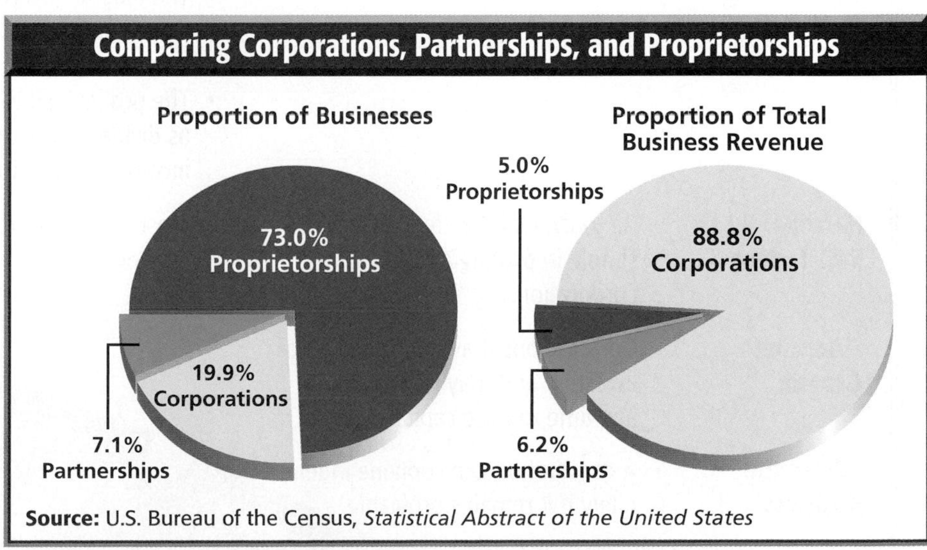

For an online update of this graph, visit ett.glencoe.com and click on ***Textbook Updates—Chapter 8.***

FIGURE 8.6

Advantages and Disadvantages of Corporations

	Advantages	Disadvantages
Profits and Losses	• Owners of the corporation–stockholders–do not have to devote time to the company to make money on their investment.	
Liability	• The corporation has limited liability. • If a corporation goes bankrupt or is sued, creditors cannot normally take personal property from stockholders to pay debts.	
Management	• Responsibility for running a corporation is divided among many. • Decisions are made by individuals trained in specific areas, such as sales, production, and so on. • Corporations can handle large and complicated operations, and can carry on many types of business activities at the same time.	• Decision making can be slow and complicated because so many levels of management are involved. • The interests of those running the corporation may not be the same as those of the stockholders, who often seek an immediate return on their investment.
Taxes		• The federal government and some state and local governments tax corporate profits. • The profits paid to stockholders as dividends are again taxed as income to those individuals.
Personal Satisfaction	• An individual may feel satisfaction simply in owning a part of a corporation.	• Most individual stockholders have little or no say in how a corporation is run.
Financing Growth	• Corporations draw on resources of investors and may issue stock at any time to raise capital.	
Life of the Business	• A corporation can continue indefinitely if it remains profitable.	

Selling Stock To raise funds for the expansion of your electronics repair business, you could sell shares of either common or preferred stock in your new corporation. **Common stock** gives the investor part ownership in the corporation, a right to a percentage of the company's future profits, and voting rights at the annual stockholders' meeting. However, it does not *guarantee* a **dividend**—a money return on the money invested in a company's stock. Holders of **preferred stock** do not have voting rights in the corporation, but they are guaranteed a certain amount of dividend each year. Plus, if the corporation goes out of business, holders of preferred stock have first claim on whatever value is left in the company after creditors have been paid.

If your corporation were to become large, you might find its stock traded in the local over-the-counter market. *Over-the-counter* means that individual brokerage firms hold quantities of shares of stock that they buy and sell for investors. Should your corporation continue to grow, its stocks may be traded on a stock exchange.

common stock: *shares of ownership in a corporation that give stockholders voting rights and a portion of future profits (after holders of preferred stock are paid)*

dividend: *portion of a corporation's profits paid to its stockholders*

preferred stock: *shares of ownership in a corporation that give stockholders a portion of future profits (before any profits go to holders of common stock), but no voting rights*

Naming a Board of Directors To become incorporated, a company must have a board of directors. You and your partners, as founders of the corporation, would select the first board for your corporation. After that, stockholders at their annual stockholders' meetings would elect the board. The bylaws of the corporation govern this election. Bylaws are a set of rules describing how stock will be sold and dividends paid, with a list of the duties of the company's officers. They are written after the corporate charter has been granted.

Economic Connection to... History

Franchises, Franchises, Everywhere!

The inventor and entrepreneur Isaac Singer began the practice of franchising in the United States. In the mid-1800s, Singer signed agreements with several merchants that allowed them to market his sewing machines.

The interstate highway system caused the practice of franchising to explode in the 1950s. Increasing automobile ownership took more Americans on the road, where they looked for familiar motels, restaurants, and gas stations they knew and trusted. Today, franchising accounts for more than 40 percent of all U.S. retail sales. Analysts estimate that franchising employs more than 8 million people in the United States. ■

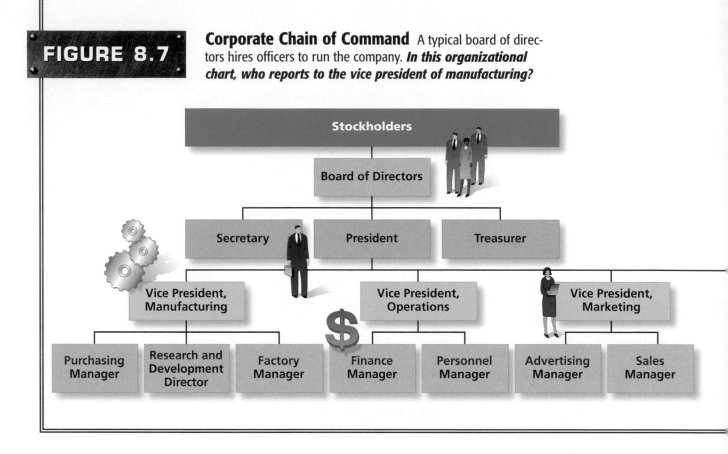

FIGURE 8.7 **Corporate Chain of Command** A typical board of directors hires officers to run the company. ***In this organizational chart, who reports to the vice president of manufacturing?***

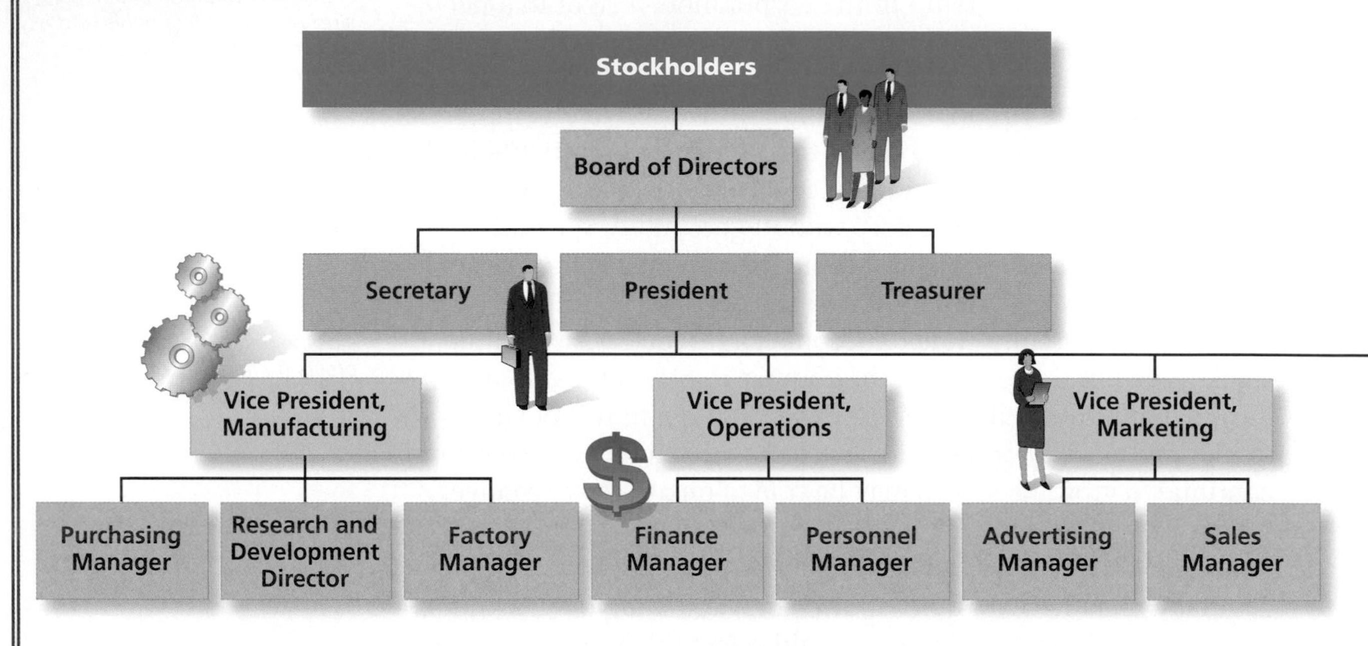

The board is responsible for supervising and controlling the corporation. It does not run business operations on a day-to-day basis. Instead, it hires officers for the company–president, vice president(s), secretary, and treasurer–to run the business and hire other employees. **Figure 8.7** shows the typical structure of a corporation.

Franchises

franchise: *contract in which one business (the franchiser) sells to another business (the franchisee) the right to use the franchiser's name and sell its products*

Many hotel, motel, gas station, and fast-food chains are franchises. A **franchise** is a contract in which a franchiser sells to another business the right to use its name and sell its products. The person or business buying these rights, called the franchisee, pays a fee that may include a percentage of all money taken in. If a person buys a motel franchise, for example, that person agrees to pay the motel chain a certain fee plus a portion of the profits for as long as his or her motel stays in business. In return, the chain will help the franchisee set up the motel. Often, the chain will have a training program to teach the franchisee about the business and set the standards of business operations.

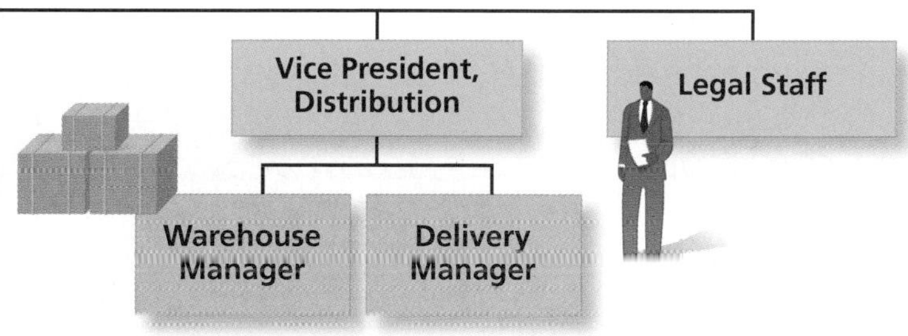

Practice and **assess** key skills with ***Skillbuilder Interactive Workbook, Level 2.***

SECTION 3 Assessment

Understanding Key Terms

1. **Define** corporation, stock, limited liability, articles of incorporation, corporate charter, common stock, dividend, preferred stock, franchise.

Reviewing Objectives

2. Analyze the advantages and disadvantages of corporations.
3. **Graphic Organizer** Create a diagram like the one below to show how corporations are typically structured.

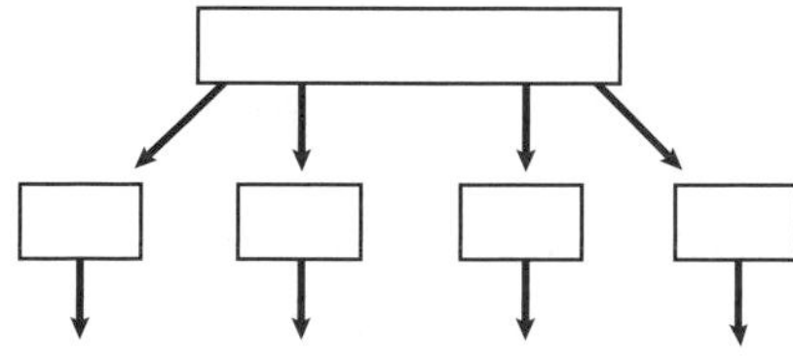

4. What types of businesses are involved in franchises?

Applying Economic Concepts

5. **Franchises** In what industry would you franchise if offered the opportunity? Explain the possible advantages and help available from other franchises in the same industry. Then describe possible disadvantages of setting up a franchise in your chosen industry.

Critical Thinking Activity

6. **Making Comparisons** Look in the financial pages of a recent newspaper to analyze how the stocks of three corporations have performed. What was the closing price for each? What were their 52-week highs? *For help in reading the financial page, see page xxiii in the Economic Handbook.*

BusinessWeek

SPOTLIGHT ON THE ECONOMY

Hate to Eat and Fly, but . . .

Check It Out! In this chapter you learned about franchises and corporations. In the following article, read to learn how one franchise has expanded its service in an unusual way.

Now that the drive-through window is a fixture of the fast-food world, Burger King is perfecting the fly-through. A Burger King in suburban London dubs the addition to its regular restaurant the "Whopper Chopper," a landing pad where helicopter pilots can drop in, grab some grub, and fly out without leaving the cockpit.

Pilots call first to alert Burger King that they are landing. An employee dashes out and calls the order in. Then it is delivered to the waiting chopper. "This is more like the old diners where someone comes out to take your order," says Jon Clarke, a Burger King spokesperson in London. "It's a bit more personal."

Pilots agree. "I think this is a great idea," says Mark Barry-Jackson, an Aeromega pilot. "Finding suitable places to stop and refuel passengers has always been difficult." The landing pad, which is under a helicopter traffic lane, was so popular it was closed over the holidays so it could be made big enough to handle military choppers, whose pilots had heard about the place. Burger King, still testing the concept, won't comment on its profitability. But the fly-through is an idea that may just take off.

–Reprinted from January 25, 1999 issue of *Business Week* by special permission, copyright © 1999 by The McGraw-Hill Companies, Inc.

Think About It

1. **How does this Burger King franchise accommodate customers who are helicopter pilots?**
2. **What do you think is positive about franchises in general? Negative?**

CHAPTER  Summary

Chapter Overview Visit the *Economics Today and Tomorrow* Web site at ett.glencoe.com and click on ***Chapter 8—Chapter Overviews*** to review chapter information.

SECTION 1 Starting a Business

- People usually decide to start a business to gain profits, to "do something on their own," or to be their own boss.
- **Entrepreneurs** must gather the relevant factors of production and decide on the form of business organization that best suits their purposes.
- For those wanting to start a small business, help is available from the government and from the Internet.
- Every business must consider four basic elements: expenses, advertising, **receipts** and record keeping, and risk.

SECTION 2 Sole Proprietorships and Partnerships

- The most basic type of business organization is the **sole proprietorship,** a business owned by one person.
- The biggest advantages of sole proprietorships are that the proprietor has full pride in owning the business and receives all the profits.
- The biggest disadvantage is that the proprietor has **unlimited liability** and can lose personal **assets** as well as the business.
- A **partnership** is a business organization owned by two or more individuals.
- A legally binding partnership agreement describes the duties of each partner, the division of profits, and the distribution of assets should the partnership end.
- In a **limited partnership,** one general partner assumes the management duties and debt responsibility, while the limited partners contribute money but have no liability.

SECTION 3 The Corporate World and Franchises

- A **corporation** can own property, pay taxes, make contracts, and sue and be sued.
- One of the major advantages of a corporation is **limited liability.**
- A major disadvantage is that corporations are taxed more heavily than other forms of business organizations.
- To form a corporation, its founders must register with the state government, sell **stock,** and elect a board of directors.
- A **franchise** is a contract in which a franchiser sells to another business the right to use its name and sell its products.

CHAPTER 8

Assessment and Activities

Self-Check Quiz Visit the *Economics Today and Tomorrow* Web site at ett.glencoe.com and click on ***Chapter 8—Self-Check Quizzes*** to prepare for the Chapter Test.

Identifying Key Terms

Identify the letter of the definition in Column B that correctly defines each term in Column A.

Column A

1. inventory
2. corporate charter
3. assets
4. franchise
5. unlimited liability
6. sole proprietorship
7. partnership
8. stock
9. joint venture
10. corporation

Column B

a. items of value
b. business owned by two or more people
c. supply of items that are used in business
d. business owned by many people, but treated as a person itself
e. contract in which a business sells the right to use its name to another business
f. business owned by one person
g. right to operate
h. temporary partnership
i. ownership shares in a business
j. legal responsibility for all debts incurred when doing business

Recalling Facts and Ideas

Section 1

1. Every business involves expenses and receipts and record keeping. What are two other elements?
2. When you calculate your profits, it is especially important for you to include the value of your time. What is this called?
3. If you need help in starting a small business, where can you look?

Section 2

4. What is the most common form of business organization?
5. Analyze the disadvantages of a sole proprietorship.
6. Explain the characteristics of a partnership and a limited partnership.
7. What is the difference between a limited partnership and a joint venture?

Section 3

8. Explain the characteristics of a corporation.
9. Who grants corporate charters?
10. Which group within a corporation chooses the board of directors?
11. How does a franchise operate?

Thinking Critically

1. **Drawing Inferences** Why do you have to include the opportunity cost of your time when you calculate your profits in your own business?
2. **Drawing Conclusions** Why would a person decide in favor of a partnership rather than a sole proprietorship?
3. **Understanding Cause and Effect** Create a diagram like the one below and identify three problems in a corporation that might be caused by its complex organizational structure.

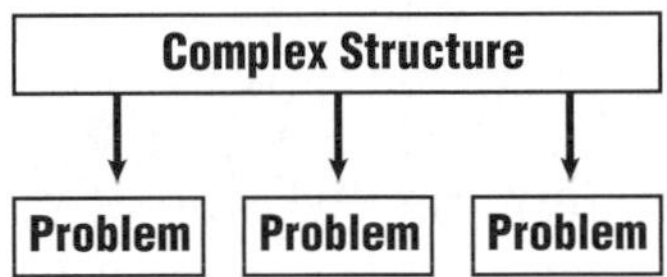

Applying Economic Concepts

Economic Institutions and Incentives In this chapter you have read about numerous advantages and disadvantages of different types of business organizations. Make a list of the following: sole proprietorship, partnership, limited partnership, joint venture, corporation, and franchise. After each type, indicate the single most important advantage that you believe this form of business organization has.

Technology Activity

Developing Multimedia Presentations Think of a product or service you would like to produce. Create a multimedia presentation promoting that product or service. Utilize video, graphics, and music in your presentation. Share your presentation with the rest of the class.

Reviewing Skills

Using the Internet Several business news magazinesÑ*Forbes, Fortune,* and *Business Week*Ñreport the top several hundred corporations in America every year. Find out what the top five corporations are, then use the Internet to locate each companyês home page. Once you have located each site, access them and use the information to prepare an oral report on each companyês (1) number of employees, (2) total sales in billions of dollars, (3) total market value as given by the stock market, and (4) change in ranking from the previous year.

Cooperative Learning Project

Working in groups of four, select a corporation listed in the financial pages of a newspaper. Then use business magazines and financial and annual reports, if possible, to determine the annual earnings, dividends, and stock prices of that corporation over the past year. Compare the corporation with those selected by other groups and discuss which stocks would have been the best investments during the past year.

Analyzing the Global Economy

Notice the labels on your clothes, shoes, and food. Find out in which countries these items were made or produced. Then research one of the top five corporations within one of those countries. Is its corporate structure similar to the structure found in American corporations? Explain.

Economics Lab

Setting Up a Business

From the classroom of Denny C. Jackson, Switzerland County High School, Vevay, Indiana

In Chapter 8 you learned about the different types of business organizations and what it takes to start a business. In this lab, you will set up a hotel business.

STEP A Tools Needed

- ✔ Hotel directories
- ✔ Hotel franchise circulars
- ✔ Vacation/travel guides (for location of the hotel)
- ✔ Drawing paper
- ✔ Colored pencils
- ✔ Clear plastic folder
- ✔ Computer with access to the Internet (optional)
- ✔ Supplies necessary to build a scale model of your hotel

STEP B Procedures to Follow

1. Work with a partner to research points 2 through 9.
2. Determine the location of your hotel. Use travel guides to identify the "generators" that will draw people to your hotel: national park, theme park, university, airport, isolated interstate, tour groups, and so on.
3. Decide whether your hotel should be an independent or a franchise. Explain your choice.
4. Determine the makeup of the hotel. How many rooms? Restaurant and lounge? Swimming pool? Gift shop? Game room and health spa?

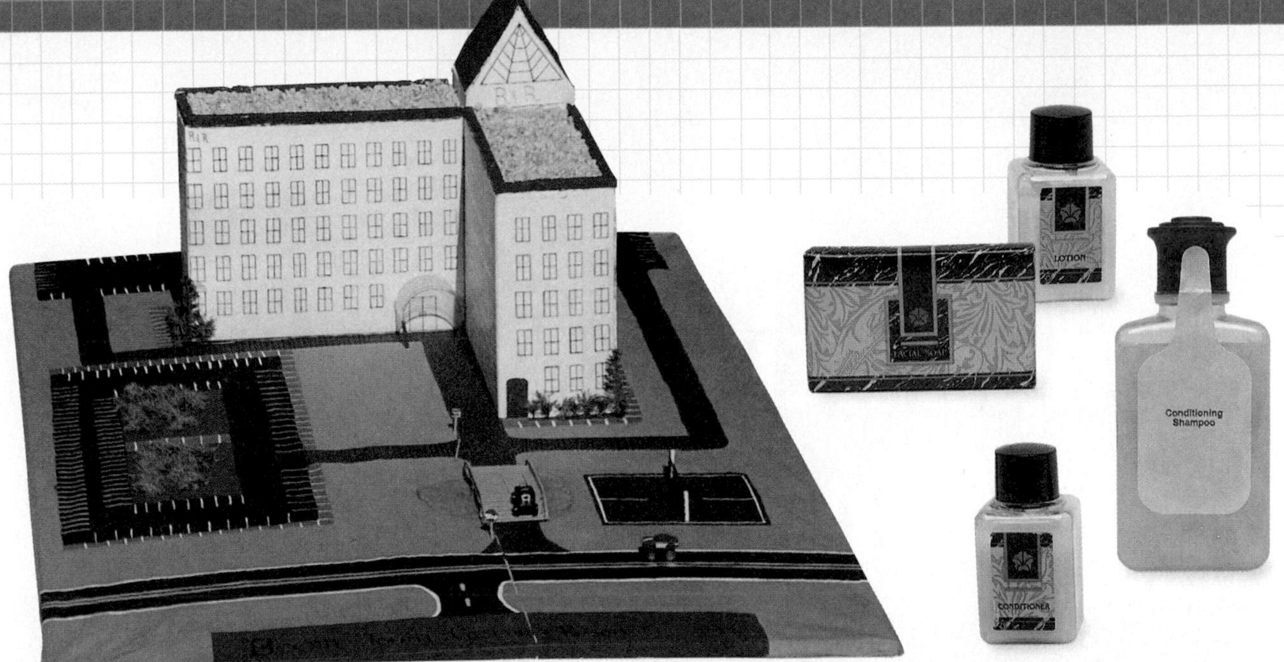

5. Decide on the number and wages of employees you will need for all shifts: a manager, assistant managers, front desk clerks, housekeeping staff, maintenance staff, restaurant staff, and so on.

6. Decide the layout of the rooms as well as their décor. Also design the exterior of the hotel, including parking facilities, subway access, and so on.

7. Determine what you will charge per room. Report on what items are included in the room (shampoo, coffee maker, satellite TV, and so on).

8. Identify and evaluate local ordinances and regulations pertaining to the establishment of the hotel.

9. Determine how you will obtain the funds needed to begin: banking institution, grant or loan from a small business incubator, etc.

STEP C Creating an Economic Model

Use the results of your research to create at least two drawings: one showing the layout of the rooms, and one showing the exterior of the hotel. Then create a scale model of your hotel. Present your drawings and model to the rest of the class.

STEP D Lab Report Analysis

After completing your presentation, answer the following questions:

1. Why did you choose an independent or franchise?
2. Why did you choose the specific location of your hotel?
3. How did you arrive at the room rate?
4. What did you decide to include in the total project?

CHAPTER 9

Competition and Monopolies

Why It's Important

How do airlines determine airfares? Why do farmers' markets often charge the same price for their produce during the summer? This chapter will explain how competition—or the lack of it—determines the prices you pay.

To learn more about competition, view the **Economics & You** *Chapter 8 video lesson:* **Competition and Monopolies**

ECONOMICS *Online*

Chapter Overview Visit the *Economics Today and Tomorrow* Web site at ett.glencoe.com and click on ***Chapter 9—Chapter Overviews*** to preview chapter information.

SECTION 1

Perfect Competition

COVER STORY

BUSINESS WEEK, MARCH 22, 1999

By December, Boston could get a lot closer to New York and Washington—at least by train. That's when Amtrak's new high-speed rail service, dubbed Acela, will start operating. With Acela, some New York–Boston trips will take just 3 hours, vs. 4½ now. And all new trains will have computer jacks and food service. Amtrak aims to compete head-on with airline shuttles.

READER'S GUIDE

Terms to Know

- market structure
- perfect competition

Reading Objectives

1. What are the five conditions of perfect competition?
2. Why is agriculture often considered an example of perfect competition?
3. How does perfect competition benefit society?

Competition—one of the basic characteristics of our market economic system—is advantageous to consumers for several reasons. First, it provides us with choices. As noted in the *Cover Story* above, people traveling from Boston to New York now have a choice of going by plane or train. Competition is advantageous for another reason as well. Having many competing suppliers of a product leads to a surplus and, thus, lower prices. As you can imagine, for this reason each supplier would like to have as little competition as possible.

Market Structure

In Chapter 8 you learned that businesses are set up based on the number of owners—sole proprietorship, partnership, corporation. In this chapter you'll learn that businesses are also categorized by **market structure**—or by the amount of competition they face. **Figure 9.1** on page 234 shows the four basic market structures in

market structure: *the extent to which competition prevails in particular markets*

FIGURE 9.1 **Comparing Market Structures** Markets that are either perfectly competitive or pure monopolies are rare. Most industries in the United States fit one of the other two forms.

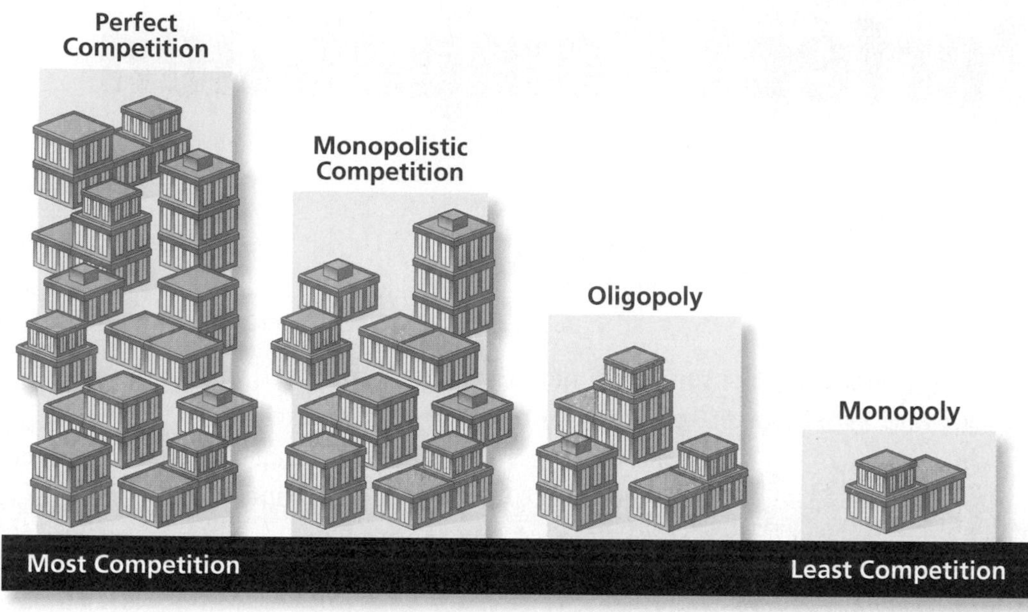

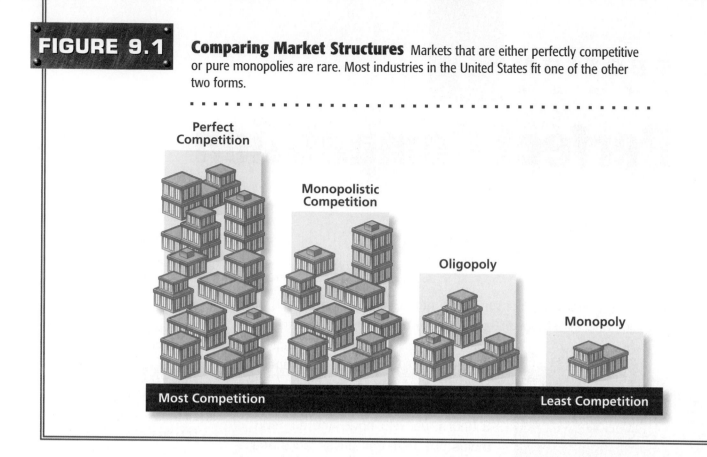

the American economy: perfect competition, monopolistic competition, oligopoly, and monopoly. In this section you'll learn about the ideal market structure of perfect competition.

Conditions of Perfect Competition

All businesses must engage in some form of competition as long as other businesses produce similar goods or services. When a market includes so many sellers of a particular good or service that each seller accounts for a small part of the total market, a special situation exists. Economists term it **perfect competition.** For perfect competition, also known as pure competition, to take place, five conditions must be met:

perfect competition: *market situation in which there are numerous buyers and sellers, and no single buyer or seller can affect price*

(1) A Large Market Numerous buyers and sellers must exist for the product.

(2) A Similar Product The good or service being sold must be nearly identical. See **Figure 9.2.**

(3) Easy Entry and Exit Sellers already in the market cannot prevent competition, or entrance into the market. In addition, the initial costs of investment are small, and the good or service is easy to learn to produce.

(4) Easily Obtainable Information Information about prices, quality, and sources of supply is easy for both buyers and sellers to obtain.

(5) Independence The possibility of sellers or buyers working together to control the price is almost nonexistent.

No Control Over Price When the above five conditions are met, the workings of supply and demand control the price, not a single seller or buyer. On the supply side, perfect competition requires a large number of suppliers of a similar product. On the demand side, perfect competition requires a large number of informed buyers who know exactly what the market price is for the good or service.

In a perfectly competitive market, the market price is the equilibrium price. Total supply and total demand are allowed to interact to reach the equilibrium price—the only price at which quantity demanded equals quantity supplied. In a world of perfect competition, each individual seller would accept that price. Because so many buyers and sellers exist, one person charging a higher or lower price would not affect the market price.

Information Is Key True perfect competition is rarely seen in the real world. Nonetheless, fierce competition does exist in many sectors of the economy. While information about prices, quality, and sources of supply might have been hard and costly to obtain in the past, that is not true today. Virtually anyone with access to the Internet can find out the lowest prices of just about anything.

Perfect Competition
Having a similar product and easy entry into the market—such as greenhouses do—are two conditions of perfect competition. ***What three other conditions must be met for perfect competition?***

Agriculture as an Example

Few perfectly competitive industries exist in the United States. The one that perhaps comes closest is the agricultural market. It is often used as an example of perfect competition because individual farmers have almost no control over the market price of their goods. **Figure 9.3** applies the five conditions of perfect competition to the wheat market.

No Control Over Wheat Prices No single farmer has any great influence on price. The interaction of supply and demand determines the price of wheat. The supply is the total supply of all the wheat that farmers produce. The demand is the total demand for all uses of wheat. The equilibrium price is the price where supply and demand intersect.

Individual wheat farmers have to accept the market price. If the price is $3 per bushel, that is the price every farmer receives. Farmers who attempt to raise their price above $3 will find that no one will buy their wheat. Farmers will not be willing to sell their wheat for less than $3 per bushel.

Unique Situation The demand for wheat and other agricultural products is somewhat different from the demand for many other products. People's demand for wheat is, for the most part, inelastic. People can use wheat in only so many ways, and people can eat only so many wheat products. So even if the price of wheat were to increase or drop dramatically, quantity demanded would not change significantly. The supply side of most agricultural markets is also unique. It is highly dependent on conditions over which farmers have little or no control, as shown in **Figure 9.4.**

FIGURE 9.3

The Wheat Market as a Perfect Competitor

1. **A Large Market** Thousands of wheat farmers grow wheat, and thousands of wholesalers buy wheat.
2. **A Similar Product** All wheat is fairly similar.
3. **Easy Entry and Exit** The costs of renting farmland are relatively low, and farming methods can be learned.
4. **Easily Obtainable Information** Information about wheat prices is fairly easy to obtain. Indeed, it can be obtained on the Internet in a few seconds.
5. **Independence** The possibility of thousands of wheat farmers banding together to control the price is very small.

Benefits to Society

The intense competition in a perfectly competitive industry forces the price down to one that just covers the costs of production plus a small profit. This price is beneficial because it means that consumers are paying only for what has been put in to make those products—the opportunity cost of the use of land, labor, capital, and entrepreneurship. The price that consumers pay for such products is a correct signal about the value of those products in society.

Perfectly competitive industries yield economic efficiency. All inputs are used in the most advantageous way possible, and society therefore enjoys an efficient allocation of productive resources.

FIGURE 9.4

Agricultural Disasters Affect Supply Variations in weather, a crop disease, or a crop-destroying insect can wipe out entire harvests. This means that farmers may have a good harvest one year and a poor harvest the next. As a result, there are widely fluctuating supplies of goods in the agricultural market.

Practice and **assess** key skills with ***Skillbuilder Interactive Workbook, Level 2.***

SECTION 1 Assessment

Understanding Key Terms

1. **Define** market structure, perfect competition.

Reviewing Objectives

2. **Graphic Organizer** Use a diagram like the one below to explain the five conditions of perfect competition.

3. Why is agriculture often considered an example of perfect competition?
4. How does perfect competition benefit society?

Applying Economic Concepts

5. **Perfect Competition** Explain how a local fast-food restaurant manager faces almost perfect competition in the demand for high school employee labor.

Critical Thinking Activity

6. **Summarizing Information** In this section, you learned that the Internet has made the United States economy more competitive. Use a search engine to find information about the market price of your favorite automobile.

Critical Thinking Skills

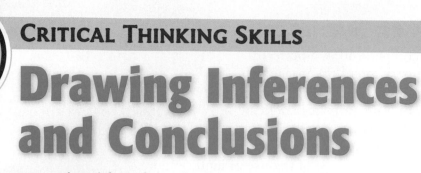

Drawing Inferences and Conclusions

To infer *means to evaluate information and arrive at a conclusion. When you make inferences, you "read between the lines," or draw conclusions that are not stated directly in the text.*

- Read carefully for stated facts and ideas.
- Summarize the information and list the important facts.
- Apply related information that you may already know to make inferences.
- Use your knowledge and insight to develop some conclusions about these facts.

Learning the Skill

To learn how to make inferences and draw conclusions, follow the steps listed on the left.

Practicing the Skill

Read the passage below, then answer the questions.

"[A] landmark 1996 bill gave farmers the freedom to plant what they wanted, when they wanted. But it also swept away much of the financial safety net of price supports for U.S. crops. . . . The next time agriculture hit a downdraft, would Washington really let the market work?

Dumb question. In 1999, Uncle Sam will dole out some $14.4 billion to farmers. . . .

This is no way to run farm policy. Indeed, it's a simple law of economics that the prospect of bailouts in times of trouble leads farmers to take more risks, such as planting additional, marginal acres. That makes the system less efficient. . . ."

—*Business Week*, June 28, 1999

1. What facts are presented in the passage?
2. What can you infer about the occupation of the passage's author? Is he or she a farmer? Explain.
3. Can you conclude that the agricultural sector is a perfectly competitive market? Explain.

Application Activity

Apply the five conditions of perfect competition to the soft drink industry. Would you conclude that it is perfectly competitive? Explain.

Practice and **assess** key skills with ***Skillbuilder Interactive Workbook, Level 2.***

SECTION 2

Monopoly, Oligopoly, Monopolistic Competition

Cover Story

Business Week, February 1, 1999

When Gillette Co. unveiled Mach3, the world's first triple-blade razor, it took a bold gamble. . . . Mach3 cartridges were to sell for around $1.60 each. Skeptics predicted the personal-care giant would soon be forced to cut that price. But the price is holding and Mach3 has become the No. 1 blade and razor.

What's the secret to pricing power? For starters, a commitment to innovation. Gillette spent nearly $1 billion on the development and initial marketing of Mach3.

Reader's Guide

Terms to Know

- monopoly
- barriers to entry
- economies of scale
- patent
- copyright
- oligopoly
- product differentiation
- cartel
- monopolistic competition

Reading Objectives

1. What are four characteristics of a pure monopoly?
2. What characterizes an oligopoly?
3. What are five characteristics of monopolistic competition?

Imagine spending $1 billion on the development and advertising of a razor blade–a common shaving tool. Would that much advertising be worth it? It would if customers paid whatever price you asked for the razors. As you read this section, you'll learn that advertising plays a major role in two types of market structures.

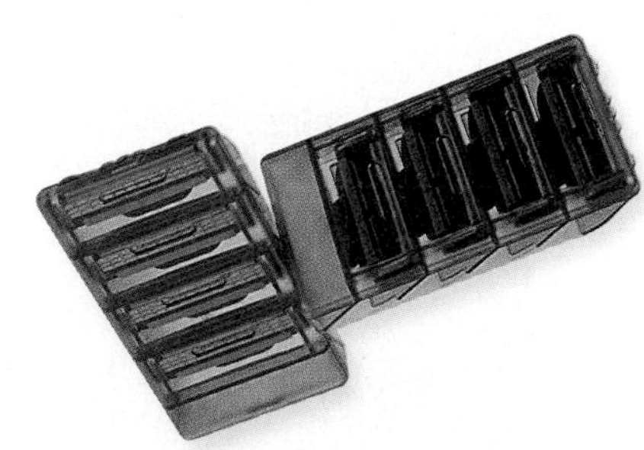

Imperfect Competition

As mentioned in Section 1, perfect competition is an ideal type of market structure. Most industries in the United States, in

FIGURE 9.5

Local Electric Companies
Because some local electric utilities are the sole providers, and the consumer has no other option, they are monopolies.

contrast, represent some form of *imperfect* competition. Economists classify these three types of imperfect market structures as monopoly, oligopoly, or monopolistic competition. They differ from one another on the basis of how much competition and control over price the seller has.

Monopoly

The most extreme form of imperfect competition is a pure **monopoly,** in which a single seller controls the supply of the good or service and thus determines the price. A few such markets do exist in the real world. As shown in **Figure 9.5,** some local electric utility companies are the sole providers for a community. The consumers have no other option but to purchase electric power from these monopolies.

monopoly: *market situation in which a single supplier makes up an entire industry for a good or service with no close substitutes*

Characteristics of a Monopoly A monopoly is characterized by four conditions:

(1) A Single Seller Only one seller exists for a good or service.
(2) No Substitutes There are no close substitutes for the good or service that the monopolist sells.
(3) No Entry The monopolist is protected by obstacles to competition that prevent others from entering the market.
(4) Almost Complete Control of Market Price By controlling the available supply, the monopolist can control the market price.

In a pure monopoly, the supplier can raise prices without fear of losing business to competitors. Unless buyers choose to pay the new price, they have nowhere else to buy the good or service. A monopolist, however, cannot charge outrageous prices. Even in a monopolistic market, the law of demand is still operating. As the price of a good or service rises, consumers buy less.

Barriers to Entry If a monopoly is collecting all the profits in a particular industry, why don't other businesses rush in to get a share of those profits? As mentioned above, a monopoly is protected by **barriers to entry**—obstacles that prevent others from entering the market.

barriers to entry: *obstacles to competition that prevent others from entering a market*

The most obvious barrier into a monopolistic market is a legal one. Some state laws, for example, prevent a competing electric, gas, or water company from operating in an area where a public utility company already provides service. The reasoning against competition in public utility industries is the fear that too much competition may lead to wasteful duplication. Imagine the inefficiency of three or four competing water companies all trying to lay water mains along your street.

Another barrier to entry is the cost of getting started. Called "excessive money capital costs," this barrier is found in industries such as cars and steel, in which initial investment is high because of the amount and cost of the equipment. See **Figure 9.6.**

Ownership of essential raw materials can also provide a barrier to entry. A good example is the diamond industry. The DeBeers Company of South Africa controls the marketing of nearly all the world's diamonds.

economies of scale: *low production costs resulting from the large size of output*

patent: *exclusive right to make, use, or sell an invention for a specified number of years*

copyright: *exclusive right to sell, publish, or reproduce creative works for a specified number of years*

Types of Monopolies Pure monopolies can be separated into four categories depending on why the monopoly exists. As shown in **Figure 9.7** on page 242, the four types of monopolies are natural, geographic, technological, and government.

In the past it was thought to be more efficient, or natural, to have just one company providing a public good or service. This belief led the government to grant exclusive rights to *natural monopolies*–providers of such things as utilities, bus service, and cable TV. The large size, or scale, of most natural monopolies seemed to give them **economies of scale**–by which they could produce the largest amount for the lowest cost. It is now being realized that advances in technology can make these industries more competitive, however. Government is making moves to deregulate and open them up for competition.

A grocery store in a remote Alaskan village is an example of a monopoly caused by geographic factors. Because the potential for profits is so small, other businesses choose not to enter, thus giving the sole provider a *geographic monopoly*. These types of monopolies are declining, however, as competition arises from mail-order and Internet catalogs and delivery services.

If you invent something, you are capable of having a *technological monopoly* over your invention. A government **patent** gives you the exclusive right to manufacture, rent, or sell your invention for a specified number of years–usually 20. Similarly, a United States **copyright** protects art, literature, song lyrics, and other creative works for the life of the author plus 70 years.

A *government monopoly* is similar to a natural monopoly, except the monopoly is held by the government itself. The construction and maintenance of roads and bridges, for example, are the responsibility of local, state, and national governments.

Barriers to Entry Huge startup costs keep some businesses from entering certain industries.

FIGURE 9.7

Types of Monopolies Monopolies exist for several reasons. ***Which type of monopoly, if any, do you think is justified? Explain your response.***

A Natural Monopoly

B Technological Monopoly

C Government Monopoly

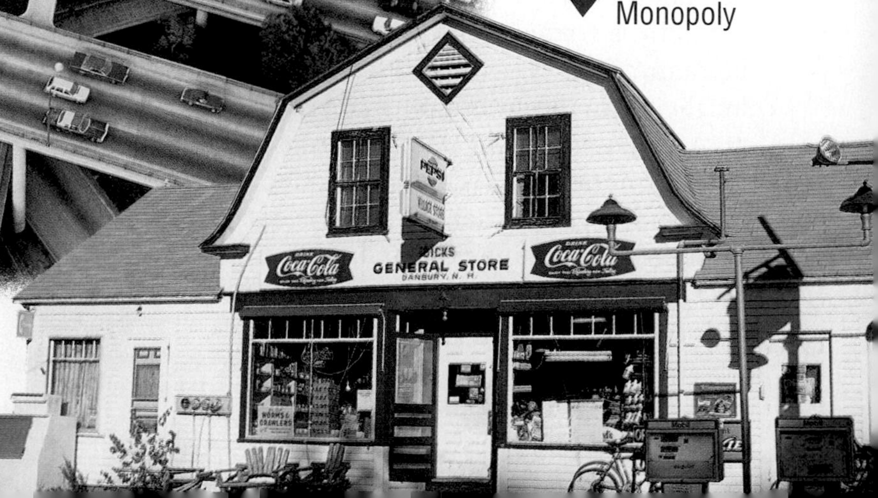

D Geographic Monopoly

How Important Are Monopolies Today? Monopolies are far less important than they once were. As noted earlier, geographic monopolies have little effect because of potential competition from mail-order businesses and electronic commerce on the Internet. Natural monopolies are being broken up by technology and government deregulation.

Technological monopolies rarely last longer than the life of the patent–if even *that* long. Why? Competitors can make and patent slight variations in new products quickly. The microcomputer revolution in the early 1980s followed such a pattern. One company copied another's product, making changes and adding features to obtain a patent of its own.

Global *Economy*

Reducing Postal Monopolies

The monopoly that national postal services have enjoyed is now being whittled away by technology. Overnight delivery companies such as Federal Express, Airborne Express, and United Parcel Service (UPS) offer faster delivery but at premium prices. And the widespread use of fax machines and electronic mail (E-mail) has virtually eliminated any remaining monopoly power that national postal services held. ■

Oligopoly

Unlike a monopoly with just one supplier, an **oligopoly** is an industry dominated by *several* suppliers who exercise some control over price. For a market structure to be labeled an oligopoly, it must meet the following conditions:

oligopoly: *industry dominated by a few suppliers who exercise some control over price*

(1) Domination by a Few Sellers Several large firms are responsible for 70 to 80 percent of the market.
(2) Barriers to Entry Capital costs are high, and it is difficult for new companies to enter major markets.
(3) Identical or Slightly Different Products The goods and services provided by oligopolists–such as airline travel, domestic automobiles, and kitchen appliances–are very similar.
(4) Nonprice Competition Advertising emphasizes minor differences and attempts to build customer loyalty.
(5) Interdependence Any change on the part of one firm will cause a reaction on the part of other firms in the oligopoly.

Figure 9.8 on page 244 shows a number of industries in which the four largest firms produce more than 80 percent of the total industry output. All of these industries are oligopolies.

Oligopolies are not considered as harmful to consumers as monopolies. Consumers may pay more than if they were buying in a perfectly competitive market. Oligopolistic markets, however, tend to have generally stable prices. They also offer consumers a wider variety of products than would a perfectly competitive industry.

FIGURE 9.8 **Oligopolies** Oligopolies exist in a number of industries throughout the United States. Here several industries are highlighted.

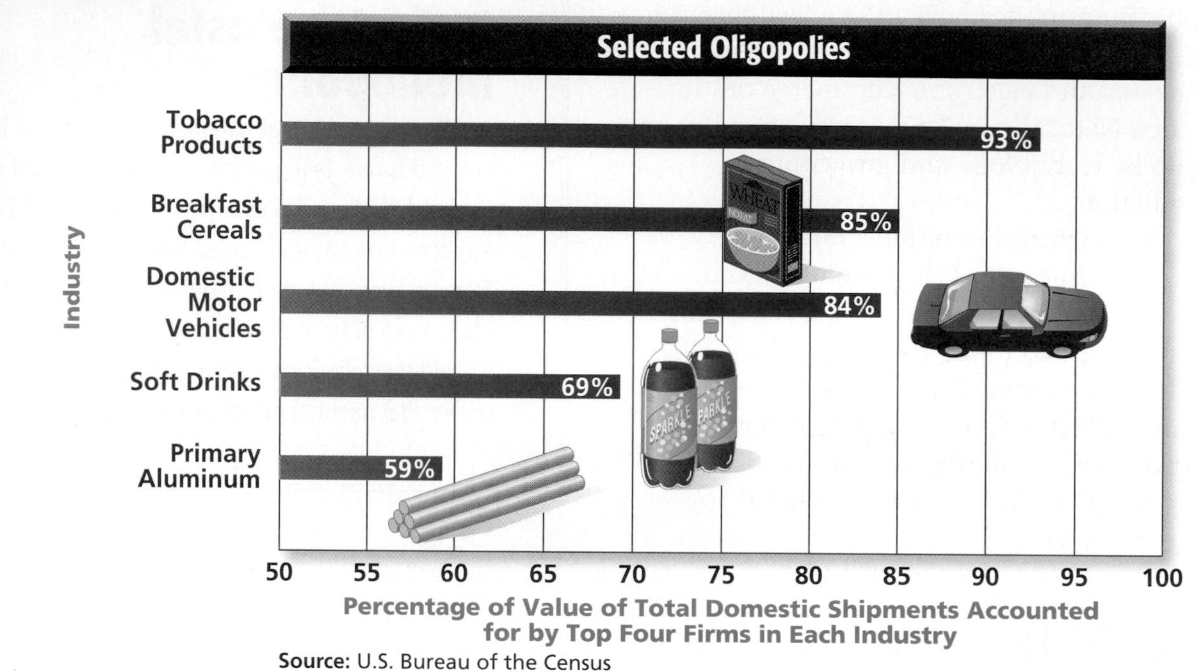

Source: U.S. Bureau of the Census

Product Differentiation We mentioned earlier that oligopolists engage in *nonprice* competition. What does this mean? Let's use automobiles as an example. Several large auto manufacturers have an oligopoly on the domestic car market. They all make cars, trucks, and sport utility vehicles. However, they spend millions, if not billions, of advertising dollars per year to differentiate their products in your mind–and to win your consumer dollars.

The price you pay for brand names is not just based on supply and demand. Rather, it is based on **product differentiation**–the real or perceived differences in the good or service that make it more valuable in consumers' eyes.

product differentiation: *manufacturers' use of minor differences in quality and features to try to differentiate between similar goods and services*

Interdependent Behavior With so few firms in an oligopoly, whatever one does, the others are sure to follow. When one airline cuts its airfares to gain market share, for example, the other major airlines lower theirs even more. Although this type of *price war* is initially good for consumers in the form of lower prices, it may force an airline out of business if prices drop too much. Fewer airlines lead to less competition, which raises prices in the long run.

In contrast, if competing firms in an oligopoly secretly agree to raise prices or to divide the market, they are performing an illegal act called *collusion*. Heavy penalties, such as fines and even prison terms, are levied against companies found guilty of collusion in the United States.

Cartels An important form of collusion is the cartel. A **cartel** is an arrangement among groups of industrial businesses, often in different countries, to reduce international competition by controlling price, production, and the distribution of goods. Such firms seek monopolistic power.

cartel: *arrangement among groups of industrial businesses to reduce international competition by controlling the price, production, and distribution of goods*

Monopolistic Competition

monopolistic competition: *market situation in which a large number of sellers offer similar but slightly different products and in which each has some control over price*

The most common form of market structure in the United States is **monopolistic competition,** in which a large number of sellers offer similar but slightly different products. Obvious examples are brand-name items such as toothpaste, cosmetics, and designer clothes. To be a monopolistic competitor, five conditions must be met:

(1) Numerous Sellers No single seller or small group dominates the market.

(2) Relatively Easy Entry Entry into the market is easier than in a monopoly or oligopoly. One drawback is the high cost of advertising.

(3) Differentiated Products Each supplier sells a slightly different product to attract customers.

(4) Nonprice Competition Businesses compete by using product differentiation and by advertising.

(5) Some Control Over Price By building a loyal customer base through product differentiation, each firm has some control over the price it charges.

Many of the characteristics of monopolistic competition are the same as those of an oligopoly. The major difference is in the number of sellers of a product. As you recall, in an oligopoly a few companies dominate an industry, and control over price is interdependent. Monopolistic competition has many firms, no real interdependence, and some slight difference among products.

CAREERS
Graphic Designer
Job Description
■ Create art using print, electronic, and film media to meet client's needs
■ Create promotional displays, marketing brochures, and television graphics
Qualifications
■ Bachelor's and/or master's degree in fine arts
■ Training in computer design techniques
Median Salary: $34,570
Job Outlook: Good
—Occupational Outlook Handbook, 2002–03

Advertising Competitive advertising is even more important in monopolistic competition than it is in oligopolies. As shown in **Figure 9.9,** advertising attempts to persuade consumers that the product being advertised is different from, and superior to, any other. When successful, advertising enables companies to charge more for their products. That's why companies like Nike, The Gap, and Procter & Gamble pour millions of dollars into their advertising budgets every year.

FIGURE 9.9

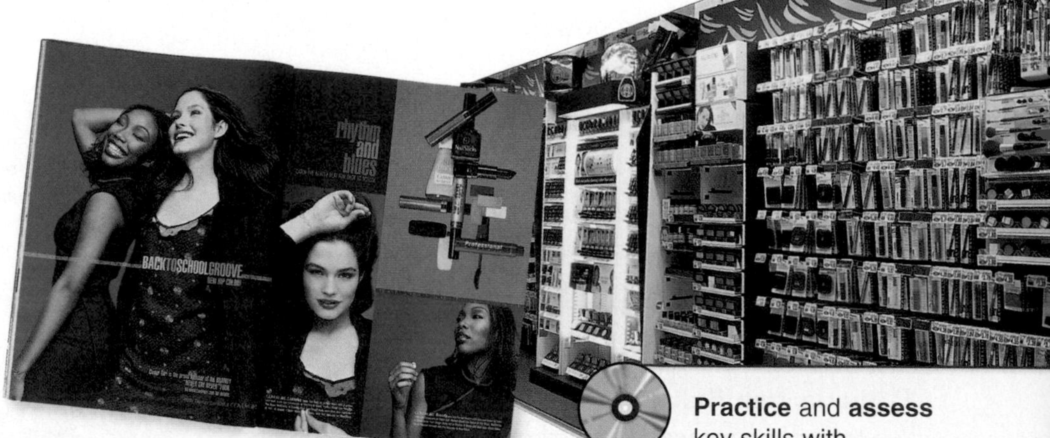

Advertising Ads lead to product differentiation and competition for consumer dollars. Businesses also compete for shelf space–space on store shelves for displaying their products and attracting buyers.

Practice and **assess** key skills with ***Skillbuilder Interactive Workbook, Level 2.***

SECTION 2 Assessment

Understanding Key Terms

1. **Define** monopoly, barriers to entry, economies of scale, patent, copyright, oligopoly, product differentiation, cartel, monopolistic competition.

Reviewing Objectives

2. What are the four characteristics of a pure monopoly?
3. What characteristics of an oligopoly allow it to have a limited control over price?
4. **Graphic Organizer** Use a chart like the one in the next column to compare a monopolistic competitor to an oligopoly in regard to these categories: number of sellers, difficulty of market entry, product differentiation, nonprice competition, and amount of control over price.

Category	Monopolistic Competition	Oligopoly

Applying Economic Concepts

5. **Product Differentiation** Give three examples of products you have bought recently based on advertising, not price. How does your consumer behavior justify product differentiation?

Critical Thinking Activity

6. **Synthesizing Information** Develop a print or video advertisement using yourself as the hardworking product. Use product differentiation to explain why an employer should "purchase" you.

BusinessWeek

Spotlight on the Economy

Celebrity Can Really Be a Gas

Check It Out! In this chapter, you learned that oligopolists and monopolistic competitors use product differentiation to attract customers. In the following article, read to learn how one celebrity puts nonprice competition to work for him.

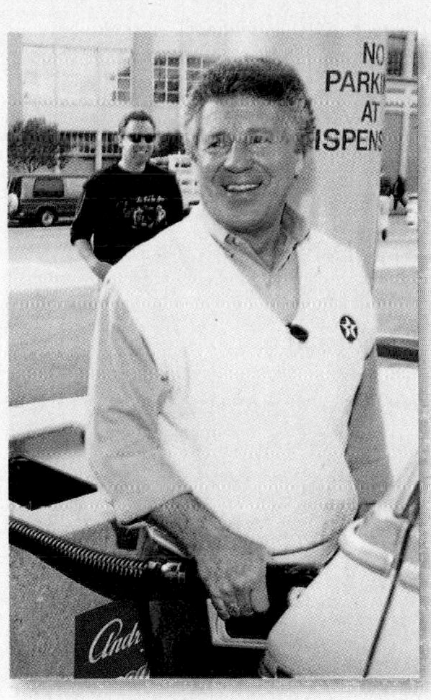

Mario Andretti

Air Jordan shoes. Martha Stewart towels. Now, how's this for the latest in celebrity branding? Mario Andretti unleaded. Yes, the 58-year-old retired racing legend is licensing his name to Texaco gas stations on the West Coast in the hopes of eventually taking the Andretti gas brand nationwide.

The first 37,000-square-foot Andretti mega-station opened in San Francisco in January. It has 10 gas pumps, as well as a Burger King and Starbucks, which lease space from Mario Andretti Petroleum LP. In coming months, Texaco will put the Andretti label on five existing California gas stations, adding "Winning Finish" car washes and "Quick Pit" service bays, branding exclusive to Andretti.

Celebrity evidently sells well. Sales at the San Francisco flagship already total 80% of first-year projected revenues of $5 million, says the partnership. The gas isn't any better than rivals', admits Andretti. But he boasts that the service is. The Indy 500 champ regularly visits his namesake station to make sure. He sometimes even lends a hand to surprised motorists. "I'll pump your gas and clean your windshield, no problem," he says. Now, if he would only drive folks home in the evening rush . . .

Think About It

1. **Are goods or services more important at Andretti's mega-station?**
2. **How does Andretti differentiate his products from others?**

SECTION 3

Government Policies Toward Competition

Reader's Guide

Terms to Know

- interlocking directorate
- antitrust legislation
- merger
- conglomerate
- deregulation

Reading Objectives

1. What is the difference between interlocking directorates and mergers?
2. What is the purpose of federal regulatory agencies?
3. How has some regulation hurt consumers?

Cover Story

Bergen Record, April 23, 1999

The Federal Trade Commission (FTC) reviews mergers to ensure that they do not substantially lessen competition. The agency certainly was busy in 1998. In that year, the number of announced mergers involving American companies exceeded 7,750. A survey conducted in 1999 suggests that the FTC's workload will not dwindle in the near future. Of the companies polled in the survey, more than one third said that they intended to acquire other companies within the year.

Historically, one of the goals of government in the United States has been to encourage competition in the economy. In this section, you'll learn about the federal laws and regulatory agencies–including the Federal Trade Commission mentioned above–that attempt to force monopolies to act more competitively.

Antitrust Legislation

The industrial expansion after the Civil War fueled the rise of big businesses. John D. Rockefeller's Standard Oil Company was the most notorious for driving competitors out of business and pressuring customers not to deal with rival oil companies. He also placed members of Standard Oil's board of directors onto the board of a competing corporation. Because the same group of people, in effect, controlled both companies, it was less tempting for them to compete with one another. This practice of creating **interlocking directorates** was perfected by Rockefeller.

interlocking directorate: *a board of directors, the majority of whose members also serve as the board of directors of a competing corporation*

Sherman Antitrust Act Public pressure against Rockefeller's monopoly, or trust, over the oil business led Congress to pass the Sherman Antitrust Act in 1890. The law sought to protect trade and commerce against unlawful restraint and monopoly. The Sherman Act was important **antitrust legislation,** or laws to prevent new monopolies or trusts from forming and to break up those that already exist.

antitrust legislation: *federal and state laws passed to prevent new monopolies from forming and to break up those that already exist*

Clayton Act Because the language in the Sherman Act was so vague, a new law was passed in 1914 to sharpen its antitrust provisions. The Clayton Act prohibited or limited a number of very specific business practices that lessened competition substantially. The Clayton Act, however, does not state what the term *substantially* means. As a result, it is up to the federal government to make a subjective decision as to whether the merging of two corporations would substantially lessen competition. **Figure 9.10** on page 250 details the Clayton Act and other antitrust legislation.

Mergers

Most antitrust legislation deals with restricting the harmful effects of mergers. A **merger** occurs when one corporation joins

merger: *a combined company that results when one corporation buys more than half the stock of another corporation and, thus, controls the second corporation*

Economic Connection to... Literature

Muckrakers

The rise of monopolies in the late 1800s contributed to the development of a new kind of journalism—muckraking. The muckrakers wrote stories exposing corruption in business and politics. One of the most famous muckrakers was Ida Tarbell. She wrote a series of articles that attacked John D. Rockefeller's monopoly, the Standard Oil Company.

In great detail, Tarbell showed how Rockefeller used unfair practices to drive his competitors out of business. She even likened Rockefeller to a crooked gambler: "Mr. Rockefeller has systematically played with loaded dice. . . . Business played in this way . . . is fit only for tricksters." Tarbell's words led to a government investigation of Standard Oil's business practices. ■

FIGURE 9.10 Antitrust Legislation

Federal Law	Function
Sherman Antitrust Act (1890)	Outlawed agreements and conspiracies that restrain interstate trade. Made it illegal to monopolize or even attempt to monopolize any part of interstate commerce.
Clayton Act (1914)	Restricted *price discrimination*—the practice of selling the same good to different buyers at different prices. Prohibited sellers from requiring that a buyer not deal with a competitor. Outlawed interlocking directorates between competitors. Outlawed mergers that lessen competition substantially.
Federal Trade Commission Act (1914)	Established the Federal Trade Commission (FTC) as an independent antitrust agency. Gave the FTC power to bring court cases against private businesses engaging in unfair trade practices.
Robinson-Patman Act (1936)	Strengthened the law against charging different prices for the same product to different buyers. An amendment to the Clayton Act of 1914.
Celler-Kefauver Antimerger Act (1950)	Strengthened the law against firms joining together to control too large a part of the market. An amendment to the Clayton Act of 1914.
Hart-Scott-Rodino Antitrust Improvements Act (1976)	Restricted mergers that would lessen competition. Required big corporations planning to merge to notify the Federal Trade Commission (FTC) and the Department of Justice, who would then decide whether to challenge the merger under the terms of the Clayton Act of 1914.

with another corporation. As shown in **Figure 9.11,** three kinds of mergers exist: horizontal, vertical, and conglomerate.

When the two corporations that merge are in the same business, a *horizontal merger* has occurred. An example of a horizontal merger occurs when Video Store A buys Video Store B. When corporations involved in a "chain" of supply merge, this is called a *vertical merger*. An example would be a paper company buying the lumber mill that supplies it with pulp or buying the office supply business that sells its paper.

conglomerate: *large corporation made up of smaller corporations dealing in unrelated businesses*

Another type of merger is the conglomerate merger. A **conglomerate** is a huge corporation involved in at least four or more unrelated businesses. Procter & Gamble is a multinational conglomerate. With operations in more than 160 countries, it produces or has acquired such businesses as Cover Girl cosmetics, Pert Plus shampoo, Clearasil skin care, Folgers coffee, Pringles potato chips, Jif peanut butter, Crest toothpaste, NyQuil cough medicine, Dawn dish soap, Cheer and Tide laundry detergent, Pampers diapers, and Charmin toilet paper.

Regulatory Agencies

Besides using antitrust laws to foster a competitive atmosphere, the government uses direct regulation of business pricing and product quality. **Figure 9.12** on page 252 lists several regulatory agencies that oversee various industries and services. These agencies exist at the federal, state, and even local levels.

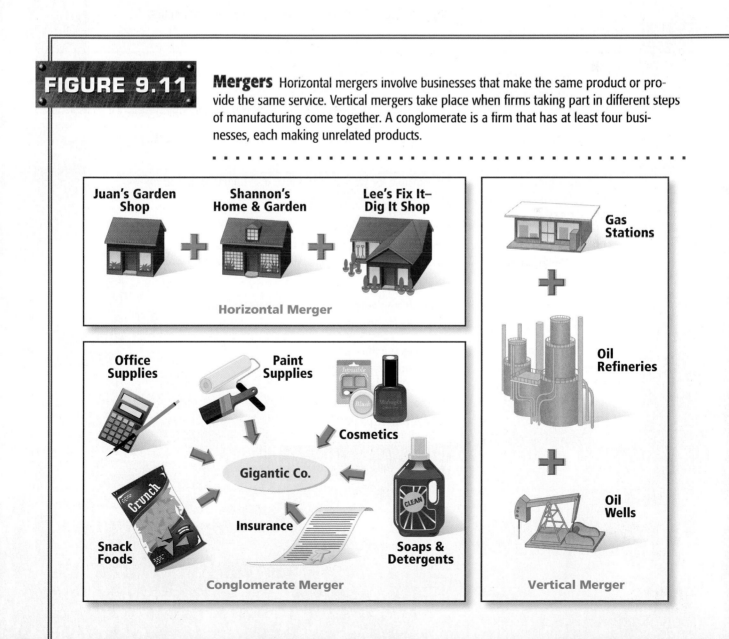

FIGURE 9.11 **Mergers** Horizontal mergers involve businesses that make the same product or provide the same service. Vertical mergers take place when firms taking part in different steps of manufacturing come together. A conglomerate is a firm that has at least four businesses, each making unrelated products.

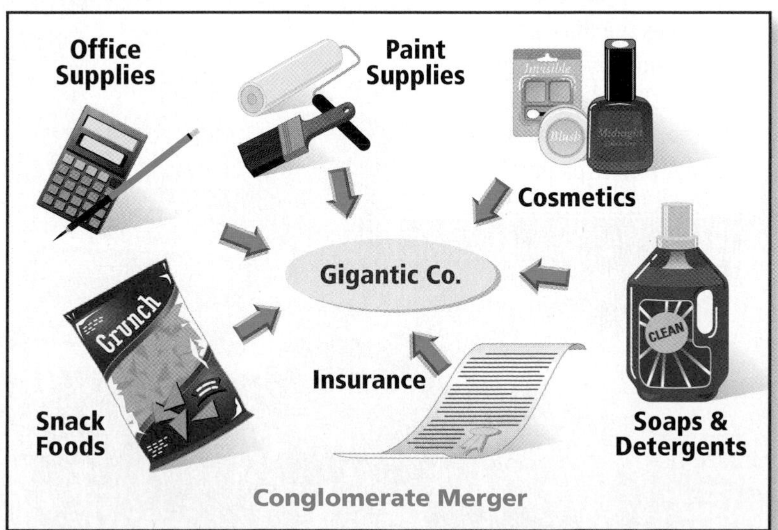

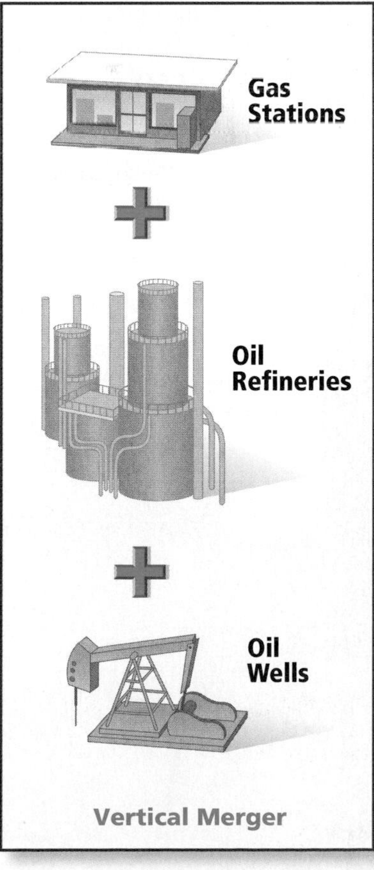

FIGURE 9.12

Federal Regulatory Agencies

Agency	Function
Federal Trade Commission (FTC) (1914)	Regulates product warranties, unfair methods of competition in interstate commerce, and fraud in advertising.
Food and Drug Administration (FDA) (1927)	Regulates purity and safety of foods, drugs, and cosmetics.
Federal Communications Commission (FCC) (1934)	Regulates television, radio, telegraph, and telephone; grants licenses, creates and enforces rules of behavior for broadcasting; most recently, partly regulates satellite transmissions and cable TV.
Securities and Exchange Commission (SEC) (1934)	Regulates the sale of stocks, bonds, and other investments.
Equal Employment Opportunity Commission (EEOC) (1964)	Responsible for working to reduce discrimination based on religion, gender, race, national origin, or age.
Occupational Safety and Health Administration (OSHA) (1970)	Regulates the workplace environment; makes sure that businesses provide workers with safe and healthful working conditions.
Environmental Protection Agency (EPA) (1970)	Develops and enforces environmental standards for air, water, and toxic waste.
Nuclear Regulatory Commission (NRC) (1974)	Regulates the nuclear power industry; licenses and oversees the design, construction, and operation of nuclear power plants.

Deregulation Although the aim of government regulations is to promote efficiency and competition, recent evidence indicates that something quite different has occurred. In the 1980s and 1990s, many industries were **deregulated**—the government reduced regulations and control over business activity. It was found that in trying to protect consumers from unfair practices, government regulations had actually *decreased* the amount of competition in the economy.

Student Web Activity Visit the *Economics Today and Tomorrow* Web site at ett.glencoe.com and click on ***Chapter 9—Student Web Activities*** to learn more about conglomerates.

As an example, the Federal Communications Commission (FCC) had for years regulated the basic channels in the television market. With deregulation came the entry of competitive pay-TV, cable, and satellite systems.

deregulation: *reduction of government regulation and control over business activity*

Many economists speculate about what would happen if the government removed its watchdog responsibility toward mergers in general. Economists assume prices would rise. If, however, the price increases caused profits to be excessive, other sellers would find ways to enter the market. Consumers would benefit eventually from a competitive supply of goods and services.

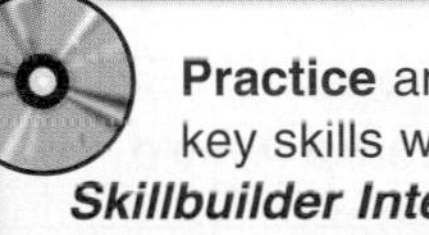

Practice and **assess** key skills with ***Skillbuilder Interactive Workbook, Level 2.***

SECTION 3 Assessment

Understanding Key Terms

1. **Define** interlocking directorate, antitrust legislation, merger, conglomerate, deregulation.

Reviewing Objectives

2. What is the difference between interlocking directorates and mergers?
3. **Graphic Organizer** Use a chart like the one below to describe the purpose of five federal regulatory agencies.

Agency	Purpose

4. How has some regulation hurt consumers?

Applying Economic Concepts

5. **Regulation** If the shampoo you just bought caused your hair to fall out, which regulatory agency should you contact to complain? Why? What agency should you contact if the new washing machine your family just bought breaks down, and the manufacturer refuses to honor the warranty?

Critical Thinking Activity

6. **Categorizing Information** Type *conglomerate* into a search engine. Research one of the conglomerates that you find, and list all the businesses or products owned by that conglomerate.

People & Perspectives

William Gates

ENTREPRENEUR (1955–)

- **Cofounder and chief executive officer of Microsoft**
- **Recipient of the 1993 Price Waterhouse Leadership Award for Lifetime Achievement**
- **"The richest man in the world" according to *Forbes Magazine*'s annual survey**

In the book *The Road Ahead* (1996), Bill Gates explains his vision of an interconnected world built around the Internet:

"Over the next decade, businesses worldwide will be transformed. Intranets will revolutionize the way companies share information internally, and the Internet will revolutionize how they communicate externally. Corporations will redesign their nervous systems to rely on the networks that reach every member of the organization and beyond into the world of suppliers, consultants, and customers. These changes will let companies be more effective and often smaller. In the longer run, as broadband networks make physical proximity to urban services less essential, many businesses will decentralize and disperse their activities, and cities may be downsized too.

Even the smallest of all businesses, the individual earning a living in a profession or as an artist, has been empowered by the PC. One person without any staff can produce reports, handle correspondence, bill customers, and maintain a credible business presence–all surprisingly easily. In field after field, the tools of the trade have been transformed by PCs and software.

All of these electronic innovations–e-mail, shared screens, videoconferencing, and video phone calls–are ways of overcoming physical separation. As they become commonplace, they'll change not just the way we work together but also the distinction we make between the workplace and everywhere else."

Checking for Understanding

1. **In Gates's opinion, what will be the long-term impact of intranets and the Internet?**
2. **How does Gates characterize electronic innovations?**

CHAPTER 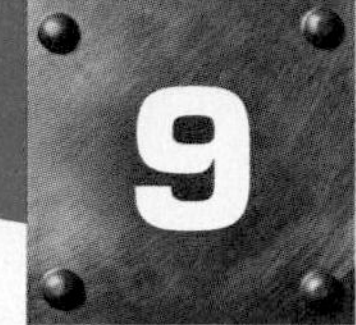 Summary

Chapter Overview Visit the *Economics Today and Tomorrow* Web site at ett.glencoe.com and click on ***Chapter 9—Chapter Overviews*** to review chapter information.

SECTION 1 Perfect Competition

- There are four basic **market structures** in the United States: **monopoly, oligopoly, monopolistic competition,** and **perfect competition.**
- Perfect competition is characterized by numerous buyers and sellers, an identical product, easy entry into the market, easy access to information about prices, and no control over price.
- The market for agricultural products is often used as an example of perfect competition because individual farmers have almost no control over the market price of their goods.
- When perfect competition exists, society benefits from its efficient allocation of productive resources.

SECTION 2 Monopoly, Oligopoly, Monopolistic Competition

- In a monopoly, a single seller controls the supply of the good or service and thus determines the price.
- A monopoly is protected by **barriers to entry,** which could be government regulations, a large initial investment, or ownership of raw materials.
- Four types of monopolies exist: natural monopoly, geographic monopoly, technological monopoly, and government monopoly.
- Natural monopolies are often advantageous in that they give the company an **economy of scale**—which means because of its size, the company can produce the largest amount for the lowest cost.
- An oligopoly is an industry dominated by several suppliers who exercise some control over price.
- Oligopolies and monopolistic competitors use **product differentiation** to make their products more valuable in consumers' eyes.
- Advertising brand names is vital in the market structure known as monopolistic competition, in which a large number of sellers offer similar but slightly different products.

SECTION 3 Government Policies Toward Competition

- The government has passed **antitrust legislation** to prevent monopolies from forming or to break up those that already exist.
- Two famous pieces of antitrust legislation are the Sherman Antitrust Act and the Clayton Act.
- Three kinds of mergers exist: horizontal, vertical, and conglomerate.
- Federal regulatory agencies oversee various types of industries to ensure fair pricing and product quality.
- **Deregulating** some industries in the 1980s and 1990s resulted in more competition among businesses.

CHAPTER 9

Assessment and Activities

Self-Check Quiz Visit the *Economics Today and Tomorrow* Web site at ett.glencoe.com and click on ***Chapter 9—Self-Check Quizzes*** to prepare for the Chapter Test.

Identifying Key Terms

Write the letter of the definition in Column B that correctly defines each term in Column A.

Column A

1. barriers to entry
2. deregulation
3. conglomerate
4. interlocking directorate
5. geographic monopoly
6. merger
7. monopolistic competition
8. oligopoly
9. government monopoly
10. antitrust legislation

Column B

a. large corporation made up of unrelated businesses
b. the joining of two corporations
c. characterized by many firms but differentiated products
d. obstacles that prevent new companies from being formed
e. removing government restrictions from industries
f. characterized by a few firms with differentiated products
g. a store located in an isolated area
h. passed to prevent monopolies
i. building and maintaining local roads and bridges
j. situation in which some of the board of directors for competing companies are the same people

Recalling Facts and Ideas

Section 1

1. In a perfectly competitive market structure, how much control does a single seller have over market price?
2. What is the relationship between the types of products that sellers sell in a perfectly competitive market?
3. What is one example of an almost perfectly competitive market?

Section 2

4. What are the three types of market structures with imperfect competition?
5. What is the difference between a geographic monopoly and a technological monopoly?
6. How much control does an oligopoly have over price?
7. In monopolistic competition, how many sellers are there?

Section 3

8. What is the difference between a horizontal merger and a vertical merger?
9. What two methods does the federal government use to keep businesses competitive?

Thinking Critically

1. **Finding the Main Idea** Explain in a paragraph how supply and demand work in the agricultural market when government controls are not operating.
2. **Making Generalizations** Re-create the spider map below, then write two ways that the free enterprise system works to break the three powers of monopolies noted.

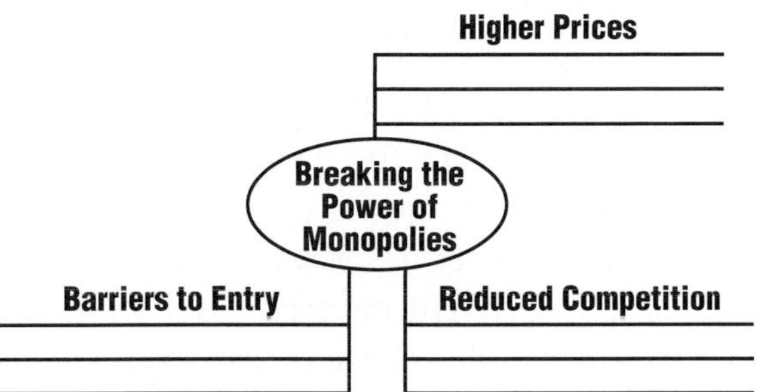

3. **Making Comparisons** What are the fundamental differences between the goals of antitrust legislation and the goals of federal government regulatory agencies?

Applying Economic Concepts

Competition and Market Structure Make a list of the four types of monopolies that exist. Under each type, list three real examples–whether at the federal, state, or local levels.

Cooperative Learning Project

Organize into groups of three–with one group member representing monopolies; another, oligopolies; and the third, monopolistic competition. Each member of each group should clip business advertisements and articles that characterize his or her market structure. As a group, compare the ads (and businesses) that each person collected. Defend your reasoning behind placing a particular company in its particular grouping.

Reviewing Skills

Drawing Inferences and Conclusions Using **Figure 9.12** on page 252, infer which federal regulatory agency would be responsible for the following "ingredients" of making pizza.

1. Checks the freshness of milk that makes mozzarella cheese.
2. Determines that shipping rates are fair for the pepperoni arriving from out-of-state.
3. Makes sure the pizza advertisement on TV is truthful.
4. Enforces safe working conditions for employees in the pizza parlor.
5. Makes sure that the pizza parlor disposes of waste in a safe manner.

Technology Activity

Using the Internet Choose a regulatory agency mentioned in this chapter and use the Internet to find the agency's homepage. Use the information to analyze the main functions of the agency and explain how the agency's regulatory actions affect the circular flow model.

Analyzing the Global Economy

Procter & Gamble was mentioned in this chapter as an example of a multinational conglomerate. Use the Internet to find out (a) in how many countries P&G has manufacturing operations; (b) how many countries buy P&G products; (c) how many people are employed by P&G; and (d) what its annual worldwide sales are. Also note the names of products used in Africa, Asia, Europe, and Latin America. Write a report about your findings, and share your report with the class.

Focus on Free Enterprise

The Home Depot

When Bernie Marcus and Arthur Blank lost their jobs at Handy Dan, a chain of home improvement stores in California, they knew what they were going to do. They would open their own home improvement store–and it would be the best in the United States. Just exactly how they were going to do this, they were not sure. It became clear to them, however, when they visited a store in Long Beach called Homeco.

A Different Approach

Homeco did not look, or work, like any other home improvement store Marcus and Blank had seen. The huge barn-like space was stacked from floor to ceiling with a vast array of home supplies. Every item was offered at a rock-bottom price. And there were tradespeople–painters, carpenters, plumbers, electricians, and so on–throughout the store ready to give shoppers help and advice. Marcus and Blank recognized that this blend of warehouse retailing and superior customer service was the way to go. They quickly asked Homeco's owner, Pat Farrah, to join them in their business venture.

Shortly after, Marcus, Blank, and Farrah moved their operations to Atlanta, Georgia. They opened their first store–called The Home Depot–there in 1978. The store operated on four simple principles. First, stock a

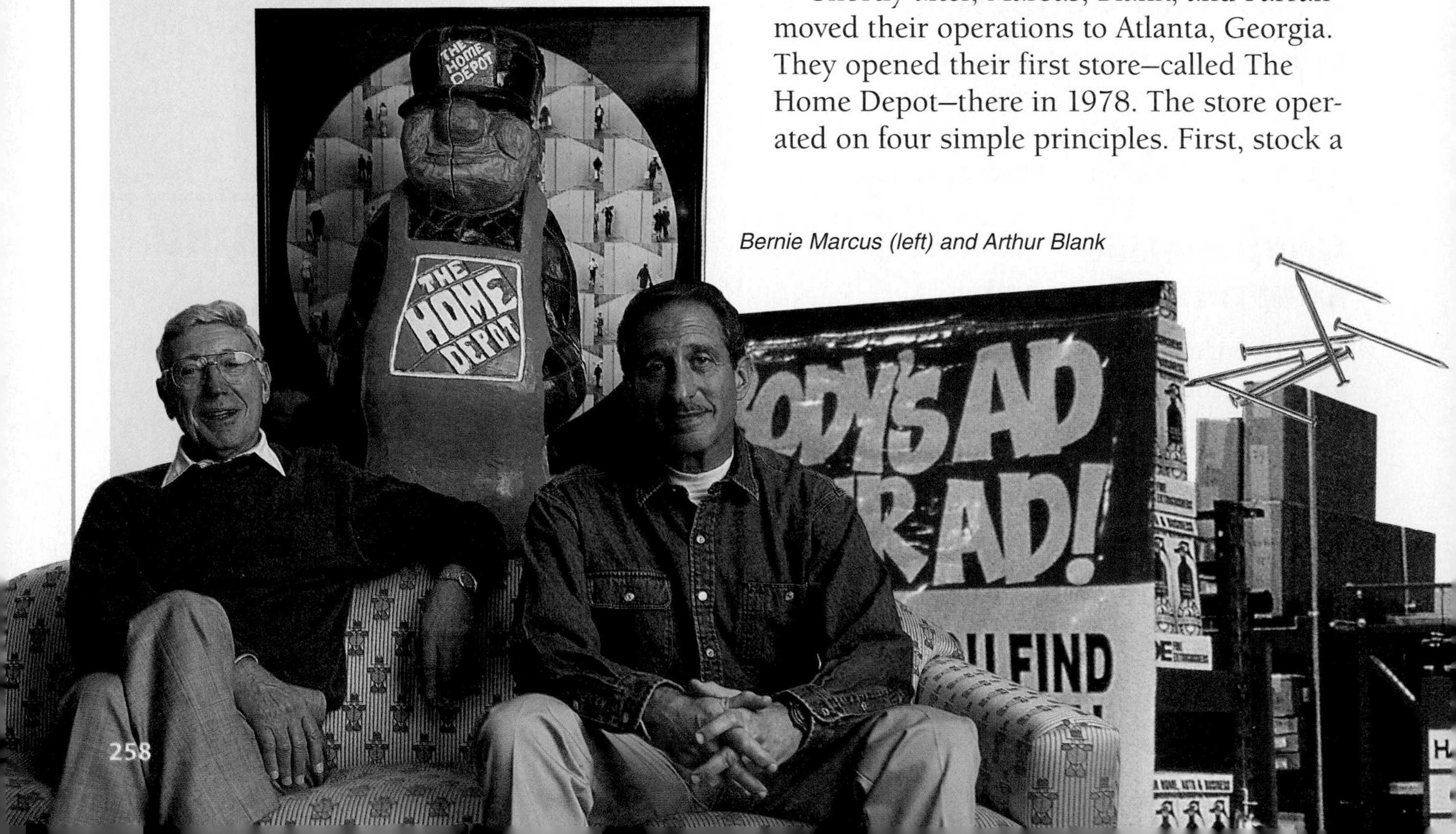

Bernie Marcus (left) and Arthur Blank

large assortment of merchandise. Second, charge the lowest prices. Third, provide excellent customer service. Finally, cater to both the do-it-yourself amateur and the construction-industry professional.

The early days were a struggle. Sometimes, the partners did not have the cash to buy supplies. So Farrah stacked the store with empty paint cans and boxes to make it look as though it were well stocked. Over time, however, business began to pick up, and Marcus, Blank, and Farrah opened several more stores.

Building an Empire

In 1981 the partners took a major step, selling shares in the company. With the $4 million they made from the sale, they began an ambitious expansion program. First, The Home Depot began to establish a foothold in other states. Then the company went international, opening stores elsewhere in the Western Hemisphere. By 1999, it had outlets in 44 states, Puerto Rico, Canada, and Chile.

Sharing the Wealth

Since its earliest days, The Home Depot has offered employees the chance to share in its success. It gives many workers the choice of taking shares instead of year-end cash bonuses. Workers also have a chance to buy shares at discount rates. This practice, Arthur Blank thinks, simply is good business. When workers own stock, he says, they "feel that they own the stores, that they own the merchandise, that they have total responsibility for the customers in their aisles, and that they create the value." Many workers certainly have benefited from the practice.

The Home Depot also makes an effort to share its good fortune with the communities in which it operates. In 2002 alone, it invested $25 million to support local communities. It also encourages its workers to volunteer for local charitable organizations. Associates invested 6 million volunteer hours in local cities and towns.

Free Enterprise in Action

1. **What new approach did The Home Depot bring to the home improvement industry?**
2. **Why does Arthur Blank think that offering stock to employees is good business practice?**

UNIT 4

Microeconomics: American Business In Action

Every year, more than 2.5 million teenagers between the ages of 16 and 19 work full time.

Chapter 10
Financing and Producing Goods

Chapter 11
Marketing and Distribution

Chapter 12
The American Labor Force

In this unit, read to FIND OUT . . .

- how businesses obtain financing and produce goods.
- how those goods are marketed and distributed to you as a consumer.
- who makes up the American labor force.

Every trading day, hundreds of millions of shares of American companies are bought and sold on the New York Stock Exchange.

Retailing in the United States is close to a $4-trillion-a-year business.
Shopping on the Internet is estimated to be a $65 billion industry, growing at nearly 26 percent a year.
The United States produces nearly 23 percent of the world's entire output of goods.
ENERGY EAST CORPORATION
COMMON STOCK
PAR VALUE $.01

CHAPTER 10

Financing and Producing Goods

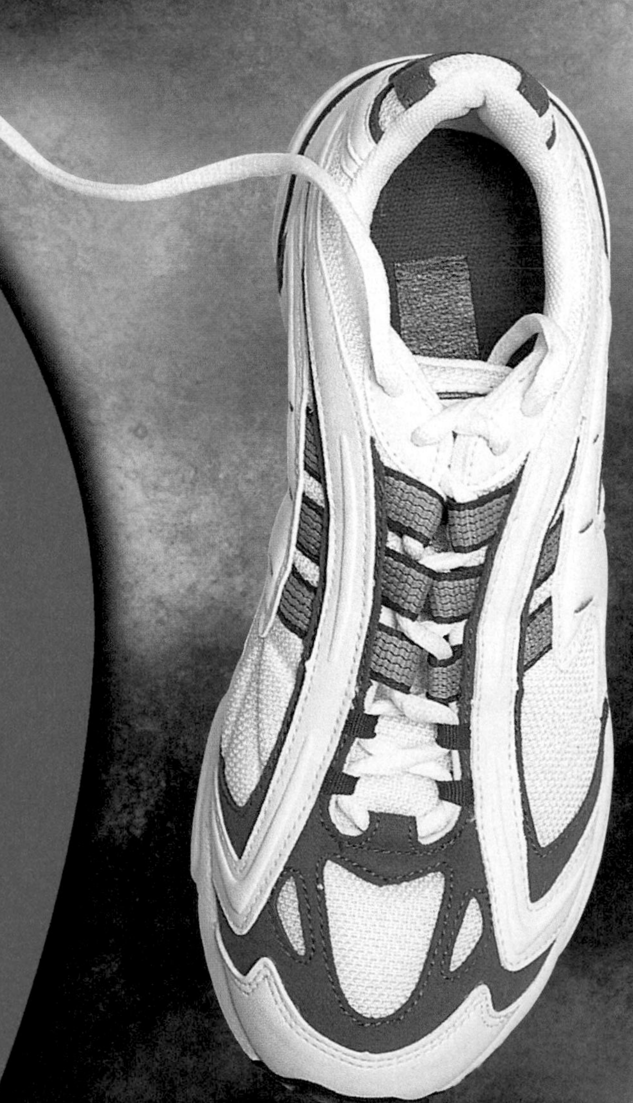

Why It's Important

How do shoe manufacturers get started? How could you get started if you wanted to open a business? This chapter will explain how companies obtain the financing needed to open for business, and how they try to work efficiently to make profits.

To learn more about factors that affect efficiency and profitability, view the **Economics & You** *Chapter 19 video lesson:* **Financing and Producing Goods**

Chapter Overview Visit the *Economics Today and Tomorrow* Web site at ett.glencoe.com and click on ***Chapter 10—Chapter Overviews*** to preview chapter information.

SECTION 1

Investing in the Free Enterprise System

Cover Story

The Chicago Tribune, May 26, 1999

Finding money for your small business is often as deflating as looking for a job. It can be an arduous process of networking, mailing people information about yourself and then calling to see what they think.

A Chicago company is using the Internet to try to streamline the money-hunting process for entrepreneurs by connecting them with venture capitalists. Venture Capital Online has signed up more than 80 venture capital firms nationwide representing $15 billion in capital. It has 200 possible deals in the pipeline. . . .

Reader's Guide

Terms to Know

- financing
- cost-benefit analysis
- revenues
- profits

Reading Objectives

1. How does a business decide whether to expand or not?
2. Why are people willing to finance business investment?
3. How does competition for financing determine how resources are allocated in a market economy?

If you were an entrepreneur, you would face many hurdles on your road to success. One hurdle would be finding sufficient financing to pay for your company's current needs–such as parts and tools–and its long-term needs–such as growth. **Financing** is the obtaining of funds, or money capital. As you read this section, you'll learn that both the short-term and long-term needs of businesses can be financed in a variety of ways.

financing: *obtaining funds or money capital for business expansion*

FIGURE 10.1

Financing Business Expansion Businesses are able to obtain financing because you and other income earners do not spend all that you earn during a year. Through saving, you and others who save make resources available to finance business expansion in the United States.

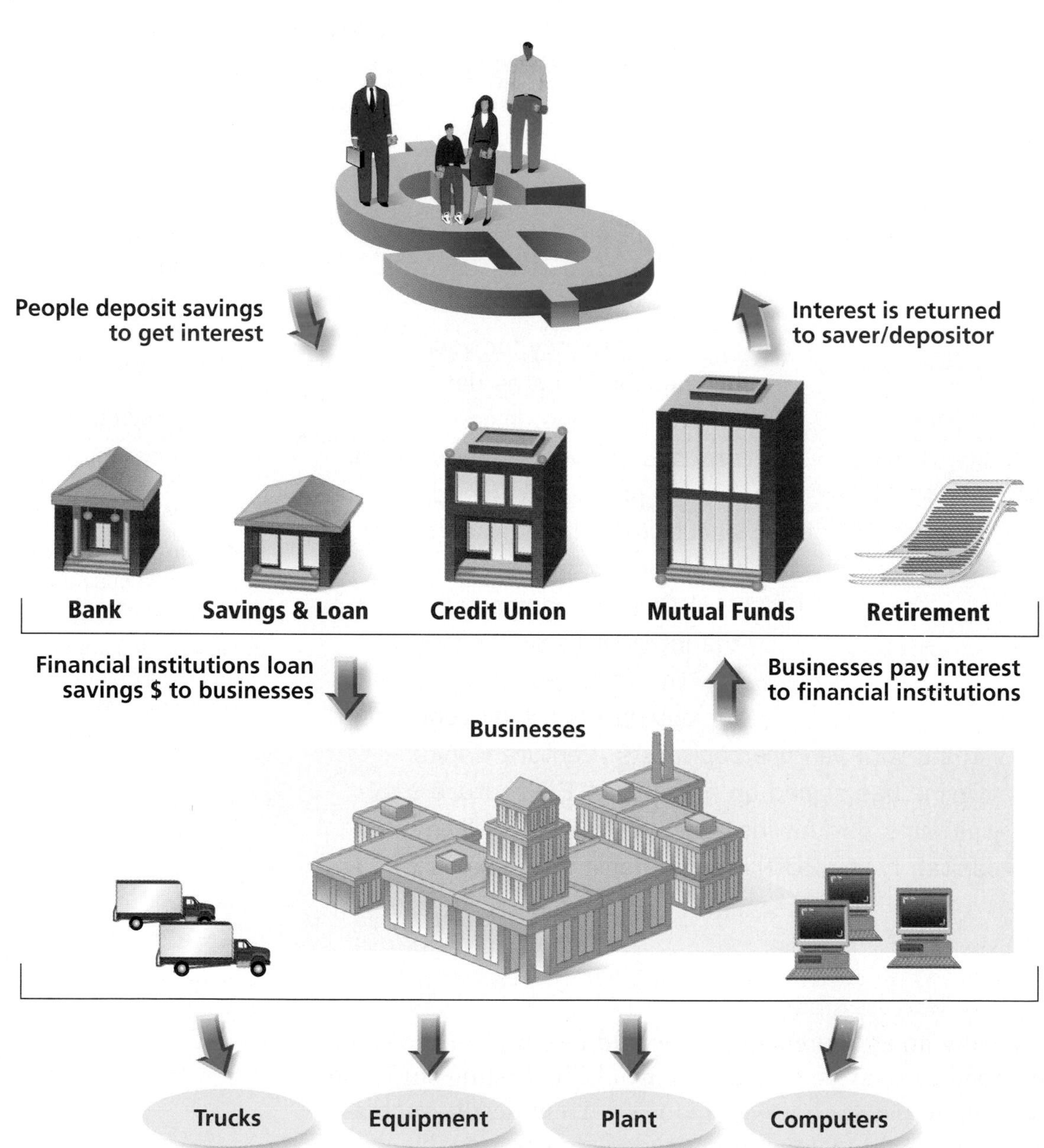

People deposit savings to get interest
Interest is returned to saver/depositor
Bank
Savings & Loan
Credit Union
Mutual Funds
Retirement
Financial institutions loan savings $ to businesses
Businesses pay interest to financial institutions
Businesses
Trucks
Equipment
Plant
Computers
Businesses use savings $ to expand and improve

Turning Savings Into Investments

Financing business operations and growth is an integral part of our free enterprise system. It all begins with people who save by depositing their funds in one of several types of financial institutions, which you learned about in Chapter 6. The financial institutions, in turn, make these deposits available to businesses to finance growth and expansion. **Figure 10.1** illustrates how people's savings become a resource available to finance business expansion in the United States.

Global *Economy*

It Started With the Dutch

In 1602, when the Dutch East India Company was founded to expand and control trade in Asia, it raised financial capital by selling shares of its expected future profits to investors. The investors thus became the owners of the company, and their ownership shares eventually became known as "shares of stock."

The company also issued notes of indebtedness, which involved borrowing money in return for interest on the funds, plus eventual repayment of the principal amount borrowed. Today we call these notes of indebtedness "bonds."

As the company prospered, some of its revenues were used to pay lenders the interest and principal owed them. Of the profits that remained, some were paid to shareholders and some were reinvested in the company. The methods of financing used by the Dutch East India Company nearly 400 years ago—stocks, bonds, and reinvestment—are still the main methods of financing for today's corporations. ■

Before You Pursue Financing

Let's assume that you own an electronics repair company that you have incorporated. You now have the opportunity to open additional repair shops in other locations, but you do not have enough extra cash to invest in the expansion. You can obtain this financing in one of many ways. These include digging into your own personal savings, asking your friends and family to loan funds to the company, borrowing from a financial institution, or selling more shares of stock. Even if you are able to finance the expansion, however, one important question remains. *Should* you expand?

Businesses usually answer this question by making a standard **cost-benefit analysis.** This analysis requires that you estimate the cost of any action and compare it with the benefits of that action. Developing a cost-benefit analysis involves five steps:

(1) Estimate the costs of expansion.
(2) Calculate expected **revenues,** or total income from sales.
(3) Calculate expected **profits,** or revenues minus costs.
(4) Calculate how much it will cost you to borrow funds to finance your proposed business expansion.
(5) If expected profits more than cover the cost of financing the expansion, then the expansion may be warranted. See **Figure 10.2** on page 266.

cost-benefit analysis: *a financial process in which a business estimates the cost of any action and compares it with the benefits of that action*

revenues: *total income from sales of output*

profits: *the money earned after a business subtracts its costs from its revenues*

The steps below show an example of cost-benefit analysis. Here is a simple numerical example: Suppose that you can borrow $1 million to finance your business expansion. Your bank will charge 10 percent per year for the loan. That equals $100,000 per year. If your expansion could generate profits of $200,000 per year, then borrowing $1 million would certainly be worthwhile.

Remember the rule that always applies: *Undertake an activity up to the point at which the additional benefit equals the additional cost.* In this case the activity is financing an expansion. The additional benefit is higher profits, and the additional cost is the cost of borrowing.

Why People Are Willing to Finance Investment

Businesses are interested in obtaining financing so that they can expand and make higher profits in the future. The people who finance such business investments—whether intentionally or

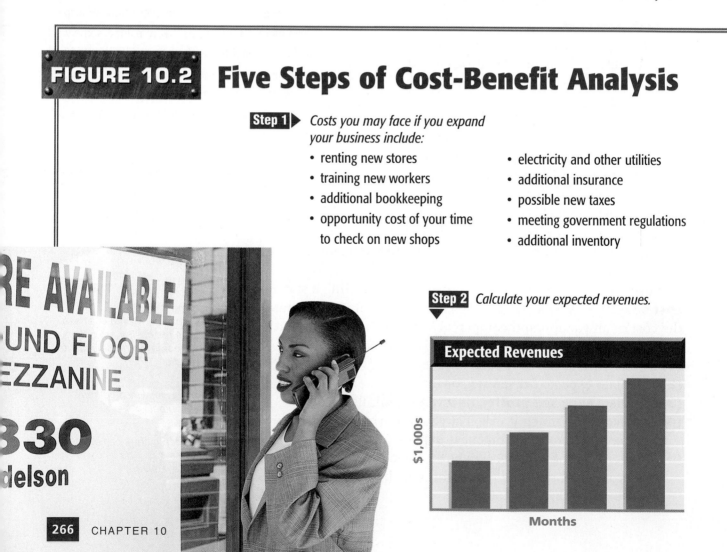

FIGURE 10.2 Five Steps of Cost-Benefit Analysis

Step 1 *Costs you may face if you expand your business include:*

- renting new stores
- training new workers
- additional bookkeeping
- opportunity cost of your time to check on new shops
- electricity and other utilities
- additional insurance
- possible new taxes
- meeting government regulations
- additional inventory

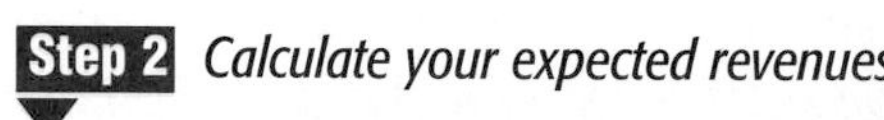

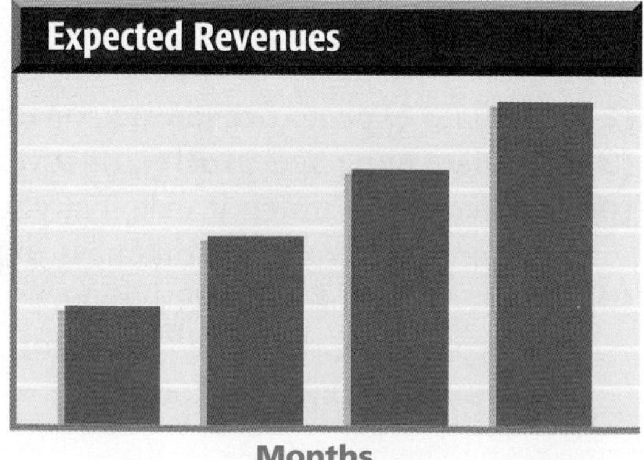

unintentionally–are also seeking rewards. Savers unintentionally finance business growth when they deposit funds in a savings account or certificate of deposit (CD). Their reward is the interest earned on the savings account or CD. For those who intentionally finance investment, the reward is the interest on a corporate bond that they purchase, or dividends from the stock that they buy in an expanding company.

Pursuing Investment Financing

In a free enterprise system, resources normally go where they generate the highest expected value. Financing investment often directs the allocation of these resources. When one business succeeds at obtaining financing, it uses funds that might have helped another business. In a market economy, each business competes for scarce financial resources. If the cost to finance business expansion is relatively high, only those businesses that believe they have the most profitable expansion projects will be willing to

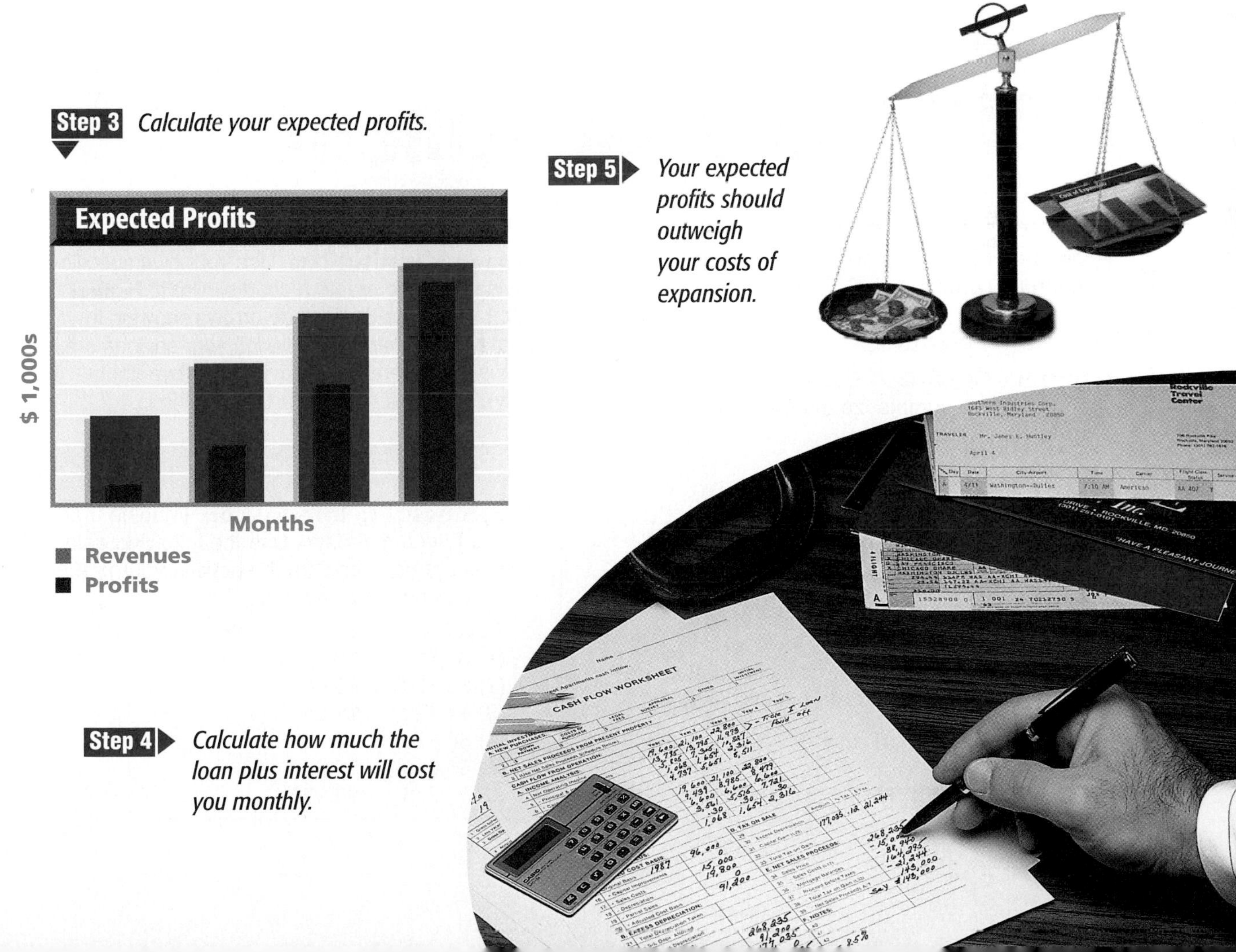

Step 3 Calculate your expected profits.
Expected Profits
$ 1,000s
Months
Revenues
Profits
Step 5 Your expected profits should outweigh your costs of expansion.
Step 4 Calculate how much the loan plus interest will cost you monthly.
CASH FLOW WORKSHEET

Student Web Activity Visit the *Economics Today and Tomorrow* Web site at ett.glencoe.com and click on ***Chapter 10—Student Web Activities*** to learn how businesses can obtain financing from the Internet.

pay the high cost of financing. If the cost of financing is relatively low, more companies will decide that they, too, can profitably engage in additional business investment. In either instance, the lending institution makes the final decision in regard to lending the business the money to expand.

Methods of Financing There are several methods of financing business expansion. As you learned in Chapter 6, corporations offer stock and may sell bonds to finance investment. Businesses, just like individuals, can also borrow from banks, finance companies, or other institutions. Today businesses can even use the Internet to obtain financing. In Section 2, you'll learn more about the types of financing for business operations.

Practice and **assess** key skills with ***Skillbuilder Interactive Workbook, Level 2.***

SECTION 1 Assessment

Understanding Key Terms

1. **Define** financing, cost-benefit analysis, revenues, profits.

Reviewing Objectives

2. **Graphic Organizer** Use a diagram like the one below to summarize the five steps in cost-benefit analysis.

Cost-Benefit Analysis

3. Why are people willing to finance business investment?
4. How does competition for financing determine how resources are allocated in our market economy?

Applying Economic Concepts

5. **Economic Institutions** Use your own specific saving habits to create a chart similar to **Figure 10.1** on page 264. Include arrows showing in what type of financial institution your savings are deposited, where those savings go (hypothetically), and what your reward for saving is.

Critical Thinking Activity

6. **Synthesizing Information** Imagine that you own a company. Use the following data to construct a bar graph showing your profits for a period of 6 months.

Revenues	*Costs*	*Profits?*
(1) $4,560	$3,990	
(2) $3,320	$3,000	
(3) $4,420	$2,250	
(4) $4,870	$2,250	
(5) $5,010	$2,880	
(6) $4,770	$3,120	

CRITICAL THINKING SKILLS

Making Generalizations

Generalizations *are judgments that are usually true, based on the facts at hand. If you say, "We have a great soccer team," you are making a generalization. If you also say that your team is undefeated, you are providing evidence to support your generalization.*

- Identify the subject matter.
- Collect factual information and examples relevant to the topic.
- Identify similarities among these facts.
- Use these similarities to form some general ideas about the subject.

LEARNING THE SKILL

To learn how to make a valid generalization, follow the steps listed on the left.

PRACTICING THE SKILL

Read the excerpt below, then identify whether each generalization that follows is valid or invalid. Explain your answers.

"At the Lintumespsan Middle School, six miles outside of Helsinki, kids as young as 10 are showing up with mobile phones. They're supposed to turn them off during class hours, but some of them always forget. What's worse, the children have their phones rigged to ring with a few bars from songs by Guns N' Roses and the Leningrad Cowboys. . . . Some 58% of all Finns own a mobile phone—the highest penetration in the world. . . . Mobile-phone subscribers can request their bank balances, weather updates, traffic reports, even the latest headlines from Cable News Network, through short-message services."

—*Business Week*, May 3, 1999

1. All Finns own mobile phones.
2. Many Finnish school children own mobile phones.
3. In Finland, mobile phones are used for more than just talking to friends.
4. Mobile-phone sales are increasing in Finland.

APPLICATION ACTIVITY

Read at least three editorials in your local newspaper. Then make a generalization about each editorial.

Practice and **assess** key skills with ***Skillbuilder Interactive Workbook, Level 2.***

SECTION 2

Types of Financing for Business Operations

Reader's Guide

Terms to Know

- debt financing
- short-term financing
- intermediate-term financing
- long-term financing

Reading Objectives

1. What are three general kinds of debt financing?
2. What four factors should companies consider in choosing the right financing?

Cover Story

Entrepreneur, July 2003

If you're thinking . . . investing in your own company is smarter than investing in the stock market, you're right. Not only have smaller company values held up better than the stock market, but right now, formerly scarce and costly items such as labor, facilities, and equipment are plentiful and cheap. . . . [E]ntrepreneurs . . . are finding that investing in their companies has the allure once restricted to Internet IPOs.

Businesses, like individuals, must undergo a certain process when borrowing funds. A business that wants to borrow must show creditworthiness by undergoing a credit check. A credit rating of good, average, or poor is then assigned to the business. Like an individual who borrows money, a business must pay interest on its loan and repay it within a stated period of time. As you read this section, you'll learn about the financing options from which businesses may choose.

Three Kinds of Financing

Raising money for a business through borrowing, or **debt financing,** can be divided into three categories: short-term, intermediate-term, and long-term financing.

debt financing: *raising money for a business through borrowing*

Short-Term Financing When a business borrows money for any period of time less than a year, it has obtained **short-term financing. Figure 10.3** describes several types of short-term

short-term financing: *money borrowed by a business for any period of time less than a year*

FIGURE 10.3 Short-Term Financing

Trade Credit

Trade credit is extended by one firm to another business buying the firm's goods. It allows the buyer to take possession of goods immediately and pay for them at some future date—usually 30 to 90 days later. Businesses often receive a discount—2 percent, for example—if they pay their bill within 10 days. If a business does not repay the bill in that amount of time, it is, in effect, paying 2 percent interest for the use of the trade credit.

Unsecured Loans

Most short-term bank credit for businesses is in the form of unsecured bank loans. These are loans not guaranteed by anything other than the promise to repay them. The borrower must sign a *promissory note* to repay the money in full by a specified time and with a specified rate of interest. The usual repayment period is one year.

Secured Loans

Secured loans are backed by *collateral*—something of value that borrowers will lose if they do not repay a loan. Businesses offer as collateral property such as machinery, inventories, or *accounts receivable*—money owed to a business by its customers.

Line of Credit

A *line of credit* is a maximum amount of money a company can borrow from a bank during a period of time, usually one year. Rather than apply each time for a loan, a company may automatically borrow up to the amount of the line of credit—$100,000, for example.

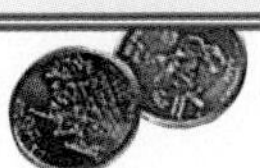

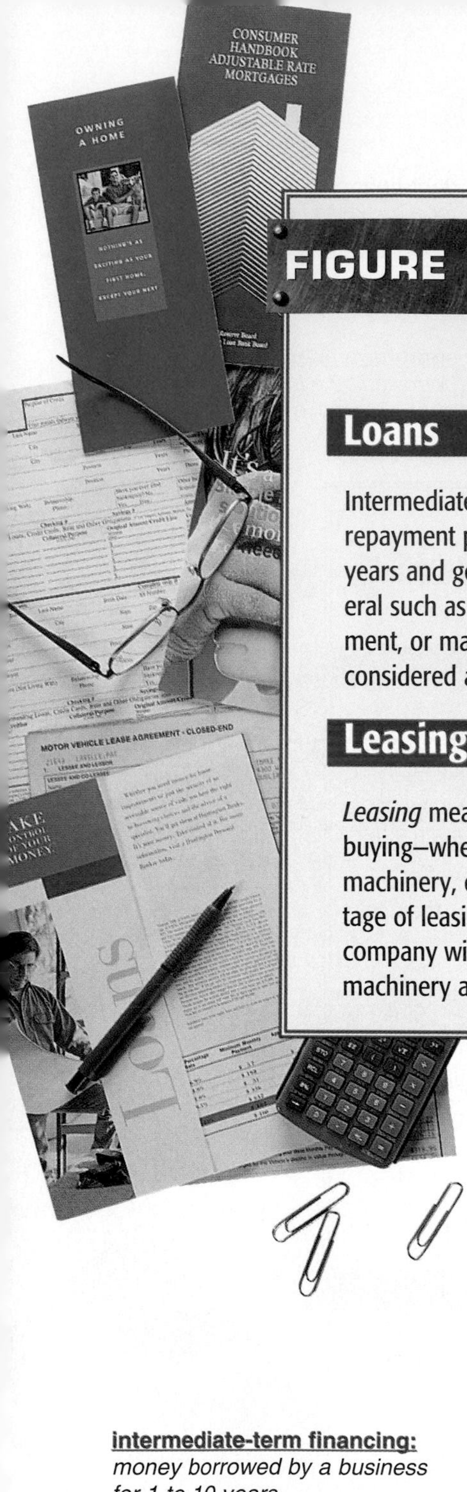

FIGURE 10.4 Intermediate-Term Financing

Loans

Intermediate-term loans have repayment periods of from 1 to 10 years and generally require collateral such as stocks, bonds, equipment, or machinery. The loan is considered a mortgage if it is secured by property such as the building in which the business is located. Sometimes large, financially sound companies may be able to get unsecured intermediate-term loans.

Leasing

Leasing means renting rather than buying–whether it is a building, machinery, or the like. One advantage of leasing is that the leasing company will often service the machinery at low cost. Another advantage is that the business may deduct a part of the money spent on a lease before figuring income taxes. A disadvantage is that a lease often costs more than borrowing to buy the same equipment.

financing. A business may seek short-term financing for many reasons. A company may have excellent business during the month but not be paid until the beginning of the following month. In the meantime, the company needs funds to pay salaries and its bills. During a growing season, a farmer may have to borrow to buy seed, repair equipment, and pay workers.

intermediate-term financing: *money borrowed by a business for 1 to 10 years*

Intermediate-Term Financing Borrowing money for 1 to 10 years is considered **intermediate-term financing.** When a company wants to expand its business by buying more land, buildings, or equipment, short-term financing generally is not adequate. For example, if you decided to expand your electronics repair business by opening another shop, you would not apply for a 90-day loan. In 90 days, you would not be able to do enough repair jobs to earn the additional revenue to repay the loan. Instead, you would look for intermediate-term financing such as described in **Figure 10.4.**

Long-Term Financing Borrowing for longer than 10 years is called **long-term financing.** Long-term financing is used for major expansion, such as building a new plant or buying expensive, long-lasting machines to replace outdated ones. For financing debts lasting 10 to 15 years or more, corporations either issue stock or sell bonds. **Figure 10.5** describes bonds and stocks as

long-term financing: *money borrowed by a business for a period of more than 10 years*

FIGURE 10.5 Long-Term Financing

Bonds

Bonds promise to pay a stated rate of interest over a stated period of time, and to repay the full amount borrowed at the end of that time.

Stocks

Selling stock is called *equity financing,* because part of the ownership, or equity, of the company is being sold. Corporations may sell either preferred or common stock. The differences between these types of stock are explained below.

Common Stock	Preferred Stock
1. Common stock is issued by all public corporations; it is the stock most often bought and sold.	1. Many corporations do not issue preferred stock.
2. Holders of common stock have voting rights in a corporation. As a group, they elect the board of directors.	2. Holders of preferred stock generally have no voting rights.
3. Common stock may pay dividends based on a corporation's performance. If the company does well, dividends may be high; if it does poorly, the dividends may be low or zero.	3. Preferred stock pays a fixed dividend. This amount must be paid before holders of common stock receive any dividends. If a company is unable to pay a fixed dividend on time, it must usually make up the missed payment at a later date.
4. The value of common stock rises and falls in relation to the corporation's performance and what investors expect it to do in the future.	4. The value of preferred stock changes in relation to how well the company is doing.
5. If a corporation fails, holders of common stock are the last to be paid with whatever money is left after paying all creditors.	5. If a corporation fails, holders of preferred stock must be paid before any holders of common stock are paid, but bondholders are paid before any stockholders.

methods of long-term financing. Usually only large corporations finance long-term debt by selling bonds. Unlike smaller companies, large corporations with huge assets appear to be better risks to investors who are interested in buying bonds.

Choosing the Right Financing

Financial managers try to obtain capital at a minimum cost to the company. To do so, they try to choose the best mix of financing. The length of a loan that a company takes out or a corporation's decision regarding whether to sell bonds or issue stock depends on four factors. These factors are the costs of interest, the financial condition of the company, the overall economic climate, and the opinions of the company's owners.

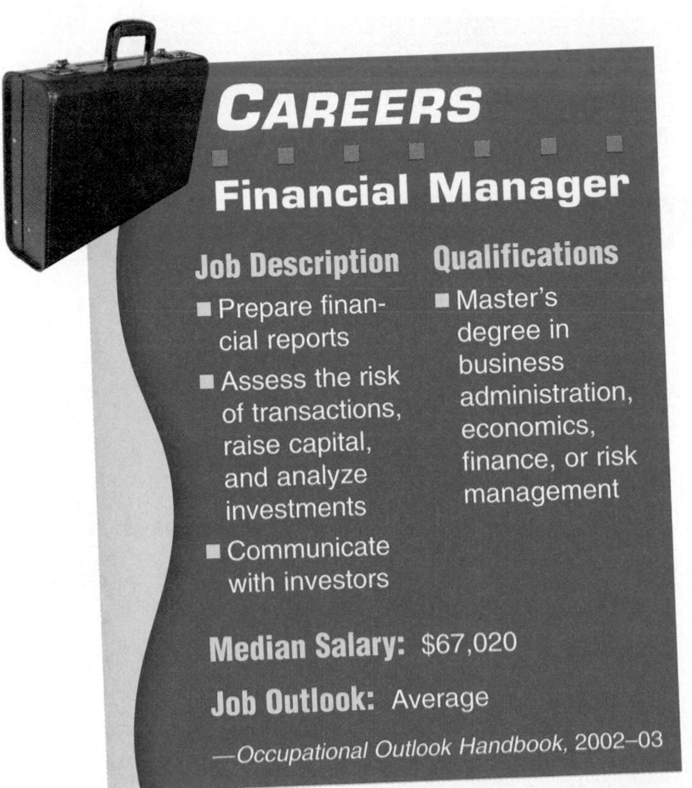

CAREERS
Financial Manager
Job Description
■ Prepare financial reports
■ Assess the risk of transactions, raise capital, and analyze investments
■ Communicate with investors
Qualifications
■ Master's degree in business administration, economics, finance, or risk management
Median Salary: $67,020
Job Outlook: Average
—Occupational Outlook Handbook, 2002–03

Interest Costs When interest rates in general are high, a business may be reluctant to take out a loan. A company may delay its expansion until it can borrow at better interest rates. Or it may take out a series of short-term loans at high rates, hoping that interest rates will drop. When that happens, the company will then take out a long-term loan.

Interest rates also affect the decision to issue bonds. When rates are high, corporations must offer high rates of interest on their bonds to attract investors. When interest rates drop overall, corporations can offer lower rates of return on their bonds.

Financial Condition of the Company A company or corporation whose sales and profits are stable or are expected to increase can safely take on more debt–if its current debt is not too large. Financial managers use cost-benefit analysis to determine if the potential profits will cover the cost of financing expansion.

Market Climate As shown in **Figure 10.6,** financial managers need to be aware of the market climate when determining whether to sell bonds or issue stock to raise financing. If economic growth in the overall market appears to be slow, investors

FIGURE 10.6

Market Climate Business managers must keep an eye on the market climate before obtaining financing. High interest rates combined with a slow economy could spell disaster for a business interested in expanding.

may prefer the fixed rate of return of bonds or preferred stock to the unknown return on common stock.

Control of the Company Bonds do not have voting rights attached to them. Most preferred stocks also do not give voting rights to shareholders. The owners of common stocks, however, do have the right to vote in company elections. When debating issues of financing, financial managers may have to gain approval from the owners of common stocks before taking action.

Practice and **assess** key skills with ***Skillbuilder Interactive Workbook, Level 2.***

SECTION 2 Assessment

Understanding Key Terms

1. **Define** debt financing, short-term financing, intermediate-term financing, long-term financing.

Reviewing Objectives

2. What are three general kinds of debt financing?
3. **Graphic Organizer** Use a diagram like the one in the next column to describe the four factors that affect a company's decision either to obtain financing in the form of loans or to sell bonds or issue stock.

Factors Affecting Loan Choices

Applying Economic Concepts

4. **Economic Institutions** If you were starting a T-shirt business with limited funds, what type of short-term financing would you pursue first? Why?

Critical Thinking Activity

5. **Making Comparisons** Write a paragraph describing the difference between secured and unsecured loans.

People & Perspectives

Thomas Sowell

ECONOMIST (1930–)

- **A Rose and Milton Friedman Senior Fellow, The Hoover Institution, Stanford University**
- **Columnist for *Forbes Magazine* and other periodicals; author of a nationally syndicated newspaper column**
- **Published books include *Conquests and Cultures* (1998), *Migrations and Cultures* (1996), and *Race and Culture: A World View* (1994)**

Economics professor and author Thomas Sowell is an outspoken commentator on political, economic, and social issues. Sowell suggests that many of the country's problems can be addressed by applying basic economic concepts to all aspects of life. In this excerpt, Sowell shows how the failure to apply inventory control or the law of supply and demand has created problems in education:

"When anyone who owns a business discovers that unsold products are piling up on the shelf or in the warehouse, it doesn't take a rocket scientist to figure out that it is time to cut back production until the inventory declines.

But no such logic applies in the academic world.

Complaints about the excess number of Ph.D.s in the humanities have gone on for years. Every year, for 12 consecutive years, American universities have broken all previous records for the number of Ph.D.s awarded. . . . Forget about supply and demand when it comes to academia.

Ironically, doctorates in science, engineering and mathematics have come down somewhat in recent years, even though American companies are recruiting engineers from India, Russia and other places. But in English, history, and other humanities fields, the graduate schools are flooding the market with people for whom there are no jobs."

—excerpted from the *Jewish World Review*, February 18, 1999

Checking for Understanding

1. **According to Sowell, how has a lack of inventory control created the situation where there are too many Ph.D.s?**
2. **Do you think the subjects university students study should be determined by economic concepts? Why or why not?**
3. **If you were in a position of authority on a college campus, how would you resolve the dilemma?**

SECTION 3

The Production Process

Cover Story

The New York Times, April 19, 1999

Each month, a purchasing agent for BOC Gases in Murray Hill, New Jersey, logs on to the Internet and looks for a bargain. In this case, the bargain involves not only the price of the product, but an entire cost-saving process set in motion when the on-screen "order" button is clicked.

Nearly 7,000 miles away from New Jersey, in a Japanese gas processing plant, a BOC supplier receives the million-dollar order. . . . And within minutes, a BOC distribution center in San Diego receives electronic notice from Japan that the shipment is on the way.

Reader's Guide

Terms to Know

- production
- consumer goods
- mechanization
- assembly line
- division of labor
- automation
- robotics

Reading Objectives

1. What are the four major steps in production operations?
2. How has technology changed production methods since the early 1800s?

After businesses obtain the necessary financing, they can begin production. **Production** is the process of changing resources into goods that satisfy the needs and wants of individuals and other businesses. As noted in the *Cover Story* above, production also involves careful planning in getting raw materials from suppliers on time. As you read this section, you'll learn about all the steps in the production process.

production: *process of changing resources into goods that satisfy the needs and wants of individuals and businesses*

Steps in Production Operations

Businesses may produce **consumer goods,** or goods sold directly to individuals to be used as they are. As you learned in Chapter 1, businesses may also produce *capital goods,* which are

consumer goods: *goods produced for individuals and sold directly to the public to be used as they are*

FIGURE 10.7

Business Location Locating a sandwich shop next to a movie theater was a wise business decision. Location is the most important planning decision in starting a retail business.

products used to make other goods. The machines used to assemble automobiles are examples of capital goods.

Besides the actual manufacturing of a good, the production process for both types of goods involves several other operations. These include planning, purchasing, quality control, and inventory control. A fifth operation, product design, will be discussed in Chapter 11.

Planning Planning includes choosing a location for the business and scheduling production. *Where* a business is located, or perhaps even more important today–*how* the business will get its products to consumers–is directly related to how successful the business will be. Among the location factors to consider are nearness to markets, raw materials, labor supply, and transportation facilities.

For example, businesses that cater to young people should locate near teen hangouts, universities, and so on. See **Figure 10.7.** Businesses that use coal should locate near their required raw material–coal fields. Businesses that require many unskilled workers should locate near urban areas with a large supply of labor. Finally, a business needs to have access to a means of delivering its products–highways, railroads, airlines, and pipelines.

Scheduling production operations involves setting start and end times for each step in the production process. It includes checking the use of labor, machinery, and materials so that production moves smoothly.

Purchasing In order to do business, a company obviously needs the raw materials to produce its goods or offer its services. It also, however, must have machinery, office supplies, telephones, and so on. The people who purchase goods for a business have to decide what to buy, from whom, and at what price. See **Figure 10.8.** To get the best

deal for the company, purchasers must find answers to such questions as:

- Is this the best price?
- Are these goods made well? Will they last?
- Does this supplier offer such services as equipment repair?
- Who pays shipping and insurance costs, and how will goods be shipped?
- How much time is there between ordering goods and receiving them?

Quality Control Quality control involves overseeing the grade or freshness of goods, their strength or workability, their construction or design, safety, adherence to federal or industry standards, and many other factors. Quality control systems can be as simple as testing one item per thousand produced or testing each product as it is finished. See **Figure 10.9** on page 280.

Inventory Control Almost all manufacturers and many service businesses, such as dry cleaners, need inventories of the materials they use in making their products or offering their services. A production line can come to a complete halt if inventory runs out. Manufacturers and businesses, such as supermarkets, also keep stockpiles of finished goods on hand for sale.

C Purchasing Shipping and Delivery Services

FIGURE 10.8

Purchasing Decisions Before purchasing goods and services from a supplier, a company must consider the price and quality of those goods as well as services, shipping, and delivery.

A Purchasing Inventory

B Purchasing Supplier Services

Inventories are costly, however. There is an opportunity cost involved in maintaining inventory. The more inventory a business has, the less capital it has for other activities. For example, it costs money to warehouse and insure goods against fire and theft. Some goods such as film and medicines spoil if kept beyond a certain period of time. Other goods such as cars and stylish clothes become obsolete, or out of date, in time.

mechanization: *combined labor of people and machines*

assembly line: *production system in which the good being produced moves on a conveyor belt past workers who perform individual tasks in assembling it*

division of labor: *breaking down of a job into small tasks performed by different workers*

automation: *production process in which machines do the work and people oversee them*

Technology and Production

Technology is the use of science to develop new products and new methods for producing and distributing goods and services. From the time of the Industrial Revolution in the late 1700s, technology has changed the methods of production.

Mechanization The Industrial Revolution—the beginning of the factory system—came about through **mechanization,** which combines the labor of people and large power-driven machines. With the introduction of spinning and weaving machines in factories, entrepreneurs replaced skilled handiwork with machines run by unskilled workers. The rate of output per labor hour greatly increased as a result.

Quality Control Trade-Off The more time spent on quality control—such as this person inspecting vacuum cleaners—the higher the production costs.

The Assembly Line An outgrowth of mechanization was the **assembly line.** An assembly line is a production system in which the good being produced moves on a conveyor belt past workers who perform individual tasks in assembling it. The Ford Motor Company developed the modern assembly-line process early in the twentieth century. Because the assembly line results in more efficient use of machines and labor, the costs of production drop.

Division of Labor Assembly-line production is only possible with interchangeable parts made in standard sizes, and with the **division of labor,** or the breaking down of a job into small tasks. A different worker performs each task.

Automation Mechanization combines the labor of people and machines. In **automation,** machines do the work and people oversee them. Automation is so common in American society that most of us don't even think about the efficiency of automated traffic signals, doors, or teller machines anymore.

Economic Connection to... Technology

No More Waiting?

In computer science terminology, a "bot" (short for "robot") is a software program that can scan E-mail messages to locate key words and phrases and respond appropriately without any human input. Companies that do business on the Internet use "bots" for all types of customer-service tasks—everything from tracking orders to offering troubleshooting tips. Many computer engineers believe that "bots" soon will be handling all routine customer questions. Waiting 20 minutes or longer on the telephone for a human customer-service representative may soon be a thing of the past! ■

Robotics ***Robotics*** refers to sophisticated, computer-controlled machinery that operates the assembly line. In some industries, robotics regulate every step of the manufacturing process—from the selection of raw materials to processing, packaging, and inventory control.

robotics: *sophisticated, computer-controlled machinery that operates an assembly line*

Practice and **assess** key skills with ***Skillbuilder Interactive Workbook, Level 2.***

SECTION 3 Assessment

Understanding Key Terms

1. **Define** production, consumer goods, mechanization, assembly line, division of labor, automation, robotics.

Reviewing Objectives

2. What are the most important steps in the production process?
3. **Graphic Organizer** Use a diagram like the one below to explain the factors that have changed production since the early 1800s.

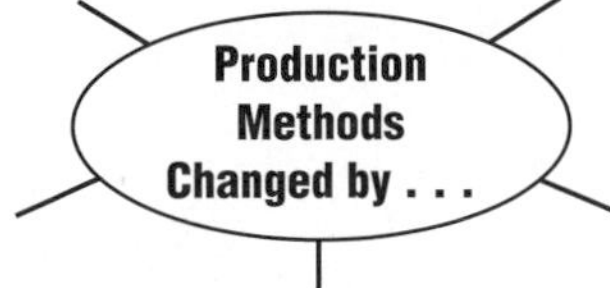

Applying Economic Concepts

4. **Productivity** Imagine that you are financially prepared to open a small ice-cream cafe. Explain the steps you would follow to begin production. Include information about your planning, purchasing, quality control, and inventory control decisions in your explanation.

Critical Thinking Activity

5. **Categorizing Information** Make a spreadsheet listing the five advances in technology discussed in this section. For one week, be aware of and count examples of each type of technology. At the end of each day, input your totals in the appropriate column of your spreadsheet. Tabulate your totals at the end of the week. Share your spreadsheet with the rest of the class.

BusinessWeek

SPOTLIGHT ON THE ECONOMY

Going All Out to Pick Up a Gig

Check It Out! In this chapter you learned that businesses must make wise decisions when selecting a supplier to ship raw materials as well as finished goods. In this article, read to learn how the Fender guitar company made a very wise decision when it selected a shipping agent.

Who says service is dead? When a big outfit like United Parcel Service is willing to hire a bunch of Dutch rockers to tune a client's guitars, you know that some companies still will do anything to keep a customer happy.

UPS Worldwide Logistics began shipping famed Fender guitars to Europe in April. As happens with stringed instruments, sometimes they arrived out of tune. Previously, the pricey guitars had been sent to 20 European distributors who tuned and tested them. But that was too costly and slow. So, to please Fender, UPS has hired four rock guitarists at its warehouse in [the city of] Roermond, the Netherlands, to do the job. "We've checked disk drives for IBM, but this was a unique challenge," says UPS project manager Ronald Klingeler.

The challenge, however, was met. In May, when the rock group Kiss played a Saturday night concert in Hamburg, it requested a new guitar on Friday—and got one, on time and in tune. Fender says the system will cut costs by 9% and delivery time from months to weeks. But life with a corporate-funded garage band is hard on some UPS guys. Says Klingeler: "When they see a really nice guitar, they always have this urge to try it out and play a song."

Think About It

1. **What did the supplier (UPS) do to help the client (Fender)?**
2. **By using UPS, how much in production costs is Fender saving?**
3. **How was Fender's delivery time improved?**

CHAPTER 10 Summary

Chapter Overview Visit the *Economics Today and Tomorrow* Web site at ett.glencoe.com and click on ***Chapter 10—Chapter Overviews*** to review chapter information.

SECTION 1 Investing in the Free Enterprise System

- **Financing** business operations and growth is an integral part of our free enterprise system. It all begins with people who save by depositing their funds in a financial institution.
- Financial institutions, in turn, make these deposits available to businesses to finance growth and expansion.
- Businesses usually perform a **cost-benefit analysis** before deciding whether to pursue financing for expansion.
- A cost-benefit analysis involves estimating costs, calculating expected **revenues,** calculating expected **profits,** and calculating the costs of borrowing.

SECTION 2 Types of Financing for Business Operations

- Raising money for a business through borrowing, or **debt financing,** can be divided into three categories based on length of time of repayment.
- **Short-term financing** is for those businesses that need funds to cover monthly or seasonal budget highs and lows.
- Borrowing money for 1 to 10 years to buy more land, buildings, or equipment is considered **intermediate-term financing.**
- **Long-term financing,** such as issuing stock and selling bonds, is used for major business expansion.
- Financial managers must examine interest costs, the market climate, and the financial condition of the company, as well as inform holders of common stock before obtaining financing.

SECTION 3 The Production Process

- **Production** is the process of changing resources into goods that satisfy the needs and wants of individuals and other businesses.
- Producing **consumer goods** and capital goods involves planning, purchasing, quality control, and inventory control.
- Planning includes choosing a location for the business and scheduling production.
- The people who purchase goods for a business have to decide what to buy, from whom, and at what price.
- Five major advances in technology—**mechanization,** the **assembly line,** the **division of labor, automation,** and **robotics**—have drastically affected the methods and costs of production.

CHAPTER 10

Assessment and Activities

Self-Check Quiz Visit the *Economics Today and Tomorrow* Web site at ett.glencoe.com and click on ***Chapter 10—Self-Check Quizzes*** to prepare for the Chapter Test.

Identifying Key Terms

Write the letter of the definition in Column B that correctly defines each term in Column A.

Column A

1. revenues
2. consumer goods
3. cost-benefit analysis
4. debt financing
5. profits
6. short-term financing
7. intermediate-term financing
8. assembly line
9. mechanization

Column B

a. the money earned after subtracting costs from revenues
b. raising money for a business through borrowing
c. trade credit and promissory notes are involved in this kind of financing
d. combining labor of people and machines
e. process that looks at actions and their benefits
f. total income from sales of output
g. enables workers to perform individual tasks more efficiently
h. sold directly to the public to be used as they are
i. leasing is typical in this kind of financing

Recalling Facts and Ideas

Section 1

1. How do individuals turn savings into investments?
2. Outline the steps you would use in reaching a necessary financial decision.

Section 2

3. What are two reasons a business may need short-term financing?
4. Issuing stocks is a form of what type of financing?
5. Do holders of common stock have any rights in a corporation? Explain.

Section 3

6. Besides quality control, what other steps are involved in the production process?
7. What does assembly-line production require?

Thinking Critically

1. **Categorizing Information** Use a diagram like the one below to describe how a saver can be both a creditor and a debtor.

2. **Synthesizing Information** Assume that you have to buy new inventory that you plan to sell off completely by the end of each month. Determine the most appropriate type of financing to use to buy this inventory.

Applying Economic Concepts

Making Financing Decisions Imagine that you own a business. List at least five business expansions you would like to make to your company that would require financing. Explain after each type of business expansion, such as buying 10 desktop computers, what the appropriate type of financing might be. Explain your choices.

Cooperative Learning Project

Organize into three groups, with each group working on one of the following topics. After the research is complete, each group will report its findings to the class.

A. **Division of Labor** The most famous example of the division of labor focuses on a pin factory, which Adam Smith discussed in his book *The Wealth of Nations*. Group A should do the following: (1) find the passage in the book about the pin factory; (2) develop a chart showing the elements of Adam Smith's arithmetic example; and (3) calculate the percentage increase in productivity due to the division of labor.

B. **Assembly-Line Techniques** This group can divide into two smaller groups. Group B1 will report on how Henry Ford developed the assembly-line process. Group B2 will look at what Eli Whitney developed with the use of interchangeable parts.

C. **Robotics** Group C will research how robotics developed and how much of American manufacturing uses robotics.

Reviewing Skills

Making Generalizations Read the following excerpt, then make a generalization based on the reading.

"Henry Ford introduced the first moving assembly line in 1913 at his Model T plant in Highland Park, Michigan. Different conveyor systems carried subcomponents to the main assembly line in a finely orchestrated manner. Before the advent of the assembly line, a Model T took more than 12 hours to produce and cost $950. By 1927, after numerous refinements, Model Ts were being turned out in less than half that time, with a price tag of $290 apiece."

—*Business Week: 100 Years of Innovation*, Summer 1999

Technology Activity

Using the Internet The Small Business Administration (SBA) was designed to help small businesses with short-term financing. Obtain information about the SBA on the Internet. Write an informative brochure for potential small business owners, describing how the SBA can help them get started.

Analyzing the Global Economy

Engineers at the University of Pennsylvania unveiled the Electronic Numerical Integrator and Computer (ENIAC) for the U.S. government in 1946 to enable artillery men to aim their guns more accurately. ENIAC was made up of 30 separate units, weighed 30 tons, occupied 1,800 square feet, had 17,468 vacuum tubes, and could do nearly 400 multiplications per second. ENIAC, however, was not the first electronic computer. Research the earlier computers built in Britain and Germany.

Global *Economy*

Worldwide Advertising Each year the United States spends over $450 billion on advertising. The map below shows advertising expenditures for five countries whose economies are at different levels of development.

Russia

Category	Spending ($millions)
Television	718.4
Radio	123.0
Print*	1,130.5
Outdoor**	58.7
Point of Purchase	374.6
Promotions***	2,773.0
Direct Mail	314.5
Other	4,117.0
Total	*$96.1 billion*
% of World Total	*10.1%*

Egypt

Category	Spending ($millions)
Television	119.7
Radio	4.8
Print*	188.4
Outdoor**	9.8
Point of Purchase	46.8
Promotions***	727.9
Direct Mail	30.3
Other	128.4
Total	*$12.6 billion*
% of World Total	*1.3%*

Kenya

Category	Spending ($millions)
Television	15.2
Radio	0.2
Print*	24.0
Outdoor**	1.2
Point of Purchase	2.0
Promotions***	88.7
Direct Mail	5.5
Other	11.5
Total	*$1.5 billion*
% of World Total	*0.16%*

Vietnam

Category	Spending ($millions)
Television	15.5
Radio	0.8
Print*	24.4
Outdoor**	1.3
Point of Purchase	0.8
Promotions***	79.7
Direct Mail	7.2
Other	10.2
Total	*$1.4 billion*
% of World Total	*0.15%*

Singapore

Category	Spending ($millions)
Television	129.7
Radio	67.0
Print*	204.2
Outdoor**	10.6
Point of Purchase	261.6
Promotions***	535.7
Direct Mail	66.3
Other	244.6
Total	*$15.2 billion*
% of World Total	*1.6%*

*newspapers and magazines
**billboards, etc.
***coupons, give-aways, etc.

Thinking Globally

1. What is the largest category of advertising for each country?

2. Which of the expenditures for specific countries surprised you the most? Explain your answer.

CHAPTER 11

Marketing and Distribution

Why It's Important

Do you think advertisements influence your buying habits? Marketers hope so—they spend billions of dollars every year toward this purpose! This chapter will explain how businesses market and distribute their goods and services.

IMPROVED

BRIGHT

To learn more about how products are marketed, view the **Economics & You** *Chapter 17 video lesson:* **Marketing and Distribution**

ECONOMICS Online

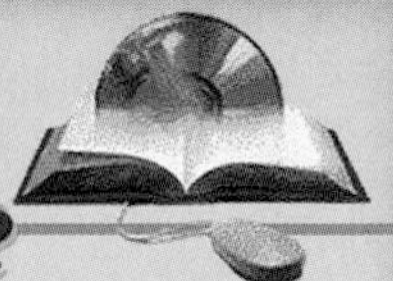

Chapter Overview Visit the *Economics Today and Tomorrow* Web site at ett.glencoe.com and click on ***Chapter 11—Chapter Overviews*** to preview chapter information.

SECTION 1

The Changing Role of Marketing

10 Reasons why you need the fast-acting

Cover Story

Business Week, June 7, 1999

Too much marketing today focuses on awareness rather than reasons to buy. In the old days, awareness advertising was more effective. There was less competition. All you had to worry about was whether or not people remembered your product. As technology and more kinds of media have come about, it's no longer enough to be remembered. The consumer has too many choices. Your marketing has to send the message that you are relevant. You need to be sending reasons to buy.

Reader's Guide

Terms to Know

- marketing
- consumer sovereignty
- utility
- market research
- market survey
- test-marketing

Reading Objectives

1. How has the role of marketing changed in the United States?
2. What elements make up market research?

In addition to financing and producing products, which you learned about in Chapter 10, businesses must promote and eventually sell their products and services. **Marketing** involves all of the activities needed to move goods and services from the producer to the consumer. As you read this section, you'll learn that these activities include market research, advertising and promotion, and distribution.

marketing: *all the activities needed to move goods and services from the producer to the consumer*

The Development of Marketing

Some economists estimate that about 50 percent of the price people pay for an item today is for the cost of marketing. The idea and importance of marketing in the United States have changed considerably since 1900. The development of marketing can be traced by analyzing what it has focused on: production, sales, advertising, and **consumer sovereignty**—or consumer as ruler. **Figure 11.1** takes you on a historical "tour" of marketing.

consumer sovereignty: *the role of the consumer as ruler of the market when determining the types of goods and services produced*

Meeting Consumer Utility Today, marketing's sole purpose is to convince consumers that a certain product will add to their utility. **Utility** is the ability of any good or service to satisfy consumer wants. Utility can be divided into four major types: form utility, place utility, time utility, and ownership utility.

utility: *the amount of satisfaction one gets from a good or service*

Form utility, created by production, is the conversion of raw materials to finished goods. Examples include transforming cotton cloth into draperies or refining crude oil into gasoline.

Place utility is created by having a good or service available where a consumer wants to buy it. Locating a gas station on a busy corner is an example of this type of utility.

FIGURE 11.1 Stages of Marketing

A The Early 1900s

Producers of consumer goods and services take advantage of new technologies to increase production. Finding that their amount of production exceeds their markets, firms begin using "announcement advertising" to introduce their goods to potential buyers statewide and even nationally. Consumers, no longer having to rely on local producers, become aware of greater choices and respond to the advertising. Less efficient local firms, or those with inferior products, wither and leave the market.

The 1920s and 1930s

Rising incomes and the increased wealth of the nation lead consumers to redefine their notions of necessities and luxuries. Greater numbers of consumers can choose among goods and services available. Producers begin to advertise in a manner extolling the virtues of their product compared to the competition. Consumers respond by favoring those companies that present themselves as having the product that best fits their needs. Firms that cannot adequately explain the benefits of their products fail.

Time utility is created by having a good or service available when a consumer wants to buy it. As shown in **Figure 11.2** on page 292, a 24-hour grocery store or all-night restaurant are examples of time utility. Catalog selling is another example of both time and place utility.

Ownership utility is the satisfaction one receives from simply owning the good or service. One might purchase a fine art painting for an exorbitant price to have the satisfaction of owning the object. Luxury cars, expensive jewelry, and lawn ornaments also provide ownership utility.

Market Research

Finding out what consumers want can be difficult. It is crucial that businesses do so, however, because many markets today are national or even global. An increase in sales of a few percentage points can result in millions of dollars in profits. Therefore,

---

C ▶ The 1950s

During the 1950s, firms began the process of creating demand. They did this by changing their advertising to convince consumers that a specific firm's product, not just a similar product, was a necessity if the consumer was to achieve a desired lifestyle. It was hoped that consumers would view the firm's particular product—whether it was laundry detergent, facial tissue, or breakfast cereal—as an important part of the American way of life.

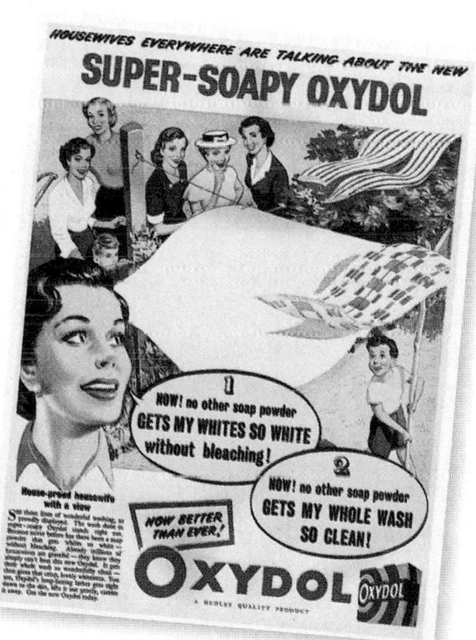

▲ E The 1990s to the Present

The emergence of the Internet allows even the smallest of firms to advertise inexpensively. Large firms producing for the masses face competition from small businesses that can produce goods and services for small groups or even individuals.

◀ D The Late 1950s to the 1980s

Large national firms find stiff competition from businesses that can imitate their products. Firms begin to research consumer tastes before production in order to be able to specifically satisfy their wants. Advertising focuses on an attempt to have the consumer identify with the person in the advertisement, rather than with the specific product being presented. The recognition that the consumer is ruler of the market—consumer sovereignty—returns. Firms ask consumers what they want and, in effect, fill the specific order much as the local blacksmith had done in the late 1800s.

FIGURE 11.2

Time Utility Businesses that are open around the clock satisfy consumers who want to be flexible in their shopping hours—also known as time utility. ***What other types of utility does marketing address?***

before a product is produced or a service is offered, businesses research their market. *Market* in this sense means the people who are potential buyers of the good or service.

Through **market research** a company gathers, records, and analyzes data about the types of goods and services that people want. From automakers to producers of frozen foods, most companies producing consumer goods invest heavily in market research. As shown in **Figure 11.3,** this cost is passed on to consumers.

market research: *gathering, recording, and analyzing data about the types of goods and services that people want*

When Should Market Research Be Done?

Market research may be done at several stages of product development. It can be done at the very beginning when the first ideas about a new product are being developed. It can be conducted again to test sample products and alternative packaging designs.

FIGURE 11.3

Cost of Marketing As Shoe has found out in the cartoon below, the cost of marketing—or "world tour"—has significantly increased the price of a cup of coffee.

SHOE

Early market research has several purposes. It helps producers determine whether there is a market for their good or service and what that market is. It can also indicate any changes in quality, features, or design that should be made before a product is offered for sale.

To investigate initial consumer response, market research is often done immediately after a product is released for sale. Some companies even test their advertising to make sure it is attracting the market segment for which the product was designed. Market researchers can also gather information about a product that has been on the market for a while. They then attempt to discover what should be done to maintain or increase sales.

Market Surveys The first step in market research is performing a **market survey,** in which researchers gather information about who might be possible users of the product. Such characteristics as age, gender, income, education, and location urban, suburban, rural–are important to a producer in deciding which market a product should target.

market survey: *information gathered by researchers about possible users of a product based on such characteristics as age, gender, income, education, and location*

A market survey typically involves a series of carefully worded questions. The questions may be administered in the form of a written questionnaire, which is mailed to consumers. Manufacturers of such small appliances as hair dryers and microwave ovens often put a questionnaire on the back of the warranty card that purchasers are to return. Another way to survey the market is by conducting individual interviews or querying focus groups. See **Figure 11.4.**

test-marketing: *offering a product for sale in a small area for a limited period of time to see how well it sells before offering it nationally*

Testing New Products As a final step before offering a product for national distribution, market researchers will often test-market a product such as a detergent or a toothpaste. **Test-marketing** means offering a product for sale in a small area, perhaps several cities, for two months to two years to see how well it sells before offering it nationally.

FIGURE 11.4

Focus Groups Members of a focus group may test and discuss what they like and dislike about similar, and often competing, products. Generally, the people chosen to be part of the focus group do not know which company has hired them to test the products. The focus group is often observed through a one-way mirror by the marketers of one of the products.

CAREERS

Market Research Analyst

Job Description

- Analyze data on past sales to predict future sales
- Design market surveys
- Analyze competitors' prices and methods of marketing

Qualifications

- Graduate degree in economics, business administration, marketing, or statistics
- Strong background in mathematics and consumer behavior

Median Base Salary: $51,190

Job Outlook: Very good

—Occupational Outlook Handbook, 2002–03

For example, before attempting to market a new granola cereal, a company might sell it in several selected areas where the product is most likely to attract the market segment that the company is seeking.

Researchers keep track of the units sold and test different prices and ad campaigns within the test markets. If the product is successful, the company will offer it nationally. If sales are disappointing, the company has two choices. It can make changes based on the data collected in the test market. Or, rather than spend more funds redesigning the product, the company can abandon the idea.

Of all the new products introduced every year in the United States, most are not profitable and do not survive in the marketplace. It is the constant lure of owning a high-profit item, however, that motivates companies to continue developing new products.

Practice and **assess** key skills with ***Skillbuilder Interactive Workbook, Level 2.***

SECTION 1 Assessment

Understanding Key Terms

1. **Define** marketing, consumer sovereignty, utility, market research, market survey, test-marketing.

Reviewing Objectives

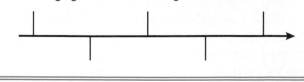

2. **Graphic Organizer** Use a diagram like the one below to make a time line tracing the changing focus of marketing in the United States.
3. What steps are involved in market research?

Applying Economic Concepts

4. **Market Surveys** Imagine that you have the task of finding the market to buy a new health-food energy bar. What are five questions you would ask consumers in a market survey?

Critical Thinking Activity

5. **Categorizing Information** Select 10 businesses in your community. Categorize each business according to the type of utility it provides.

SPOTLIGHT ON THE ECONOMY

Generation Y

Check It Out! In this chapter, you learned how important it is for advertisers to know their market. In this article, read to learn how advertisers are marketing their products toward *your* generation.

Today's teens may force marketers to toss their old tricks. Born during a baby bulge that demographers locate between 1979 and 1994, they are as young as 5 and as old as 20. And at 60 million strong, they're the biggest thing to hit the American scene since the 72 million baby boomers. They go by a host of taglines: Generation Y, Echo Boomers, or Millennium Generation.

Indeed, though the echo boom rivals its parents' generation in size, in almost every other way it is very different. This generation is more racially diverse: One in three is not Caucasian. One in four lives in a single-parent household. Three in four have working mothers.

"Most marketers perceive them as kids. When you do that, you fail to take in what they are telling you about the consumers they're becoming," said J. Walker Smith, who specializes in generational marketing. "This is not about teenage marketing. It's about the coming of age of a generation."

Smith and others believe that behind the shift in Gen Y labels lies a shift in values on the part of Gen Y consumers. The marketers that capture Gen Y's attention do so by bringing their messages to the places these kids congregate, whether it's the Internet, a snowboarding tournament, or cable TV. The ads may be funny or disarmingly direct. What they don't do is suggest that the advertiser knows Gen Y better than these savvy consumers know themselves.

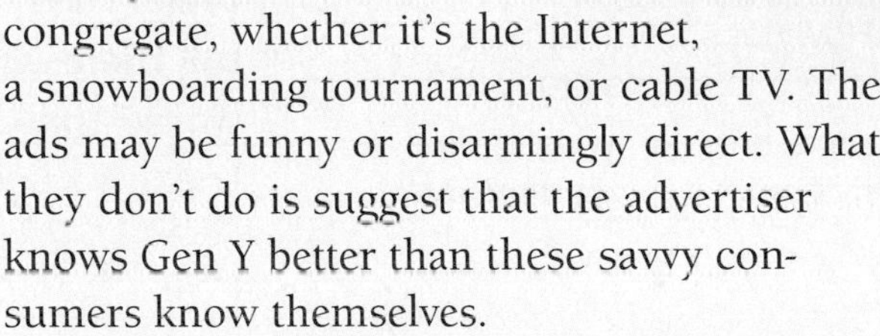

Instead, Gen Yers respond to humor, irony, and the (apparently) unvarnished truth. . . .

Marketers who don't bother to learn the interests and obsessions of Gen Y are apt to run up against a brick wall of distrust and cynicism.

–Reprinted from February 15, 1999 issue of *Business Week* by special permission, copyright © 1999 by The McGraw-Hill Companies, Inc.

Think About It

1. **What market does "Generation Y" make up?**
2. **According to the article, how can advertisers reach Gen Yers?**

SECTION 2

The Marketing Mix

Reader's Guide

Terms to Know

- price leadership
- penetration pricing
- promotion
- direct-mail advertising
- product life cycle

Reading Objectives

1. What is the importance of product identification?
2. Which market strategies depend on price?
3. How does a firm decide where to sell its products?
4. What are four types of promotion that a firm may use?

Cover Story

The Washington Post, February 1, 1999

"Tommy Hilfiger has created a marketing phenomenon by speaking the language of teens," says the company's vice president of worldwide marketing. "Tommy Hilfiger's employees comb the streets, campuses, and nightclubs to see what teenagers are wearing. What teens really dislike is having someone older tell them what to wear. There's nothing worse than a bunch of 35- to 40-year-olds trying to figure out what teenagers want."

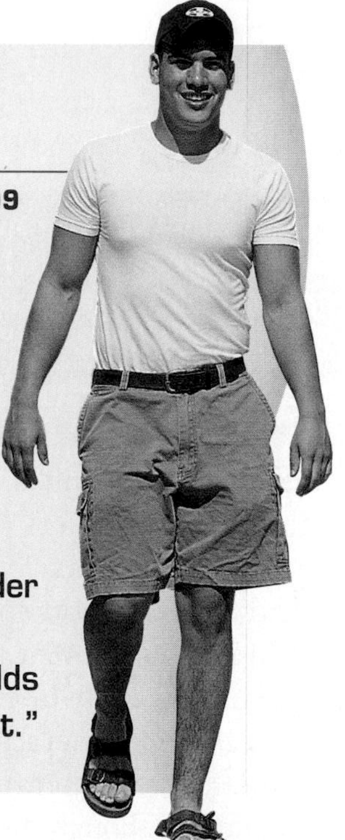

In today's highly competitive world, simply producing a product and offering it for sale is not enough. Through their marketing departments, companies plan a marketing strategy, which details how the company will sell the product effectively. As you read this section, you'll learn that a marketing strategy, or plan, combines the "four Ps" of marketing: product, price, place, and promotion. Decisions about each are based on the data collected through the company's market research. See **Figure 11.5.**

Product

Market research helps determine *what* good or service to produce. It also helps a company determine what services to offer with the product, how to package it, and what kind of product identification to use.

Additional services that accompany a product often help make a sale. Warranties are customary with many manufactured products, but some manufacturers offer special services free or for a small charge. For example, if you buy a camera, you may be able to purchase from the manufacturer a 2-year extended warranty in addition to the 1-year warranty given by the store in which you bought the camera. Automakers used to offer 1-year or 12,000-mile warranties on new cars. Today a 3-year or 36,000-mile warranty is a common offer.

Packaging is also an important factor in selling a product. The "right" packaging combines size, design, and color to attract potential consumers. Compact discs, books, and food are especially dependent on packaging. Such words as *New and Improved* or *Economy Size* are used to attract customers. For economy-minded shoppers, manufacturers add cents-off coupons and rebate offers to their packages.

FIGURE 11.5

The Four Ps of Marketing

A Product
From the Pillsbury Dough Boy to the familiar Cheerios logo, all of these items are good examples of packaging that achieves product identification.

D Promotion
Product promotion includes the use of advertising to inform customers about a new or improved product. It also dictates where and how a product is physically displayed.

C Place
A marketing department must decide where its company's product should be sold—whether in a specialty store, on the Internet, or through a catalog.

B Price
Although the laws of supply and demand will ultimately determine the price at which a product sells, a new product often will be priced low to attract customers away from better-known products.

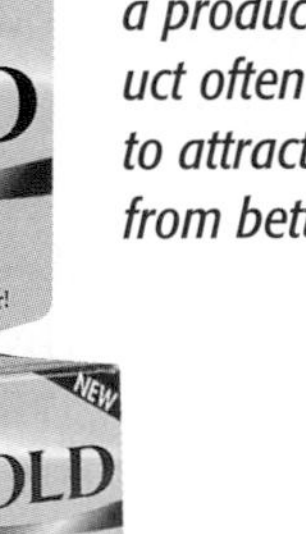

Economic Connection to...

Advertising-to-Sales Ratio

Companies measure the effectiveness of their advertising through the advertising-to-sales ratio. This number is calculated by dividing the dollar amount spent on advertising by the dollar amount of sales generated by that advertising. For example, if a $1 million advertising campaign generated $4 million in sales, the advertising-to-sales ratio would be 0.25.

Companies also use the ratio to see which type of advertising—direct mail, television, the Internet, and so on—is most effective. Below are recent advertising-to-sales ratios for the types of advertising most used by businesses. Smaller numbers indicate a greater return on each advertising dollar.

Newspapers	.087
Direct Mail	.096
Magazines	.120
Internet	.143
Radio	.172
Television	.204 ■

Coupons are used to persuade consumers to make a repeat purchase and develop the habit of buying the product.

Once a product is offered for sale, *product identification* becomes important. Product identification is meant to attract consumers to look at, buy, and remember a particular product. It can involve the use of a logo or certain colors on a package. It can also involve a song or jingle, a certain type of packaging, or anything that can be associated with and identify the product.

Price

Supply and demand ultimately determine the price of a good or service. Because of the laws of supply and demand, the price at which a product sells may help determine whether it is successful in attracting buyers while still being profitable to its maker. In setting a price, a company has to consider the costs of producing, advertising, selling, and distributing the product, as well as the amount of profit it hopes to make.

price leadership: *practice of setting prices close to those charged by other companies selling similar products*

penetration pricing: *selling a new product at a low price to attract customers away from an established product*

Often companies sell similar goods at similar prices. This practice is known as **price leadership.** For example, one major airline may lower its prices, which causes all of the other major airlines to follow by lowering their fares.

Selling a new product at a low price is another marketing strategy called **penetration pricing.** The low price is meant to attract customers away from an established product.

Place

Where the product should be sold is another decision of the marketing department. Should it be sold through the mail, by telephone, in department stores, in specialty shops, in supermarkets, in discount stores, door-to-door, or on the Internet? Usually the answer is obvious because of past experience with similar products. A cereal company, for example, would most likely market a new cereal in supermarkets. Another company might decide that its goods would appeal to a limited market. Therefore, it may choose to sell its goods only in specialty shops and on the Internet.

Promotion

promotion: *use of advertising to inform consumers that a new or improved product or service is available and to persuade them to purchase it*

Promotion is the use of advertising and other methods to inform consumers that a new or improved product or service is available and to convince them to purchase it. See **Figure 11.6.** Businesses spend billions of dollars each year to advertise through direct-mail pieces and in newspapers, magazines, radio, and television. Increasingly, businesses are also advertising on the World Wide Web.

direct-mail advertising: *type of promotion using a mailer that usually includes a letter describing the product or service and an order blank or application form*

Types of Promotion The particular type of promotion that a producer uses depends on three factors: (1) the product, (2) the type of consumer that the company wants to attract, and (3) the amount of money the company plans to spend. Magazines and catalogs, credit card companies, and insurance companies often use **direct-mail advertising.** The mailer usually includes a letter describing the product or service and an order blank.

Other promotional efforts include free samples, cents-off coupons, gifts, and rebates. Where and how a product is displayed

FIGURE 11.6

Promotion Product promotion is done in many ways, including having celebrities endorse the product's fine features, as Hawthorne is doing in the cartoon below. ***What are other types of promotion?***

SHERMAN'S LAGOON

are important to promotion as well. For example, magazines are often placed next to checkout lines where people wait.

ECONOMICS Online

Student Web Activity Visit the *Economics Today and Tomorrow* Web site at ett.glencoe.com and click on ***Chapter 11—Student Web Activities*** to see how Web marketing has become serious business.

Product Life Cycle

Most products go through what is known as a **product life cycle.** This cycle is a series of stages from first introduction to complete withdrawal from the market. The four stages of a typical product life cycle include introduction, growth, maturity, and decline.

product life cycle: *series of stages that a product goes through from first introduction to complete withdrawal from the market*

People involved in marketing products need to understand the stages of each product's life cycle because marketing programs are different for each stage. A product in its introductory stage has to be explained and promoted much differently than one in its maturity stage. Also, pricing can vary depending on the stage. Prices of products tend to be relatively high during the growth stage.

Many marketers attempt to extend the life of old products. They may redesign the packaging or find new uses for the product. Advertisements attempt to persuade consumers that they need the product for its new uses.

Practice and **assess** key skills with ***Skillbuilder Interactive Workbook, Level 2.***

SECTION 2 Assessment

Understanding Key Terms

1. **Define** price leadership, penetration pricing, promotion, direct-mail advertising, product life cycle.

Reviewing Objectives

2. How does packaging contribute to product identification?
3. What two marketing strategies depend on price?
4. How does a firm decide where to sell its products?
5. **Graphic Organizer** Use a diagram like the one in the next column to explain four ways a firm may promote a product.

Applying Economic Concepts

6. **Marketing Strategy** Design an advertisement for a new cereal box. Keep in mind that packaging and product identification are two of the most important factors in selling a product.

Critical Thinking Activity

7. **Distinguishing Fact From Opinion** Analyze the validity of 10 print advertisements in newspapers or magazines. Identify the facts and bias found in each one.

People & Perspectives

- **President and chief executive officer of eBay Inc., an Internet auction house**
- **Ranked as the richest woman CEO in the world**
- **Voted one of the top 25 "Women on the Web" by a leading women's Internet association**

Margaret Whitman

ENTREPRENEUR (1957–)

Margaret "Meg" Whitman has served as the chief executive officer of eBay, the Internet auction house, since March 1998. She is one of the new breed of Internet CEOs whose background is in marketing rather than computer technology. Whitman explains eBay's marketing strategy:

"We started with commerce, and what grew out of that was a community. So we think of ourselves as a sort of community-commerce model. And what we've basically done is put in place a venue where people can be successful dealing and communicating with one another. But we also want to expand the kinds of merchandise sold on eBay. . . .

[W]e . . . want to get into the kind of merchandise that is not necessarily shippable because it's not economic to ship or you want to see it before you buy it–cars, boats, RVs, things like that. We're also looking at the kind of merchants who sell on eBay. In the beginning, this was strictly about individuals doing business with one another. What happened is that some of those individuals actually became small dealers. . . . Now, we have a lot of merchants who keep their storefronts but in fact their most profitable distribution channel is eBay.

We are looking at storefronts as something to think about. Now, all our selling on eBay is in an auction format. And the question is: Are there other formats both our buyers and sellers would want? There are people who don't necessarily like to buy in an auction, and there are sellers who want to sell some of their goods in an auction and some in a storefront . . ."

Checking for Understanding

1. **Whitman refers to a community-commerce model. Why do you think she uses this characterization?**
2. **What changes in marketing strategy does Whitman foresee for eBay?**

SECTION 3

Distribution Channels

READER'S GUIDE

Terms to Know

- channels of distribution
- wholesalers
- retailers
- e-commerce

Reading Objectives

1. What is the difference between wholesale and retail distribution?
2. What are two new types of distribution channels?

COVER STORY

BUSINESS WEEK, FEBRUARY 15, 1999

A rose is a rose is a rose, wrote Gertrude Stein. But don't tell that to flower sellers who are trying to differentiate themselves from their fellow petal-pushers.

To stand out in a crowd, U.S.A. Floral Products, the nation's biggest flower distributor, is test-marketing a plan to sell flowers sporting a tag telling consumers the last date the flowers can be sold for maximum freshness—the equivalent of a "sell by" date on a quart of milk.

Decisions about distribution, or moving goods from where they are produced to the people who will buy them, is another function of marketing. As you read this section, you'll learn about **channels of distribution,** or the routes by which goods are moved. **Figure 11.7** shows the various distribution channels for different types of goods.

<u>channels of distribution:</u> *routes by which goods are moved from producers to consumers*

Wholesalers and Retailers

Some consumer goods, such as clothing and farm products, are usually sold by a producer to a wholesaler and then to a retailer, who sells them to consumers. Other consumer goods, such as automobiles, are normally sold by the producer directly to a retailer and then to consumers. With each transaction, or

FIGURE 11.7 Channels of Distribution

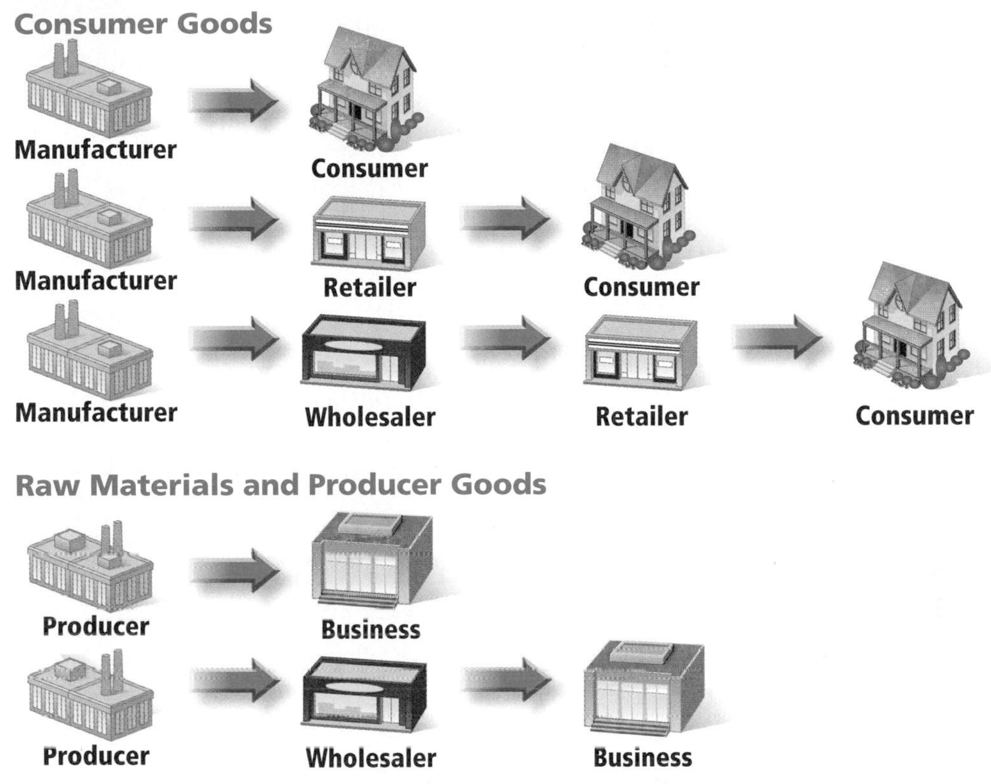

business deal, the price increases. Few goods go directly from producer to consumer; an example of this would be vegetables sold at a farmer's roadside stand. See **Figure 11.8** on page 304.

Wholesalers Businesses that purchase large quantities of goods from producers for resale to other businesses (not to consumers) are called **wholesalers.** Various types of wholesalers exist. Some may buy goods from manufacturers and sell them to retail stores that then deal directly with consumers. Others may also buy and sell raw materials or capital goods to manufacturers.

wholesalers: *businesses that purchase large quantities of goods from producers for resale to other businesses*

Retailers Businesses that sell consumer goods directly to the public are **retailers.** You are probably familiar with many of them: department stores, discount stores, supermarkets, mail-order houses, specialty stores such as bookshops, and so on.

Traditional retailers have also "set up shop" on the World Wide Web. More and more, there are **e-commerce** retailers that have no physical store anywhere. They are "virtual companies." You'll read more about e-commerce in Chapter 22.

retailers: *businesses that sell consumer goods directly to the public*

e-commerce: *business transactions conducted over computer networks, in particular the World Wide Web*

Storage and Transportation

Part of the distribution process includes storing goods for future sales. The producer, wholesaler, or retailer may perform this function. Most retailers keep some inventory on hand for immediate sales. Many have a two- to three-month supply, depending on the type of merchandise.

Transportation involves the physical movement of goods from producers and/or sellers to buyers. In deciding the method of transportation, businesspeople must consider the type of good, such as perishable food. The size and weight of the good are also important. Airfreighting tons of wheat is impractical, but airfreighting small machine parts is not. Speed may be necessary to fulfill a sale or to get fresh fruit to a food plant. The cost of the different types of transportation helps determine how to ship items.

Distribution Channels

In the last 15 to 20 years, distribution channels have expanded rapidly due to the growth of club warehouse stores and direct marketing.

Club Warehouse Stores A typical club warehouse store requires a membership fee—about $35 a year for individuals and more for businesses. Individual club members usually have to be part of a larger group such as a teacher's union or a credit union.

FIGURE 11.8

Wholesalers Versus Retailers Wholesalers add value to the product by providing time utility and place utility. The consumer benefits from wholesaler networks, but also ends up paying for these services in the final price of the product. In contrast, a local farmer may act as both "manufacturer" and retailer, and prices may be lower. The trade-off is that consumers usually must go out of their way to purchase the product.

The club warehouse formula is to buy a limited number of models and brands of each product in such huge quantities that the warehouse gets very favorable prices from the manufacturers. Some of the biggest club warehouses are Costco and Sam's Club (a division of Wal-Mart).

Direct Marketing Direct marketing is done mainly through catalogs and over the Internet. Advertising called "space ads" in newspapers and magazines is also direct marketing. Catalog shopping has become a popular distribution channel to avoid state sales taxes. The purchaser normally does not pay sales tax if the catalog company is located in another state. The same holds true for goods purchased through the Internet, although this may change in the future.

Shopping on the Internet has become increasingly popular because of the ease with which it can be done. Anybody with access to the Internet and a valid credit card can order just about anything on the Web.

Kmart Shoppers

On any given weekend day, 15,000 people come to Guam's hottest spot—Kmart. Reported to be the world's biggest and perhaps busiest Kmart store, its opening drove down prices of everything from shampoo to Cheerios to stereo sets with its famous discounts.

Little shops on this small island always were able to charge high amounts, jacking up prices to cover high shipping costs into the middle of the Pacific Ocean. Shoppers are now grateful for 89-cent cans of Campbell's soup. They must, however, plan their day around getting in and out of the store. It is so big that customers take cell phones so they don't lose their companions in the aisles. ■

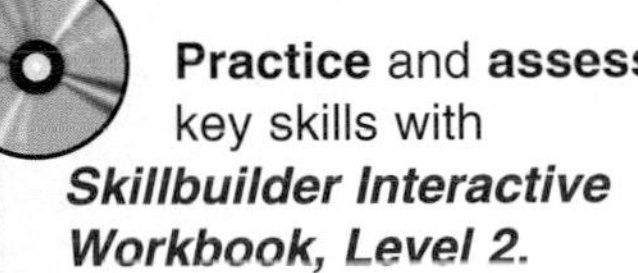

Practice and **assess** key skills with ***Skillbuilder Interactive Workbook, Level 2.***

SECTION 3 Assessment

Understanding Key Terms

1. **Define** channels of distribution, wholesalers, retailers, e-commerce.

Reviewing Objectives

2. What is the difference between wholesalers and retailers?
3. **Graphic Organizer** Create a diagram like the one below to list and describe four distribution channels for merchandise.

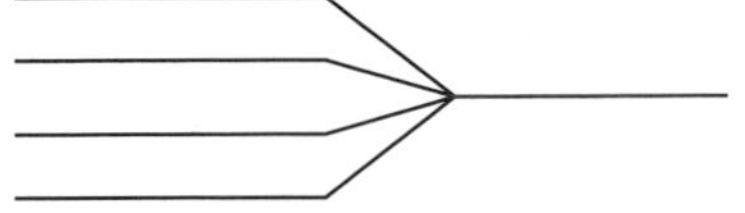

Applying Economic Concepts

4. **The Role of Government** Research the debate of taxing versus not taxing goods purchased through catalog orders and those purchased on the Internet. What issues are involved, and how many sales tax dollars are estimated to be lost?

Critical Thinking Activity

5. **Summarizing Information** Type *e-commerce* into your search engine. Research and write a paragraph on the advantages or disadvantages of this type of retailing.

Technology Skills

Developing Multimedia Presentations

Your economics teacher has assigned a presentation about the history of commercials and advertising. You want to develop a presentation that really holds your classmates' attention.

- Which forms of media do I want to include? Video? Sound? Animation? Photographs? Graphics?
- Which kinds of media equipment are available at my school or local library?
- What types of media can I create to enhance my presentation?
- Which of the media forms does my computer support?

Learning the Skill

A multimedia presentation involves using several types of media, including photographs, videos, or sound recordings. The equipment can range from simple cassette players, to overhead projectors, to VCRs, to computers, and beyond.

Multimedia, as it relates to computer technology, is the combination of text, video, audio, and animation in an interactive computer program. You need certain tools to create multimedia presentations on a computer, including computer graphics tools and draw programs, animation programs, and authoring systems that tie everything together. Your computer manual will tell you which tools your computer can support.

Practicing the Skill

Plan and create a multimedia presentation on a topic found in the chapter, such as product promotion. List three or four major ideas you would like to cover. Then think about how multimedia resources could enhance your presentation. Use the questions listed on the left as a guide when planning your presentation.

Application Activity

Choose an economist from the twentieth century and create a multimedia presentation analyzing the importance of his or her theories. Share your presentation with the class.

Various equipment that can be used in multimedia presentations

CHAPTER 11 Summary

Chapter Overview Visit the *Economics Today and Tomorrow* Web site at ett.glencoe.com and click on ***Chapter 11—Chapter Overviews*** to review chapter information.

SECTION 1 The Changing Role of Marketing

- **Marketing** involves all of the activities needed to move goods and services from the producer to the consumer.
- In today's economy, marketing's sole purpose is to convince consumers that a certain product or service will add to their **utility.**
- Utility—the ability of any good or service to satisfy consumer wants—can be divided into four major types: form utility, place utility, time utility, and ownership utility.
- Through **market research** a company gathers, records, and analyzes data about the types of goods and services that people want.
- The first step in market research is performing a **market survey.**
- Before offering a product for national distribution, market researchers will often **test-market** a product.

SECTION 2 The Marketing Mix

- A marketing plan combines the "four Ps" of marketing: product, price, place, and promotion.
- "Product" means determining what services to offer with the product, how to package it, and what kind of product identification to use.
- In setting a price, a company has to consider the costs of producing, advertising, selling, and distributing, as well as the amount of profit it hopes to make.
- "Place" means determining where a product should be sold.
- **Promotion** is the use of advertising and other methods to inform consumers that a new product is currently available and to convince them to buy it.

SECTION 3 Distribution Channels

- Deciding what **channels of distribution** to use is another function of marketing.
- Businesses that purchase large quantities of goods from producers for resale to other businesses are called **wholesalers.**
- Businesses that sell consumer goods directly to the public are **retailers.**
- In the last 10 to 15 years, distribution channels have expanded due to the growth of club warehouse stores and direct marketing, including catalog shopping and **e-commerce.**

CHAPTER 11

Assessment and Activities

Self-Check Quiz Visit the *Economics Today and Tomorrow* Web site at ett.glencoe.com and click on ***Chapter 11—Self-Check Quizzes*** to prepare for the Chapter Test.

Identifying Key Terms

Write the letter of the definition in Column B that correctly defines each term in Column A.

Column A

1. test-marketing
2. penetration pricing
3. price leadership
4. retailer
5. promotion

Column B

a. use of advertising to inform consumers about a product and to persuade them to purchase it
b. business that sells goods directly to the consumer
c. selling a new product at a low price to attract new customers away from an established product
d. offering a product in a small area for a limited time to see how well it sells
e. setting prices close to those of competing companies

Recalling Facts and Ideas

Section 1

1. What is the relationship between marketing and utility?
2. What are the historic stages in the development of marketing in the United States?
3. How is market research conducted?

Section 2

4. List and describe the "four Ps" of planning a marketing strategy.
5. How are goods and services promoted?
6. What does *place* mean, when referring to marketing?
7. What are the last two stages of a typical product life cycle?

Section 3

8. What are distribution channels?
9. How does a club warehouse store differ from a standard retail outlet?
10. Who may perform the storage function of distribution?
11. What are the factors that a business must consider in choosing a method of transporting goods?

Thinking Critically

1. **Sequencing Information** Suppose you must do a market survey for a new type of running shoe. Use a chart like the one in the next column to list the questions you would ask, and whom and where you would ask the questions.

Questions	Whom?	Where?

2. **Making Generalizations** What are alternative ways to extend the life of an old product that is in its declining stage?

Applying Economic Concepts

The Rising Opportunity Cost of Time When individuals earn higher incomes, by definition the opportunity cost of their time increases. Economic theory says that they will react in a predictable way—reducing the amount of time they spend shopping. Make a list of the various methods that people can use to reduce the time they spend when they shop for (1) presents for various holidays, Mother's Day, birthdays, etc., (2) food, and (3) photographic and stereo equipment.

Cooperative Learning Project

Organize into six groups, with each group choosing a particular product from the following categories of consumer goods: home electronics, food, clothing, electric humidifiers, automobiles, computers.

After each group has chosen one product or brand within one of the above categories, research the following:

- product packaging
- pricing strategies
- the place where the product is sold
- how the product is promoted
- the product life cycle.

Each group should write a summary of the research results, preferably in graphic form. When the results of each group are completed, compare and contrast the differences in the five categories across the various products.

Reviewing Skills

Developing a Multimedia Presentation Working with a partner, create an advertisement that you think will successfully market a new product. Use multimedia to develop a video commercial, then show the commercial to the rest of the class. Based on your advertising, would they buy the product? Why or why not? (See page 311 for more information on types of advertising appeals.)

Technology Activity

Using E-Mail The club warehouse phenomenon has been around the United States since the 1970s. E-mail 10 friends and relatives to survey their use of club warehouse stores. What percentage patronizes this type of store? What are their reasons for doing so? Did you receive any negative E-mails about warehouse stores (forcing small retailers out of business, for example)? Assemble your responses and summarize them in a paragraph.

Analyzing the Global *Economy*

Contact the foreign language teachers in your school to see if they have any advertising materials (print or video) showing commercials from other countries. (Many cable television channels carry foreign stations, too.) Even without translating the language spoken or written, can you understand the purpose of the advertisement? Write several paragraphs describing how marketing in other countries does or does not achieve the same goals as marketing in the United States.

Economics Lab

Analyzing and Creating Advertisements

From the classroom of Stephanie Felix, Glendora High School, Glendora, California

In Chapter 11 you learned about marketing and distribution. A function of marketing is product promotion–convincing consumers to buy the product. In this lab, you will examine many advertising techniques used by companies. Then you will develop and market your own product by creating a commercial demonstrating various types of advertising techniques.

STEP A Tools Needed

- ✔ paper
- ✔ poster board and markers
- ✔ video camera (optional)
- ✔ props for your commercial

STEP B Procedures to Follow

1. Working in groups of no more than four people, come up with an idea for a product. As a group, submit a one-page typed paper describing your product and answering these questions:
   - What does it do?
   - What is the price?
   - Who is your target market?
   - How are you going to promote your product?
2. On poster board, design the packaging of your product. Include the product's name and any special logos or phrases for product identification.
3. Next, analyze the chart listing **Advertising Techniques** on page 311. Select at least three techniques to incorporate into a commercial about your product.
4. Create a commercial at least 2 minutes long. All members of your group must be included in the commercial.
5. Perform your commercial for the class, or videotape it and bring it to class for viewing.

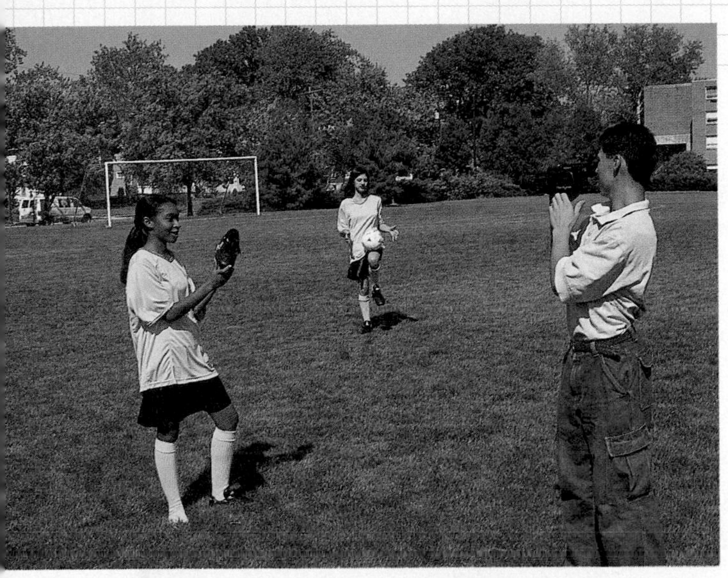

STEP C Creating an Economic Model

Analyze all groups' commercials. Identify and count the types of advertising techniques used in each. As a class, draw a series of bar graphs showing the number of times each technique was used.

Advertising Techniques

ADVERTISING TECHNIQUE	DESCRIPTION
Youthful/Fun	"Use our product and you'll feel like a kid again!"
Plain/Humble	"Our product will make you feel natural and simplify your life."
Expert Testimony	"I'm a doctor, and I recommend this product."
Famous Person	[If Michael Jordan uses the product, it must be cool.]
Fear	"If you don't use this, you may regret it."
Statistics	"Nine out of ten dentists use this product."
Everyone Has One	"Molly the doctor drives this car, and Joe the student does, too."
Senses	[Mouth-watering pizza, steaming hot cocoa, sizzling burgers]
Snob	"It may be more expensive, but aren't you worth it?"
Happy Family	"This diaper makes Susie happy, and if she's happy, I'm happy."
Humor	[When you're shopping, you may remember laughing and buy the product.]
New and Improved	"Obviously, we made the product better just for you!"
Symbol	[Majestic bald eagle, solid Rock of Gibraltar, proud American flag]
Overexposure	[News clips, fast speed, quick shots]
Healthy	"This product is *good* for you."
Attractiveness	"This product will make you attractive."

STEP D Lab Report Analysis

After studying each group's commercial, answer the questions below.

1. Which type of advertising technique was used most often?
2. What technique(s) do you think is the most subtle? The most obvious?
3. Which techniques, if any, carry the most validity? Explain your answer.

CHAPTER 12

The American Labor Force

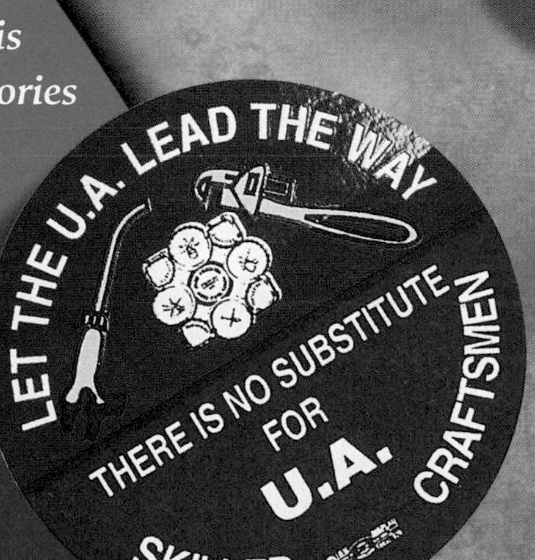

Why It's Important

Do you have a part-time job? Who determines how much you get paid? How can you earn more? This chapter will explain the major categories of the labor force and the factors that affect wages.

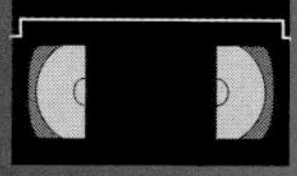

To learn more about workers in the United States, view the **Economics & You** *Chapter 14 video lesson:* **The American Labor Force**

Chapter Overview Visit the *Economics Today and Tomorrow* Web site at ett.glencoe.com and click on ***Chapter 12—Chapter Overviews*** to preview chapter information.

SECTION 1

Americans at Work

Cover Story

The Columbus Dispatch, March 17, 1999

Baseball player, president, and cowboy—great jobs, right? Wrong. Try Web site manager, computer systems analyst, and software engineer.

Low stress, short workweeks, and room for advancement put those professions near the top of the list in *Jobs Rated Almanac,* a book ranking 250 of the best and worst jobs in the country.

Nine of the top 10 jobs were in computer or math-related fields. Physical labor fared worst in the rankings, with oil field "roustabouts," lumberjacks, and fishermen taking the final three spots on the list.

Reader's Guide

Terms to Know

- civilian labor force
- blue-collar workers
- white-collar workers
- service workers
- unskilled workers
- semiskilled workers
- skilled workers
- professionals
- minimum wage law

Reading Objectives

1. How are workers categorized according to skill level and training?
2. How do skill, type of job, and location affect supply and demand in the labor market?

Everyone–from a factory worker to the president of a corporation–belongs to the productive resource known as labor. As you read this section, you'll learn how workers are categorized, how wages are determined, and why employers need to pay more to get (and keep) good workers.

The Civilian Labor Force

When discussing labor, economists use the term *labor force* in a specific way. The **civilian labor force** is the total number of people 16 years old or older who are either employed or actively

civilian labor force: *total number of people 16 years old or older who are either employed or actively seeking work*

FIGURE 12.1

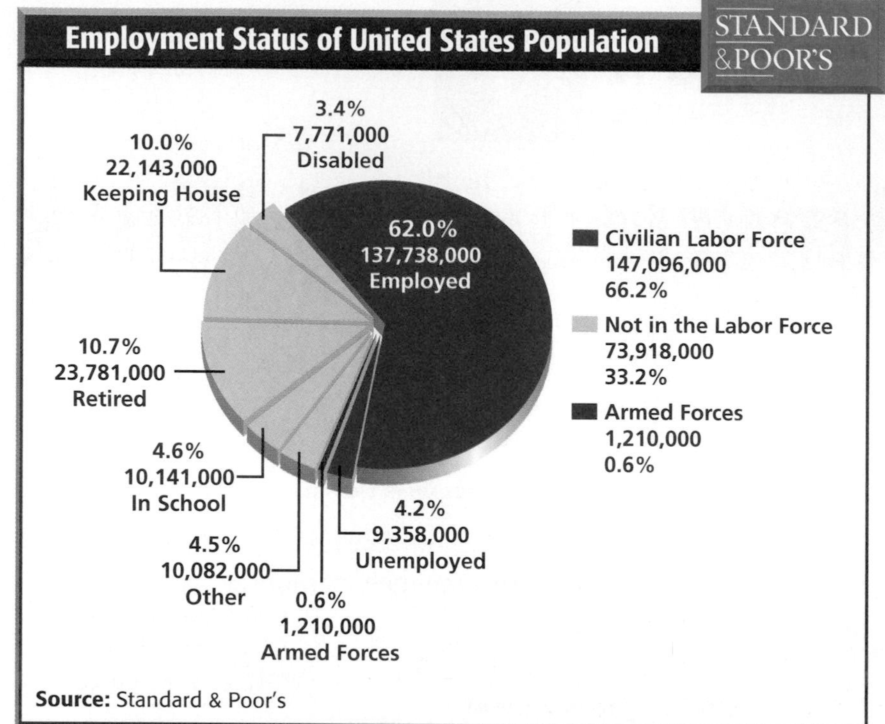

Total Workforce 16 Years and Older The number of people age 16 and older who are not in the labor force is not the same number as the nation's unemployment rate. ***Why?***

For an online update of this graph, visit ett.glencoe.com and click on ***Textbook Updates—Chapter 12.***

seeking work. Individuals not able to work, such as disabled people or those in prisons or mental institutions, are not included in the civilian labor force. People in the armed forces or those not looking for a paying job, such as full-time students and homemakers, are excluded as well. **Figure 12.1** shows the civilian labor force in comparison to the total working-age population.

Categories of Workers

Workers in the United States are categorized in several ways. One way is to group them according to the type of work they perform. Another way is by the level of training or education their jobs require.

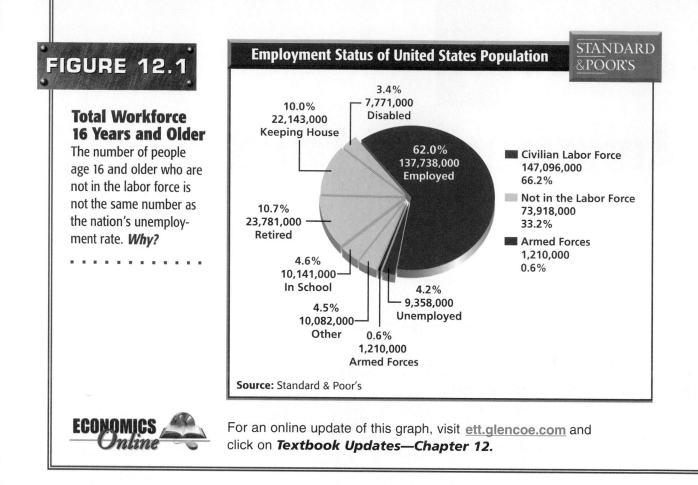

Blue-Collar, White-Collar, and Service Workers During the late 1800s and early 1900s, many farmworkers moved to cities. This migration occurred in part because the increased use of farm machinery required fewer agricultural workers. Higher wages paid to workers in the growing industries of urban areas also lured farmworkers there. Displaced farmers, and others who entered the workforce because of higher wages, often became **blue-collar workers**—craft workers, workers in manufacturing, and nonfarm laborers.

The largest sector of the labor force is **white-collar workers.** Office workers, salespeople, and highly trained individuals such as physicians and engineers are classified as white-collar workers. This sector experienced steady growth throughout the twentieth century.

In recent years, a shift away from farm work and blue-collar jobs to the service sector of the economy has occurred. **Service workers** are those who provide services directly to individuals. Cooks, piano tuners, health-care aides, and barbers are all service workers. See **Figure 12.2.**

blue-collar workers: *category of workers employed in crafts, manufacturing, and nonfarm labor*

white-collar workers: *category of workers employed in offices, sales, or professional positions*

service workers: *people who provide services directly to individuals*

Worker Categories by Type of Job Economists sometimes classify workers by their type of occupation, regardless of the skills necessary to perform the job.

A *White-collar workers include office workers, salespeople, and highly trained individuals such as engineers.*

B *Blue-collar workers include craft workers, workers in manufacturing, and nonfarm laborers.*

C *Service workers provide services—haircuts, food service, child care, and so on—directly to individuals.*

unskilled workers: *people whose jobs require no specialized training*

semiskilled workers: *people whose jobs require some training, often using modern technology*

skilled workers: *people who have learned a trade or craft either through a vocational school or as an apprentice to an experienced worker*

professionals: *highly educated individuals with college degrees and usually additional education or training*

Jobs Categorized by Skill Level Another way to categorize workers is by the skills required to perform their occupation. **Unskilled workers** are those whose jobs require no specialized training. Jobs such as waiting on tables and custodial work are considered unskilled, although obviously these types of work require skills such as patience and the ability to pace oneself or to work according to a schedule. Such jobs may also demand the ability to work well with people.

Semiskilled workers are those whose jobs require some training, often using modern technology. The job of nurse's aide, for example, is considered a semiskilled occupation.

Someone who has learned a trade or craft, either through a vocational school or as an apprentice to an experienced worker, is considered a **skilled worker.** Police officers and masons hold skilled occupations.

Professionals are those with college degrees and usually additional education or training. Also classified as white-collar workers, people who hold professional jobs include teachers, architects, and accountants. As shown in **Figure 12.3,** workers may move from one skill level to another as they gain training and experience.

Worker Categories by Skill

This woman moved from a semiskilled position–lumberjack–to a skilled position–manager of the lumberyard.

Supply and Demand in the Labor Market

The labor market, like other markets, is affected by supply and demand. Suppliers are the workers who offer their services, while the demand comes from employers who require workers.

Supply and Demand Factors That Affect Wages Three major factors affect how supply and demand determine prices, or in this case wages, in the labor market. These factors include skill, type of job, and location.

The first factor, *skill,* is the ability a person brings to a job. It may come from talent, initiative, education and/or training, or experience. Because the demand for highly talented individuals is usually high, whereas the supply of such employees is often scarce, a shortage occurs. As you remember from Chapter 7, a shortage usually results in high prices–or high wages. A highly educated brain surgeon and a talented major league home-run hitter, for example, both are paid large sums of money because their skills are in high demand relative to supply.

A worker's initiative also plays a large role in determining wages. Overall, a worker's wages will reflect the value of the

Economic Connection to... *Literature*

Shakespeare as Business Guru?

If you want to succeed in business, study the masters: Warren Buffett. Lee Iacocca. Bill Gates. And William Shakespeare.

Shakespeare's plays deal with people in positions of power and responsibility. A workshop at Shakespeare's Globe Theater teaches business leaders to read Shakespeare's works for wisdom that can be applied in the work world.

To weather acts of betrayal, you might turn to *Julius Caesar*. Newly promoted leaders can find parallels with Shakespeare's *Henry V*, who struggles to gain respect in his new role as king. Consider *Hamlet* when you're facing indecision and action. And *Macbeth* teaches how to avoid becoming obsessed with power for its own sake. ■

—*The Columbus Dispatch,* May 27, 1999

product that the worker produces. The worker's productivity will be the major factor in determining his or her success. An employee whose value is easily and generally recognized cannot be underpaid for long by a firm, because another firm will soon entice that worker away with a higher salary.

The *type of job* also affects the amount an employer is willing to pay and a potential employee is willing to accept. Jobs that are unpleasant or dangerous, such as coal mining, often pay higher wages compared to other jobs requiring equal levels of skill. Again, the demand for workers is high, but the supply of laborers willing to do the work may be low.

In contrast, some jobs are enjoyable or prestigious or desirable enough that people are willing to take them even at low wages. Many people take lower-paying jobs in industries such as filmmaking and publishing for these reasons. In these cases, the demand for workers is low, whereas the supply of individuals waiting for prestigious positions is high.

The *location* of both jobs and workers is the third factor in determining wages. If workers are relatively scarce in an area, companies may have to pay high wages to attract workers to move there. Alaska, for example, has the highest wages per person in the country. In contrast, a company in a highly populated area often can hire people

Student Web Activity Visit the *Economics Today and Tomorrow* Web site at ett.glencoe.com and click on ***Chapter 12—Student Web Activities*** to see how the Internet can help you find a job.

at relatively low wages. Even professionals in such a location may not receive high wages. See **Figure 12.4.**

Restrictions on Wages If the labor market were perfectly competitive, the changing supply and demand for labor would result in constantly shifting wage rates. The labor market, however, is not perfectly competitive. For one reason, the flow of information about

FIGURE 12.4

Supply and Demand Factors Affecting Wages

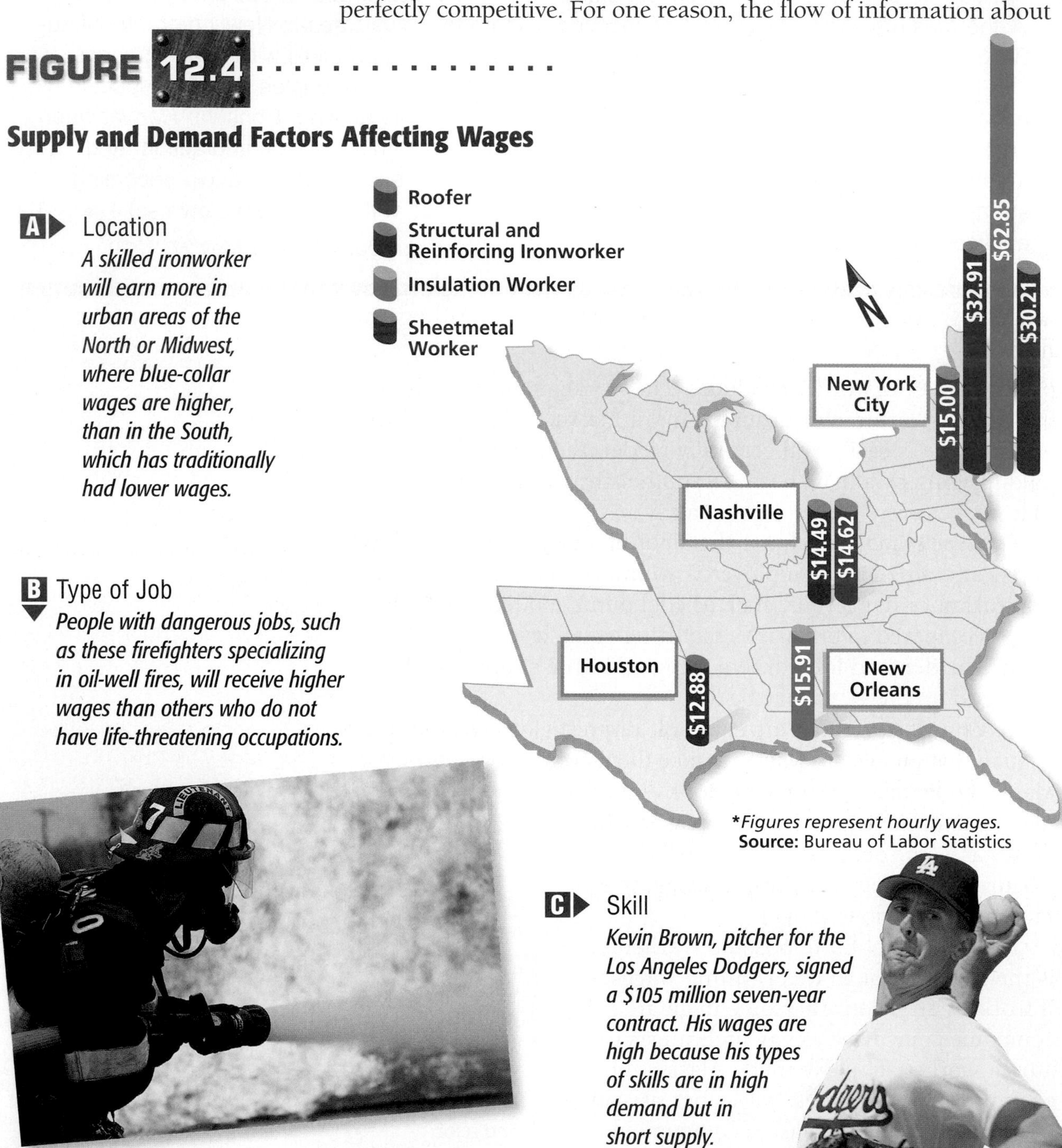

A Location

A skilled ironworker will earn more in urban areas of the North or Midwest, where blue-collar wages are higher, than in the South, which has traditionally had lower wages.

B Type of Job

People with dangerous jobs, such as these firefighters specializing in oil-well fires, will receive higher wages than others who do not have life-threatening occupations.

**Figures represent hourly wages.*
Source: Bureau of Labor Statistics

C Skill

Kevin Brown, pitcher for the Los Angeles Dodgers, signed a $105 million seven-year contract. His wages are high because his types of skills are in high demand but in short supply.

jobs is imperfect. Workers cannot know exactly what all other employers will pay for their services. Employers, for their part, do not know what all workers are willing to accept. Economists call this lack of information a *market failure.*

Two other factors restrict supply and demand in terms of their influence on wages. One is the federal **minimum wage law,** which sets the lowest legal hourly wage rate that may be paid to certain types of workers. Although the purpose of the minimum wage is to help workers, some studies have shown that the opposite often occurs. An increase in the minimum wage causes some firms to hire fewer low-skilled workers. This can delay the acquisition of job skills by teenagers and minorities and reduce their subsequent attractiveness in the labor force.

minimum wage law: *federal law that sets the lowest legal hourly wage rate that may be paid to certain types of workers*

Another factor that restricts the influence of supply and demand on wages is the process of wage negotiations between organized labor (unions) and management. Supply and demand have less influence on wage negotiations than do such things as the company's ability to pay higher wages, the length of the negotiated contract, and seniority—length of time on the job. You'll learn more about organized labor in Sections 2 and 3.

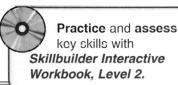

Practice and **assess** key skills with ***Skillbuilder Interactive Workbook, Level 2.***

SECTION 1 Assessment

Understanding Key Terms

1. **Define** civilian labor force, blue-collar workers, white-collar workers, service workers, unskilled workers, semiskilled workers, skilled workers, professionals, minimum wage law.

Reviewing Objectives

2. What are four categories of workers as determined by skill level and education?
3. **Graphic Organizer** Create a diagram like the one below to describe how skill, type of job, and location affect supply and demand in the labor market.

Applying Economic Concepts

4. **The Civilian Labor Force** Are you technically a member of the civilian labor force? Explain why you are or are not considered part of this group.

Critical Thinking Activity

5. **Understanding Cause and Effect** Draw two line graphs showing (1) how the labor supply would change in a highly remote location if very high wages were offered to prospective employees, and (2) how the demand for labor would change in a firm that just invested in robotics. *For help in using line graphs, see page xv in the Economic Handbook.*

BusinessWeek

Spotlight on the Economy

Pink Slips with a Silver Lining

Check It Out! In Section 1, you learned how supply and demand affect wages. In this article, read to learn how one company's laid-off workers are offered an alternative when their positions are in short supply.

If layoffs can have happy endings, this may be one case: Cisco Systems (CSCO), which dismissed 6,000 full-time workers in April, got creative about its severance package–and decided to help charity. The San Jose (Calif.) company is allowing the pink-slipped who agree to work for a local nonprofit organization for a year, to collect one-third of their salaries, plus benefits and stock options–and be first in line for rehire once the economy recovers.

Nonprofits, of course, are delighted. "It's going to allow us to move ahead faster on technology projects," says Dave Sandretto, director of the food bank for Santa Clara and San Mateo counties. He's interviewing Cisco candidates for five accounting and computer-related positions.

OPTIONS EXTENSION. So far, 150 ex-Ciscoans are participating. The company is also offering workers nine months longer than usual to exercise their (currently underwater) stock options.

Carol Cone, who runs Boston-based strategic marketing firm Cone Inc., says Cisco is wisely maintaining ties to its talent pool while helping tech-challenged nonprofits: "It's really a fascinating and very visionary approach to a layoff." Hear that, Human Resources?

Think About It

1. **According to the article, how can nonprofit organizations benefit from the help of former Cisco employees?**
2. **Why do you think Cisco came up with this program? How does the company benefit from it?**

SECTION 2

Organized Labor

COVER STORY

1884 GOVERNMENT REPORT DESCRIBING WORKING CONDITIONS FOR WOMEN IN A SMALL FACTORY, BOSTON

The work is dangerous . . . [and they] are liable to get their fingers jammed under the bench, or caught in the die when it comes down to press the parts of the buttons together. A man (although not a surgeon) is provided to dress wounds three times for each individual without charge; afterwards, the person injured must pay all expenses. There are 35 machines in use, and accidents are of very frequent occurrence.

READER'S GUIDE

Terms to Know

- labor union
- strike
- craft union
- industrial union
- local union
- closed shop
- union shop
- agency shop
- right-to-work laws

Reading Objectives

1. What obstacles did labor unions face when they began to organize in the 1800s?
2. How do closed shops, union shops, and agency shops differ?

To have some control over the wages they receive as well as over other working conditions, many American workers formed labor unions. A **labor union** is an association of workers organized to improve wages and working conditions for its members. As you read this section, you'll learn that unions are based on the idea that workers as a group will have more influence on management than will individual workers acting alone. (In discussing labor-management relations, the term *management* refers to those in charge of a company—the executives and managers.)

labor union: *association of workers organized to improve wages and working conditions for its members*

FIGURE 12.5 **Labor's Early Struggle for Recognition** The major weapon for workers to use against management was the strike. More often than not, however, striking unions were viewed as dangerous by the public, who turned against them.

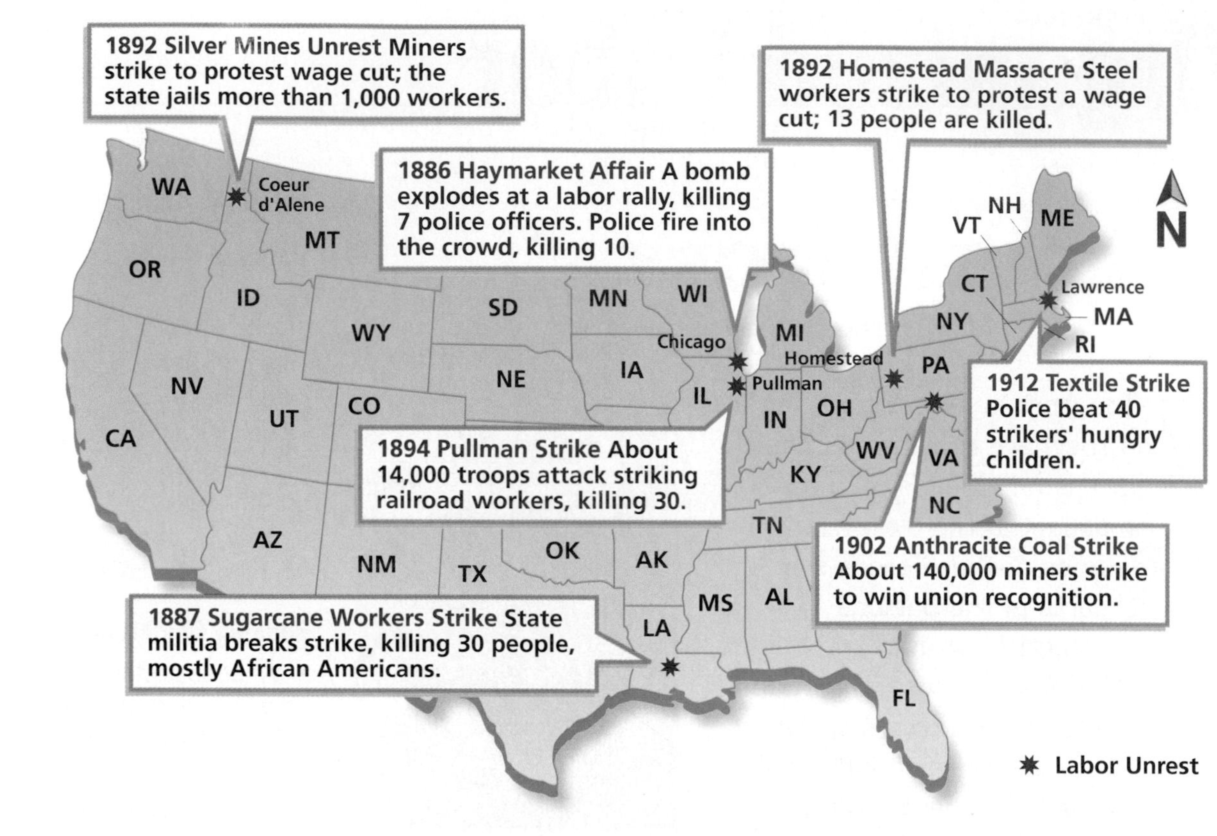

1892 Silver Mines Unrest Miners strike to protest wage cut; the state jails more than 1,000 workers.
1892 Homestead Massacre Steel workers strike to protest a wage cut; 13 people are killed.
1886 Haymarket Affair A bomb explodes at a labor rally, killing 7 police officers. Police fire into the crowd, killing 10.
1894 Pullman Strike About 14,000 troops attack striking railroad workers, killing 30.
1912 Textile Strike Police beat 40 strikers' hungry children.
1902 Anthracite Coal Strike About 140,000 miners strike to win union recognition.
1887 Sugarcane Workers Strike State militia breaks strike, killing 30 people, mostly African Americans.
WA
Coeur d'Alene
MT
OR
ID
WY
SD
MN
WI
MI
NV
UT
CO
NE
IA
Chicago
Homestead
Pullman
IL
IN
OH
PA
NY
VT
NH
ME
CT
Lawrence
MA
RI
CA
AZ
NM
TX
OK
AK
KY
WV
VA
NC
TN
MS
AL
LA
FL
N
Labor Unrest

Development of Labor Unions

Working conditions in the 1800s were very different from those of today. Buildings were often poorly lighted and ventilated, and the machinery was sometimes dangerous to operate. The workweek was long, and wages were low. No unemployment insurance helped those who were out of work until they found new jobs. Health-care benefits, sick leave, and paid vacations and holidays did not exist.

Workers began to form unions to force employers to improve wages and working conditions, shorten the workday, and end child labor. Unionism, however, met with strong resistance. In the 1800s, state legislatures—influenced by business interests—passed laws against unions, and courts upheld them.

Many businesses refused to hire union members or deal with unions. Workers who were found trying to organize unions were fired and blacklisted–kept from being employed. **Strikes,** or deliberate work stoppages by workers to force an employer to give in to their demands, often resulted in violence between strikers and police, as described in **Figure 12.5.** Not until the mid-1930s did Congress begin to pass laws to regulate labor-management relations. Several of these laws are explained in **Figure 12.6.**

strike: *deliberate work stoppage by workers to force an employer to give in to their demands*

The American Labor Movement For much of its history, organized labor in the United States has been split into two groups: craft unions and industrial unions. A **craft union** is made up of skilled workers in a specific trade or industry, such as carpentry or printing. The first permanent federation, or organization of national labor unions, was the American Federation of Labor (AFL), composed of craft unions and led by Samuel Gompers. See **Figure 12.7** at right.

craft union: *union made up of skilled workers in a specific trade or industry*

FIGURE 12.7

The AFL Samuel Gompers established the American Federation of Labor and served as its president from 1886 to 1924. Among other causes, he fought for the eight-hour workday.

FIGURE 12.6 Labor-Management Legislation

Legislation	Description
Norris-LaGuardia Act, 1932	Limits the power of the courts to stop picketing and boycotts, and makes yellow-dog contracts illegal. This type of contract is the practice whereby employers require that employees pledge not to join a union.
Wagner Act, 1935	Guarantees labor's right to organize and bargain collectively. Sets up National Labor Relations Board (NLRB) to oversee the establishment and operation of unions.
Taft-Hartley Act, 1947	Outlaws certain strike tactics, permits states to pass laws making union shops illegal, and allows the President to delay a strike if it will threaten the nation's health and safety.
Landrum-Griffin Act, 1959	Increases government control over unions and guarantees union members certain rights, such as freedom of speech in union activities and control over union dues.

industrial union: *union made up of all the workers in an industry regardless of job or skill level*

An **industrial union** is made up of all the workers in an industry regardless of job or level of skills. Attempts to organize industrial unions date to the late 1800s and the leadership of Eugene V. Debs, founder of the American Railway Union. The first significant effort to unionize unskilled and semiskilled workers did not begin, however, until the formation of the Congress of Industrial Organizations (CIO) in 1938.

The AFL-CIO During the late 1930s and early 1940s, both the AFL and the CIO launched organizing campaigns that made the lines between industrial and craft unions less clear. AFL unions began recruiting semiskilled and unskilled workers, while the CIO began organizing workers in the skilled trades. The resulting rivalry cost both union federations time and effort.

By the mid-1950s, union leaders realized that the labor movement would make greater gains if craft and industrial unions worked together. As a result, the two federations merged in 1955 to form the present AFL-CIO.

Global Economy

Improving Working Conditions Worldwide

Overseas factories drew attention in the 1990s after human-rights groups disclosed that clothing sold in Wal-Mart was produced in a Honduran sweatshop. The Vietnamese factory making Nike products was accused of having dangerous levels of chemicals. The White House convened manufacturers and human-rights groups in 1996 to address such abuses.

Since then, Nike and other companies have taken steps to improve conditions for workers. At Nike's Vietnamese factory, for example, ventilation has been improved and workers are using a less toxic glue. Federal contractors are required to certify that no abusive child labor went into the goods they buy. ■

How Unions Are Organized

Organized labor operates at three levels: the local union, the national or international union, and the federation.

local union: *members of a union in a particular factory, company, or geographic area*

Local Unions A **local union** consists of the members of a union in a particular factory, company, or geographic area. The local deals with a company by negotiating a contract and making sure the terms of the contract are kept. The influence that a local has often depends on the type of membership policy it has negotiated with management.

closed shop: *company in which only union members could be hired*

union shop: *company that requires new employees to join a union after a specific period of time*

agency shop: *company in which employees are not required to join the union, but must pay union dues*

Not all local unions are alike. Membership requirements and the ways in which management relates to union members vary from one kind of shop to another. In a **closed shop**, companies could hire only union members. The Taft-Hartley Act of 1947 outlawed closed shops, however. In a **union shop,** a new employee must join the union after a specific period of time, usually three months. In an **agency shop,** employees are not required to join the union, but they must pay union dues.

Supporters of union shops and agency shops argue that employees in companies that are unionized should be required to pay union dues because they benefit from contracts the union negotiates. Opponents believe that a person should not be required to join a union.

Since 1947 a number of states, as shown in **Figure 12.8,** have passed **right-to-work laws** that forbid union shops. These laws allow workers to continue working in a particular job without joining a union. The benefits negotiated by the union must be made

right-to-work laws: *state laws forbidding unions from forcing workers to join and pay union dues*

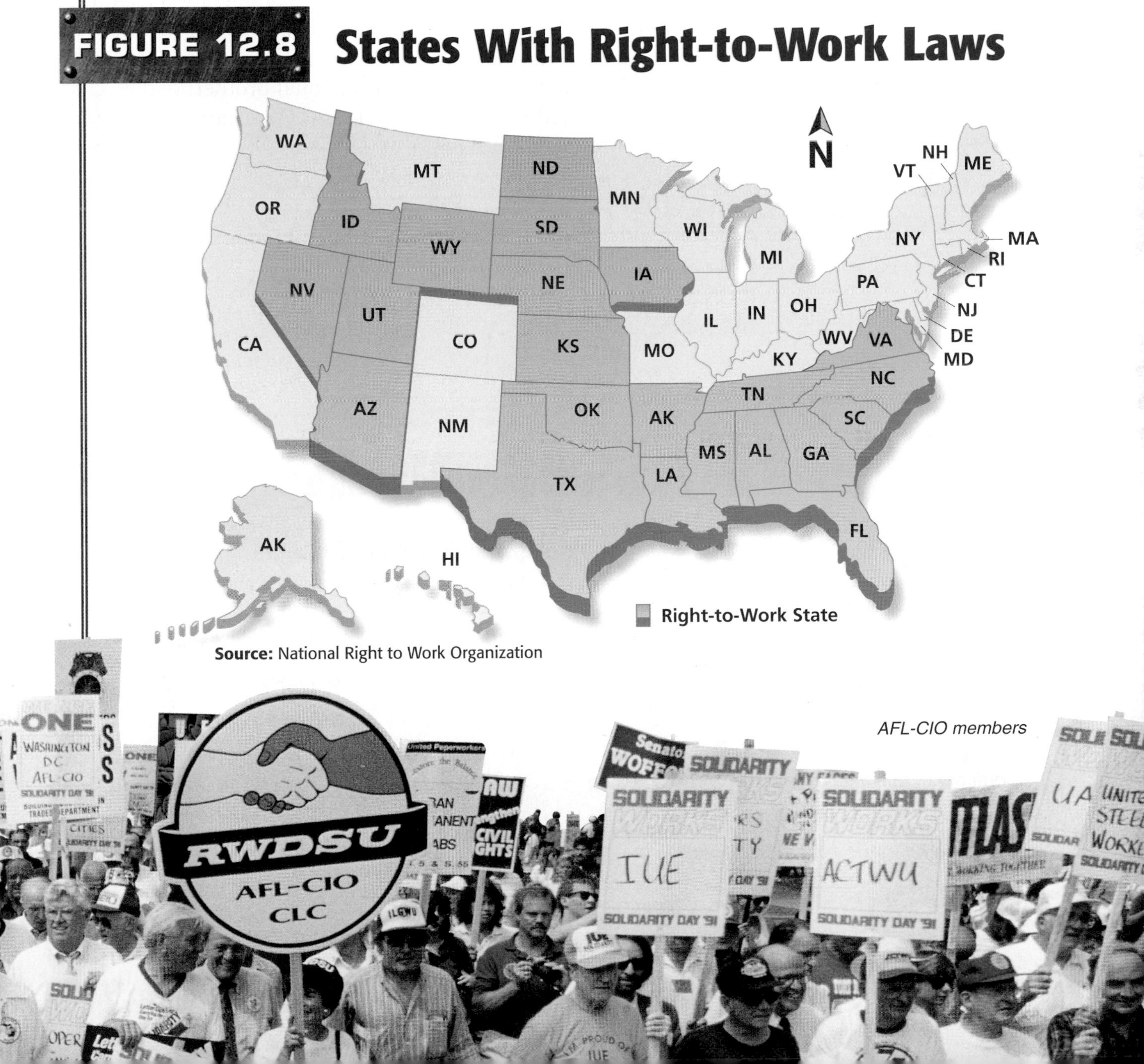

FIGURE 12.8 **States With Right-to-Work Laws**

Source: National Right to Work Organization

AFL-CIO members

available to workers who do not join the union. Unions have less power in states with right-to-work laws than in other states.

National Unions Above the locals are the national unions. These organizations are the individual craft or industrial unions that represent locals nationwide. Those unions that also have members in Canada or Mexico are often called international unions.

National unions send in organizers to help employees organize campaigns to set up locals. To help in negotiating a contract between a local and a particular company, the nationals provide lawyers and other staff members. In certain industries such as steel and mining, the national union negotiates the contract for the entire industry. After the majority of union members accept the contract, all the locals within the industry must work under the contract. Some of the largest unions are the International Brotherhood of Teamsters, the United Automobile Workers (UAW), and the United Steelworkers of America (USW).

Federation Level At the federation level is the AFL-CIO, which is made up of national and international unions. More than 65 unions with about 13 million members are associated with the AFL-CIO.

Practice and **assess** key skills with ***Skillbuilder Interactive Workbook, Level 2.***

SECTION 2 Assessment

Understanding Key Terms

1. **Define** labor union, strike, craft union, industrial union, local union, closed shop, union shop, agency shop, right-to-work laws.

Reviewing Objectives

2. What obstacles did labor unions face when they began to organize in the 1800s?
3. **Graphic Organizer** Create a chart like the one below to summarize the differences among closed shops, union shops, and agency shops.

Type of Union	Summary

Applying Economic Concepts

4. **Economic Institutions** List and evaluate the four pieces of legislation highlighted in **Figure 12.6** on page 323. Rate the acts as follows: "+" for acts that benefited unions, "–" for acts that harmed unions, "0" for acts that had a mixed impact on unions.

Critical Thinking Activity

5. **Synthesizing Information** According to **Figure 12.8** on page 325, is your state a right-to-work state? How do right-to-work laws affect unions? Do you agree or disagree with right-to-work laws? Explain your answer.

People & Perspectives

Walter Reuther

LABOR LEADER (1907–1970)

- **President of the United Automobile Workers (UAW), 1946–1970**
- **President of the Congress of Industrial Organizations (CIO), 1952–1955**
- **Helped to bring about the merger of the American Federation of Labor (AFL) and the CIO in 1955**
- **Posthumously awarded the Presidential Medal of Freedom for distinguished civilian service in peacetime in 1995**

Walter Reuther ranks among the greatest American labor leaders of the twentieth century. A driving force in the union-organizing movement of the 1930s and 1940s, he was the first union leader to negotiate for, and win, benefits that workers today take for granted—cost-of-living raises, pension plans, employer-funded health insurance, and profit sharing. Reuther was also deeply involved in the civil rights and environmental movements. As another union leader noted, "Walter Reuther was on the front lines of the battle for a better world." In the excerpt below, Reuther explains his philosophy of unionism:

"My main point is that the labor movement is about that problem we face 'tomorrow morning'. . . . The guys have a right to expect the labor movement to deal with that problem. I can't give them some philosophical baloney and say: Well, fellows, you know we're operating way up here in the stratosphere and you shouldn't get excited about these little problems that are bothering you every morning.

But to make that the sole purpose of the labor movement is to miss the main target. The labor movement is about changing society. I mean, I don't think I am eloquent when I say to a guy: What good is a dollar an hour more in wages if your neighborhood is burning down? What good is another week's vacation if the lake you used to go to, where you've got a cottage, is polluted and you can't swim in it and the kids can't play in it? What good is another $100 pension if the world goes up in atomic smoke?"

Checking for Understanding

1. **What do you think Reuther meant by the "little problems that [bother workers] every morning"?**
2. **What did Reuther think was the main "target" of the labor movement?**

SECTION 3

Collective Bargaining

Reader's Guide

Terms to Know

- collective bargaining
- cost-of-living adjustment (COLA)
- mediation
- arbitration
- picketing
- boycott
- lockout
- injunction

Reading Objectives

1. What are the major issues over which union contracts are negotiated?
2. What workers' actions and management responses may accompany a strike?
3. How has collective bargaining in the United States changed in recent years?

Cover Story

The Denver Post, July 23, 2003

With the signings of NHL unrestricted free agents coming infrequently and in some cases at "bargain" salaries this summer, it has been natural to wonder if the owners might be undercutting themselves.

The collective bargaining agreement between the Players' Association and the league expires in September 2004, and a possible work stoppage looms as the NHL hopes to rearrange the financial landscape.

collective bargaining: *process by which unions and employers negotiate the conditions of employment*

Collective bargaining, as mentioned above, is the process by which unions and employers negotiate the conditions of employment. At the center of the collective bargaining process is compromise. The company wants to keep wages and benefits low to hold its labor costs down and remain competitive in the market. The union wants to increase wages and benefits for its members as much as possible. As you read this section, you'll learn that both sides must be prepared to give and take a little.

Negotiations

Negotiations take place when labor and management meet to discuss in detail a wide range of contract issues. **Figure 12.9** on page 330 lists the most important issues that labor and management may negotiate, including working hours, fringe benefits, and a **cost-of-living adjustment (COLA).** In most cases, negotiations are friendly and result in an agreement that satisfies all parties.

cost-of-living adjustment (COLA): *provision calling for an additional wage increase each year if the general level of prices rises*

mediation: *a neutral person tries to get both sides to reach an agreement during negotiations*

arbitration: *union and management submit the issues they cannot agree on to a third party for a final decision*

Mediation

If negotiations become hostile or compromise breaks down, labor and management may try mediation. **Mediation** occurs when a neutral person steps in and tries to get both sides to reach an agreement. The mediator suggests possible solutions and works to keep the two sides talking with each other.

The federal government, through the Federal Mediation and Conciliation Service (FMCS), provides a mediator free of charge upon request of either union or management. In a typical year, FMCS mediators are involved in thousands of negotiations. A number of state and private mediators also help resolve disputes.

Arbitration

If mediation fails, the negotiation process may go one step further to arbitration. In **arbitration,** the two sides submit the issues they cannot agree on to a third party for a final decision. Both sides agree in advance to accept the arbitrator's decision, although one or both sides may not be completely happy with the outcome. The FMCS often helps in these cases by providing labor and management with a list of private arbitrators in their area.

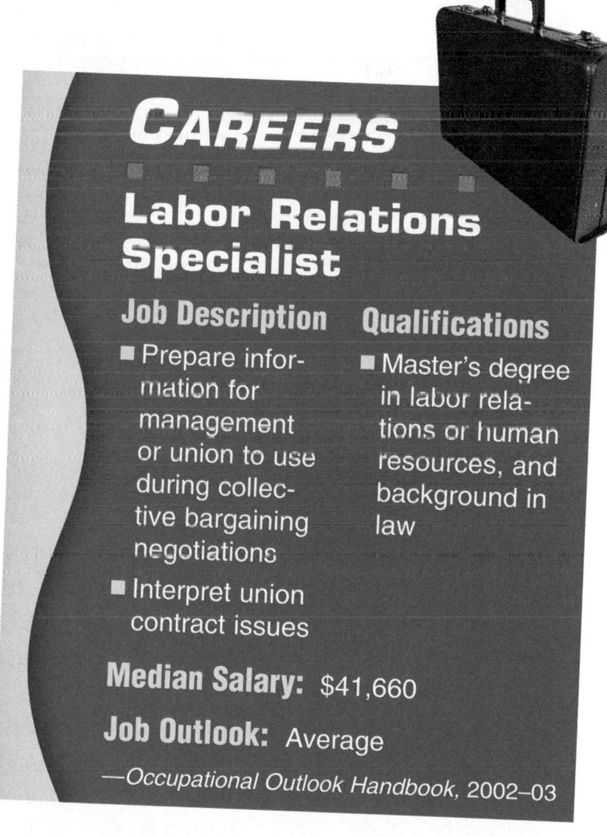

CAREERS
Labor Relations Specialist
Job Description
Prepare information for management or union to use during collective bargaining negotiations
Interpret union contract issues
Qualifications
Master's degree in labor relations or human resources, and background in law
Median Salary: $41,660
Job Outlook: Average
—Occupational Outlook Handbook, 2002–03

Strikes and Management

Most contracts are settled at the bargaining table. Sometimes, however, negotiations break down and a strike results. The number of strikes in the United States has declined sharply since the 1970s, as shown in **Figure 12.10** on page 331.

Strikers usually walk up and down in front of their workplace carrying picket signs that state their disagreement with the company. **Picketing** is meant to discourage workers from crossing the picket line to work for the employer. It is also aimed at embarrassing the company and building public support for the strike.

picketing: *action of strikers who walk in front of a workplace carrying signs that state their disagreement with the company*

FIGURE 12.9 Union Contract Issues

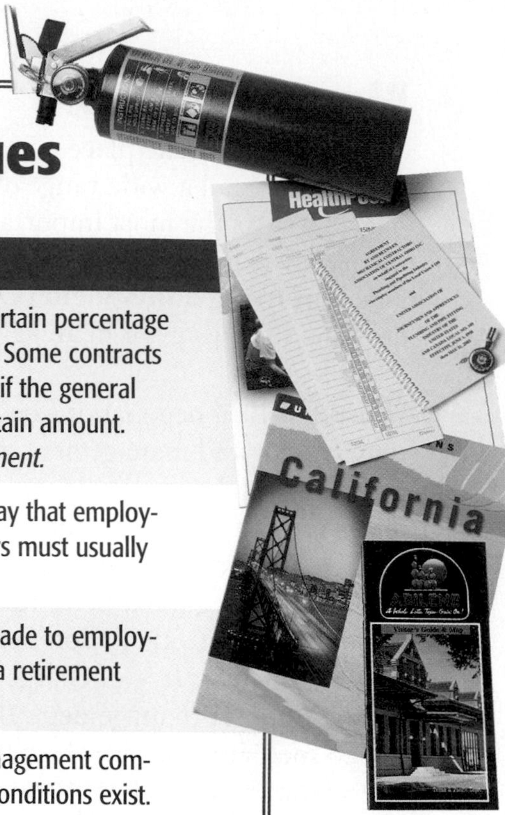

Issue	Description
Wages	Most contracts provide for wage increases of a certain percentage for each worker during each year of the contract. Some contracts also provide for an additional increase each year if the general level of prices in the economy rises beyond a certain amount. This provision is known as a *cost-of-living adjustment.*
Working Hours	The contract establishes the number of hours a day that employees must work. Employees who work longer hours must usually be paid extra wages, called *overtime pay.*
Fringe Benefits	Fringe benefits are payments other than wages made to employees. These can include health and life insurance, a retirement plan, and time off for vacations and holidays.
Working Conditions	Contracts often provide for a joint union and management committee to ensure that safe and pleasant working conditions exist. Working conditions are a particularly important issue to employees in industries that deal with poisonous substances or dangerous machinery.
Job Security	At issue under job security is protection against layoffs because of technological change or a slowdown in business. Most contracts do not forbid layoffs, but rather set up rules that the employer must follow when laying off workers. For example, those with the least *seniority*—amount of time spent with the company—are usually laid off first.
Grievance Procedures	Grievance procedures are a set of formal rules used to resolve a dispute between union members and management. A *grievance,* or complaint, may be filed if one side feels that the other is not living up to the terms of the contract. If the union and the company cannot settle the grievance, a third party will often be asked to judge the matter objectively.

Striking unions may also use a boycott to exert more economic pressure against a firm. In a **boycott,** unions urge the public not to purchase goods or services produced by a company. In addition, unions may ask politicians to push management for a settlement or to publicly support the union's demands.

boycott: *economic pressure exerted by unions urging the public not to purchase the goods or services produced by a company*

Strikes can drag on for months and even years. After a long period of time, strikers sometimes become discouraged. Some may decide to go back to work without gaining what they wanted. In most cases, however, strikes are settled as management and labor return to the negotiating table and work out an agreement.

Lockouts When faced with a strike, management has methods of its own to use against strikers. One is the **lockout,** which occurs when management prevents workers from returning to work until they agree to a new contract. Another tactic is to bring in strikebreakers, called *scabs* by strikers. These are people willing to cross a picket line to work for the terms the company offers.

lockout: *situation that occurs when management prevents workers from returning to work until they agree to a new contract*

FIGURE 12.10 **Strikes** Compare the trend in strikes with what is happening in union membership. ***How do you think the two are related?***

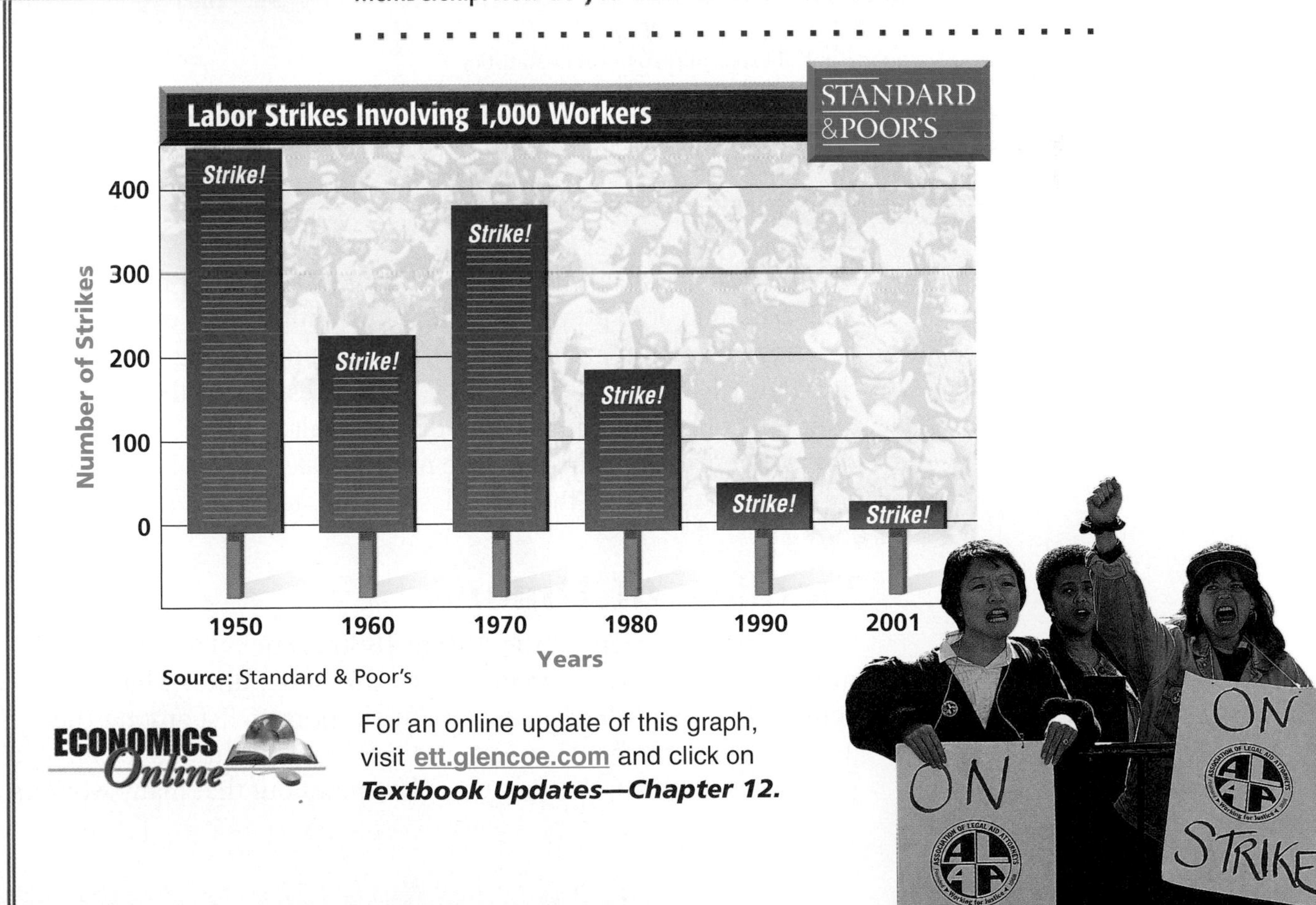

Source: Standard & Poor's

ECONOMICS Online

For an online update of this graph, visit ett.glencoe.com and click on ***Textbook Updates—Chapter 12.***

FIGURE 12.11

Declining Union Membership The labor movement today faces many problems. The percentage of union members among the labor force reached a high in the mid-1940s and has been declining since 1955.

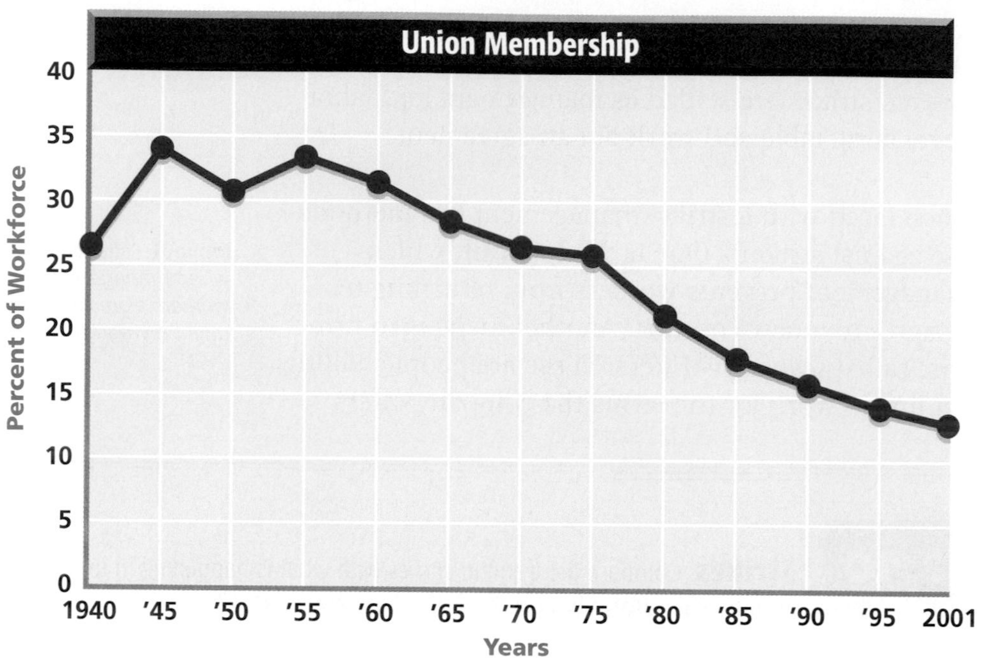

Source: U.S. Department of Labor, Bureau of Labor Statistics

For an online update of this graph, visit ett.glencoe.com and click on ***Textbook Updates—Chapter 12.***

injunction: *court order preventing some activity*

Injunctions Management sometimes requests a court injunction to limit picketing or to prevent a strike from continuing or even occurring. An **injunction** is a legal order of a court preventing some activity. Under the Taft-Hartley Act of 1947, the President of the United States can obtain an injunction to delay or halt a strike for up to 80 days if the strike will endanger the nation's safety or health. During this cooling-off period, the two sides must try to reach a settlement.

Decline of Unions

The establishment of the AFL in 1886 is considered the beginning of the modern union era. Since that time, unions have achieved many of their goals. Union supporters list among their accomplishments better wages and working conditions for all employees—union and nonunion. They point out that many workers now enjoy a sense of security that helps to maintain some control over their jobs and lives.

Union supporters also note that the collective bargaining process has brought more order and fairness to the workplace. It has made clear the rights and responsibilities of both management and labor.

Because working conditions have improved so dramatically over the years, nonunion workers often see little to gain from joining a union. **Figure 12.11** shows how much union membership has declined since the 1940s. In addition, the nature of the economy itself is changing. More jobs are opening in the white-collar and service sectors, whereas blue-collar jobs are decreasing due to automation.

Critics The labor movement also has its critics. Some opponents charge that unions have grown so large and bureaucratic that they are out of touch with their members' needs. Others claim that increased wages are passed on to consumers in the form of higher prices.

Employers often argue that union rules decrease productivity. They point to rules that slow the introduction of new technology or require more employees than necessary to do a job. In addition, corruption among some labor leaders has damaged the reputation of organized labor with the public.

Practice and **assess** key skills with ***Skillbuilder Interactive Workbook, Level 2.***

SECTION 3 Assessment

Understanding Key Terms

1. **Define** collective bargaining, cost-of-living adjustment (COLA), mediation, arbitration, picketing, boycott, lockout, injunction.

Reviewing Objectives

2. **Graphic Organizer** Create a chart like the one below to list and describe the major issues over which union contracts are negotiated.

Issue	Description

3. What workers' actions and management responses may accompany a strike?
4. How has collective bargaining in the United States changed in recent years?

Applying Economic Concepts

5. **Labor Unions** What is your opinion of the influence of unions today? How is your opinion similar to or different from the information given in the text concerning the decline of unionism?

Critical Thinking Activity

6. **Making Generalizations** Write two newspaper accounts of a fictional local strike. One account should be from the perspective of a union member. The other account should be written from the standpoint of management.

Study & Writing Skills

Using Library Resources

Your teacher has assigned a major research report, so you go to the library. As you wander the aisles surrounded by books, you wonder: Where do I start my research? Which reference works should I use?

- **Encyclopedia:** set of books containing short articles on many subjects arranged alphabetically
- **Biographical dictionary:** brief biographies listed alphabetically by last names
- **Atlas:** collection of maps and charts
- **Almanac:** annually updated reference that provides current statistics and historical information on a wide range of subjects
- **Card catalog:** listing of every book in the library, either on cards or computerized; search for books by author, subject, or title
- **Periodical guide:** set of books listing topics covered in magazines and newspaper articles
- **Computer database:** collections of information organized for rapid search and retrieval

Learning the Skill

Libraries contain many resources. Listed on the left are brief descriptions of important ones.

Practicing the Skill

Suppose you are assigned a research report dealing with the famous labor leaders Samuel Gompers and Eugene V. Debs. Read the questions below, then decide which of the sources described on the left you would use to answer each question and why.

1. During which years did the men lead their unions?
2. What were the most famous labor actions each dealt with?
3. How did the public react to the labor unions' activities?
4. What benefits do we enjoy today as a result of these two labor leaders?

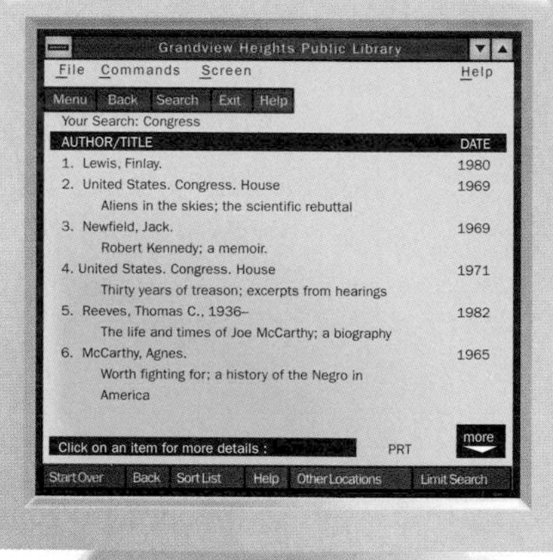

Computerized card catalog

Application Activity

Using library resources, research the origins and important leaders of the American Federation of Labor. Present the information you find to the class.

Practice and **assess** key skills with ***Skillbuilder Interactive Workbook, Level 2.***

CHAPTER 12 Summary

Chapter Overview Visit the *Economics Today and Tomorrow* Web site at ett.glencoe.com and click on ***Chapter 12—Chapter Overviews*** to review chapter information.

SECTION 1 Americans at Work

- The **civilian labor force** is the total number of people 16 years old or older who are either employed or actively seeking work.
- Workers in the United States are categorized according to the type of work they perform—**blue-collar, white-collar,** or **service worker.**
- Another way to categorize workers is by the skills required to perform their occupation—**unskilled, semiskilled, skilled,** or **professional.**
- Three major factors—skill, type of job, and location—affect how supply and demand determine prices, or in this case wages, in the labor market.
- Factors that restrict supply and demand in terms of their influence on wages include **minimum wage laws** and organized labor.

SECTION 2 Organized Labor

- A **labor union** is an association of workers organized to improve wages and working conditions for its members.
- Workers began to form unions to force employers to improve working conditions, shorten the workday, and end child labor.
- For much of its history, organized labor in the United States has been split into two groups: **craft unions** and **industrial unions.**
- Organized labor operates at three levels: the **local union,** the national or international union, and the federation.
- Local unions may negotiate a **union shop** or an **agency shop.**

SECTION 3 Collective Bargaining

- **Collective bargaining** is the process by which unions and employers negotiate the conditions of employment.
- Labor and management may negotiate working hours, wages, fringe benefits, and a **cost-of-living adjustment (COLA).**
- If negotiations become hostile or compromise breaks down, labor and management may try **mediation** or **arbitration.**
- Striking unions may use **picketing** or a **boycott** to exert economic pressure against a firm.
- When faced with a strike, management may use a **lockout** or an **injunction** against strikers.
- The percentage of union members among the labor force reached a high in the mid-1940s and has been declining since 1955.

CHAPTER 12

Assessment and Activities

Self-Check Quiz Visit the *Economics Today and Tomorrow* Web site at ett.glencoe.com and click on ***Chapter 12—Self-Check Quizzes*** to prepare for the Chapter Test.

Identifying Key Terms

Identify the letter of the definition in Column B that correctly defines each term in Column A.

Column A

1. unskilled workers
2. agency shop
3. arbitration
4. injunction
5. right-to-work law
6. closed shop
7. boycott

Column B

a. company in which employees are not required to join a union but must pay union dues
b. refusal to purchase the goods and services of a company
c. court order preventing some activity, often a strike
d. those having no special training in job-related skills
e. procedure for settling undecided issues between labor and management by giving them to a third party for a final decision
f. company in which only union members could be hired (now illegal)
g. forbids contracts that require employees to join a union

Recalling Facts and Ideas

Section 1

1. Which category of worker has a higher-education degree as well as additional training?
2. What is the difference between blue-collar and white-collar workers?
3. What factors determine how much a person is paid for his or her work?

Section 2

4. What are the major kinds of labor unions?
5. What two union federations merged in 1955?
6. How do right-to-work laws affect workers who do not belong to unions?

Section 3

7. Wages are one of the most important major issues in collective bargaining negotiations. What are other important issues?
8. If management and labor have reached a bargaining deadlock, they may try to engage in mediation. If mediation fails, what is the next possible "friendly" step?
9. What do union workers do when they go on strike?
10. What has been the most recent trend in the importance of labor unions in America?

Thinking Critically

1. **Determining Cause and Effect** Explain why workers with more education and training generally get paid higher wages.
2. **Predicting Consequences** Create a diagram like the one below to explain the factors that may cause a decline in union membership in the future.

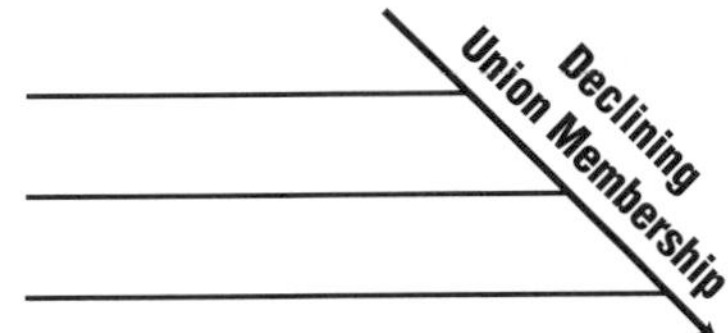

Applying Economic Concepts

Economic Costs and Benefits There are costs and benefits for every activity. Strikes are no exception. Many workers believe that the benefits exceed the costs or they would not strike. List the benefits to workers of going on strike. Then list the costs of going on strike.

Reviewing Skills

Using Library Resources Use library resources to research one of the following labor strikes: Baltimore & Ohio Railroad Workers, 1877; Haymarket Riot, 1886; Homestead Strike, 1892; Pullman Strike, 1894; Anthracite Coal Strike, 1902; Textile Strike in Lawrence, Massachusetts, 1912; Ludlow Massacre in Ludlow, Colorado, 1914. Write a report describing the people or groups involved, the conditions that led to the incident, what happened, and the conclusion.

Cooperative Learning Project

Analyze the data that follow for the number of unemployed persons over a five-year period. Working in groups, compute the *mean average* number of unemployed.

1996	7,236,000
1997	6,739,000
1998	6,210,000
1999	5,880,000
2000	5,655,000

Now compute the *median average* unemployment rate for the seven years listed below.

1994	6.1
1995	5.6
1996	5.4
1997	4.9
1998	4.5
1999	4.2
2000	4.0

For help in determining averages, see page xx in the Economic Handbook.

Technology Activity

Using a Spreadsheet Keep track of the employed individuals with whom you come into contact over a one-week period. Write down the types of jobs they do. Then use these jobs as the basis of a spreadsheet showing the training, average salary, and prospects for growth for each job. Use the Internet or sources such as the *Occupational Outlook Handbook* or *O*Net* to find this information.

Analyzing the Global *Economy*

France's trucking union struck in 1997, parking their vehicles on roads and highways leading into Paris. Research and report on the reasons for the strike, how long it lasted, the effect on the economy of Paris, and the result of the strike.

CASE STUDY

Focus on Free Enterprise

eBay, Inc.

Star Wars™ toys

One night in 1995, while Pierre Omidyar and his fiancée were having dinner, the subject of Pez™ dispensers came up. She was an avid collector of these colorful little candy servers. Where, she wondered, might she meet people with a similar passion to talk and trade? Omidyar, a pioneer of online commerce, knew the place—the Internet.

Pierre Omidyar and Meg Whitman

The Online Auctioneer

Omidyar's idea was fairly simple: set up a Web site where people with similar interests could buy and sell unique items—the equivalent of an Internet flea market. The site—called eBay—opened in September 1995. A few days later, eBay held its first auction.

An eBay auction follows a set pattern. First, a seller places a description of the item to be sold, often accompanied by photographs, on the Web site. Next, buyers check in and make bids on the item. After a set period of time, usually three to seven days, the auction is closed and the item goes to the highest bidder. eBay earns its revenues by charging customers fees and commissions.

Slow Start

At first, business was slow. Just 10 people registered to use eBay's services in 1995. In time, however, more and more people visited the Web site, attracted by the opportunity of finding a bargain. In 1996, eBay made a profit of $150,000. By 1998, profits hit $2.4 million.

Fiesta®

eBay's success was no accident, mostly due to people Omidyar recruited to run the company. He hired Meg Whitman as chief executive officer of eBay in 1998. Today she is the richest female CEO in the world.

eBay has about 30 million registered customers. It has hurtled past being an auction room for Pez™ dispensers and other odd collectibles. It now offers millions of items in thousands of categories—everything from Star Wars™ toys to antique pottery.

The eBay "Community"

Each day, eBay hosts millions of online auctions. In 2002, these transactions added up to more than $14.9 billion. The close interaction that takes place between buyers and sellers during these auctions has helped to create a sense of community among eBay users. In fact, eBay has become a way of life for many.

Ironing Out Some Wrinkles

With so much activity, it is not surprising that eBay has experienced some instances of fraud. eBay's management, however, has established a system called Safe Harbor to protect buyers from fraudulent transactions. It offers such services as product authentication and transaction insurance. Also, through Safe Harbor feedback, members can report on their experiences during auctions. Any person who receives a poor feedback rating may be "vaporized"—expelled from eBay.

Expanded Services

eBay offers other services in addition to online auctions. Through eBay Professional Services, small businesses can find professionals and freelancers for a variety of business needs, including Web design, accounting, writing, and technical support.

eBay Premier is a specialty site featuring fine art, antiques, and rare collectibles from leading auction houses and dealers around the world.

eBay Motors, the largest online auction-style marketplace for buying and selling vehicles, also provides online services such as financing, auto insurance, title and registration, and even a lemon check!

Free Enterprise in Action

1. **Why might fraud be a problem for a business like eBay? What steps has eBay taken to combat fraud?**
2. **How has eBay responded to the competition provided by other Internet auction sites?**

Pez™

UNIT 5

Macroeconomics: The Nation's Economy

Chapter 13
Measuring the Economy's Performance

Chapter 14
Money and Banking

Chapter 15
The Federal Reserve System and Monetary Policy

Chapter 16
Government Spends, Collects, and Owes

Chapter 17
Stabilizing the National Economy

This is the universal seal for the Federal Reserve System—the central bank of the United States.

The microprinted words "USA 100" appear in the lower left numeral.

In this unit, read to FIND OUT . . .

- what statistics measure the economy's health.
- how the American banking system works.
- the role of government in the economy.

FRANKLIN
AB
Secretary of
The portrait is off-center, leaving room for a watermark and reducing wear and tear on the portrait.
A vertically embedded security thread with the words "USA 100" glows red under ultraviolet light.
The microprinted words "United States of America" appear in the lapel of Franklin's collar.
A watermark identical to the portrait is visible from both sides when held up to a light.

CHAPTER 13

Measuring the Economy's Performance

Why It's Important

Inflation, GDP, the consumer price index—what do the headlines mean? This chapter will explain what these terms indicate about the state of the economy.

To learn more about economic statistics, view the **Economics & You** *Chapter 20 video lesson:* **Measuring the Economy's Performance**

ECONOMICS Online

Chapter Overview Visit the *Economics Today and Tomorrow* Web site at ett.glencoe.com and click on ***Chapter 13—Chapter Overviews*** to preview chapter information.

SECTION 1

National Income Accounting

Cover Story

The Columbus Dispatch, June 8, 1999

Oregon and New Hampshire enjoyed the fastest economic growth among the states in 1997, and California's economy remained the biggest, the government said. . . .

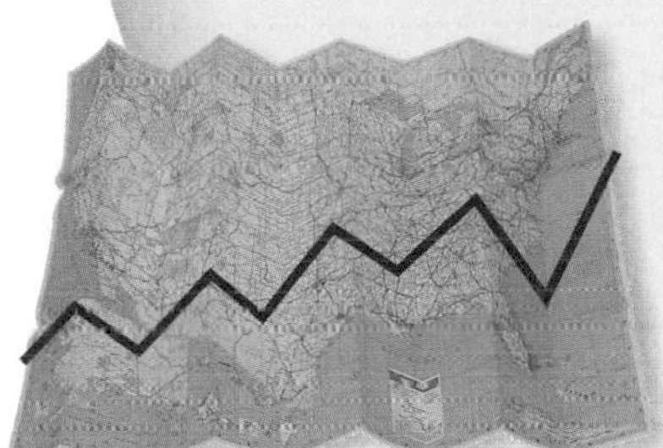

A Commerce Department report broke down the nation's gross domestic product, the total output of goods and services, to show the amount contributed by each state.

Reader's Guide

Terms to Know

- national income accounting
- gross domestic product (GDP)
- net exports
- depreciation
- net domestic product (NDP)
- national income (NI)
- personal income (PI)
- transfer payments
- disposable personal income (DI)

Reading Objectives

1. What four categories of economic activity are used to measure GDP?
2. How do the three measurements of income—national, personal, and disposable—differ?

People can measure how successful they are economically by the amount of their incomes and by their standard of living, including how much their spendable income will buy. In this section, you'll learn that the success of the overall economy is measured in a similar way.

National Income Accounting

To determine how healthy the American economy is, economists constantly measure such factors as the amount of goods and services produced yearly by the nation and the amount of income people have to spend. The measurement of the national economy's performance is called **national income accounting.** This area of economics deals with the overall economy's output, or production, and its income.

national income accounting: *measurement of the national economy's performance, dealing with the overall economy's output and income*

Five major statistics measure the national economy. These are gross domestic product, net domestic product, national income, personal income, and disposable personal income. Each will be examined separately, starting with the largest overall measurement—gross domestic product. **Figure 13.1** shows gross domestic product and the other four measurements in descending order of value.

Measuring GDP

gross domestic product (GDP): *total dollar value of all final goods and services produced in a nation in a single year*

The broadest measure of the economy's size is **gross domestic product (GDP).** This is the total dollar value of all *final* goods and services produced in the nation during a single year. This

FIGURE 13.1

STANDARD &POOR'S

GDP and Its Components Economists start with GDP and subtract various items until they reach the figure measuring disposable personal income–the amount of money people have left to spend after they pay taxes. ***What is the difference in dollars between gross domestic product and disposable personal income?***

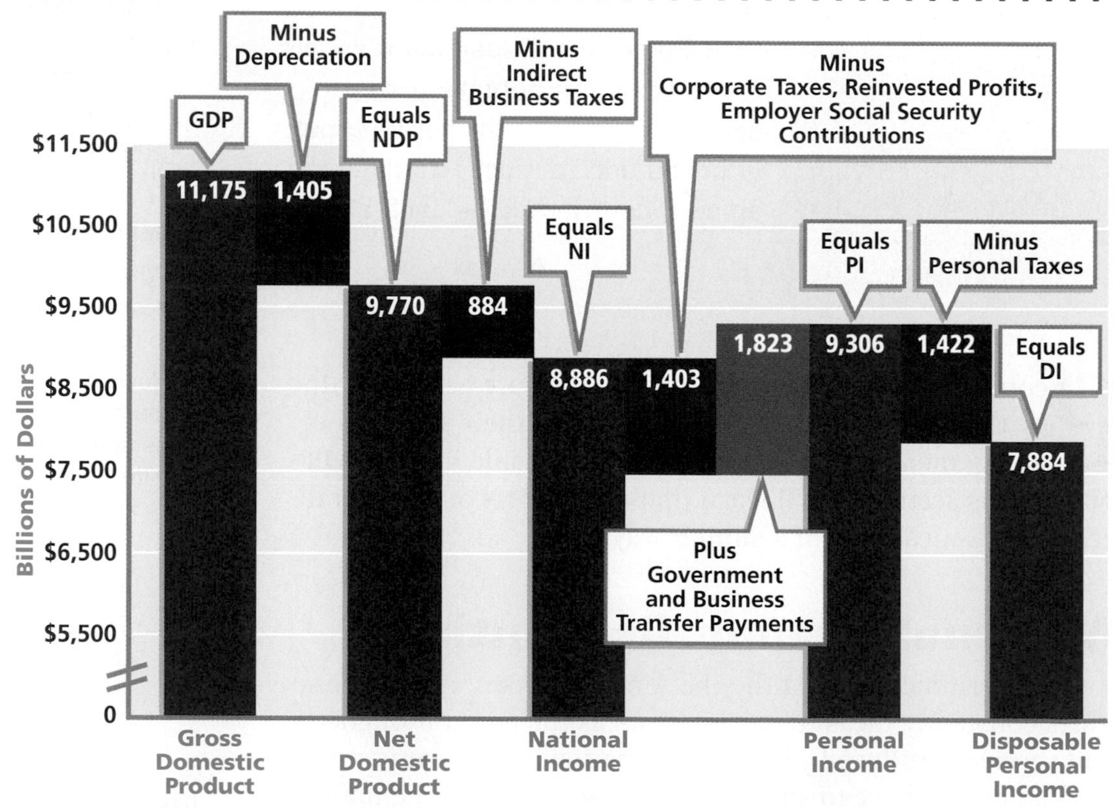

Source: Standard & Poor's

For an online update of this graph, visit ett.glencoe.com and click on ***Textbook Updates—Chapter 13.***

figure tells the amount of goods and services produced within the country's borders and made available for purchase in that year.

Measuring Value

Note the word *value* in the definition. Simply adding up the *quantities* of different items produced would not mean much. Can we really measure the strength of the economy, for example, if we know that 3 billion safety pins and 2 space shuttles were produced?

What we need to know is the total *value* of the items, using some common measure. Economists use the dollar as this common measure of value. As a result, GDP is always expressed in dollar terms. For example, in 2002, GDP for the United States totaled more than $11 trillion.

FIGURE 13.2

Avoiding Double Counting When calculating GDP, economists count only the value of the final product. The intermediate products that go into making a loaf of wheat bread–wheat that was milled into wheat flour–are not counted in GDP. Only the price of the loaf of bread is counted.

Measuring Final Goods and Services

The word *final* in the definition of GDP is also important. Measuring the economy's performance accurately requires that economists add up only the value of final goods and services to avoid *double counting*. For example, GDP does not add the price of computers and memory chips and motherboards if those chips and motherboards are installed in computers for sale. The final price to the buyer already includes the price of the memory chips and motherboards.

Also, only new goods are counted in GDP. The sale price of a used car or a secondhand refrigerator is not counted as part of GDP. Such a sale is not due to the production of the nation, but only transfers an existing product from one owner to another. If a new battery is put in an old car, however, that new battery is counted as part of GDP. **See Figure 13.2.**

Computing GDP

To total the amount of GDP, economists add the expenditures made in four categories of the economy. The first category is the *consumer sector (C)*, or those goods and services bought by consumers for their direct use. The second category is the *investment sector (I)*, or business purchases of tools, machines, buildings, and so on, used to produce other goods. This area also includes money spent on business inventories.

Student Web Activity Visit the *Economics Today and Tomorrow* Web site at ett.glencoe.com and click on ***Chapter 13—Student Web Activities*** to learn about your gross state product.

FIGURE 13.3

Four Categories of GDP To compute GDP, economists add the total amount of expenditures from the consumer sector, the investment sector, the government sector, and net exports.

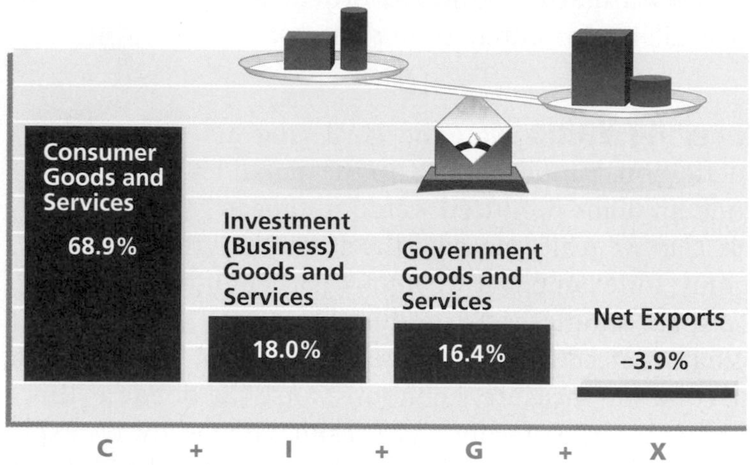

Source: *Economic Indicators*, May 2002

For an online update of this graph, visit ett.glencoe.com and click on ***Textbook Updates—Chapter 13.***

The *government sector (G)* makes up the third category added to GDP. The goods and services bought by federal, state, and local governments range from paper clips to jets. The final category is **net exports** *(X)*, or the difference between what the nation sells to other countries (exports) and what it buys from other countries (imports). This figure may be a plus or minus depending on whether the nation sells more or less to other nations than it buys from them. See **Figure 13.3.**

net exports: *difference between what the nation sells to other countries and what it buys from other countries*

Weaknesses of GDP The statistics used in computing GDP are accurate only to a point. Statistics about easily measurable things, such as government purchases, are reliable. Some workers, however, are given food, fuel, or housing as part of their

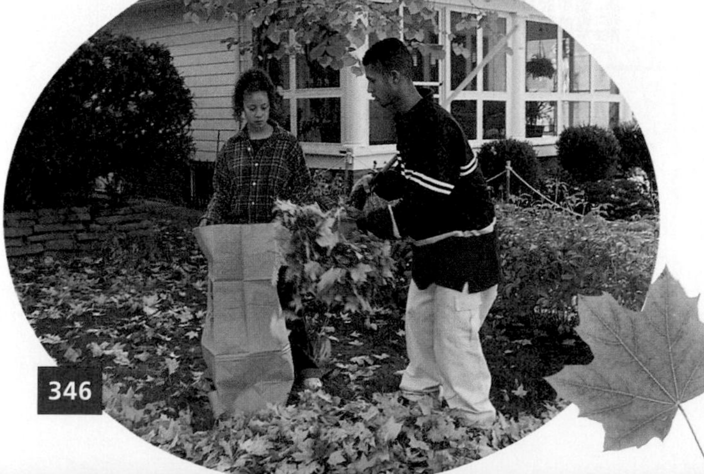

Non-GDP Work Unpaid work is not counted as part of GDP, even though it adds to the nation's output. This category includes lawn mowing, maintenance work on a home, baby-sitting, and so on. The government cannot estimate the value of this work accurately.

wages. GDP can include only an estimate of the value of such goods and services. Moreover, as **Figure 13.4** shows, GDP omits certain areas of economic activity such as unpaid work.

Net Domestic Product

The loss of value because of wear and tear to durable goods, such as automobiles and refrigerators, is called **depreciation.** The same concept applies to capital goods–machines and equipment. GDP disregards depreciation. It does not take into account that some production merely keeps machines and equipment in working order and replaces them when they wear out.

depreciation: *loss of value because of wear and tear to durable goods and capital goods*

net domestic product (NDP): *value of the nation's total output (GDP) minus the total value lost through depreciation on equipment*

Net domestic product (NDP)–another way of measuring the economy–accounts for the fact that some production is only due to depreciation. NDP takes GDP and subtracts the total loss in value of capital goods caused by depreciation.

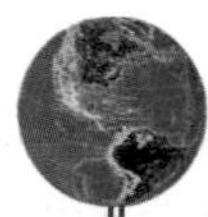

Global Economy

Per Capita GDP

One picture of a country's standard of living comes from computing its real GDP per capita–or GDP divided by the total population. This is a measure of the average GDP per resident of a country. Listed below are the 10 nations with the highest per capita GDP.

Luxembourg	$42,922
Japan	$37,546
Norway	$36,021
United States	$35,619
Switzerland	$33,326
Denmark	$30,489
Iceland	$30,462
Sweden	$25,818
United Kingdom	$23,887
Finland	$23,437

Measurements of Income

So far, you've learned about GDP and NDP–two major measurements of the nation's output. Three additional measurements look at income–national income, personal income, and disposable personal income.

National Income The total amount of income earned by everyone in the economy is called **national income (NI).** NI includes those who use their own labor to earn an income as well as those who make money through the ownership of the other factors of production. NI is equal to the sum of all income resulting from five different areas of the economy. These include wages and salaries, income of self-employed individuals, rental income, corporate profits, and interest on savings and other investments.

national income (NI): *total income earned by everyone in the economy*

If you look again at **Figure 13.1** on page 344, you'll see that national income is equal to NDP minus indirect business taxes, which includes such items as sales taxes and license fees.

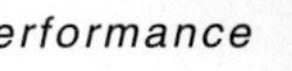

personal income (PI): *total income that individuals receive before personal taxes are paid*

Personal Income The total income that individuals receive before personal taxes are paid is called **personal income (PI).** PI can be derived from NI through a two-step process. First, several items are subtracted: corporate income taxes, profits that businesses reinvest in business to expand, and Social Security contributions employers make. These items are subtracted because they represent income that is not available for individuals to spend.

transfer payments: *welfare and other supplementary payments that a state or the federal government makes to individuals*

Then transfer payments are added to NI. **Transfer payments** are welfare payments and other assistance payments—unemployment compensation, Social Security, and Medicaid—that a state or the federal government makes to individuals. These transfer payments add to an individual's income even though they are not exchanged for any current productive activity.

disposable personal income (DI): *income remaining for people to spend or save after all taxes have been paid*

Disposable Personal Income The income that people have left after taxes, including Social Security contributions, is called **disposable personal income (DI).** DI equals PI minus personal taxes. DI is an important indicator of the economy's health because it measures the actual amount of money income people have available to save and spend.

Practice and **assess** key skills with ***Skillbuilder Interactive Workbook, Level 2.***

SECTION 1 Assessment

Understanding Key Terms

1. **Define** national income accounting, GDP, net exports, depreciation, NDP, NI, PI, transfer payments, DI.

Reviewing Objectives

2. What four categories of economic activity are used to measure GDP?
3. **Graphic Organizer** Create a diagram like the one below to show what must be subtracted from and added to national income to determine personal income.

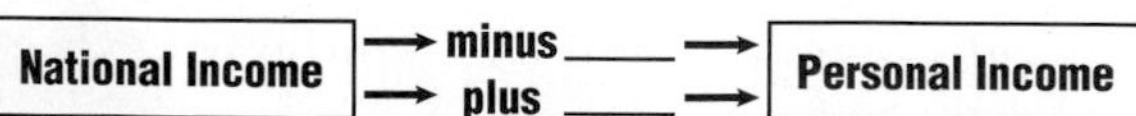

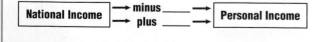

Applying Economic Concepts

4. **Gross Domestic Product** List five items you have recently purchased. Explain why they should or should not be counted in GDP. Use the terms *value, final,* and *double counting* in your explanations.

Critical Thinking Activity

5. **Synthesizing Information** Reconstruct **Figure 13.1** on page 344 in the form of a spreadsheet. Start with the dollar figure for GDP, then subtract the dollar figure of depreciation to get NDP. Continue until you have tabulated DI.

Study & Writing Skills

Taking Notes

Effective note taking involves more than just writing facts in short phrases. It involves breaking up much of the information into meaningful parts so that it can be understood and remembered.

- When taking notes on material presented in class, write the key points and important facts and figures in a notebook.
- Writing quickly and neatly, use abbreviations and phrases.
- Copy words, statements, or diagrams drawn on the chalkboard.
- Ask the teacher to repeat important points you have missed or do not understand.
- When studying textbook material, organize your notes into an outline (see page 406 for hints on outlining).
- For a research report, take notes on cards. Note cards should include the title, author, and page number of sources.

Learning the Skill

To learn how to take good notes, follow the steps listed on the left.

Practicing the Skill

Suppose you are writing a research report on the United States GDP. First, identify main-idea questions about this topic, such as "What does GDP measure?" "What components make up GDP?" and "What are the weaknesses of using GDP to measure the economy?" Then find material about each main-idea question.

Using this textbook as a source, read the material in Section 1 and prepare notes like this:

Main Idea: What does GDP measure?
1. GDP is prt of nat'l inc. acct.
2. NIC measrs amt of gds & serv prducd yrly
3. GDP = tot $ vlu of final gds & srvs prdcd in U.S. in 1 yr.

Main Idea: What components make up GDP?
1.
2.
3.

Application Activity

Scan a local newspaper for a short editorial or article about the nation's GDP. Take notes by writing the main idea and supporting facts. Summarize the article using only your notes.

Practice and **assess** key skills with ***Skillbuilder Interactive Workbook, Level 2.***

SECTION 2

Correcting Statistics for Inflation

READER'S GUIDE

Terms to Know

- inflation
- purchasing power
- deflation
- consumer price index (CPI)
- market basket
- base year
- producer price index (PPI)
- GDP price deflator
- real GDP

Reading Objectives

1. What is the relationship between the purchasing power of money and the rate of inflation?
2. How do the consumer price index and the producer price index differ in what they measure?

COVER STORY

BUSINESS WEEK, MAY 31, 1999

In Wall Street's galaxy, the Phantom Menace is inflation. It's the Dark Side of the economy's Force. The financial markets know that [nonexistent] inflation is the single most important factor supporting the economy's amazing performance of recent years. . . .

That's why the May 14 news of an unexpected 0.7% jump in the April consumer price index, the largest monthly rise in more than nine years, looked as scary as Darth Maul wielding his light saber.

INFLATION

In Section 1, you learned how GDP statistics measure the economy. You also learned that GDP figures can be unreliable because they do not measure unpaid work or depreciation. Another factor that skews GDP figures is **inflation,** or a prolonged rise in the general price level of goods and services. As mentioned in the *Cover Story* above, the presence of inflation can pose a threat to the economy. In this section, you'll learn how inflation affects the current dollar value of GDP as well as your ability to purchase goods and services.

inflation: *prolonged rise in the general price level of goods and services*

The Purchasing Power of Money

When is a dollar not a dollar? When inflation occurs, the prices of goods and services rise. Therefore, the **purchasing power** of the dollar goes down. A dollar's purchasing power is the real goods and services that it can buy. In other words, a dollar cannot buy the same amount as it did before inflation.

purchasing power: *the real goods and services that money can buy; determines the value of money*

How does a drop in the dollar's purchasing power skew GDP? The higher GDP figures that result from inflation do not represent any increase in output. For example, last year an ice-cream cone may have cost $1.00. This year it may cost $1.95. The physical output–in this case, one ice-cream cone–has not changed; only its money value has. To get a true measure of the nation's output in a given year, inflation must be taken into account. **Deflation,** a prolonged *decline* in the general price level, also affects the dollar value of GDP, but deflation rarely happens.

deflation: *prolonged decline in the general price level of goods and services*

Measures of Inflation

The government measures inflation in several ways. The three most commonly used measurements are the consumer price index, the producer price index, and the implicit GDP price deflator.

Consumer Price Index (CPI) Every month, the government measures the change in price of a specific group of goods and services that the average household uses. This measurement is the **consumer price index (CPI).** The group of items that are

consumer price index (CPI): *measure of the change in price over time of a specific group of goods and services used by the average household*

Economic Connection to...

Compiling the CPI

When compiling the CPI, the Bureau of Labor Statistics (BLS) does not record every price of every product bought by everyone in the United States. The BLS instead tries to get a *representative* picture of the prices paid by consumers for all products. A national sample of some 29,000 families provides the BLS with information on their spending habits. This enables the BLS to put together the market basket and to "weight" items according to consumer spending. For example, housing items are given more weight, or importance, than recreation items because most consumers spend more on housing than on recreation. ■

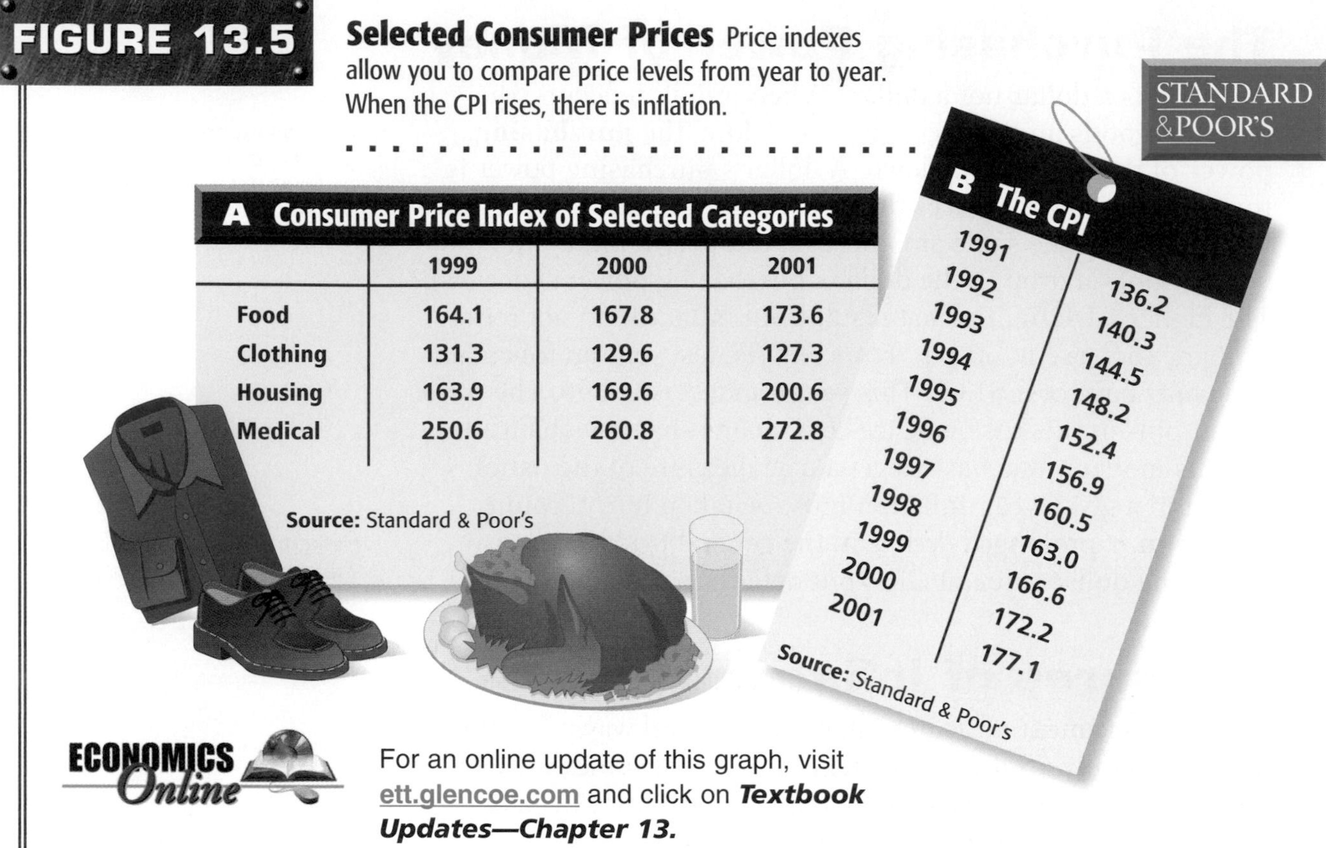

FIGURE 13.5 **Selected Consumer Prices** Price indexes allow you to compare price levels from year to year. When the CPI rises, there is inflation.

A Consumer Price Index of Selected Categories

	1999	2000	2001
Food	164.1	167.8	173.6
Clothing	131.3	129.6	127.3
Housing	163.9	169.6	200.6
Medical	250.6	260.8	272.8

Source: Standard & Poor's

B The CPI

1991	136.2
1992	140.3
1993	144.5
1994	148.2
1995	152.4
1996	156.9
1997	160.5
1998	163.0
1999	166.6
2000	172.2
2001	177.1

Source: Standard & Poor's

For an online update of this graph, visit ett.glencoe.com and click on ***Textbook Updates—Chapter 13.***

market basket: *representative group of goods and services used to compile the consumer price index*

priced, called a **market basket,** includes about 80,000 specific goods and services under general categories such as food, housing, transportation, apparel, education, recreation, medical care, and personal care. About every 10 years, the market basket is updated to include new products and services and to reflect more current spending patterns. *Part A* of **Figure 13.5** has broken down the CPI into several major categories, whereas *Part B* shows the overall CPI for several years.

base year: *year used as a point of comparison for other years in a series of statistics*

Employees at the federal Bureau of Labor Statistics (BLS) compile the CPI monthly. They start with prices from a **base year** so that they have a point of comparison for current-day prices. For example, if you paid $1.00 for an ice-cream cone in 2001, and the price of the cone increased to $1.95 in 2003, the cost of an ice-cream cone has risen 95 cents (and in this case, 95 percent) since 2001 ($1.95 − 1.00 = .95).

In compiling the CPI, the BLS's base year is really the average of prices that existed for the three years 1982 to 1984. This base is given a value of 100. CPI numbers for later years indicate the percentage that the market basket price has risen since the base year.

For example, the 2001 CPI of 177.1 means that the average price of goods and services in the market basket has risen 77.1 percent since the period 1982–1984 (177.1 − 100 = 77.1). The price level, therefore, rose 77.1 percent since 1982–1984. The CPI can also be used to calculate inflation for any period, as shown in **Figure 13.6.**

producer price index (PPI): *measure of the change in price over time that United States producers charge for their goods and services*

GDP price deflator: *price index that removes the effect of inflation from GDP so that the overall economy in one year can be compared to another year*

real GDP: *GDP that has been adjusted for inflation by applying the price deflator*

Producer Price Index Another important measure of inflation is the **producer price index (PPI).** The PPI is actually a group of indexes that measures the average change in prices that United States producers charge their customers–whether these customers are other producers buying crude materials for further processing or wholesalers who will sell the products to retailers or directly to consumers. Most of the producer prices included in the PPIs are in mining, manufacturing, and agriculture.

The PPIs usually increase before the CPI. Apple producers, for example, may experience a weak harvest. Because of the shortage of apples, the price of apples rises. A bakery that buys apples will eventually increase the price of its apple pies to cover the higher price of apples. Eventually the CPI will increase because consumers will have to pay more for the final products–in this case, apple pies. Therefore, changes in the PPIs often are watched as a hint that inflation and the CPI are going to increase.

GDP Price Deflator Government economists account for inflation by issuing another measure of price changes in GDP, called the **GDP price deflator.** This index removes the effects of inflation from GDP so that the overall economy in one year can be compared to another year. When the price deflator is applied to GDP in any year, the new figure is called **real GDP.**

The federal government uses 1995 as its base year to measure real GDP. Each year the price deflator is used to change current, or nominal, GDP into real GDP. For example, GDP in current dollars for 2002 was $10,446.2 billion. To find real GDP for 2002, the government divides 2002 GDP by the 2002 price deflator (110.66) and multiplies the result by 100:

$$\$10{,}446.2 \div 110.66 \times 100 = \$9{,}439.9$$

Real GDP for 2002 was $9,439.9 billion. This figure may now be compared to 1996 nominal GDP of $7,813.2 billion. This is a more meaningful comparison than comparing 2002 GDP in nominal dollars to 1996 GDP. **Figure 13.7** on page 354 shows both current GDP and real GDP over time.

FIGURE 13.6

Calculating Inflation At the end of 1991, the CPI was 136.2. In May 2001 it was 177.7, which is a difference of 41.5 (177.7 − 136.2 = 41.5). If we now use 1991 as the base year, we can find out by what percentage consumer prices on average rose from 1991 to 2001. We do this by dividing 41.5 by 136.2, which gives us 0.3047 (41.5 ÷ 136.2). When we multiply by 100 to give the result as a percent, we get 30.47 percent.

FIGURE 13.7 **GDP in Current and Chained (1996) Dollars** Real GDP has been adjusted for inflation using 1996 as a base year.

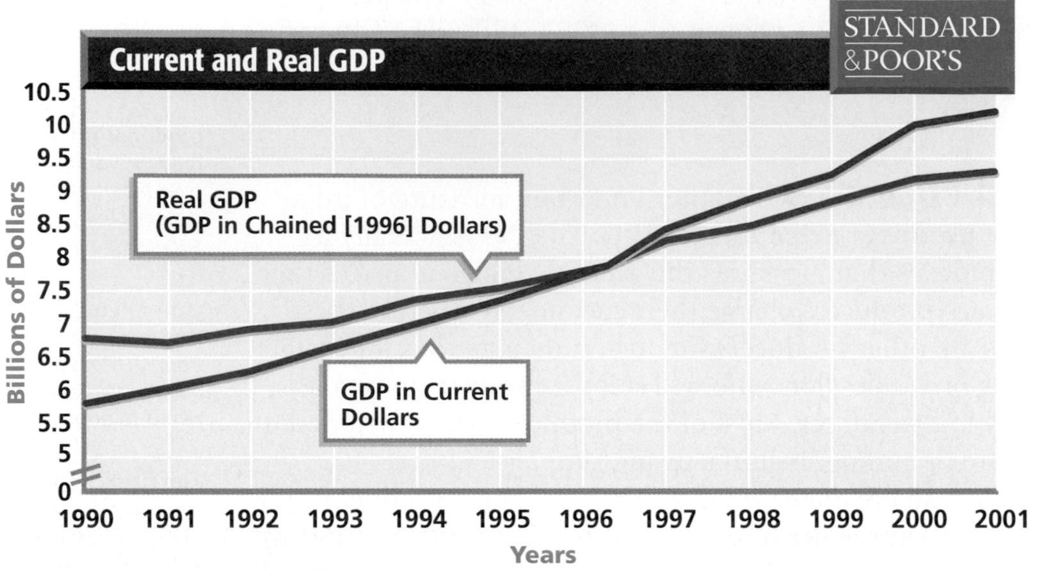

Source: Standard & Poor's

For an online update of this graph, visit ett.glencoe.com and click on ***Textbook Updates—Chapter 13.***

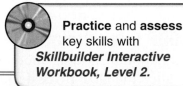

Practice and **assess** key skills with ***Skillbuilder Interactive Workbook, Level 2.***

SECTION 2 Assessment

Understanding Key Terms

1. **Define** inflation, purchasing power, deflation, consumer price index, market basket, base year, producer price index, GDP price deflator, real GDP.

Reviewing Objectives

2. What is the relationship between the purchasing power of money and the rate of inflation?
3. **Graphic Organizer** Use a chart like the one in the next column to show the difference between what the CPI and the PPI measure.

Index	What It Measures

Applying Economic Concepts

4. **Market Basket** If you were to construct a market basket of goods and services that students typically consume, what would you select?

Critical Thinking Activity

5. **Making Predictions** If the PPIs measuring crude oil, agricultural products, and lumber decrease for three months in a row, what prediction could you make about the CPI?

BusinessWeek

Spotlight on the Economy

Unveiling the Secrets of the CPI

Check It Out! In this chapter you learned about the consumer price index (CPI). In this article, read to learn about several weaknesses of the CPI and how the Bureau of Labor Statistics (BLS) tries to overcome these weaknesses.

The government tracks inflation in various forms. For instance, the producer price index (PPI) captures changes in prices charged by U.S. goods producers. . . . For the best inflation reading, however, markets look to the CPI. It is the most comprehensive indicator because it covers all goods and services purchased by households. It's the timeliest because the report is released . . . about two weeks after the end of each month. The CPI does include sales and excise taxes.

The CPI is not perfect. The elderly complain that the CPI, although used for adjusting Social Security checks, misses price hikes on drugs. Increases in property taxes show up only indirectly when the BLS calculates rents. And if your employer increases your health-insurance premium, the CPI won't reflect it.

The BLS counters that the consumer price index's aim is to measure prices for a specific basket of goods and services that the average household buys, according to surveys done from 1993 to 1995. This set basket leads to the biggest rap on the CPI: It does not allow for substitution. Say, a drought in Washington means a price jump for Red Delicious apples. Consumers might buy cheaper Granny Smiths. But the CPI would still give more weight to the price of Red Delicious apples.

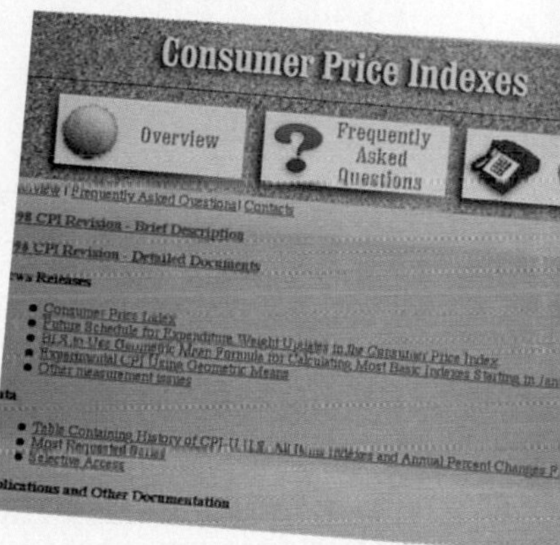

In the mid-1990s, economists criticized the CPI for overestimating inflation. . . . For one thing, said economists, the BLS took too long to include new products, and thus the CPI failed to capture the price reductions that take place in the first years of a product's lifetime. Cell phones, for instance, were costly to use when they were introduced in the 1980s. But competition brought the connection fees down rapidly. However, the BLS did not include cellular phones in the CPI until 1998.

Quality adjustment is another problem. How does the BLS account for air bags in cars, which add costs but save lives?

Think About It

1. **What does the CPI measure?**
2. **What are three criticisms of the CPI?**

SECTION 3

Aggregate Demand and Supply

Reader's Guide

Terms to Know
- aggregates
- aggregate demand
- aggregate demand curve
- aggregate supply
- aggregate supply curve

Reading Objectives
1. Why is there an inverse relationship between aggregate quantity demanded and the price level?
2. What causes the aggregate supply curve to slope upward?
3. How do you use aggregate demand and supply analysis to determine the equilibrium price level?

Cover Story

Akron Beacon Journal, August 12, 2003

[M]onths after the official end of the recession in November 2001, the number of jobs in the United States continues to decline.

Economists call it a "growth recession," in which the economy grows so slowly that it doesn't add jobs.

Economists are focusing on two fundamental economic changes . . . the use of technology to produce more goods and services . . . and the movement of a greater variety of jobs overseas.

As alluded to in the *Cover Story* above, the laws of supply and demand can be applied to the economy as a whole, as well as to individual consumer decisions. Economists are interested in the demand by all consumers for all goods and services, and the supply by all producers of all goods and services. When we look at the economy as a whole in this way, we are looking at **aggregates**—the summing up of all the individual parts in the economy. As you'll learn in this section, we call these sums aggregate demand and aggregate supply.

aggregates: *summation of all the individual parts in the economy*

Aggregate Demand

Aggregate demand is the total quantity of all goods and services in the entire economy demanded by all people. How can we find out the aggregate quantity of goods and services that all

aggregate demand: *total quantity of goods and services in the entire economy that all citizens will demand at any single time*

FIGURE 13.8

Aggregate Demand Curve Although the curve for aggregate demand resembles that for simple demand, it is for the entire economy, not just one good or service. Aggregate demand may increase (curve shifts to the right) if consumers collectively spend more and save less or if better economic conditions are forecast. Aggregate demand may decrease (curve shifts to the left) if higher taxes are imposed on the overall economy or if bleak economic conditions are forecast.

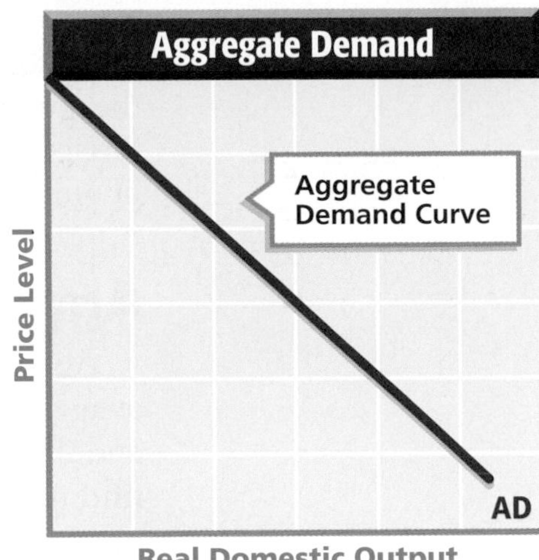

citizens will demand at any single point in time? To answer this question, we have to relate aggregate demand to something else. As you remember from Chapter 7, the basic law of demand relates the quantity demanded of a specific product to its price. When discussing aggregates, however, we are talking about *all* products. Because there are millions of different prices for all products, aggregate demand cannot be related to prices.

Instead, aggregate demand is related to the *price level*—the average of all prices as measured by a price index. If we use the implicit GDP price deflator as our index, our measure of aggregate demand will be based on real (adjusted for inflation) domestic output. You can see this relationship in **Figure 13.8.** It is called the **aggregate demand curve.**

aggregate demand curve: *a graphed line showing the relationship between the aggregate quantity demanded and the average of all prices as measured by the implicit GDP price deflator*

Notice the similarity between the aggregate demand curve labeled AD in **Figure 13.8** and the individual demand curve you studied in Chapter 7 (page 179). Both of these curves slope downward, showing an inverse relationship. As the price level in the nation's economy goes down, a larger quantity of real domestic output is demanded per year. This change in quantity demanded is shown as a movement *along* the AD curve.

There are two main reasons for this inverse relationship. One involves the real purchasing power of your cash, and the other concerns the relative price of goods and services sold to other countries.

Consider the first reason. Inflation causes the purchasing power of your cash to go down. Deflation causes your purchasing power to go up. Therefore, when the price level goes down, the purchasing power of any cash that you hold will go up. You and everyone else will feel slightly richer because you are able to buy more goods and services.

As for the second reason, when the price level goes down in the United States, our goods become relatively better deals for foreigners who want to buy them. Foreigners then demand more of our goods as exports.

Aggregate Supply

Aggregate demand is only one side of the picture. Let us look at aggregate supply. As the price of a specific product goes up, and if all other prices stay the same, producers of that product find it profitable to produce more. The same is true for all producers in the economy over a short period of time. If the price level goes up and wages do not, overall profits will rise. Producers will want to supply more to the marketplace–they offer more real domestic output as the price level increases. The reverse is true as the price level falls. This is called **aggregate supply.** You can see this positive relationship in **Figure 13.9**–the **aggregate supply curve.**

aggregate supply: *real domestic output of producers based on the rise and fall of the price level*

aggregate supply curve: *a graphed line showing the relationship between the aggregate quantity supplied and the average of all prices as measured by the implicit GDP price deflator*

Putting Aggregate Demand and Aggregate Supply Together

Just as we are able to compare demand and supply for a given product to find an equilibrium price and quantity, we can

FIGURE 13.9

Aggregate Supply Curve Similar to the individual supply curve, the aggregate supply curve shows the amount of real GDP that could be produced at various price levels. Aggregate supply increases (curve shifts to the right) when all firms experience lower costs of production due to lower taxes or interest rates or lower prices for foreign oil, for example. Aggregate supply decreases (curve shifts to the left) for the opposite reasons: higher taxes, higher interest rates, higher prices for foreign oil.

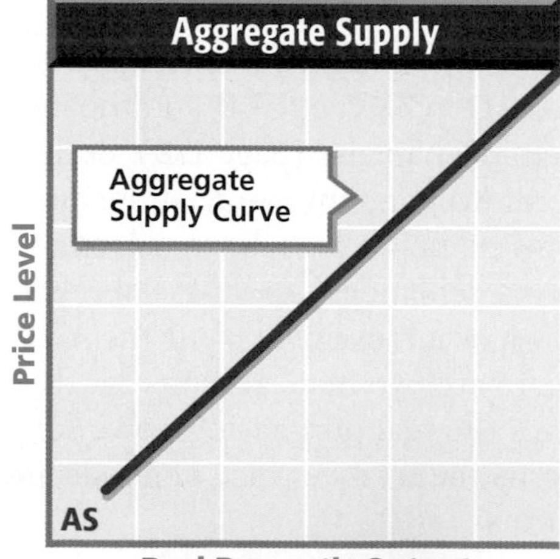

▼ Producers

FIGURE 13.10

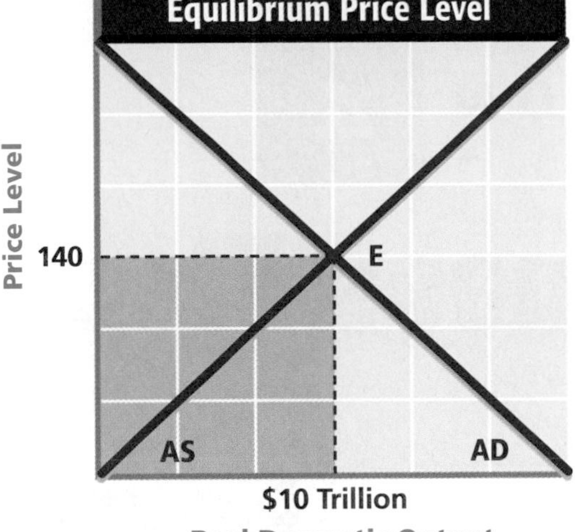

National Output and the Price Level The intersection of aggregate demand and aggregate supply gives the equilibrium price level and national output (real domestic output).

compare aggregate demand and aggregate supply. We do this in **Figure 13.10.**

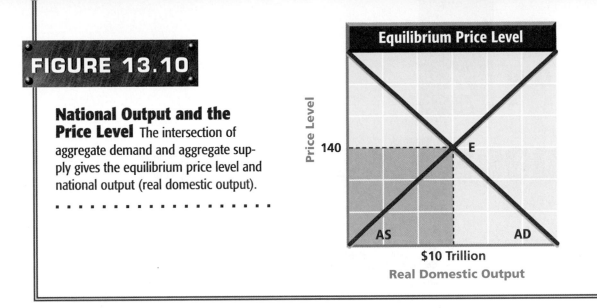

The equilibrium price level in our example is determined where the aggregate demand curve crosses the aggregate supply curve, or at a GDP price deflator of 140. The equilibrium quantity of real GDP demanded and supplied is $10 trillion. As long as nothing changes in this situation, the economy will produce $10 trillion of real domestic output, and the price level will remain at 140—there will be neither inflation nor deflation.

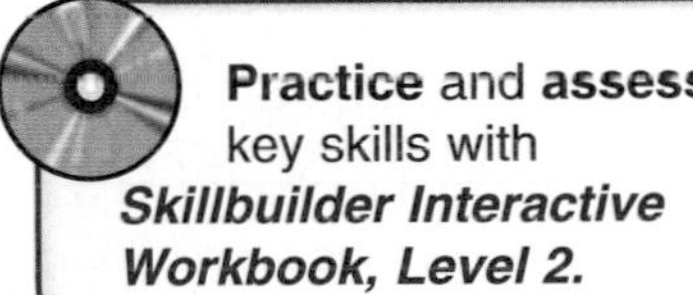

Practice and **assess** key skills with ***Skillbuilder Interactive Workbook, Level 2.***

SECTION 3 Assessment

Understanding Key Terms

1. **Define** aggregates, aggregate demand, aggregate demand curve, aggregate supply, aggregate supply curve.

Reviewing Objectives

2. **Graphic Organizer** Create a diagram like the one below to show why there is an inverse relationship between aggregate quantity demanded and the price level.

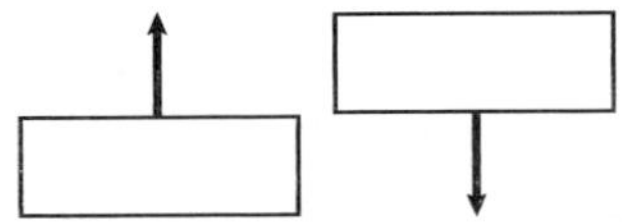

3. What causes the aggregate supply curve to slope upward?
4. How do you use aggregate demand and supply analysis to determine the equilibrium price level?

Applying Economic Concepts

5. **Aggregate Demand** What would happen to the aggregate demand curve if there was a massive tax cut?

Critical Thinking Activity

6. **Synthesizing Information** Draw a graph showing both an aggregate demand curve and an aggregate supply curve. Now assume that the price level increases. What happens to aggregate demand and aggregate supply?

SECTION 4

Business Fluctuations

Reader's Guide

Terms to Know
- business fluctuations
- business cycle
- peak
- boom
- contraction
- recession
- depression
- trough
- expansion
- recovery

Reading Objectives
1. What are the phases of a typical business cycle?
2. What have been the three most severe downturns in the United States economy since the 1920s?

Cover Story

Business Week, August 27, 2001

Does the New Economy exist? Not long ago, with growth strong and markets booming, the answer seemed an obvious yes. But then came the bust. In the first half of this year, output grew at an annual rate of just 1%—and there's still a chance of an outright recession.... Those who thought the New Economy meant good times forever have been mugged by reality.

Some years inflation is high; other years it is not. The same holds true for unemployment, world trade, and taxes. We have fluctuations in virtually all aspects of our economy. The ups and downs in an economy are called **business fluctuations.** Some people associate these ups and downs in business activity with what has been called the **business cycle**–irregular changes in the level of total output measured by real GDP.

business fluctuations: *ups and downs in an economy*

business cycle: *irregular changes in the level of total output measured by real GDP*

Model of the Business Cycle

Figure 13.11 shows an idealized business cycle. According to this model, the phases of a business cycle begin with growth leading to an economic **peak** or **boom**–a period of prosperity. New businesses open, factories are producing at full capacity, and everyone who wants work can find a job.

Eventually, however, real GDP levels off and begins to decline. During this part of the cycle, a **contraction** of the economy

peak/boom: *period of prosperity in a business cycle in which economic activity is at its highest point*

contraction: *part of the business cycle during which economic activity is slowing down* occurs. Business activity begins to slow down. If the contraction lasts long enough and is deep enough, the economy can continue downward until it slips into a recession.

A **recession** is any period of at least two quarters—six months—during which real GDP does not grow. In a recession, business activity starts to fall at a rapid rate economy-wide. Factories cut back on production and lay off workers. Consumers, with less income, cut back on purchases. Faced with a worsening economy, fewer new businesses open and some existing ones fail. If a recession becomes extremely bad, it deepens into a **depression.** Then millions of people are out of work, many businesses fail, and the economy operates far below capacity.

recession: *part of the business cycle in which the nation's output (real GDP) does not grow for at least six months*

depression: *major slowdown of economic activity*

At some point, the downward direction of the economy levels off in a **trough.** A trough is the lowest point in the business cycle. It occurs when real GDP stops going down, levels off, and slowly begins to increase. The increase in total economic activity that follows is called an **expansion** or **recovery.** Consumer spending picks up, signaling factories to hire workers and increase production to meet demand. New businesses begin to open. The recovery continues until the economy hits another peak, and a new cycle begins.

trough: *lowest part of the business cycle in which the downward spiral of the economy levels off*

expansion/recovery: *part of the business cycle in which economic activity slowly increases*

Ups and Downs of Business

In the real world, as you can see from **Figure 13.12** on page 362, the business cycles are not as regular as the model shows. The peaks and troughs are clear, however.

FIGURE 13.11

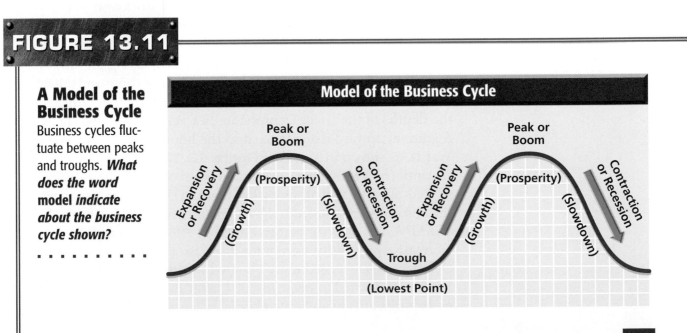

A Model of the Business Cycle
Business cycles fluctuate between peaks and troughs. ***What does the word*** **model** ***indicate about the business cycle shown?***

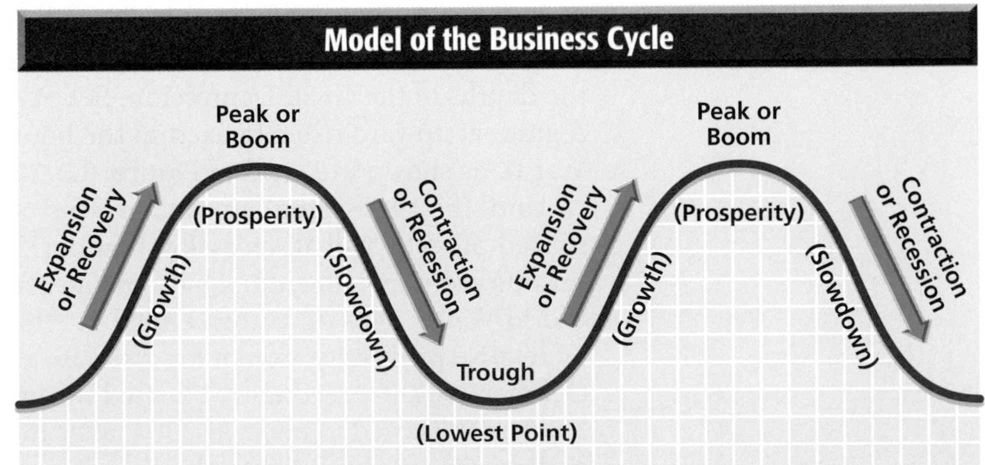

FIGURE 13.12 **Business Activity** American business activity declined about 50 percent during the Great Depression, yet bounced back to new highs after World War II.

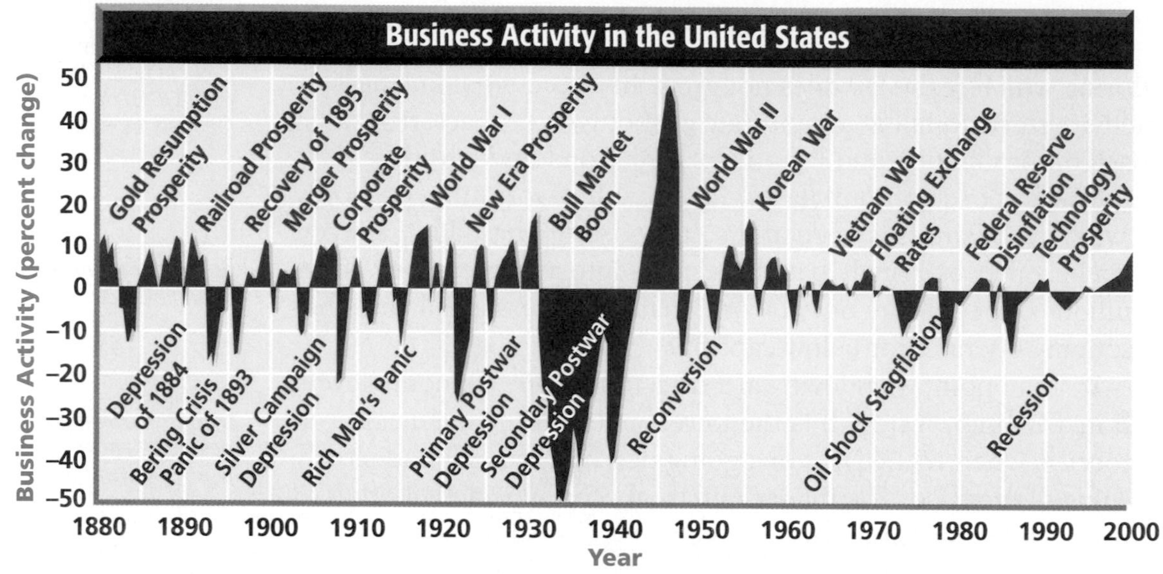

Sources: *American Business Activity from 1790 to Today,* 67th ed., AmeriTrust Co., January 1996; plus author's projections

The largest drop that eventually resulted in a depression followed the stock market crash in October 1929. The preceding years had been a time of widespread prosperity, as shown in *Part A* of **Figure 13.13.** By September 1929, heavy speculation had driven stock prices to an all-time peak. Then stock prices started to fall in early October and continued to fall. Suddenly, on October 29, there was a stampede to unload stocks. In one day the total value of all stocks fell by $14 billion.

Not long after the stock market crash, the United States fell into a serious recession. Factories shut down, laying off millions of workers. Businesses and banks failed by the thousands. Real GDP fell sharply over the next few years, pushing the nation into the depths of the Great Depression. See *Part B* of **Figure 13.13.** A gradual upward rise climaxed in the boom period after World War II, as shown in *Part C* of **Figure 13.13.**

Until the 1980s, small ups and downs occurred. The 1980s started off with a small recession that developed into the most serious economic downturn by some measurements since World War II. This downturn ended in 1982 and was followed by relative prosperity, except for a severe stock market crash in October 1987. The economy boomed during the last half of the 1990s, but started to falter in 2001, after the disruption caused by terrorist attacks in September.

FIGURE 13.13 Prosperity, Depression, and Boom

Prosperity Before the Crash A
The 1920s had been a decade in which Americans began buying increasing numbers of radios, stoves, and automobiles. During these years, prices remained stable, and the standard of living rose about 3 percent per year.

B Depression Conditions
The Great Depression of the 1930s forced millions of Americans out of work. Used to the prosperity of the 1920s, Americans during the bust era of the Depression often relied on handouts.

War Boom C
The United States economy grew rapidly during World War II. There were 17 million new jobs created, and farmers shared in the prosperity as crop prices doubled between 1940 and 1945.

Practice and **assess** key skills with ***Skillbuilder Interactive Workbook, Level 2.***

SECTION 4 Assessment

Understanding Key Terms

1. **Define** business fluctuations, business cycle, peak or boom, contraction, recession, depression, trough, expansion or recovery.

Reviewing Objectives

2. What are the phases of a typical business cycle?
3. **Graphic Organizer** Create a time line like the one below to describe the three most severe downturns in the United States economy since the 1920s.

Applying Economic Concepts

4. **Business Fluctuations** Write three headlines that might have appeared in a newspaper during the years of the Great Depression. Then write three headlines that might have appeared during the expansion of the 1990s. Explain why you chose to write those particular headlines for those time periods.

Critical Thinking Activity

5. **Understanding Cause and Effect** What actions and reactions throughout the economy may cause a recession to deepen into a depression?

SECTION 5

Causes and Indicators of Business Fluctuations

READER'S GUIDE

Terms to Know

- innovations
- economic indicators
- leading indicators
- coincident indicators
- lagging indicators

Reading Objectives

1. What are some of the potential causes of business fluctuations?
2. What are the three broad categories of economic indicators?

COVER STORY

COMPTON'S ONLINE ENCYCLOPEDIA, "BUSINESS CYCLE"

Economists, politicians, and others have been puzzled by business cycles since at least the early 19th century. One of the more unusual explanations was proposed by English economist William Stanley Jevons in the 19th century. He believed the ups and downs of an economy were caused by sunspot cycles, which affected agriculture and caused cycles of bad and good harvests. This hypothesis is not taken seriously today.

For as long as booms and recessions have existed, economists have tried to explain why business fluctuations occur. If they could understand the causes, they reason, then the government could take actions to smooth out business fluctuations. No single theory, however, seems to explain past cycles or to serve as an adequate measure to predict future ones. The difficulty arises because at any given time, several factors are working together to create business fluctuations.

Causes of Business Fluctuations

For many years economists believed that business fluctuations occurred in regular cycles. Later, economists believed that business fluctuations were related to changes in the rate of saving and investing. Today economists tend to link business fluctuations to four main forces: business investment, government activity, external factors, and psychological factors.

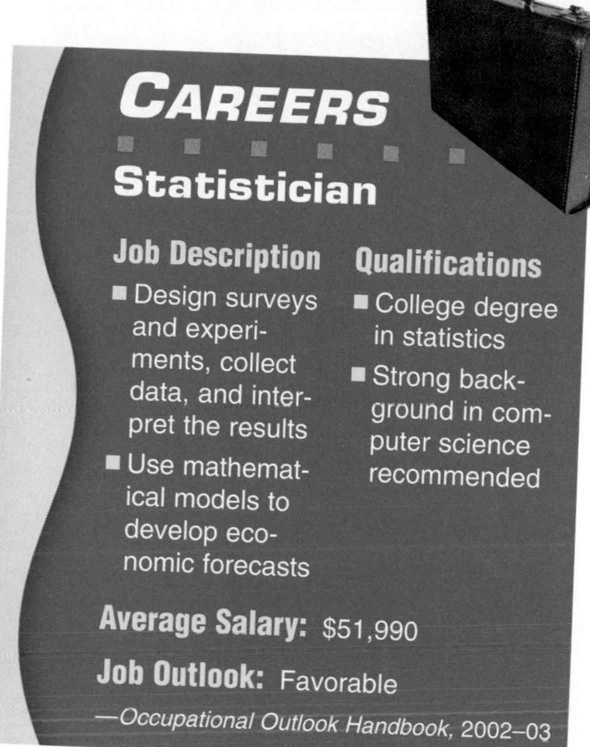

Business Investment Some economists believe that business decisions are the key to business fluctuations. Suppose a firm believes that prospects for future sales are good. Probably it will increase its capital investment: buy new machines, build new factories, expand old ones, and so on. This expansion will create new jobs and more income for consumer spending.

Innovations–inventions and new production techniques–can have a similar effect on the economy. When one firm begins to use an innovation, others must imitate the product or production method in order to become competitive again.

When businesses anticipate a downturn in the economy, they cut back on their capital investment and inventories. Producers, in turn, cut back on production to prevent a surplus. Enough inventory cutbacks could lead to a recession.

innovations: *inventions and new production techniques*

Government Activity A number of economists believe that the changing policies of the federal government are a major reason for business cycles. The government affects business activity in two ways: through its policies on taxing and spending, and through its control over the supply of money available in the economy. You'll learn more about these government actions in Chapters 15 and 16.

External Factors Factors outside a nation's economy also influence the business cycle. As you can see from **Figure 13.14**,

FIGURE 13.14

External Factors War, natural and environmental disasters, and crime waves are some external factors that affect business cycles.

FIGURE 13.15 Major Economic Indicators

Leading Indicators

1. Average weekly hours for production workers in manufacturing
2. Weekly initial claims for unemployment insurance
3. New orders for consumer goods
4. Speed with which companies make deliveries (the busier a company, the longer it will take to fill orders)
5. Number of contracts and orders for plants and equipment
6. Number of building permits issued for private housing units
7. Stock prices
8. Changes in money supply in circulation
9. Changes in interest rates
10. Changes in consumer expectations

Coincident Indicators

1. Number of nonagricultural workers who are employed
2. Personal income minus transfer payments
3. Rate of industrial production
4. Sales of manufacturers, wholesalers, and retailers

Lagging Indicators

1. Average length of unemployment
2. Size of manufacturing and trade inventories
3. Labor cost per unit of output in manufacturing
4. Average interest rate charged by banks to their best business customers
5. Number of commercial and industrial loans to be repaid
6. Ratio of consumer installment debt to personal income
7. Change in consumer price index for services

wars in particular have an important impact. This impact results from the increase in government spending during wartime.

Another external factor—the availability of raw materials such as oil—may also have an effect on the economy. New sources of raw materials may lower operating costs for certain industries. The sudden loss of raw materials and the resulting higher prices, however, can have the opposite effect.

Psychological Factors

Finally, it is possible that people's psychological reactions to events also cause business fluctuations. Consider one important example. The United States and much of the world were already entering into what seemed to be a mild recession in the fall of 2001. After the horrible terrorists' attacks on New York City and Washington, D.C., on September 11, 2001, consumers and businesses pulled back all over the world. Consumers spent less, and business managers reduced investment-spending plans.

Economic Indicators

Every day, business leaders are faced with the dilemma of trying to predict what will happen to the economy in the coming months and years. To aid decision makers, government and private economists study a number of economic indicators—listed in **Figure 13.15**—to learn about the current and possible future state of the economy. **Economic indicators** are statistics that measure variables in the economy, such as stock prices or the dollar amount of loans to be repaid. Each month, the U.S. Department of Commerce compiles statistics for 78 economic indicators covering all aspects of the state of the U.S. economy.

economic indicators: *statistics that measure variables in the economy*

Leading Indicators Statistics that point to what will happen in the economy are called **leading indicators.** They seem to lead to a change in overall business activity—whether it is an upward or a downward trend. The Commerce Department keeps track of numerous leading indicators, but the ten listed in **Figure 13.15** are the ones that most concern American economists.

leading indicators: *statistics that point to what will happen in the economy*

Coincident Indicators Other economic indicators, which usually change at the same time as changes in overall business activity, also help economists. When these **coincident indicators** begin a downswing, they indicate that a contraction in the business cycle has begun. If they begin an upswing, they indicate that the economy is picking up and a recovery is underway.

coincident indicators: *economic indicators that usually change at the same time as changes in overall business activity*

Lagging Indicators A third set of indicators seems to lag behind changes in overall business activity. For example, it may be six months after the start of a downturn before businesses reduce their borrowing. The amount of change in these **lagging indicators,** whether up or down, gives economists clues as to the duration of the phases of the business cycle.

lagging indicators: *indicators that seem to lag behind changes in overall business activity*

Practice and **assess** key skills with ***Skillbuilder Interactive Workbook, Level 2.***

SECTION 5 Assessment

Understanding Key Terms

1. **Define** innovations, economic indicators, leading indicators, coincident indicators, lagging indicators.

Reviewing Objectives

2. **Graphic Organizer** Create a diagram similar to the one here to explain four of the potential causes of business fluctuations.

3. What are the three broad categories of economic indicators?

Applying Economic Concepts

4. **Business Fluctuations** What innovation do you think has had the most influence on expanding the American economy? Why?

Critical Thinking Activity

5. **Making Predictions** Identify two events that would cause you to predict a contraction of the economy.

People & Perspectives

Janet Yellen

ECONOMIST (1946–)

- **Chair of President Clinton's Council of Economic Advisers, 1997–99**
- **Member of Federal Reserve Board of Governors, 1994–97**
- **Member of Congressional Budget Office's Panel of Economic Advisers**
- **Professor at the University of California at Berkeley; also held teaching positions at Harvard University and the London School of Economics**

During her career, Janet Yellen has investigated a wide variety of economic issues. She has paid special attention to wages, prices, and unemployment–issues that directly affect ordinary Americans. In her Senate confirmation hearings for the position of governor of the Federal Reserve Board, Yellen stated that she hoped to keep her eye on the people behind the numbers.

"I think stabilization policy is important–to avoid huge swings in unemployment. When you have the kind of recession we had in 1982 and 1983, for example, you can see the visible toll it takes on households. Perhaps because the causes and consequences of unemployment have been a focus of my research, I consider it easy to remain mindful of the people behind the numbers. In order to avoid high unemployment we must be careful not to push the economy below the NAIRU [Non-Accelerating Inflation Rate of Unemployment–the minimum rate of unemployment consistent with stable inflation], allowing inflation to rise and to become embedded in expectations. Because when that happens, it takes a period of above normal unemployment to lower inflation. That's the painful lesson of the '70s. Even when it comes to inflation we have to remember that prices [in themselves] do not affect social welfare. Inflation matters because of its repercussions on a country's economic performance, which in turn affects the welfare of individuals. Why are we in this business? It seems to me that it's to promote the well-being of American households. That's what it's all about."

Checking for Understanding

1. **According to Yellen, why is stabilization policy important?**
2. **Why is it dangerous to let inflation get out of hand?**

CHAPTER 13 Summary

Chapter Overview Visit the *Economics Today and Tomorrow* Web site at ett.glencoe.com and click on ***Chapter 13—Chapter Overviews*** to review chapter information.

SECTION 1 National Income Accounting

- The measurement of the national economy's performance is called **national income accounting**—and includes five statistical measures.
- **Gross domestic product (GDP)** is the total dollar value of all final goods and services produced in the nation during a single year.
- When **depreciation** is subtracted from GDP, you get a statistic called **net domestic product.**
- Three additional measurements—**national income, personal income,** and **disposable personal income**—look at how much money is available to be spent by businesses and individuals.

SECTION 2 Correcting Statistics for Inflation

- When **inflation** occurs, the **purchasing power** of the dollar declines.
- Inflation skews GDP by making it appear that more output was produced, when in reality only the prices of goods and services have increased.
- To find **real GDP,** the government measures inflation's effect on current GDP.
- Three common measurements of inflation are the **consumer price index,** the **producer price index,** and the **GDP price deflator.**

SECTION 3 Aggregate Demand and Supply

- **Aggregate demand** and **aggregate supply** relate the total quantity of all goods and services in the entire economy to the price level.
- Equilibrium exists where the **aggregate demand curve** intersects the **aggregate supply curve,** thus resulting in neither inflation nor deflation.

SECTION 4 Business Fluctuations

- The economy experiences **business fluctuations.**
- A **business cycle** begins with a **peak** or **boom,** then continues with a **contraction** toward a **recession** (and perhaps even a **depression**). The downward spiral hits a **trough,** then increases again in an **expansion** or **recovery.**
- The Great Depression was the worst economic crisis in United States history.

SECTION 5 Causes and Indicators of Business Fluctuations

- Economists link business fluctuations to four main forces: business investment, government activity, external factors, and psychological factors.
- To help business and government leaders in making economic decisions for the future, economists create and update **economic indicators.**

CHAPTER 13

Assessment and Activities

Self-Check Quiz Visit the *Economics Today and Tomorrow* Web site at ett.glencoe.com and click on ***Chapter 13—Self-Check Quizzes*** to prepare for the Chapter Test.

Identifying Key Terms

Write the letter of the definition in Column B below that correctly defines each term in Column A.

Column A

1. base year
2. trough
3. economic indicators
4. expansion
5. real GDP
6. business cycle

Column B

a. point when economic activity is at its lowest
b. figures for the nation's total production that have been corrected for inflation
c. measurement of specific aspects of the economy such as stock prices
d. used as a point of comparison for other years in a series of statistics
e. periodic ups and downs in the nation's economic activity
f. business recovery period, when economic activity increases

Recalling Facts and Ideas

Section 1

1. Net exports and government goods are two components of GDP. What are the other two components?
2. What five categories of income make up national income?
3. If you were given the statistic on disposable personal income, what other information would you need to derive personal income?

Section 2

4. What are the most commonly used price indexes?
5. What is the difference between inflation and deflation?
6. How would you determine real GDP if you knew only GDP?

Section 3

7. Why does the aggregate demand curve slope downward and the aggregate supply curve slope upward?
8. What is determined at the intersection of the aggregate supply and aggregate demand curves?
9. What would cause the AD curve to shift to the right?

Section 4

10. What are the four main phases of a business cycle?
11. When the economy enters a recession, what normally happens?
12. When was the most serious downturn in economic activity in the United States?

Section 5

13. How might psychological factors affect the business cycle?
14. What two aspects of government activity affect business cycles?

Thinking Critically

1. **Making Generalizations** How might knowledge of nationwide economic statistics help you?
2. **Summarizing Information** Create a diagram like the one below to summarize national income accounting. Start with the lowest statistic, disposable personal income, and work your way up to GDP—adding and subtracting the appropriate items.

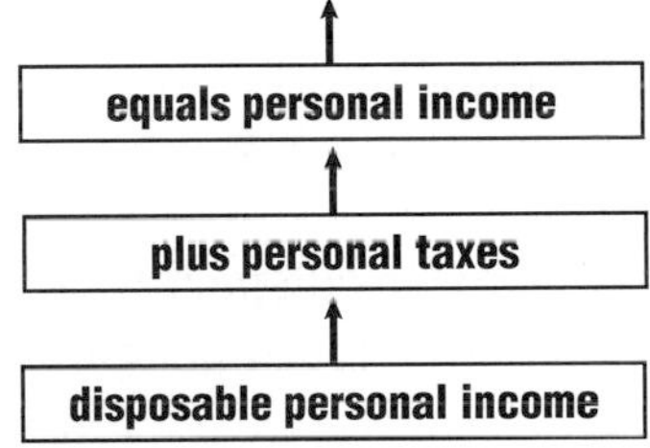

Applying Economic Concepts

Business Cycles Try to analyze what you think occurs throughout the economy during a recession. Make a list of some of the things that business owners may do to react to a recession, such as reduce employees' overtime hours.

Cooperative Learning Project

To make comparisons between the prices of things in the past and those of today, you have to make the distinction between current prices (often called *nominal values*), and prices adjusted for inflation *(real values)*. Working with a partner, use the following statistics and equation to find real 2000 GDP.

2000 nominal GDP = $10.223 trillion
2000 price deflator = 107.7
nominal GDP ÷ implicit price deflator × 100 = real GDP

Reviewing Skills

Taking Notes Research lagging indicators, coincident indicators, and leading indicators. Take notes on your research using the following guidelines:

- For each type of indicator, what are the various subgroups?
- How long has the indicator been reported in the United States?
- Can you find instances when the indicator was wildly inaccurate?

From your notes, write a paragraph describing how useful any of these indicators might be in accurately predicting changes in the nation's overall economic activity.

Technology Activity

Using the Internet Use the Internet to find the latest edition of the *Statistical Abstract of the United States*. Locate the tables in the "Prices" section that give price indexes for consumer goods for selected cities and metropolitan areas. Construct a line graph showing the rise in the index for "all items" over the last six years.

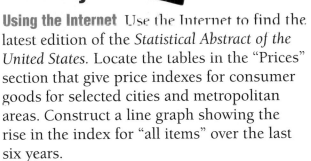

Analyzing the Global Economy

Use the Internet or a source in the library to find out the 10 countries with the highest real GDP. Then compare this list with the 10 countries with the highest real GDP per capita, found in the Global Economy feature on page 347.

Economics Lab

Constructing a Market Basket

From the classroom of Rochelle Tuchman, Shulamith High School, Brooklyn, New York

In Chapter 13 you learned how the consumer price index compares prices for a market basket of about 80,000 goods and services in order to adjust GDP for inflation. In this lab, you'll construct your own market basket and price index.

STEP A Tools Needed

- ✔ notebook
- ✔ pencil
- ✔ calculator
- ✔ transportation to local supermarket

STEP B Procedures to Follow

1. Survey students in your school to see what kinds of food their families eat the most.
2. Identify five categories of food that are purchased most often (and that are available in a supermarket): frozen pizza, pasta, soda, and so on.
3. Then identify three specific items in each category, including brand name and size (16 ounces, for example).
4. Also identify the locations of supermarkets in your community where the items can be purchased.
5. Now price your specific items on a per-week basis for one month. You must price the same product(s) in the same supermarket on the same day each week.
6. After the first visit to the supermarket, add up the total amount of the 15 items in your market basket. This number will signify your base year.
7. After each of the remaining three visits to the supermarket, add up the total amount of your market basket again, and compare the new totals to your base year.

STEP C Creating an Economic Model

Use your totals to construct a price index. It should begin with a listing of your market basket contents and quantities. Week 1, your base year, will have a value of 100. Index numbers for Weeks 2, 3, and 4 will show the percentage that the market basket price has risen since the "base year." Remember, to calculate the percentage of change, subtract 100 (base year value) from the new figure: [Week 2 figure] − 100 = percent change of market basket.

STEP D Lab Report Analysis

Study the price index you created in Step C, then answer the questions below.

1. What was the total amount of your market basket in your base year?
2. By how much did your price index change from your base year (Week 1) to Week 4?
3. Were you surprised by the results of your price index? Explain.

CHAPTER 14

Money and Banking

Why It's Important

Why are these coins considered money? Besides coins and cash, what other kinds of money exist? This chapter will explain what makes our currency money and how banks work to keep money in circulation.

To learn more about the supply of money in the United States, view the **Economics & You** *Chapter 18 video lesson:* **Money and Banking**

Chapter Overview Visit the *Economics Today and Tomorrow* Web site at ett.glencoe.com and click on ***Chapter 14—Chapter Overviews*** to preview chapter information.

SECTION 1

The Functions and Characteristics of Money

Cover Story

Discover, October 1998

[W]ealthy citizens [in Mesopotamia] were flaunting money at least as early as 2500 B.C. and perhaps a few hundred years before that. "There's just no way to get around it," says Marvin Powell, a historian at Northern Illinois University in De Kalb. "Silver in Mesopotamia functions like our money today. It's a means of exchange. People use it for a storage of wealth, and they use it for defining value."

Reader's Guide

Terms to Know

- money
- medium of exchange
- barter
- unit of accounting
- store of value
- commodity money
- representative money
- fiat money
- legal tender

Reading Objectives

1. What are the three functions of money?
2. What are the six major characteristics of money?

For thousands of years, money has made it possible for businesses to obtain easily what they need from suppliers and for consumers to obtain goods and services. What, however, is money? As you read this section, you'll learn the answer to this question.

The Functions of Money

The basis of the market economy is voluntary exchange. In the American economy, the exchange usually involves money in return for a good or service. Most Americans think of money as bills, coins, and checks. Historically, though, and in other economies, money might be shells, gold, or even goods such as sheep.

money: *anything customarily used as a medium of exchange, a unit of accounting, and a store of value*

medium of exchange: *use of money in exchange for goods or services*

barter: *exchange of goods and services for other goods and services*

unit of accounting: *use of money as a yardstick for comparing the values of goods and services in relation to one another*

Figure 14.1 shows several items that have been used as money. For example, Native Americans used wampum—beads made from shells. People in the Fiji Islands have used whales' teeth.

Economists identify money by certain functions. Anything that is used as a medium of exchange, a unit of accounting, and a store of value is considered **money.** See **Figure 14.2.**

Medium of Exchange To say that money is a **medium of exchange** simply means that a seller will accept it in exchange for a good or service. Most people are paid for their work in money, which they then can use to buy whatever they need or want. Without money, people would have to **barter**—exchange goods and services for other goods and services.

Barter requires what economists call a double coincidence of wants. Each party to a transaction must want exactly what the other person has to offer. This situation is rare. As a result, people in societies that barter for goods spend great amounts of time and effort making trades with one another. Bartering works only in small societies with fairly simple economic systems.

Unit of Accounting Money is the yardstick that allows people to compare the values of goods and services in relation to one another. In this way, money functions as a **unit of accounting.** Each nation uses a basic unit to measure the value of goods, as it uses the foot or meter to measure distance. In the United States, this base unit of value is the dollar. In Japan, it is the yen; in much of Europe, the euro. An item for sale is marked with a price that indicates its value in terms of that unit.

By using money prices as a factor in comparing goods, people can determine whether one item is a better bargain than another. A single unit of accounting also allows people to keep accurate financial records—records of debts owed, income saved, and so on.

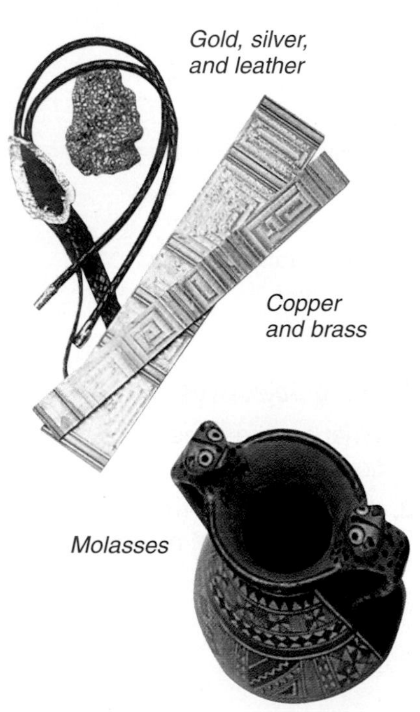

FIGURE 14.1

Selected Items Used as Money These items are just a sample of the various things that have been used as money.

FIGURE 14.2

Three Functions of Money All money serves three functions. The money this woman holds is serving as a medium of exchange; the vendor will accept it in exchange for a pizza. The money is also a unit of accounting–the products in the market are all priced in dollars, so the woman can compare values of different items. Finally, the money serves as a store of value–the woman has stored her purchasing power in the form of dollars.

Store of Value Money also serves as a **store of value.** You can sell something, such as your labor, and store the purchasing power that results from the sale in the form of money for later use. People usually receive their money income once a week, once every two weeks, or once a month. In contrast, they usually spend their income at different times during a pay period. To be able to buy things between paydays, a person can store some of his or her income in cash and some in a checking account. It is important to note that in periods of rapid and unpredictable inflation, money is less able to act as a store of value.

store of value: *use of money to store purchasing power for later use*

Characteristics of Money

Anything that people are willing to accept in exchange for goods can serve as money. At various times in history, cattle, salt, animal hides, gems, and tobacco have been used as mediums of exchange. Each of these items has certain characteristics that make it better or worse than others for use as money. Cattle, for example, are difficult to transport, but they are durable. Gems are easy to carry, but they are not easy to split into small pieces to use.

Figure 14.3 on page 378 lists the characteristics that to some degree all items used as money must have. Almost

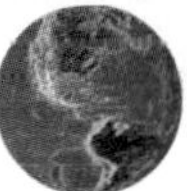

Global Economy

Russia's Barter Economy

Because Russian currency is not trusted, real money plays a fairly small part in Russia's economy today. Most business is conducted by barter or with IOUs. For example, workers rarely receive wages in the form of cash. A bicycle factory outside the city of Perm pays its workers in bicycles! To get cash, the workers have to sell their "paychecks." More often than not, they simply trade the bicycles for the products they want. ■

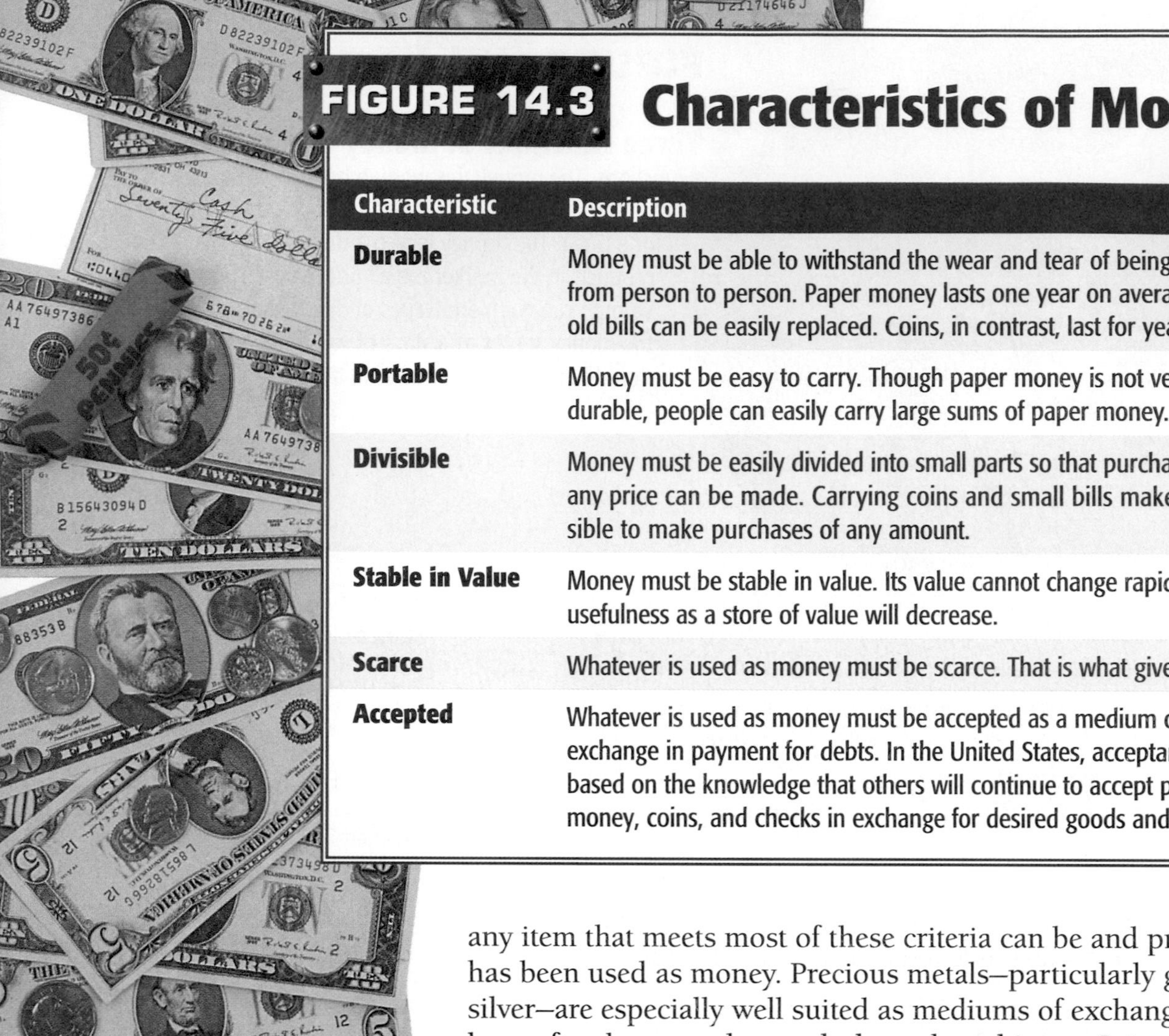

FIGURE 14.3 Characteristics of Money

Characteristic	Description
Durable	Money must be able to withstand the wear and tear of being passed from person to person. Paper money lasts one year on average, but old bills can be easily replaced. Coins, in contrast, last for years.
Portable	Money must be easy to carry. Though paper money is not very durable, people can easily carry large sums of paper money.
Divisible	Money must be easily divided into small parts so that purchases of any price can be made. Carrying coins and small bills makes it possible to make purchases of any amount.
Stable in Value	Money must be stable in value. Its value cannot change rapidly or its usefulness as a store of value will decrease.
Scarce	Whatever is used as money must be scarce. That is what gives it value.
Accepted	Whatever is used as money must be accepted as a medium of exchange in payment for debts. In the United States, acceptance is based on the knowledge that others will continue to accept paper money, coins, and checks in exchange for desired goods and services.

any item that meets most of these criteria can be and probably has been used as money. Precious metals–particularly gold and silver–are especially well suited as mediums of exchange, and have often been used as such throughout history. It is only in more recent times that paper money has been widely used as a medium of exchange.

Types of Money

commodity money: *a medium of exchange such as cattle or gems that has value as a commodity or good aside from its value as money*

representative money: *money that is backed by an item of value, such as gold or silver*

Mediums of exchange such as cattle and gems are considered **commodity money.** They have a value as a commodity, or good, aside from their value as money. Cattle are used for food. Gems are used for jewelry.

Representative money is money backed by—or exchangeable for—a valuable item such as gold or silver. Typically, the amount of representative money in circulation, or in use by people, was limited because it was linked to some scarce good, such as gold.

At one time, the United States government issued representative money in the form of silver and gold certificates. In addition, private banks accepted deposits of gold bars or silver ingots

Economic Connection to... History

A Chocolate Lover's Dream

The Aztec in Central America used cacao beans, from which chocolate is made, as money. Prices varied from a few beans for a piece of fruit to several thousand for an enslaved person.

Aztec merchants had to take care when selling expensive items. Payment usually came stored in sacks, and the sacks might contain counterfeit money—bean husks filled with mud. ■

(called bullion) in exchange for paper money called banknotes. The notes were a promise to convert the paper money back into coin or bullion on demand. These banks were supposed to keep enough gold or silver in reserve—on hand—to redeem their banknotes. That did not always happen, however.

Today all United States money is **fiat money,** meaning that its face value occurs through government fiat, or order. It is in this way declared **legal tender.**

fiat money: *money that has value because a government fiat, or order, has established it as acceptable for payment of debts*

legal tender: *money that by law must be accepted for payment of public and private debts*

Practice and **assess** key skills with ***Skillbuilder Interactive Workbook, Level 2.***

SECTION 1 Assessment

Understanding Key Terms

1. **Define** money, medium of exchange, barter, unit of accounting, store of value, commodity money, representative money, fiat money, legal tender.

Reviewing Objectives

2. What are the three functions of money?
3. **Graphic Organizer** Create a diagram like the one below to describe the six major characteristics of money.

Characteristics of Money

Applying Economic Concepts

4. **Money** Imagine that you live in a bartering society. List 10 items that you use frequently, and then identify alternative goods that you would be willing to trade for them.

Critical Thinking Activity

5. **Making Comparisons** Make a chart with five columns. In the first column, list Commodity Money, Representative Money, and Fiat Money. In the other four columns, write Description, Example, Advantage, and Disadvantage. Fill in the chart, comparing the three types of money. *(For help in using charts, see page xvii in the Economic Handbook.)*

Critical Thinking Skills

Synthesizing Information

Synthesizing information involves combining information from two or more sources. Information gained from one source often sheds new light upon other information.

- Analyze each source separately to understand its meaning.
- Determine what information each source adds to the subject.
- Identify points of agreement and disagreement between the sources. Ask: Can Source A give me new information or new ways of thinking about Source B?
- Find relationships between the information in the sources.

Learning the Skill

To learn how to synthesize information, follow the steps listed on the left.

Practicing the Skill

Study the sources below, then answer the questions.

Source A “*At present 60% to 70% of all dollars in circulation are used abroad. Today Panama is the best-known country that is 'dollarized,' but 11 others use the U.S. dollar. The best route for the emerging market countries is to unilaterally dollarize. . . . [T]he dollar could serve as the linchpin of a new global financial architecture, one that would eliminate currency crises, lower interest rates, and stimulate growth.*”

–*Forbes*, May 3, 1999

Source B “*When a country abandons its currency, it surrenders a central symbol of national identity. . . . We are courting trouble if many countries dollarize. They would blame us for their problems; and they would try to influence U.S. policies, pushing for either lower or higher interest rates.*”

–*Newsweek*, May 17, 1999

1. What is the main subject of each source?
2. Does Source B support or contradict Source A? Explain.
3. Summarize what you learned from both sources.

Application Activity

Find two sources of information on banking practices. What are the main ideas in the sources? How does each source add to your understanding of the topic?

Practice and **assess** key skills with ***Skillbuilder Interactive Workbook, Level 2.***

SECTION 2

History of American Money and Banking

Cover Story

The Economist, August 21, 2003

Who wants to buy a Japanese bank? They are barely profitable, and they are weighed down by $1.25 trillion of bad debts. . . . Yet several, mostly foreign, groups are out shopping. A handful of private-equity groups from America have bought bankrupt regional banks. The best-known foreign purchase was made by Ripplewood Holdings in 2000.

Reader's Guide

Terms to Know

- overdraft checking
- electronic funds transfer (EFT)
- automated teller machine (ATM)

Reading Objectives

1. What are some of the most important events in the history of American money and banking?
2. What are six services provided by banks and savings institutions?
3. How has electronic banking changed banking services?

American banking has included everything from wampum to "virtual" money—banking in cyberspace on the Internet. In this section, you'll learn about the development of and changes in the United States banking industry.

History of American Banking

Because the history of money in the United States is so closely tied to the development of the banking system, the time line in **Figure 14.4** on pages 382–383 describes both. During the colonial period, England did not permit the American colonies to print money or mint coins. Bartering for goods was common.

Time Line of American Money and Banking

Years	Events
1780s	The new nation has no reliable medium of exchange. National leaders disagree on a type of banking system. One group, led by Alexander Hamilton, believes a national banking system is necessary for development. The opposition, led by Thomas Jefferson, argues that only states should have the right to charter banks.
1791	Congress establishes the First Bank of the United States and gives it a 20-year charter. The bank is a private business, although the government supplies one-fifth of its starting capital. It serves as a depository for government funds, makes loans to the government and private individuals and businesses, and regulates the activities of banks with state charters. It also issues banknotes backed by gold.
1792	Congress passes the Coinage Act, which organizes a mint and establishes the dollar as the basic unit of currency for the nation. The Act also places the nation on a bimetallic monetary standard—the value of the dollar is fixed according to specific quantities of both silver and gold.
1811	Congress refuses to renew the charter of the First Bank because of questions about its legality and fears that it is gaining too much power. Without federal controls, dozens of state-chartered banks lend money and issue banknotes freely, many of which are not backed by enough gold or silver reserves.
1816	Congress establishes the Second Bank of the United States after the financial confusion caused by the War of 1812. Like the First Bank, it brings some order to the banking system. It pressures state-chartered banks to limit lending and to keep enough gold and silver in reserve to redeem their banknotes. Opposition to a strong national bank remains, however. In 1832 President Andrew Jackson vetoes legislation to extend the Second Bank's charter.
1830s–1860s	The end of the Second Bank brings another rapid rise in state-chartered banks. The amount of money in circulation varies widely. Such shifts in the amount of money available result in major fluctuations in business activity and prices.
Civil War	To help pay for the war, the United States issues fiat money—the first time since the Revolutionary War. These United States notes, called *greenbacks,* change in value as confidence in the Union army rises or falls. Difficulties in raising money for the war make clear the need for a better monetary and banking system. In 1863 and 1864, Congress passes the National Bank acts. These acts establish a system of federally chartered private banks, called *national banks.* The government also sets up a safe, uniform currency by requiring that all national banknotes be fully backed by government bonds. The *Comptroller of the Currency* is created to grant charters for national banks and to oversee their activities.

Years	Events
Late 1860s–Early 1900s	The nation shifts to a gold monetary standard in 1869. The federal government begins redeeming early 1860s greenbacks for gold coins. Despite the new banking system, problems remain. There is no simple way to regulate the amount of national banknotes in circulation, so periodic shortages of money occur. Financial panics occur in 1873, 1884, 1893, and 1907. Many banks with low reserves are forced to close.
1913	To control the amount of money in circulation, Congress establishes the Federal Reserve System. It serves as the nation's central bank with power to regulate reserves in national banks, make loans to member banks, and control the growth of the money supply. In 1914 the system begins issuing paper money called *Federal Reserve notes*. These notes soon become the major form of currency in circulation.
1929	The Great Depression begins. Stocks and other investments lose much of their value. Bankrupt businesses and individuals are unable to repay their loans.
1929–1934	A financial panic causes thousands of banks to collapse. When President Franklin Roosevelt takes office in March 1933, he declares a "bank holiday," closing all banks. Each bank is allowed to reopen only after it proves it is financially sound. Congress passes the Glass-Steagall Banking Act in June, establishing the Federal Deposit Insurance Corporation (FDIC). This new agency helps restore public confidence in banks by insuring funds of individual depositors in case of a bank failure. The nation switches from a gold standard to a fiat monetary standard. The government stops converting greenbacks into gold, calls in all gold coins and certificates, and prohibits private ownership of gold.
1930s–1960s	Banking reforms of the 1930s allow banks to enter a period of long-term stability, in which few banks fail.
Late 1960s–1970s	Congress passes a series of laws to protect consumers in dealing with financial institutions. The Truth in Lending Act of 1968, the Equal Credit Opportunity Act of 1974, and the Community Reinvestment Act of 1977 make clear the rights and responsibilities of banks and consumers. Banks begin using computers to transfer money electronically and to handle many banking activities. Congress passes the Electronic Funds Transfer Act of 1978 to protect consumers using these new services.
1980s–present	As part of the general move toward deregulation of business, Congress passes the Depository Institutions Deregulation and Monetary Control Act in 1980. Deregulation allows the savings and loan industry to make risky loans. Many S&Ls face bankruptcy. Congress passes the Financial Institutions Reform, Recovery, and Enforcement Act of 1989. The full cost of bailing out the S&Ls is $300 billion, or about $4,000 per United States family in future taxes. The FDIC takes over regulation of the thrift institutions industry. Banking continues to evolve, incorporating technology such as e-cash on the Internet.

Student Web Activity Visit the *Economics Today and Tomorrow* Web site at ett.glencoe.com and click on ***Chapter 14—Student Web Activities*** to see how online banking works.

Though scarce, some European gold and silver coins also circulated in the colonies. The Spanish *dolár,* later called the "dollar" by colonists, was one of the more common coins.

The Revolutionary War brought even more confusion to the already haphazard colonial money system. To help pay for the war, the Continental Congress issued bills of credit, called Continentals, that could be used to pay debts. So many of these notes were issued that they became worthless, and people often refused to accept them. The phrase "not worth a Continental" became a way of describing something of little value.

After the war, establishing a reliable medium of exchange became a major concern of the new nation. The Constitution, ratified in 1788, gave Congress the power to mint coins, although private banks were still allowed to print banknotes representing gold and silver on deposit.

Banking Services

Banks and savings institutions today offer a wide variety of services, including checking accounts, interest on certain types of checking accounts, automatic deposit and payment, storage of valuables, transfer of money from one person to another, and overdraft checking. **Overdraft checking** allows a customer to write a check for more money than exists in his or her account. The bank lends the needed amount and the customer pays the money back, usually at a relatively high rate of interest.

overdraft checking: *checking account that allows a customer to write a check for more money than exists in his or her account*

In general, the types of banking services are the same across the country. The exact terms and conditions of the services, however, vary from state to state according to each state's banking laws. When choosing a bank or savings institution, you should investigate the bank's service charges.

Electronic Banking

One of the most important changes in banking began in the late 1970s with the introduction of the computer. With it came **electronic funds transfer (EFT),** a system of putting onto computers all the various banking functions that in the past had to be handled on paper. One of the most common features

electronic funds transfer (EFT): *system of putting onto computers all the banking functions that in the past were handled on paper* of EFT is **automated teller machines (ATMs).** These units let consumers do their banking without the help of a teller.

Today you can even do your banking from home. You can see your account balances, transfer funds from a savings account to a checking account, and often even apply for a loan—all on the Internet.

automated teller machine (ATM): *unit that allows consumers to do their banking without the help of a teller*

EFT Concerns Although EFT can save time, trouble, and costs in making transactions, it does have some drawbacks. The possibility of tampering and lack of privacy are increased because all records are stored in a computer. A person on a computer terminal could call up and read or even alter the account files of a bank customer in any city, if he or she knew how to get around the safeguards built into the system. In response to these and other concerns, the Electronic Fund Transfer Act of 1978 describes the rights and responsibilities of participants in EFT systems. For example, EFT customers are responsible for only $50 in losses when someone steals or illegally uses their ATM cards, if they report the cards missing within two days. If they wait more than two days, they could be responsible for as much as $500. Users are also protected against computer mistakes.

Practice and **assess** key skills with ***Skillbuilder Interactive Workbook, Level 2.***

SECTION 2 Assessment

Understanding Key Terms

1. **Define** overdraft checking, electronic funds transfer (EFT), automated teller machine (ATM).

Reviewing Objectives

2. **Graphic Organizer** Create a time line like the one below to list and describe at least five of the most important events in the history of American money and banking. See **Figure 14.4** on pages 382–383 for information.

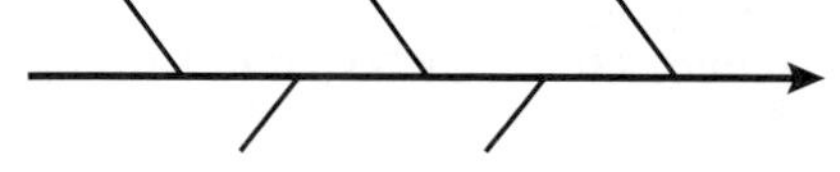

3. What are six services offered by banks and savings institutions?
4. How has electronic banking changed banking services?

Applying Economic Concepts

5. **Money** In 1934 the government stopped backing paper money with gold. Some experts have proposed a return to the gold standard. Do you think this would be a good idea? Why or why not?

Critical Thinking Activity

6. **Drawing Inferences** Why do you think coins have been a more desirable form of money than paper currency throughout American history?

BusinessWeek

SPOTLIGHT ON THE ECONOMY

How Higher Fees Hurt Banks

Check It Out! In this chapter you learned about banking services. In this article, read to learn how consumers are reacting to higher bank fees for those services.

Anyone who has maintained a checking account over the past decade knows that the rules of the game have been dramatically changing. Specifically, your once friendly bank or thrift institution has probably been imposing a lot more fees and restrictions on your account–in an understandable effort to save money and wring even more profits from your need for its services.

Among other things, many banks now try to save money on handling canceled checks–either by not returning them at all or, more likely, charging either a set monthly amount for all returned checks or a per-check fee. Some also charge customers for using live tellers instead of ATMs. And many have been raising their fees considerably for handling bounced checks and for using other banks' ATMs.

Ironically, reports economist Joanna Stavins in a recent issue of the Federal Reserve Bank of Boston's *New England Economic Review*, most of the gambits don't seem to be paying off. In a study of checking accounts at some 250 banks around the nation in 1997, she found that only two of the features described above appeared to be producing higher revenues: increased charges for bounced checks and higher fixed monthly fees for returning canceled checks.

In all other cases, raising fees or tightening restrictions tended to induce depositors to switch to other institutions–thus lowering the banks' take. Consumers, it seems, are a lot more sensitive to such practices than banks realize.

Think About It

1. **What actions are banks taking to earn more profits?**
2. **Analyze the consequences of a bank's decision to raise its fees.**

SECTION 3

Types of Money in the United States

Cover Story

Kiplinger's Personal Finance Magazine, July 2000

To get its new Sacajawea dollar into circulation, the U.S. Mint has issued more than 500 million of the golden coins since the end of January, not only to banks, but also to Wal-Mart and Sam's Club stores. But in what may be the greatest coin trick ever, the dollars have all but vanished. People are making them into jewelry, auctioning them off on eBay, and leaving them under pillows on behalf of the tooth fairy—anything but spending them. . . . The Mint expects Sacajawea to be back in circulation by year-end, when more than a billion of the dollars will have been minted and the novelty, it hopes, will have worn off.

Reader's Guide

Terms to Know

- checking account
- checkable deposits
- thrift institutions
- debit card
- near moneys
- M1
- M2

Reading Objectives

1. What is the difference between money and near moneys?
2. What does the M2 definition of money include?

Randy L'Teton, model for the Sacajawea coin

When you think of money, you may think only of coins and paper bills. As you read this section, you'll learn that money is more than just cash.

Money and Near Moneys

Money in use today consists of more than just currency. It also includes deposits in checking and savings accounts, plus certain other investments.

Currency All United States coins in circulation today are token coins. The value of the metal in each coin is less than its exchange value. A quarter, for example, consists of a mixture of copper and nickel. The value of the metal in a quarter, however, is much less than 25 cents. The Bureau of the Mint, which is part of the Treasury Department, makes all coins. About 5 percent of the currency in circulation in the United States today is in the form of coins.

Most of the nation's currency is in the form of Federal Reserve notes issued by Federal Reserve banks. The Bureau of Engraving and Printing, also part of the Treasury Department, prints all Federal Reserve notes. They are issued in denominations of $1,

FIGURE 14.5

Writing a Check and Balancing Your Checkbook Always fill out your checks completely and clearly in ink. See the sample check in Part A. After you write a check to someone or make a deposit into your checking account, write the number, date, and amount in your check register. See the sample register in Part B.

Then, when you receive your monthly bank statement, balance your checkbook by following these steps:

1. Sort your checks by number. Check off each one in your checkbook.
2. Check off your deposit slips.
3. Deduct service charges and bank fees from your checkbook balance.
4. Add to the bank statement balance any deposits that have not cleared.
5. Total the amount of checks that have not cleared. Subtract this total from the amount on your bank statement.

The sample checkbook register in Part B shows that you have a running total of $191.36 in your account. Balance this total against the bank statement in Part C.

A

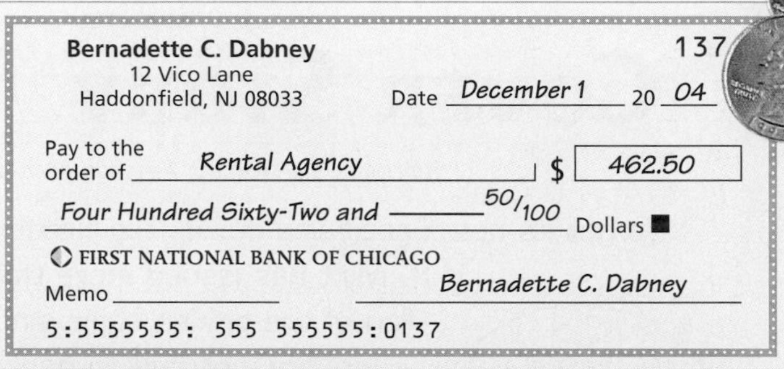

Bernadette C. Dabney
12 Vico Lane
Haddonfield, NJ 08033
137
Date December 1 20 04
Pay to the order of Rental Agency $ 462.50
Four Hundred Sixty-Two and 50/100 Dollars
FIRST NATIONAL BANK OF CHICAGO
Memo
Bernadette C. Dabney
5:5555555: 555 555555:0137

B

Number	Date	Description	Payment of Debt	Fee	Deposit of Credit	Balance
						$ 827.91
132	10/25	Fashion Shop	$ 73.16		$	$ 754.75
133	11/1	Rent	462.50			292.25
134	11/7	Phone	83.00			209.25
135	11/14	Cash	50.00			159.25
136	11/15	J.W. Little	10.00			149.25
—	11/22	John's check			4.00	153.25
—	11/23	Paycheck			500.61	653.86
137	12/1	Rent	462.50			191.36

C

FIRST NATIONAL BANK OF CHICAGO

Bernadette C. Dabney
12 Vico Lane
Haddonfield, NJ 08033

123-456-7
Account Number
1 Dec. 2004
Statement Date

Summary of Accounts

Account Number	Previous Balance	Total Credits	Total Debits	Total Charges	Current Balance
123-456-7	827.91	504.61	674.66	3.00	660.86

Previous Balance	827.91	Current Balance	660.86

Debits	Credits	Balance
Nov. 4 132 73.16		754.75
8 133 462.50		292.25
15 134 83.00		209.25
135 50.00		159.25
	Nov. 22 4.00	163.25
	23 500.61	663.86
SC 3.00		660.86

$2, $5, $10, $20, $50, and $100. (Larger notes used to be printed, but the practice was stopped to make it harder for criminals to hide large amounts of cash.)

The Treasury Department has also issued United States notes in several denominations. These bills have the words *United States Note* printed across the top and can be distinguished from Federal Reserve notes by a red Treasury seal. United States notes make up less than 1 percent of the paper money in circulation. Both Federal Reserve notes and United States notes are fiat money, or legal tender.

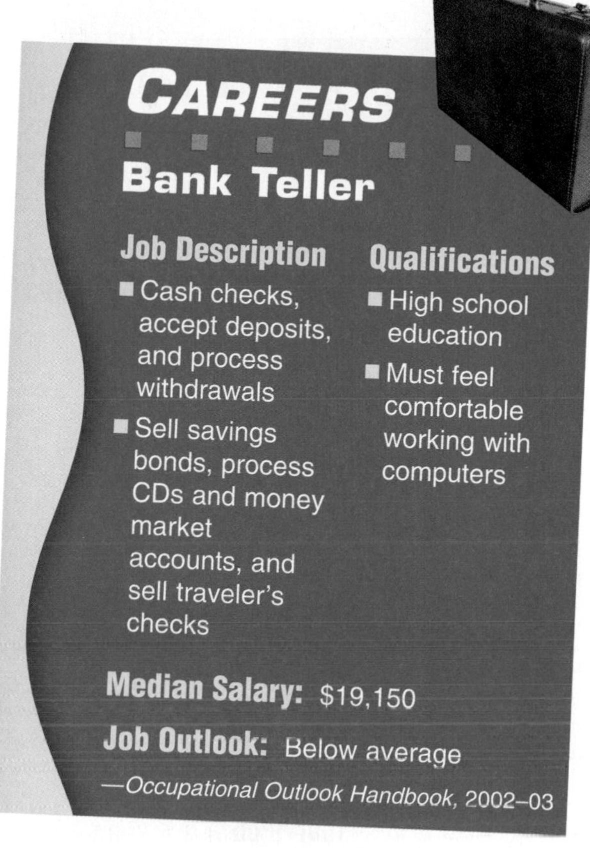

Checks A **checking account** is money deposited in a bank that a person can withdraw at any time by writing a check. The bank must pay the amount of the check on demand, or when it is presented for payment. Such accounts used to be called *demand deposits.* Today we call these **checkable deposits,** and a variety of financial institutions offer them.

Commercial banks used to be the only financial institutions that could offer checkable deposits. Today all **thrift institutions**–mutual savings banks, savings and loan associations (S&Ls), and credit unions–offer checkable deposits. In addition, many brokerage houses offer the equivalent of checking accounts. Merrill Lynch and Fidelity Investments are two examples.

The largest part of the money supply in the United States consists of checkable accounts. **Figure 14.5** shows how to write a check and balance a checkbook.

checking account: *account in which deposited money can be withdrawn at any time by writing a check*

checkable deposits: *money deposited in a bank that can be withdrawn at any time by presenting a check*

thrift institutions: *mutual savings banks, S&Ls, and credit unions that offer many of the same services as commercial banks*

Credit Cards and Debit Cards Even though many people use their credit cards to purchase goods and services, the credit card itself is not money. It acts neither as a unit of accounting nor as a store of value. The use of your credit card is really a loan to you by the issuer of the card, whether it is a bank, retail store, gas company, or American Express. Basically, then, credit card "money" represents a future claim on funds that you will have later. Credit cards defer rather than complete transactions that ultimately involve the use of money.

A **debit card** automatically withdraws money from a checkable account. When you use your debit card to purchase something, you are in effect giving an instruction to your bank to

debit card: *device used to make cashless purchases; money is electronically withdrawn from the consumer's checkable account and transferred directly to the store's bank account*

FIGURE 14.6 **M1 and M2** With the deregulation of banking services in the early 1980s, the definition of the money supply was enlarged to include the new types of accounts.

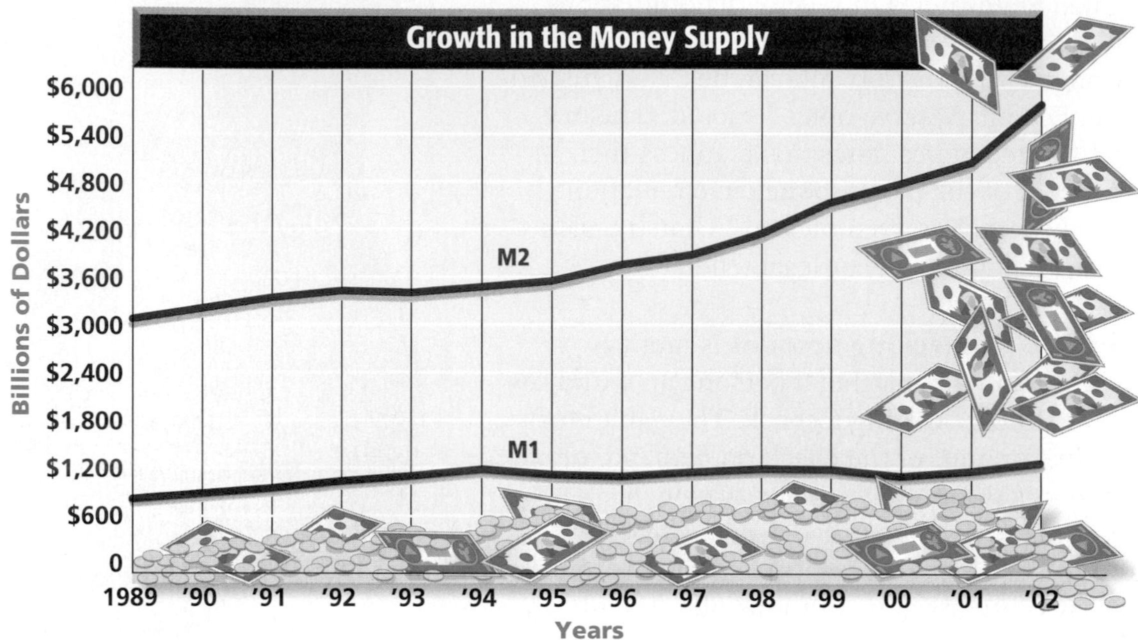

Source: Board of Governors of the Federal Reserve System

For an online update of this graph, visit ett.glencoe.com and click on ***Textbook Updates—Chapter 14.***

transfer money directly from your bank account to the store's bank account. The use of a debit card does not create a loan. Debit card "money" is similar to checkable account money.

near moneys: *assets, such as savings accounts, that can be turned into money relatively easily and without the risk of loss of value*

Near Moneys Numerous other assets are almost, but not exactly, like money. These assets are called **near moneys.** Their values are stated in terms of money, and they have high liquidity in comparison to other investments, such as stocks. Near moneys can be turned into currency or into a means of payment, such as a check, relatively easily and without the risk of loss of value. For example, if you have a bank savings account, you cannot write a check on it. You can, however, go to the bank and withdraw some or all of your funds. You can then redeposit these funds in your checking account or spend it all as cash.

Time deposits and savings account balances are near moneys. Both pay interest, and neither can be withdrawn by check. Time deposits require that a depositor notify the financial institution within a certain period of time, often 10 days, before withdrawing money. Savings accounts do not usually require such notification.

The Money Supply

How much money is there in the United States today? That question is not so easy to answer. First, the definition of *money supply* must be agreed upon. Currently, two basic definitions are used, although others exist. The first is called M1, and the second M2.

M1 includes all currency (bills and coins), all checkable deposits, and traveler's checks. **M2** includes everything in M1 plus savings deposits, time deposits, small-denomination certificates of deposit, money market deposit accounts, money market mutual fund balances, and other more specialized account balances. **Figure 14.6** shows the growth of M1 and M2 from 1989 to 2002.

M1: *narrowest definition of the money supply; consists of moneys that can be spent immediately and against which checks can be written*

M2: *broader definition of the money supply; includes all of M1, plus such near moneys as money market mutual fund balances, certificates of deposit, and Eurodollars*

Practice and **assess** key skills with ***Skillbuilder Interactive Workbook, Level 2.***

SECTION 3 Assessment

Understanding Key Terms

1. **Define** checking account, checkable deposits, thrift institutions, debit card, near moneys, M1, M2.

Reviewing Objectives

2. **Graphic Organizer** Create a chart like the one below to explain the difference between money and near moneys.

Money	Near Moneys	Differences

3. What does the M2 definition of money include?

Applying Economic Concepts

4. **Exchange, Money, and Interdependence** What various forms or types of money and near moneys do you use?

Critical Thinking Activity

5. **Summarizing Information** Use a search engine to find the Bureau of Engraving and Printing Web site. Find out how currency is printed and what security measures are taken to avoid counterfeiting. What steps would you suggest to minimize counterfeiting?

People & Perspectives

- **Administrator of the United States Small Business Administration (SBA)**
- **Served as chairman of the board for the Latin Business Association and as a board member for the Minority Business Opportunity Committee in Los Angeles**
- **Founded his own company, Barreto Insurance and Financial Services, which specialized in providing financial services to California's Latino population**

Hector Barreto

GOVERNMENT OFFICIAL (1961-)

In 2001 President George W. Bush appointed Hector Barreto as Administrator of the Small Business Administration (SBA). The SBA oversees the development and delivery of financial and business programs to aid small businesses. Barreto outlined some benefits of small businesses:

"... Small business in the United States remains the swiftest and surest way of achieving the American Dream, regardless of your beginnings. [It] is the largest employer in the United States. [It] remains the most effective market laboratory for new ideas and innovations. Small business is the place where ideas are conceived, tested, and proved. Small business tax revenues are the backbone of our local, state, and national governments, and the reason our nation can do so much for so many."

Barreto shares the impact of small business on his life:

"... I have always lived the benefit of small business on a personal level. It has empowered my family to achieve the American Dream. Through my national small business relationships, I have come to appreciate the power and importance of small business on a national and international level."

Barreto believes the SBA will evolve to meet the needs of U.S. small businesses:

"... Through my small business ownership and relationships, I have [spoken] with many entrepreneurs. I have gained some insight into the special challenges and barriers to entry that negatively impact today's entrepreneurs.... [S]uccessful small business requires a sound business plan, relationships, and opportunity.... A successful Agency empowers small business to achieve its goals."

Checking for Understanding

1. **According to Barreto, what are some of the benefits of small businesses?**
2. **How does Barreto plan to help small businesses achieve their goals?**

CHAPTER  Summary

Chapter Overview Visit the *Economics Today and Tomorrow* Web site at ett.glencoe.com and click on ***Chapter 14—Chapter Overviews*** to review chapter information.

SECTION 1 The Functions and Characteristics of Money

- **Money** has three functions. It can be used as a **medium of exchange,** a **unit of accounting,** and a **store of value.**
- Anything serving as money must be durable, portable, divisible, stable in value, scarce, and accepted as a medium of exchange in payment for debts.
- Money that has an alternative use as a commodity—cattle, gems, and tobacco, for example—is considered **commodity money.**
- Money that is backed by—or can be exchanged for—gold or silver is known as **representative money.**
- Today all United States money is **fiat money,** or **legal tender.**

SECTION 2 History of American Money and Banking

- Throughout American history, people have used commodity money, European coins, privately printed banknotes, and many other forms of notes.
- To control the amount of money in circulation, Congress established the Federal Reserve System in 1913. It serves as the nation's central bank. In 1914 the system began issuing paper money called Federal Reserve notes, which soon became the major form of currency.
- The Constitution of the United States gave Congress the power to mint coins. It was not until the Civil War that the government set up a safe, uniform currency.
- In 1934 the nation switched from a gold standard to a fiat money standard.
- **Electronic funds transfer** has revolutionized the banking industry, with customers using **automated teller machines** and even the Internet to do their banking.

SECTION 3 Types of Money in the United States

- Money today consists of more than just currency. It also includes deposits in **checking accounts** as well as **debit cards** and **near moneys.**
- Economists measure the amount of money in the economy by adding up **M1**—currency, all **checkable deposits,** and traveler's checks. Then they calculate **M2**—all the items in M1 plus savings deposits, time deposits, small-denomination certificates of deposit, and other account balances.

CHAPTER 14

Assessment and Activities

Self-Check Quiz Visit the *Economics Today and Tomorrow* Web site at ett.glencoe.com and click on ***Chapter 14—Self-Check Quizzes*** to prepare for the Chapter Test.

Identifying Key Terms

Write the letter of the definition in Column B that correctly defines each term in Column A.

Column A

1. fiat money
2. checkable deposits
3. M1
4. commodity money
5. near moneys
6. legal tender
7. electronic funds transfer

Column B

a. money that by law must be accepted for payment of debts
b. currency in circulation, traveler's checks, plus checking-type deposits
c. money in a bank that can be withdrawn at any time
d. money that has value because the government has established it as acceptable payment for debts
e. computerized banking functions that previously were handled on paper
f. assets that can be turned into money fairly easily
g. money that has value aside from its value as money

Recalling Facts and Ideas

Section 1

1. What is the alternative to using money?
2. Money should be durable and divisible. What other characteristics should money have?
3. Is the type of money used in the United States commodity money, representative money, or fiat money?

Section 2

4. What type of system did the early colonists use when they bought and sold goods and services?
5. When was the most serious banking panic of the twentieth century?
6. Electronic banking is increasingly common today. What form of this system do most consumers use?

Section 3

7. What are the only denominations of paper currency being issued today by the federal government?
8. Why were checking accounts formerly called demand deposits?
9. What is the distinction between money and near moneys?
10. Why is M1 considered a narrower definition of the money supply than M2?

Thinking Critically

1. **Making Comparisons** Create a diagram like the one below to compare the costs and benefits of engaging in barter to the costs and benefits of using money.

	Costs	Benefits
Barter		
Money		

2. **Making Generalizations** Why are debit cards similar to money, whereas credit cards are not?

Applying Economic Concepts

The Functions of Money The three functions of money are as a medium of exchange, a unit of accounting, and a store of value. Keep track of any time you use money, see money used, or see dollar values written out somewhere. Try to determine in each instance what function the money is serving. For example, if you see a headline that says "Microsoft Corporation Sales Increased to $10 Billion," you know that money is being used as a unit of accounting.

Cooperative Learning Project

During the 1930s, the United States underwent a tragic economic depression. Work in groups to research the following aspects of daily life.

- What happened to incomes and prices?
- What happened to savings accounts?
- What happened to the availability of jobs?

Each member of each group should research one question. Summarize the group's notes to develop a lecture that describes what actually happened during the Great Depression.

Reviewing Skills

Synthesizing Information Imagine that the country is returning to privately issued banknotes. Design the currency you would like to see in circulation.

Use information from the Bureau of Engraving and Printing's Web site to gather data about the exact measurements of existing currency. Then make a list of items, ideas, people, and so on that are important to you. Utilize your list to help create your currency. Share your design with the rest of the class.

Technology Activity

Using a Database Analyze the currency in your possession. List the features that appear on the front and back of each bill or coin, noting the similarities and differences between the various currencies.

Create a database that could be accessed by foreign visitors to describe the specific features and purposes of each bill and coin. Create fields such as portrait, paper/coin, value, Federal Reserve Bank, watermarks, colors, etc.

Analyzing the Global Economy

Analyze several foreign coins and paper currencies. Use a magnifying glass if necessary. Make a chart listing the following items noted on each currency: Country of Origin, Monetary Unit, Year of Origin, Watermarks, Identity of People Pictured, Symbols, Natural Features, Buildings or Animals Shown, Other. Compare the foreign currency to United States currency, and share your chart with the rest of the class.

A Brief History of Money Over the centuries such items as cattle, salt, large stones, seashells, metals, beads, tea, coffee, tobacco, fishhooks, and furs have served as money. Some of the more important developments in the history of money are described here.

Two Bits

Do you know why people sometimes call a quarter "two bits"? The origin of this term dates back to colonial times. The American colonists used Spanish silver dollar coins called pieces of eight. Each coin was divided into eight pieces—or bits—so that it could be broken to make change. Four bits was equal to half a dollar, while two bits equaled a quarter.

Rings and Ingots

Perhaps as early as 2500 B.C. the people of ancient Egypt and Mesopotamia—the land between the Tigris and Euphrates Rivers—were using gold and silver as money. The money took the form of rings, small ornaments, and ingots, or bars.

The First Coins

The Lydians, who lived in what is now western Turkey, probably made the first coins during the 600s B.C. These coins were made of electrum, a mix of gold and silver, and were stamped with pictures of gods or emperors. The Greeks, Persians, and Romans adopted Lydian coining techniques and, in time, the use of coins spread throughout much of Western Europe.

The First Paper Banknotes

The Chinese may have begun to make coins around the same time as the Lydians. These coins were made of bronze and often had holes in them so that they could be carried on a string. The Chinese also began using paper banknotes—printed on paper made from mulberry bark—in the A.D. 800s.

Cowrie Shells

Cowrie shells have been used as money throughout Asia, Africa, and Oceania. The cowrie was still in use in some African countries as recently as the mid-1900s. The name for Ghana's monetary unit, the cedi, comes from the Ghanaian word meaning "cowrie shell."

Thinking Globally

1. **Where did the use of coins develop?**
2. **What developments in the history of money took place in China?**
3. **How is the history of money in Africa reflected in the currency of Ghana?**

CHAPTER 15

The Federal Reserve System and Monetary Policy

Why It's Important

Who determines how much money exists in the United States? This chapter will explain who's in charge of the money supply and how they decide what amount to put into circulation.

To learn more about the money supply, view the **Economics & You** *Chapter 22 video lesson:* **The Federal Reserve System and Monetary Policy**

ECONOMICS Online

Chapter Overview Visit the *Economics Today and Tomorrow* Web site at ett.glencoe.com and click on ***Chapter 15—Chapter Overviews*** to preview chapter information.

SECTION 1 Organization and Functions of the Federal Reserve System

COVER STORY

THE WASHINGTON POST, FEBRUARY 10, 1999

The Federal Reserve cannot put a dollar in anyone's pocket, provide jobs for very many people, or buy more than a tiny amount of goods and services that the nation produces. But the 86-year-old government bank can have an enormous impact on how you spend, invest, or borrow money. . . . That is because the Fed . . . is in charge of the nation's monetary policy, taking actions almost daily to help determine how much money is available, how easily it may be borrowed, and how costly it will be.

READER'S GUIDE

Terms to Know

- Fed
- monetary policy
- Federal Open Market Committee
- check clearing

Reading Objectives

1. How is the Federal Reserve System in the United States organized?
2. What are the functions of the Fed?

Congress created the Federal Reserve System in 1913 as the central banking organization in the United States. Its major purpose was to end the periodic financial panics (recessions) that had occurred during the 1800s and into the early 1900s. Over the years, many other responsibilities have been added to the Federal Reserve System, or **Fed,** as it is called. In this section, you'll learn how the Fed is organized to carry out its functions.

Fed: *the Federal Reserve System created by Congress in 1913 as the nation's central banking organization*

Organization of the Federal Reserve System

The Federal Reserve System is made up of a Board of Governors assisted by the Federal Advisory Council, the Federal Open Market Committee, 12 Federal Reserve district banks, 25 branch banks, and about 4,000 member banks. As its name states, the Fed is a system, or network, of banks. Power is not concentrated in a single central bank but is shared by the governing board and the 12 district banks. **See Figure 15.1.**

The Fed is responsible for monetary policy in the United States. **Monetary policy** involves changing the rate of growth of the supply of money in circulation in order to affect the amount of credit, thereby affecting business activity in the economy.

monetary policy: *policy that involves changing the rate of growth of the supply of money in circulation in order to affect the cost and availability of credit*

Board of Governors The *Board of Governors* directs the operations of the Fed. It supervises the 12 Federal Reserve district banks and regulates certain activities of member banks and all other depository institutions.

FIGURE 15.1

Organization of the Fed Since the change in banking regulations in the early 1980s, nonmember banks are also subject to control by the Federal Reserve System.

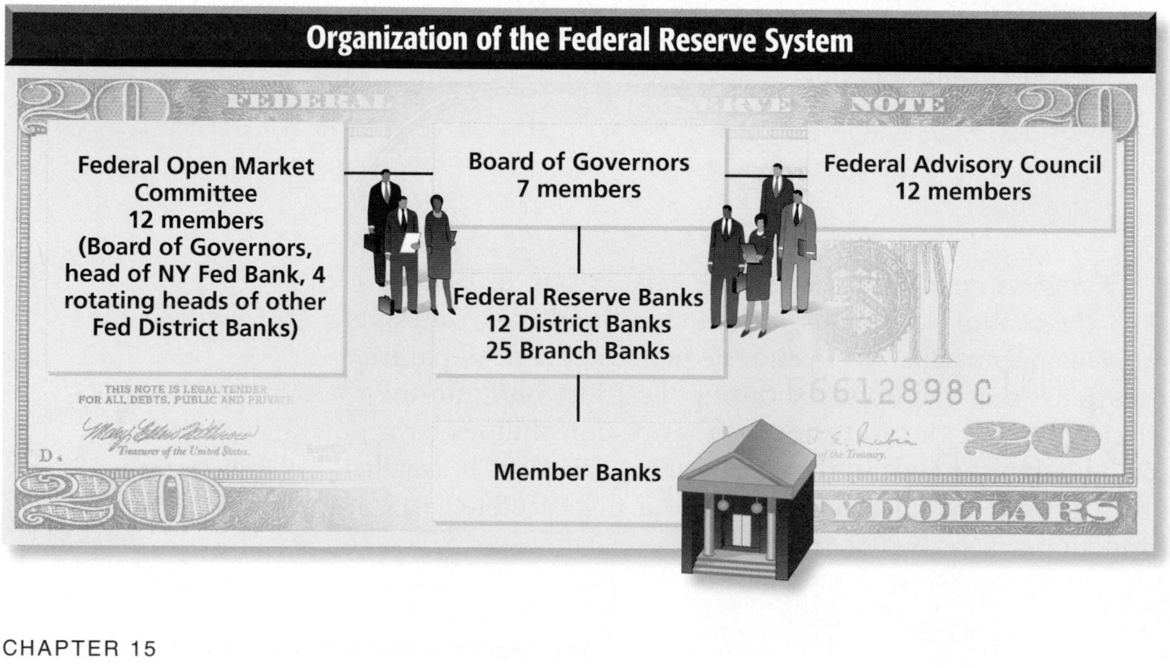

Economic Connection to... History

The First Central Bank

The Bank of Amsterdam was established in Holland in 1609. At that time, Amsterdam was a center of world trade. More than 340 different kinds of silver coins and about 500 types of gold coins circulated throughout the city. Dutch merchants had little idea of how much these coins were worth, so the Bank of Amsterdam was set up under a charter from the city to standardize the currency.

The Bank of Amsterdam operated as Holland's central bank for more than 200 years. After making a series of bad loans, however, it failed and went out of business in 1819—almost 100 years *before* America's central bank was founded. ■

The 7 full-time members of the Board of Governors are appointed by the President of the United States with the approval of the Senate. The President chooses one member as a chairperson. Each member of the board serves for 14 years. The terms are arranged so that an opening occurs every 2 years. Members cannot be reappointed, and their decisions are not subject to the approval of the President or Congress. Their length of term, manner of selection, and independence in working frees members from political pressures.

Student Web Activity Visit the *Economics Today and Tomorrow* Web site at ett.glencoe.com and click on ***Chapter 15—Student Web Activities*** to see how the Federal Reserve System functions.

Federal Advisory Council The Board of Governors is assisted by the *Federal Advisory Council (FAC)*. It is made up of 12 members elected by the directors of each Federal Reserve district bank. The FAC meets at least 4 times each year and reports to the Board of Governors on general business conditions in the nation.

Federal Open Market Committee The 12 voting members on the **Federal Open Market Committee (FOMC)** meet 8 times a year to decide the course of action that the Fed should take to control the money supply. The FOMC determines such economic decisions as whether to raise or lower interest rates. It is this committee's actions that have a resounding effect throughout the financial world.

Federal Open Market Committee: *12-member committee in the Federal Reserve System that meets 8 times a year to decide the course of action that the Fed should take to control the money supply*

Federal Reserve Banks As shown in **Figure 15.2,** the nation is divided into 12 Federal Reserve districts, with each district having a Fed district bank. Each of the 12 district banks is set up as a corporation owned by its member banks. A 9-person board of directors—made up of bankers and businesspeople—supervises each Federal Reserve district bank.

The system also includes 25 Federal Reserve branch banks (also shown in **Figure 15.2**). These smaller banks act as branch offices and aid the district banks in carrying out their duties.

FIGURE 15.2

The Federal Reserve System The 12 Federal Reserve district banks that serve the nation's banks are distributed throughout the country. Trillions of dollars a year pass through the Fed as it processes billions of checks. Note that the Fed is headquartered in Washington, D.C. ***In what cities are the 12 Federal Reserve district banks located?***

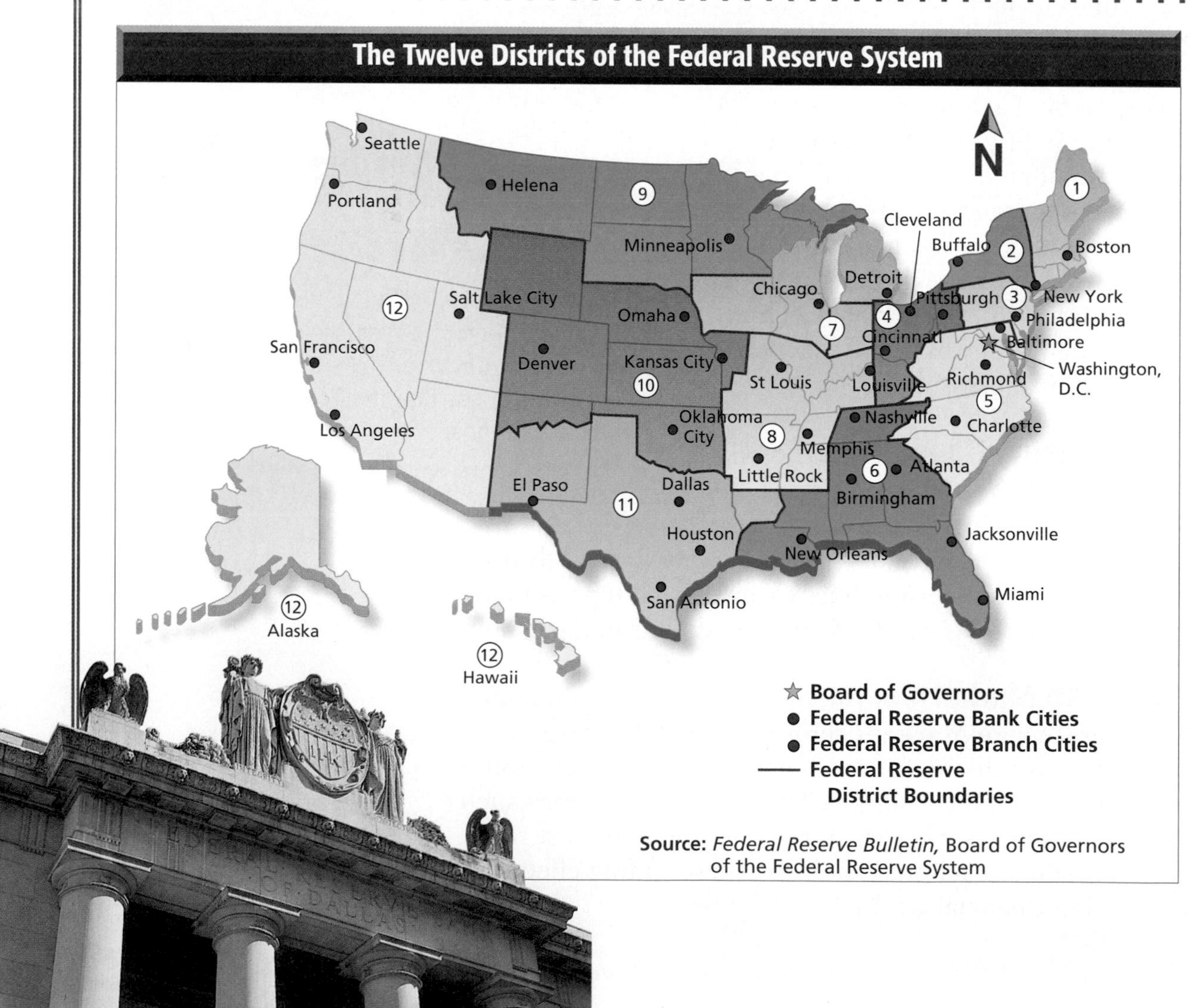

Source: *Federal Reserve Bulletin,* Board of Governors of the Federal Reserve System

FIGURE 15.3 **Check Clearing** All depository institutions may use the Federal Reserve's check-clearing system. The reserve accounts mentioned in the diagram refer to a bank's account in its Federal Reserve district bank.

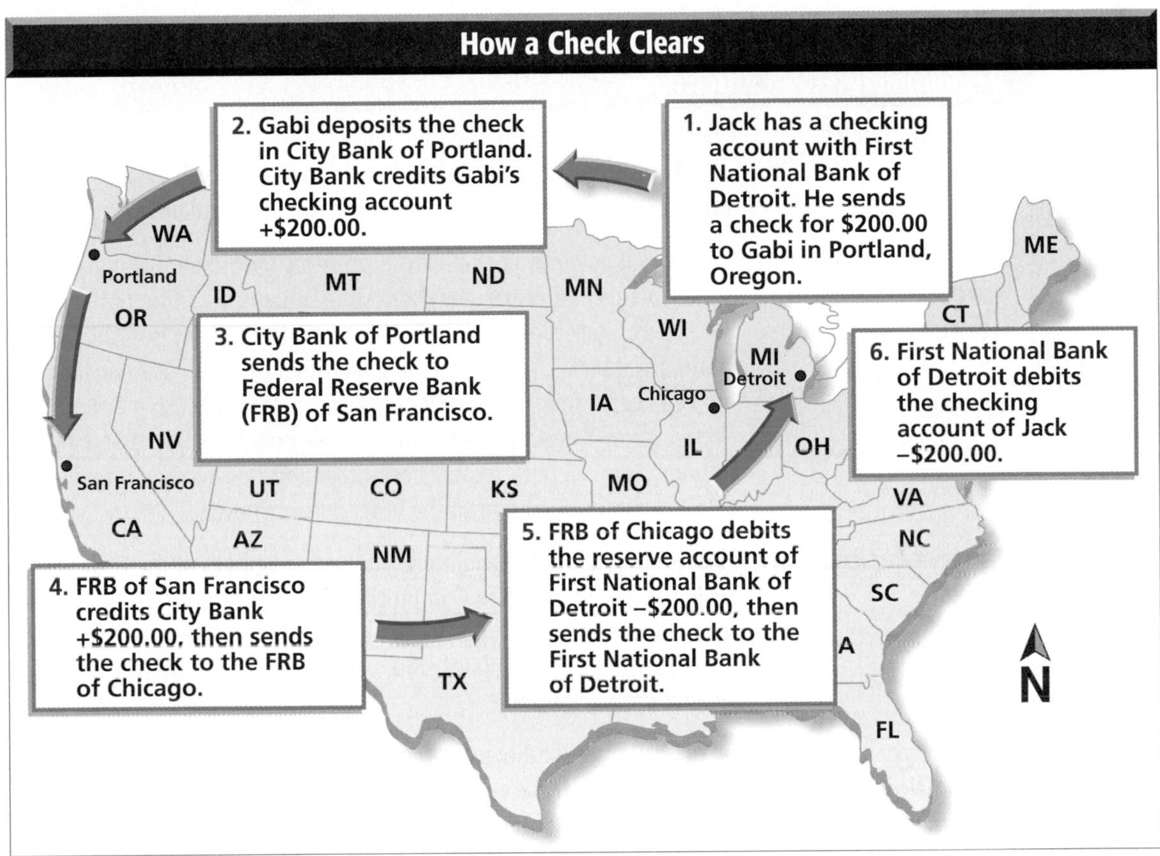

How a Check Clears
1. Jack has a checking account with First National Bank of Detroit. He sends a check for $200.00 to Gabi in Portland, Oregon.
2. Gabi deposits the check in City Bank of Portland. City Bank credits Gabi's checking account +$200.00.
3. City Bank of Portland sends the check to Federal Reserve Bank (FRB) of San Francisco.
4. FRB of San Francisco credits City Bank +$200.00, then sends the check to the FRB of Chicago.
5. FRB of Chicago debits the reserve account of First National Bank of Detroit –$200.00, then sends the check to the First National Bank of Detroit.
6. First National Bank of Detroit debits the checking account of Jack –$200.00.
WA
Portland
OR
ID
MT
ND
MN
WI
MI
Detroit
Chicago
IA
IL
OH
NV
San Francisco
CA
UT
CO
KS
MO
AZ
NM
TX
VA
NC
SC
A
FL
ME
CT
N

Member Banks All national banks—those chartered by the federal government—are required to become members of the Federal Reserve System. Banks chartered by the states may join if they choose to do so. To become a member bank, a national or state bank buys stock in its district's Federal Reserve bank.

In the past, only member banks were required to meet Fed regulations, such as keeping a certain percentage of their total deposits as cash in their own vaults or as deposits in their Federal Reserve district bank. Now all institutions that accept deposits from customers must keep reserves in their Fed district bank. See **Figure 15.3.** Fed services are also available to all depository institutions—member or nonmember—for a fee.

Today, the major advantage of membership in the Fed is that member banks, as stockholders in their district bank, receive

FIGURE 15.4 Functions of the Federal Reserve

Responsibility	Description
Clearing checks	Check clearing is the method by which a check that has been deposited in one depository institution is transferred to the depository institution on which it was written. **Figure 15.3** (on page 403) explains this process.
Acting as the federal government's fiscal agent	The federal government collects large sums of money through taxation, and it spends and distributes even more. It deposits some of this money in the Federal Reserve banks and distributes the rest among thousands of commercial banks. As the federal government's fiscal, or financial, agent, the Fed keeps track of these deposits and holds a checking account for the United States Treasury. Checks for such payments as Social Security, tax refunds, and veterans' benefits are drawn on this account. The Fed also acts as a financial adviser to the federal government.
Supervising member banks	The Fed regulates the state banks that are members of the Federal Reserve System. The Office of the Comptroller of the Currency (OCC) regulates federally chartered commercial banks. The Federal Deposit Insurance Corporation (FDIC) regulates state banks that are not members of the Federal Reserve System.
Holding reserves and setting reserve requirements	All depository institutions are required by law to keep a certain percentage of their deposits in reserve. Each of the 12 Federal Reserve banks holds reserves of member and nonmember depository institutions in its district. By raising or lowering the percentage required, within the limits set by Congress, the Fed can change the amount of money in circulation.
Supplying paper currency	Since 1914 the Fed has been responsible for maintaining much of the nation's paper money. All Federal Reserve notes are printed in Washington, D.C., at the Bureau of Printing and Engraving. Each note, however, has a code number indicating which of the 12 Federal Reserve banks issued it. The money is shipped from the bureau to the appropriate bank to be put into circulation. Much of this money simply replaces old bills. However, each Fed bank must have on hand a sufficient amount of currency to meet the demand–especially during holidays when depositors withdraw large amounts of currency.
Regulating the money supply	The primary responsibility of the Fed is determining the amount of money in circulation, which, in turn, affects the amount of credit and business activity in the economy.

dividends on their stock in the district bank. Member banks also are able to vote for 6 of the district bank's 9 board members.

Functions of the Fed

The Federal Reserve has a number of functions, as shown in **Figure 15.4.** Among them are check clearing, acting as the federal government's fiscal agent, supervising member state banks, holding reserves, supplying paper currency, and regulating the money supply. The most important function of the Fed is regulating the money supply, which you'll learn about in Section 3. As you already noted in **Figure 15.3** on page 403, however, **check clearing**–the transferring of funds from one bank to another when you write or deposit a check–is also an important and complex function.

check clearing: *method by which a check that has been deposited in one institution is transferred to the issuer's depository institution*

Consumer Protection The Fed also sets standards for certain types of consumer legislation, mainly truth-in-lending legislation. By law, sellers of goods and services must make some kinds of information available to people who buy on credit. This information includes the amount of interest and size of the monthly payment to be paid. The Federal Reserve System decides what type of financial information must be supplied to consumers.

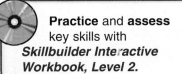

Practice and **assess** key skills with ***Skillbuilder Interactive Workbook, Level 2.***

SECTION 1 Assessment

Understanding Key Terms

1. **Define** Fed, monetary policy, Federal Open Market Committee, check clearing.

Reviewing Objectives

2. How is the Fed organized?
3. **Graphic Organizer** Create a diagram like the one below to explain the functions of the Fed.

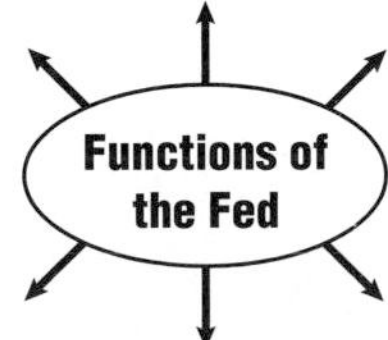

Applying Economic Concepts

4. **Monetary Policy** Explain why you agree or disagree with the following statement: The independence of the Federal Reserve System is essential to the health of the economy.

Critical Thinking Activity

5. **Summarizing Information** Learn more about the functions of the Fed district banks. Choose one of the 12 banks, then use the Internet to reach its home page. Write a summary of the information presented on the bank's Web site.

Study & Writing Skills

Outlining

Outlining may be used as a starting point for a writer. The writer begins with the rough shape of the material and gradually fills in the details in a logical manner. You may also use outlining as a method of note taking and organizing information as you read.

- Read the text to identify the main ideas. Label these with Roman numerals.
- Write subtopics under each main idea. Label these with capital letters.
- Write supporting details for each subtopic. Label these with Arabic numerals.
- Each level should have at least two entries and should be indented from the level above.
- All entries should use the same grammatical form, whether phrases or complete sentences.

Learning the Skill

There are two types of outlines–informal and formal. An informal outline is similar to taking notes–you write words and phrases needed to remember main ideas. A formal outline has a standard format. To formally outline material, follow the steps on the left.

Practicing the Skill

On a separate sheet of paper, copy the following outline for a main idea of Section 1. Then use your textbook to fill in the missing subtopics and details.

I. Organization of the Fed
- **A.** Board of Governors
  - **1.** Directs operations of Fed
    - **a.** Supervises 12 Fed district banks
    - **b.** Regulates member banks and depository institutions
  - **2.** ____________________
- **B.** Federal Advisory Council
  - **1.** ____________________
  - **2.** ____________________
- **C.** ____________________
- **D.** ____________________

II. Functions of the Fed
- **A.** ____________________
  - **1.** ____________________
  - **2.** ____________________
- **B.** ____________________

Application Activity

Following the guidelines above, prepare an outline for Section 2 of this chapter.

Practice and **assess** key skills with ***Skillbuilder Interactive Workbook, Level 2.***

SECTION 2

Money Supply and the Economy

Cover Story

Business Week, July 23, 2001

...[Federal Reserve] Chairman Alan Greenspan decided seven years ago to publicize the central bank's interest-rate moves once they were made. Now, each meeting of the Fed—whether the central bank changes rates or not—triggers a chorus of instant analysis of what it means for the economy and the financial markets.

Reader's Guide

Terms to Know

- loose money policy
- tight money policy
- fractional reserve banking
- reserve requirements

Reading Objectives

1. What are the differences between loose money and tight money policies?
2. What is the purpose of fractional reserve banking?
3. How does the money supply expand?

As you learned in Section 1, the jobs of the Fed today range from processing checks to serving as the government's banker. As you read this section, you'll learn that the Fed's most important function, however, involves control over the rate of growth of the money supply.

Loose and Tight Money Policies

You may have read a news report in which a business executive complained that money is "too tight." You may have run across a story about an economist warning that money is "too loose." In these cases, the terms *tight* and *loose* are referring to the monetary policy of the Fed. *Monetary policy,* as you recall, involves changing the rate of growth of the money supply in order to affect the cost and availability of credit.

Credit, like any good or service, has a cost. The cost of credit is the interest that must be paid to obtain it. As the cost of credit increases, the quantity demanded decreases. In contrast, if the cost of borrowing drops, the quantity of credit demanded rises.

loose money policy: *monetary policy that makes credit inexpensive and abundant, possibly leading to inflation*

tight money policy: *monetary policy that makes credit expensive and in short supply in an effort to slow the economy*

Figure 15.5 shows the results of monetary policy decisions. If the Fed implements a **loose money policy** (often called "expansionary"), credit is abundant and inexpensive to borrow. If the Fed follows a **tight money policy** (often called "contractionary"), credit is in short supply and is expensive to borrow.

A loose money policy is implemented to encourage economic growth. You may be wondering why any nation would want a tight money policy, however. The answer is to control inflation. If money becomes too plentiful too quickly, prices increase and the purchasing power of the dollar decreases.

Fractional Reserve Banking

fractional reserve banking: *system in which only a fraction of the deposits in a bank is kept on hand, or in reserve; the remainder is available to lend*

reserve requirements: *regulations set by the Fed requiring banks to keep a certain percentage of their deposits as cash in their own vaults or as deposits in their Federal Reserve district bank*

Before you can understand how the Fed regulates the nation's money supply, you need to understand the basis of the United States banking system and the way money is created. The banking system is based on what is called **fractional reserve banking.**

Since 1913 the Fed has set specific **reserve requirements** for many banks. This means that they must hold a certain percentage of their total deposits either as cash in their own vaults or as deposits in their Federal Reserve district bank. Banks must hold

FIGURE 15.5

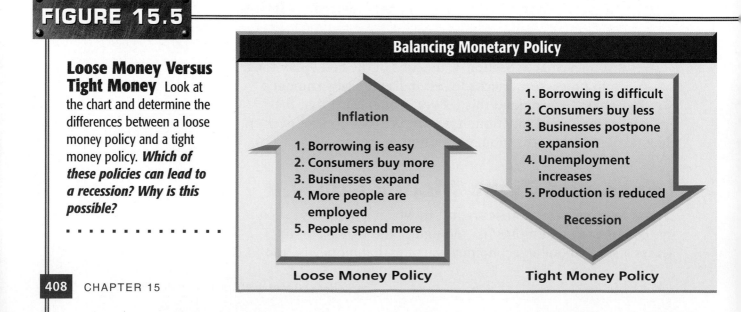

Loose Money Versus Tight Money Look at the chart and determine the differences between a loose money policy and a tight money policy. ***Which of these policies can lead to a recession? Why is this possible?***

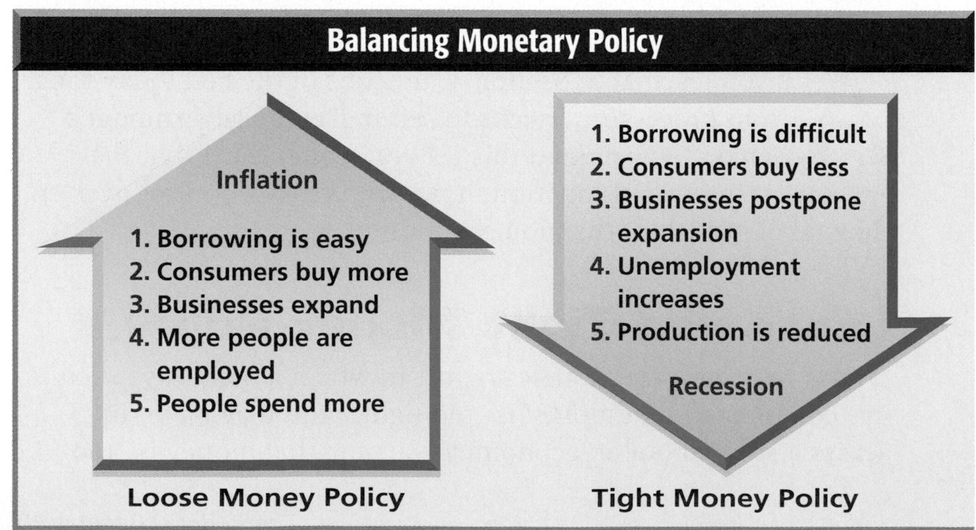
Balancing Monetary Policy
Inflation
1. Borrowing is easy
2. Consumers buy more
3. Businesses expand
4. More people are employed
5. People spend more
Loose Money Policy
1. Borrowing is difficult
2. Consumers buy less
3. Businesses postpone expansion
4. Unemployment increases
5. Production is reduced
Recession
Tight Money Policy

these reserves in case one or more banking customers decide to withdraw large amounts of cash from their checking accounts. Currently, many financial institutions must keep 10 percent of their checkable deposits as reserves with the Fed.

Money Expansion

Currency is a small part of the money supply. A larger portion consists of funds that the Fed and customers have deposited in banks. Because banks are not required to keep 100 percent of their deposits in reserve, they can use these excess reserves to create what is, in effect, new money. See **Figure 15.6.**

FIGURE 15.6 Expanding the Money Supply

- The chart shows how $1,000 in new reserves expands to $5,000 by simple loans. In Round 1, the Fed deposits $1,000 in Bank A. With a 20 percent reserve requirement, Bank A must hold $200 of the new deposit on reserve. This leaves the bank with $800 of excess reserves.
- In Round 2, Mr. Jones applies to Bank A for an $800 loan to buy a computer. Bank A finds him creditworthy and credits his account with $800. Mr. Jones writes a check to Computer World, which deposits the money at Bank B. Bank B's reserves increase by $800. Of this amount, $160 (20 percent of $800) are required reserves, and the remaining $640 are excess reserves.
- In Round 3, Bank B–to earn profits–loans its excess reserves to Ms. Wang, who wants to borrow $640. She, in turn, buys something from Mr. Diaz, who does his banking at Bank C. He deposits the money from Ms. Wang. Bank C now has $640 in new deposits, of which $128 are required reserves. Bank C now loans $512 of excess reserves to Mrs. Fontana, who buys something from Mrs. Powers, and so on.

Round	Deposited by	Amount of Deposit	Required Reserves (20%)	Excess Reserves (80%)	Loaned to	Paid to
1	the Fed (Bank A)	$1,000	$200	$800	Mr. Jones	Computer World
2	Computer World (Bank B)	$800	$160	$640	Ms. Wang	Mr. Diaz
3	Mr. Diaz (Bank C)	$640	$128	$512	Mrs. Fontana	Mrs. Powers
4	Mrs. Powers (Bank D)	$512	$102.40	$409.60	Mr. Gibbs	Mr. Santana
5	Mr. Santana (Bank E)	$409.60	$81.92	$327.68		
6	All Others					
Eventual Totals		$5,000	$1,000			

Suppose Bank A sells a government bond to the Fed and receives $1,000. This is $1,000 in "new" money because the Fed simply creates it by writing a check. With a 20 percent reserve requirement, the bank must hold $200 of that money in reserve. The bank is free to lend the remaining $800.

Suppose a customer asks the same bank for an $800 loan. The bank creates $800 simply by transferring $800 to the customer's checking account. The bank must keep in reserve 20 percent of this new deposit–$160–but now it can lend the remaining $640. This $640 is, in turn, treated as a new deposit. Eighty percent of it–$512–can again be lent. The process continues, with each new deposit giving the bank new funds to continue lending. The original $1,000 becomes $5,000.

Of course, a bank usually does not lend and receive back the same money. Its customers will probably withdraw money and spend it or deposit it in another bank. As the money finds its way into a second and third bank, and so on, each bank can use the non-required reserve portion of the money to make more loans. This process is known as the *multiple expansion of the money supply.*

Practice and **assess** key skills with ***Skillbuilder Interactive Workbook, Level 2.***

SECTION 2 Assessment

Understanding Key Terms

1. **Define** loose money policy, tight money policy, fractional reserve banking, reserve requirements.

Reviewing Objectives

2. **Graphic Organizer** Create a chart to describe the effect of loose money and tight money policies on the actions listed below.

Effect on . . .	Loose Money Policy	Tight Money Policy
Borrowing		
Consumer buying		
Businesses		
Employment		
Production		

3. What is the purpose of fractional reserve banking?
4. How does the money supply expand?

Applying Economic Concepts

5. **Monetary Policy** If there is a 10 percent reserve requirement, by how much does the money supply expand if the Fed injects $100 of new money? By how much does it expand if the reserve requirement is raised to 20 percent?

Critical Thinking Activity

6. **Synthesizing Information** Analyze **Figure 15.6** on page 409. Create a similar scenario showing the expansion of the money supply. Begin the expansion by depositing $200 into Bank A. Assume that the reserve requirement is 20 percent.

BusinessWeek

Spotlight on the Economy

Why the Fed's Open-Mouth Policy Works

Check It Out! In this chapter you learned that the Federal Open Market Committee decides whether to raise or lower interest rates to control inflation. In this article, read to learn how the FOMC announces its decisions.

Not too many years ago, Federal Reserve officials conducted monetary policy as if they were members of the Politburo plotting behind the thick walls of the Kremlin. The Fed's reasoning: Secrecy was essential if central bankers were to avoid political pressure from those who would like to influence Fed policy on interest rates.

But for the past five years, Fed Chairman Alan Greenspan has been dismantling those Kremlin walls, brick by brick. On May 18, we saw the results of his efforts. Instead of waiting six weeks or more to let the markets know what it thought, the policy-setting Federal Open Market Committee broadcast the outcome of its meeting immediately: Yes, the Fed will adopt a tightening bias in light of rising inflation risks. The markets, which had reeled on news of a surprisingly high consumer price index for April, took the news in stride–relieved to see that the Fed was not yet ready to raise rates.

It all worked beautifully. Alan Greenspan, who is a great believer in free markets, loves it when traders do the Fed's work–raising and lowering bond yields to keep the domestic economy on course. As the reaction to the Fed's May 18 announcement shows, the markets are fully capable of taking direction from the Fed.

. . . Now, everyone from home buyers in North Dakota to executives in Florida . . . gets the same information–and the right information–at exactly the same time.

Think About It

1. **How did Alan Greenspan change the way the FOMC announces its decisions?**
2. **What are the benefits of a transparent monetary policy?**

SECTION 3

Regulating the Money Supply

READER'S GUIDE

Terms to Know

- discount rate
- prime rate
- federal funds rate
- open-market operations

Reading Objectives

1. How can the Fed use reserve requirements to alter the money supply?
2. How does the discount rate affect the money supply?
3. How does the Fed use open-market operations?
4. What are some of the difficulties of carrying out monetary policy?

COVER STORY

THE COLUMBUS DISPATCH, JULY 1, 1999

Like a driver applying a quick tap of the brakes, the Federal Reserve yesterday raised the cost of borrowing to keep the U.S. economy from running ahead too fast.

As a result, consumers can expect to pay a little more when buying homes, cars, and other big-ticket items, as well as when carrying credit-card balances.

The main goal of the Federal Reserve is to keep the money supply growing steadily and the economy running smoothly without inflation. As you'll learn in this section, the Fed uses several tools to achieve a smoothly running economy.

Changing Reserve Requirements

The Federal Reserve can choose to control the money supply by changing the reserve requirements of financial institutions. The lower the percentage of deposits that must be kept in reserve, the more dollars are available to loan. The reverse is also true.

Figure 15.7 explains how changes in the reserve requirement affect the nation's money supply.

As *Part C* of **Figure 15.7** shows, the Fed may raise reserve requirements. To build up its reserves to meet the new requirement, a bank has several possibilities. It can call in some loans, sell off securities or other investments, or borrow from another bank or from the Federal Reserve. Obviously, because all banks would have to increase their reserves, this action would decrease the amount of money in the economy. Raising reserve requirements, then, could be used to help slow down the economy if it were expanding too rapidly.

Even small changes in the reserve requirement can have major effects on the money supply. As a result, some believe that this tool is not precise enough to make frequent small adjustments to the money supply. In recent years, changing the reserve requirement has not been used to regulate the money supply.

FIGURE 15.7 Raising and Lowering Reserve Requirements

Bank Deposits	Reserve Requirement	$ Amount Bank May Loan	Fed Action
Part A **$1,000,000**	10% (10% × $1,000,000 = $100,000)	$900,000	Suppose a bank has $1 million in deposits, and the reserve requirement is 10 percent. The bank must keep at least $100,000 in reserves.
Part B **$1,000,000**	5% (5% × $1,000,000 = $50,000)	$950,000	If the Fed wanted to increase the money supply, it could lower the reserve requirement to 5 percent, for example. The bank would then need to keep only $50,000 in reserves. It could lend out the other $950,000. This additional $50,000 would expand the money supply many times over as it was lent and redeposited. This could help pull the economy out of a recession.
Part C **$1,000,000**	15% (15% × $1,000,000 = $150,000)	$850,000	Suppose instead that the Fed wanted to decrease the money supply, or at least slow down its rate of growth. It could do this by increasing the reserve requirement from 10 to 15 percent. The bank in this example would then need to keep $150,000 on reserve–$50,000 more than with a 10% reserve requirement.

Changing the Discount Rate

Sometimes a bank will find itself without enough reserves to meet its reserve requirement. This situation may occur if customers unexpectedly borrow a great deal of money or if depositors suddenly withdraw large amounts. The bank must then borrow funds to meet its reserve requirement. One of the ways it can do this is to ask its Federal Reserve district bank for a loan. The district bank, like any other bank, charges interest. The rate of interest the Fed charges its member banks is called the **discount rate.**

discount rate: *interest rate that the Fed charges on loans to member banks*

If the bank does borrow from the Fed, this newly created money would then be available for lending to individuals or businesses, thus increasing the money supply. If the discount rate is high, the bank passes its increased costs on to customers in the form of higher interest rates on loans. For example, it might raise its **prime rate**—the interest rate it charges its best business customers. High discount rates, which discourage borrowing, might keep down the growth of the money supply.

prime rate: *rate of interest that banks charge on loans to their best business customers*

In contrast, if the discount rate is low, even a bank with sufficient reserves might borrow money. The loan will raise the bank's reserves and increase its ability to make loans. Thus, a reduction in the discount rate may increase the total money supply.

Changing the discount rate, like changing the reserve requirement, is rarely used by the Fed as a tool of monetary policy. Rather, either through its chair or its Federal Open Market Committee, the Fed periodically states that it is going to change "the" interest rate. Because there are many interest rates in the economy, which one does the Fed mean?

Worldwide Influence

Decisions made by the Federal Open Market Committee (FOMC) may have an impact far beyond the American economy. Immediately after the FOMC announces its actions, American financial markets respond. Traders consider how these actions will affect the economy, and they buy or sell stocks and bonds accordingly. As a result, stock and bond prices rise or fall, sometimes sharply.

By the end of the business day in the United States, financial markets in Asia are opening. Traders and investors there read the Fed's actions and note the response of the American markets, often following the example of their American counterparts. A comparable situation develops a few hours later in Europe, when financial markets open there. As one American financial expert has noted, "The Fed has become the dominant central bank in the world." ■

Federal Funds Rate When the media discusses a rate hike or reduction by the Fed, they are referring to the federal funds rate, or the interest rate that banks charge each other for overnight loans. ***How does an increase in the federal funds rate affect you as a banking customer?***

FOX TROT

Federal Funds Rate The interest rate the Fed is referring to is the **federal funds rate.** This is the interest rate that banks charge each other for short-term loans (usually overnight). Why would one bank need to borrow from another? Suppose a customer walks into Bank A late in the day and withdraws a large amount. In order to provide funds to the customer, the bank must dip into its required reserves. Before the banking day ends, Bank A must raise its reserves to the required amount or pay a penalty to the Fed.

federal funds rate: *interest rate that banks charge each other on loans (usually overnight)*

Bank A could borrow money from the Fed as discussed earlier, but the discount rate may be too high. Instead, Bank A approaches Bank B for a loan. Bank B happens to have excess reserves that day, so it loans Bank A the money it needs at the federal funds rate. This federal funds market is active—billions of dollars of reserves are borrowed and loaned each business day.

If the Fed causes the federal funds rate to drop from 5.25 percent to 5 percent, banks will borrow more and, thus, lend more. This increases business activity in the economy. In contrast, the chairman of the Fed may publicly state the opposite—that the Fed is causing the federal funds rate to rise from, say, 5.5 percent to 5.75 percent. At this higher rate, banks will reduce their borrowing from other banks as well as raise the interest rates they charge their own customers. Economic activity will contract. See **Figure 15.8.**

Open-Market Operations

open-market operations: *buying and selling of United States securities by the Fed to affect the money supply*

Buying and selling government securities, called **open-market operations,** is the major tool the Fed uses to control the money supply. As you may remember from Chapter 6, securities are government IOUs such as Treasury bills, notes, and bonds. The term *open market* is used because these securities are bought and sold in the open market through dealers who specialize in buying and selling government securities. An open market is one that is open to private businesses and not controlled or owned by the government.

When the Fed buys securities–such as Treasury bills–it pays for them by making a deposit in the account of the security dealer's bank. This deposit increases the bank's reserves and therefore the amount of money it can lend, thus increasing the money supply. Remember the *multiple expansion of money* that you learned about in Section 2? When the Fed adds even a relatively small amount of new reserves into the banking system, banks can create money by holding on to required reserves and loaning out the rest.

In contrast, when the Fed sells Treasury bills to a dealer, the dealer's bank must use its deposits to purchase the securities. This action means that banks have fewer reserves to support loans and must reduce their lending. The multiple expansion of money works in reverse by taking more money out of circulation than just the initial withdrawal.

Difficulties of Monetary Policy

Economists sometimes describe the Fed's control over the money supply as similar to a driver's control over a car. Like a driver, the Fed can accelerate or brake, depending on what phase of the business cycle the economy is in. In reality, the Fed cannot control the money supply as quickly and as surely as a driver can control a car.

One problem is the difficulty in gathering and evaluating information about M1 and M2. As you know, the money supply is measured in terms of M1–currency, traveler's checks, and checkable accounts–and M2–which is M1 plus certain near moneys. In recent years, new savings and investment opportunities have appeared. Keeping track of the growth of M1 and M2 becomes more difficult as money is shifted from savings accounts into interest-paying checkable accounts or from checkable accounts into money market deposit accounts. The increased use of debit cards and electronic funds transfer has also changed the way money circulates through the economy.

Throughout its history, the Fed's monetary policies have been criticized. In some instances of rising inflation, the Fed increased the amount of money in circulation, thereby worsening inflation. During other periods when the economy was slowing down and going into recession, the Fed decreased the money supply. This action made the recession worse.

To prevent such misjudgments, some critics of the Fed have requested that the money supply simply be increased at the same rate every year. They recommend that the Fed *not* engage in monetary policy.

Although the Fed is protected from direct political pressure, it nonetheless still receives conflicting advice from many directions. In addition, the Fed is not the only force working to affect the economy. The spending and taxing policies of the federal government are also at work. The Fed's task is to consider all of these factors as it plots a course for the growth of the economy as well as one that ensures price stability.

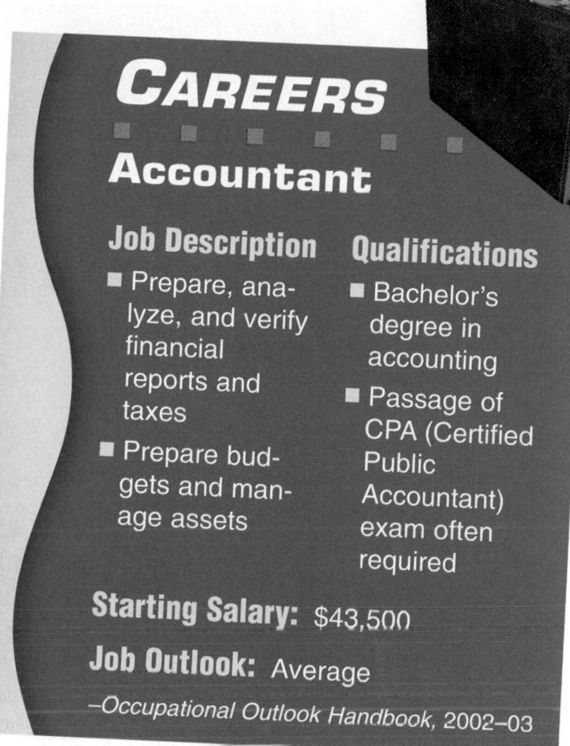

CAREERS
Accountant
Job Description
■ Prepare, analyze, and verify financial reports and taxes
■ Prepare budgets and manage assets
Qualifications
■ Bachelor's degree in accounting
■ Passage of CPA (Certified Public Accountant) exam often required
Starting Salary: $43,500
Job Outlook: Average
–Occupational Outlook Handbook, 2002–03

Practice and assess key skills with ***Skillbuilder Interactive Workbook, Level 2.***

SECTION 3 Assessment

Understanding Key Terms

1. **Define** discount rate, prime rate, federal funds rate, open-market operations.

Reviewing Objectives

2. How can the Fed use reserve requirements to alter the money supply?
3. How does the discount rate affect the money supply?
4. What are some of the difficulties of carrying out monetary policy?
5. **Graphic Organizer** Create a diagram like the one in the next column to show how the Fed uses open-market operations to change the money supply.

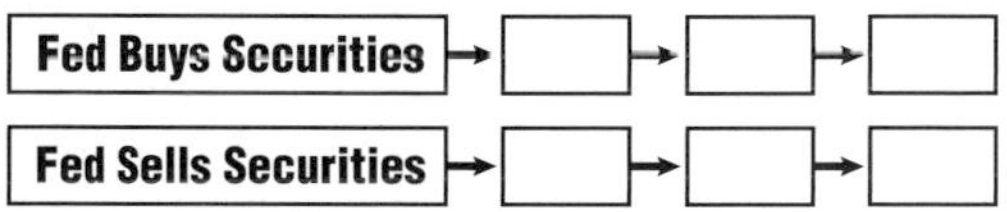

Applying Economic Concepts

6. **Monetary Policy** If you were responsible for controlling the nation's money supply, which tool would you use? Why?

Critical Thinking Activity

7. **Synthesizing Information** Imagine that you are the chairman of the Fed. Write a paragraph to the general public explaining why you are raising the federal funds rate. Include the words "inflation" and "recession" in your explanation.

People & Perspectives

Alan Greenspan

ECONOMIST (1926–)

- **Chairman of the Federal Reserve Board since 1987**
- **Chairman of the Council of Economic Advisers under President Gerald Ford**
- **Member of the Economic Policy Advisory Board under President Ronald Reagan**

As Chairman of the Federal Reserve Board, Alan Greenspan monitors developments in the United States economy—the impact of new technologies, for example. In this excerpt, Greenspan discusses the economic impact of information technology.

"The American economy, clearly more than most, is in the grip of what the eminent Harvard professor, Joseph Schumpeter, many years ago called 'creative destruction,' the continuous process by which emerging technologies push out the old. Standards of living rise when incomes created by the productive facilities employing older, increasingly [outdated], technologies are marshaled to finance the newly produced capital assets that embody cutting-edge technologies.

. . . Of course, large remnants of imprecision still persist, but the remarkable surge in the availability of real-time information in recent years has sharply reduced the degree of uncertainty confronting business management. This has enabled businesses to remove large swaths of now unnecessary inventory, and dispense with [redundant use of] worker[s] and capital. . . . As a consequence, growth in output per work hour has accelerated, elevating the standard of living of the average American worker.

. . . Moreover, technological innovations have spread far beyond the factory floor and retail and wholesale distribution channels. Biotech, for example, is revolutionizing medicine and agriculture, with far-reaching consequences for the quality of life not only in the United States but around the world."

Checking for Understanding

1. **What does Greenspan mean by the term "creative destruction"?**
2. **How, according to Greenspan, have technological innovations fundamentally changed the economy?**

CHAPTER  Summary

ECONOMICS Online

Chapter Overview Visit the *Economics Today and Tomorrow* Web site at ett.glencoe.com and click on ***Chapter 15—Chapter Overviews*** to review chapter information.

SECTION 1 Organization and Functions of the Federal Reserve System

- Congress created the Federal Reserve System, or **Fed,** in 1913 as the central banking organization in the United States.
- The Fed is made up of a Board of Governors assisted by the Federal Advisory Council, the **Federal Open Market Committee,** 12 district banks, 25 branch banks, and thousands of member banks.
- Among the Fed's functions are **check clearing,** acting as the federal government's fiscal agent, supervising member state banks, holding reserves, supplying paper currency, and carrying out **monetary policy.**

SECTION 2 Money Supply and the Economy

- The most important function of the Fed is monetary policy, or controlling the rate of growth of the money supply.
- With a **loose money policy,** credit is abundant and inexpensive to borrow. With a **tight money policy,** credit is in short supply and is expensive to borrow.
- The banking system is based on **fractional reserve banking,** in which banks hold a certain percentage of their total deposits either as cash in their vaults or in Fed banks.
- After banks meet the **reserve requirement,** they can loan out the rest to create what is, in effect, new money.

SECTION 3 Regulating the Money Supply

- The Fed can control the money supply by changing the reserve requirements of financial institutions. Lowering the requirement allows banks to loan more, thus increasing the money supply.
- Other tools the Fed can use are changing the **discount rate** and **federal funds rate,** which also affect the **prime rate.** By making borrowing more expensive, banks and consumers are discouraged from spending, which halts the growth of the money supply.
- The main tool the Fed uses to control the money supply is **open-market operations**—buying and selling government securities. By depositing money in the banking system (buying securities), the money supply grows. By withdrawing money from the banking system (selling securities), the money supply decreases.

CHAPTER 15

Assessment and Activities

Self-Check Quiz Visit the *Economics Today and Tomorrow* Web site at ett.glencoe.com and click on ***Chapter 15—Self-Check Quizzes*** to prepare for the Chapter Test.

Identifying Key Terms

Write the letter of the definition in Column B that correctly defines each term in Column A.

Column A

1. Fed
2. prime rate
3. tight money policy
4. reserve requirements
5. monetary policy
6. open-market operations
7. discount rate
8. loose money policy
9. federal funds rate
10. check clearing

Column B

a. means of changing the growth rate of the money supply
b. central banking system in the United States
c. purchases and sales of United States securities by the Fed
d. method by which a check deposited in one bank is transferred to another bank
e. the interest paid by banks when they borrow reserves among themselves
f. situation in which credit is expensive to borrow
g. the interest paid by banks when they borrow from a Fed district bank
h. situation in which credit is inexpensive to borrow
i. the interest rate that banks charge their best customers for loans
j. rule that banks keep a certain percentage of their deposits as cash

Recalling Facts and Ideas

Section 1

1. What does the Board of Governors do within the Fed?
2. How many Fed banks and branches are there?
3. Which agency of the federal government supplies paper currency to the economy?

Section 2

4. What are the two basic types of monetary policies?
5. In a 10 percent fractional reserve banking system, what happens to the money supply when the Fed injects $100 of new money into the American economy?
6. Why do banks have to keep money in reserve accounts?

Section 3

7. The Fed can change the money supply in circulation by changing reserve requirements. What are two other methods that it can use to do this?
8. If the Fed wants to decrease the money supply, what can it do?

9. Why is it difficult for the Fed to gather and evaluate information about M1 and M2?
10. Why do some of the Fed's critics think the Fed should not engage in monetary policy?

Thinking Critically

1. **Understanding Cause and Effect** Create a flowchart like the one below to show how the banking system creates money.

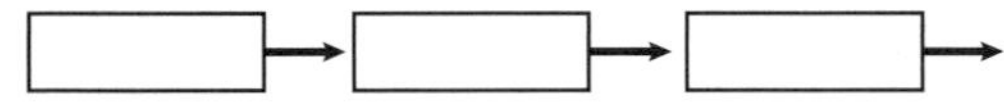

2. **Making Comparisons** What is the advantage for banks to be members of the Federal Reserve today? How does this differ from the past?
3. **Identifying Alternatives** How do you think the Fed would operate differently if it were under the control of the executive branch?

Applying Economic Concepts

Monetary Policy Look at **Figure 15.2** on page 402. Use the map to answer the following questions.

1. In what federal district do you live?
2. What is the Federal Reserve Bank city of district 9?
3. What is the Federal Reserve Bank city of district 4? What are district 4's branch cities?
4. What are the branch cities of district 11?
5. To what district bank would checks written in Hawaii go first?

Cooperative Learning Project

Working in groups, imagine that you are members of the Federal Open Market Committee. Eight times a year, you meet to discuss whether changes in the supply of money are necessary. The research staff presents information about the state of the economy. Write a list of the different types of information you think the members of the FOMC should have during their meetings.

Reviewing Skills

Outlining Reread and outline Section 3 of this chapter, using the following as your skeleton:

I. Regulating the Money Supply
   A. Changing reserve requirements
   B. Changing the discount rate
   C. Open-market operations
   D. The difficulties of monetary policy

After outlining the information, develop a convincing argument in favor of one monetary tool over the use of the other two monetary tools. Summarize your argument and present that summary in a short speech to the class using your outline.

Technology Activity

Using the Internet On the Internet, check the most recent issue of the *Federal Reserve Bulletin* for the current reserve requirements and discount rate. Check the same month's issue for the last four years to see how often they have changed and by how much. Track these data on a chart.

Analyzing the Global Economy

Select a nation and research its central banking organization. Does the country have a "central bank"? If so, how does it regulate the money supply? If not, what controls does the country have in place to avoid inflation or recessions? Present your findings to the class.

CHAPTER 16

Government Spends, Collects, and Owes

Why It's Important

Who owns national parks and museums? How are tax dollars and your high school related? This chapter will explain why the government collects tax dollars from you, and what it spends those funds on.

To learn more about the federal government's debt, view the **Economics & You** *Chapter 15 video lesson:* **How Government Spends, Collects, and Owes**

Chapter Overview Visit the *Economics Today and Tomorrow* Web site at ett.glencoe.com and click on ***Chapter 16—Chapter Overviews*** to preview chapter information.

SECTION 1

Growth in the Size of Government

Cover Story

The New York Times, April 14, 1999

The [White House] is expected to announce as early as next week requirements for cleaner gasoline and tougher pollution standards for the nation's automobiles. The expected regulations would also force sport utility vehicles and pickup trucks to meet the stricter standards for passenger cars for the first time.

Environmentalists are pleased, but the oil and auto industries say gasoline prices for all drivers and the costs of sport utility vehicles and pickup trucks would be increased.

Reader's Guide

Terms to Know

- public-works projects
- Medicare

Reading Objectives

1. What are two measurements of government growth?
2. What do some economists believe caused the growth of government?

As you learned in Chapter 2, the United States is not a pure market economy. In addition to the market forces of supply and demand, other forces affect the distribution of resources throughout the economy. As revealed in the *Cover Story* above, the government is one of the most important of these forces. As you read this section, you'll learn that government at every level–local, state, and federal–is involved in almost every aspect of the United States economy.

Government Growth

Government has grown considerably in the last 70 years or so. In 1929, just before the Great Depression began, government at all levels employed slightly more than 3 million civilian workers. During the Depression, however, there was a demand for more government services.

Today, about 2.9 million people work for the federal government alone. If you add local and state employees, the government employs over 20 million civilian workers. This figure represents more than a sixfold increase during a period in which the population a little more than doubled.

The number of government workers has increased because the number of government functions has risen. **Figure 16.1** shows one way of looking at the government activities that affect our lives.

Figure 16.2 on page 426 shows another way of looking at the economy. As you can see from the graph, the different levels of government have grown at different rates. During the late 1960s, state and local governments spent less than the federal government. The federal government paid for national defense; the salaries of

Government Involvement in the Economy Government plays a major role in most aspects of our lives. Some individuals believe that government has grown too large and that the private sector should provide goods and services without government intervention. Others argue that government should be even larger.

B Education
Your school probably receives some form of aid from the local, state, or federal government.

A Transportation
When you travel on a highway, you are using a resource financed by federal and state moneys.

members of Congress, federal judges, and the employees of executive departments such as the State Department; and public-works projects. **Public-works projects** are publicly used facilities such as schools and highways that are built and paid for with tax dollars.

public-works projects: *publicly used facilities, such as schools and highways, built by federal, state, or local governments with public money*

This situation continued until about 1970. At that time, federal funds diminished, while state and local government spending for such items as sewers, roads, and schools increased rapidly.

Why Has Government Grown?

Economists have often tried to explain the huge growth in government spending. During the Great Depression, there appeared to be a need for more government services. In the 1940s, the government spent billions of dollars to pay for World War II. Why has the government continued to grow since then?

One theory is that as the nation became richer, especially in the late 1960s and early 1970s, people demanded more government services to even out certain income inequities. Today, total government *purchases* represent about 18 percent of GDP. This figure does not include such items as interest payments on the national debt and transfer payments such as welfare programs. If you add these items, total government *outlays* easily exceed one-third of GDP. See **Figure 16.3** on page 426.

C Product Safety
Many goods that you buy are produced in accordance with local, state, and federal regulations.

D Worker Safety
If you have a job, government safety and other regulations often determine your working conditions.

E Taxation
If you own property, buy goods, or earn money income, you probably pay taxes that help pay for many government activities.

The True Size of Government The size of government cannot be measured merely by the cost of government spending. Any discussion of the government's size must include *where* government spends this money.

Medicare: *government program that provides health care for the aged*

When the government taxes you to provide you with a particular service, such as **Medicare** (health care for the aged), this cost of government is included in government spending. What if the

FIGURE 16.2

Government Consumption Expenditures and Gross Investment

Government Consumption Expenditures and Gross Investment Government purchases of goods and services (excluding Social Security and other welfare payments and interest) corrected for inflation show an increase in all levels of government spending.

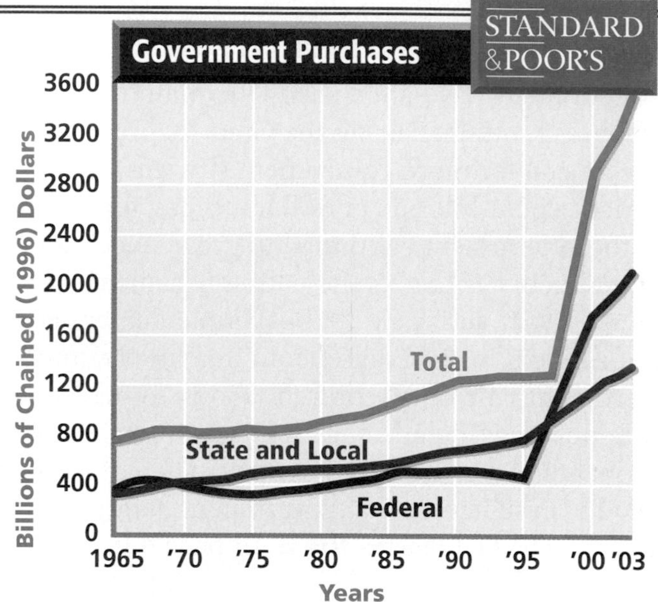

Source: Standard & Poor's

For an online update of this graph, visit ett.glencoe.com and click on ***Textbook Updates—Chapter 16.***

FIGURE 16.3

Government Spending as a Percentage of GDP Total government expenditures–including Social Security and other welfare payments, as well as interest payments–expressed as a percentage of GDP have grown from 1965 to the present.

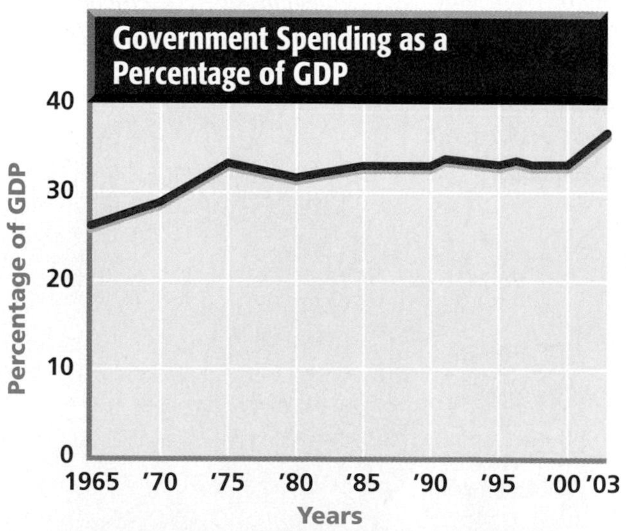

Source: *Economic Report of the President*, 2003

government also requires that your employer provide that same service? State governments are doing just that. In Massachusetts, for example, employers with six or more employees must provide medical insurance for each employee. So, the federal government taxes employees to pay for government-provided health insurance, and a state government requires that employers provide health insurance directly. The true size of government, then, may be even greater than government estimates show because some "private sector" spending is required by law.

The Growth of Government—Good or Bad? We know that government in the United States grew throughout the 1900s. Can we say whether this is good or bad for society? Although no one can know how much government is good for society, a general rule to remember is that government taxing and spending has opportunity costs. Government activity displaces private economic decision making along the production possibilities curve, which you learned about in Chapter 1. This private decision making involved in buying and selling is at the core of wealth creation and a rising standard of living for all citizens.

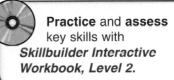

CAREERS

City Manager

Job Description

- Elected to enforce laws, oversee budgets, and ensure that programs are carried out
- Encourages business investment and economic development

Qualifications

- Master's degree in public administration recommended
- Courses in planning, budgeting, and civil engineering

Median Salary: $75,000

Job Outlook: Below average

—*Occupational Outlook Handbook*, 2002–03

Practice and **assess** key skills with ***Skillbuilder Interactive Workbook, Level 2.***

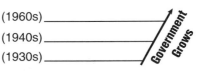

SECTION 1 Assessment

Understanding Key Terms

1. **Define** public-works projects, Medicare.

Reviewing Objectives

2. What are two measurements of government growth?
3. **Graphic Organizer** Create a diagram like the one shown in the next column to explain what has caused the growth of government since the 1930s.

(1960s) __________
(1940s) __________
(1930s) __________
Government Grows

Applying Economic Concepts

4. **The Role of Government** Do you think it is easier to increase or decrease government spending? Why?

Critical Thinking Activity

5. **Synthesizing Information** According to **Figure 16.2,** by how much did government spending at all levels increase since 1970?

People & Perspectives

John Maynard Keynes

ECONOMIST (1883–1946)

- **Educated and later taught at Cambridge University**
- **Served as adviser to the British government in the 1930s and 1940s**
- **Keynesian economics named after him**
- **Most influential publication was *The General Theory of Employment, Interest, and Money* (1936)**

John Maynard Keynes originated the school of economic thought referred to as Keynesian economics, which supports the use of government spending and taxing to help the economy. Keynes believed that there was a need for government intervention, in part because an economy may reach an equilibrium level of employment that is below full employment.

Keynes added that the equilibrium level of employment depends on the level of investment. If the level of investment is low, full employment cannot be achieved:

"Thus, to justify any given amount of employment there must be an amount of current investment sufficient to absorb the excess of output over what the community chooses to consume when employment is at a given level. . . . It follows, that . . . the equilibrium level of employment, [that is] the level at which there is no inducement to employers as a whole either to expand or contract employment, will depend on the amount of current investment."

Keynes believed that his theory explained why large pockets of poverty exist in otherwise rich communities or nations:

". . . This analysis supplies us with an explanation of the paradox of poverty in the midst of plenty.

. . . Moreover the richer the community, the wider will tend to be the gap between its actual and its potential production; and therefore the more obvious and outrageous the defects of the economic system."

Checking for Understanding

1. **According to Keynes, what is the relationship between employment and current investment?**
2. **According to Keynes, what is the equilibrium level of employment?**

SECTION 2

The Functions of Government

Cover Story

The News Star, August 12, 2003

Louisiana's senior U.S. senator believes senior citizens may have prescription drug coverage through Medicare by early next year.

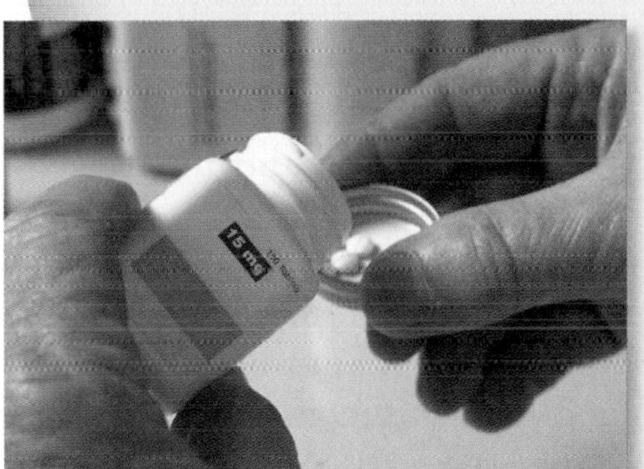

Senator John Breaux told a group of senior citizens . . . that a congressional overhaul of the nation's Medicare program will likely include for the first time prescription drug coverage in the aging Medicare program.

Medicare was created in 1965 and has not kept pace with the changing face of health care, Breaux said.

Reader's Guide

Terms to Know

- public goods
- income redistribution
- social insurance programs
- Social Security
- workers' compensation
- public-assistance programs
- welfare
- Supplemental Security Income
- Temporary Assistance for Needy Families
- Medicaid
- externalities

Reading Objectives

1. What are public goods?
2. Through what two general categories does government redistribute income?
3. What are some criticisms of government involvement in the economy?

The general purpose of government in the United States is to protect individual rights, to promote a stable legal environment for economic activity, and to promote policies that support the general well-being of all citizens. In this section, you'll learn that government tries to accomplish this purpose in four ways: (1) providing public goods, (2) redistributing income, (3) regulating economic activity, and (4) ensuring economic stability.

Providing Public Goods

public goods: *goods or services that government supplies to its citizens; can be used by many individuals at the same time without reducing the benefit each person receives*

Public goods are a special type of goods or services that government tries to supply to its citizens. Many people can use public goods—such as streetlights—at the same time, without reducing the benefit each person receives.

National defense is one of the few public goods only the federal government provides. Usually, the different levels of government share responsibility for other types of public goods—the legal system, for example. Federal, state, and some local governments maintain separate systems of courts, correctional institutions, and law-enforcement agencies.

The most important public good that only government can provide is a sound system of property rights. In such a system, individuals have the right to own factors of production, to risk investment, and to discover new ways of production.

Merit Goods In any society, certain goods and services are considered to have special merit. A *merit good* is one that is deemed socially desirable by government leaders—museums, ballets, and classical music concerts, for example. The government may subsidize such goods by requiring all taxpayers to support them. This allows everyone to enjoy such goods for less than the full market price. See **Figure 16.4.**

Demerit Goods The opposite of merit goods are *demerit goods.* These are goods that elected government officials have deemed socially undesirable, such as gambling and injurious drugs. The government exercises its role in the area of demerit goods by taxing, regulating, or prohibiting the manufacture, sale, and use of such goods. For example, governments justify very high taxes on alcohol and tobacco products because they are demerit goods.

THE CITIZENS
OF GEORGIA
WELCOME YOU
TO THEIR PARK

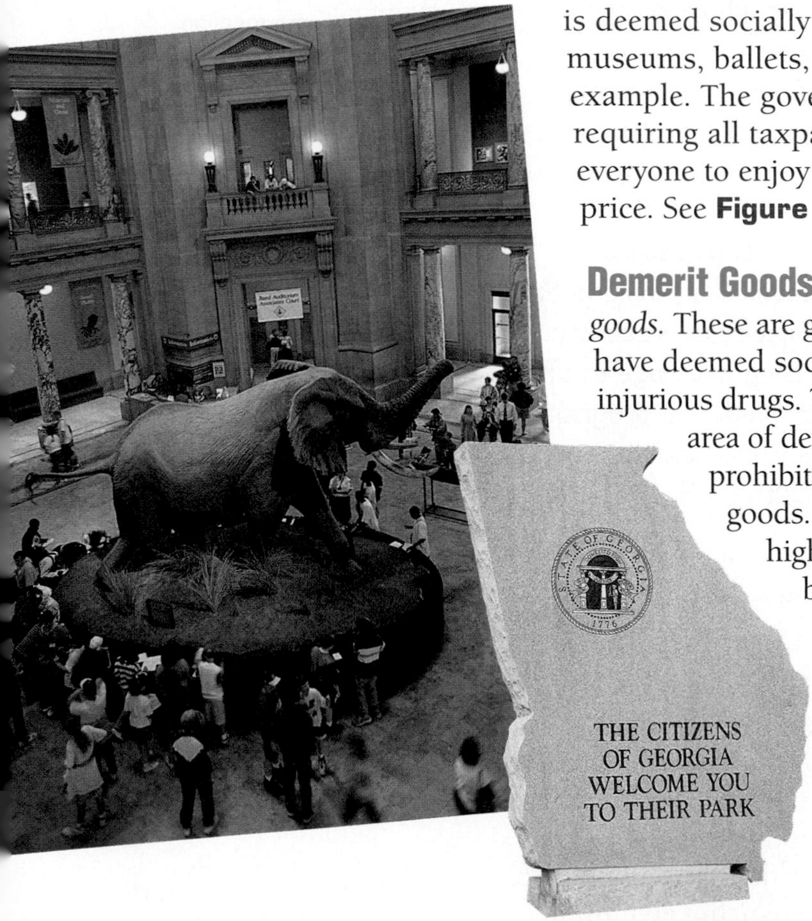

FIGURE 16.4

Merit Goods Museums and parks fall under the government function of providing merit goods.

Redistributing Income

Some Americans do not have many of the factors of production. Therefore they are on the bottom of the distribution of income in this country. These people profit from another function of government: to provide for the public well-being by assisting specific groups. These groups include the aged, the ill, and the poor. Through their elected representatives, Americans have chosen to see that almost everyone in the nation is provided with a certain minimum level of income and health-care support. This task is accomplished primarily through **income redistribution,** or using tax receipts to assist citizens in need. Tax dollars are used to subsidize two general categories of assistance: social insurance programs and public-assistance programs.

income redistribution: *government activity that takes income from some people through taxation and uses it to help citizens in need*

Social Insurance Programs

When you receive a paycheck, you will notice that a portion of your pay has been withheld by various levels of government. Some of this money is earmarked for **social insurance programs**–programs that pay benefits to retired and disabled workers, their families, and the unemployed. These benefits are financed by taxes that you, other workers, and employers pay into the programs. Examples of social insurance programs include **Social Security,** a federal program that provides monthly payments to people who are retired or unable to work. Upon retirement, you are also eligible for Medicare, a federal program that provides low-cost health care for the aged.

Another social insurance program is **workers' compensation**, a state program that provides payments for medical care to workers injured on the job. People who have lost jobs altogether can receive payments through *unemployment insurance.*

social insurance programs: *government programs that pay benefits to retired and disabled workers, their families, and the unemployed*

Social Security: *federal program that provides monthly payments to people who are retired or unable to work*

workers' compensation: *government program that extends payments for medical care to workers injured on the job*

Public-Assistance Programs

Public-assistance programs, often called **welfare,** are different from social insurance programs. Public-assistance programs make payments to individuals based on need, regardless of whether a person has paid taxes into the program.

Included in this category are **Supplemental Security Income,** a federally financed and administered program that makes payments to the aged, blind, and disabled; and **Temporary Assistance for Needy Families,** a state-run program that provides assistance and work opportunities to needy families raising young children. **Medicaid,** a state and federal program that helps pay health care costs for low-income and disabled persons, is another public-assistance program.

public-assistance programs/ welfare: *government programs that make payments to citizens based on need*

Supplemental Security Income: *federal programs that include food stamps and payments to the disabled and aged*

Temporary Assistance for Needy Families: *state-run program that provides assistance and work opportunities to needy families*

Medicaid: *state and federal public-assistance program that helps pay health care costs for low-income and disabled persons*

Government Regulations Government under the American free enterprise system regulates certain aspects of the economy.

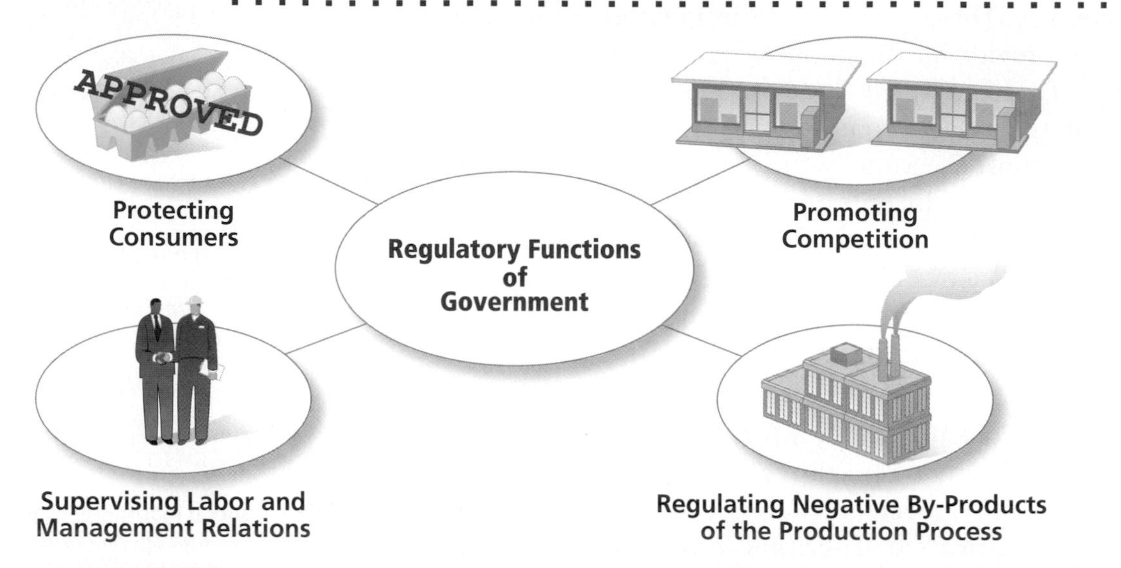

Regulating Economic Activity

Figure 16.5 illustrates four ways in which the government intervenes in economic activity. One of the most important regulatory functions concerns the side effects of the production process–also called **externalities.** When a steel mill produces steel, for example, the resulting pollution from the smokestacks may cause health problems in the surrounding area. In the absence of legal rules that limit such pollution, the steel mill does not have to correct these negative externalities. Government has often stepped in to require plants to install equipment that will reduce pollution.

externalities: *economic side effects or by-products that affect an uninvolved third party; can be negative or positive*

Ensuring Economic Stability

Ensuring economic stability has meant smoothing the ups and downs in the nation's overall business activity. Such intervention has been sought to shield citizens from the harmful effects of business fluctuations, including unemployment, high inflation, recessions, and even depressions. In Chapter 17, you'll learn more about the government's attempt to stabilize the economy.

Critics of Government Involvement

There are many critics of government involvement in the economy. They point out that merit goods, for example, should be provided by private organizations. If people pay fewer taxes, they have more disposable income and can choose to fund symphonies or other merit goods if they really want such services.

Opponents of redistribution programs think that most government assistance discourages personal initiative, affects incentives, and harms self-development. Critics of government regulations argue that most regulations raise the prices of goods and services. A better approach, these critics say, would be to encourage market solutions to such problems as pollution.

Global *Economy*

Working in Britain

In the mid-1940s, the British government established a welfare system designed to provide its citizens with economic security "from cradle to grave." Over the years, the system grew and now accounts for more than 30 percent of the government's annual budget. Almost half of all Britons receive some form of assistance–from retirement pensions to housing benefits.

In 1999 Prime Minister Tony Blair called for an overhaul of the system. "If you can work," he stated, "you should work." He suggested that people who receive welfare assistance would have to actively seek employment or risk losing their benefits: "The days of an automatic right to benefit will go." ■

Practice and **assess** key skills with ***Skillbuilder Interactive Workbook, Level 2.***

SECTION 2 Assessment

Understanding Key Terms

1. **Define** public goods, income redistribution, social insurance programs, Social Security, workers' compensation, public-assistance programs, welfare, Supplemental Security Income, Temporary Assistance for Needy Families, Medicaid, externalities.

Reviewing Objectives

2. What are public goods?
3. **Graphic Organizer** Create a chart like the one below to list the programs through which government redistributes income.

Social Insurance Programs	Public-Assistance Programs

4. What are some criticisms of government involvement in the economy?

Applying Economic Concepts

5. **The Role of Government** List five ways that local, state, and federal government are involved in your daily life. Provide specific examples in your list.

Critical Thinking Activity

6. **Summarizing Information** In a paragraph, list at least three activities or "goods" that you think should be considered merit goods, or goods that are deemed socially desirable by government leaders. Then describe why you think the government should or should not be involved in providing merit goods to society.

BusinessWeek

Spotlight on the Economy

Social Security Is Aptly Named

Check It Out! In this chapter you learned that one function of government is to provide for the public well-being. In this article, read to learn how distributing income through Social Security can increase the well-being of the elderly.

One result of the current Social Security debate has been to concentrate the public's mind on the true economic condition of the elderly—and to give the lie to those who describe them as "greedy geezers." While the top 20% of seniors are relatively affluent, reports the Center on Budget & Policy Priorities, almost all of the rest are highly dependent on Social Security.

In 1997, the average Social Security retirement benefit was just $765 a month, and the average check to 65-year-olds was $819 a month—a tidy sum, but hardly a bonanza. Yet, according to the center's analysis, the program provided at least half of the total income of more than 55% of senior citizens and at least 75% of the total income of more than a third.

Social Security's impact on poverty among older Americans is equally revealing. Based on 1997 Census Bureau data, the center finds that the retirement program lifted 11.4 million seniors—or nearly half of the 65-and-older population—out of poverty, cutting the elderly's poverty rate from 47.6% to 11.9%. Means-tested programs, such as Supplemental Security Income, lowered the rate still further to 10.5%—bringing it close to that of other adult Americans.

Think About It

1. **What percentage of senior citizens rely on Social Security to provide half of their income?**
2. **How many seniors were lifted out of poverty by Social Security payments?**

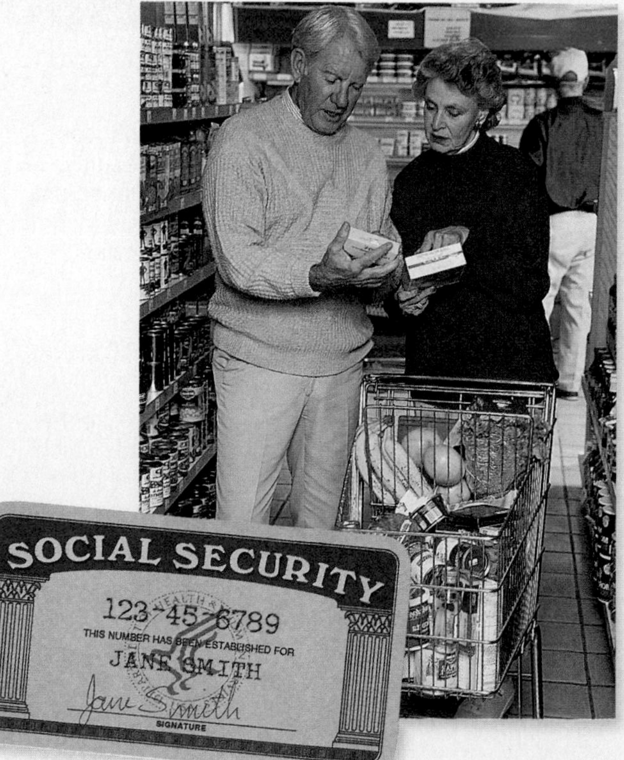

SECTION 3

The Federal Budget and the National Debt

COVER STORY

THE NEW YORK TIMES, JANUARY 31, 1999

The federal budget deficit is gone, transformed by a strong economy into a string of projected surpluses that should grow larger for years to come. . . .

Eliminating the deficit is hardly the end of the government's financial troubles, however. . . . [T]he national debt was built up over decades of deficit spending—the federal government has not run steady surpluses since the 1920s—and it remains an economic millstone of considerable proportions.

Debt

READER'S GUIDE

Terms to Know

- fiscal year
- budget deficit
- deficit financing
- national debt
- budget surplus

Reading Objectives

1. What are the steps in the federal budget-making process?
2. What are the five largest federal expenditures?
3. What are the five largest state and local government expenditures?
4. How does deficit spending increase the national debt?

To carry out all of its functions, government must spend huge sums of money. As a result, the federal budget is huge and has numerous categories. Because all resources are scarce, an increase in spending in one area will cause a decrease in spending in some other area. *Parts A* and *B* of **Figure 16.6** on page 436 show the major areas in which the federal, state, and local governments spend their money. As you read this section, you'll learn how the government prepares its budget and decides where to spend its funds.

FIGURE 16.6

Part A Federal Spending The federal budget is based on a fiscal year, rather than the calendar year. Spending is calculated from the beginning of the budget year on October 1 of one year to September 30 of the next year.

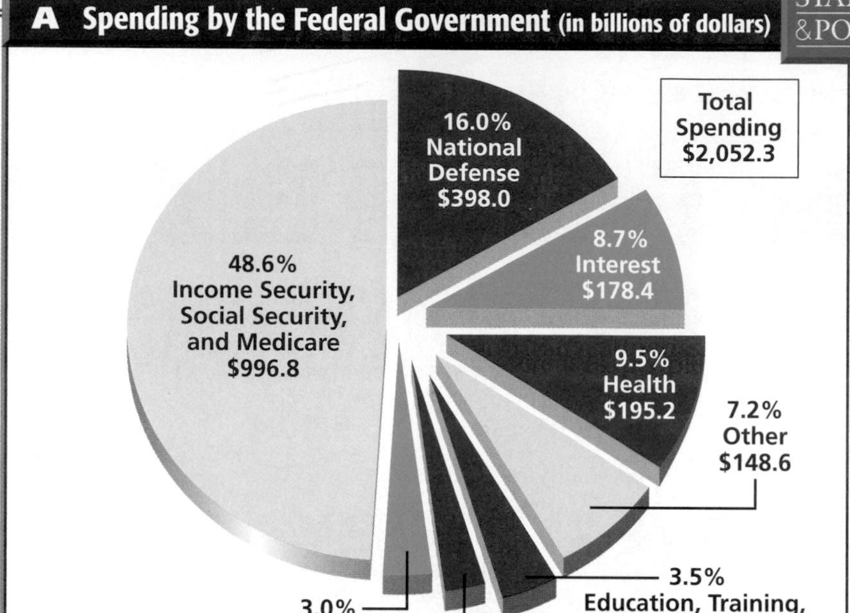

Part B State and Local Government Spending State and local government expenditures have increased in recent years, as these governments cover the rising costs of social welfare programs.

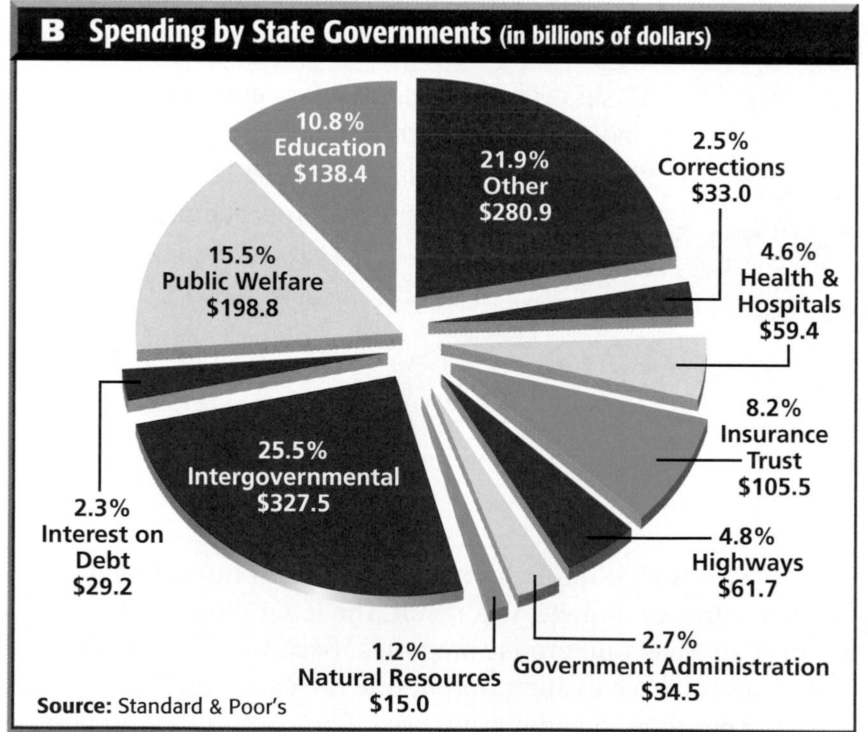

For online updates of these graphs, visit ett.glencoe.com and click on ***Textbook Updates—Chapter 16.***

FIGURE 16.7

The Federal Budget-Making Process The Office of Management and Budget (OMB) starts the budget process, with the advice of the Council of Economic Advisers and the Treasury Department.

Part B of **Figure 16.6** shows how state and local governments spend the tax revenues they collect. The largest single category by far in state and local expenditures is education. The "other" expenditure includes expenditures for such things as state parks, sewers, and libraries.

The Budget-Making Process

Considerable debate and compromise are necessary in preparing an annual budget. A complicated budget-making process goes on every year, not just in Washington, D.C., but in every state and local government unit as well.

The Federal Budget About 18 months before the **fiscal year** begins on October 1, the executive branch of the government begins to prepare a budget, as **Figure 16.7** shows. Working with the President, the Office of Management and Budget (OMB) makes an outline of a tentative budget for the next fiscal year. The various departments and agencies receive this outline and usually start bargaining with the OMB for a larger allocation of federal funds.

Steps in the Budget Process

February–September 2003
Executive branch agencies develop requests for funds and submit them to the Office of Management and Budget (OMB).

September–December 2003
The President and OMB review the requests and make the fiscal decisions on what goes in the budget. The budget is printed and formally sent to Congress.

January–September 2004
The House and Senate Budget Committees review the President's proposed budget. By April 15, these committees prepare an initial resolution for the budget that goes to the entire Congress for debate. By September 25, the congressional budget should be finalized and passed by the House of Representatives, which approves spending and revenue bills.

October 1, 2004
The fiscal year begins.

October 1, 2004–September 30, 2005
Agency program managers implement the budget and disburse funds.

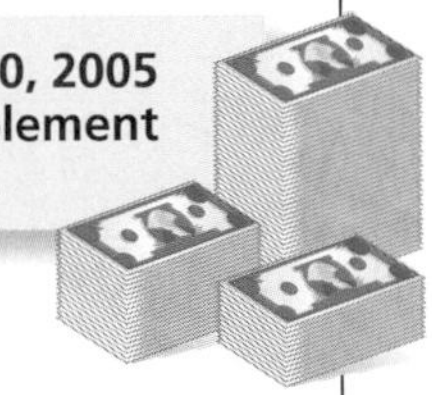

October–November 2005
Data on actual spending and receipts for the completed fiscal year become available, and the General Accounting Office audits the fiscal-year outlays.

fiscal year: *year by which accounts are kept; for the federal government, October 1 to September 30 of the next year*

FIGURE 16.8

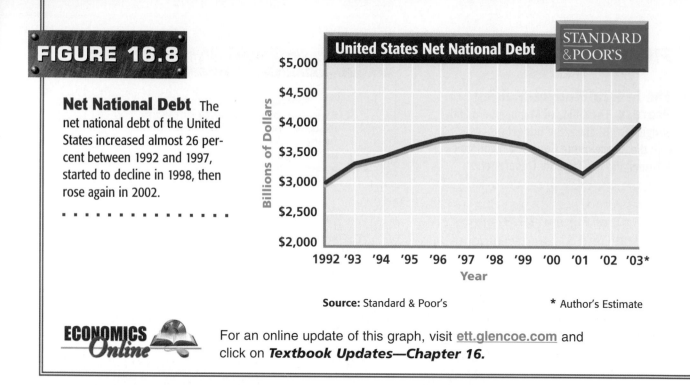

Net National Debt The net national debt of the United States increased almost 26 percent between 1992 and 1997, started to decline in 1998, then rose again in 2002.

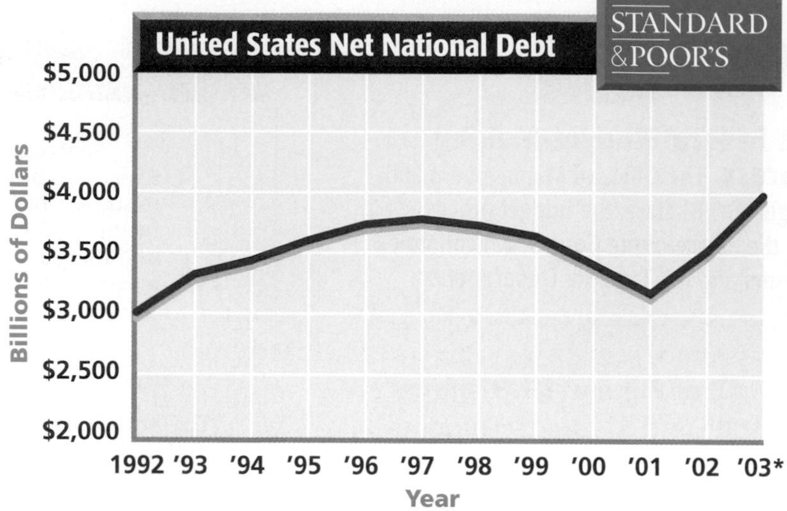

Source: Standard & Poor's

* Author's Estimate

For an online update of this graph, visit ett.glencoe.com and click on ***Textbook Updates—Chapter 16.***

The President reviews and approves the budget plan. The budget is printed, and the President submits the budget to Congress by January. Then various committees and subcommittees of Congress examine the budget's proposals, while the Congressional Budget Office (CBO) advises the committees about different aspects of the budget. Throughout the year, each committee holds a series of discussions.

Congress is supposed to pass two budget resolutions that set binding limits on spending and taxes for the upcoming fiscal year. In practice, however, the required budget resolutions often do not get passed on time. Moreover, when they are passed, the resolutions are not always treated as binding. As a result, the fiscal year sometimes starts without a budget, and the government must operate on the basis of a continuing congressional resolution. Agencies that allocate funds can continue spending as they spent the year before until the new budget resolution is passed.

Deficit Spending and the National Debt

budget deficit: *situation when the amount of government spending exceeds its receipts during the fiscal year*

In spite of the budget process outlined above, federal government revenues have not always been equal to government expenditures. Most years, the federal government spent more than it collected in taxes, causing a **budget deficit.** When a budget deficit occurs, the government must raise the extra funds through borrowing. This borrowing is similar to an individual overspending his or her income and using credit. The government's overspending is called **deficit financing.**

deficit financing: *government policy of spending more money than it is able to bring in through revenues*

Government Borrowing Government borrows money to cover the deficit by selling securities to individuals and businesses. Federal securities include Treasury bonds, notes, and bills. When you buy United States savings bonds, you are also lending funds to the federal government. In addition, individual agencies of the federal government, such as the Tennessee Valley Authority, are authorized to sell bonds. State and local governments can borrow by selling bonds to finance some of their activities.

Each year the federal government creates new debt by issuing new securities. At the same time, it retires old debt by paying off bonds, notes, and bills as they come due. The total amount of outstanding debt for the federal government is called the **national debt,** or public debt.

national debt: *total amount of outstanding debt for the federal government*

As you can see from **Figure 16.8,** from 1992 until 1997, the amount of the net national debt grew. The government began to run a **budget surplus**—government revenues exceeded government expenditures during the fiscal year—in 1998. However, the planned surpluses of 2001 and later years seemed unlikely to occur after terrorism struck the United States in September 2001. The federal government had to spend more to fight terrorism.

budget surplus: *situation when the amount of government receipts is larger than its expenditures during the fiscal year*

Practice and **assess** key skills with ***Skillbuilder Interactive Workbook, Level 2.***

SECTION 3 Assessment

Understanding Key Terms

1. **Define** fiscal year, budget deficit, deficit financing, national debt, budget surplus.

Reviewing Objectives

2. **Graphic Organizer** Create a diagram like the one below to describe the steps in the federal budget-making process.

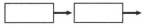

3. What are the five largest federal expenses?
4. What are the five largest state and local expenses?
5. How does deficit spending increase the size of the national debt?

Applying Economic Concepts

6. **Trade-Offs** If you had to reduce spending at the state and local levels, which categories shown in *Part B* of **Figure 16.6** would you reduce? Why?

Critical Thinking Activity

7. **Categorizing Information** What is your share of the national debt today? Search the Internet under *national debt* for the debt total, then divide that number by an estimate of the current population.

SECTION 4 Taxation

Reader's Guide

Terms to Know

- benefits-received principle
- ability-to-pay principle
- proportional tax
- progressive tax
- regressive tax

Reading Objectives

1. What are the two principles of taxation?
2. What effect do the three forms of taxation have on taxpayers?

Cover Story

The Washington Post, April 12, 1999

"We'll cut your taxes" is the most repeated campaign promise in the history of American politics. Yet somehow it is still considered visionary, worth a fight. Worth, indeed, a crusade.

Why? It's in our blood. Historically, Americans have hated taxes, and not merely because we had to pay them. We've hated taxes because we've perceived them to be an infringement on our liberty—and the source of big, powerful, and mischievous government. This was true from the beginning. It wasn't just "taxation without representation" that bothered us so much. It was taxation. Period.

You, the American taxpayer, are the source of most of the money the government spends. Almost all federal, state, and local government revenue comes from taxes. In this section, you'll learn about the major kinds of taxes paid in this country.

Principles of Taxation

Figure 16.9 lists the major taxes that the various levels of government use to raise revenue. Taxes are usually justified according to one of two major principles. Under the **benefits-received principle,** those who use a particular government service should support it with taxes in proportion to the benefit they receive. Those who do not use a service do not pay taxes for it. A gasoline

benefits-received principle: *system of taxation in which those who use a particular government service support it with taxes in proportion to the benefit they receive; those who do not use a service do not pay taxes for it*

FIGURE 16.9 Major Taxes

Tax	Description	Type
Personal income	Tax is a percentage of income and a major source of federal revenue; many state governments also levy	Progressive at the federal level, but is sometimes proportional at the state level
Social insurance	Taxes covered by the Federal Insurance Contributions Act (FICA); second-largest source of federal revenue	Proportional up to income of $80,400 in 2001, regressive above that (as estimated by the Social Security Administration)
Corporate income	Federal tax as a percentage of corporate profits; some states also levy	At the federal level, progressive up to $18.3 million, proportional above that
Excise	Tax paid by the consumer on the manufacture, use, and consumption of certain goods; major federal taxes are on alcohol, tobacco, and gasoline; some states also levy	Regressive if people with higher incomes spend a lower proportion of income on taxed items
Estate	Federal tax on the property of someone who has died; some states also levy	Progressive; rate increases with the value of the estate
Inheritance	State tax paid by those who inherit property	Varies by state
Gift	Federal tax paid by the person who gives a large gift	Progressive; rate increases with the value of the gift
Sales	Tax paid on purchases; almost all states as well as many local governments levy; rate varies from state to state and within states; items taxed also vary	Regressive if people with higher incomes spend a lower proportion of income on taxed items
Property	State and local taxation of the value of property; both real property (such as buildings and land) and personal property (such as stocks, bonds, and home furnishings) may be taxed	Proportional; rate is set by state and local governments
Customs duties	Tax on imports; paid by the importer	Proportional

Economic Connection to... History

The Constitution and Taxes

Article 1, Section 8 of the Constitution states that "Congress shall have the power to lay and collect taxes. . ." for the purpose of paying debts and providing for the nation's defense and general welfare. Any taxes imposed must apply equally to all parts of the United States. The Constitution also made direct taxes, such as income taxes, difficult to impose because they had to be in proportion to each state's population. This meant the states with more people would pay higher taxes. The 16th Amendment, passed in 1913, enabled the federal government to impose income taxes on individuals. ■ *Why does the Constitution give Congress the power to tax? How have the original restrictions on taxation been changed?*

tax to pay for highway construction and repair is based on the benefits-received principle. Frequent users of the highways often buy more gasoline and, therefore, pay more in gasoline taxes.

A tax based on the benefits-received principle is useful in raising funds to pay for a service only certain individuals use. Many government services–national defense, for example–benefit everyone equally, however. Also, those who most require services, such as the aged and poor, are the individuals least able to pay taxes.

ability-to-pay principle: *principle of taxation in which those with higher incomes pay more taxes than those with lower incomes, regardless of the number of government services they use*

Under the **ability-to-pay principle,** those with higher incomes pay more taxes than those with lower incomes, regardless of the number of government services they use. For example, in most cities all property owners, even those without school-aged children, must pay property taxes to support the local school system. Property taxes are calculated as a percentage of the value of a person's home. Thus, wealthier people with more expensive homes pay more property taxes.

Student Web Activity Visit the *Economics Today and Tomorrow* Web site at ett.glencoe.com and click on ***Chapter 16—Student Web Activities*** to learn how the federal government spends your tax dollars.

Forms of Taxation

Actual taxes are classified according to the effect they have on those who are taxed. In the United States today, these classifications include proportional, progressive, and regressive taxes.

Proportional Tax A **proportional tax** is the easiest type of tax to understand. The taxes you owe are simply a proportion of the money income you have earned. If there is a tax of 10 percent on all income and you earn $1,000, then you pay $100 in taxes. If you earn $10,000, you pay $1,000 in taxes, and so on.

proportional tax: *tax that takes the same percentage of all incomes; as income rises, the amount of tax paid also rises*

Progressive Tax With a **progressive tax,** when an individual earns a higher income, his or her taxes increase more than in proportion to the increase in money income. A good example of a progressive tax is our federal individual income tax system. As you make more reported income, you pay an increasingly higher percentage of that additional income in taxes to the federal government. A progressive income tax has often been justified on the basis of the ability-to-pay principle.

progressive tax: *tax that takes a larger percentage of higher incomes than lower incomes; justified on the basis of the ability-to-pay principle*

Regressive Tax As you might expect, a **regressive tax** is the opposite of a progressive tax. The percentage that you pay in taxes actually goes down as you make more money income. Some economists believe that a good example of a regressive tax is the sales tax on food. They point out that poorer families spend a larger proportion of their income on food. Therefore, the sales tax they pay on food takes up a larger proportion of their total income than a wealthier family pays.

regressive tax: *tax that takes a larger percentage of lower incomes than of higher incomes*

Practice and **assess** key skills with ***Skillbuilder Interactive Workbook, Level 2.***

SECTION 4 Assessment

Understanding Key Terms

1. **Define** benefits-received principle, ability-to-pay principle, proportional tax, progressive tax, regressive tax.

Reviewing Objectives

2. What are the two principles of taxation?
3. **Graphic Organizer** Create a chart like the one in the next column to explain the three forms of taxation and their effect on taxpayers.

Type of Tax	Effect on Taxpayer	Example

Applying Economic Concepts

4. **Taxation** List and describe the kinds of taxes you personally pay.

Critical Thinking Activity

5. **Making Comparisons** Which of the two principles of taxation do you think is the more equitable? Explain your answer.

Technology Skills

Using E-Mail

Electronic mail, or E-mail, refers to communicating at a distance through the use of a computer. A computer is ready to "talk" to other computers after two things are added to it: (a) a modem—a device that allows communication through a telephone line, and (b) communications software, which lets your computer prepare and send information to the modem.

1. Select the "Message" function from your communications software.
2. Type in your message, and proofread it for errors.
3. Type in the E-mail address of the recipient. and select the "Send" button.
4. The E-mail system places the message in the receiver's electronic mailbox. He or she may read the message at any time, and send you a return message.
5. When you receive E-mail, the sender's address is on the message—add it to your electronic address book at that time.

Learning the Skill

To send an E-mail message, follow the steps listed on the left.

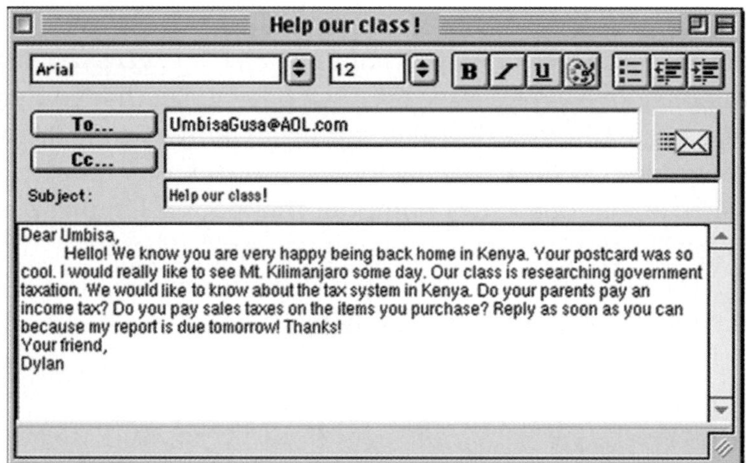

Help our class!
Arial
12
B
I
U
To...
UmbisaGusa@AOL.com
Cc...
Subject:
Help our class!
Dear Umbisa,
Hello! We know you are very happy being back home in Kenya. Your postcard was so cool. I would really like to see Mt. Kilimanjaro some day. Our class is researching government taxation. We would like to know about the tax system in Kenya. Do your parents pay an income tax? Do you pay sales taxes on the items you purchase? Reply as soon as you can because my report is due tomorrow! Thanks!
Your friend,
Dylan

After you type in your message, you may send it, forward it, and even save it to a file.

Practicing the Skill

Select a current issue concerning government taxation to research. Then browse the Internet to obtain the E-mail address of a federal official concerned with the issue. E-mail the official, sharing opinions about the issue, asking questions about the issue, and requesting information.

Application Activity

E-mail a classmate. Forward the information you received from the government official concerning the issue above. Working together, write a summary of the E-mail correspondence with the official.

CHAPTER  Summary

Chapter Overview Visit the *Economics Today and Tomorrow* Web site at ett.glencoe.com and click on ***Chapter 16—Chapter Overviews*** to review chapter information.

SECTION 1 Growth in the Size of Government

- Government at every level—local, state, and federal—is involved in almost every aspect of the United States economy.
- All levels of government employ about 20 million civilian workers.
- Government finances highways, education, and other **public-works projects.** It also regulates product and worker safety.
- Total government outlays, including actual purchases as well as transfer payments, exceed one-third of GDP.

SECTION 2 The Functions of Government

- One function of government is to provide **public goods,** such as national parks and national defense.
- Another function of government is to provide for the public well-being through **social insurance programs**—such as **Social Security, Medicare,** and **workers' compensation**—and **public-assistance programs**—such as **Supplemental Security Income** and **Medicaid.**
- A third function of government is to regulate the negative **externalities** of the production process.
- A fourth function—ensuring economic stability—has meant smoothing the ups and downs in the nation's overall business activity.

SECTION 3 The Federal Budget and the National Debt

- The federal government's largest expenditures include Social Security/Medicare/income security, national defense, interest on the national debt, and health.
- The executive and legislative branches prepare a federal budget for each **fiscal year.**
- Spending more in a fiscal year than it collects in taxes results in the government running a **budget deficit.**
- The total amount accumulated by annual budget deficits is the **national debt.**

SECTION 4 Taxation

- Under the **benefits-received principle,** people who use a particular government service support it with taxes in proportion to the benefit they receive.
- Under the **ability-to-pay principle,** those with higher incomes pay more taxes than those with lower incomes, regardless of the number of government services they use.
- Major types of taxes include personal income, social insurance, corporate income, sales, and property taxes.
- Taxes are classified according to the effect they have on those who are taxed: **proportional, progressive,** or **regressive.**

CHAPTER 16

Assessment and Activities

Self-Check Quiz Visit the *Economics Today and Tomorrow* Web site at ett.glencoe.com and click on ***Chapter 16—Self-Check Quizzes*** to prepare for the Chapter Test.

Identifying Key Terms

Write the letter of the definition in Column B that correctly defines each term in Column A.

Column A

1. benefits-received principle
2. public goods
3. ability-to-pay principle
4. income redistribution
5. national debt
6. Medicare
7. Social Security
8. Medicaid

Column B

a. public-assistance program that provides free health care to low-income persons
b. taking tax dollars from some to give to others in the form of aid
c. system by which those with higher incomes pay higher taxes
d. provides monthly payments to the retired
e. payment for a particular government service by those who use the service
f. goods and services whose use by one person does not reduce use by another
g. provides health care for the aged
h. amount of money the government owes

Recalling Facts and Ideas

Section 1

1. In what ways has the government grown since the Great Depression?
2. What percent of GDP is accounted for by total government purchases?

Section 2

3. What are government's main functions?
4. Give five examples of public goods.
5. What would be a negative externality of having an airport built near your home? What would be a positive externality?

Section 3

6. About how long does it take the federal government to prepare a budget?
7. What causes the nation's public debt?

Section 4

8. What are the principal taxes that exist in the United States today?
9. If all income were taxed at exactly the same rate, what type of tax would be in existence?

Thinking Critically

1. **Analyzing Information** Look at **Figure 16.2** on page 426. When did federal government purchases drop below state and local purchases? Why do you think this situation occurred?

2. **Drawing Conclusions** Create a diagram like the one below to explain how you think taxes can encourage or discourage consumer and business behaviors.

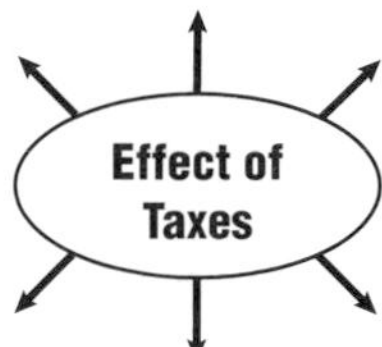

Applying Economic Concepts

Principles of Taxation You learned about two principles of taxation, one of which was the benefits-received principle. Assume that you want to use this principle to justify a progressive income tax system. Write a list of the reasons explaining why, as a person's income goes up, that person receives more benefits from the government and therefore should be taxed progressively.

Cooperative Learning Project

Work in groups representing at least three regions of the United States. Each member should choose one or more states in the group's region to research. Determine which states in the region have the highest tax rate. The information needed will be:

- Highest tax rate applied to personal income
- Highest tax rate applied to corporate income
- Sales tax rate

Share your information with the rest of your group, and then have the groups present the information to the rest of the class. Which state in which region has the highest tax rate? Which region in general has the highest tax rate?

Reviewing Skills

Using E-Mail Using your communications software, type a message asking 10 registered voters for their opinions on the national debt. In your E-mail, ask the recipients questions such as the following:

1. How serious do you think the national debt is for the future of the United States?
2. What measures, if any, should the federal government take to reduce the national debt?
3. If we do not reduce the national debt, what consequences do you foresee, particularly for the generation currently attending high school?
4. What sacrifices do you think you would be willing to make to help reduce the debt?

Technology Activity

Developing Multimedia Presentations Develop a video tracing your daily routine and examining each part of your life in which the government is involved. For example, if you take a bus to school, videotape the bus and explain that this is an example of property taxes being used to fund school transportation. Continue filming throughout the day as you come in contact with other government services. Show your completed video to the class.

Analyzing the Global Economy

Compare the federal income tax rate of the United States to other industrialized nations, including the Netherlands, Germany, Sweden, Japan, and France. Which nation has the highest tax rate?

CASE STUDY

Focus on Free Enterprise

The Trek Bicycle Corporation

On July 27, 2003, American Lance Armstrong rode through the streets of Paris, France, greeted by thousands of wildly cheering spectators. He was on his way to his fifth consecutive victory in the Tour de France—the world's greatest bicycle race. Armstrong is the first American to have won the tour more than two times in a row. The race lasts about three weeks and covers more than 2,000 miles. It was an "all-American" victory, for Armstrong was riding an American-made bike—a Trek.

Lance Armstrong

The Bike Barn

Trek bikes got their start in Waterloo, Wisconsin, more than 25 years ago. Richard Burke and his friends loved tinkering with bicycles, even making their own bike frames. When other people started admiring their handiwork, they realized they had a real business opportunity.

In 1976 Burke and his friends set up Trek Bicycle Corporation in a rented barn in Waterloo. The company had just five workers and made one product—hand-built steel bike frames. Over time, Trek Bicycle expanded its business, making its own road bicycles using quality parts from American manufacturers. In the early 1980s, Trek introduced a line of mountain bikes. By the end of the decade, Trek was producing bicycle clothing, safety equipment, and children's bikes.

As a result, Trek expanded its production facilities, building three factories in Wisconsin—one right next door to the barn in Waterloo. It also opened facilities in Europe and Japan. Today Trek employs about 1,500 people worldwide

Police patrol on Y bikes

and has yearly sales in excess of $550 million. It ranks as one of the world's leading quality bicycle manufacturers.

Building a Better Bike

Trek Bicycle's success is due to its commitment to product improvement. Trek has continually made research and development one of its top priorities. This focus has resulted in many innovations in bicycle construction. Their carbon fiber frame is one example. Weighing less than 2.5 pounds, it was designed using the same technology that developed the Stealth fighter.

Another example is the aluminum-frame Y bike. The technology used in its construction combined the comfort of mountain bikes with the quickness of road bikes. The Y bike is popular in an unusual market–law enforcement. Many police forces use the Y bike for their bicycle units. Even the President's Secret Service squad patrols the White House grounds on specially designed Y bikes!

Trek's innovations also are popular with people in the industry. In 1995 the Trek engineers who designed the Y bike won *Popular Mechanics* magazine's Design Engineer of the Year Award. In 1996 the Industrial Designers Society of America gave Trek's Y bike its Gold Industrial Excellence Award.

Future Plans

Trek Bicycle plans to continue developing new and exciting products for cycling enthusiasts. The most recent is a line of bikes built especially for riding in the city—the Urban Assault Vehicle. Trek also wants to solidify itself as an American operation. At present, some 70 percent of Trek bikes are made at the company's Wisconsin facilities. In the next few years, Trek hopes to push this figure higher. For Richard Burke and other Trek executives, "Made in America" is an important and proud boast.

Free Enterprise in Action

1. **What is the key to Trek Bicycle Corporation's success?**
2. **How do Trek Bicycle's future plans show that the company takes the statement "Made in America" seriously?**

CHAPTER 17

Stabilizing the National Economy

Why It's Important

Why is it important for the economy to be balanced, or stabilized? This chapter will explain the factors that destabilize the economy, and what actions are taken to adjust it.

To learn more about unemployment and inflation, view the **Economics & You** *Chapter 23 video lesson:* **Economic Growth and Stability**

Chapter Overview Visit the *Economics Today and Tomorrow* Web site at ett.glencoe.com and click on ***Chapter 17—Chapter Overviews*** to preview chapter information.

SECTION 1

Unemployment and Inflation

Cover Story

CNN/Money, August 7, 2003

Despite a recent wave of rosy reports on the U.S. economy and much optimism about the direction of growth, businesses still aren't hiring—and some economists worry the labor market slump, if it doesn't end soon, could nip the recovery in the bud.

NOTICE OF EMPLOYMENT TERMINATION
NAME:
JOB TITLE:
EFFECTIVE DATE:
Signed,

Economic news Thursday from the Labor Department highlighted the promise and the danger for the job market. Weekly jobless claims stayed below a critical level for the third straight week, a sign things might be getting better.

Reader's Guide

Terms to Know

- stabilization policies
- unemployment rate
- full employment
- underground economy
- demand-pull inflation
- stagflation
- cost-push inflation

Reading Objectives

1. What are two problems the government faces in measuring unemployment?
2. What are the four kinds of unemployment?
3. How does demand-pull inflation differ from cost-push inflation?

When people are unemployed, they experience uncertainty. In the same way, unemployment in general causes uncertainty in the American economy. To keep the economy healthy and to make the future more predictable for planning, saving, and investing, the federal government uses monetary and fiscal policies. Together these are called **stabilization policies.** Unfortunately, neither policy is always successful in

stabilization policies: *attempts by the federal government to keep the economy healthy; includes monetary and fiscal policies*

Student Web Activity Visit the *Economics Today and Tomorrow* Web site at ett.glencoe.com and click on ***Chapter 17—Student Web Activities*** to learn how to write an online resume.

solving the complex problems of the economy. As you read this section, you'll learn that two of the biggest threats to a nation's economic stability are high unemployment and inflation.

Measuring Unemployment

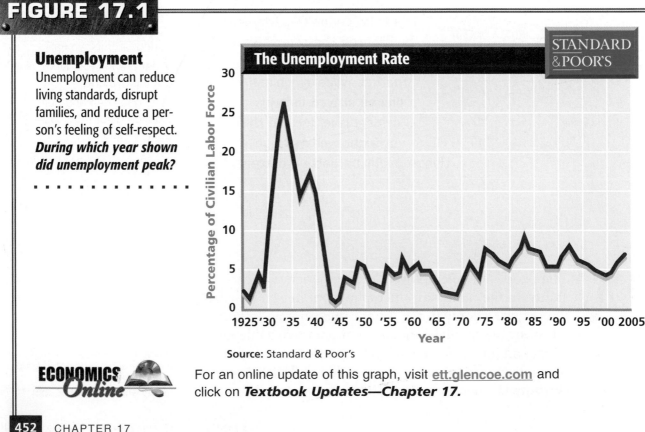

Expert economists advise the President and Congress, but they often disagree about the causes and cures of the economic problems that periodically face the nation. One statistic they all look at, however, is the **unemployment rate**–the percentage of the civilian labor force that is without jobs but that is actively looking for work. See **Figure 17.1.**

unemployment rate: *percentage of the civilian labor force that is unemployed but is actively looking for work*

High unemployment is usually a sign that all is not well with the economy. Moreover, the waste of human resources that unemployment causes is an extremely serious problem. As a result, maintaining a low unemployment rate is one of the major goals in stabilizing the economy.

FIGURE 17.1

Unemployment
Unemployment can reduce living standards, disrupt families, and reduce a person's feeling of self-respect. ***During which year shown did unemployment peak?***

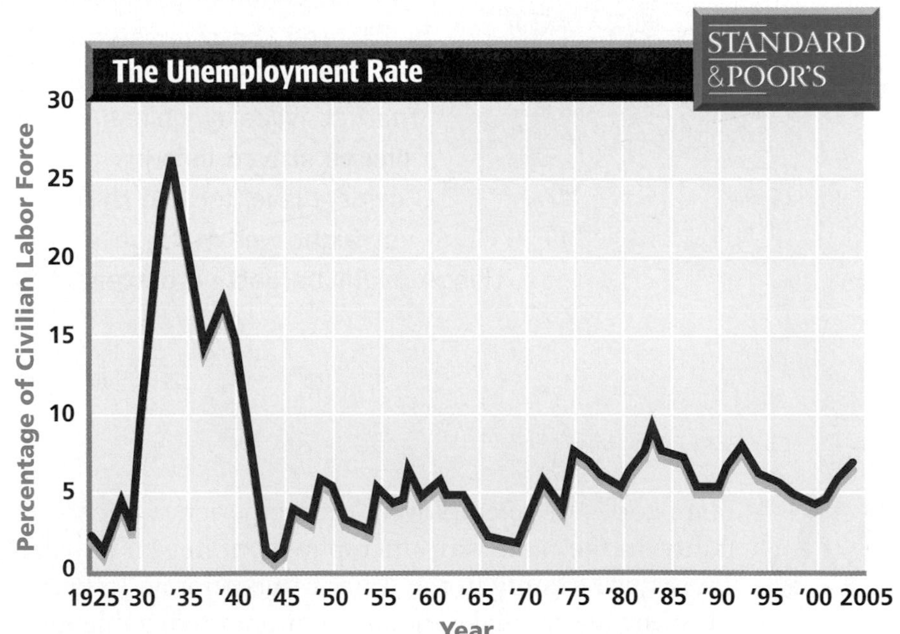

Source: Standard & Poor's

For an online update of this graph, visit ett.glencoe.com and click on ***Textbook Updates—Chapter 17.***

FIGURE 17.2 Types of Unemployment

Type	Definition	Characteristics
Cyclical	Unemployment associated with up or down fluctuations in the business cycle	Rises during recessions and depressions; falls during recoveries and booms
Structural	Unemployment caused by changes in the economy, such as technological advances or discoveries of natural resources	Can result when workers are replaced by computers or other machines or when cheaper natural resources are found elsewhere; often affects less skilled workers
Seasonal	Unemployment caused by changes in the seasons or weather	Affects construction workers, particularly in the Northeast and Midwest; also affects farmworkers needed only during certain months of the growing season
Frictional	Temporary unemployment between jobs because of firings, layoffs, voluntary searches for new jobs, or retraining	Always exists to some degree because of the time needed between jobs to find new work and the imperfect match between openings and applicants

Types of Unemployment Many types of unemployment exist. **Figure 17.2** describes these kinds of unemployment. Some people work in seasonal jobs or jobs that are sensitive to technological advances or to changes in the marketplace. As a result, not all unemployment can or should be eliminated. Moreover, economists disagree over what the level of full employment should be. Economists today generally have come to consider the economy at **full employment** when the unemployment rate is less than 5 percent.

full employment: *condition of the economy when the unemployment rate is lower than a certain percentage established by economists' studies*

It is important to remember that the unemployment rate is only an estimate. The unemployment rate does not include people who are unemployed and have stopped looking for work. Nor does it include people who work in family businesses without receiving pay.

Unemployment is difficult to measure accurately because government statisticians cannot possibly interview every person in and out of the labor force. Survey results are also imperfect because of the existence of the **underground economy.** The underground economy consists of people who do not follow federal and state laws with respect to reporting earnings. Examples might include tax avoiders, gamblers, and drug traffickers.

underground economy: *transactions by people who do not follow federal and state laws with respect to reporting earnings*

Global Economy

Unemployment

How do United States unemployment statistics compare to those of other industrialized nations?

U.S.	Japan	France	Germany
Unemployment Rate			
6.1%	5.4%	8.8%	8.4%
% of Average Wage Received in Benefits			
35%	48%	63%	44%
Length of Time Benefits Are Paid			
39 weeks	13 mo.	25 mo.	47 mo.

Source: *The World Factbook*, 2003

Inflation

A second major problem that may face any nation is inflation. The economy can usually adapt to gradually rising prices. If prices rise about 3 percent every year, for example, everyone comes to expect and understand that. Unpredictable inflation, however, has a destabilizing effect on the economy.

During periods of unpredictable high inflation, creditors raise interest rates to maintain the level of profits they had before inflation began to rise rapidly. This, in turn, may have a slowing effect on the economy's growth.

Inflation may also affect consumers' standard of living. Suppose you receive a 5 percent pay raise in a year in which inflation has risen 8 percent. Your real (adjusted for inflation) income has decreased. Inflation is a particularly serious problem for people who live on *fixed incomes,* such as those who are retired.

Not all economists agree on a single explanation of why inflation occurs. Two competing ideas have developed: the demand-pull theory (prices are *pulled* up by high demand) and the cost-push theory (prices are *pushed* up by high production costs and wages).

demand-pull inflation: *theory that prices rise as the result of excessive business and consumer demand; demand increases faster than total supply, resulting in shortages that lead to higher prices*

Demand-Pull According to the theory of **demand-pull inflation,** prices rise as the result of excessive business and consumer demand. If economy-wide, or aggregate, demand increases faster than total supply, the resulting shortage will lead to the bidding up of prices.

Demand-pull inflation can occur for several reasons. If the Federal Reserve causes the money supply to grow too rapidly, individuals will spend the additional dollars on a limited supply of goods and services. This increased demand will cause prices to rise. Increases in government spending and in business investment can also increase overall demand. Aggregate demand can also increase if taxes are reduced or consumers begin saving less.

Cost-Push The demand-pull theory assumes that increased demand will increase output and reduce unemployment. Experience, however, has shown that rising prices and unemployment

FIGURE 17.3

Effects of Inflation As Ziggy notes, inflation lowers the purchasing power of people, especially those on fixed incomes.

ZIGGY

..WITH THE HIGH COST OF THINGS NOWADAYS,
..I'M FINDING IT MORE AND MORE DIFFICULT TO GRASP THE CONCEPT OF "PETTY" CASH!
PAY
BILL
PAST DUE
© 1999 Ziggy and Friends, Inc./Dist. by Universal Press Syndicate

can occur at the same time. This combination of inflation and low economic activity is sometimes called **stagflation.**

According to some economists, stagflation is a result of cost-push inflation at work in the economy. The theory of **cost-push inflation** states that the wage demands of labor unions and the excessive profit motive of large corporations push up prices. When businesses have to pay higher wages, their costs increase. To maintain their profit level, businesses must raise the prices of the goods and services they produce.

During periods of cost-push inflation, unemployment can remain high. Prices are being adjusted for higher wages and profits—not because of increased aggregate demand. Without additional aggregate demand, producers have no reason to increase output by hiring new workers.

stagflation: *combination of inflation and low economic activity*

cost-push inflation: *theory that higher wages and profits push up prices*

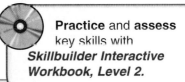

Practice and **assess** key skills with ***Skillbuilder Interactive Workbook, Level 2.***

SECTION 1 Assessment

Understanding Key Terms

1. **Define** stabilization policies, unemployment rate, full employment, underground economy, demand-pull inflation, stagflation, cost-push inflation.

Reviewing Objectives

2. What are two problems the government faces in measuring unemployment?
3. **Graphic Organizer** Create a diagram like the one below to describe the four kinds of unemployment.

Types of Unemployment

4. How does demand-pull inflation differ from cost-push inflation?

Applying Economic Concepts

5. **Inflation and Deflation** Name some factors that could cause the price of each of the following to go up or down: oil, medical care, orange juice, automobiles.

Critical Thinking Activity

6. **Understanding Cause and Effect** Construct a table that identifies the causes of inflation. List four causes under demand-pull inflation in column 1 and three causes under cost-push inflation in column 2. *For help in constructing tables, see page xvii in the Economic Handbook.*

BusinessWeek

SPOTLIGHT ON THE ECONOMY

Your Next Job

Check It Out! In this chapter you learned about the four kinds of unemployment. In this article, read to learn how the United States job market looked at the end of the twentieth century.

Employers across the country are facing a newly emboldened American work force. We're living through the tightest U.S. labor market in three decades—a hiring bonanza that is transforming the nature of work. The current hypergrowth in jobs can't last forever; fast-food restaurants won't be paying signing bonuses during the next recession. But the most remarkable changes in the workplace—and our attitudes toward it—will redefine careers well into the 21st century. Just as the Great Depression produced a generation of frugal worry-warts, those of us benefiting from the long jobs boom of the 1990s sport an often brazen self-confidence about how we connect to our jobs. . . .

What is worth knowing? That more Americans are creating entirely new styles of employment. They're found in the expanding ranks of self-employed Free Agents who find financial and professional independence in everything from personal training to urban planning. Or they are the new Nomads, workers who never seem to stop job hunting. There's an emerging class of Globalists, too—those have-laptop-will-travel workers who straddle time zones in today's borderless economy. . . .

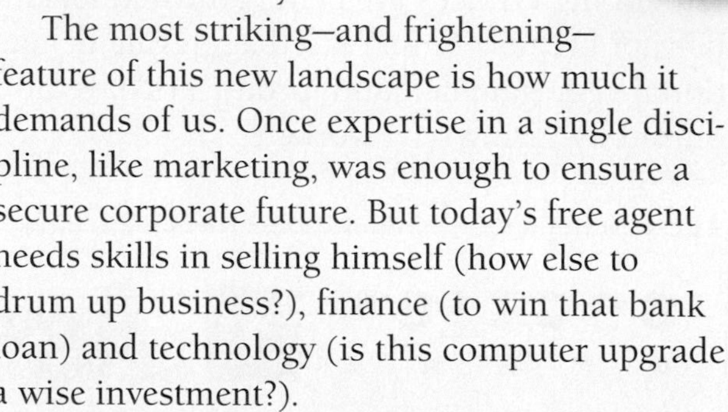

The most striking—and frightening—feature of this new landscape is how much it demands of us. Once expertise in a single discipline, like marketing, was enough to ensure a secure corporate future. But today's free agent needs skills in selling himself (how else to drum up business?), finance (to win that bank loan) and technology (is this computer upgrade a wise investment?).

Think About It

1. **According to the article, why are workers so confident about their jobs?**
2. **How have the new styles of employment changed what is demanded of workers?**

SECTION 2

The Fiscal Policy Approach to Stabilization

Cover Story

The New York Times, July 14, 1999

For all the recent talk of cutting taxes, Congress rarely cuts them when the economy is growing robustly, as it is now, and unemployment is low. The worry among economists is that the extra money in people's pockets may make an already strong economy too strong, finally stoking inflation after a long period of relatively stable prices.

Reader's Guide

Terms to Know

- fiscal policy
- circular flow of income

Reading Objectives

1. How does income flow between businesses and consumers?
2. How can the federal government use fiscal policy to combat unemployment?

Most economists belong to one of two groups on the question of stabilization. One group emphasizes the role of the Federal Reserve in stabilizing the economy, which you learned about in Chapter 15. In this section, you'll learn that the other group concentrates more on the use of **fiscal policy,** the federal government's deliberate use of its taxation rates and expenditures to affect overall business activity.

fiscal policy: *federal government's use of taxation and spending policies to affect overall business activity*

John Maynard Keynes

John Maynard Keynes developed fiscal policy theories during the Great Depression. Keynes believed that the forces of aggregate supply and demand operated too slowly in a serious recession, and that government should step in to stimulate aggregate demand.

The Circular Flow of Income

circular flow of income: *economic model that pictures income as flowing continuously between businesses and consumers*

To understand Keynesian theory, you must first understand what is known as the **circular flow of income**. You learned about this model in Chapter 2. The model pictures income as flowing from businesses to households as wages, rents, interest, and profits. Income flows from households to businesses as payments for consumer goods and services.

Not all income, however, follows this circular flow. Some of it is removed from the economy through consumer saving and government taxation. Economists use the term *leakage* to refer to this removal of money income. **Figure 17.4** shows these leakages. Offsetting leakages of income are injections of income into the economy. Injections occur through business investment and government spending.

FIGURE 17.4

Circular Flow Government occupies a central position in the circular flow of income. By using fiscal policy, the federal government partially controls the levels of leakages and injections. This, in turn, may control the overall level of economic activity.

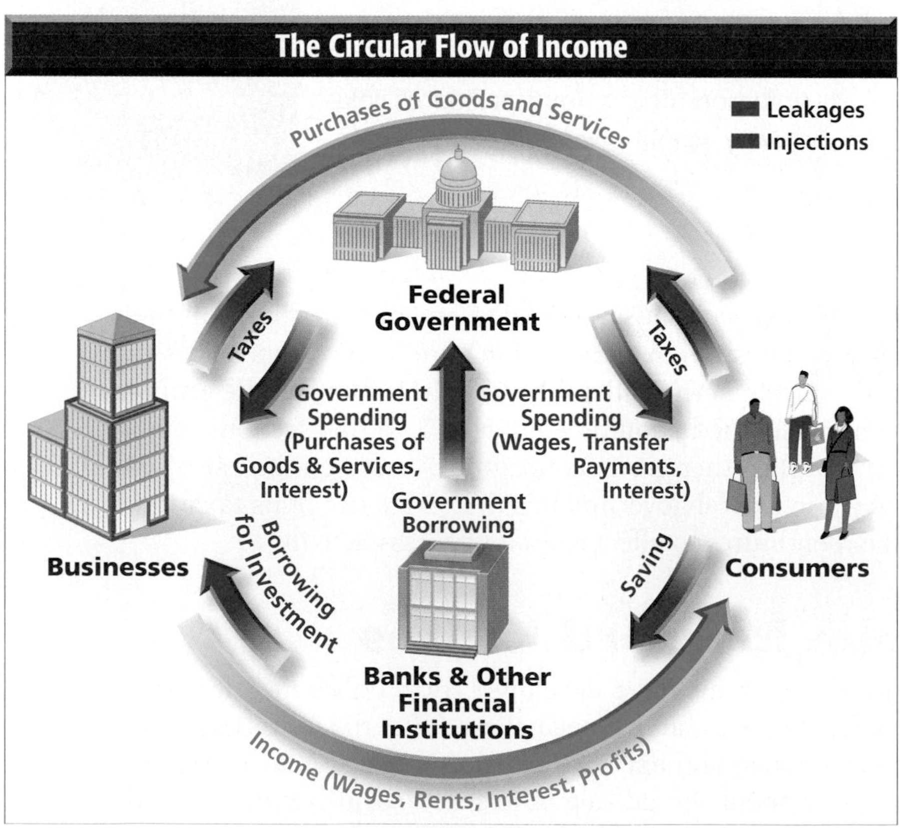

FRANK & ERNEST

FRANK & ERNEST reprinted by permission of Newspaper Enterprise Association, Inc.

FIGURE 17.5 **Equilibrium** The customer above is unhappy that his income and outgo are in equilibrium. Keynesian economists, however, want injections and leakages (income and outgo) to balance in the circular flow of economic activity.

Ideally, leakages and injections balance each other. See **Figure 17.5.** In this state of equilibrium, the income that households save is reinjected through business investment. Income taken out through taxes is returned through government spending.

Fiscal Policy and Unemployment

Many public officials and labor leaders have suggested starting jobs programs to reduce unemployment and stimulate the economy. Several suggestions for forming new government-sponsored jobs programs to bring down unemployment rates were made in the early 1980s and again in 1992 and 1993.

Cuts in federal taxes are another way in which fiscal policy has been used in an attempt to speed up economic activity and fight unemployment. Giving businesses tax credits on investments allows them to deduct from their taxes some of the costs of new capital equipment. The goal is to encourage businesses to expand production and hire more workers.

Fiscal Policy and Supply-Side Effects

Some argue that tax cuts lead to more work, saving, and investment. These are called supply-side effects because they affect the supply of key ingredients of economic growth. President Bush used this supply-side argument to promote his Jobs and Growth Tax Act of 2003.

Economic Connection to... History

Jobs Programs

Jobs programs were created by the federal government during the 1930s. The Federal Art Project employed artists to depict American history and everyday life in public buildings. These artists created more than 2,500 murals and 17,700 sculptures.

The Federal Writers Project employed writers who worked on many different publications. The best known was the *American Guide* series—tour guides that included information on the history, geography, industry, and culture for each of the 48 states. ■

CCC and WPA posters

Many features of this act were aimed at increasing economic growth. Tax rates that were to be phased in over several years instead became effective in January 2003. The highest tax rate fell from 39.6 percent to 35 percent. Investors got a big break, too. The tax rate applied to dividends–income payments to shareholders of corporations–fell from as high as 39.9 percent to 15 percent. The tax rate on long-term capital gains (see Chapter 6) dropped from 20 percent to 15 percent. For some low-income earners, this rate fell to 5 percent.

Practice and **assess** key skills with ***Skillbuilder Interactive Workbook, Level 2.***

SECTION 2 Assessment

Understanding Key Terms

1. Define fiscal policy, circular flow of income.

Reviewing Objectives

2. **Graphic Organizer** Create a diagram like the one below to show what types of income flow from businesses to consumers in the circular flow.

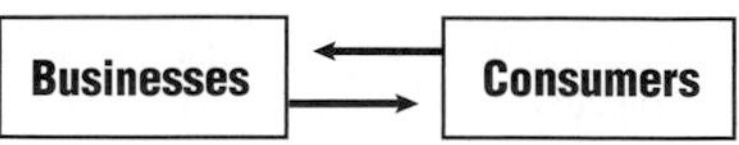

3. How can the federal government use fiscal policy to combat unemployment?

Applying Economic Concepts

4. **Fiscal Policy** Explain how the government policy of increasing federal, state, or local taxes could eventually lower inflation.

Critical Thinking Activity

5. **Evaluating Primary and Secondary Sources** Research the Depression-era writings of Studs Terkel and photographs of Dorothea Lange. Write a report describing the economic conditions of the early 1930s and what actions you think the government should have taken to ease the crisis.

Critical Thinking Skills

Summarizing Information

Have you ever read something and just a short time later forgotten what it was all about? Summarizing information—reducing many sentences to just a few well-chosen phrases—helps you remember the main ideas and important facts contained in a longer reading selection.

- Your summary should be much shorter than the reading selection.
- Your summary should contain the main ideas of the reading selection.
- Your summary should not contain your opinion. It should contain only the opinion of the person who wrote the selection.
- Your summary sentences and phrases should not be copied word for word from the selection. Write a summary in your own words to be sure that you understand the main ideas of the selection.

Learning the Skill

To learn how to summarize information, follow the guidelines listed on the left.

Practicing the Skill

Read the excerpt below, then answer the questions.

"Tomorrow's school, it turns out, may remind parents more of a sleek shopping mall than of the long, chalk-choked corridors of their youth. Retailers and health clubs of today 'have got it figured out,' says Paul Hansen, the principal architect in charge of a $118 million retrofit of Sandburg High School [Chicago]. The new Sandburg will incorporate some of the hottest ideas in school design: a central library that resembles a Barnes & Noble superstore, a gym with updated amenities like a rock-climbing wall, and a food court to replace the cafeteria. . . . Schools of the future will be wired to the hilt. Fiber optics, internal computer networks, videoconferencing, and the like are musts."

—*Newsweek*, December 14, 1998

1. What is the main idea of this paragraph?
2. What are the supporting details of the main idea?
3. Write a short summary that will help you remember what the paragraph is about.

Application Activity

Spend 15 minutes reading and summarizing two articles on the front page of today's newspaper. Circle the articles and have a classmate ask you questions about them. How much were you able to remember after summarizing the information?

Practice and **assess** key skills with ***Skillbuilder Interactive Workbook, Level 2.***

SECTION 3

Monetarism and the Economy

READER'S GUIDE

Terms to Know
- monetarism
- monetarists
- monetary rule
- time lags

Reading Objectives
1. What do monetarists think the government and the Fed should do to stabilize the economy?
2. Why do monetarists criticize fiscal policy?

COVER STORY

ROCKY MOUNTAIN NEWS, AUGUST 19, 2003

The amount of money in the banking system may soar after the Federal Reserve responded to the worst blackout in North American history by adding the most cash since the September 11, 2001, terrorist attacks.

The central bank added $20 billion of reserves on Friday, the day after an electrical failure . . . shut down New York City and cut off power in other major cities including Detroit. Monday the Fed added $12 billion to help meet the demand for cash through Wednesday.

monetarism: *theory that deals with the relationship between the amount of money the Fed places in circulation and the level of activity in the economy*

monetarists: *supporters of the theory of monetarism, often linked with Milton Friedman*

In this section, you'll learn about **monetarism,** the theory that deals with the relationship between the amount of money the Federal Reserve places in circulation and the level of activity in the economy. The supporters of this theory are called **monetarists.**

The Theory of Monetarism

Monetarism is often linked with economist Milton Friedman (see page 466). As you remember from Chapter 15, the Federal Reserve can change the growth rate of the money supply. Friedman and many other economists believe that the Fed should increase the money supply at a smooth, given percent each year. They argue that when the amount of money in circulation expands too rapidly, people spend more. If the economy is operating below capacity, this extra demand will lead to a rise in output. To produce more, businesses will have to hire more workers, and unemployment will decrease. If there is already full employment, however, the increased aggregate demand will lead to a rise in prices—inflation.

Government Policy According to Monetarists

Friedman and his monetarist followers believe the economy is so complex and so little understood that government does more harm than good in trying to second-guess businesspeople and consumers. As a result, monetarists generally oppose using fiscal policy to stimulate or slow the economy.

For example, they do not believe the government should operate with budget deficits each year in an attempt to stimulate the economy. Instead, monetarists believe that the government should balance the federal budget. This action would keep government from competing with private business to borrow money in the credit market. It would also reduce the amount of interest that the government must pay each year.

CAREERS
Social Worker
Job Description
■ Assist families dealing with unemployment, illness, or serious conflicts
■ Refer clients to specialists
Qualifications
■ Bachelor's degree in social work
■ State licensing certification
Median Salary: $31,470
Job Outlook: Above average
—Occupational Outlook Handbook, 2002–03

The Fed, according to monetarists, should also stop trying to smooth the ups and downs in the economy. Rather, the Fed should follow a **monetary rule,** or allow the money supply to grow smoothly and consistently at a rate of perhaps 3 to 5 percent per year. Monetarists believe that a steady growth in the money supply within strict guidelines (or targets, as they are called) is the best way to provide businesses and consumers with more certainty about the future. According to monetarism, this policy would result in a controlled expansion of the economy without rapid inflation or high unemployment.

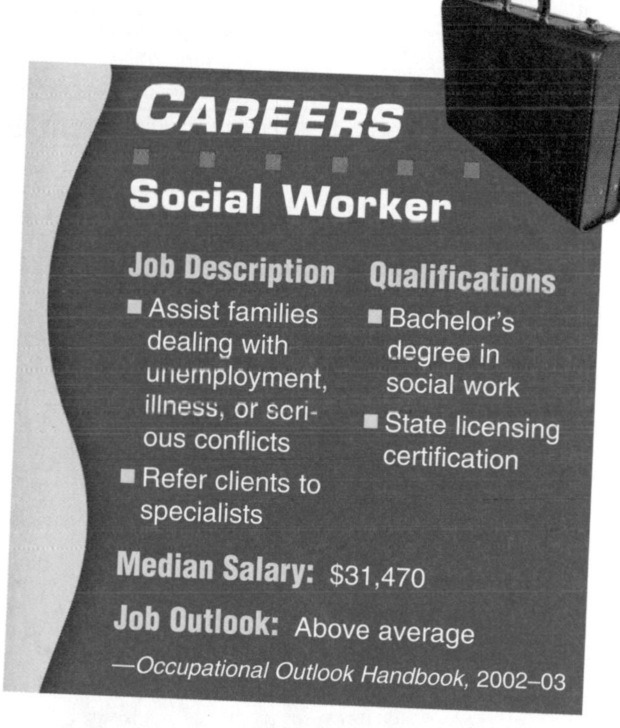

monetary rule: *monetarists' belief that the Fed should allow the money supply to grow at a smooth, consistent rate per year and not use monetary policy to stimulate or slow the economy*

Monetarist Theory and the Federal Reserve Monetarist theory had a major influence on Federal Reserve policies in the 1980s. You can trace the changing monetary policies of the Fed in **Figure 17.6** on page 464.

Monetarists' Criticism of Fiscal Policy

Monetarists believe that the theory of fiscal policy never matches the reality of fiscal policy. Two reasons account for this discrepancy. The first reason concerns the political process of fiscal policy. Monetarists point out that no single government body

FIGURE 17.6

Changing Fed Policies To monetarists, the reduction in the amount of money in circulation can mean only one thing–a reduction in aggregate demand. With less aggregate demand, fewer workers are needed and unemployment increases. ***What happened to the unemployment rate when Fed policies began to lower inflation from 1980–1982?***

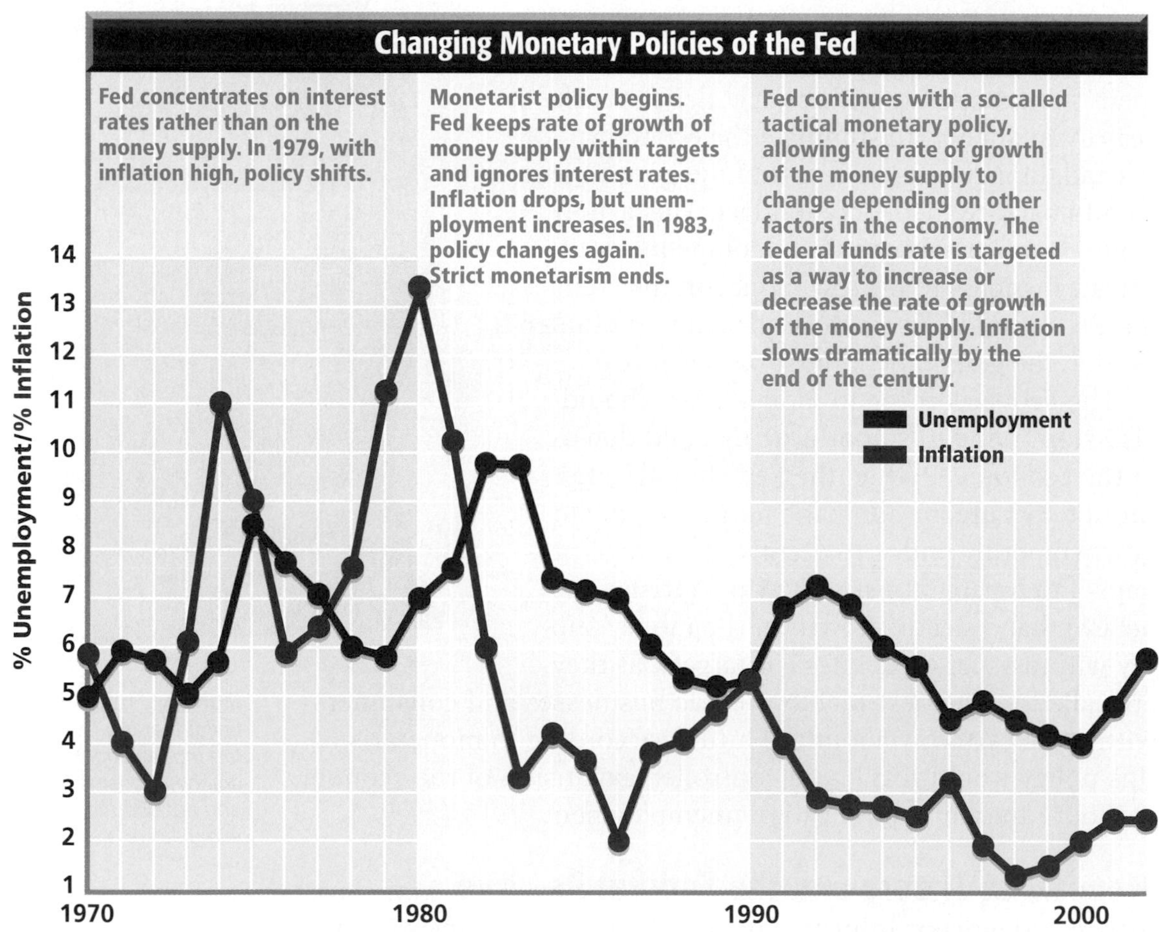

Changing Monetary Policies of the Fed
Fed concentrates on interest rates rather than on the money supply. In 1979, with inflation high, policy shifts.
Monetarist policy begins. Fed keeps rate of growth of money supply within targets and ignores interest rates. Inflation drops, but unemployment increases. In 1983, policy changes again. Strict monetarism ends.
Fed continues with a so-called tactical monetary policy, allowing the rate of growth of the money supply to change depending on other factors in the economy. The federal funds rate is targeted as a way to increase or decrease the rate of growth of the money supply. Inflation slows dramatically by the end of the century.
Unemployment
Inflation
% Unemployment/% Inflation
14
13
12
11
10
9
8
7
6
5
4
3
2
1
1970
1980
1990
2000

Sources: *Economic Report of the President,* 2001; Bureau of Economic Analysis

designs and implements fiscal policy. The President, with the aid of the director of the Office of Management and Budget (OMB), the secretary of the Treasury, and the Council of Economic Advisers, designs yet only *recommends* the desired mix of taxes and government expenditures.

Congress, with the aid of many committees (the House Ways and Means Committee, the Senate Finance Committee, and the Senate Budget Committee, to name a few), actually enacts fiscal policy. One built-in organizational problem is that the power to enact fiscal policy does not rest with a single government institution. Disagreement as to the proper fiscal policy emerges among members of Congress and between Congress and the President. Furthermore, being politicians, they have incentives to take actions that will look good today and help them get reelected, but which may hurt the economy in the long run.

Monetarists also point out that even if fiscal policy could be enacted when the President wanted, there are various **time lags** between when it is enacted and when it becomes effective. It takes many months, if not years, for fiscal policy stimuli to cause employment to rise in the economy. Consequently, a fiscal policy designed to combat a recession might not produce results until the economy is already experiencing inflation. In this event, the fiscal policy could worsen the situation.

time lags: *periods between the time fiscal policy is enacted and the time it becomes effective*

Practice and **assess** key skills with ***Skillbuilder Interactive Workbook, Level 2.***

SECTION 3 Assessment

Understanding Key Terms

1. **Define** monetarism, monetarists, monetary rule, time lags.

Reviewing Objectives

2. **Graphic Organizer** Create a diagram like the one below to analyze what monetarists think the government and the Fed should do to stabilize the economy.

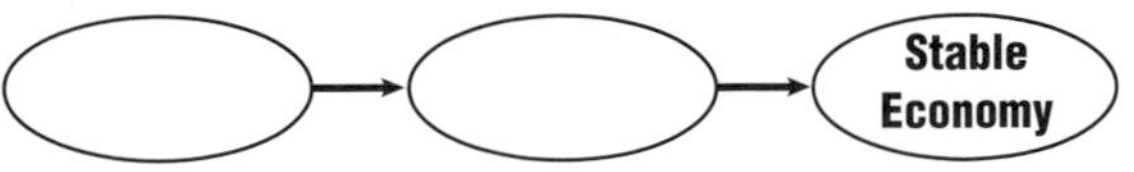

3. Why do monetarists criticize fiscal policy?

Applying Economic Concepts

4. **Monetarism** Do you agree or disagree with the theory of monetarism? Explain your response.

Critical Thinking Activity

5. **Making Comparisons** Describe in your own words the difference between monetarism and monetary policy. Share your description with a classmate, making sure he or she understands the difference.

People & Perspectives

- **Won Nobel Prize for Economics in 1976**
- **Leading supporter of monetarism**
- **Publications include *The Monetary History of the U.S. 1867–1960* with Anna J. Schwartz (1963), *Capitalism and Freedom* (1962), and *Free to Choose* with Rose Friedman (1980)**

Milton Friedman

ECONOMIST (1912–)

Milton Friedman has written extensively on the monetary history of the United States. Here, Friedman explains why he does not approve of the Fed and gives a possible alternative solution to regulating the money supply:

"The establishment of the Federal Reserve System . . . established a separate official body charged with explicit responsibility for monetary conditions, and supposedly clothed with adequate power to achieve monetary stability or, at least, to prevent pronounced instability. It is therefore instructive to compare experience as a whole before and after its establishment–say, from just after the Civil War to 1914 and from 1914 to date.

. . . The stock of money, prices, and output was decidedly more unstable after the establishment of the Reserve System than before. . . .

. . . Any system which gives so much power and so much discretion to a few men that mistakes–excusable or not–can have such far-reaching effects is a bad system. It is a bad system to believers in freedom just because it gives a few men such power without any effective check by the body politic–this is the key political argument against an 'independent' central bank.

. . . My choice at the moment would be . . . instructing the monetary authority to achieve a specified rate of growth in the stock of money. . . . I would specify that the Reserve System shall see to it that the total stock of money so defined rises . . . at an annual rate of X percent, where X is a number between 3 and 5."

Checking for Understanding

1. **What is Friedman's argument against an "independent" central bank?**
2. **What rule does Friedman propose to govern decisions of the Federal Reserve System?**

CHAPTER  Summary

Chapter Overview Visit the *Economics Today and Tomorrow* Web site at ett.glencoe.com and click on ***Chapter 17—Chapter Overviews*** to review chapter information.

SECTION 1 Unemployment and Inflation

- Two of the biggest threats to the nation's economic stability are high unemployment and inflation.
- Maintaining a low **unemployment rate** is a goal of **stabilization policies.**
- The four types of unemployment are cyclical, structural, seasonal, and frictional.
- According to the theory of **demand-pull inflation,** prices rise because excessive business and consumer demand increases faster than total supply.
- The theory of **cost-push inflation** states that the wage demands of labor unions and the excessive profit motive of large corporations push up prices.

SECTION 2 The Fiscal Policy Approach to Stabilization

- Some economists believe economic stabilization can be met with **fiscal policy**—the federal government's deliberate use of taxation and spending to affect overall business activity.
- John Maynard Keynes developed fiscal policy theories during the Great Depression.
- Keynesian theory states that leakages out of and injections into the **circular flow of income** affect aggregate demand, and should be counteracted by government taxing and spending policies.
- To bring down unemployment, Keynesian economists believe in forming government-sponsored jobs programs and cutting federal taxes.

SECTION 3 Monetarism and the Economy

- **Monetarists** believe in using the growth rate of the money supply to stabilize the economy.
- The theory of **monetarism** is often linked with economist Milton Friedman.
- Friedman and his supporters believe that the Fed should follow a **monetary rule** by increasing the money supply at a smooth, given percent per year.
- Monetarists criticize fiscal policy because of the political arena in which it is developed, and because **time lags** between enactment and implementation of fiscal policies may worsen the situation.

CHAPTER 17

Assessment and Activities

Self-Check Quiz Visit the *Economics Today and Tomorrow* Web site at ett.glencoe.com and click on ***Chapter 17—Self-Check Quizzes*** to prepare for the Chapter Test.

Identifying Key Terms

Write a one-sentence explanation of each of the following terms.

1. unemployment rate
2. full employment
3. underground economy
4. demand-pull inflation
5. stagflation
6. cost-push inflation
7. fiscal policy
8. monetarism
9. monetary rule
10. time lags

Recalling Facts and Ideas

Section 1

1. What are the four types of unemployment?
2. What causes demand-pull inflation?
3. What causes cost-push inflation?

Section 2

4. What are the leakages out of the circular flow of income?
5. What are the injections of income into the circular flow of income?
6. What do Keynesian economists think the federal government should do to reduce unemployment?

Section 3

7. Who is the economist most often linked to monetarism?
8. What do monetarists believe the Fed should do in terms of monetary policy?

Thinking Critically

1. **Making Generalizations** Analyze why full employment cannot be defined as zero unemployment.
2. **Understanding Cause and Effect** Create a diagram like the one below to explain why the unemployment rate might rise if fiscal policy were used to combat inflation.

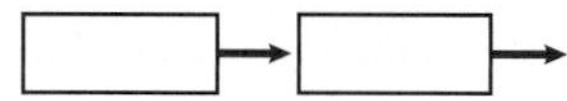

Technology Activity

Using the Internet Choose a contemporary economic issue such as unemployment or inflation to investigate. Using a search engine, type in *unemployment* or *inflation* to locate current statistics on your chosen topic. Visit a government Web site to learn about the most up-to-date statistics. Write a one-page summary of your findings.

Applying Economic Concepts

Unanticipated Versus Anticipated Inflation Unanticipated inflation may affect you in many ways. For example, when inflation is high, banks charge higher interest rates to compensate for inflation. If you borrowed money at the high interest rates and then the rate of inflation fell, you would be worse off. You would be paying too much interest on that borrowed money. Make a list of other problems that you might encounter if there were a change in the rate of inflation that you did not anticipate.

Reviewing Skills

Summarizing Information Read the excerpt below, then answer the questions that follow.

> *"In recent years–as the second-longest economic expansion on record has spread its impact–most of the country has experienced a shortage of workers.*
>
> *What's most perplexing is this: Tight labor markets are not affecting the economy the way textbooks say they should.*
>
> *Normally, in the organic life of an economy, tight labor leads to higher wages, which triggers inflation, which leads to higher interest rates, which cause the economy to slow, which then eases the demand for labor.*
>
> *For years now, economists have expected this chain of events to play out. But the scenario has been nipped from the start. Tight labor has not led to spiraling wages."*
>
> –*The Columbus Dispatch*, August 23, 1999

1. According to the article, what should happen when there is a shortage of workers?
2. Summarize what the article states about the economy.

Cooperative Learning Project

Organize into four groups. The first three groups will each track one of the following: government fiscal policies, monetary policies, and major economic indicators. The last group will create visuals from the information that is collected.

Using the front page of 10 consecutive issues of the *Wall Street Journal,* three groups will record a summary of news in each of their categories. Fiscal policy includes taxes and government spending. Monetary policy includes central bank interest rates, money supply, open-market operations, and reserve requirements. Economic indicators include such measurements as the consumer price index, industrial production, producer prices, retail sales, stocks and bonds, and unemployment. Each item should include the category, the date of the news, and a brief summary of the news.

As the information is being gathered by the first three groups, the last group should begin creating headlines that place the events in chronological order on a bulletin board. To conclude this project, the class should discuss the state of the economy as reflected in the headlines.

Analyzing the Global *Economy*

Scan the international section of a newspaper or business magazine. Keep track of the number of times that you read about the topics of unemployment and inflation in other countries. Create a table listing the specific countries and the specific topics. After each entry, indicate whether the economic news was positive or negative.

UNIT 6

The International Scene

Chapter 18
Trading With Other Nations

Chapter 19
Converging Economic Systems

Chapter 20
Economic Growth in Developing Nations

Chapter 21
The Global Economy

Chapter 22
Cybernomics

In this unit, read to FIND OUT . . .

- how the United States trades with the rest of the world.
- why many of the world's nations are moving toward a free enterprise economic system.
- how the world is becoming smaller through the Internet.

Most new jobs in the world will change from agricultural to service and professional specialties.

Experts continue to predict increases in worldwide Internet use.

Two hundred years ago, the United States was a developing nation.
The amount of global travel is expected to double in the next 25 years.
Many of the world's economies are converging toward the same kind of system we have in the United States.
PASSPORT
SAUDI ARABIA
AFRICA
SUDAN
EGYPT
IRAN
PAKISTAN
ETHIOPIA
SOMALIA
YEMEN
TANZANIA
ANGOLA
KAZAKHSTAN
American Map Corporation

CHAPTER 18

Trading With Other Nations

Why It's Important

What percent of goods in American stores are foreign-made? What happens to the dollars Americans spend outside the United States? This chapter will explain the importance of international trade, and how you benefit from it.

To learn about foreign exchange and trade surpluses and deficits, view the **Economics & You** *Chapter 24 video lesson:* **International Trade**

ECONOMICS *Online*

Chapter Overview Visit the *Economics Today and Tomorrow* Web site at ett.glencoe.com and click on ***Chapter 18—Chapter Overviews*** to preview chapter information.

SECTION 1

The Benefits of World Trade

Cover Story

The Washington Post, February 15, 1999

Mickey makes it to Beijing. Getting [the Disney movie] 'Mulan' into Chinese theaters was seen as an essential part of Disney's business plan for this nation of 1.3 billion, with a growing middle class and eager young customers. The film, about a courageous heroine who disguises herself as a man and secretly takes her ailing father's place in battle against the invading Huns, is based on a 1,500-year-old Chinese legend, and the story is as familiar here as Cinderella or Snow White in the United States. 'Mulan' has earned $299 million worldwide.

Reader's Guide

Terms to Know

- imports
- exports
- absolute advantage
- specialization
- comparative advantage

Reading Objectives

1. What are the benefits of international trade?
2. What is the difference between absolute advantage and comparative advantage?

As you read this section, ask yourself what would happen if the United States could no longer sell goods to other countries or buy goods in return. Before you answer, you should be aware that the value of **imports**—goods bought from other countries for domestic use—is about 14 percent of GDP in the United States. That figure may not seem large, but many inconveniences would result without imports.

imports: *goods bought from other countries for domestic use*

We would have no coffee, chocolate, or pepper. Consider also that more than 60 percent of the radios, television sets, and motorcycles sold in the United States are imported. Many raw materials also come from foreign sources. Nearly 100 percent of the nation's bauxite, from which aluminum is made, is imported.

Benefits of Trade

exports: *goods sold to other countries*

Imports tell only half the story. Many American workers are employed in industries that export their products overseas. **Exports** are goods sold to other countries. For example, more than 40 percent of the nation's engineering and scientific instruments are sold to consumers overseas. In addition, nearly one-half of the wheat produced in the United States is shipped abroad.

Made in the U.S.A.? Sometimes it is hard to distinguish between goods made in America and those purchased abroad, as shown in **Figure 18.1.** In short, international trade affects you whether you know it or not. We have truly entered the age of a global economy, so learning about international trade is simply learning about everyday life.

Differences Among Nations Nations benefit through world trade because each differs in the type and amount of the factors of production it has available for use. The availability of natural resources is one of the most important of these differences.

The type and amount of labor and capital available to a nation are equally important. For example, much of the economy of the United States is based on high-technology production. A highly skilled labor force and large amounts of capital–in the form of advanced equipment and machinery–make this possible. Another nation–with the same natural resources but without the same labor and capital resources–could have a very different economy.

FIGURE 18.1

Who Made the Parts?
Consider the Boeing 777. This plane is hardly "made in America." International suppliers provide rudders, elevators, outboard flaps, wingtip assemblies, engines, nose-landing gears, nose-landing gear doors, and main-landing gears. Japanese suppliers, in particular, provide cargo doors, fuselage panels, and passenger doors. The complicated Boeing 777 jet aircraft is a jigsaw puzzle in which the pieces come from all over the world.

Economic Connection to... 

Comparative Advantage

Adam Smith's *Wealth of Nations* supplied powerful arguments for free trade. In the early 1800s, British economist David Ricardo expanded on Smith's ideas by observing that it pays to specialize and trade–even if some potential trading partner is more productive in all economic activities. His work was vital in developing the idea of comparative advantage as an argument in support of free trade.

According to Ricardo's theory, a country does not have to be best at anything to gain from trade. If a country is relatively better at making Product A than Product B, it makes sense to put more resources into Product A and to trade Product A to pay for imports of Product B. Benefits come from specializing in those economic activities which, at world prices, the country is relatively better at, even though it may not possess an absolute advantage in them. The two countries can both gain from trade, provided that they trade along the lines of comparative advantage. ■

Absolute vs. Comparative

If the United States could produce everything *more cheaply* than every other nation, it might not want to import anything. We know this situation does not exist for any nation, however, because of opportunity cost. All nations must make choices in how they use their scarce resources.

Absolute Advantage The particular distribution of resources in a nation often gives it an advantage over another nation in the production of one or more products. Brazil's tropical climate and inexpensive labor make it ideally suited for growing bananas. A country with a moderate climate, such as France, would produce far fewer bananas. Brazil, therefore, has an absolute advantage in banana production over France. A country has an **absolute advantage** when it can produce a product more efficiently (i.e., with greater output per unit of input) than can another country.

A nation often finds it profitable to produce and export a limited assortment of goods for which it is particularly suited. This concept is known as **specialization.** See **Figure 18.2** on page 476. For example, Japan's specialization in consumer electronics has led many nations to import these types of products from Japan.

absolute advantage: *ability of one country to produce a product more efficiently (i.e., with greater output per unit of input) than can another country*

specialization: *concept that a nation should produce and export a limited assortment of goods for which it is particularly suited in order to remain profitable*

Comparative Advantage A nation doesn't need to have an absolute advantage in the production of a certain good to find it

FIGURE 18.2

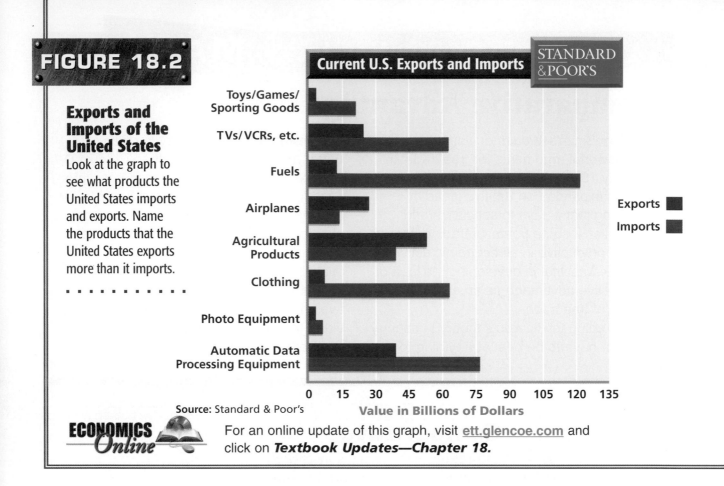

Exports and Imports of the United States

Look at the graph to see what products the United States imports and exports. Name the products that the United States exports more than it imports.

Current U.S. Exports and Imports

STANDARD & POOR'S

Toys/Games/ Sporting Goods

TVs/VCRs, etc.

Fuels

Airplanes

Agricultural Products

Clothing

Photo Equipment

Automatic Data Processing Equipment

Exports

Imports

0 15 30 45 60 75 90 105 120 135

Value in Billions of Dollars

Source: Standard & Poor's

ECONOMICS Online

For an online update of this graph, visit ett.glencoe.com and click on ***Textbook Updates—Chapter 18.***

profitable to specialize and then to trade with other countries. For example, consider two imaginary nations, Alpha and Beta. Assume that each country produces only soybeans and corn.

When producing only soybeans, Alpha produces 10 million bushels, while Beta produces only 8 million. The next year, suppose the two countries decide to grow only corn. Alpha produces 50 million bushels, while Beta produces 25 million. According to this example, Alpha has an absolute advantage in the production of both soybeans and corn.

Does this mean that Alpha will produce both crops and, therefore, have no reason to trade with Beta? No. Alpha can produce slightly more soybeans than Beta. In contrast, it can produce a great deal more corn. It would make little sense for Alpha to take land, labor, and capital resources away from the efficient production of corn and use them for the less efficient production of soybeans. Alpha's opportunity cost–what it gives up to get something else–would be less if it invested all its resources in the production of corn. It could export its surplus corn and use the revenues it receives to import soybeans from Beta.

comparative advantage: *ability of a country to produce a product at a lower opportunity cost than another country*

Alpha has a comparative advantage in corn production. **Comparative advantage** is the ability of a country to produce a

product at a *lower opportunity cost* than another country. Beta has a comparative advantage in soybean production. It can produce about the same amount of soybeans as Alpha, but only half as much corn. By using its resources to grow only soybeans, Beta is just giving up the relatively inefficient production of corn. Beta, then, has a lower opportunity cost for soybean production than does Alpha. Beta should produce the maximum amount of soybeans, export soybeans to Alpha, and import corn. Both countries benefit when each country concentrates on that production for which it is relatively most efficient.

Practice and **assess** key skills with ***Skillbuilder Interactive Workbook, Level 2.***

SECTION 1 Assessment

Understanding Key Terms

1. **Define** imports, exports, absolute advantage, specialization, comparative advantage.

Reviewing Objectives

2. How important is international trade to the United States economy?
3. **Graphic Organizer** Create a diagram like the one below to explain the difference between absolute advantage and comparative advantage.

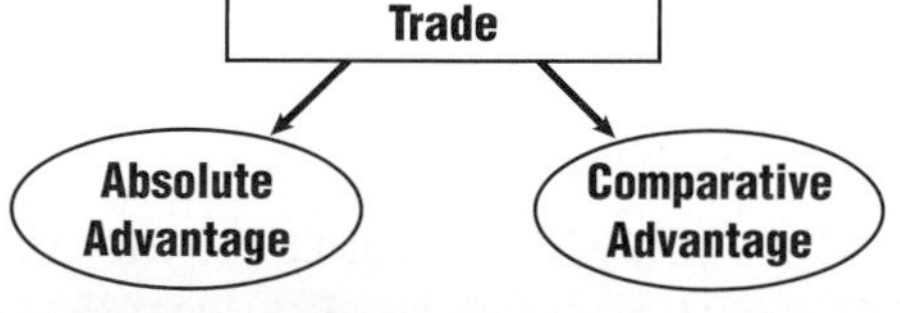

Applying Economic Concepts

4. **Comparative Advantage** List at least three activities in your daily life in which you have a comparative advantage (such as cooking or lawn maintenance). Describe how you and those who live at your house could use comparative advantage in order to "trade" to get more accomplished.

Critical Thinking Activity

5. **Synthesizing Information** Use **Figure 18.2** to answer the following question: In what two products do trading partners seem to have the greatest absolute advantage or comparative advantage over the United States? Explain.

Study & Writing Skills

Applying the Writing Process

Researching and writing allow you to organize your ideas in a logical manner. The writing process involves using skills you have already learned, such as taking notes, outlining, and synthesizing information.

- Select an interesting topic. Do preliminary research to determine whether your topic is too broad or too narrow.
- Write a thesis statement that defines what you want to prove, discover, or illustrate in your writing. This will be the focus of your entire paper.
- Research your topic by formulating a list of main ideas and preparing note cards listing facts and source information for each main idea.
- Your report should have an introduction, a body, and a conclusion summarizing and restating your findings.
- Each paragraph should express one main idea in a topic sentence. Additional sentences support or explain the main idea by using details and facts.

Practice and **assess** key skills with ***Skillbuilder Interactive Workbook, Level 2.***

Learning the Skill

Use the guidelines listed on the left to help you apply the writing process.

Practicing the Skill

Suppose you are writing a report on international trade. Answer the following questions about the writing process.

1. How could you narrow this topic?
2. What are three main ideas that should be included in this report?
3. Name three possible sources of information about international trade.
4. What maps, charts, and graphs might you include with your report?

Application Activity

Research and write a short report on the manufacturing of your favorite automobile. What parts, if any, were imported?

SECTION 2

Financing World Trade

Cover Story

The Columbus Dispatch, September 7, 1999

If the price of buying a car starts rising in the United States, consumers may need to look no further than the dollar's recent slide against major foreign currencies.

On the other hand, economically depressed Midwestern farmers may find it easier to sell surplus grain overseas if a weak dollar makes it cheaper for foreigners to buy U.S. goods.

The dollar spent much of last week on the skids, flirting with its lowest level of the year against the Japanese yen. . . . It also has lost ground to the euro.

Reader's Guide

Terms to Know

- exchange rate
- foreign exchange markets
- fixed rate of exchange
- International Monetary Fund (IMF)
- devaluation
- flexible exchange rates
- depreciation
- balance of trade

Reading Objectives

1. Why do nations need a system of currency exchange rates?
2. How do the forces of supply and demand determine flexible exchange rates?
3. How do exchange rates affect the balance of trade?

The United States uses the dollar as its medium of exchange; Mexico, the peso; India, the rupee; and Japan, the yen. As you read this section, you'll learn that to engage in world trade, people must have a way of knowing the **exchange rate**—what the price of their currency is in terms of another nation's currency. They must also be able to exchange one type of currency for another. Why is this so?

exchange rate: *the price of one nation's currency in terms of another nation's currency*

A Japanese digital video disk (DVD) manufacturer who exports DVD systems to the United States probably does not want American dollars in payment. The firm needs Japanese currency to pay its workers and suppliers. Fortunately, international

foreign exchange markets: *markets dealing in buying and selling foreign currency for businesses that want to import goods from other countries*

trade is organized so that individuals and businesses can easily and quickly convert one currency to another. **Foreign exchange markets** allow for these conversions. People in these markets deal in buying and selling foreign currency for businesses that want to import goods from other countries. Some of the currency trading also takes place through banks. **Figure 18.3** shows you what information a typical exchange rate lists on a given day.

Fixed Exchange Rates

fixed rate of exchange: *system under which a national government sets the value of its currency in relation to a single standard*

From 1945 to the early 1970s, the foreign exchange market operated with a **fixed rate of exchange.** Under this system, national governments set the value of their currency in relation to a single standard—usually the amount of gold held in reserve. With a fixed rate of exchange, a government could compare its

FIGURE 18.3 Foreign Exchange Rate Listing

In the second column of this listing, on a particular day one British pound costs 1.62 American dollars. The third column shows that one United States dollar is worth .62 British pounds.

Country (currency)	U.S. $ Equivalent	Currency per U.S. $
Australia (Dollar)	.6478	1.5438
Brazil (Real)	.5299	1.8870
Britain (Pound)	1.6185	.6179
Canada (Dollar)	.6720	1.4882
Euro	1.0599	.9435
India (Rupee)	.02299	43.495
Japan (Yen)	.009005	111.06
Mexico (Peso)	.1069	9.3510
South Africa (Rand)	.1645	6.0790
Venezuela (Bolivar)	.001607	622.25

FIGURE 18.4

Effects of Devaluation These charts show how devaluation of the Japanese yen affects consumers in the United States. ***Do you think an American consumer would prefer to buy a DVD system before or after devaluation? Why?***

Effects of Official Devaluation of Japanese Yen

Before Devaluation	After Devaluation
Japanese DVD costs 20,000 yen	Japanese DVD costs 20,000 yen
Exchange Rate: 100 yen = $1 U.S.	Exchange Rate: 200 yen = $1 U.S.
$\text{DVD} = \frac{20{,}000 \text{ yen}}{100 \text{ yen per \$}} = \$200.00$	$\text{DVD} = \frac{20{,}000 \text{ yen}}{200 \text{ yen per \$}} = \$100.00$
An American would have to pay $200 for the Japanese DVD	An American would have to pay $100 for the Japanese DVD

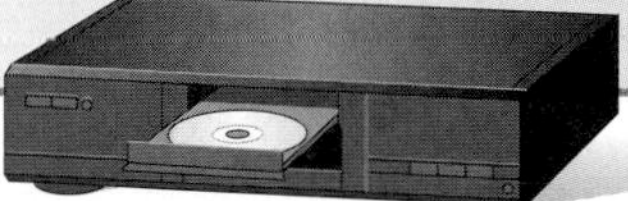

currency to that of other countries. The **International Monetary Fund (IMF)** supported a fixed exchange rate system. Member governments of the IMF (including the United States) were obligated to keep their foreign exchange rates more or less fixed.

International Monetary Fund (IMF): *agency whose member governments once were obligated to keep their foreign exchange rates more or less fixed; today it offers monetary advice and provides loans to developing nations*

A fixed rate of exchange had some advantages for world trade. Importers and exporters knew exactly how much of a foreign currency they could purchase with their own nation's money. Also, the system allowed central banks to affect the level of exports and imports in their country by devaluing the currency. **Devaluation** means lowering a currency's value in relation to other currencies by government order. **Figure 18.4** shows how the cost of a Japanese DVD system would decrease if Japan devalues its yen by one-half.

devaluation: *lowering a currency's value in relation to other currencies by government order*

This system of fixed exchange rates eventually proved impractical. The basic problem was the difficulty of holding exchange rates fixed in an international economic climate that was constantly changing. Suppose one nation such as the United States suffered from high inflation, and a trading partner such as Japan did not. Then American goods would become very costly for the Japanese to buy. Because the price of Japanese goods would not be rising, Americans could use their inflated, or "cheaper," dollars to buy more Japanese products. The United States would be importing huge quantities of Japanese goods but exporting little to Japan.

Student Web Activity Visit the *Economics Today and Tomorrow* Web site at ett.glencoe.com and click on ***Chapter 18—Student Web Activities*** to learn about increased efficiency in international trade.

Flexible Exchange Rates

flexible exchange rate: *arrangement in which the forces of supply and demand are allowed to set the price of various currencies*

On August 15, 1971, President Richard Nixon officially announced what would become the end of fixed American exchange rates. Most of the world's nations turned to a **flexible exchange rate** system. Under this arrangement, the forces of supply and demand are allowed to set the price of various currencies. With flexible exchange rates, a currency's price may change, or float, up or down a little each day. For example, Japanese currency might be trading at 115.6 yen to the dollar on one day and 118.2 yen to the dollar on the next.

depreciation: *fall in the price of a currency through the action of supply and demand*

The forces actually determining exchange rates are the supply and demand of goods and services that can be bought with a particular currency. For example, suppose the amount of dollars wanted by Japanese exporters is greater than the quantity of dollars supplied by Americans who want to buy Japanese goods. Because the quantity demanded exceeds that supplied, the American dollar will become more expensive in relation to the yen. It will take more yen to equal one dollar. In contrast, if the quantity of dollars American importers supplied is more than the quantity demanded by Japanese exporters, the price of a dollar will become cheaper in relation to the yen. Fewer yen will equal one dollar.

When the price of a currency falls through the action of supply and demand, it is termed **depreciation.** As with devaluation, depreciation of a country's currency improves its competitive edge in foreign trade.

Besides import-export transactions, political or economic instability within a country may encourage people to exchange their currency for a more stable currency, often the United States dollar. In that case, the value of the dollar would rise in relation to the other nation's currency. A country that is experiencing rapid inflation will find its currency falling in value in relation to other currencies.

Global *Economy*

The Big Mac Index

One way to see whether a currency is devalued or overvalued against the U.S. dollar is to use the "Big Mac Index" developed by *The Economist.* Economists compare the price of a Big Mac hamburger in the United States to what it costs in another country's local currency. Converting the foreign price to U.S. dollars shows whether the price of a Big Mac is undervalued or overvalued against the U.S. dollar. For example, a Big Mac may cost $2.49 in the United States and 262 yen in Japan (which converts to $2.01 in U.S. currency). The Japanese yen, therefore, is undervalued against the U.S. dollar. ■

Country	Big Mac Prices in local currency	in U.S. dollars	Percent under (–) or over (+) valued against dollar
U.S. (Dollar)	2.49	$2.49	---
Brazil (Real)	3.60	1.55	–38
China (Yuan)	10.50	1.27	–49
Israel (Shekel)	12.00	2.51	+1
Mexico (Peso)	21.90	2.37	–5
Russia (Ruble)	39.00	1.25	–50

FIGURE 18.5 **Balance of Trade** This graph shows how the United States has had a negative balance of trade for the most part since the 1970s.

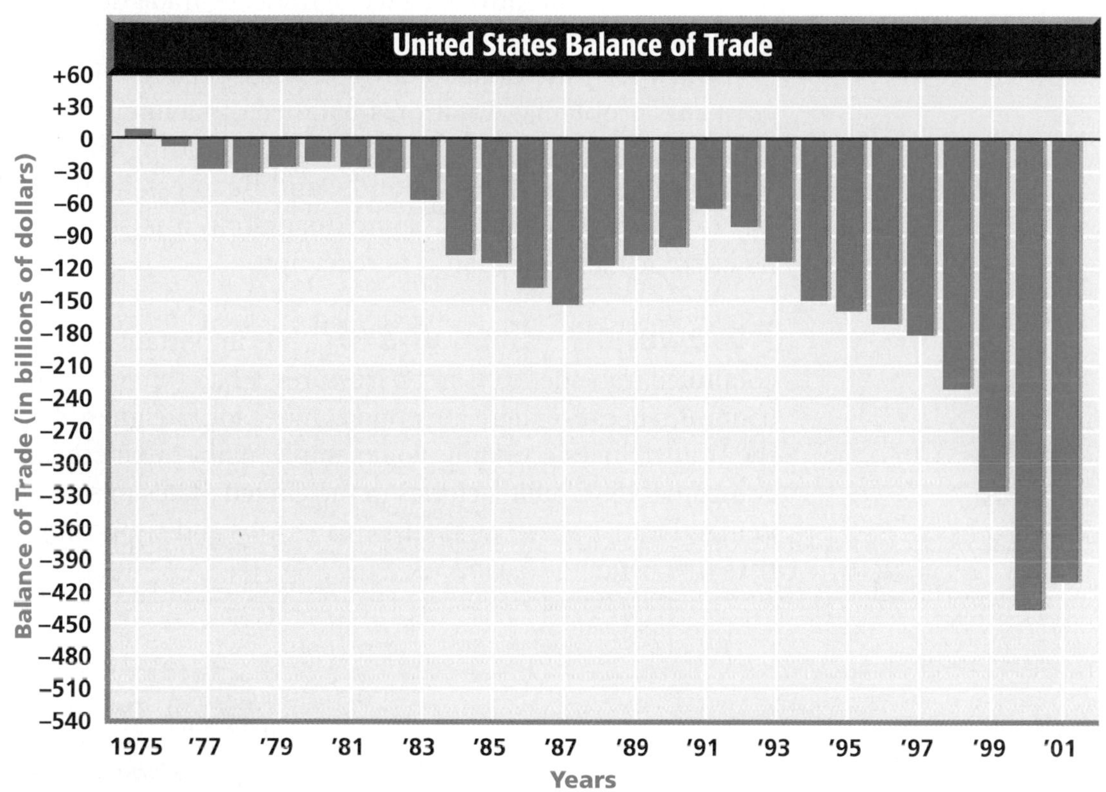

Source: *Statistical Abstract of the United States*, 2002

For an online update of this graph, visit ett.glencoe.com and click on ***Textbook Updates—Chapter 18.***

Balance of Trade

A currency's exchange rate can have an important effect on a nation's **balance of trade.** See **Figure 18.5.** The balance of trade is the difference between the value of a nation's exports and its imports. If a nation's currency depreciates, or becomes "weak," the nation will likely export more goods because its products will become cheaper for other nations to buy. If a nation's currency increases in value, or becomes "strong," the amount of its exports will decline.

balance of trade: *difference between the value of a nation's exports and its imports*

When the value of goods leaving a nation exceeds the value of those coming in, a positive balance of trade is said to exist. In this case, the nation is bringing in more money as payments for goods than it is paying out. A negative balance of trade exists when the value of goods coming into a country is greater than the value of those going out. This situation is called a *trade deficit*. The United States has had a negative balance of trade, or trade deficit, for many years beginning in the 1970s.

Typically, trade deficits have been associated with *balance of payments* problems. A nation's balance of payments takes into account all international transactions, including the buying and selling of services, stocks, bonds, and business interests. When a nation has a balance of payments deficit, it is sending more of its currency abroad than it is receiving.

Trade Deficit—Good or Bad? It is important to realize that a continued trade deficit is not necessarily a bad thing. A trade deficit continues because there are opportunities for foreigners to invest in the United States economy. For example, many Japanese automobile companies have built factories in the United States to satisfy the U.S. demand for Japanese cars. This creates jobs and supporting industries that benefit U.S. citizens.

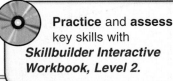

Practice and **assess** key skills with ***Skillbuilder Interactive Workbook, Level 2.***

SECTION 2 Assessment

Understanding Key Terms

1. **Define** exchange rate, foreign exchange markets, fixed rate of exchange, International Monetary Fund (IMF), devaluation, flexible exchange rates, depreciation, balance of trade.

Reviewing Objectives

2. Why do nations need a system of currency exchange rates?
3. How do the forces of supply and demand determine flexible exchange rates?
4. **Graphic Organizer** Create a diagram like the one in the next column to explain how exchange rates affect the balance of trade.

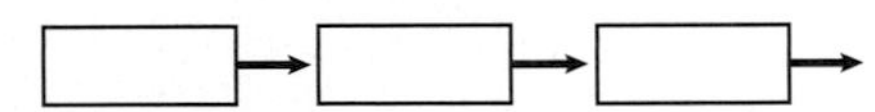

Applying Economic Concepts

5. **Flexible Exchange Rates** In what ways does depreciation of a country's currency improve that country's competitiveness in foreign trade?

Critical Thinking Activity

6. **Synthesizing Information** How does a weak American dollar affect you as a consumer? How does a strong American dollar affect you?

People & Perspectives

James Tobin

ECONOMIST (1918–2002)

- **Member of John F. Kennedy's Council of Economic Advisers, 1961–1962**
- **Awarded the Nobel Prize in Economics in 1981**
- **Author/editor of 16 books and more than 400 articles on economics**
- **Holds the position of Sterling Professor of Economics Emeritus at Yale University**

Nearly 30 years ago, economist James Tobin suggested that a tax should be imposed on foreign exchange transactions to discourage speculation in the foreign exchange markets. With the rise of the global economy and the Internet, economists are reviewing the issue of foreign exchange speculation—and the "Tobin tax"—once again. In the following paragraphs, Tobin explains what the Tobin tax is and how it would work.

"There are 1.3 trillion dollars a day in foreign exchange transactions. Those transactions would be taxed, at a very low rate, something like one tenth of one percent per dollar per transaction. The taxes would be levied by each country on transactions that originate in the country, and collected by the usual tax authority of that country.

If people are involved in making a lot of transactions every day, every week, they would have to pay the tax a lot of times. So they are discouraged from doing that just by the existence of the tax."

Even though there is discussion among economists about the Tobin tax, Tobin himself is doubtful that it will ever be implemented:

"I am not optimistic about that. I don't think the financial community, including ministers of finance in major countries and the central banks of those countries, have any use for those taxes. They don't want it. . . . The International Monetary Fund is not going to go for it.

People do not like to be taxed. They think it is an interference with the free market."

Checking for Understanding

1. **What is the Tobin tax? What is its purpose?**
2. **Why, according to Tobin, will the Tobin tax not be implemented?**

SECTION 3

Restrictions on World Trade

Reader's Guide

Terms to Know

- tariff
- revenue tariff
- protective tariff
- import quota
- embargo
- protectionists
- General Agreement on Tariffs and Trade (GATT)
- World Trade Organization (WTO)
- North American Free Trade Agreement (NAFTA)
- European Union (EU)

Reading Objectives

1. How can a nation restrict imports?
2. What are three arguments for and against free trade?
3. What are some current international and regional trade agreements?

Cover Story

Business Week, January 18, 1999

The mood was giddy just about everywhere on the Continent as Europe's new currency, the euro, made its grand debut. . . . After years of skepticism from critics on the Continent and abroad, Europe has its common currency.

The long-term effects of melding an 11-nation, $6.5 trillion, 290 million-person region into one economic and financial bloc are giving Continental Europe new [power]. Companies around the world are eager to exploit what they hope will become a true single market.

To trade or not to trade? The difficulties that different currencies cause are only one problem of world trade. There are also natural barriers, which include the differences in languages and cultures between various trading partners. As you read this section, you'll learn that some nations may set restrictions to discourage or limit trade.

Three Ways to Restrict Imports

Three major barriers to world trade are tariffs, quotas, and embargoes. The most commonly used barrier to free trade is the **tariff**, a tax on imports.

tariff: *tax placed on an imported product*

Tariffs Two types of tariffs can be applied to an import. A **revenue tariff** is used primarily to raise government revenue without restricting imports. Although tariffs today account for less than 2 percent of the federal government's income, they were the major sources of federal funding until the early 1900s.

A **protective tariff** is one designed to raise the cost of imported goods and thereby protect domestic producers. Some protective tariff rates have been as high as 62 percent of the value of the imported goods.

revenue tariff: *tax on imports used primarily to raise government revenue without restricting imports*

protective tariff: *tax on imports used to raise the cost of imported goods and thereby protect domestic producers*

Quotas An alternative method for restricting imports is the quota system. An **import quota** usually restricts the number of units of a particular good that can be brought into the country. The United States has placed quotas on imports of sugar, dairy products, various types of apparel, and cloth.

import quota: *restriction imposed on the number of units of a particular good that can be brought into the country*

Embargoes An **embargo** is a complete restriction on the import or export of a particular good. Often embargoes are enacted for political reasons. For example, in 1998 an embargo was ordered against Serbia for its actions in neighboring Kosovo.

The United States has also ordered embargoes on goods *from* certain countries. An embargo on trade with Cuba has been in place for more than four decades because that country's leader is Communist.

embargo: *complete restriction on the import or export of a particular good*

protectionists: *people who argue for trade restrictions to protect domestic industries*

Arguments Against Free Trade

The pros and cons of trade restrictions are still often the subject of intense public debate. **Protectionists** are those who argue *for* trade restrictions. There are three main arguments for trade protection.

Job Security Protectionists argue that many domestic workers will be unemployed if foreign competitors sell goods at lower prices than American firms. In the 1980s, for example, American steel mills laid off many workers because of foreign competition.

National Economic Security Protectionists argue that certain industries are crucial to the economy of the United States. They believe that

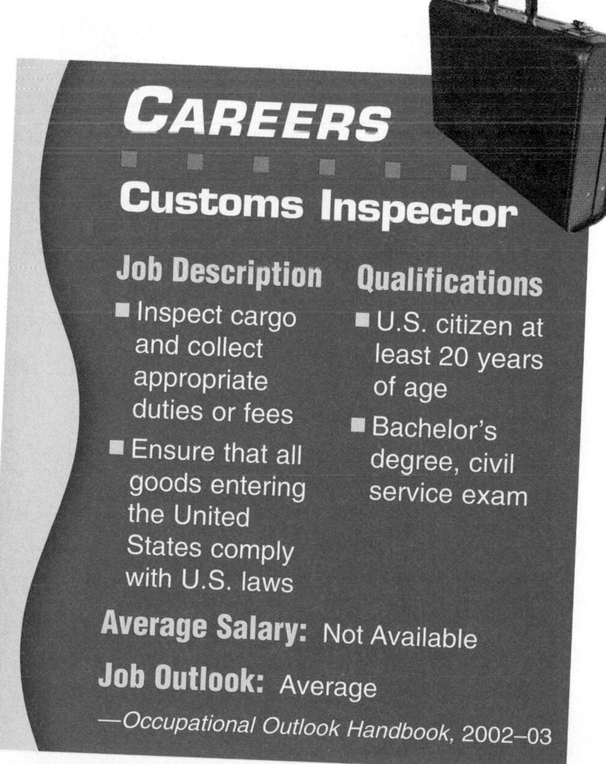
CAREERS
Customs Inspector
Job Description
■ Inspect cargo and collect appropriate duties or fees
■ Ensure that all goods entering the United States comply with U.S. laws
Qualifications
■ U.S. citizen at least 20 years of age
■ Bachelor's degree, civil service exam
Average Salary: Not Available
Job Outlook: Average
—Occupational Outlook Handbook, 2002–03

entire industries, such as oil, should be protected against foreign competition. See **Figure 18.6.**

FIGURE 18.6

National Security
Protectionists believe that certain industries, such as those that are energy-based, should be protected so that the United States is not vulnerable to other nations during times of crises.

Infant Industries Protectionists believe that tariffs and quotas are needed as temporary protection for new, infant industries. If foreign competition is restricted for a time, a young industry may become strong enough to compete in the world market.

Arguments For Free Trade

People who argue for free trade believe that exports and imports should not be restricted. There are three main arguments in support of free trade.

Improved Products Foreign competition encourages United States firms to improve their technology and production methods. As you learned in Chapter 7, better technology increases the production and supply of goods and services available, which raises our standard of living.

Export Industries American workers involved in export industries are hurt or may become unemployed when trade restrictions are implemented. One reason is that when the United States imports fewer goods, there is less American money available outside the United States to buy American exports. Another reason is that when the United States restricts imports, other nations may retaliate and restrict their own imports.

Specialization and Comparative Advantage Those in favor of free trade admit that too much economic specialization allows the country to be at the mercy of world demand. However, some specialization benefits consumers because comparative advantage in production results in more goods at lower prices.

Trade Agreements

After World War II, numerous bilateral trade agreements were brought together in the **General Agreement on Tariffs and Trade (GATT).** Under GATT, countries met periodically to negotiate tariff reductions that were mutually advantageous to all members. In 1994, GATT members signed a treaty establishing the **World Trade Organization (WTO)**, which came into being the following year with 76 member nations. The WTO constitutes the most far-reaching global trade agreement in history.

General Agreement on Tariffs and Trade: *trade agreement under which countries met periodically to negotiate tariff reductions that were mutually advantageous to all members*

World Trade Organization: *world's largest trade agreement currently with more than 140 nations*

Regional Trade Agreements In many parts of the world, regional trade agreements have been reached in order to increase free trade. Certain nations in Southeast Asia as well as in Central and South America have such regional trade agreements. The United States formed one with Canada and Mexico called the **North American Free Trade Agreement (NAFTA).** The U.S. Congress approved NAFTA in 1993. Since then, trade has increased among the 3 nations to the general benefit of all.

Perhaps the most important regional trade agreement in the world today is the **European Union (EU).** Currently, the EU consists of France, Germany, Great Britain, Denmark, Italy, Spain, Greece, Portugal, Luxembourg, Belgium, the Netherlands, Finland, Sweden, Austria, and Ireland. Starting in 2004, 10 additional countries planned to join the EU. On January 1, 1993, the EU began eliminating most of its restrictions on trade among its member countries. On January 1, 1999, 11 of the 15 member nations started putting into place the euro as a common currency. Those 11 nations and Greece abandoned their own national currencies as of January 1, 2002. Eventually, the EU will have a common currency for over 370 million European consumers. It will rival the United States in market size. See pages 494–495.

North American Free Trade Agreement: *trade agreement designed to reduce and gradually eliminate tariff barriers among Mexico, Canada, and the United States*

European Union: *organization of European nations whose goal is to encourage economic integration as a single market*

Practice and **assess** key skills with ***Skillbuilder Interactive Workbook, Level 2.***

SECTION 3 Assessment

Understanding Key Terms

1. **Define** tariff, revenue tariff, protective tariff, import quota, embargo, protectionists, General Agreement on Tariffs and Trade, World Trade Organization, North American Free Trade Agreement, European Union.

Reviewing Objectives

2. How can a nation restrict imports?
3. What are three arguments for and against free trade?
4. **Graphic Organizer** Create a chart like the one below to list and describe at least three trade agreements.

Agreement	Purpose

Applying Economic Concepts

5. **Free Trade** Assume you are (a) a startup computer software producer, (b) the owner of a retail dress shop, (c) a steelworker whose company just closed, (d) a student working in fast-food service. Write a short argument for or against free trade from the standpoint of each individual.

Critical Thinking Activity

6. **Summarizing Information** Research the benefits and costs of the North American Free Trade Agreement (NAFTA) on the Internet. Scan several articles to identify which groups support NAFTA and which groups oppose the trade agreement. Evaluate the reasons each group gives for supporting or opposing NAFTA.

BusinessWeek

Spotlight on the Economy

Mexican Makeover

Check It Out! In this chapter you learned about regional trade agreements. In this article, read to learn how NAFTA has helped to create the world's newest industrial power.

Mexico's economy is undergoing a stunning transformation. Five years after the launch of the North American Free Trade Agreement (NAFTA), it is fast becoming an industrial power. Free trade with the U.S. and Canada is turning the country from a mere assembler of cheap, low-quality goods into a reliable exporter of sophisticated products, from auto brake systems to laptop computers. Since 1993, exports have more than doubled, to $115 billion. Manufactured goods now make up close to 90% of Mexico's sales abroad, up from 77% five years ago. . . .

Mexico's industrial surge also means that North America is winning back thousands of jobs that had been lost to Asia as U.S. and Canadian companies shifted production to lower-cost production sites in the last decade. Now, for example, IBM is making computer components in Guadalajara that were formerly made in Singapore. And clothing retailers such as Gap Inc. and Liz Claiborne are increasingly buying garments from Mexican contractors, who can offer faster delivery than Asians. . . .

But the makeover of Mexican industry goes far beyond export and investment numbers. From small entrepreneurs to executives of the country's new multinationals, Mexican managers are becoming more confident as they respond to heightened competition at home and to the tough demands of foreign customers.

–Reprinted from December 21, 1998 issue of *Business Week* by special permission, copyright © 1998 by The McGraw-Hill Companies, Inc.

Think About It

1. **How has NAFTA affected Mexico's exports?**
2. **How has NAFTA affected Mexico's entrepreneurs?**

CHAPTER 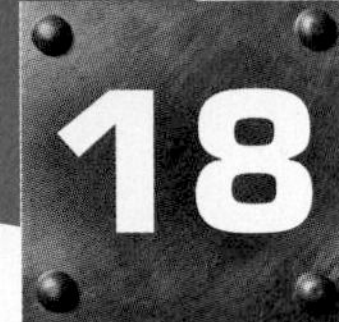 Summary

Chapter Overview Visit the *Economics Today and Tomorrow* Web site at ett.glencoe.com and click on ***Chapter 18—Chapter Overviews*** to review chapter information.

SECTION 1 The Benefits of World Trade

- Trade is important because **imports** supply us with many goods and natural resources, and many American workers are employed in industries that **export** products abroad.
- **Absolute advantage** is the ability of one country, using the same amount of resources as another country, to produce a particular product at a lower absolute cost.
- **Comparative advantage** is the ability of a country to produce a product at a lower opportunity cost than another country.

SECTION 2 Financing World Trade

- **Foreign exchange markets** allow businesses around the world to exchange their currency for another currency.
- Under a **fixed exchange rate,** a nation's currency was tied to a certain standard—usually the amount of gold the nation held in reserve.
- Under a **flexible exchange rate** system, the forces of supply and demand are allowed to set the price of various currencies.
- The rate at which a currency is being exchanged can have an important effect on a nation's **balance of trade.**
- If a nation's currency **depreciates,** the nation will likely export more goods and services. If a nation's currency increases in value, the amount of its exports will decline.

SECTION 3 Restrictions on World Trade

- Three major barriers to world trade are **tariffs, quotas,** and **embargoes.**
- **Protectionists** are in favor of trade restrictions to protect American jobs, to protect national security, and to protect infant industries.
- Those who argue for free trade believe that competition results in better products at lower prices and that restricting imports hurts export industries.
- Recent trade agreements such as the **World Trade Organization,** the **North American Free Trade Agreement,** and the **European Union** have worked to lower trade restrictions.

CHAPTER 18

Assessment and Activities

Self-Check Quiz Visit the *Economics Today and Tomorrow* Web site at ett.glencoe.com and click on ***Chapter 18—Self-Check Quizzes*** to prepare for the Chapter Test.

Identifying Key Terms

Write the letter of the definition in Column B that correctly defines each term in Column A.

Column A

1. absolute advantage
2. comparative advantage
3. embargo
4. protectionists
5. balance of trade
6. devaluation
7. depreciation
8. revenue tariff
9. exchange rate

Column B

a. price of one country's currency in relation to another country's currency
b. lowering of a currency's value in relation to other currencies
c. complete restriction on the import or export of a particular good
d. difference between the value of a nation's exports and its imports
e. ability of a nation to produce a product more efficiently than can another country
f. drop in the price of a currency in response to supply and demand
g. ability of a country to use the same amount of resources as another to produce a product at less cost
h. those who oppose the relaxation of trade restrictions
i. tax on imports to raise money

Recalling Facts and Ideas

Section 1

1. How does a country determine whether it has a comparative advantage in the production of certain goods?
2. What does the United States gain from international trade?
3. "America can produce more DVDs per labor hour than can any other country in the world." Is this an example of an absolute advantage or a comparative advantage?

Section 2

4. Why are foreign exchange markets necessary?
5. Why was it difficult to maintain a system of fixed rates of exchange?

Section 3

6. What is the difference between a revenue tariff and a protective tariff?
7. What are three arguments against free trade?
8. What is also affected when restrictions are put on imports?

Thinking Critically

1. **Making Predictions** If the value of the dollar fell in relation to other currencies, what would you expect to happen to American exports?
2. **Understanding Cause and Effect** Create a diagram like the one below to show how protecting infant industries will allow them to grow.

Applying Economic Concepts

International Trade Although international trade accounts for only about 13 percent of the American economy, it affects all Americans. To understand how international trade affects you, try to describe what your world would be like if international trade were outlawed. You can do this by writing a list of all the products you would *not* be able to purchase or whose price would go up dramatically without international trade.

Cooperative Learning Project

Working in groups of four, concentrate on one or more countries from the following list:

- Mexico
- Kenya
- Canada
- Morocco
- Japan

Each member of the group will research one of the following items:

- The size of the international sector within each country (i.e., the percentage of GDP accounted for by imports or exports)
- The natural resource base of the nation
- The top three items that are exported
- The top three items that are imported

Each group will decide what the relationship is between the natural resource base and what is exported and imported. Finally, each group will write a summary of how life in each country would be different if international trade were prohibited.

Reviewing Skills

Applying the Writing Process There are virtually no restrictions on trade within the 50 states, mainly because the Constitution of the United States forbids it. Write a one-page description of problems that might have arisen if the Constitution had been silent on trade among the states. Include in your paper the section or sections in the Constitution that prohibit at least one restriction on international trade.

Technology Activity

Developing Multimedia Presentations Study the list of topics below. Choose one of the topics and explain how you would use at least three types of media in a presentation to best teach the topic to your class.

1. U.S. Exports and Imports
2. Foreign Exchange Markets
3. U.S. Balance of Trade
4. North American Free Trade Agreement

Analyzing the Global *Economy*

Use the Internet to find out more about international trade. Type *international trade* into your search engine. From the list of Web sites that appears on the monitor, select at least three. Read and summarize your findings.

Global *Economy*

The European Union The European Union (EU) is an organization of 15 independent European nations whose goal is to create a unified and strong market. The map below shows the value of trade between the EU and other world regions.

North America
Imports from EU = $172.1 million
Exports to EU = $177.4 million

Latin America
Imports from EU = $53.4 million
Exports to EU = $42.4 million

Beginning January 1, 2002, the currency used in all EU member countries except Denmark, Great Britain, and Sweden is the euro. After 2002, coins in the national currencies of the 12 countries adopting the euro will have no value. People will be able to exchange their bills for euros for many years, however.

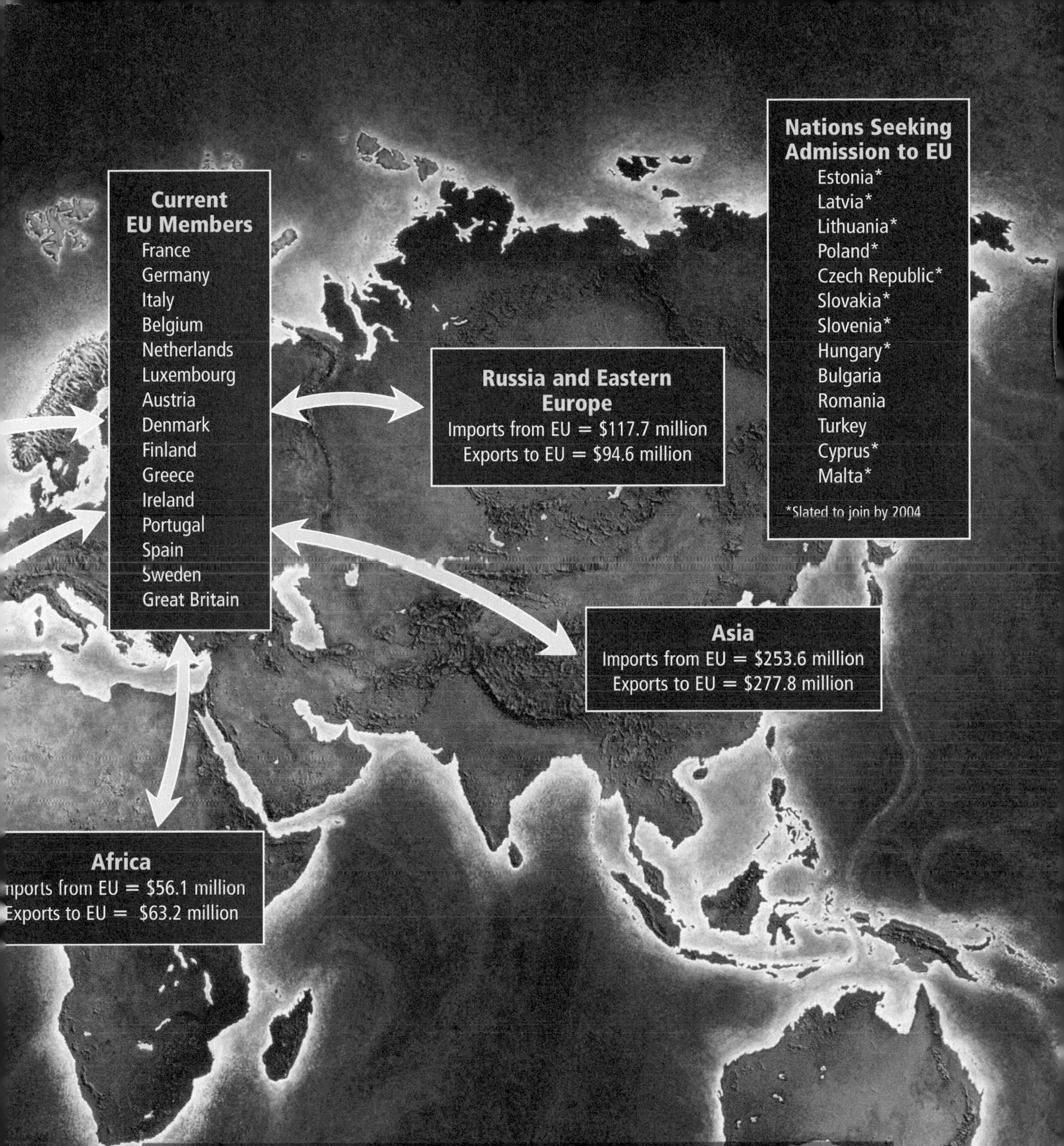

Current EU Members
France
Germany
Italy
Belgium
Netherlands
Luxembourg
Austria
Denmark
Finland
Greece
Ireland
Portugal
Spain
Sweden
Great Britain

Nations Seeking Admission to EU
Estonia*
Latvia*
Lithuania*
Poland*
Czech Republic*
Slovakia*
Slovenia*
Hungary*
Bulgaria
Romania
Turkey
Cyprus*
Malta*

*Slated to join by 2004

Russia and Eastern Europe
Imports from EU = $117.7 million
Exports to EU = $94.6 million

Asia
Imports from EU = $253.6 million
Exports to EU = $277.8 million

Africa
nports from EU = $56.1 million
Exports to EU = $63.2 million

Thinking Globally

1. With which regions of the world does the EU have a trade surplus? A trade deficit?

2. Which region is the EU's biggest trade partner?

CHAPTER 19

Converging Economic Systems

Why It's Important

Why do people in some countries pay much higher taxes than Americans do? How do other nations' economies work? This chapter explains the differences between capitalism and socialism—and why many nations are moving toward free enterprise.

To learn more about the differences between socialism and capitalism, view the **Economics & You** *Chapter 25 video lesson:* **Comparative Economic Systems**

Chapter Overview Visit the *Economics Today and Tomorrow* Web site at ett.glencoe.com and click on ***Chapter 19—Chapter Overviews*** to preview chapter information.

SECTION 1

Comparing Capitalism and Socialism

Cover Story

Business Week, July 19, 1999

For more than 15 years, the handful of foreign automakers allowed into China have dutifully assembled the cars and trucks prescribed by Beijing [China's capital]—even if those vehicles didn't make the most economic sense.

. . . For years, China has tightly restricted market access, especially for passenger cars. The government limited the number of players, set production volumes and prices, and dictated what types of vehicles could be made and where. Foreign carmakers have ended up making outmoded vehicles that are too expensive for most Chinese.

Reader's Guide

Terms to Know

- proletariat
- communism
- democratic socialism
- authoritarian socialism

Reading Objectives

1. What are the three characteristics of pure market capitalism?
2. What are the key characteristics of pure socialism?
3. How did socialism develop?
4. What are the benefits of capitalism?

Some government intervention occurs in the American economy, but generally the marketplace answers the three basic economic questions of WHAT, HOW, and FOR WHOM goods and services should be produced. In command economies, however, the government (not the market) answers these three basic questions.

In this chapter you will study different economic systems. The system that we know best in the United States is market capitalism. The opposite of this system is pure command socialism.

FIGURE 19.1

A Characteristics of Pure Capitalism

1. Pure capitalism is a system in which prices seek their own level as determined by the forces of supply and demand.
2. Resources, including labor, are free to move in and out of industries in competing geographic locations. The movement of resources follows the lure of profits—higher expected profits create an incentive for more resources to go where those profits are expected to occur.
3. Private property rights exist, are legal, and are enforced by the government, or the rule of law.
4. Those who take risks may be rewarded by higher profits. When those risks turn out to be bad business decisions, the risk takers lose money.
5. The three basic economic questions are all decided in a decentralized way by individuals.

B Characteristics of Pure Socialism

1. Most prices are set by the state, rather than by forces of supply and demand.
2. The movement of resources, particularly labor, is strictly controlled. The central planning authority makes all the decisions.
3. Most of the major factors of production are owned by the state. Private property rights are strictly limited to small tools that an individual needs for an occupation.
4. Individual risk taking is not allowed. The state takes all of the risk when it decides which new companies shall be formed. All citizens pay for unsuccessful risk taking.
5. Economic decisions about what, how, and for whom to produce are all made by state officials through central planning agencies and other administrative units.
6. Taxation is often used to redistribute income.

Pure Market Capitalism

In its purest theoretical form, market or pure capitalism operates on the basis of the *three Ps:* Prices, Profits, and Private Property. See *Part A* of **Figure 19.1.** Government in a pure capitalist system is limited to providing such public goods as national defense and police protection.

Pure Socialism

Pure socialism is an economic system in which there is little private property and the state owns virtually all the factors of production. Few examples of pure command socialism exist. Perhaps the most extensively controlled economies are in North Korea and Cuba. *Part B* of **Figure 19.1** lists the characteristics of pure socialism.

The Marxian View of Socialism Socialism as a modern economic system grew out of protests against the problems caused by the Industrial Revolution of the 1800s. Karl Marx viewed history as a continual struggle between various groups, or classes, in society. In his own day, he saw this struggle as going on between capitalists–owners of the land, machines, and factories–and the **proletariat**, or workers. Marx believed capitalists exploited the proletariat, or used them unfairly. According to Marx, the value of goods depends only on how much labor is used in producing them. When capitalists sold a good and kept the profit, they were taking income that rightly belonged to the proletariat.

proletariat: *term used by Karl Marx referring to workers*

Despite capitalism's dominance in the nineteenth century, Marx believed it was doomed to fail. He outlined the collapse of capitalism, as shown in **Figure 19.2**, and predicted the

FIGURE 19.2 The Change From Capitalism to Socialism According to Marx

The End of Capitalism Clearly Marx did not accurately predict what would happen in capitalist nations. Indeed, the opposite has proven to be true.

The Change From Capitalism to Socialism According to Marx

Step 1
Capitalism would suffer extreme recessions and depressions that would harm workers. A few rich capitalists would have all industrial power.

Step 2
The wide gap between the rich and the poor would cause workers to unite and overthrow capitalism.

Step 3
The victorious workers would establish a new socialist system. Workers, through the state, would own and control the means of production.

Step 4
The system would evolve into pure communism. Workers would contribute to society to their full abilities and, in return, take only what they needed.

Leaders of the 1917 Russian Revolution

Economic Connection to... History

Socialist Party of America

Several political parties that promoted socialism developed in the United States during the late 1800s and early 1900s. The most successful of these, the Socialist Party of America, was founded in 1901. By 1912 party membership had grown to about 118,000. And in the presidential election of that year, the Socialist candidate, Eugene V. Debs, received more than 900,000 votes. ■

communism: *term used by Karl Marx for his ideal society in which no government is necessary*

evolution of socialism into **communism**–an ideal system with no need for a government. Today *communism* has come to mean any authoritarian socialist system that supports revolution as a means to overthrow capitalism and bring about socialist goals. Instead of "no government," communist systems historically have demonstrated that a central government controls the entire economy.

democratic socialism: *system that works within the constitutional framework of a nation to elect socialists to office; the government usually controls only some areas of the economy*

authoritarian socialism: *system that supports revolution as a means to overthrow capitalism and bring about socialist goals; the entire economy is controlled by a central government; also called* communism

Socialism Since Marx In the twentieth century, socialism split into two major trends: democratic socialism and authoritarian socialism. **Democratic socialism** is a type of socialist system that works within the constitutional framework of a nation to elect socialists to office. In democratic socialist nations, government usually controls only some areas of the economy.

Authoritarian socialism, in contrast, more closely follows Marx's beliefs. Its supporters advocate revolution as the means to overthrow capitalism and bring about socialist goals. In authoritarian socialist nations, a central government controls the entire economy. *Communism,* the term Marx applied to his ideal society, came to mean any authoritarian socialist system.

The Benefits of Capitalism

Many economists like to compare the advantages and disadvantages of capitalism and socialism. Often such comparisons are based on individual values. Those who place a high value on personal freedom, initiative, and individuality prefer capitalism. Critics of socialism point out that it brings extensive government intervention in all parts of the economy and, by necessity, in people's personal lives.

Supporters of capitalism point out that capitalism allows for more efficiency in the marketplace and for greater rates of economic growth. Indeed, considerable evidence shows that unregulated economic systems—those that are closer to pure capitalism—have *much higher* rates of economic growth.

All Economies Are Planned It is often said that pure socialism requires centralized planning, and pure capitalism does not. In reality, all economies are planned in one way or another. The United States has a highly planned economy. The difference between economic planning here versus in socialist countries is *who* does the planning. Private firms, individuals, and elected government officials do the planning in the American economy. In pure socialist systems, central planners make decisions on behalf of everyone.

Real-world capitalism has some problems. Critics note that income is unequally distributed throughout the economy. They also say that although capitalist nations have enough government-provided goods such as highways, they do not have enough schools and museums for the general public. Such critics clearly value the political goals of socialism.

Practice and **assess** key skills with ***Skillbuilder Interactive Workbook, Level 2.***

SECTION 1 Assessment

Understanding Key Terms

1. **Define** proletariat, communism, democratic socialism, authoritarian socialism.

Reviewing Objectives

2. What are the three characteristics of pure market capitalism?
3. What are the key characteristics of pure socialism?
4. **Graphic Organizer** Create a diagram like the one below to show the major steps in the development of socialism.

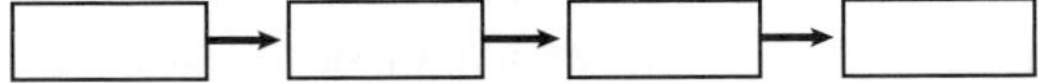

5. What are the benefits of capitalism?

Applying Economic Concepts

6. **Authoritarian Socialism** Imagine that you live in an authoritarian socialist nation. What arguments might you make to change the economic and political systems?

Critical Thinking Activity

7. **Making Comparisons** Create a table that compares how each of the following functions is handled under capitalism and democratic socialism: setting price of goods; ownership of production; economic planning; business failures. *For help in creating tables, see page xvii in the Economic Handbook.*

People & Perspectives

Karl Marx

ECONOMIST (1818–1883)

- **Born and educated in Germany, but spent much of his adult life in exile in Great Britain**
- **Deeply influenced by the German philosopher Georg Hegel**
- **Publications include *The Communist Manifesto* (1848), *Critique of Political Economy* (1859), and *Das Kapital* (1867)**

Karl Marx outlined his view of socialism in *The Communist Manifesto,* a pamphlet that he wrote with colleague Friedrich Engels in 1848. In the following excerpt, Marx answers two questions: Who are the Communists? What is their basic theory?

"The Communists do not form a separate party opposed to other working-class parties. They have no interests separate and apart from the proletariat as a whole.

. . . The immediate aim of the Communists is the same as that of all other proletarian parties: Formation of the proletariat into a class, overthrow of the bourgeois supremacy, conquest of political power by the proletariat.

. . . The distinguishing feature of communism is not the abolition of property generally, but the abolition of bourgeois property. But modern bourgeois private property is the final and most complete expression of the system of producing and appropriating products that is based on class antagonisms, on the exploitation of the many by the few.

In this sense, the theory of the Communists may be summed up in the single sentence: Abolition of private property.

. . . It has been objected that upon the abolition of private property, all work will cease, and universal laziness will overtake us. According to this, bourgeois society ought long ago to have gone to the dogs through sheer idleness; for those of its members who work, acquire nothing, and those who acquire anything, do not work. The whole of this objection is but another expression of the tautology [needless repetition of an idea]: There can no longer be any wage labor when there is no longer any capital."

Checking for Understanding

1. **According to Marx, what phrase sums up communist theory?**
2. **Why was the incentive to work an issue Marx had to address?**

SECTION 2

Changing Authoritarian Socialism—The Case of China

COVER STORY

MANCHESTER GUARDIAN WEEKLY, MARCH 21, 1999

China took another big step towards opening itself up to private enterprise last week when it changed its constitution to raise the status of the burgeoning business sector.

The landmark decision by the National People's Congress, the country's parliament, allows the private sector to become an important component of what is still referred to as the socialist economy.

READER'S GUIDE

Terms to Know

- five-year plans
- World Trade Organization (WTO)

Reading Objectives

1. How did the Chinese economic system develop following World War II?
2. What have been two major problems in China's attempt to move to capitalism?

The People's Republic of China remains the largest nation that has some form of command socialism. As you read this section, however, you'll learn that a growing area of China has an economic system that is much closer to that of the United States.

Development of China's Economic System

The Communists won China's civil war following World War II. The new government started an economic system based on

so-called **five-year plans.** The first such five-year plan, implemented in 1953, failed to fully meet expectations. Starting in the mid-1950s, the Chinese began to alter their strict centralized planning.

In 1957 they reformed their system to give some decision-making powers to local government rather than restricting them to the central government. The national planning system was transformed into a regional planning system. These reforms did not transform the Chinese economy, however, because it was still not governed by capitalism's *three Ps*—Prices, Profits, and Private Property. Economic conditions worsened after 1958.

In 1978 Chinese leaders designed a reform to motivate people to work harder. Private individuals were permitted to rent land for up to 15 years. Each peasant household became responsible for its own plot of land. Whatever it produced in excess of a minimum amount required by the state remained the property of the household. The results were impressive. Between 1979 and 1984, overall farm productivity increased dramatically.

five-year plans: *centralized planning system that was the basis for China's economic system; eventually was transformed to a regional planning system leading to limited free enterprise*

Another set of reforms and a restructuring of the economy occurred in the mid-1980s. These reforms are continuing today. Managers in state-owned businesses are allowed much more decision-making power than before. After they fulfill state production requirements, they can set production according to market demand. They also are allowed to sell part of their output to whomever they choose at market prices. See **Figure 19.3.**

FIGURE 19.3

The Shift to a Free Market
China—after the failure of command economies throughout the world—has begun to allow free enterprise.

The Transition Toward a Mixed Economy

Student Web Activity Visit the *Economics Today and Tomorrow* Web site at ett.glencoe.com and click on ***Chapter 19—Student Web Activities*** to learn more about China's evolving economy.

As you may recall, one of the most important aspects of pure capitalism is well-defined private property rights. In China, the state still owns large parts of the economy, especially urban industries. In the countryside, provincial governors are still held accountable for ensuring that each province grow as much grain as it consumes. The government still leases land for 15-year intervals to farmers. Without complete property rights, farmers are therefore not interested in investing in farm equipment and making improvements to the land.

Establishing the Rule of Law Countries shifting from non-capitalist to capitalist systems all face the same problem—how to establish the rule of law. When no specific property rights exist, the unavoidable result is corruption. Throughout China there is an atmosphere of lawlessness and unpredictability for anyone in the business world. This is particularly true for foreign investors. Because army and government officials still control many resources, they continue to seek bribes. Thus, such individuals still influence the way business is conducted in China.

Only very gradually is China becoming a nation of laws, rather than of men and women. The notion of property rights is slow to be accepted because communist dogma has for decades criticized private property as detrimental to the state. For example, compact disc factories in China routinely "pirate" CDs. The Chinese government supported this practice, but at one point shut down the factories because of international pressure. The pirates reopened a few years later, however. Chinese government officials ignored the fact that singers and musicians were being denied royalties. See **Figure 19.4.**

FIGURE 19.4

China's Black Market In China, consumers can buy Nike T-shirts for less than $2, DVDs for under $3, and music CDs for a fraction of their cost in the United States. Many Chinese "entrepreneurs" produce and sell American brand-name products very inexpensively because they do not pay royalties on the brands they counterfeit.

Prospects for China's Economic Future

A foreigner visiting Beijing or Shanghai or another large city in China would have difficulty knowing he or she was in the People's Republic of China. There are McDonald's restaurants, business executives with cellular phones and pagers, and advertisements for Levi's clothing, 7Up, Heinz products, and Head & Shoulders shampoo everywhere.

World Trade Organization (WTO): *world's largest trade agreement—currently includes more than 140 nations*

In 2000 that foreign presence began expanding. In that year, the United States agreed to allow China to join the **World Trade Organization (WTO),** which regulates trade among more than 140 nations. This action had far-reaching effects for both China and the rest of the world.

China is an enormous market for foreign companies eager to sell their products to the nation's 1.3 billion people. As a result of being admitted to the WTO, the inefficient state-owned industries draining China's economy were forced to face many economic reforms. As a member of the WTO, China also has *Normal Trade Relations (NTR)* status with the United States. (formerly called *Most Favored Nation status*). WTO membership has increased the prospects for a more prosperous, democratic, and stable China.

Practice and **assess** key skills with ***Skillbuilder Interactive Workbook, Level 2.***

SECTION 2 Assessment

Understanding Terms

1. **Define** five-year plans, World Trade Organization (WTO).

Reviewing Objectives

2. How did the Chinese economic system develop following World War II?
3. **Graphic Organizer** Create a diagram like the one below to explain two major problems China is facing in its move toward capitalism.

Problem	Cause	Effect

Applying Economic Concepts

4. **International Trade** Research the World Trade Organization on the Internet. Find and summarize the issues involved in admitting China as a member of the World Trade Organization.

Critical Thinking Activity

5. **Synthesizing Information** Explain how government involvement in setting production quotas for industries could lead to either a surplus or a shortage of goods and services. Incorporate real-world examples in your explanation.

BusinessWeek

Spotlight on the Economy

China's Transformation to a Market Economy

Check It Out! In this chapter you learned about China's evolving economy. In this article, read to learn about the changes that the Chinese people will need to make as their economy moves toward free enterprise.

Much of what has defined life for China's 1.2 billion people is in flux. [The Premier's] efforts to turn around tens of thousands of money-losing state enterprises will mean the shutting of countless factories. More than 10 million workers . . . will be laid off over the next few years. Some will find jobs in the proliferation of private enterprises, from new computer factories to roadside restaurants.

If they are fortunate, thanks to new social-services programs, they will make up for the perks that they forfeit, from company housing to free cradle-to-grave health care. Private-sector workers, Chinese leaders hope, will form the vast base of middle-class consumers that will power the economy for decades to come.

The other transformation facing China will be its greater opening to the outside world. . . . [S]ectors from high-tech manufacturing to banking and telecom services will open to foreign investors as never before. Companies will flock to places with the most flexible policies, such as Shanghai.

That is the vision. But for millions of Chinese, the transition will be wrenching. The purging of most of socialism's last vestiges will throw many into a desperate search for work and shelter. The income gap between those with the skills required to thrive in an open economy and those without will widen. But whether the changes bring prosperity or hardship, . . . most Chinese are determined to seize the opportunity.

Think About It

1. **What changes will Chinese workers face with the transformation to a free enterprise economy?**
2. **What do you think will change the most as the Chinese have more contact with the outside world?**

SECTION 3

Nations Move Toward the Market System

Reader's Guide

Terms to Know

- privatization
- welfare state

Reading Objectives

1. How has Russia changed since privatization?
2. How has the Swedish economy been changing?
3. What changes have recently occurred in Latin American economies?

Cover Story

Business Week, April 26, 1999

It's a bizarre and oddly flexible economic model. Some economists call it the "virtual economy," because real money, real goods, and real output play such a small role. It is, in fact, a three-tier economy. The Russian currency, the ruble, is used mainly to buy necessities such as food. IOUs, barter, and "surrogate currencies" are used in most dealings involving companies. Instead of paying cash wages, [one company] issues its employees cards that can be used in company-owned shops and the city department stores. Russians, meanwhile, keep their savings in dollars.

Economics textbooks written 15 or 20 years ago included information on the Soviet Union and its satellite countries in Eastern Europe. The centralized command economy lasted for 74 years in the Soviet Union, and more than 40 years in Eastern Europe. From the revolution in 1917 until the economic and political system collapsed in December 1991, the Soviet Union experienced five-year plans, central-planning commissions, and hundreds of other types of commissions. In this section you'll learn about Russia's—and other nations'—hard road to capitalism.

Privatization in Russia

Privatization simply means the change from state ownership of business, land, and buildings to private ownership. The private owners can be partnerships, domestic or foreign corporations, or individuals, as shown in **Figure 19.5.** Sometimes workers even buy the companies that employ them, and foreign companies have purchased formerly state-owned companies.

privatization: *change from state ownership of business, land, and buildings to private ownership*

Resistance to Privatization When a state enterprise is sold to a private interest, disruptions can occur. In particular, workers may find themselves out of a job. One of the problems with state-owned firms is that they are inefficiently run. When private owners take over, they often modernize the equipment and streamline the production processes. As a result, they sometimes require fewer workers. Because of the possibility of increased unemployment, many sectors of the population have resisted privatization. Some workers even demanded that old-style centralized planning be brought back to Russia.

Reforming the Price System Until the 1990s in Russia, prices were not determined by supply and demand. Rather, government officials set prices—often too low—which resulted in severe shortages of nearly everything the Russians needed.

Currently, most prices in Russia are set by the forces of supply and demand, just as they are in the United States and other capitalist countries. As you remember, when overall demand increases, the prices of goods and services increase. Consumers in Russia still end up "going without" because now they are unable to afford the high prices that the market system has set.

Russian Economic Changes Russia and the other republics that had centrally planned economies are now all moving at different rates toward market capitalism. One of the ways they are doing this is by privatizing formerly state-owned industries.

Challenges Still Remain Besides the inefficiency of many Russian factories, capitalism there is not yet the same as it is in the United States. Private capital is often steered into projects controlled by small groups in power, usually government power.

The Russian economy fell into serious decline in 1998. It was discovered that many formerly state-owned businesses had been sold at bargain-basement prices to "friends" of the government. It was also discovered that at least half of the economy was operating on a barter system. Businesses bartered because they had no faith in the Russian currency. Another reason they bartered was to avoid paying taxes. The expensive Russian tax

Global Economy

Learning About Capitalism

Many Russian children learn about capitalism by reading a textbook that was published in 1997. Its title is *Economics for Little Ones, or How Misha Became a Businessman*. It's a story about a bear that opens a honey, berry, and nut store in the forest. ■

system prevented businesses from paying all their legally owed taxes and still staying in business.

Changes in Sweden

Sweden has been labeled a **welfare state**—a blend of capitalism and socialism. It combines private ownership of the means of production and competitive allocation of resources with the goal of social equality for its citizens. The so-called Swedish model helped transform what was an underdeveloped country in 1870 into a modern nation with one of the highest per-capita incomes in the world a century later.

welfare state: *country that has a blend of capitalism and socialism, combining private ownership of the means of production with the goal of social equality for its citizens*

Currently, government expenditures (and taxes) account for about 51.3 percent of Sweden's annual economic activity. As recently as 1960, this figure was little more than 30 percent. See **Figure 19.6.**

The Swedish government passed an employment security bill in the 1970s that almost guarantees lifelong employment. It also passed a law requiring labor union participation in company decision making. Full employment has existed for a number of

FIGURE 19.6

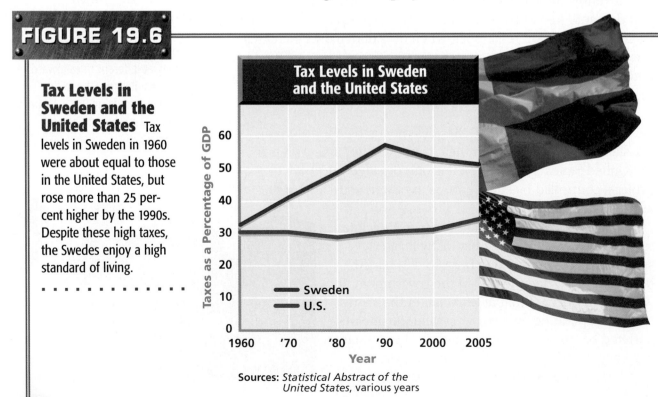

Tax Levels in Sweden and the United States Tax levels in Sweden in 1960 were about equal to those in the United States, but rose more than 25 percent higher by the 1990s. Despite these high taxes, the Swedes enjoy a high standard of living.

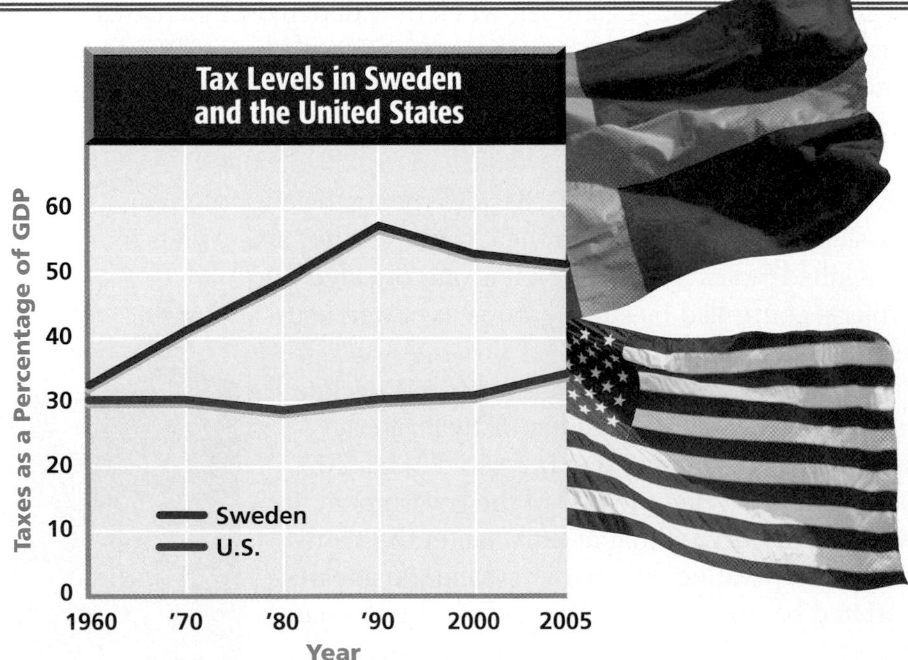

Sources: *Statistical Abstract of the United States*, various years

years because the government took over many large industries and firms, such as steelworks.

Now Sweden has initiated changes in its economic system of capitalism combined with welfare socialism. In the 1990s, the government started to cut taxes and eliminate some public jobs. It also eased business regulations and approved foreign ownership of certain companies. The government ended the monopoly in both the taxicab and the airline industries and has plans to move further toward a market system in the future.

Changes in Latin America

Many nations in Latin America—especially Mexico, Venezuela, Chile, Brazil, and Argentina—have experienced high rates of growth since the mid-1980s. Though virtually all Latin American countries have economic systems that operate under market capitalism, most have had large government sectors. Since 1985, however, many government enterprises have been privatized.

Mexico is a good example. Other countries in Latin America are trying to follow the Mexican model, but infighting among various political parties has made this difficult. Nonetheless, Chile has privatized its airlines, phones, utilities, and pension funds. The Argentinean government has sold state-run oil fields, waterworks, petrochemical plants, and even army housing.

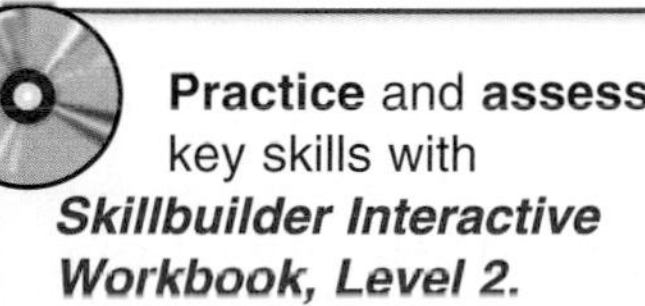

Practice and **assess** key skills with ***Skillbuilder Interactive Workbook, Level 2.***

SECTION 3 Assessment

Understanding Terms

1. **Define** privatization, welfare state.

Reviewing Objectives

2. **Graphic Organizer** Create a diagram like the one below to list and explain how Russia's economy has changed since privatization.

3. How has the Swedish economy been changing?
4. What changes have recently occurred in Latin American economies?

Applying Economic Concepts

5. **Welfare State** Explain some of the advantages and disadvantages of living in Sweden prior to reforms that began in the 1990s.

Critical Thinking Activity

6. **Evaluating Primary and Secondary Sources** Use the Internet to find a primary and secondary account of the privatization of Russia's economy. Write a report analyzing and evaluating the validity of information from each source for bias, propaganda, point of view, and frame of reference.

Critical Thinking Skills

Making Predictions

Predicting future events can be difficult and sometimes risky. The more information you have, however, the more accurate your predictions will be.

- Gather information about the decision or action.
- Use your knowledge of history and human behavior to identify what consequences could result.
- Analyze each of the consequences by asking: How likely is it that this will occur?

Learning the Skill

To help you make predictions, follow the steps listed on the left.

Practicing the Skill

Read the passage below, then answer the questions.

"Anyone who assumes the Internet is still a novelty in China has been asleep at the mouse. The communist giant's state-owned factories and political system may seem frozen in another era. But when it comes to cyberindustry, China is moving at Net speed. Driven by soaring computer sales, rapid expansion of China's telecom networks, and the encouragement of reformist leaders, Internet use is growing explosively. Two years ago, only 640,000 Chinese were connected. Now, more than 4 million are. By 2001, estimates International Data Corp., the online population should hit 27 million–perhaps bigger than Japan's. And while only $42 million in E-commerce transactions are expected this year, they could near $4 billion by 2003."

–*Business Week*, August 2, 1999

1. What trend does the passage show?
2. Do you think this trend is likely to continue?
3. On what do you base this prediction?
4. What are three possible consequences of this trend?

Application Activity

Analyze three articles in the business section of the newspaper. Predict three consequences of the actions in the articles. On what do you base your predictions?

Practice and **assess** key skills with ***Skillbuilder Interactive Workbook, Level 2.***

CHAPTER  Summary

ECONOMICS *Online*

Chapter Overview Visit the *Economics Today and Tomorrow* Web site at ett.glencoe.com and click on ***Chapter 19—Chapter Overviews*** to review chapter information.

SECTION 1 Comparing Capitalism and Socialism

- Pure capitalism operates on the basis of the *three Ps:* Prices, Profits, and Private Property.
- Pure socialism is an economic system in which there is little private property and the state owns virtually all the factors of production.
- Karl Marx predicted that a class struggle between the capitalists and the **proletariat** would evolve into a system of **communism.**
- In **democratic socialism,** government usually controls only some areas of the economy.
- **Authoritarian socialists** advocate revolution as a means to overthrow capitalism and bring about socialist goals.

SECTION 2 Changing Authoritarian Socialism—The Case of China

- The People's Republic of China remains the largest nation that has some form of command socialism.
- After World War II, the Chinese government based the centralized economy on **five-year plans.**
- Reforms in the 1970s and 1980s gave individuals more decision-making power and the ability to sell part of their goods and services for a profit.
- Incomplete property rights, the lack of the rule of law, and resulting corruption are problems that China faces today.
- China's economy is starting to open to the rest of the world.

SECTION 3 Nations Move Toward the Market System

- When Russia moved toward **privatization,** many workers lost their jobs, prices skyrocketed, and the Russian economy fell into serious decline.
- Many hardships face the Russian people as they make the transition to free enterprise.
- As a **welfare state,** Sweden has very high taxes that support the nation's people from cradle to grave.
- Sweden has recently initiated changes in its welfare socialist economic system.
- Many Latin American countries have privatized their transportation and energy industries.

CHAPTER 19

Assessment and Activities

Self-Check Quiz Visit the *Economics Today and Tomorrow* Web site at ett.glencoe.com and click on ***Chapter 19—Self-Check Quizzes*** to prepare for the Chapter Test.

Identifying Key Terms

Write a short paragraph about the different types of socialism using all of the following terms:

- communism
- proletariat
- democratic socialism
- authoritarian socialism
- welfare state
- five-year plans
- privatization

Recalling Facts and Ideas

Section 1

1. What is the role of supply and demand in pure market capitalism?
2. Why do we call pure capitalism a price system?
3. Can individuals take business risks under pure socialism? Explain.
4. What term did Karl Marx apply to his ideal society?
5. How do pure market capitalism and pure socialism differ in regard to private property rights?

Section 2

6. What evidence shows that China is moving toward capitalism?
7. What two problems exist in China's movement toward capitalism?

Section 3

8. Describe the main economic change that is occurring in the former Soviet Union.
9. Why has Sweden been labeled a welfare state?
10. In what way have Latin American countries moved closer to market capitalism?

Thinking Critically

1. **Making Comparisons** Compare the type of planning used in a decentralized capitalist system with that used in a centralized command socialist system.
2. **Understanding Cause and Effect** Create a diagram like the one below to explain why farmers generally are unwilling to invest in farm equipment and land improvement in China.

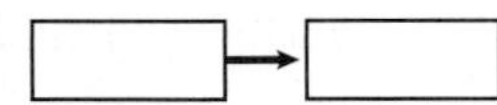

3. **Drawing Inferences** What is the relationship between privatization and decentralization of an economy?

Applying Economic Concepts

Economic Incentives In communist dogma, striving for profits is viewed negatively. Yet free market theory tells us that profits are necessary as a type of signal in our economic system. Make a list of what profits signal in our economy and the results of those signals. Then list some of the things that might happen if profits were outlawed or at least severely restricted.

Cooperative Learning Project

Organize into two groups. One group will represent former communist governments attempting to change to a capitalist system. The other group will represent officials from the United States trying to aid the transition. Each group should meet separately to choose a solution. The groups should then meet to implement a solution and evaluate its effectiveness.

Reviewing Skills

Making Predictions Analyze the graph below, then answer the questions that follow.

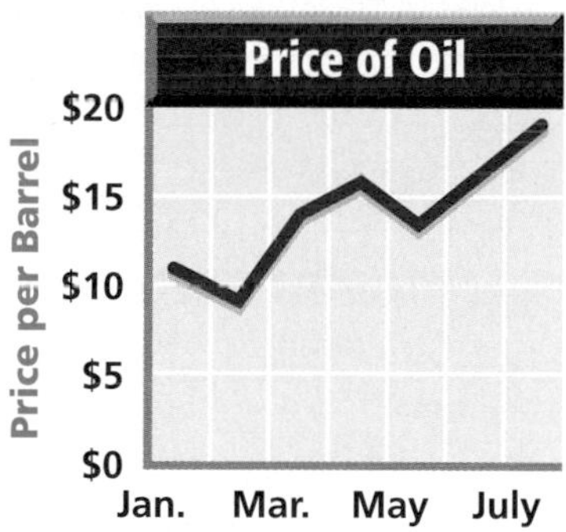

1. What trend does the graph show?
2. What do you predict will happen to Russia's oil exports as a result of this trend?
3. What do you predict will happen to the amount of oil available to Russian consumers?
4. On what do you base the prediction you made in question 3?

Technology Activity

Using a Database Prepare a database gathering information about the advantages and disadvantages of pure capitalism, pure socialism, authoritarian socialism, and market capitalism. First, reread the chapter and consider the advantages and disadvantages of each economic system. Then use resources at your school or local library or on the Internet to find other characteristics to include in your database. Share your database with the class.

Analyzing the Global *Economy*

Research privatization efforts in one of the following areas:

- Russia
- the other republics of the former Soviet Union
- Hungary
- Romania
- Bulgaria
- Poland
- Czech Republic
- Slovakia
- European Union
- Latin America
- People's Republic of China

Answer the following questions about your selected area. Report your findings to the class.

- How much of the region's government-owned businesses and property is being privatized?
- How fast it is being privatized?
- What are the benefits of privatization?
- What problems are associated with privatization?
- How popular are the privatization efforts?

CHAPTER 20

Economic Growth in Developing Nations

Why It's Important

How can developing countries become industrialized? Why should Americans be concerned about the economies of these countries? This chapter will explain how developing countries work to become part of the global economy.

To learn more about the economic challenges of developing nations, view the **Economics & You** *Chapter 26 video lesson:* **Developing Countries**

ECONOMICS *Online*

Chapter Overview Visit the *Economics Today and Tomorrow* Web site at ett.glencoe.com and click on ***Chapter 20—Chapter Overviews*** to preview chapter information.

SECTION 1

Characteristics of Developing Nations

Cover Story

The Columbus Dispatch, June 30, 1999

For coffee drinkers with a social conscience, a share of each coffee dollar now goes to fill the pockets of poor farmers instead of corporations. An importer called Equal Exchange pays coffee growers [in developing countries] a guaranteed minimum price for their beans, while cutting out middlemen to deliver the coffee from tree to table.

Before they began selling to Equal Exchange, some farmers earned as little as 20 cents a pound for their coffee. . . . Now they receive a minimum price of $1.26 a pound, plus a 15-cent premium for coffee grown without the use of chemicals.

Reader's Guide

Terms to Know

- developed nations
- developing nations
- subsistence agriculture
- infant mortality rate

Reading Objectives

1. About how many nations in the world are considered developed?
2. What are five economic characteristics of developing nations?
3. Why have poorly defined property rights been a problem in developing countries?

Many Americans may not realize it, but even the poorest families in the United States usually have an income far above the average income in much of the rest of the world. About one-half of the world's population lives at or close to subsistence, with just enough to survive. As you read this section, you'll learn about the characteristics of these *developing countries*.

Developed vs. Developing Nations

developed nations: *nations with relatively high standards of living and economies based more on industry than on agriculture*

developing nations: *nations with little industrial development and relatively low standards of living*

Of the more than 192 nations in the world, only about 35 are considered **developed nations.** These nations include the United States, Canada, all European countries, Japan, Australia, and New Zealand.

The remaining parts of the world's population live in **developing nations.** These are nations with less industrial development and a relatively low standard of living. Within this general definition, however, nations differ in many ways. **Figure 20.1** compares two developing nations, Madagascar and Mexico. The average income per person in Mexico is only about 30 percent that of the United States. Yet Mexico is much more developed and prosperous than almost all other developing nations.

Religion influences economic policies in some developing countries. This is not new. During the Middle Ages, the Church influenced many economic decisions throughout Europe. In colonial America, various churches influenced economics. Today some developing countries forbid lending money with interest. As a result, foreign investment in these countries is low.

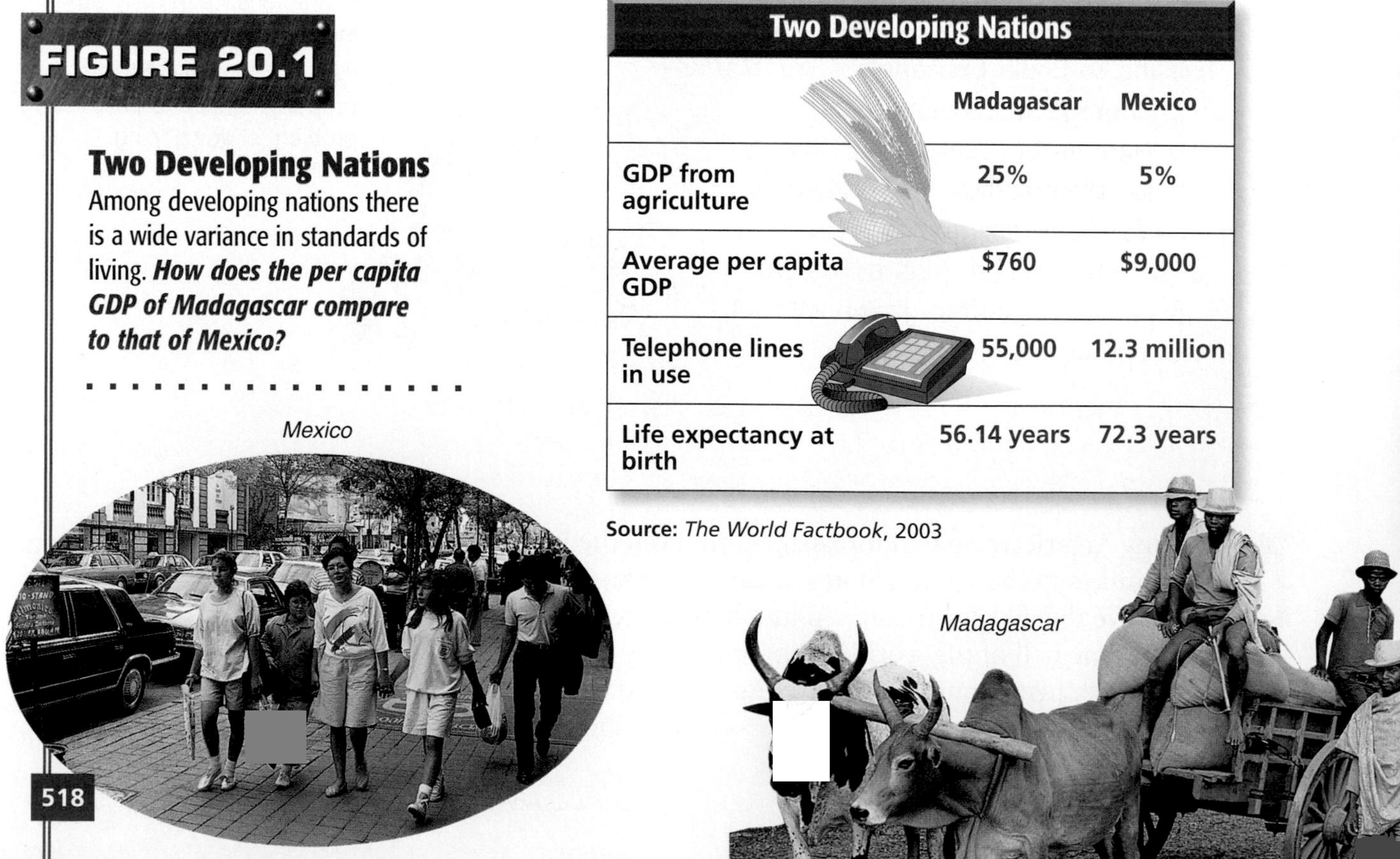

FIGURE 20.1

Two Developing Nations
Among developing nations there is a wide variance in standards of living. ***How does the per capita GDP of Madagascar compare to that of Mexico?***

Two Developing Nations

	Madagascar	Mexico
GDP from agriculture	25%	5%
Average per capita GDP	$760	$9,000
Telephone lines in use	55,000	12.3 million
Life expectancy at birth	56.14 years	72.3 years

Source: *The World Factbook*, 2003

FIGURE 20.2

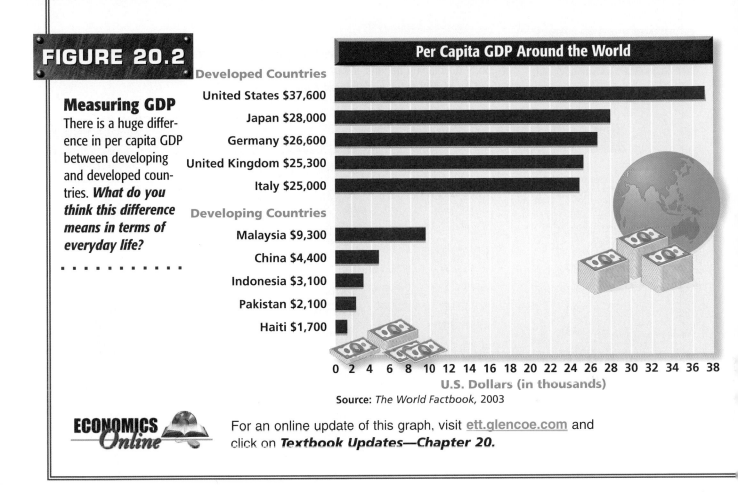

Measuring GDP
There is a huge difference in per capita GDP between developing and developed countries. ***What do you think this difference means in terms of everyday life?***

Per Capita GDP Around the World

Developed Countries
- United States $37,600
- Japan $28,000
- Germany $26,600
- United Kingdom $25,300
- Italy $25,000

Developing Countries
- Malaysia $9,300
- China $4,400
- Indonesia $3,100
- Pakistan $2,100
- Haiti $1,700

0 2 4 6 8 10 12 14 16 18 20 22 24 26 28 30 32 34 36 38
U.S. Dollars (in thousands)

Source: *The World Factbook,* 2003

For an online update of this graph, visit ett.glencoe.com and click on ***Textbook Updates—Chapter 20.***

Economic Characteristics

Economists often use per capita GDP as a rough measure of a nation's prosperity. Estimates of per capita GDP in the United States and other industrial nations range from $15,000 to about $35,000 per year.

Low GDP Per capita GDP in developing nations, in contrast, is considerably less, and in the world's poorest nations it is extremely low. Look at **Figure 20.2,** which shows per capita GDP for a number of developing countries. While developing nations may have many natural and human resources, they lack the equipment, financing, and knowledge necessary to put those resources to use.

An Agricultural Economy Agriculture is central to the economies of developing nations. Much of the population exists through **subsistence agriculture,** in which each family grows just enough to take care of its own needs. This means that no crops are available for export or to feed an industrial workforce.

subsistence agriculture: *growing of just enough food by a family to take care of its own needs; no crops are available for export or to feed an industrial workforce*

FIGURE 20.3

Comparing Nations Basic needs such as food and shelter are not met in many developing nations. ***What relationship between literacy rates and infant mortality rates is apparent from the chart?***

Economic and Social Statistics for Selected Nations				
Life expectancy at birth	Infant mortality: deaths per 1,000 live births	Country	Literacy (% of people who can read & write)	Population (in millions)
77	7	United States	97	290.3
81	3	Japan	99	127.2
80	5	Australia	100	19.7
79	7	Israel	95	6.1
79	6	Italy	99	58.0
72	25	China	86	1,287.0
72	24	Mexico	92	104.9
71	32	Brazil	86	182.0
63	60	India	60	1,050.0
31	199	Mozambique	48	17.5
61	66	Bangladesh	43	138.4
41	103	Ethiopia	43	66.6

Source: *The World Factbook*, 2003

For an online update of this graph, visit ett.glencoe.com and click on ***Textbook Updates—Chapter 20.***

Poor Health Conditions Poor health conditions are also common in many developing nations. Many people die from malnutrition or illness due to lack of food. Developing nations may also suffer from a shortage of modern doctors, hospitals, and medicines. The result is often a high **infant mortality rate** and a low life expectancy among adults. See **Figure 20.3.**

infant mortality rate: *death rate of infants who die during the first year of life*

Low Literacy Rate A fourth characteristic of developing nations is a low adult literacy rate–the percentage of people who are able to read and write. Governments have few resources to build and maintain schools. Many children miss school to help their families farm. The lack of a large pool of educated workers makes it difficult to train the population for needed technical and engineering jobs.

Rapid Population Growth A fifth characteristic of developing nations–rapid population growth–is often the source of many other problems, such as lack of food and housing. The population in the United States grows at a rate of about 1 percent a year. The growth rate in many developing nations is three and sometimes four times this rate. With a growth rate of 3.6 percent, a nation may double its population in about 20 years.

Weak Property Rights

Perhaps the most important aspect of many developing nations is weak property rights. Economists have generally found that governments in developing countries do not support a system of strong, well-defined private property rights.

A good example is Peru. Only 20 percent of Peru's land is legally owned. On the remaining 80 percent–which has no true legal ownership–peasant farmers till the land as they have done for generations. Without specifically defined private property rights, individuals cannot exchange land. As a result, no large-scale farming has occurred in Peru, and peasant families have little incentive to improve the value of the property on which they farm.

Practice and **assess** key skills with ***Skillbuilder Interactive Workbook, Level 2.***

SECTION 1 Assessment

Understanding Key Terms

1. **Define** developed nations, developing nations, subsistence agriculture, infant mortality rate.

Reviewing Objectives

2. About how many nations in the world are considered developed?
3. **Graphic Organizer** Create a diagram like the one below to explain five economic characteristics of developing nations.

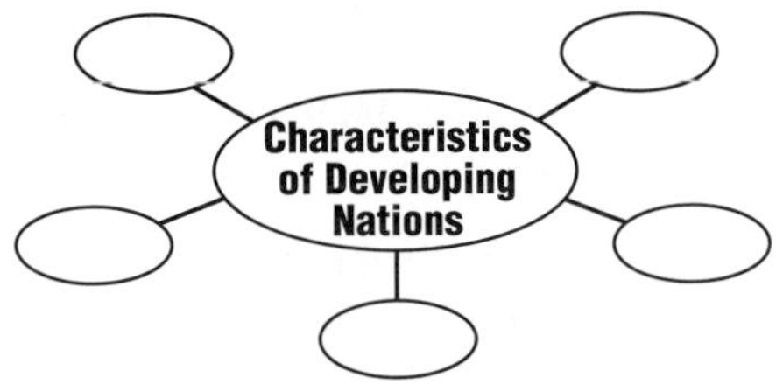

4. Why have poorly defined property rights been a problem in developing countries?

Applying Economic Concepts

5. **Developing Nations** Of the five characteristics of developing nations, which do you think would be most difficult to change? Why?

Critical Thinking Activity

6. **Categorizing Information** Using **Figure 20.3** for your data, input the information in a database. Sort the data by infant mortality, by life expectancy, and then by access to safe drinking water. Print out the new tables. Which country in your database has the highest infant mortality rate? Which country has the lowest life expectancy? Which two countries' populations have the highest access to safe drinking water?

People & Perspectives

Thomas Malthus

ECONOMIST (1766–1834)

- **Professor of political economy and modern history at the college of the East India Company at Haileybury from 1805 until his death**
- **Served briefly as an Anglican minister in the late 1700s and early 1800s**
- **Major publications include *An Essay on the Principle of Population* (1798), *An Inquiry Into the Nature and Progress of Rent* (1815), and *Principles of Political Economy* (1820)**

Thomas Malthus foresaw future world problems caused by a world population that was growing faster than food production. In *An Essay on the Principle of Population,* Malthus concludes that population growth will always outpace the supply of food:

"... I say, that the power of population is infinitely greater than the power in the earth to produce subsistence for man.

Population, when unchecked, increases in a geometrical ratio. Subsistence increases only in an arithmetical ratio. A slight acquaintance with numbers will show the immensity of the first power in comparison of the second.

By that law of our nature which makes food necessary to the life of man, the effects of these two unequal powers must be kept equal."

Malthus argues that people will always struggle to survive, and no social system can improve this condition:

"... This natural inequality of the two powers of population and of production in the earth and that great law of our nature which must constantly keep their effects equal form the great difficulty that to me appears insurmountable in the way to the perfectibility of society. All other arguments are of slight and subordinate consideration in comparison of this. I see no way by which man can escape from the weight of this law which pervades all animated nature. . . . And it appears, therefore, to be decisive against the possible existence of a society, all the members of which should live in ease, happiness, and comparative leisure; and feel no anxiety about providing the means of subsistence for themselves and families."

Checking for Understanding

1. **What is Malthus's principle, stated simply?**
2. **According to Malthus, why can there be no happy, worry-free society?**

SECTION 2

The Process of Economic Development

COVER STORY

THE COLUMBUS DISPATCH, SEPTEMBER 14, 1999

After a turbulent year in which the International Monetary Fund disbursed a record $30 billion to help beleaguered countries cope with economic troubles, the agency says the global financial crisis finally seems to be ebbing.

In its annual report, the 182-nation lending organization said that there have been encouraging signs, including a resumption of growth in some of the hardest hit nations.

INTERNATIONAL MONETARY FUND

READER'S GUIDE

Terms to Know

- nationalization
- foreign aid
- economic assistance
- technical assistance
- military assistance

Reading Objectives

1. Where do developing countries obtain outside sources of financing for economic development?
2. What agencies channel aid from major industrial nations to developing nations?
3. Why do nations give foreign aid?

Most nations pass through three stages of economic development. The first is the agricultural stage, when most of the population has jobs in farming. The second is the manufacturing stage, when much of the population has jobs in industry. In the third stage, many workers shift into the service sector–sales, food service, repair work, and computer and Internet services. As you read this section, you'll learn how developing nations use foreign investment and aid to move through the three stages of economic development.

FIGURE 20.4

The Agricultural Stage Many developing nations have a large labor force and the natural resources necessary for an industrial economy. They sometimes lack the financing, capital, and trained personnel to put these resources to work, however. ***What are two basic needs of nations in the agricultural stage?***

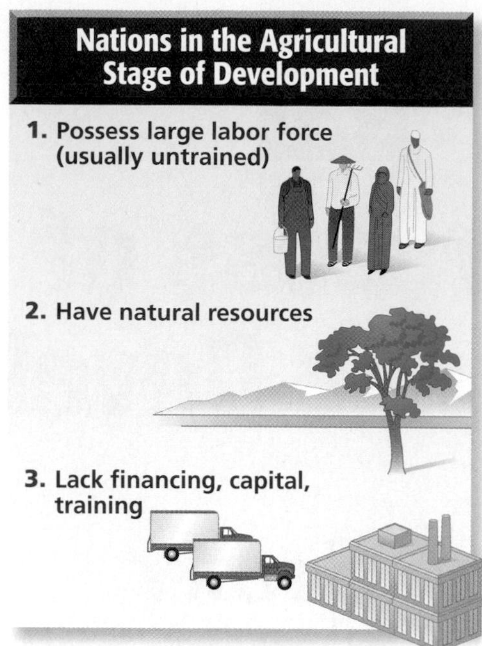

Nations in the Agricultural Stage of Development
1. Possess large labor force (usually untrained)
2. Have natural resources
3. Lack financing, capital, training

Financing Economic Development

Most developing nations are still in the agricultural stage. As **Figure 20.4** shows, three factors are evident in this stage. A basic problem for many developing nations is how to finance the equipment and training necessary to improve their standard of living.

One source of money capital is domestic savings. Many people believe that citizens of developing nations cannot save because they are barely subsisting. In fact, even very poor people do save something for their future. For example, in a traditional economy, saving may involve storing grain that can later be traded for other goods. Although this is saving, it does not provide a pool of money capital from which businesses can borrow for investment. Therefore, many developing nations must look to outside sources for investment capital. The two major outside sources of capital are investment by foreign businesses and foreign aid from developed nations.

FIGURE 20.5

Corporate Control Over Foreign Resources During the late 1970s, the Gulf and Western Corporation (later Paramount) owned 264,000 acres, or 8 percent, of the Dominican Republic's available farmland. It produced one-third of the nation's sugar and had investments in livestock, tobacco, and fruit and vegetable production as well. The corporation was accused of converting farmland used for local crops to the more profitable production of sugarcane.

Foreign Investment: Attractions and Risks

Investors are attracted to developing countries because of their low wage rates, few regulations, and abundant raw materials. Investment may include a corporation's setting up branch offices and fully owned companies, or buying into companies already established in developing nations.

Besides attractions, there are also risks to investing in developing countries. Political instability within a nation's borders leads to uncertainty. If the government changes often, or if terrorist groups threaten stability, foreign businesses may lose their investment. In some cases, the government in developing nations has taken control of private firms—a practice called **nationalization**—forcing the firm's owners out of the country.

Problems exist from the developing nation's viewpoint as well. In nations with heavy foreign investment, citizens often criticize the economic control these foreign companies have over their resources. See **Figure 20.5.** What these critics may not consider is that factors of production remain idle unless such firms organize the materials and skills of the country's inhabitants.

Economic Assistance

nationalization: *placement of industries under government ownership*

Foreign Aid Foreign aid is a second type of financing available to nations. Sometimes it plays an important role in economic development. **Foreign aid** is the money, goods, and services given by governments and private organizations to help other nations and their citizens. Several kinds of foreign aid exist.

foreign aid: *money, goods, and services given by governments and private organizations to help other nations and their citizens*

Economic assistance consists of loans and outright grants of money or equipment to other nations. One use of such aid is to help build transportation and communications systems. A second use for economic assistance is to purchase basic producer goods, including machinery that will increase a nation's productivity.

economic assistance: *loans and outright grants of money or equipment to other nations*

Technical assistance includes providing professionals such as engineers, teachers, technicians, and consultants to teach skills. Such training is designed to strengthen a nation's human resources in the same way economic assistance increases a nation's capital resources.

technical assistance: *aid in the form of engineers, teachers, and technicians to teach skills to individuals in other nations*

Military assistance involves giving either economic or technical assistance to a nation's armed forces. For example, a country may lend a developing nation the money to purchase airplanes or tanks, or it might make a gift of such goods.

military assistance: *aid given to a nation's armed forces*

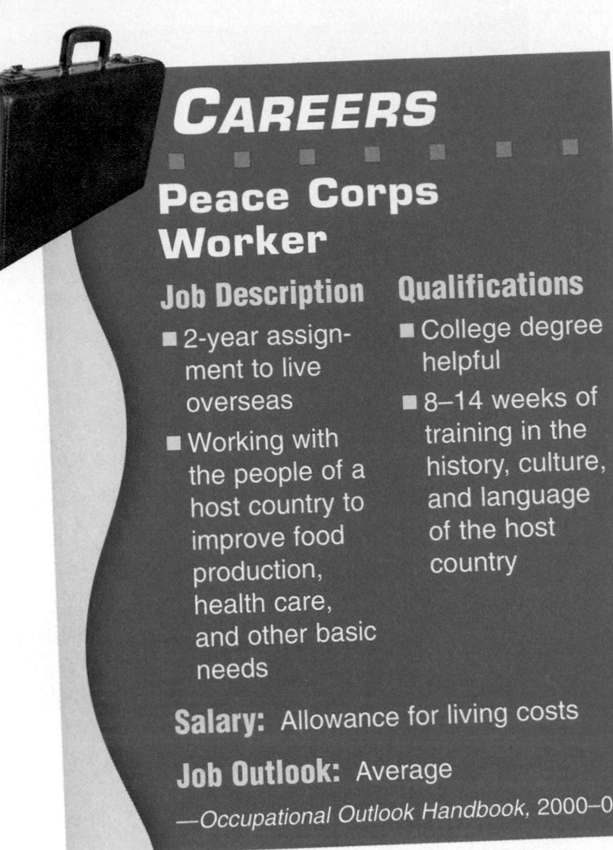

Emergency shipments of food, clothing, and medical supplies to victims of drought, earthquakes, floods, and other disasters are also considered foreign aid. Governments, many private organizations, and several agencies of the United Nations provide such assistance. This type of foreign aid, however, is not directed toward economic development.

Who Supplies Foreign Aid?

Many of the developed nations offer some type of foreign aid to developing nations. After World War II, the United States devoted most of its foreign assistance to help rebuild Europe's war-torn economy through the Marshall Plan. Today, most American foreign aid is sent to developing nations in the Middle East and Southeast Asia. Nations in Africa receive about 11 percent, Latin America about 14 percent, and East Asia and the Pacific about 5 percent.

Comparing Aid Many other major industrial nations also give foreign aid. France and Great Britain, for example, have concentrated most of their aid programs on their former colonies in Africa and Asia. Germany and Japan both began giving aid to developing nations after their own economies had recovered from World War II.

The dollar amount of American foreign aid may sound high—$7.4 billion in 2001. When viewed as a percentage of GDP, however, that amount is just a fraction of what many other nations give in foreign aid. Norway's foreign aid, for example, is 0.9 percent of that nation's GDP. By comparison, foreign aid given by the United States is less than 0.1 percent of its GDP.

Student Web Activity Visit the *Economics Today and Tomorrow* Web site at ett.glencoe.com and click on ***Chapter 20—Student Web Activities*** to keep abreast of developments in foreign aid.

Channels of Aid The United States channels much of its foreign aid to other nations through the U.S. Agency for International Development (USAID). Funds are also channeled through United Nations agencies, including the International Bank for Reconstruction and Development—usually called the World Bank. Founded in 1944, the World Bank provides loans and other services to developing nations. Two affiliates of the bank are the International Development Association (IDA), which lends money to nations that are the least able to obtain financing from other sources, and the International Finance Corporation (IFC), which encourages private investment in developing nations.

Recently, the International Monetary Fund (IMF) has become a major foreign aid agency. It has offered a variety of loans to Russia, Thailand, South Korea, Indonesia, Malaysia, Brazil, and Mexico.

These foreign aid agencies have grown increasingly alarmed as many developing nations find themselves unable to repay their foreign debts. By the late 1990s, the level of indebtedness had become extremely high, with about 40 of the most heavily indebted nations owing the IMF and World Bank more than $127 billion. In 1999 the leaders of the major industrial nations proposed a plan that would cancel some of this debt. By 2001, 23 countries had received $54 billion in debt relief under this plan.

Reasons for Giving Foreign Aid

Humanitarianism is the basis of some foreign aid. The relief of human suffering is a major goal in particular of many private aid organizations. See **Figure 20.6** on page 528. At least three other reasons are also given for providing government-sponsored foreign aid.

The first reason involves economics. It is usually in the best interests of developed nations to encourage international trade. Foreign aid expands a nation's markets for exports and provides new opportunities for private investment.

Politics is also a reason for giving foreign aid. From 1947–1991, an important objective of American foreign aid was to enhance the appeal of democracy and prevent Communists from coming to

Global *Economy*

Leading Suppliers of Foreign Aid

Data collected by the Organization for Economic Cooperation and Development (OECD) shows that the top five suppliers of foreign aid—in total dollars—for 2002 were as follows:

United States	$12.9 billion
Japan	$9.2 billion
Germany	$5.4 billion
France	$5.2 billion
Great Britain	$4.7 billion

When foreign aid is presented as a percentage of GDP, however, the "top five" table has a very different look:

Denmark	0.99%
Norway	0.92
Netherlands	0.83
Sweden	0.77
Luxembourg	0.71

FIGURE 20.6

Humanitarianism Many industrialized nations have decided that they have a responsibility to help end world hunger and disease.

power. The United States has also used foreign aid to build political friends that will support it in such international bodies as the United Nations.

A final reason for providing foreign aid is to help protect a nation's own security. Economic aid is often a down payment on a military alliance with a developing nation. Through alliances, the United States has gained overseas military bases and observation posts that it can use to gather information about other nations. This type of plan can backfire, however, if a friendly government loses power. In such a situation, the military equipment given to that nation would fall into the hands of the new government, one that may be hostile.

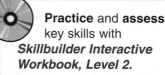

Practice and **assess** key skills with ***Skillbuilder Interactive Workbook, Level 2.***

SECTION 2 Assessment

Understanding Key Terms

1. **Define** nationalization, foreign aid, economic assistance, technical assistance, military assistance.

Reviewing Objectives

2. Where do developing countries obtain outside sources of financing for economic development?
3. What agencies channel aid from major industrial nations to developing nations?
4. **Graphic Organizer** Create a diagram like the one in the next column to explain why nations give foreign aid.

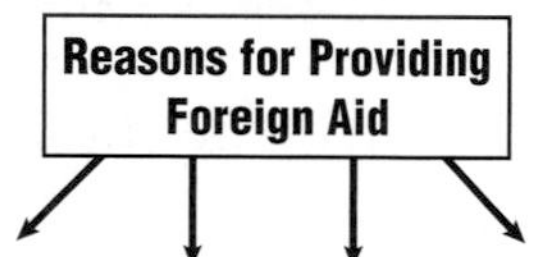

Applying Economic Concepts

5. **Foreign Aid** Why do you think United States foreign aid—as a percentage of its GDP—has declined in recent years?

Critical Thinking Activity

6. **Distinguishing Fact From Opinion** Based on the information under the heading "Reasons for Giving Foreign Aid," write an opinion article titled "The Most Important Reason for Giving Foreign Aid."

SECTION 3

Obstacles to Growth in Developing Nations

Cover Story

Business Week, September 20, 1999

Although the sheer numbers of people living in poverty seem overwhelming—at least 3 billion subsist on less than $2 a day—[economist] Amartya Sen is optimistic that real progress can be made over the next few generations. . . .

The world's "rich" nations can help by moving ahead with debt-pardoning schemes. . . . But governments in developing countries also must cut back on military spending and corruption and spend more on health and education, especially for women.

Reader's Guide

Terms to Know

- bureaucracies
- capital flight

Reading Objectives

1. What are the main obstacles to economic growth in developing nations?
2. Why did Indonesia fail to sustain rapid economic growth?

The successful rebuilding of Europe's economy following World War II convinced many economists that injections of money capital into a nation could achieve rapid economic growth. As a result, billions of dollars flowed into developing nations during the 1950s and 1960s. Aid to many of these nations, however, failed to produce the same growth as Europe experienced. In this section, you'll learn why developing nations have not followed the same path of recovery as Europe did in the 1940s.

Four Obstacles to Growth

Many developing nations face a number of obstacles to growth that are not immediately solved by injections of money capital.

Economic Connection to... Geography

The World's People

There are now over 6 billion people living on the earth. More than 80 percent live in the less developed nations, and demographers (scientists who study population) say the imbalance will get worse.

Population in developing nations is growing at a rate of 1.7 percent a year—or nearly 82 million people. In contrast, the population of developed nations is increasing at a growth rate of 0.1 percent—which adds 1.5 million people annually. If growth rates remain unchanged, demographers project that the world's population will grow by some 2 billion over the next 25 years. ■

Europe's rapid recovery after World War II was a special case. In 1945 countries in Europe already had skilled labor forces, advanced organizations such as corporations and trade groups, and experienced government **bureaucracies,** or specialized offices and agencies. This is not the case in developing nations.

bureaucracies: *offices and agencies of the government that each deal with a specific area*

Attitudes and Beliefs One obstacle to economic growth resides in people's attitudes and beliefs, which are usually slow to change. In many developing nations, people live and work much as their ancestors did hundreds of years before. Innovation of any sort is often viewed with suspicion. Farmers, for example, may be reluctant to accept a new way of plowing, even though it means better soil conservation and a larger harvest.

Continued Rapid Population Growth A high population growth rate may reduce the rate of growth of a nation's standard of living. Even if a nation's economy is growing, per capita GDP will decrease if its population is growing at a faster rate.

Misuse of Resources Development in some nations has been slowed by the misuse of resources. For example, aid to the military instead could be spent on agricultural development or on training.

Corruption among government and military leaders also weakens the economies of many developing nations. Local currency may be legally exported or illegally sent from the country into leaders' private bank accounts, a practice known as **capital flight.** Even if new, honest leaders take over, they may have inherited crushing debts from previously corrupt regimes.

capital flight: *the legal or illegal export of currency or money capital from a nation by that nation's leaders*

Trade Restrictions To develop domestic industries, many developing nations have used import restrictions such as quotas and tariffs. These trade restrictions prevent consumers from purchasing cheaper foreign substitutes.

Gecko from Indonesia's rain forest

Case Study: Indonesia

When Indonesia won independence from the Netherlands in 1949, it seemed well equipped for economic growth. It was the world's sixth most populous nation. It was also rich in minerals, and had vast oil reserves as well as valuable farmland and rain forests. During his regime, President Achmed Sukarno obtained foreign aid totaling more than $2 billion from both capitalist and communist nations. Yet Indonesia's economy was a disaster.

The reasons behind this failure reveal some of the problems of trying to bring rapid growth to developing nations. One problem involved attitudes. Indonesians lacked a sense of national identity. The country had been formed from several former Dutch colonies, and its people were divided by nationality, religion, and politics. The major blame for economic failure, however, can be placed on Sukarno's economic policies. See **Figure 20.7.**

FIGURE 20.7

Indonesia's Economy Under Sukarno and Suharto

President Sukarno's Regime (1949–1965)	General Suharto's Regime (1965–1998)
1. Loss of foreign aid from the United States resulted from strong opposition to capitalism.	1. Control of the money supply was tightened and confidence in government increased. Initially, corruption was reduced and bureaucracy decreased.
2. Foreign aid from former Soviet Union and others was often wasted on projects for the rich such as sports stadiums and department stores. Mineral resources were not developed, and decaying roads and rail lines went without repairs.	2. Alliances with some Western nations were made.
3. Nationalization of businesses placed them under government ownership, discouraging foreign investment.	3. Foreign aid and investment increased, and resources were focused on improving agricultural output and oil production.
4. Heavy regulation of business, a huge government bureaucracy, and widespread corruption hurt the economy.	4. Industry was developed. More funds could be spent on industry because fewer funds were needed to import food.
5. Inflation soared out of control. The nation's price index rose from 100 in 1953 to 3,000 only 10 years later. By the mid-1960s, the national debt was $2.5 billion.	5. A system of "crony" capitalism developed—family members and close friends owned or controlled major businesses.
	6. The economy declined dramatically in 1998, forcing the resignation of General Suharto as the nation's leader. He was replaced by B.J. Habibie.

Subsequent improvements in Indonesia's economy were credited to General Suharto, who assumed power in 1965. Suharto's initial economic policies, as listed in **Figure 20.7** on page 531, made Indonesia one of the fastest-growing economies among developing nations by the end of the 1970s.

Unfortunately, Indonesia found that reliance on a few products could be dangerous. In the early 1980s, the world "oil glut" cut deeply into the nation's trade income. When an economic crisis hit Southeast Asia in 1997–1998, Indonesia's economy tumbled. Riots ensued and General Suharto resigned.

Indonesia's value as a case study lies in the variety of lessons it teaches about foreign aid. It illustrates that simply pouring money capital into a developing nation will not guarantee economic growth. Indonesia also shows that growth *can* occur if government restrictions on economic activity are reduced.

Foreign aid must be used wisely in combination with domestic savings, foreign investment, and government policies that ensure economic stability. Finally, the case study points out that growth of a developing nation's economy may prove temporary if it depends on only one or two products.

Practice and **assess** key skills with ***Skillbuilder Interactive Workbook, Level 2.***

SECTION 3 Assessment

Understanding Key Terms

1. **Define** bureaucracies, capital flight.

Reviewing Objectives

2. **Graphic Organizer** Create a diagram like the one below to explain the main obstacles to economic growth in developing nations.

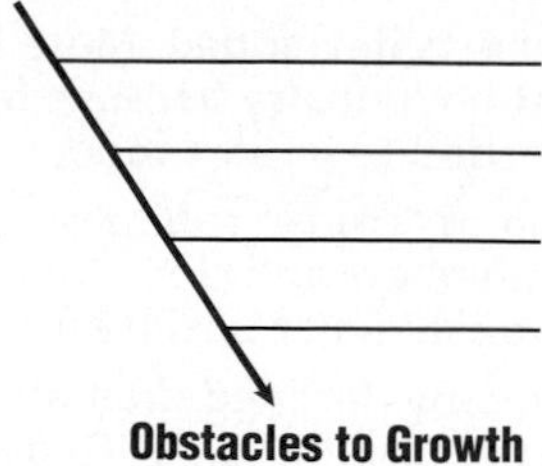

3. Why did Indonesia fail to sustain rapid economic growth?

Applying Economic Concepts

4. **Economic Policy** What economic policies exhibited by a foreign government would discourage you from investing money capital in that nation's businesses?

Critical Thinking Activity

5. **Understanding Cause and Effect** Explain why import restrictions are an obstacle to growth in a developing nation. Why do developing nations impose import restrictions such as quotas and tariffs in the first place?

BusinessWeek

SPOTLIGHT ON THE ECONOMY

Indonesia—A Pariah State?

Check It Out! In this chapter you learned about Indonesia's struggle to become a developed nation. In this article, read to learn about the economic backlash it faced as a result of a 1999 government-approved massacre against civilians in Indonesia's former province of East Timor.

Indonesian military

Whatever the motives of the hardened men who run Indonesia, it is clear that the damage to this Asian giant will be immense. Nothing is certain any longer—the country's passage into democracy, its economic recovery, even who is running the government now. With relations with the International Monetary Fund already inflamed over a banking scandal, Indonesia is on the verge of being cut off from new loans that are needed to stabilize the financial system. Economists have lowered forecasts for this fiscal year, from 2% growth to negative 0.8%. Ethnic Chinese businessmen, still traumatized by deadly rioting in 1998, are moving funds offshore again. As the international backlash mounts, Indonesia is close to being branded a pariah state.

Looting in East Timor

. . . The buildup of anger does not bode well for business in Indonesia. Standard & Poor's has downgraded Indonesia's currency rating, citing political tension and the risk that international aid may be cut. On Sept. 10, a group of ethnic Chinese businessmen from Indonesia met in Singapore to compare notes on how much capital they were pulling out.

Think About It

1. **What economic actions resulted from Indonesia's massacre of East Timor citizens?**
2. **Why is it significant that capital is being removed from Indonesia?**

SECTION 4

Industrialization and the Future

READER'S GUIDE

Terms to Know
- vicious cycle of poverty

Reading Objectives
1. What are four problems of rapid industrialization in developing nations?
2. In addition to poverty, what factors influence economic development?
3. What is the relationship between the increased flow of information and international economic cooperation?

COVER STORY

HOOVER'S COMPANY PROFILES, JULY 8, 2003

Yanzhou Coal Mining Co. is helping fuel China's industrialization. The company, a leader in coal production in eastern China, produces more than 34 metric tons per year and had about 2 billion metric tons in proven and probable reserves. . . . It also owns major rail transport assets.

The high standard of living of any developed nation is usually a result of its high level of industrialization. As you read earlier in this chapter, industrialization is the second stage of economic development. As a result, many developing nations have tried to improve their standard of living by shifting their resources away from agriculture to industry. As you read this section, however, you'll learn that attempts at *rapid* industrialization can prove a wasteful use of scarce resources.

Problems of Rapid Industrialization

There are four problems of rapid industrialization: investing unwisely, not adapting to change, using inappropriate technology, and rushing through the stages of development.

Unwise Investments Some developing nations have invested in steel factories and automobile plants. These nations do not necessarily have a comparative advantage in producing steel or automobiles, however. As a result, the people in these nations are worse off. Citizens receive less economic value from their resources than they would have received from other investments. In India, for instance, steel mills produced steel 2–3 times more expensively than what it would have cost if it had been imported.

Not Adapting to Change Rapid economic change also can be harmful if a nation's population does not have time to adapt to new patterns of living and working. Suppose much of a nation is converted from subsistence farming to growing one crop for export. This may displace large numbers of people who are no longer needed for farming. Unable to find work in the countryside, many will migrate to already overcrowded cities.

Using Inappropriate Technology Another aspect of industrialization and balanced growth is the need to use technology that is appropriate, or suitable, to a culture. See **Figure 20.8.** For example, instead of buying tractors, it may be better for a nation using wooden plows to first replace them with ones made of steel. The benefits of modernization can be distributed more widely because steel plows are cheaper than tractors.

Rushing Through the Stages of Development Many economists believe industrialization is generally more beneficial if it comes about naturally. Time allows nations to adapt successfully to one stage of development before moving on to the next. Gradually, the developing nation increases its income and savings and its number of skilled and educated workers. Economic conditions reach the point where businesspeople freely decide to build factories instead of increasing farm output.

Technological Change Many people fear change. These storekeepers in Russia still use an abacus to tally receipts as they move slowly toward capitalism.

FIGURE 20.9

Factors Influencing Economic Development Three major factors affect how nations develop economically.

A Supportive Political Structure

Typically, in countries in which government-owned business accounts for a small percentage of GDP, more economic development can be found. If, however, the political system supports and enforces any types of price controls, there will be less incentive for entrepreneurs to enter business.

B Appropriate Incentive Structure

The incentive structure in any economy determines how fast that economy will grow and develop. For example, developing countries need tax rates that are not too high and a legal system that protects private property rights.

C Trade With the Outside World

The more a country trades with the outside world, the faster it will grow. Therefore, developing nations can develop more quickly if they stop restricting trade.

Economic Development

Several major factors influence economic development, as shown in **Figure 20.9.** These include trade with the outside world, an appropriate incentive structure, and a supportive political structure. Natural resources such as trees and minerals and reduced population growth are important factors as well.

Not having one of these factors, however, does not mean that a less developed country will be trapped in underdevelopment or in the **vicious cycle of poverty.** This theory states that developing nations are poor because they cannot save and invest, but they cannot save and invest *because* they are poor.

vicious cycle of poverty: *situation in which a less-developed country with low per capita incomes cannot save and invest enough to achieve acceptable rates of economic growth and thus is trapped*

Economic development normally depends on entrepreneurs who are able to perceive opportunities and then take advantage of those opportunities. The political system must be such that risk-taking entrepreneurs are rewarded, however. That requires well-established property rights and no fear of government nationalization of business.

The more certain private property rights are, the more investment there will be. When people have property rights that are supported and enforced by the government, they feel confident about making investments.

Information Leads to Cooperation

Because of the media and the Internet, information about the higher standards of living of developed countries is known today even in the most remote villages of developing nations. One effect of this increased flow of information has been to convince developing nations of the benefits of working together. These nations have come to realize that, compared to large developed nations such as the United States, each developing nation has little influence over world trade. Together, however, the developing nations can and do have power in the international economic community.

A second trend in recent years has been toward more cooperation between developed and developing nations. Since 1981, leaders of both developing and developed nations have met many times. A major purpose of these meetings is to establish global negotiations aimed at a more equal distribution of the world's wealth and resources. Some suggestions to achieve this goal have included low tariffs for developing nations and an "income tax" on developed nations to pay for international assistance programs.

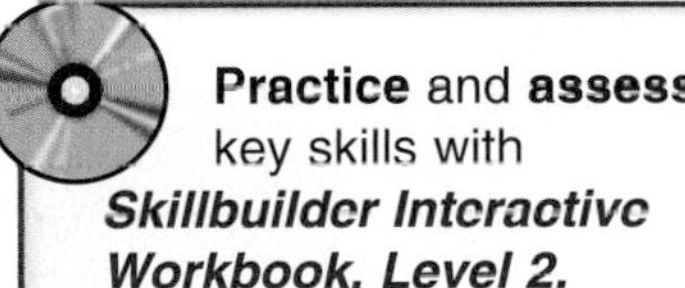

Practice and **assess** key skills with ***Skillbuilder Interactive Workbook, Level 2.***

SECTION 4 Assessment

Understanding Key Terms

1. **Define** vicious cycle of poverty.

Reviewing Objectives

2. **Graphic Organizer** Create a diagram like the one below to describe four problems of rapid industrialization in developing nations.

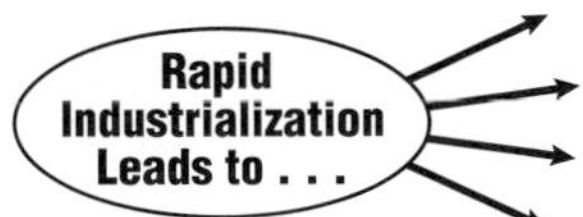

3. In addition to poverty, what factors influence economic development?
4. What is the relationship between the increased flow of information and international economic cooperation?

Applying Economic Concepts

5. **Economic Development** Assume that you are the president of a developing country. What policies would you propose to improve the nation's chances of attracting entrepreneurs?

Critical Thinking Activity

6. **Understanding Cause and Effect** How do you think the economic growth and development of developing countries will affect you in the future?

Study & Writing Skills

Taking a Test

Learning how to take a test is an important skill. Whether you are in school or looking for a job, you will be asked to take many tests during your life.

- Start studying several days before the test. In particular, review your notes and become familiar with new vocabulary terms.
- Read the test directions and the questions carefully.
- Pace yourself so that you leave enough time to answer all of the questions.
- Skip the more difficult questions, then come back to them after you've answered the other questions.
- Do not leave any answer blank. A good guess may be the correct answer.
- Some essay questions start with the words *discuss, describe,* or *explain.* This means that you must give full answers, usually written in complete sentences.

Learning the Skill

When your teacher announces that you will be tested soon, follow the guidelines for taking a test listed on the left.

Practicing the Skill

On a separate sheet of paper, answer the following questions.

1. The most important rule in taking a test is to
  a. read the directions and the questions carefully;
  b. work as fast as you can;
  c. answer all the questions.

2. Which of the following may be caused by the other three?
  a. failure on a test;
  b. not enough studying;
  c. going to bed late the night before a test;
  d. taking poor notes in class.

3. True or False? A true or false question is false if any part of it is false.

Application Activity

Learning the proper way to take a test is important, but writing the actual test questions yourself is an effective way to study for the test. Reread Section 4—Industrialization and the Future—in this chapter. Practice writing five multiple-choice questions and five true/false questions for this section.

Practice and **assess** key skills with ***Skillbuilder Interactive Workbook, Level 2.***

CHAPTER 20 Summary

ECONOMICS Online

Chapter Overview Visit the *Economics Today and Tomorrow* Web site at ett.glencoe.com and click on ***Chapter 20—Chapter Overviews*** to review chapter information.

SECTION 1 Characteristics of Developing Nations

- **Developing nations** are those with less industrial development and a relatively low standard of living.
- Five characteristics of developing nations include a low GDP, an economy based on **subsistence agriculture,** poor health conditions (including a high **infant mortality rate**), a low literacy rate, and rapid population growth.
- Many developing nations have governments that do not support private property rights.

SECTION 2 The Process of Economic Development

- The three stages of economic development are the agricultural stage, the manufacturing stage, and the service sector stage.
- A basic problem for developing nations is how to finance the equipment and training necessary to improve their standard of living.
- Developing nations receive financing through foreign investment and **foreign aid.** Foreign aid can be given in the form of **economic assistance, technical assistance,** and/or **military assistance.**
- International agencies, including the World Bank and the International Monetary Fund, channel funds to developing nations.
- Developed countries provide foreign aid for humanitarian, economic, political, and military reasons.

SECTION 3 Obstacles to Growth in Developing Nations

- Four obstacles hamper economic growth in developing nations: traditional attitudes and beliefs, continued rapid population growth, a misuse of resources (including **capital flight**), and trade restrictions.
- The economic failure of Indonesia highlights some of the problems associated with rapid economic growth—lack of a national identity, massive government corruption and **bureaucracies,** reliance on a single product, and government interference in trade.

SECTION 4 Industrialization and the Future

- There are four problems of rapid industrialization: unwise investments, not enough time to adapt to new patterns of living and working, use of inappropriate technology, and inadequate time to move through the stages of development.
- Factors that spur economic growth include trade with the outside world, an appropriate incentive structure, a supportive political structure, natural resources, and reduced population growth.
- Developing countries can get out of the **vicious cycle of poverty** if their political system rewards entrepreneurs and promotes private property rights.

CHAPTER 20

Assessment and Activities

Self-Check Quiz Visit the *Economics Today and Tomorrow* Web site at ett.glencoe.com and click on ***Chapter 20—Self-Check Quizzes*** to prepare for the Chapter Test.

Identifying Key Terms

Write the letter of the definition in Column B that correctly defines each term in Column A.

Column A

1. foreign aid
2. subsistence agriculture
3. developing nations
4. technical assistance
5. developed nations
6. bureaucracies
7. nationalization

Column B

a. raising enough food sufficient for family needs only
b. nonindustrialized countries
c. money, goods, and services given by governments and private organizations to help other nations and their citizens
d. aid in the form of professional expertise from engineers, doctors, teachers, and other specialists
e. placement of railroads, businesses, and other industries under government ownership
f. nations with relatively high standards of living and economies based more on industry than on agriculture
g. offices and agencies of the government that each deal with a specific area

Recalling Facts and Ideas

Section 1

1. The per capita income in countries such as the United States, Japan, and Germany is approximately how many thousands of dollars?
2. What characteristics identify most developing nations?

Section 2

3. List two affiliates of the World Bank.
4. What is the difference between military assistance and technical assistance?
5. In what stage of development are most developing nations?
6. What are some reasons for giving foreign aid?

Section 3

7. How is rapid population growth an obstacle to economic development?
8. How do international trade restrictions hinder economic growth in developing nations?

Section 4

9. Why are property rights a factor in economic development?
10. How can a developing nation's government influence foreign investment?

Thinking Critically

1. **Making Inferences** Is an abundance of natural resources required in order for a country to have economic growth and development? Explain.
2. **Determining Cause and Effect** Create a diagram like the one below to explain the relationship between well-defined and government-enforced private property rights and the incentive structure for investment in a nation.

Applying Economic Concepts

Foreign Aid Developed countries gave much foreign aid to Russia during the 1990s. Use the information you have obtained in this chapter about the problems facing developing countries and the difficulty of using foreign aid wisely. Make a list of the obstacles that Russia faces in putting to good use the foreign aid it receives.

Cooperative Learning Project

Organize into at least five groups. Each group will study one part or region of the world, such as northern Africa, central Africa, Southeast Asia, Central America, or Western Europe.

The goal of each group is to determine the percentage of the economy devoted to agriculture and the percentage devoted to industry. Each member of each group will obtain the relevant information for one or more countries in his or her chosen region. Compare the information obtained, selecting one person to prepare summary statistics for your group's region.

Reviewing Skills

Taking a Test Write 10 questions that could be used on a test for this chapter. Write 3 multiple-choice questions, 3 true/false questions, 3 matching questions, and 1 short-answer question. Include short directions for each type of question. Exchange your test with another student. After taking each other's test, analyze the questioning strategies used. Were wrong choices obvious? Which type of questions were the most difficult to answer? Why?

Technology Activity

Using E-Mail Choose a developing country to investigate. E-mail the embassy of that country in Washington, D.C. To do so, you will first need to use the Internet to locate the embassy's E-mail address. Using a search engine, type in the name of the country. Then explore the sites listed until you find the E-mail address. Finally, write an E-mail asking for information on the country's history as well as current statistics on the country's economic development. Share the responses you receive with the class.

Analyzing the Global *Economy*

Select a developing nation and write a research report about the economic and social conditions of that nation by collecting facts on housing, food production, transportation, medical care, and the role of the government. The most reliable sources are the International Monetary Fund Reports, United Nations reports, and government statistical bulletins.

The Global Economy

Why It's Important

Why do foreigners invest in the United States? Should we be worried about foreigners investing in our country? This chapter will explain how global integration is now a fact of life.

To learn more about the challenges and opportunities of a global economy, view the **Economics & You** *Chapter 27 video lesson:* **Global Economic Challenges**

Chapter Overview Visit the *Economics Today and Tomorrow* Web site at ett.glencoe.com and click on ***Chapter 21—Chapter Overviews*** to preview chapter information.

SECTION 1

Reasons for and Results of Global Integration

Cover Story

The Economist, May 3, 2003

Those who believe that globalization throttles democracy, gouges the poor and fouls the environment are bound to regard today's mostly open markets for international capital as evil.

. . . No serious economist questions the case for international integration through flows of goods and services, though there is a lively argument over how integration through trade can best be brought about. Trade is good. But even the most enthusiastic advocate of economic integration may be starting to wonder whether unimpeded flows of capital are quite such a blessing.

Reader's Guide

Terms to Know

- global integration
- telecommunications

Reading Objectives

1. How has improved telecom munications affected global integration?
2. What kinds of financial investments are traded in global markets?

In the United States, it is not unusual to ride on a bus that was made in Germany or drive a Japanese-made car. A Canadian may own a local restaurant. Some of the restaurant's food perhaps has been imported from Mexico, France, and Spain. Interest rates may fall because political upheavals in other countries have caused businesses there to invest their money capital in politically stable America. In this section, you'll learn that we now live not just as Americans, but as part of the global economy.

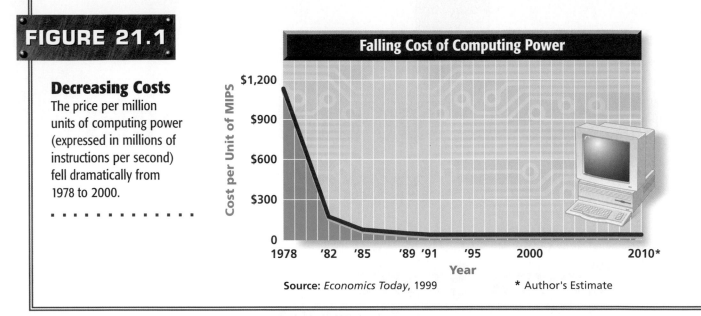

FIGURE 21.1

Decreasing Costs
The price per million units of computing power (expressed in millions of instructions per second) fell dramatically from 1978 to 2000.

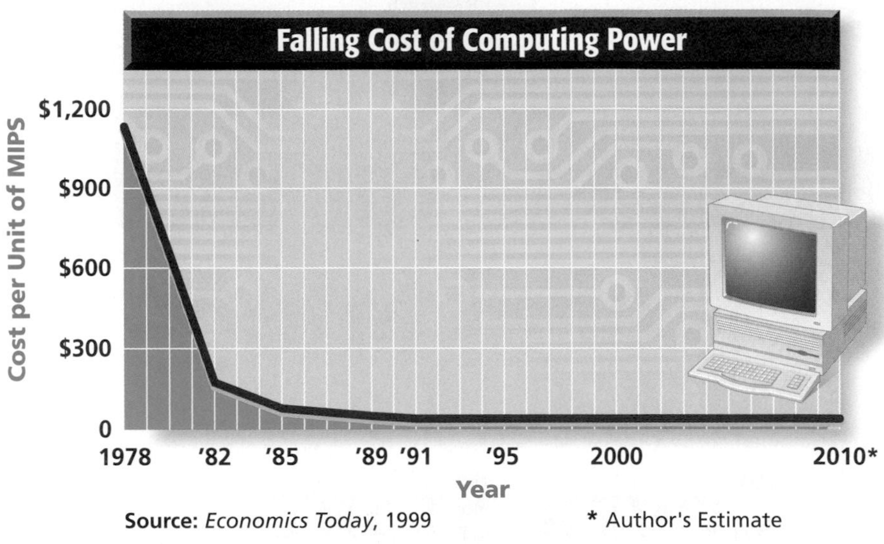

Improved Telecommunications

global integration: *interdependency among the countries of the world, especially within financial markets and telecommunications*

telecommunications: *long-distance communication, usually electronic, using communications satellites and fiber-optic cables*

Global integration—the interdependency among countries—has increased dramatically over the past several decades. Many reasons explain this increase. One reason is improved **telecommunications,** or long-distance electronic communication.

The first transatlantic telegraph cable was completed in 1866. Before then it took two weeks to find out the price of the dollar in London. The telegraph cable reduced that time to two minutes. With the invention of the semiconductor—the computer chip—telecommunications grew rapidly. Look at **Figure 21.1,** which shows how much the price of computing power has fallen in just the last few years.

Several other inventions and factors have influenced the rapid improvement in worldwide telecommunications. Communications satellites circle the earth day and night. Radio and television waves, beamed up to them, are reflected down to other parts of the earth. On the earth's surface, fiber-optic cables are being placed throughout much of North America and already exist in parts of Europe. The rapid expansion of the Internet has also been an important aspect of the worldwide communications system.

Consider some of the ways cheap and readily available satellite television has transformed the information received in the Eastern Hemisphere. Before the 1990s virtually all of the television (and radio) available in the Eastern Hemisphere was both state-run and state-controlled. Viewers saw few programs and advertisements from other parts of the world. Today, people in Asia receive sports, music, soap operas, news, and advertisements via satellite that are free of government control. See **Figure 21.2.**

How does this increase in communications affect the rest of the world, particularly Asia? Viewers in other nations are changing their cultural tastes and buying habits. In India, viewers buy copies of outfits worn by popular music television personalities. Viewers demand foreign products they see advertised on television, which increases exports from the originating nations. In addition, because many popular television programs are transmitted in English, more of the world's people want to learn English as a second language.

The Globalization of Financial Markets

Because of the speed and power of computers and the affordability of telecommunications, the world has become one financial market. This globalization started in the 1970s and 1980s, when United States banks developed worldwide branch networks for loans and foreign exchange trading. Today money and financial capital markets are truly global, and many stocks and bonds are traded on them.

United States government securities (bonds that the United States government sells), foreign exchange, and shares of stocks are now traded continuously in vast quantities around the world. Trading in United States government securities is the world's fastest growing 24-hour market. Foreign exchange—the buying and selling of foreign currencies—became a 24-hour worldwide market in the 1970s. Markets also exist worldwide in commodities such as grains, gold and silver, and stocks. The worldwide stock market, started in the mid-1970s, however, has some problems.

FIGURE 21.2

Satellite Communications More people in controlled societies, such as Cuba, are seeing how the rest of the world looks, thinks, and operates.

CAREERS

Computer Programmer

Job Description
- Write, test, and maintain programs—or instructions for the computer to follow—and code the instructions in a programming language
- Update, repair, modify, and expand existing programs

Qualifications
- 4-year degree in computer science commonly required
- 2-year degree or substantial specialized experience needed

Median Salary: $57,590

Job Outlook: Average

—*Occupational Outlook Handbook*, 2002–03

Problems With the Worldwide Stock Market The United States economy represents a major part of the world economy. So, when the U.S. stock market falters, so do the stock markets worldwide. For example, on October 19, 1987, the United States stock market suffered one of its worst days ever. The Dow Jones Industrial Average dropped over 500 points. It took two years for the United States stock market to recover, but many foreign stock markets took even longer.

On September 11, 2001, one of the most devastating acts of terrorism in history occurred. The World Trade Towers in New York City were destroyed, and thousands lost their lives. When the stock market reopened on September 17, the Dow fell by almost 700 points. In the meantime, stock markets worldwide had already fallen in response. Fortunately, both in the United States and elsewhere, stock markets started to recover within a few months.

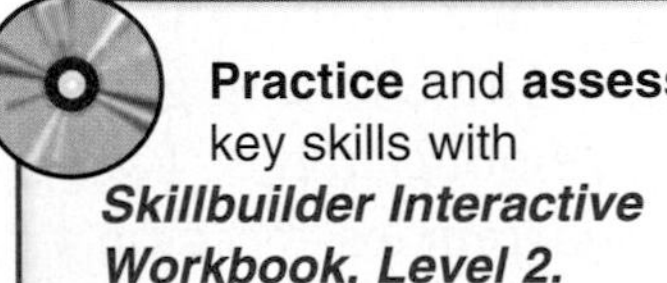

Practice and **assess** key skills with ***Skillbuilder Interactive Workbook, Level 2.***

SECTION 1 Assessment

Understanding Key Terms

1. **Define** global integration, telecommunications.

Reviewing Objectives

2. **Graphic Organizer** Create a diagram like the one below to explain how improved telecommunications has affected global integration.

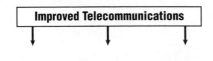

Improved Telecommunications		
↓	↓	↓

3. What kinds of financial investments are traded in global markets?

Applying Economic Concepts

4. **Global Financial Markets** Why should an individual be cautious about investing heavily in the global financial market?

Critical Thinking Activity

5. **Summarizing Information** List five telecommunications inventions and/or events that helped create a global financial market.

BusinessWeek

SPOTLIGHT ON THE ECONOMY

Does Globalization Get a Bad Rap?

Check It Out! In this chapter you learned about the globalization of financial markets and how the United States stock market crash in 1987 caused foreign markets to crash as well. Read to learn how globalization affects other parts of the world.

The poor shall always be with us, cautions the Bible. Maybe not, argues Indian economist and former World Bank staffer Surjit S. Bhalla in a provocative new book, *Imagine There's No Country: Poverty, Inequality and Growth in the Era of Globalization*. . . . [T]he book is a must-read for anyone seriously interested in the debate about whether globalization is good for the poor. . . .

Antiglobalization advocates claim that the free-market, pro-globalization policies of the past two decades have made the world worse for the poor. Even the World Bank has joined in the fray, professing concern that the number of people in poverty has fallen only slowly.

. . . Look again, urges Bhalla. He contends that the past 20 years have been a time of "fantastic" opportunity for the world's poorest people. Poverty has fallen at the fastest rate in history. Average annual growth in developing countries has been almost double that of the industrialized world–3.1% vs. 1.6%. For each 10% rise in consumption by the nonpoor, consumption by poor people rose 18%. . . .

The most important implication, if Bhalla is right, is that the pro-market policies of the last 20 years are working just fine. It's an illusion to look for policies that will be more pro poor, because no formula in history has ever been more pro-poor. In essence, he's saying the search for an elusive Third Way of global development that lifts all the fortunes of the poor can be abandoned because it has already been found.

Think About It

1. **According to antiglobalization advocates, what is an adverse effect of globalization?**
2. **According to the article, what is the best way of lifting the fortunes of the poor?**

SECTION 2 Direct Foreign Investment—Should We Be Worried?

Reader's Guide

Terms to Know

- direct foreign investment (DFI)

Reading Objectives

1. What concerns do some people have about direct foreign investment?
2. Why do some people argue in favor of more direct foreign investment?

Cover Story

The News Tribune, June 23, 2003

The Frank Russell Co. could emerge as one of the winners in a new tax battle . . . but it would likely come at the expense of two other Washington state corporations—Boeing and Microsoft. Russell . . . has tried to persuade Congress to eliminate a tax that discourages foreign investment in U.S. mutual funds.

The tax bill, however, also could result in a financial blow to Boeing and Microsoft. The bill would end a tax break that has provided them and 4,000 other companies with billions of dollars in tax relief designed to boost U.S. exports.

Who owns whom? Nothing seems more American than Burger King or the Pillsbury Dough Boy, right? Not quite, for those companies are now owned by the British. In addition, the Japanese own about 20 percent of the office space in downtown Los Angeles. A Thailand-based firm owns Chicken of the Sea Tuna, and a German company owns A&P Supermarkets. Throughout the world, American companies have likewise purchased foreign firms. As you read this section, you'll learn that foreign investment has grown considerably in the past decade.

Foreign Investment, Then and Now

There is a long history of foreign investment in the United States. For example, Great Britain was the biggest foreign investor in American railroads in the late 1800s and early 1900s. At the beginning of World War I, the United States owed more money to foreign lenders than any other country in the world.

In the United States today, however, **direct foreign investment (DFI)**—the purchase of real estate and businesses by foreigners—has increased to the point where some Americans want to restrict it. In any single year, foreigners purchase billions of dollars of American real estate and businesses. Anytime political upheaval strikes in another part of the world, foreign investment in the United States increases because we remain a politically stable country.

Global *Economy*

Leading Foreign Investors

Who are the leading foreign investors in the United States? The table below shows the top 10 countries, ranked according to revenues from American holdings in 1999.

Germany	$221 billion
United Kingdom	$219 billion
Japan	$111 billion
Netherlands	$98 billion
Switzerland	$70 billion
France	$59 billion
Canada	$58 billion
China	$50 billion
Sweden	$29 billion
Belgium	$18 billion ■

Foreign Control of American Companies Many people argue against foreign ownership of American companies because they worry about foreign control. Is foreign control important? Presumably, foreign investors purchase American assets in order to maximize profits. Foreigners' interests in running a corporation would seem to be identical to the interest of any domestic investor who owned the same corporation. The profit-making behavior of a corporation does not depend on the nationality of that corporation. If the British took over a hotel on Miami Beach, would the service necessarily be any different in the long run? Economists do not think so.

direct foreign investment (DFI): *the purchase by foreigners of real estate and businesses in another country*

What about the foreign investors' influence over the United States government? Foreigners own over 30 percent of all United States government securities that now exist. Can they use this to control United States foreign policy? Probably not. Foreigners purchase United States government securities when they think the rate of return is higher than they can get elsewhere. Remember that whenever foreigners buy United States government securities or private corporate securities, they free up United States financial capital for other productive uses.

FIGURE 21.3

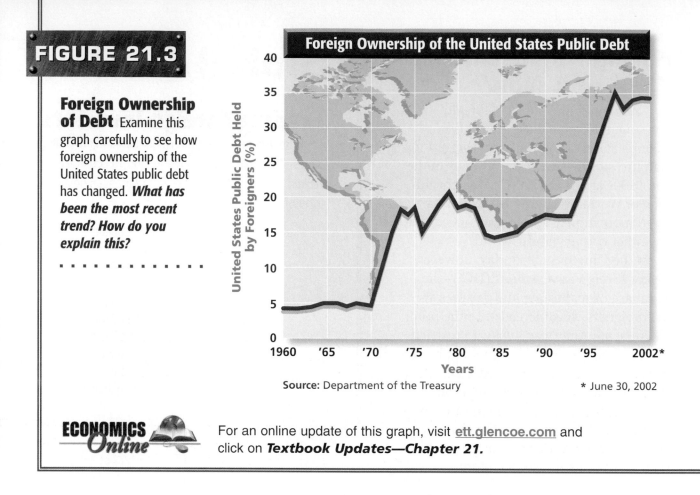

Foreign Ownership of Debt Examine this graph carefully to see how foreign ownership of the United States public debt has changed. ***What has been the most recent trend? How do you explain this?***

Source: Department of the Treasury

* June 30, 2002

For an online update of this graph, visit ett.glencoe.com and click on ***Textbook Updates—Chapter 21.***

In reality, the United States government has more control over foreigners. Because they own about 35 percent of the United States public debt, as you can see in **Figure 21.3,** foreign investors are subject to United States government policy. For example, the federal government, through its Federal Reserve System, could create tremendous inflation. In doing so, it would wipe out the real value of the United States government debt that foreigners own.

In a larger sense, foreign corporations may *indirectly* influence our government. Our government cannot make the business climate in America too difficult for these corporations or they will take their investments elsewhere. The positive side of this situation is that domestic corporations benefit from the hands-off approach of government toward foreign-owned businesses.

Investment Here and Abroad

Despite the concern some have about foreigners "owning" the United States, the total share of foreign ownership of American industries is about 6 percent. Although foreign investment here is readily visible as shown in **Figure 21.4,** foreign investment is relatively low when compared to that of other nations. In Great Britain, for example, more than 20 percent of total sales comes from companies owned by foreigners.

How much investing do American companies carry out abroad? The United States's share of worldwide direct investment is more than 40 percent. Indeed, throughout the world many people fear that United States culture has taken over everyone else's culture. Some people have called this *economic imperialism*.

Most consumers in the world, however, have little knowledge about who ultimately owns the company that provides the goods or services they purchase—and they do not really care. Some even argue that we should *encourage* direct investment and debt purchases by foreigners. Why? Foreigners then would have an increased incentive for the American economy to remain strong, for real estate prices *not* to collapse, for the legal structure to stay on a stable course, and for United States businesses to compete effectively by providing goods and services that consumers want.

FIGURE 21.4

Visible Foreign Investment Unlike Burger King or other companies that are not obviously owned by foreigners, there are some companies that are clearly visible as being foreign-owned. Toyota is one of these.

Practice and **assess** key skills with ***Skillbuilder Interactive Workbook, Level 2.***

SECTION 2 Assessment

Understanding Key Terms

1. **Define** direct foreign investment (DFI).

Reviewing Objectives

2. **Graphic Organizer** Create a diagram like the one below to explain the concerns that some Americans have about direct foreign investment.

3. Why do some people argue in favor of more direct foreign investment?

Applying Economic Concepts

4. **Direct Foreign Investment** Would you buy a more expensive American-made product to prevent a trade deficit that could eventually lead to more foreign ownership of American business? Why or why not?

Critical Thinking Activity

5. **Making Comparisons** Use a recent *Statistical Abstract of the United States,* under the table "Foreign Commerce and Aid," to find the amount of direct investment of two European countries in the United States during the past 5 years. How much did the United States invest in those two countries during the same period?

CRITICAL THINKING SKILLS

Recognizing Bias

Most people have a point of view, or bias. This bias influences the way they interpret and write about events. Recognizing bias helps you judge the accuracy of what you hear or read.

- Examine the author's identity, especially his or her views and particular interests.
- Identify statements of fact.
- Identify any expressions of opinion or emotion.
- Determine the author's point of view.
- Determine how the author's point of view is reflected in the work.

LEARNING THE SKILL

To learn how to recognize bias, follow the steps listed on the left.

PRACTICING THE SKILL

Read the passage below, then answer the questions that follow.

The Global Corporation Becomes the Leaderless Corporation

"*In the 20th century, the Soviet Union collapsed because its command-and-control economy couldn't keep up with the West's free market. In the 21st century, the same fate will befall companies whose CEOs [chief executive officers] attempt to control everything. In a world that is becoming ever more chaotic and dependent on brainpower, teams at the top will make more sense than a single outrageously paid CEO who sits behind a 'buck stops here' plaque.*"

–*Business Week*, August 30, 1999

1. What statements of fact are presented in this passage?
2. What opinions are stated?
3. What is the purpose of this passage?
4. What evidence of bias do you find?

APPLICATION ACTIVITY

Find an editorial in the newspaper that deals with a topic of specific interest to you. Apply the steps for recognizing bias to the editorial. Write a paragraph summarizing your findings.

Practice and **assess** key skills with ***Skillbuilder Interactive Workbook, Level 2.***

SECTION 3

Multinationals and Economic Competition

Cover Story

Business Week, July 30, 2003

For most industries, the rivalry between China and India hasn't been much of a contest. China is tops in manufacturing, with multinationals pouring billions of dollars of direct investment into the country. . . .

With far less foreign direct investment and a vastly inferior infrastructure, India is an also-ran to China in manufacturing achievements. But the service industry? That's a different story. India boasts world-class software service companies, . . . and multinationals have made India the top choice for outsourced software development, call centers, and other business operations.

Reader's Guide

Terms to Know

- multinationals
- foreign affiliates

Reading Objectives

1. About how many multinationals exist in the world today?
2. What is a cross-border investment?
3. What are the advantages of corporate alliances?
4. How have recent patterns of immigration to the United States increased the need for tolerance?

Much international or cross-border investing is undertaken by **multinationals,** firms that do business or have offices or factories in many countries. In the past, critics argued that because these firms are so large, they may come to dominate the world economy. Such firms were seen as ruthless companies that would exploit the poor and manipulate governments. Few people hold such opinions today. In this section you'll learn that multinationals usually set up operations on a regional basis, often forming alliances in the process.

multinationals: *firms that do business and have offices or factories in many countries*

The Size and Number of Multinationals

foreign affiliates: *branches of multinational firms*

In the 1970s, many people predicted that a few hundred multinationals would control 80 percent of the world's production by the mid-1980s. By 2003, there were about 60,000 multinational corporations, with about 620,000 **foreign affiliates,** or branches of their firms. The foreign affiliates of the world's top nonfinancial companies accounted for about $2.3 trillion in assets. **Figure 21.5** lists the top 25 American-owned multinationals.

Worldwide Ownership The top 100 multinationals are very important, accounting for almost 50 percent of all cross-border assets. This means nothing, however, without comparing these assets to the worldwide total. In 2003, the 500 companies with the highest revenues in the world had combined sales of $9 trillion. What this means is that the top 100 multinationals account for less than 20 percent of the world's productive assets—hardly an overwhelmingly dominant share.

It is also true today that the United States and Great Britain no longer dominate multinationals. Of the 7,000 multinationals identified by the United Nations in 1970, the Americans and the British owned more than 50 percent. Today Americans, Japanese, Germans, and the Swiss own a little more than half of all multinationals. Numerous multinationals are based in the industrializing nations of Asia, such as Taiwan, South Korea, and Malaysia.

Economic Connection to... History

Ancient Multinationals

Economic historians suggest that multinationals may have existed nearly 4,000 years ago in the ancient kingdom of Assyria. Information on writing tablets found in central Turkey indicates that a thriving trade existed between this region and Assur, the Assyrian capital. Private companies in Assur shipped tin and textiles to the town of Kanesh in central Turkey. Assyrian merchants there traded the textiles for other goods to be sent back to Assur. Furthermore, Assyrian-owned businesses in Turkey used the tin to make finished bronze goods to be sold in Assyria. ■

FIGURE 21.5 The Largest American Multinationals

Rank/Company	Revenue ($Mil)	Net Income ($Mil)	Assets ($Mil)	Market Value ($Mil)
1. Citigroup	93,101	14,536	1,136,973	211,173
2. General Electric	130,483	14,829	583,634	286,838
3. American Intl. Group	70,272	5,493	591,809	150,974
4. ExxonMobil	195,465	15,860	162,495	243,130
5. Bank of America	46,690	9,494	679,765	111,155
6. Fannie Mae	53,128	5,351	913,264	72,507
7. Verizon Communications	67,529	6,338	172,053	104,088
8. Wal-Mart Stores	246,282	8,248	96,473	230,731
9. Berkshire Hathaway	44,255	5,100	169,616	108,980
10. Intl. Business Machines	83,221	3,771	95,720	152,133
11. Altria Group	60,706	10,923	89,900	83,626
12. General Motors	189,100	2,991	382,922	33,320
13. Freddie Mac	36,773	5,764	721,739	41,112
14. JP Morgan Chase & Co.	43,869	2,081	755,156	66,747
15. Wells Fargo	28,879	5,823	369,669	80,908
16. SBC Communications	41,078	8,301	100,798	84,588
17. Morgan Stanley	31,844	3,132	559,436	49,744
18. ChevronTexaco	101,490	2,523	81,302	75,788
19. Microsoft	31,375	9,597	74,482	264,219
20. Merck	53,009	7,235	48,954	124,629
21. Wachovia	23,455	3,693	348,064	54,049
22. Pfizer	33,151	11,858	52,928	244,886
23. Merrill Lynch	26,877	2,741	455,587	40,137
24. Bank One	21,844	3,326	287,864	42,679
25. Johnson & Johnson	37,376	6,833	41,994	161,355

Source: *Forbes*, July 21, 2003

FIGURE 21.6

Japan's Major Investment Like most countries, Japan invests most heavily in itself. Downtown Tokyo shows evidence of how strongly Japanese companies dominate that nation's capital.

Regional Cross-Border Investments

Although many of the biggest multinationals invest all over the world, most do not. Most invest in regions that are closest to home. The European Union plus Switzerland conduct more direct foreign investment in western Europe than anywhere else, for example.

In a world in which borders matter less, the line separating sales at home and those abroad becomes less important. The most appropriate way to look at patterns of direct investment is to include direct domestic sales as a part of regional sales. European firms principally invest in western Europe. American firms principally invest in the United States, Canada, Mexico, and South America. Japanese firms principally invest in Japan, South Korea, China, and Southeast Asia. **Figure 21.6,** for example, shows Japanese investment in Tokyo.

Beyond Multinationals—Alliances

In addition to multinational direct investments in other countries, firms in different countries are forming *alliances.* These may be joint ventures or licensing deals. Indeed, many foreign governments have insisted that multinationals enter their markets through joint ventures with local firms in the hope that locals will capture some of the profits.

Most alliances have been between firms from industrialized countries. Alliances are even popular within nations like the United States. International Business Machines (IBM), for example, developed its personal computer in alliance with Microsoft (for the software), Intel (for the central processing unit), and Lotus. In the late 1980s, IBM entered into an alliance with Siemens of Germany to work on memory chips. In the 1990s, IBM entered into an alliance with Apple Computers, once its archrival.

Student Web Activity Visit the *Economics Today and Tomorrow* Web site at ett.glencoe.com and click on ***Chapter 21—Student Web Activities*** to see how one multinational corporation operates.

Alliances can be seen as each firm's acceptance of its own limitations, whether they are financial, technological, or geographical. Alliances can be used to help a firm leapfrog its competitors or catch up to them. Such a strategy is particularly effective in industries that have seen rapid changes, such as software.

The Global Village and Tolerance

One of the social results of the globalization of our world is increased immigration. America has become a truly multicultural society because of such immigration. In many cities the combined number of African Americans, Hispanics, Asians, and other minorities now constitutes a majority of the population.

In the 1980s, the Asian population in America increased more than 100 percent. In 2003, Hispanics became the largest minority group in the United States. With so many immigrants, public schools are more diverse. This diversity means that the need for tolerance and open-mindedness is more important today than it ever has been. For Americans, this includes learning one or more foreign languages and maintaining friendships with those of different ethnic, cultural, national, and/or religious backgrounds.

Practice and **assess** key skills with ***Skillbuilder Interactive Workbook, Level 2.***

SECTION 3 Assessment

Understanding Key Terms

1. **Define** multinationals, foreign affiliates.

Reviewing Objectives

2. How many multinationals exist in the world today?
3. What is an example of a cross-border investment?
4. **Graphic Organizer** Create a diagram like the one below to list and explain the advantages of corporate alliances.

5. How have recent patterns of immigration to the United States increased the need for tolerance?

Applying Economic Concepts

6. **Corporate Alliances** If you owned an American business and wanted to enter a foreign market, what should you consider before agreeing to a joint venture with a small firm in that market?

Critical Thinking Activity

7. **Synthesizing Information** Use the information in **Figure 21.5** on page 555 to build a database. Input the top 10 corporations listed as well as information from the following columns: Foreign Revenue, Total Revenue, Foreign Assets. Then sort the database by each column and print out the new tables.

People & Perspectives

- **Vice chair of the Federal Reserve Board, 1996–99**
- **Director of the White House Office of Management and Budget, 1994–96**
- **First director of the Congressional Budget Office, 1975–1983**
- **Staff member at the Brookings Institution, a public policy research group**

Alice Rivlin

ECONOMIST (1931–)

Alice Rivlin has been involved in government as an economist for many years. One task she has tried to fulfill throughout her career is to help the general public develop a better understanding of economics:

"Without a basic understanding of how the economy works, what the essential terms and concepts are, the average citizen is likely to feel completely left out of any conversation . . . about what is happening in the economy and what to do about it.

Feeling left out is frustrating and alienating. If talk is unintelligible–if the listener is without keys or clues or a basic framework into which to fit what is being said–then it is natural for the listener to tune out and to feel powerless. . . .

In order to feel included and empowered, a citizen needs to have a basic understanding of how the world works–in this case how the economic world works–that will provide a basis for asking pertinent questions, obtaining more information and eventually figuring out what the issues are all about and what ought to be done.

Economic literacy is [like] having a working knowledge of a foreign language. If you are with a group of foreigners and don't speak their language at all, . . . you tune out. You feel excluded, perhaps uneasy. If you have a rudimentary working knowledge of the language, you can at least follow the drift of the conversation, ask a few questions and feel that, even if you are not getting the fine points, you are not totally left out and you have a basis for acquiring more knowledge. That, it seems to me, is what economic literacy means–a rudimentary working knowledge of the concepts and language of economic activity and economic policy."

Checking for Understanding

1. **What, according to Rivlin, is the impact of not having a basic understanding of how the economy works?**
2. **To what does Rivlin compare economic literacy?**
3. **How does Rivlin define economic literacy?**

CHAPTER  Summary

Chapter Overview Visit the *Economics Today and Tomorrow* Web site at ett.glencoe.com and click on ***Chapter 21—Chapter Overviews*** to review chapter information.

SECTION 1 Reasons for and Results of Global Integration

- **Global integration** has increased dramatically over the past several decades, mainly because of improved **telecommunications.**
- Because of the increase in communications, people in other nations are changing their cultural tastes and buying habits, which also affects exports and language.
- The world has become one financial market, with government securities, foreign exchange, and shares of stock traded 24 hours a day.
- A globalized financial market now causes everyone everywhere to feel the effects of a financial panic.

SECTION 2 Direct Foreign Investment—Should We Be Worried?

- There is a long history of foreign investment in the United States.
- **Direct foreign investment** in the United States has increased to the point where some Americans want to restrict it.
- Many people argue against foreign ownership of American companies because they worry about foreign control.
- Economists believe that foreigners purchase American assets in order to maximize profits.
- The total share of foreign ownership of American industries is about 6 percent.
- The United States's share of worldwide direct investment is more than 40 percent.

SECTION 3 Multinationals and Economic Competition

- Much international or cross-border investing is undertaken by **multinationals.**
- By the late 1990s, there were an estimated 63,000 multinationals with about 690,000 **foreign affiliates.**
- The top 100 multinationals account for about 15 percent of the world's productive assets.
- Most multinationals invest in regions that are closest to home.
- Multinationals often form alliances in the form of joint ventures or licensing deals.
- One of the results of the globalization of our world is increased immigration and diversity, which means that the need for tolerance and open-mindedness is more important today than it ever has been.

CHAPTER 21

Assessment and Activities

Self-Check Quiz Visit the *Economics Today and Tomorrow* Web site at ett.glencoe.com and click on ***Chapter 21—Self-Check Quizzes*** to prepare for the Chapter Test.

Identifying Key Terms

Write a short paragraph about the global economy using all of the following terms.

- global integration
- telecommunications
- direct foreign investment
- foreign affiliates
- multinationals

Recalling Facts and Ideas

Section 1

1. Why has improved telecommunications led to increased global integration?
2. What happened elsewhere in the world when the United States stock market crashed in 1987?
3. What language is the leading second language in the world? Why is this so?

Section 2

4. What foreign nation's investors own much of the office space in downtown Los Angeles?
5. Why do foreigners purchase United States government securities?
6. What is the United States's share of worldwide direct investment?

Section 3

7. How can multinationals help developing countries?
8. What four countries own about half of the 63,000 multinationals that exist today?
9. Why do firms in different countries form alliances with one another?

Thinking Critically

1. **Understanding Cause and Effect** Although cheap telecommunications is widespread in industrialized nations, it is not so widespread in developing nations. What will happen to global integration as developing nations catch up to the developed nations?
2. **Drawing Conclusions** A foreign company buys an American company. Explain why that company might not necessarily be run any differently from other American companies.
3. **Making Generalizations** Create a diagram like the one below to list possible advantages and disadvantages of multinationals.

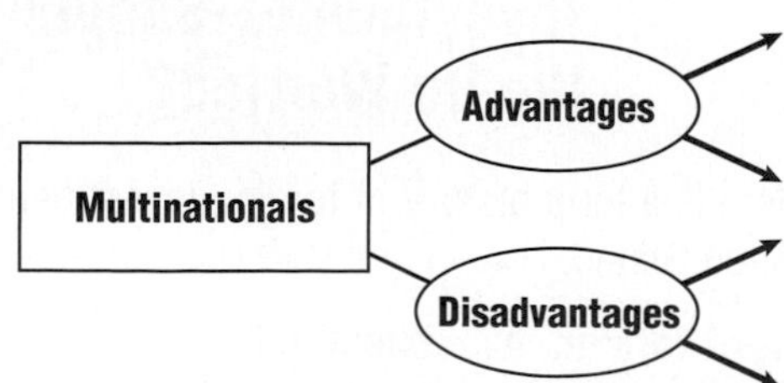

Applying Economic Concepts

Investment Incentives Make a list of the reasons that people give for why they are afraid of direct foreign investment in the United States. For each reason, present a counterargument.

Cooperative Learning Project

Working in groups of four, research the following innovations:

- the fax machine
- overnight delivery service (for example, Federal Express and Airborne Express)
- plain-paper copy machines
- high-speed computer modems
- satellite television
- portable cellular phones
- the Internet

Each team member will be responsible for one or more of the following:

a. Explaining what the innovation involves
b. Information on when it was first used and how much it cost then
c. How the innovation changed the way business is done
d. The future of the innovation

Reviewing Skills

Recognizing Bias Read the passage below, then answer the questions that follow.

"Does anybody remember tiddlywinks? Kids these days seem to crave electronic games, from Nintendo's handheld Gameboy to Sony's dazzling PlayStation to the shoot-'em-up antics of video arcades. They're not just for kids, of course–much of Sony's new software is geared toward adults. But the software, hardware, and portables still appeal most to youthful buyers, who could push U.S. retail sales in this industry as high as $7 billion this year. Experts say kids can actually get something worthwhile out of this–reflex skills sure get a workout."

–*Business Week: 100 Years of Innovation*, Summer 1999

1. What statements of fact are presented?
2. What opinions are stated?
3. What is the purpose of this passage?
4. What evidence of bias do you find?

Technology Activity

Developing Multimedia Presentations Identify a foreign-owned business in the United States. Use library resources or the Internet or visit the business and ask for information about the history of the business, its size, its organization, and its plans for the future. Then use this information to prepare a multimedia presentation about the business. Share your presentation with the rest of the class.

Analyzing the Global Economy

Choose a country other than the United States and investigate how much direct foreign investment occurs there each year. (United Nations and World Bank publications are useful sources.) Try to establish the dollar volume of such direct foreign investment, what percentage of total investment this represents, and the major foreign countries that do the investing. Write a summary of your results.

Economics Lab

Buying a New Car

From the classroom of Rick Johnson, New Harmony High School, New Harmony, Indiana

In this unit you have learned about global integration. In Chapter 21 you learned that automobile corporations are among the largest of the multinational firms. In this lab, you will research the financing needed to purchase an automobile. You'll find the best interest rates for a new car, compare interest rates over different terms, and compare leasing a vehicle versus buying.

STEP A Tools Needed

- ✔ Newspaper advertisements for new vehicles
- ✔ Access to the Internet (optional)
- ✔ Spreadsheet software

STEP B Procedures to Follow

1. Organize into groups of four.
2. As a group, decide what type of new vehicle you wish to purchase.
3. Obtain the price of the vehicle either by newspaper, the Internet, or a phone call to a dealer.
4. Three people in your group should each contact a lending institution to obtain loan interest rates for new cars over a 3-, 4-, and 5-year term. One lending institution should be a bank, one a credit union, and the other a mutual bank or savings and loan.

5. The fourth group member will obtain information about a 3-year lease agreement, which should include monthly payments, down payment, maximum miles, and residual value.

6. Next, find the monthly payments and total payment of the loan for each term (3, 4, or 5 years) for each lending institution. This is done by using an amortization schedule. Many banking institutions have online loan calculators. Insert the loan amount (principal), the term either in months or years, and the interest rate, then click *compute*.

STEP C Creating an Economic Model

After you accumulate all the information from the lending institutions, enter it on a spreadsheet and convert it to a creative graph like the one below. The graphs from all group members should be put on poster board for a class presentation.

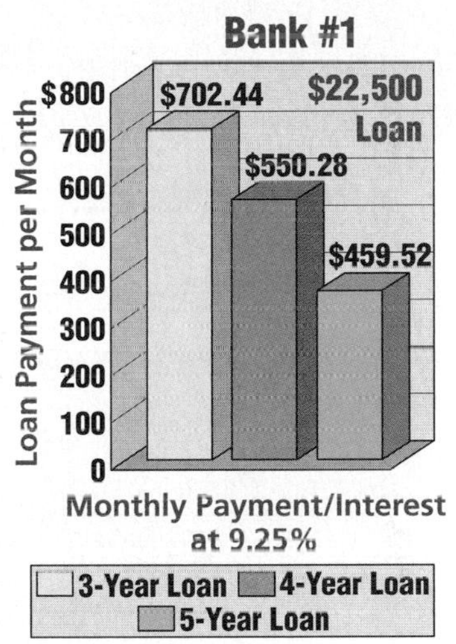

STEP D Lab Report Analysis

Analyze the graphs that you created in step C, then answer the questions below.

1. How much did the monthly payment vary among the three terms and among the lending institutions?

2. How different was the lease payment compared to the purchase payment?

3. Were you surprised by the information you received? Explain.

CHAPTER 22

Cybernomics

Why It's Important

Electronic communications enable us to access information, purchase goods and services, and share ideas instantly around the globe. New technologies continue to accelerate the rate of economic change. This chapter will help you understand the new economic environment.

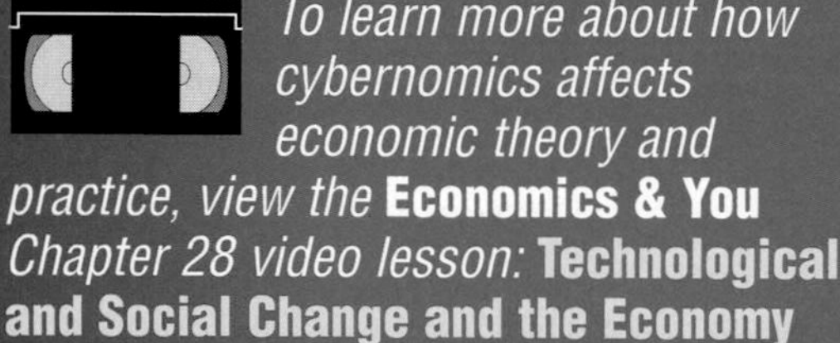

To learn more about how cybernomics affects economic theory and practice, view the **Economics & You** *Chapter 28 video lesson:* **Technological and Social Change and the Economy**

ECONOMICS *Online*

Chapter Overview Visit the *Economics Today and Tomorrow* Web site at ett.glencoe.com and click on ***Chapter 22—Chapter Overviews*** to preview chapter information.

SECTION 

The Growth of E-Commerce

Cover Story

Business Week, March 22, 1999

In certain Levi Strauss & Co. stores, you can plug in your measurements at a Web kiosk and have custom-made jeans delivered to your home in about two weeks. On cable-TV's Disney Channel, little bug-like creatures called Zoogs tell kids to log onto Disney's Web site to send fan mail to their favorite stars. What is going on here? Both cases illustrate a combination of traditional and cyberspace marketing.

Reader's Guide

Terms to Know

- microchip
- cybernomics
- Internet
- World Wide Web
- Web sites
- e-commerce
- frequency marketing

Reading Objectives

1. How is the Internet affecting the way companies do business?
2. Why are marketers collecting information about your purchases?
3. How does e-commerce benefit the consumer?

Most people have 20 digits, better known as fingers and toes. Numbers, also called digits, are so vital to our lives today that people have labeled our era "the digital age." We identify ourselves by credit card numbers, PINs (personal identification numbers), and Social Security numbers. Numbers measure and track everything from blood pressure to national opinion, from personal checking accounts to the federal debt.

The invention that brought us the digital age also helps institutions manage all this information. The **microchip**, or integrated circuit—smaller than a thumbnail—is one of the most remarkable inventions of our lifetime. This chapter will explain

microchip: *a tiny electronic circuit that processes and digitally transfers information*

FIGURE 22.1

Microchips Microchips, the building blocks of our electronic age, are made up of tiny rectangles of silicon circuits constructed with thousands, perhaps millions, of transistors. An electronic marketplace is made possible by millions of microchips, shown being manufactured here. ***Why is our economy sometimes called a "digital economy"?***

how microchips in a network of interconnected computers are changing how we communicate, produce, consume, educate, and entertain ourselves. See **Figure 22.1.** Some economists believe we have entered the age of **cybernomics**–economics driven by a huge digital machine, the Internet.

Business on the Internet

cybernomics: *an economic system driven by Internet commerce*

Internet: *a worldwide system of interconnected computers that store, process, and share information*

World Wide Web: *part of the Internet, used for communications among consumers, business, governments, and other organizations*

Web sites: *electronic World Wide Web locations that store information to be viewed or downloaded*

The **Internet** is a network of computers that enables people everywhere to access and exchange information instantaneously. Its growth has been remarkable. **Figure 22.2** shows how the spread of computer and Internet use compares to the spread of earlier technologies.

Use of the Internet accelerated as the prices of computers and Internet access fell. Meanwhile, the store of information on the **World Wide Web**–the most popular use of the Internet–grew both in the amount of information available and the number of Web sites. **Web sites** are electronic locations on the World Wide Web that store information which may be viewed or downloaded onto another computer.

E-Commerce Web sites connecting businesses, private organizations, government offices, and educational institutions make locating information and global communication extraordinarily easy. The Internet provides businesses in particular with the opportunity to directly reach suppliers and consumers. By 2010 e-commerce is expected to bring in revenues of more than $1 trillion in the United States alone. No one really knows just how quickly this market will continue to develop.

The entire business landscape is changing. Companies that have painstakingly built their supply chains suddenly find that anyone using the Web can bypass their chains. New companies spring up nearly overnight, competing with well-known businesses that have spent years building their customer bases. *Business Week* magazine called **e-commerce,** or electronic business, "perhaps the most sweeping transformation of the corporate landscape in decades."

e-commerce: *electronic commerce on the Internet (also referred to as e-business)*

E-commerce is both enticing and risky. Companies with intelligent e-commerce plans can reap huge profits, while less thoughtful business planners may waste billions of dollars and precious time. Planners must decide among a bewildering array of possible business models. Various combinations of advertising, subscriptions, commissions, fees, and direct sales can generate increased electronic business revenue—or cause huge losses. What works well for one company may be the wrong choice for another. Competition is fierce because both the market and the competitors encompass the whole world.

FIGURE 22.2

Spread of Technology It took about 95 years for 90 percent of American households to own a telephone. ***About how long did it take for 30 percent of American households to own an automobile? A television? A personal computer?***

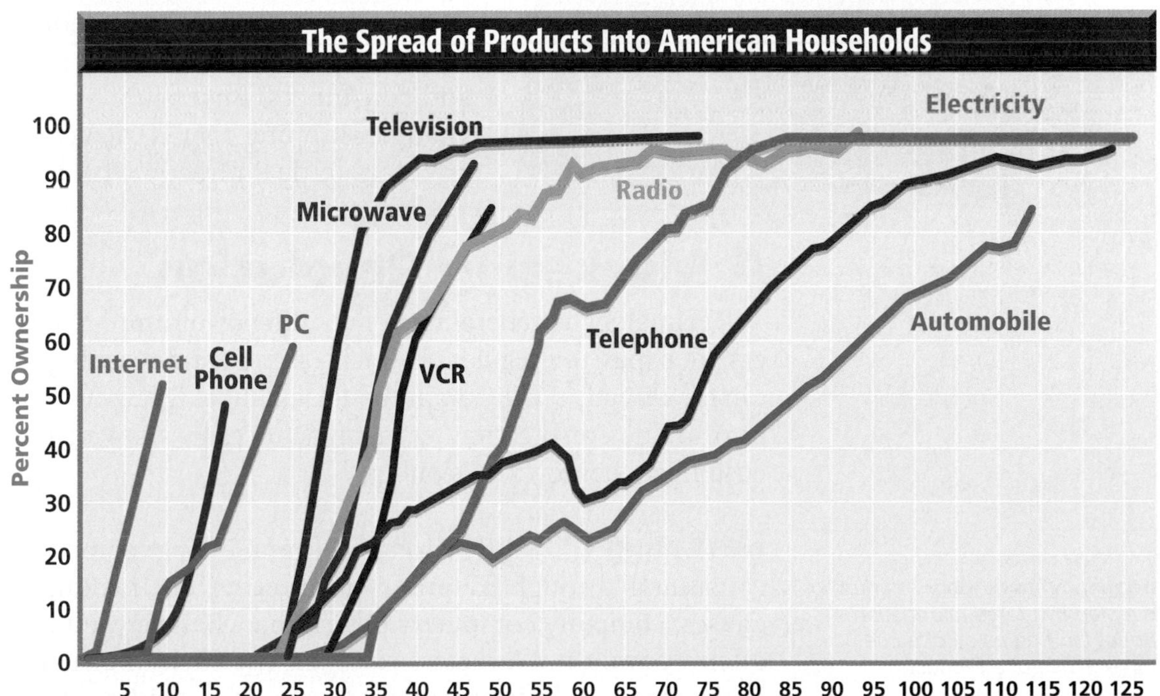

Sources: Bureau of the Census; *The World Almanac;* Cellular Telecommunications Industry Association

By the late 1990s, many businesses began to realize that they really did not have a choice whether to go online. A competitor on the Web could grab customers, causing investors to flock to the more innovative company and sending the rival company's stock into a tailspin.

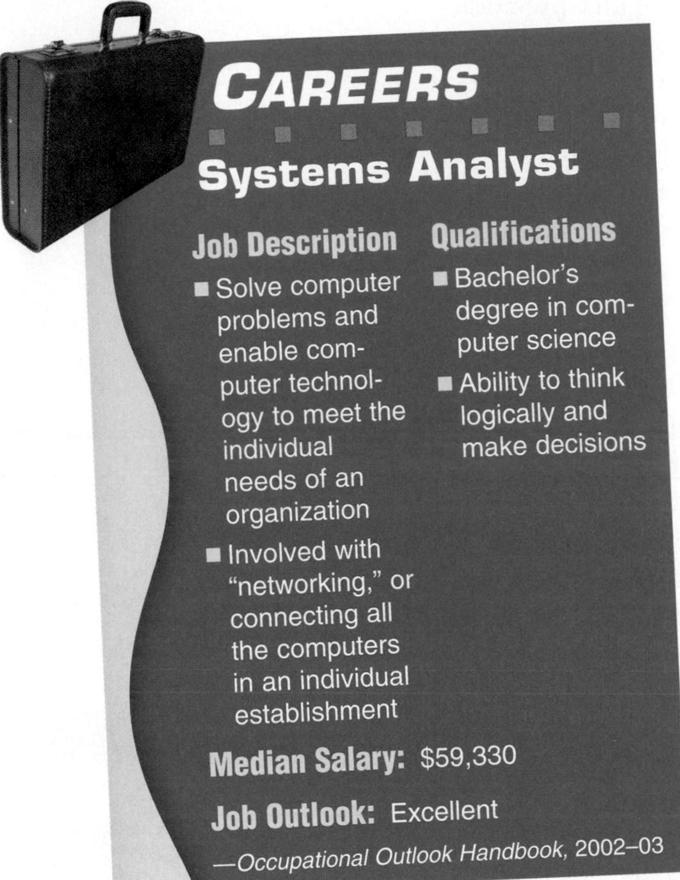

The Customer Wins

Whether it is a business-to-business transaction or a retail sale, e-commerce shifts the balance of power to the customer. This happens because the Web reduces distances. Instead of spending hours driving around comparison shopping, a Web shopper can quickly gather information about products and vendors almost anywhere.

Businesses have found that the virtual distance between producers and consumers has disappeared. In this new world of cybernomics, the buyer is ruler. If one seller cannot deliver a superior product at a competitive price in real time, another seller will. The realization that any business can directly reach a final consumer is changing the relationships among producers, wholesalers, distributors, retailers, and consumers. Buyers are driving this change, skipping agents, dealers, and distributors to deal directly with producers.

A Marketing Revolution

Technology is generating a marketing revolution. Many producers are bypassing regular channels of trade and reaching out to customers directly. Dell Computer, for example, grew twice as fast as other personal computer manufacturers by allowing buyers to customize their own PCs online.

Marketing Changes Today computers help companies serve consumers through **frequency marketing.** By tracking our purchases, company computers determine what we want and how often we want it. Marketers can then use such information stored in databases to build customer loyalty by providing the precise goods and services we demand. For example, Amazon.com's Web

frequency marketing: *marketing directed by stored information about the frequency of a customer's use of a product* site automatically suggests a list of books based on the types of books the customer ordered the last time he or she visited the site. More than ever before, marketing is consumer driven.

Cybercommunities Is e-commerce a new kind of self-service that creates an impersonal relationship between buyer and seller? Not necessarily. Savvy Web managers are finding that the best way to build a customer base is to establish a cybercommunity. People around the world are beginning to associate in virtual communities on the Web. Assembling people with common interests and needs, and serving those needs, is the new direction for businesses, especially those that add a personal touch to selling. Companies are also developing creative ways of responding to customer E-mail, providing answers to questions, and offering customers technical assistance.

For example, The Home Depot has become a virtual service provider as well as a store that offers home supplies. It gives small contractors access to its Web site where they can order materials, tell the supplier when and where to deliver them, find a plumber or an electrician, and learn how to schedule work.

Practice and **assess** key skills with ***Skillbuilder Interactive Workbook, Level 2.***

SECTION 1 Assessment

Understanding Key Terms

1. **Define** microchip, cybernomics, Internet, World Wide Web, Web sites, e-commerce, frequency marketing.

Reviewing Objectives

2. Analyze how the Internet is affecting the way companies do business.
3. Why are marketers collecting information about your purchases?
4. **Graphic Organizer** Create a diagram like the one below to explain how e-commerce benefits the consumer.

Applying Economic Concepts

5. **Market Structure** E-commerce has helped the consumer in many ways, particularly by reducing the time it takes to comparison shop. Another benefit is lower prices. Why is it less likely that businesses can control the prices of goods or services when they sell on the Internet?

Critical Thinking Activity

6. **Making Comparisons** Select three well-known retail stores in which you have shopped. Search the Internet to find out if they are using the Web for advertising, promotions, or sales services. Make a chart rating the Internet services for all three. Share your chart with the rest of the class.

BusinessWeek

SPOTLIGHT ON THE ECONOMY

Chips That Mimic the Human Senses

Check It Out! In this chapter you learned how computers, using microchips, are affecting industry, commerce, and economic choices. In this article, read to learn how digital-signal processing chips will soon affect the convergence of computers, telecommunications, and consumer electronics.

You may not have realized it, but you've probably used digital-signal processing chips a dozen times today. Listening to a compact-disk over breakfast was one instance. So was using a modem to check your E-mail. Driving your car involved several electronic systems powered by these specialized chips. They are also found in cell phones, personal-computer sound systems, digital cameras–and the list goes on.

But that's nothing compared with what's coming. Industry experts predict that by 2005, the convergence of computers, telecommunications, and consumer electronics will push demand for digital-signal processing (DSP) to 10 times what it is today. These chips will then be at the heart of almost every electronic gadget you touch, from new stereo systems and smart home appliances to office machines and factory equipment. DSP chips that can understand speech will replace touchpads and push-buttons on all kinds of products–including VCRs that you can program by telling them what to record.

What makes these chips so special? Well, DSP could stand for digital sensory perception, because these slices of silicon are the nerve cells that connect electronic devices to the real world. They're honed to deal with things like sounds, images, pressure, temperature, electrical currents, and radio waves. They chop these analog signals into digital bits, then perform specialized operations, such as compressing the bits gushing through telephone lines. And they do this at blinding speed.

Think About It

1. **What will cause the demand for DSP chips to increase dramatically in the next few years?**
2. **Why, according to the article, could DSP stand for digital sensory perception?**

SECTION 2

A New Economy?

Cover Story

The Boston Globe, June 25, 2003

The question . . . is whether the political, business, and civic communities can cooperate with the universities to deliver the maximum benefit. . . . The stakes are clear. In the new global economy, the key to global success is knowledge. The asset with the greatest leverage in a knowledge economy is the modern research university, an asset Greater Boston possesses in abundance.

. . . [Boston] universities actually added jobs in the last two years, a claim no other sector can make.

Reader's Guide

Terms to Know

- telecommunications
- Information Age
- knowledge economy
- weightless economy
- innovation

Reading Objectives

1. What changes caused the new environment called the Information Age?
2. How does the knowledge economy differ from the industrial economy?
3. How does innovation affect economic growth?

During the nineteenth century, the Industrial Revolution began to dramatically change society, especially in the Western world. The introduction of steam power produced both a social and economic revolution.

In the 1900s, discoveries and inventions in **telecommunications**, or electronic communications, brought us radio, television, satellite uplinks, and cable access. The computer revolutionized information storage and manipulation. When telecommunications and computer technologies began to merge, the immediate results were dramatic. Will the new environment, now being called the **Information Age**, have as great an effect on human life as did the Industrial Revolution? Many people believe it will.

telecommunications: *communications over long distances, assisted by technology*

Information Age: *the period when telecommunications and computer technology gave information significant economic value*

Global *Economy*

Web Site Challenges

Although the United States leads the world in Internet usage, many American companies face cultural, legal, and linguistic challenges in setting up Web sites in other countries. Experts note that many Europeans feel that American sites have too many distracting "bells and whistles." European sites are more plain and consumer-oriented. Something as simple as the colors used on the Web sites could turn off users. In America, for example, red is the color of love. In Spain, however, it is associated with socialism. ■

The Knowledge Economy

New terms are springing up to describe the economic changes that we see today. The **"knowledge economy"** and the **"weightless economy"** describe an environment in which ideas and information are at least as valuable as more tangible goods. There are many elements in this new economy: information and communications technology; intellectual property, such as patents and brand names; technical information, such as biotechnology and engineering; and stored data in libraries, databases, and videos.

knowledge economy: *economy in which information is the key to growth*

weightless economy: *term coined to identify an economy based on products that are not tangible*

Knowledge Products What are the differences between the knowledge economy and the industrial economy? First, knowledge products are not used up physically by consumers. Unlike a candy bar or a pair of shoes, computer software is not consumed by use. In fact, the more often it is used, the more valuable it may be to the consumer.

Second, a knowledge product knows no spatial boundary or geographical distance. Two people on opposite sides of the globe can simultaneously be using the same software transmitted by a satellite circling high above the earth. Third, knowledge products consist of both the product and the idea behind it. When you buy a database program, for example, you are purchasing both the disk (the product) as well as the computer programming that allows you to organize your data into fields and records (the idea).

Finally, the development of knowledge products requires creative minds and highly trained technicians. After the prototype or original is built, however, thousands of copies are easily and cheaply reproduced.

Student Web Activity Visit the *Economics Today and Tomorrow* Web site at ett.glencoe.com and click on ***Chapter 22—Student Web Activities*** to learn more about the knowledge economy.

A Change or a Revolution?

A number of leading economists believe that the "new" economy is not really so revolutionary. They believe that other factors, such as shifts in the labor market and declining wages, explain why the United States had fuller employment without inflation in the 1990s. They point out that periods of rapid growth in productivity have generally accompanied fundamental innovations. The harnessing of electricity and the inventions of the automobile, radio, and television each spurred a period of expansion, for example.

Most economists do agree that innovation is a significant factor in the world's changing economy. **Innovation** is the introduction of new products and/or delivery systems that dramatically affect large segments of the population. See **Figure 22.3.**

innovation: *development of new products, systems, or processes that have wide-ranging effects*

Waves of Innovation For years economists assumed that the output of an economy could be measured by the effect of two basic inputs–capital and labor. The exception was the law of diminishing returns–at some point adding more inputs gave a smaller and smaller increase. Yet, this explanation did not account for several large bursts of economic growth during certain periods of history. Until recently, economists had not included innovation in their equation of economic output. Innovation intrigues economists because it can affect national growth and GDP in unpredictable ways. For instance, who would have guessed before 1920 that the automobile would change America's economic and social environment the way that it did?

Innovation Highly trained technicians create products that contribute to a growing economy. ***How do innovations affect economic growth?***

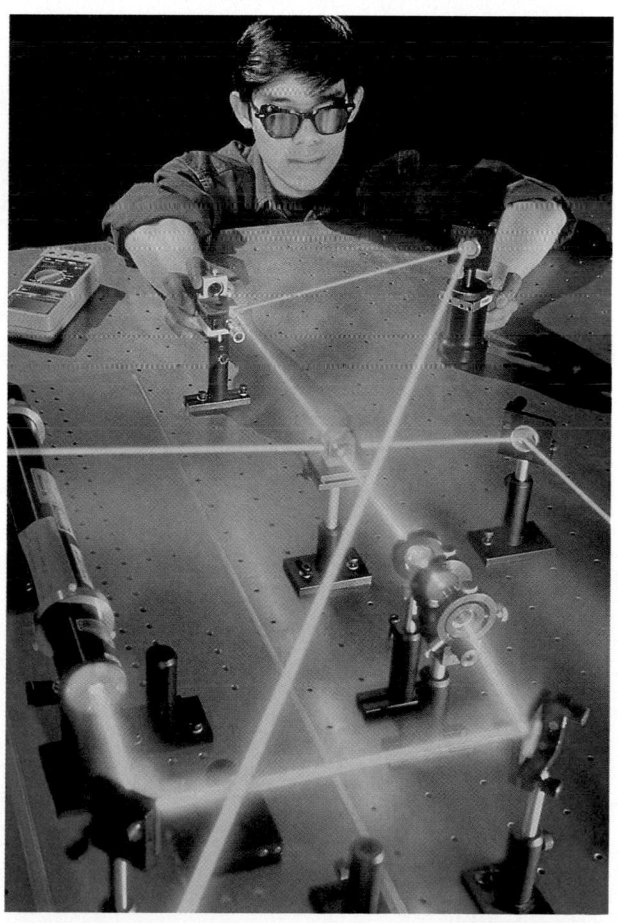

Schumpeter Cycles Economist Joseph Schumpeter was the first to suggest that a normal healthy economy would never be in equilibrium because entrepreneurs would sometimes disrupt it by innovations. Schumpeter studied the history of long business cycles and concluded that each new cycle starts when a set of innovations comes into general use. Each upswing stimulates investment and expansion, as shown in **Figure 22.4** on page 574.

The significance of the knowledge economy may be measured by its effect on individuals and nations. Information and communications technology firms are the growth leaders in the United States economy. The Bureau of Labor Statistics forecasts that computer-related jobs will average more than a 70 percent increase in a ten-year period. Whether the "new economy" is really revolutionary or simply the old economy plus the innovation factor, however, economists today face compelling challenges. You will learn more about these challenges in Section 3.

FIGURE 22.4

Schumpeter's Waves Schumpeter's waves or cycles included the innovations of waterpower for producing textiles (1785); the age of steam locomotives (1845); and the introduction of electricity accompanied by the internal-combustion engine (1900). After he died in 1950, other economists using Schumpeter's model added two more waves—the age of petrochemicals, electronics, and aviation (1950) and the current convergence of telecommunications and computers (1990).

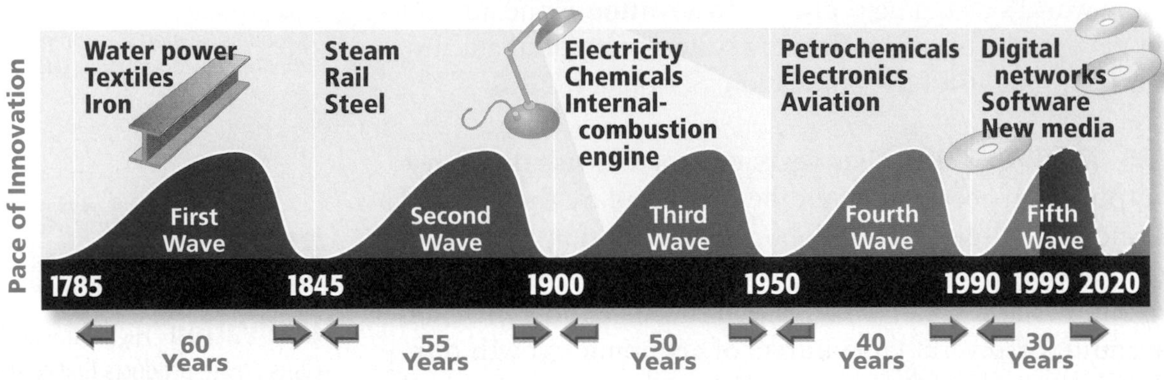

Practice and **assess** key skills with ***Skillbuilder Interactive Workbook, Level 2.***

SECTION 2 Assessment

Understanding Key Terms

1. **Define** telecommunications, Information Age, knowledge economy, weightless economy, innovation.

Reviewing Objectives

2. What changes caused the new environment called the Information Age?
3. How does the knowledge economy differ from the industrial economy?
4. **Graphic Organizer** Create a chart like the one below, then list and give examples of "products" of the knowledge economy.

Knowledge Product	Example(s)

5. How does innovation affect economic growth?

Applying Economic Concepts

6. **Knowledge Economy** What evidence suggests that the knowledge economy will have a significant impact on United States GDP?

Critical Thinking Activity

7. **Drawing Conclusions** Develop a questionnaire concerning the significance of the knowledge economy to your future. For example, you might ask such questions as: How will the knowledge economy affect career choices in the future? How will it affect entertainment and transportation? Survey your classmates with the questionnaire, then enter the results into a database. What conclusions can you draw from the responses you received?

Critical Thinking Skills

Evaluating Primary and Secondary Sources

Primary sources *are original records of events made by people who witnessed them. They include letters, journals, legal documents, drawings, photographs, and artifacts.* Secondary sources *are documents created after an event occurred. They pull together many sources and provide an overview of events.*

- Identify the author of the document.
- Identify when and where the document was written.
- Read the document for its content.
- Identify the author's opinions and bias.
- Determine what kind of information the document provides and what is missing.

Learning the Skill

To interpret primary and secondary sources, follow the steps listed on the left.

Practicing the Skill

Read these excerpts about the Chicago World's Fair of 1893, then answer the questions below.

> *"The Fair helped change Americans' reactions to technology. It became the vehicle for the hopes and dreams of Americans, as they saw in it a reflection of their own progressive nature and bright future. . . . Visitors were meant to see that one of the most potent agents of change in their society–electricity–was not to be feared, but celebrated."*
>
> –*World's Columbian Exposition,* xroads.virginia.edu

> *"Men who . . . had never touched an electric battery–never talked through a telephone, and had not the shadow of a notion what amount of force was meant by a watt . . . had no choice but to sit down on the steps . . . ashamed of [our] childlike ignorance. . . . Chicago asked in 1893 for the first time the question whether the American people knew where they were driving."*
>
> –Henry Adams, *The Education of Henry Adams,* 1907

1. Which document is a primary source? Why?
2. Which document is a secondary source? Why?
3. How does each source view technology?

Application Activity

Look through the letters to the editor in your local newspaper. Summarize any primary sources cited.

Practice and **assess** key skills with ***Skillbuilder Interactive Workbook, Level 2.***

SECTION 3

Issues in Cybernomics

READER'S GUIDE

Terms to Know

- day trading
- intellectual property
- consumer-credit laws
- distance education

Reading Objectives

1. Why is some trading on the Internet considered risky?
2. How is intellectual property being stolen?
3. What is being done to protect consumers' privacy?

COVER STORY

THE CAPITAL TIMES & WISONSIN STATE JOURNAL, JULY 3, 2003

American consumers fundamentally misunderstand how Internet companies use their personal information, according to a new survey that concludes tougher federal privacy laws are needed. The study . . . said 86 percent of surveyed adults believe companies should be required by law to standardize the promises they make on Web sites about how personal information will be protected.

You Are About to Lose Your Privacy

The findings renewed demands for fresh U.S. privacy laws even as the threat of terrorism and heightened security to meet it have supplanted privacy as a cornerstone for technology policy debates in Washington.

Today's policy makers face momentous issues that will determine our future economic environment. Many of these issues are the result of rapidly changing technology.

Ensuring Safe Internet Trade

The Internet has reduced the cost of entry for companies willing to sell goods electronically. Little or no inventory, a small staff, and a modest outlay of capital for the server is all it takes to start a business. How can you trust startup companies that you know only through the Internet? Internet users themselves may provide the best answer. Because of the ease of communication, news of unscrupulous dealings spreads rapidly across the Web and into the electronic media.

One of the fastest-growing forms of online trade is in securities, because electronic brokers have substantially lowered the cost of such trade. Securities trading on the Internet can be very risky, however. The urge to gamble by purchasing stock online has led people into financial trouble.

The term that describes rapid stock trading going on in cyberspace is **day trading.** Unlike brokerage firms, day-trading firms do not really execute customer trades. Instead they set up Internet connections and computers that let the clients come to their "offices" and trade among themselves. Day-trading firms get a commission on all sales, so they encourage people to make trades.

day trading: *buying and selling securities directly over the Internet*

Some people make money day trading. Many others, however, lose money fast. The Securities and Exchange Commission receives hundreds of complaints about online investing, including those of discouraged small investors who lost student loan money or retirement funds. The government must balance the consumer's right to a free market with the need for consumer protection.

Protecting Intellectual Property

Copyright laws are supposed to protect **intellectual property**—a creation whose source is someone's intellect, rather than physical property. Recorded music is an example of intellectual property that has been difficult to protect. Pirating of recorded CDs has been widespread. Some people pirate intellectual property for profit, while other Internet users share software and music at no charge.

intellectual property: *creations of a person's intellect that are protected by copyright; for example, written works and music*

Economic Connection to... Geography

Learning Knows No Boundaries

Students in Australia's outback have for years learned via radio waves. The vast distances in Australia and sparse population in the outback prevented typical schools from operating. At one time, this type of schooling seemed highly unconventional.

Today, however, online learning has spread throughout the United States and other countries. The number of people taking undergraduate and graduate courses online is expected to increase to 2.81 million in 2005, accounting for 20 percent of all higher-education students. For people who don't have the time for in-class learning, or who live across the country from their favorite university, online learning is the answer. ■

In 1999 a coalition of more than 110 music, computer, and consumer-electronics firms published a standard for future players of online music files. The standard blocks the playing of illegal copies of newly released songs and does not allow their distribution over the Internet.

A future digital-rights system could let the publisher decide what rights go with the product. The controls would be both in the software and hardware. For example, digital "tags" in the software represent certain rights, such as the right to transfer the information to another device. Future personal computers–hard-wired with a copyright chip–would interpret the "tag."

Protecting Consumer Privacy

The computer has invaded people's privacy. Advances in computing have made it possible for institutions to collect all kinds of personal information that used to be unrecorded, such as credit card or bank debt, telephone calls, items bought at particular stores, and the movement of one's automobile. Hospitals and schools are constructing vast databases with information ranging from your report card to your DNA. See **Figure 22.5.**

The potential abuses of databases are troubling. Who is watching out for your privacy? National and state government privacy statutes have been in place for many years. **Consumer-credit laws** gave individuals the right to examine their credit beginning in the 1970s, for example. Today an entire industry is growing around security. Software programs are being developed to keep hackers and thieves from infiltrating Web bank accounts, E-mails, and corporate purchasing networks.

consumer-credit laws: *laws passed to protect consumers by giving them access to their credit records*

Developing Nations

How will the information revolution affect developing economies? Some economists believe that information and communications technologies can enable developing countries to "leapfrog" stages of development, thus narrowing the gap between rich and poor.

For example, many countries are rapidly expanding cellular telephone and wireless technology, thereby shortening the time that might have been required to reach rural areas via wired networks. Developing countries can also take advantage of **distance education,** which connects teachers to students through telecommunications. Wireless technology can bring education to remote areas much more quickly and economically than traditional systems.

distance education: *education provided via telecommunications technology*

FIGURE 22.5

Privacy When you visit the doctor or go to school, personal data are collected. New laws may regulate the distribution of such data. ***How could a file of personal data be misused against an individual?***

The wide gap in schooling between developing and industrialized nations, however, is dramatic in the area of computer education. In addition, developing nations often have little appreciation for intellectual property rights. These facts support those economists who believe that the information revolution will widen the divergence between developing and industrialized countries.

It is vital that we keep up with the issues discussed in this section, because an informed citizenry affects leadership. The Information Age provides us with a way to do this. The new technology allows us to keep in touch, both with the issues and with our leaders to influence the critical decisions that will create a challenging cybernomic future.

Practice and **assess** key skills with ***Skillbuilder Interactive Workbook, Level 2.***

SECTION 3 Assessment

Understanding Key Terms

1. **Define** day trading, intellectual property, consumer-credit laws, distance education.

Reviewing Objectives

2. Why is some trading on the Internet considered risky?
3. How is intellectual property being stolen?
4. **Graphic Organizer** Create a diagram like the one in the next column to explain ways that government and business are helping to protect consumer privacy.

Government → Consumer Privacy
Business → Consumer Privacy

Applying Economic Concepts

5. **International Growth and Stability** Do you think the gap between rich and poor nations will widen in the future? Why or why not?

Critical Thinking Activity

6. **Making Predictions** What do you think will be the privacy issues of the next few years as telecommunications and computing power increase?

People & Perspectives

Steven Spielberg

ENTREPRENEUR (1947–)

- **One of Hollywood's most successful directors and producers: credits include *Jaws, Raiders of the Lost Ark, E.T. The ExtraTerrestrial, Jurassic Park, The Color Purple, Back to the Future, Schindler's List, Amistad, Saving Private Ryan, A.I.***
- **Attended California State University at Long Beach**

Combining advances in technology with a great gift for storytelling has made Steven Spielberg an extraordinarily successful entrepreneur and resulted in millions of happy moviegoers. He attributes many of his biggest movie hits to early childhood memories. Spielberg's movie *Close Encounters of the Third Kind* was inspired by watching a meteor shower with his father, a fervent science-fiction fan. Reflecting on his creative gift, Spielberg explains:

> *"Once a month the sky falls on my head, I come to, and I see another movie I want to make. Sometimes I think I've got ball bearings for brains; these ideas are slipping and sliding across each other all the time. My problem is my imagination won't turn off. I wake up so excited I can't eat breakfast. I've never run out of energy. . . . I got it from my mom."*

Spielberg's interests, however, are not limited to movies. Much of Spielberg's attention today is focused on DreamWorks SKG, a studio that he created with Jeffrey Katzenberg and David Geffen. DreamWorks created a joint venture with Sega and Universal Studios to satisfy Spielberg's interest in video arcades. Steven Spielberg draws inspiration from his seven children:

> *"There are films that I feel that I need to make, for a variety of reasons, for personal reasons, for reasons that I want to have fun, that the subject matter is cool, that I think my kids will like it."*

Checking for Understanding

1. **What personal characteristics make Steven Spielberg a successful entrepreneur?**
2. **As part of the "knowledge economy," how may movies affect future innovation?**

CHAPTER 22 Summary

Chapter Overview Visit the *Economics Today and Tomorrow* Web site at ett.glencoe.com and click on ***Chapter 22—Chapter Overviews*** to review chapter information.

SECTION 1 The Growth of E-Commerce

- Numbers, also called digits, are so vital to our lives today that people have labeled our era "the digital age."
- **Microchips** in a network of interconnected computers are changing how people communicate, produce, consume, educate, and entertain themselves.
- Some economists believe we have entered the age of **cybernomics**—economics driven by a huge digital machine, the **Internet.**
- **Web sites** connecting businesses, private organizations, government offices, and educational institutions make locating information and global communication extraordinarily easy. The Internet provides businesses in particular with the opportunity to directly reach suppliers and consumers.
- **E-commerce** is expanding rapidly, affecting both business-to-business relationships and consumers.
- In this new world of cybernomics, the buyer is ruler. If one seller cannot deliver a superior product at a competitive price in real time, another seller will.
- Marketers can now track purchases electronically and organize cybercommunities of people whose needs they serve.

SECTION 2 A New Economy?

- The **Information Age** may be as significant as was the Industrial Revolution in affecting human society.
- The **knowledge economy** includes communications technology, intellectual property, and stored data.
- Some economists believe that new concepts are needed to explain how the knowledge economy differs from earlier economic concepts and principles.
- Most economists agree that **innovation** affects economic growth cycles.

SECTION 3 Issues in Cybernomics

- Cybernomics has raised important issues. Decisions being made by policy makers today will help determine your economic future.
- Among the important issues today are ensuring safe Internet trade, securing **intellectual property** rights, protecting consumer privacy, and helping developing nations catch up with the rapidly changing global economy.
- Communications technology provides access to knowledge and **distance education,** but we must make wise choices that help create a better economic future.

CHAPTER 22

Assessment and Activities

Self-Check Quiz Visit the *Economics Today and Tomorrow* Web site at ett.glencoe.com and click on ***Chapter 22—Self-Check Quizzes*** to prepare for the Chapter Test.

Identifying Key Terms

Write a paragraph about cybernomics using all of the following terms.

- microchip
- cybernomics
- Internet
- World Wide Web
- e-commerce
- intellectual property
- frequency marketing
- innovations

Recalling Facts and Ideas

Section 1

1. Why is e-commerce on the Internet considered both enticing and risky?
2. How has e-commerce shifted the balance of power to the customer?
3. How do computers help marketers know what products you want?

Section 2

4. What revolution changed people's way of life in the nineteenth century?
5. What elements are included in the knowledge economy?
6. Why are knowledge products called weightless?
7. How does the use and consumption of knowledge products differ from traditional products?
8. Over what issues do economists studying the information revolution disagree? On what do most economists agree?
9. How did economist Joseph Schumpeter explain the several large bursts of economic growth during certain periods of history?

Section 3

10. Give an example of intellectual property that has been difficult to protect.
11. Who is most at risk in day trading on the Internet?
12. How has the computer invaded people's privacy?
13. What are the two positions that economists have taken regarding how the information revolution will affect developing economies?

Thinking Critically

1. **Understanding Cause and Effect** Why did many businesses feel compelled to go on the Internet in the 1990s?
2. **Making Generalizations** Write a paragraph expressing whether you believe the Information Age will have as far-reaching effects on society as did the Industrial Revolution.

3. **Categorizing Information** On a table like the one below, rank the four issues presented in Section 3 according to the level of their importance to you. Then rank the same issues according to how they affect the global economy.

Issues as they affect me	Issues as they affect the global economy
1.	1.
2.	2.
3.	3.
4.	4.

Applying Economic Concepts

The Role of Government Choose one of the following areas and write a short position statement on what, if anything, the federal government should be doing about it:

- Assuring personal privacy
- Regulating telecommunications
- Protecting intellectual property
- Regulating securities trading on the Internet

Cooperative Learning Project

Scarcity of resources means that even governments must consider trade-offs and opportunity costs. Organize into four groups, each representing a congressional committee charged with addressing one of the four issues mentioned in Section 3 of this chapter. Prepare an argument supporting your issue and seeking resources to study and resolve it. Present your arguments to the class.

Reviewing Skills

Evaluating Primary and Secondary Sources
Read the excerpt in the next column, then answer the questions that follow.

"In 1984, when I got a job as a field service marketing manager for a large computer manufacturer, I thought I was the only dummy on the block, that everyone else was a genius. But I found out that a lot of people in techie jobs had nontechnical backgrounds–just like me.

Unless you're designing software or are in research and development, where technical degrees are necessary, you can find good jobs in technology. Fear of technology is a waste of time. Dump the fear."

–William A. Schaffer, European development manager for software and technology at Sun Microsystems, 1999

1. Is this a primary or a secondary source? How do you know?
2. When was this document written?
3. What was the general feeling of the person who wrote this document?
4. What kind of information is missing from this passage?

Technology Activity

Using the Internet Probably the most information about privacy for Internet users is to be found on the Net itself. Use a search engine to find out what is being written. Key in *privacy* and/or *encryption* and scroll down through the articles. Make a list of the kinds of sites and news articles that are available.

Analyzing the Global Economy

Visit the United Nation's UNESCO Web site. Open the Yearbook and click on "Culture and Communications." Reference tables here will help you compare the progress of communications technology around the world. Print out a chart, study it, and write a summary report.

Focus on Free Enterprise

Industrial Light & Magic

Chewbacca, C3PO, Darth Vader, Jar Jar Binks, R2-D2, and Yoda. These memorable characters, and the world they inhabit, sprang from the fertile imagination of filmmaker George Lucas. When Lucas first thought up the world of* Star Wars*, he had an idea of what everything should look like. It took Lucas's special effects company, Industrial Light & Magic (ILM), however, to transfer this idea to the movie screen.

C3PO

George Lucas

Beginnings

When George Lucas first took the idea of *Star Wars* to Hollywood studios, he had no luck in getting their backing. Science-fiction movies rarely made money. Finally, 20th Century Fox agreed to back the movie, providing a budget of $9 million. One area in which Fox offered little help was special effects. So in 1975 Lucas set up his own company called Industrial Light & Magic to develop special effects for *Star Wars*.

Unconventional Working Environment

ILM was unlike other companies–either in the movie business or business in general. Except for a few managers, the vast majority of employees were straight out of college. There were no set working hours–ILM was essentially open 24 hours a day. There were few hard-and-fast job descriptions. As well as doing their own jobs, design artists might also be called upon to make models and operate cameras.

Although ILM's work practices were unconventional, they proved very effective. In less than 18 months, the ILM team had completed the *Star Wars* special effects. Although Lucas expressed disappointment with the finished product, the public did not agree. The movie became a huge box-office success.

Building a Reputation

Lucas immediately plowed his profits from the movie into two more episodes of *Star Wars*. While working on these movies, the ILM team began to use computers to control cameras and generate images. Over time, ILM became the industry's leader in applying the most recent technology to moviemaking.

Velociraptor

Digital Effects

In 1993, ILM changed moviegoers' expectations forever with the digital effects it used in the film *Jurassic Park*. Audiences were stunned when they first viewed the digitally created dinosaurs on the big screen—nothing so realistic had ever been done before. Nearly everyone who saw the movie wandered out of the theater asking, "How did they *do* that?"

Steven Spielberg, who directed the film, had seen early digital footage created by the artists at ILM. He immediately scrapped plans to use stop-animation dinosaurs, instead urging ILM to create all the dinosaur scenes using computer graphics. Artists at ILM studied animal behavior and movement, filmed themselves running around their parking lot, and generally dove into the "minds" of dinosaurs to create the most believable special effects ever.

This technological innovation, along with dazzling artistic creativity, soon won ILM the attention of other moviemakers. Many times when a movie required stunning visual effects, ILM was called in—earning the company critical and financial success. ILM has won 14 Academy Awards for Best Visual Effects. In addition, ILM has provided the special effects for more than half of the top 15 box-office hits of all time.

T-rex

Free Enterprise in Action

1. **How was ILM different from most other companies in the movie business?**
2. **What attracted other moviemakers to ILM?**

REFERENCE HANDBOOK

Contents

Reference Atlas A1
Standard & Poor's Databank A14
Glossary A30
Spanish Glossary A42
Spanish Chapter Summaries A55
Index A77

HONORING AMERICA

Flag Etiquette

Over the years, Americans have developed rules and customs concerning the use and display of the flag. One of the most important things every American should remember is to treat the flag with respect.

- The flag should be raised and lowered by hand and displayed only from sunrise to sunset. On special occasions, it may be displayed at night, but it should be illuminated.
- The flag may be displayed on all days, weather permitting, particularly on national and state holidays and on historic and special occasions.
- No flag may be flown above the American flag or to the right of it at the same height.
- The flag should never touch the ground or floor beneath it.
- The flag may be flown at half-staff by order of the president, usually to mourn the death of a public official.
- The flag may be flown upside down only to signal distress.
- When the flag becomes old and tattered, it should be destroyed by burning. According to an approved custom, the Union (stars on blue field) is first cut from the flag; then the two pieces, which no longer form a flag, are burned.

★ ★ ★ ★ ★ ★ ★ ★

The Star-Spangled Banner

O! say can you see, by the dawn's early light,
What so proudly we hail'd at the twilight's last gleaming,
Whose broad stripes and bright stars through the perilous fight,
O'er the ramparts we watched, were so gallantly streaming?
And the Rockets' red glare, the Bombs bursting in air,
Gave proof through the night that our Flag was still there;
O! say, does that star-spangled banner yet wave
O'er the Land of the free and the home of the brave!

The Pledge of Allegiance

I pledge allegiance to the Flag of the United States of America and to the Republic for which it stands, one Nation under God, indivisible, with liberty and justice for all.

Reference Atlas

World: Political	A2
United States: Political	A4
World: Land Use	A6
United States: Land Use	A8
World GDP Cartogram	A10
World Population Cartogram	A12

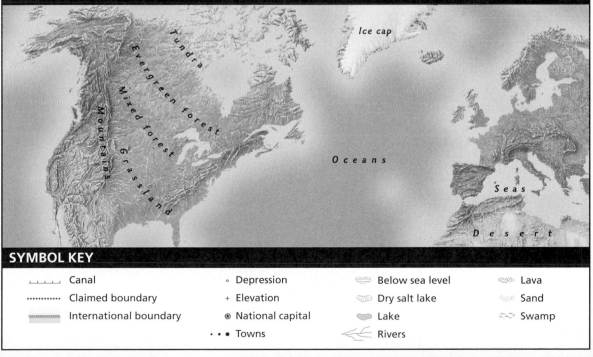

ATLAS KEY

Ice cap
Tundra
Evergreen forest
Mixed forest
Mountains
Grassland
Oceans
Seas
Desert

SYMBOL KEY

- Canal
- Claimed boundary
- International boundary
- Depression
- Elevation
- National capital
- Towns
- Below sea level
- Dry salt lake
- Lake
- Rivers
- Lava
- Sand
- Swamp

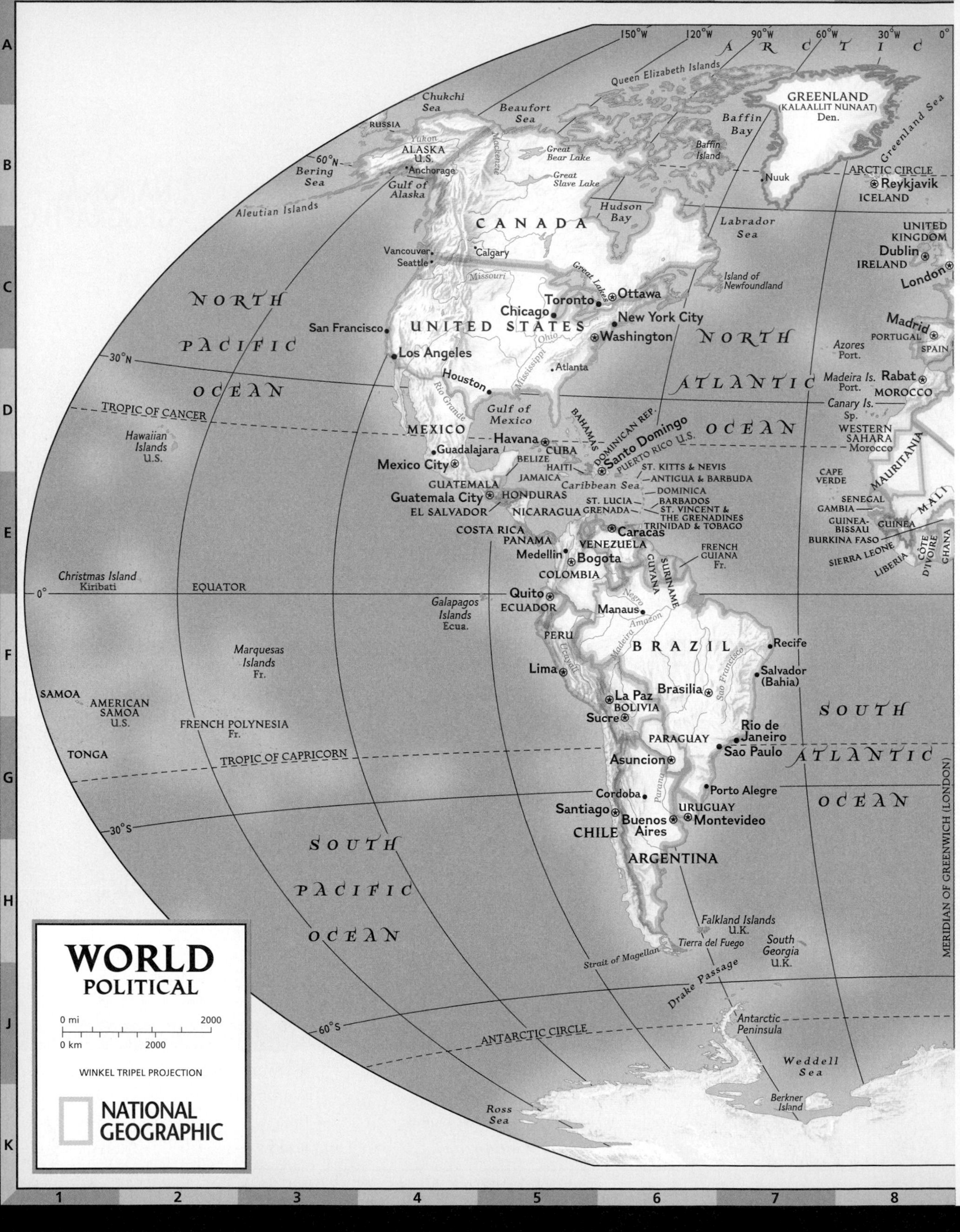
WORLD
POLITICAL
0 mi 2000
0 km 2000
WINKEL TRIPEL PROJECTION
NATIONAL GEOGRAPHIC
ARCTIC
GREENLAND (KALAALLIT NUNAAT) Den.
Queen Elizabeth Islands
Chukchi Sea
Beaufort Sea
Baffin Bay
Greenland Sea
RUSSIA
ALASKA U.S.
Anchorage
Bering Sea
Gulf of Alaska
Aleutian Islands
Great Bear Lake
Great Slave Lake
Baffin Island
Nuuk
ARCTIC CIRCLE
Reykjavik
ICELAND
Hudson Bay
Labrador Sea
CANADA
UNITED KINGDOM
Dublin
IRELAND
London
Vancouver
Seattle
Calgary
Great Lakes
Island of Newfoundland
NORTH PACIFIC OCEAN
Toronto
Ottawa
Chicago
New York City
San Francisco
UNITED STATES
Washington
NORTH ATLANTIC OCEAN
Madrid
PORTUGAL
SPAIN
Azores Port.
Los Angeles
Atlanta
Houston
Madeira Is. Port.
Rabat
MOROCCO
Canary Is. Sp.
TROPIC OF CANCER
Gulf of Mexico
BAHAMAS
DOMINICAN REP.
Santo Domingo
PUERTO RICO U.S.
MEXICO
Havana
CUBA
WESTERN SAHARA Morocco
MAURITANIA
Hawaiian Islands U.S.
Guadalajara
BELIZE
HAITI
ST. KITTS & NEVIS
ANTIGUA & BARBUDA
Mexico City
JAMAICA
Caribbean Sea
DOMINICA
CAPE VERDE
GUATEMALA
Guatemala City
HONDURAS
ST. LUCIA
BARBADOS
ST. VINCENT & THE GRENADINES
SENEGAL
GAMBIA
MALI
EL SALVADOR
NICARAGUA
GRENADA
TRINIDAD & TOBAGO
GUINEA-BISSAU
GUINEA
COSTA RICA
Caracas
PANAMA
VENEZUELA
BURKINA FASO
SIERRA LEONE
LIBERIA
CÔTE D'IVOIRE
GHANA
Medellin
Bogota
GUYANA
SURINAME
FRENCH GUIANA Fr.
COLOMBIA
Christmas Island Kiribati
EQUATOR
Quito
ECUADOR
Galapagos Islands Ecua.
Negro
Manaus
Amazon
PERU
Madeira
BRAZIL
Recife
Marquesas Islands Fr.
Ucayali
Lima
Salvador (Bahia)
Brasilia
Sao Francisco
SAMOA
AMERICAN SAMOA U.S.
La Paz
BOLIVIA
SOUTH ATLANTIC OCEAN
Sucre
FRENCH POLYNESIA Fr.
Rio de Janeiro
PARAGUAY
TONGA
Sao Paulo
TROPIC OF CAPRICORN
Asuncion
Parana
Porto Alegre
Cordoba
URUGUAY
Santiago
Buenos Aires
Montevideo
CHILE
SOUTH PACIFIC OCEAN
ARGENTINA
MERIDIAN OF GREENWICH (LONDON)
Falkland Islands U.K.
Tierra del Fuego
South Georgia U.K.
Strait of Magellan
Drake Passage
Antarctic Peninsula
ANTARCTIC CIRCLE
Weddell Sea
Ross Sea
Berkner Island
150°W
120°W
90°W
60°W
30°W
0°
60°N
30°N
0°
30°S
60°S
1 2 3 4 5 6 7 8
A B C D E F G H J K
Missouri
Ohio
Mississippi
Rio Grande
Yukon
Mackenzie

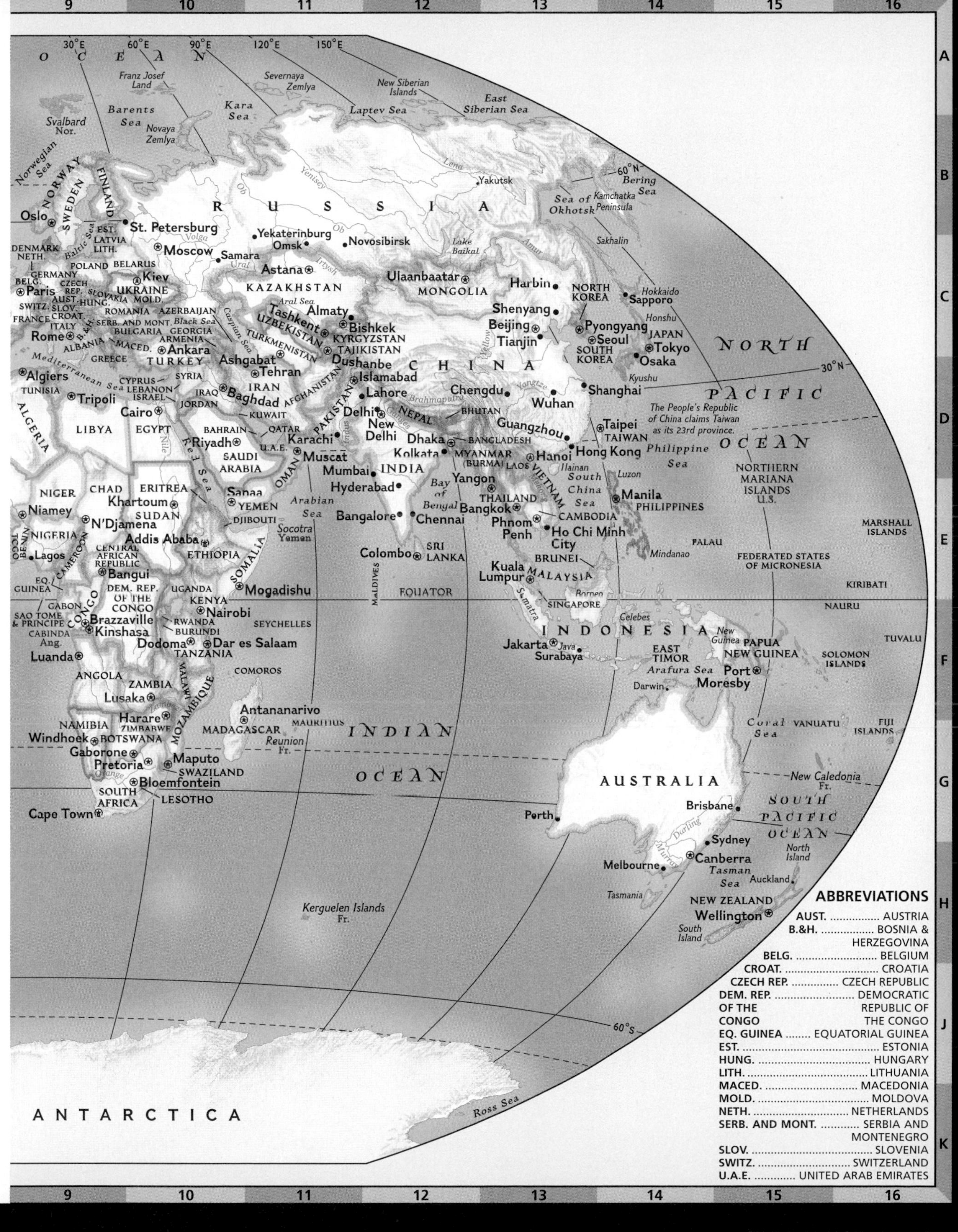

9 10 11 12 13 14 15 16
A B C D E F G H J K
30°E 60°E 90°E 120°E 150°E
OCEAN
Franz Josef Land
Severnaya Zemlya
New Siberian Islands
East Siberian Sea
Laptev Sea
Kara Sea
Barents Sea
Svalbard Nor.
Novaya Zemlya
Norwegian Sea
NORWAY
SWEDEN
FINLAND
60°N
Bering Sea
Yakutsk
Sea of Okhotsk
Kamchatka Peninsula
RUSSIA
Oslo
St. Petersburg
Baltic Sea
EST.
LATVIA
LITH.
Moscow
Volga
Yekaterinburg
Omsk
Novosibirsk
Ob
Yenisey
Lena
Lake Baikal
Amur
Sakhalin
DENMARK
NETH.
POLAND
BELARUS
GERMANY
BELG.
CZECH REP.
Paris
Kiev
UKRAINE
AUST.
HUNG.
SLOVAKIA
MOLD.
SWITZ.
SLOV.
CROAT.
FRANCE
ROMANIA
ITALY
B.&H.
SERB. AND MONT.
BULGARIA
Rome
ALBANIA
MACED.
GREECE
Samara
Ural
Astana
Irtysh
KAZAKHSTAN
Ulaanbaatar
MONGOLIA
Harbin
NORTH KOREA
Hokkaido
Sapporo
AZERBAIJAN
Black Sea
GEORGIA
ARMENIA
Caspian Sea
Aral Sea
Tashkent
Almaty
Bishkek
KYRGYZSTAN
UZBEKISTAN
TURKMENISTAN
TAJIKISTAN
Ankara
TURKEY
Ashgabat
Dushanbe
CHINA
Shenyang
Beijing
Tianjin
Pyongyang
Seoul
SOUTH KOREA
Honshu
JAPAN
Tokyo
Osaka
Kyushu
NORTH
30°N
Mediterranean Sea
Algiers
TUNISIA
CYPRUS
SYRIA
LEBANON
ISRAEL
Tehran
IRAN
Islamabad
IRAQ
Baghdad
AFGHANISTAN
Lahore
Brahmaputra
Chengdu
Yangtze
Wuhan
Shanghai
PACIFIC
The People's Republic of China claims Taiwan as its 23rd province.
Tripoli
ALGERIA
Cairo
JORDAN
KUWAIT
PAKISTAN
Delhi
New Delhi
NEPAL
BHUTAN
Guangzhou
Taipei
TAIWAN
Hong Kong
LIBYA
EGYPT
Nile
BAHRAIN
QATAR
U.A.E.
Riyadh
Karachi
Indus
Ganges
Dhaka
BANGLADESH
Kolkata
MYANMAR (BURMA)
LAOS
Hanoi
Philippine Sea
OCEAN
Red Sea
SAUDI ARABIA
Muscat
OMAN
Mumbai
INDIA
Bay of Bengal
Yangon
VIETNAM
Hainan
South China Sea
Luzon
NORTHERN MARIANA ISLANDS U.S.
NIGER
CHAD
ERITREA
Sanaa
YEMEN
Hyderabad
Manila
PHILIPPINES
Khartoum
SUDAN
Arabian Sea
THAILAND
Bangkok
CAMBODIA
Niamey
N'Djamena
DJIBOUTI
Socotra Yemen
Bangalore
Chennai
Phnom Penh
Ho Chi Minh City
MARSHALL ISLANDS
NIGERIA
BENIN
TOGO
Addis Ababa
ETHIOPIA
SOMALIA
SRI LANKA
Colombo
PALAU
Mindanao
Lagos
CAMEROON
CENTRAL AFRICAN REPUBLIC
Bangui
BRUNEI
FEDERATED STATES OF MICRONESIA
Kuala Lumpur
MALAYSIA
EQ. GUINEA
DEM. REP. OF THE CONGO
UGANDA
KENYA
Mogadishu
MALDIVES
EQUATOR
Sumatra
Borneo
SINGAPORE
KIRIBATI
GABON
CONGO
Nairobi
NAURU
SAO TOME & PRINCIPE
Brazzaville
Kinshasa
RWANDA
BURUNDI
SEYCHELLES
Celebes
INDONESIA
New Guinea
PAPUA NEW GUINEA
CABINDA Ang.
Dodoma
Dar es Salaam
TANZANIA
Jakarta
Java
Surabaya
EAST TIMOR
TUVALU
Luanda
Arafura Sea
Port Moresby
SOLOMON ISLANDS
ANGOLA
COMOROS
Darwin
ZAMBIA
MALAWI
Lusaka
MOZAMBIQUE
Antananarivo
Zambezi
NAMIBIA
Harare
ZIMBABWE
MADAGASCAR
MAURITIUS
INDIAN
Coral Sea
VANUATU
FIJI ISLANDS
Windhoek
BOTSWANA
Reunion Fr.
Gaborone
Maputo
Pretoria
SWAZILAND
Orange
OCEAN
New Caledonia Fr.
Bloemfontein
AUSTRALIA
SOUTH AFRICA
LESOTHO
Brisbane
SOUTH PACIFIC OCEAN
Cape Town
Perth
Darling
Sydney
Murray
Canberra
North Island
Melbourne
Tasman Sea
Auckland
Tasmania
NEW ZEALAND
Wellington
South Island
Kerguelen Islands Fr.
60°S
Ross Sea
ANTARCTICA
ABBREVIATIONS
AUST. .... AUSTRIA
B.&H. .... BOSNIA & HERZEGOVINA
BELG. .... BELGIUM
CROAT. .... CROATIA
CZECH REP. .... CZECH REPUBLIC
DEM. REP. OF THE CONGO .... DEMOCRATIC REPUBLIC OF THE CONGO
EQ. GUINEA .... EQUATORIAL GUINEA
EST. .... ESTONIA
HUNG. .... HUNGARY
LITH. .... LITHUANIA
MACED. .... MACEDONIA
MOLD. .... MOLDOVA
NETH. .... NETHERLANDS
SERB. AND MONT. .... SERBIA AND MONTENEGRO
SLOV. .... SLOVENIA
SWITZ. .... SWITZERLAND
U.A.E. .... UNITED ARAB EMIRATES

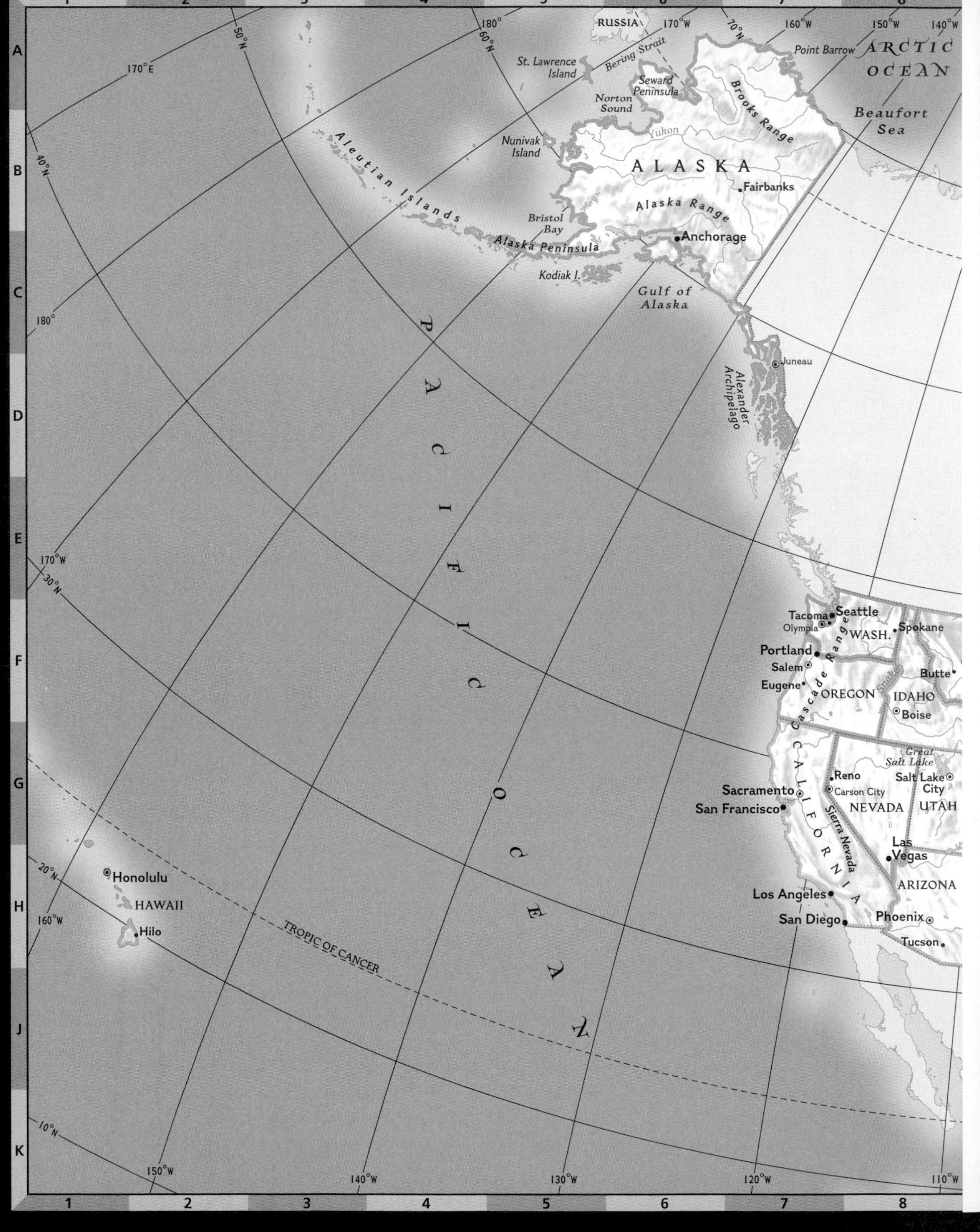
RUSSIA
St. Lawrence Island
Bering Strait
Seward Peninsula
Norton Sound
Point Barrow
ARCTIC OCEAN
Brooks Range
Beaufort Sea
Yukon
Nunivak Island
ALASKA
Fairbanks
Alaska Range
Aleutian Islands
Bristol Bay
Alaska Peninsula
Anchorage
Kodiak I.
Gulf of Alaska
Juneau
Alexander Archipelago
PACIFIC OCEAN
Tacoma
Seattle
Olympia
WASH.
Spokane
Portland
Salem
Eugene
Cascade Range
OREGON
Snake
IDAHO
Boise
Butte
Great Salt Lake
Salt Lake City
UTAH
Reno
Carson City
NEVADA
Sacramento
San Francisco
CALIFORNIA
Sierra Nevada
Las Vegas
ARIZONA
Los Angeles
San Diego
Phoenix
Tucson
Honolulu
HAWAII
Hilo
TROPIC OF CANCER
170°E
180°
170°W
160°W
150°W
140°W
130°W
120°W
110°W
70°N
60°N
50°N
40°N
30°N
20°N
10°N
1 2 3 4 5 6 7 8
A B C D E F G H J K

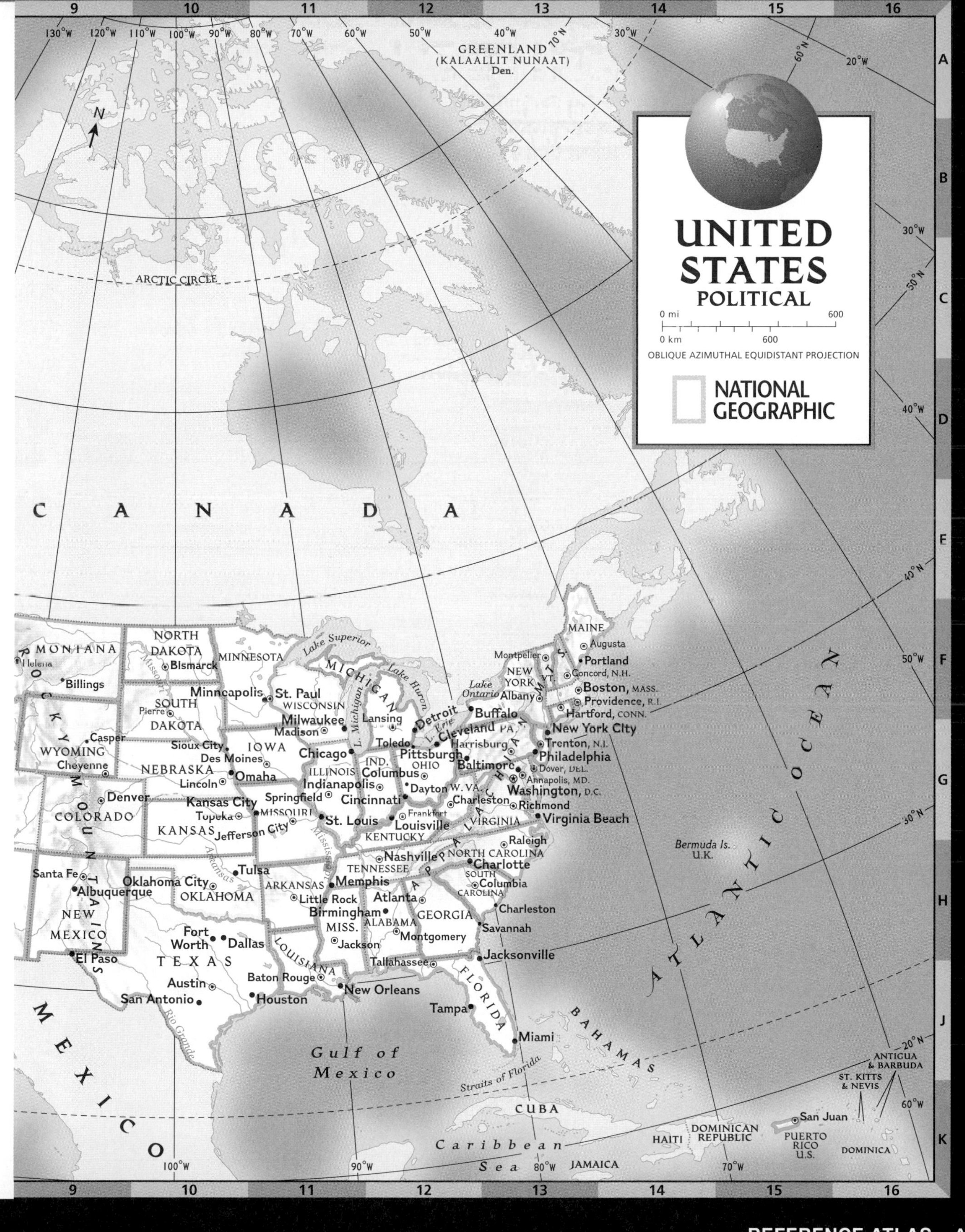
UNITED STATES
POLITICAL
0 mi 600
0 km 600
OBLIQUE AZIMUTHAL EQUIDISTANT PROJECTION
NATIONAL GEOGRAPHIC
GREENLAND (KALAALLIT NUNAAT) Den.
ARCTIC CIRCLE
CANADA
ATLANTIC OCEAN
Gulf of Mexico
MEXICO
Caribbean Sea
CUBA
HAITI
DOMINICAN REPUBLIC
JAMAICA
PUERTO RICO U.S.
San Juan
BAHAMAS
Bermuda Is. U.K.
ANTIGUA & BARBUDA
ST. KITTS & NEVIS
DOMINICA
Straits of Florida
ROCKY MOUNTAINS
APPALACHIAN MTS.
MONTANA
Helena
Billings
NORTH DAKOTA
Bismarck
MINNESOTA
Minneapolis
St. Paul
SOUTH DAKOTA
Pierre
WYOMING
Casper
Cheyenne
NEBRASKA
Lincoln
Omaha
IOWA
Des Moines
Sioux City
WISCONSIN
Madison
Milwaukee
MICHIGAN
Lansing
Detroit
Lake Superior
Lake Michigan
Lake Huron
Lake Erie
Lake Ontario
ILLINOIS
Chicago
IND.
Indianapolis
OHIO
Columbus
Toledo
Cleveland
Dayton
Cincinnati
PA.
Pittsburgh
Harrisburg
Philadelphia
NEW YORK
Buffalo
Albany
New York City
Trenton, N.J.
Dover, DEL.
Baltimore
Annapolis, MD.
Washington, D.C.
W. VA.
Charleston
VIRGINIA
Richmond
Virginia Beach
MAINE
Augusta
Portland
Montpelier
VT.
N.H.
Concord, N.H.
Boston, MASS.
Providence, R.I.
Hartford, CONN.
COLORADO
Denver
KANSAS
Topeka
Kansas City
MISSOURI
Springfield
Jefferson City
St. Louis
KENTUCKY
Frankfort
Louisville
TENNESSEE
Nashville
Memphis
NORTH CAROLINA
Raleigh
Charlotte
SOUTH CAROLINA
Columbia
Charleston
GEORGIA
Atlanta
Savannah
ALABAMA
Birmingham
Montgomery
MISS.
Jackson
ARKANSAS
Little Rock
OKLAHOMA
Oklahoma City
Tulsa
NEW MEXICO
Santa Fe
Albuquerque
El Paso
TEXAS
Fort Worth
Dallas
Austin
San Antonio
Houston
LOUISIANA
Baton Rouge
New Orleans
FLORIDA
Tallahassee
Jacksonville
Tampa
Miami
Missouri
Mississippi
Arkansas
Rio Grande

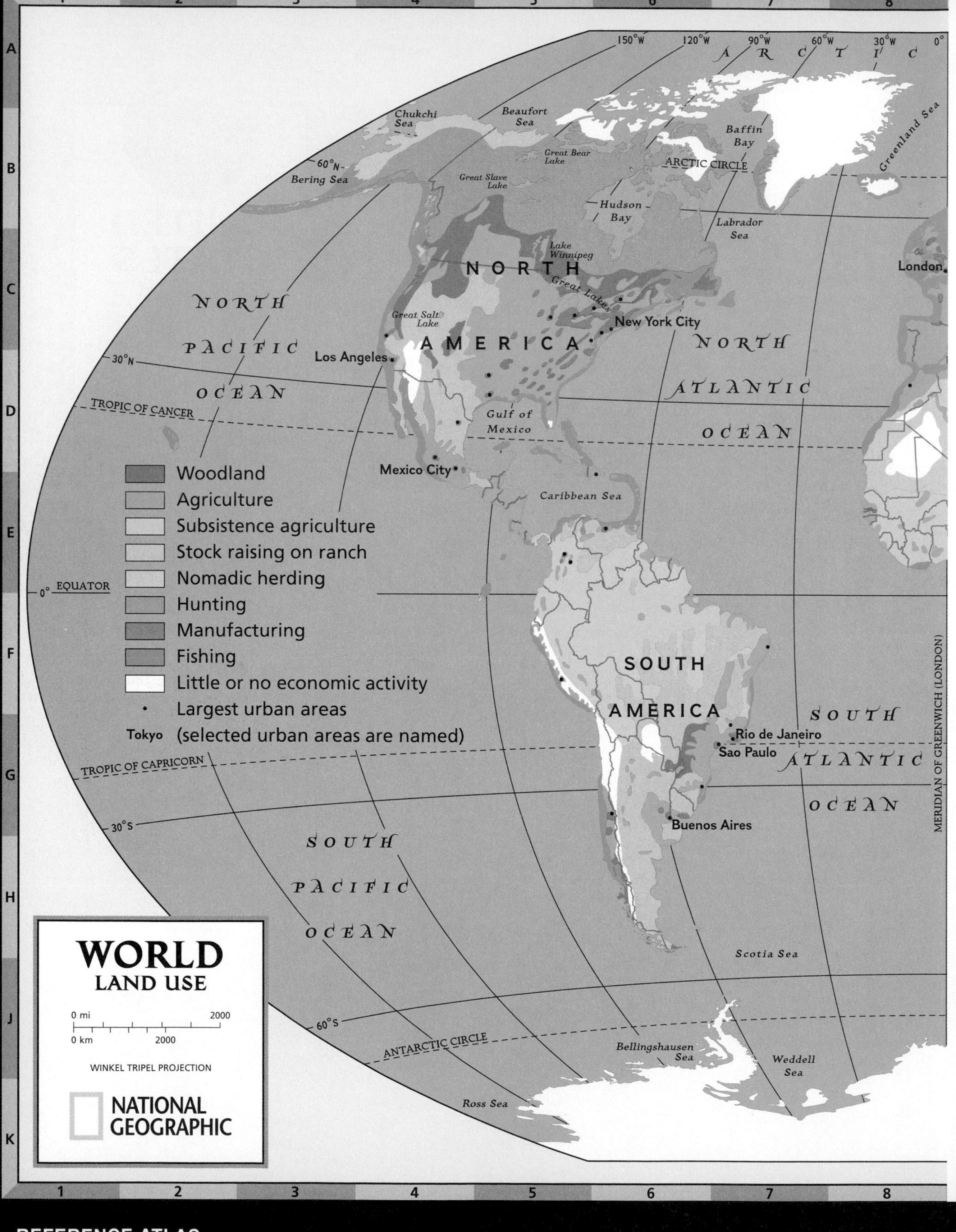

WORLD
LAND USE
Woodland
Agriculture
Subsistence agriculture
Stock raising on ranch
Nomadic herding
Hunting
Manufacturing
Fishing
Little or no economic activity
Largest urban areas
Tokyo (selected urban areas are named)
0 mi 2000
0 km 2000
WINKEL TRIPEL PROJECTION
NATIONAL GEOGRAPHIC
NORTH AMERICA
SOUTH AMERICA
NORTH PACIFIC OCEAN
SOUTH PACIFIC OCEAN
NORTH ATLANTIC OCEAN
SOUTH ATLANTIC OCEAN
ARCTIC
Chukchi Sea
Beaufort Sea
Bering Sea
Great Bear Lake
Great Slave Lake
Baffin Bay
Greenland Sea
Hudson Bay
Labrador Sea
Lake Winnipeg
Great Lakes
Great Salt Lake
New York City
Los Angeles
London
Gulf of Mexico
Mexico City
Caribbean Sea
Rio de Janeiro
Sao Paulo
Buenos Aires
Scotia Sea
Bellingshausen Sea
Weddell Sea
Ross Sea
ARCTIC CIRCLE
TROPIC OF CANCER
EQUATOR
TROPIC OF CAPRICORN
ANTARCTIC CIRCLE
MERIDIAN OF GREENWICH (LONDON)
150°W
120°W
90°W
60°W
30°W
0°
60°N
30°N
0°
30°S
60°S
1 2 3 4 5 6 7 8
A B C D E F G H J K

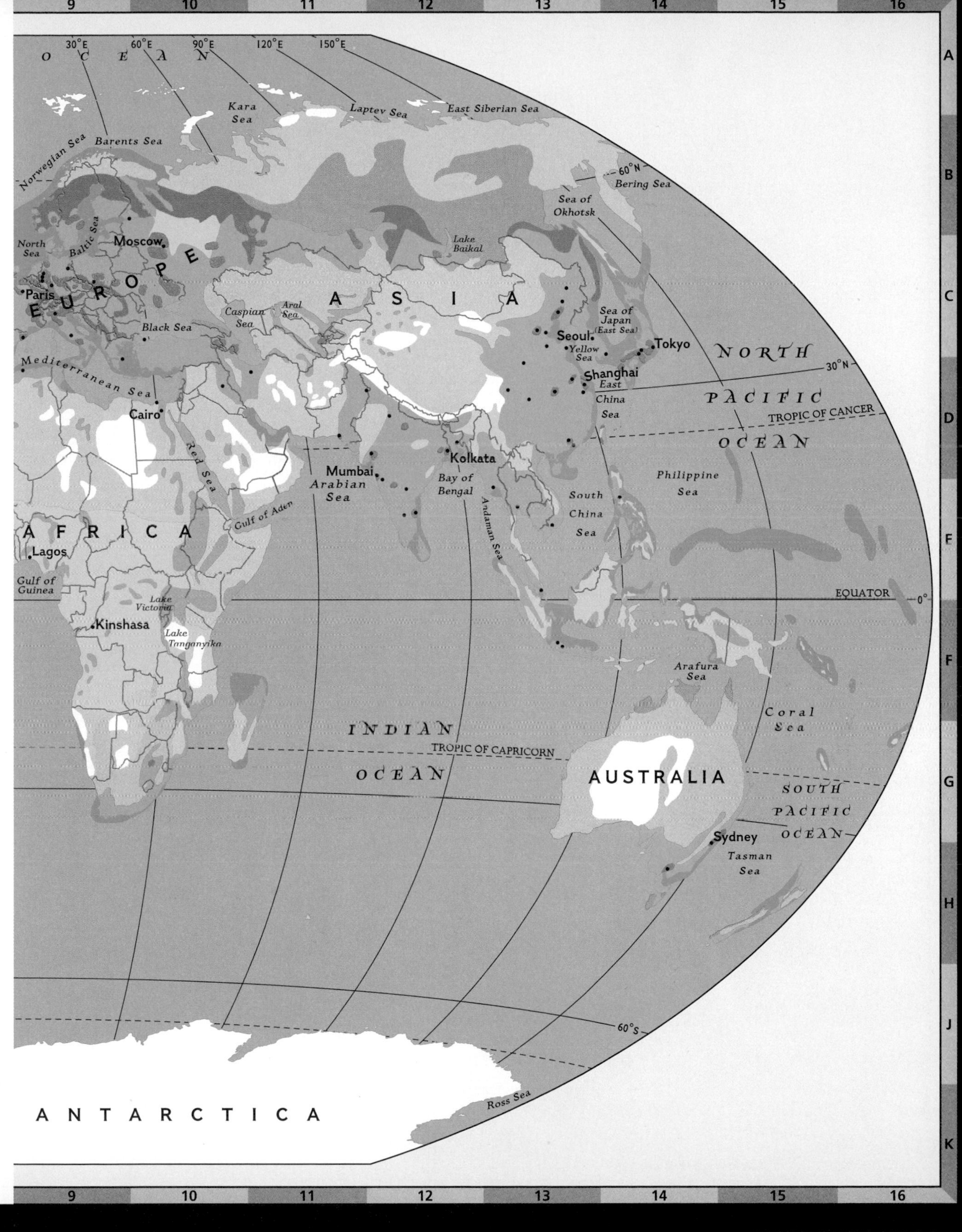

9
10
11
12
13
14
15
16
A
B
C
D
E
F
G
H
J
K
30°E
60°E
90°E
120°E
150°E
O C E A N
Kara Sea
Laptev Sea
East Siberian Sea
Norwegian Sea
Barents Sea
60°N
Bering Sea
Sea of Okhotsk
North Sea
Baltic Sea
Moscow
Lake Baikal
EUROPE
ASIA
Paris
Caspian Sea
Aral Sea
Sea of Japan (East Sea)
Black Sea
Seoul
Tokyo
Yellow Sea
NORTH
Mediterranean Sea
Shanghai
30°N
East China Sea
PACIFIC
Cairo
TROPIC OF CANCER
OCEAN
Red Sea
Kolkata
Mumbai
Arabian Sea
Bay of Bengal
Philippine Sea
South China Sea
Andaman Sea
Gulf of Aden
AFRICA
Lagos
Gulf of Guinea
Lake Victoria
EQUATOR
0°
Kinshasa
Lake Tanganyika
Arafura Sea
Coral Sea
INDIAN
TROPIC OF CAPRICORN
OCEAN
AUSTRALIA
SOUTH
PACIFIC
OCEAN
Sydney
Tasman Sea
60°S
Ross Sea
ANTARCTICA

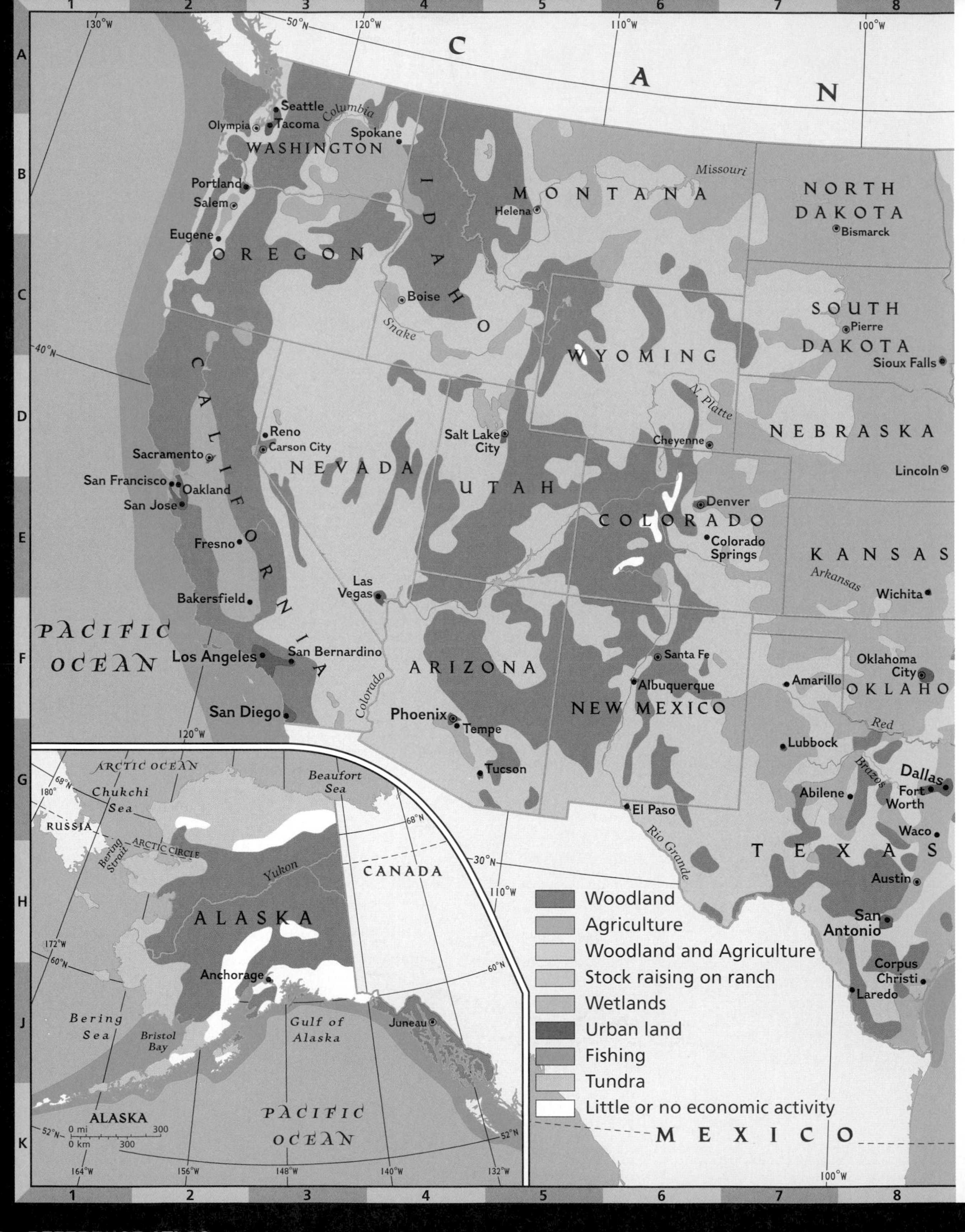

CANADA
WASHINGTON
Seattle
Tacoma
Olympia
Spokane
Columbia
OREGON
Portland
Salem
Eugene
IDAHO
Boise
Snake
MONTANA
Helena
Missouri
NORTH DAKOTA
Bismarck
SOUTH DAKOTA
Pierre
Sioux Falls
WYOMING
N. Platte
Cheyenne
NEBRASKA
Lincoln
CALIFORNIA
Sacramento
San Francisco
Oakland
San Jose
Fresno
Bakersfield
Los Angeles
San Bernardino
San Diego
NEVADA
Reno
Carson City
Las Vegas
UTAH
Salt Lake City
COLORADO
Denver
Colorado Springs
KANSAS
Arkansas
Wichita
ARIZONA
Colorado
Phoenix
Tempe
Tucson
NEW MEXICO
Santa Fe
Albuquerque
El Paso
Rio Grande
OKLAHOMA
Oklahoma City
Red
Amarillo
Lubbock
TEXAS
Brazos
Dallas
Fort Worth
Abilene
Waco
Austin
San Antonio
Corpus Christi
Laredo
PACIFIC OCEAN
MEXICO
ARCTIC OCEAN
Chukchi Sea
Beaufort Sea
RUSSIA
Bering Strait
ARCTIC CIRCLE
Yukon
ALASKA
CANADA
Anchorage
Juneau
Bering Sea
Bristol Bay
Gulf of Alaska
PACIFIC OCEAN
ALASKA
0 mi 300
0 km 300
Woodland
Agriculture
Woodland and Agriculture
Stock raising on ranch
Wetlands
Urban land
Fishing
Tundra
Little or no economic activity

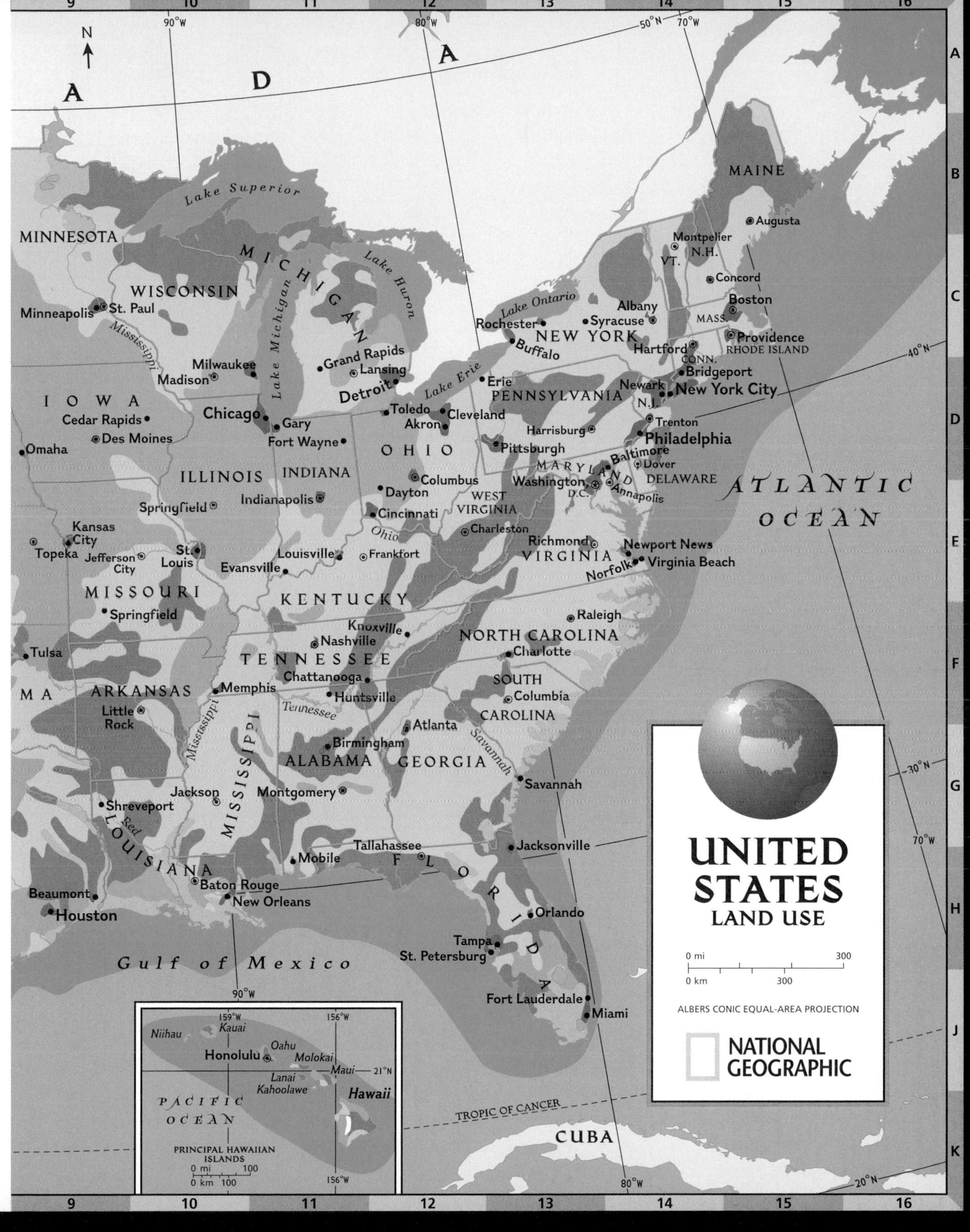

UNITED STATES
LAND USE
0 mi 300
0 km 300
ALBERS CONIC EQUAL-AREA PROJECTION
NATIONAL GEOGRAPHIC
ATLANTIC OCEAN
Gulf of Mexico
CUBA
TROPIC OF CANCER
PRINCIPAL HAWAIIAN ISLANDS
PACIFIC OCEAN
Niihau
Kauai
Oahu
Honolulu
Molokai
Maui
Lanai
Kahoolawe
Hawaii
MINNESOTA
WISCONSIN
MICHIGAN
IOWA
ILLINOIS
INDIANA
OHIO
PENNSYLVANIA
NEW YORK
MAINE
N.H.
VT.
MASS.
RHODE ISLAND
CONN.
N.J.
DELAWARE
MARYLAND
WEST VIRGINIA
VIRGINIA
KENTUCKY
MISSOURI
TENNESSEE
NORTH CAROLINA
SOUTH CAROLINA
ARKANSAS
MISSISSIPPI
ALABAMA
GEORGIA
LOUISIANA
FLORIDA
Lake Superior
Lake Michigan
Lake Huron
Lake Erie
Lake Ontario
Mississippi
Ohio
Tennessee
Savannah
Red
Minneapolis
St. Paul
Milwaukee
Madison
Chicago
Gary
Grand Rapids
Lansing
Detroit
Toledo
Cleveland
Akron
Erie
Buffalo
Rochester
Syracuse
Albany
Montpelier
Augusta
Concord
Boston
Providence
Hartford
Bridgeport
Newark
New York City
Trenton
Philadelphia
Harrisburg
Pittsburgh
Baltimore
Dover
Annapolis
Washington, D.C.
Cedar Rapids
Des Moines
Omaha
Fort Wayne
Columbus
Dayton
Indianapolis
Springfield
Cincinnati
Charleston
Richmond
Newport News
Norfolk
Virginia Beach
Kansas City
Topeka
Jefferson City
St. Louis
Louisville
Frankfort
Evansville
Springfield
Raleigh
Knoxville
Nashville
Charlotte
Tulsa
Memphis
Chattanooga
Huntsville
Columbia
Little Rock
Atlanta
Birmingham
Montgomery
Jackson
Shreveport
Savannah
Jacksonville
Tallahassee
Mobile
Baton Rouge
New Orleans
Beaumont
Houston
Orlando
Tampa
St. Petersburg
Fort Lauderdale
Miami

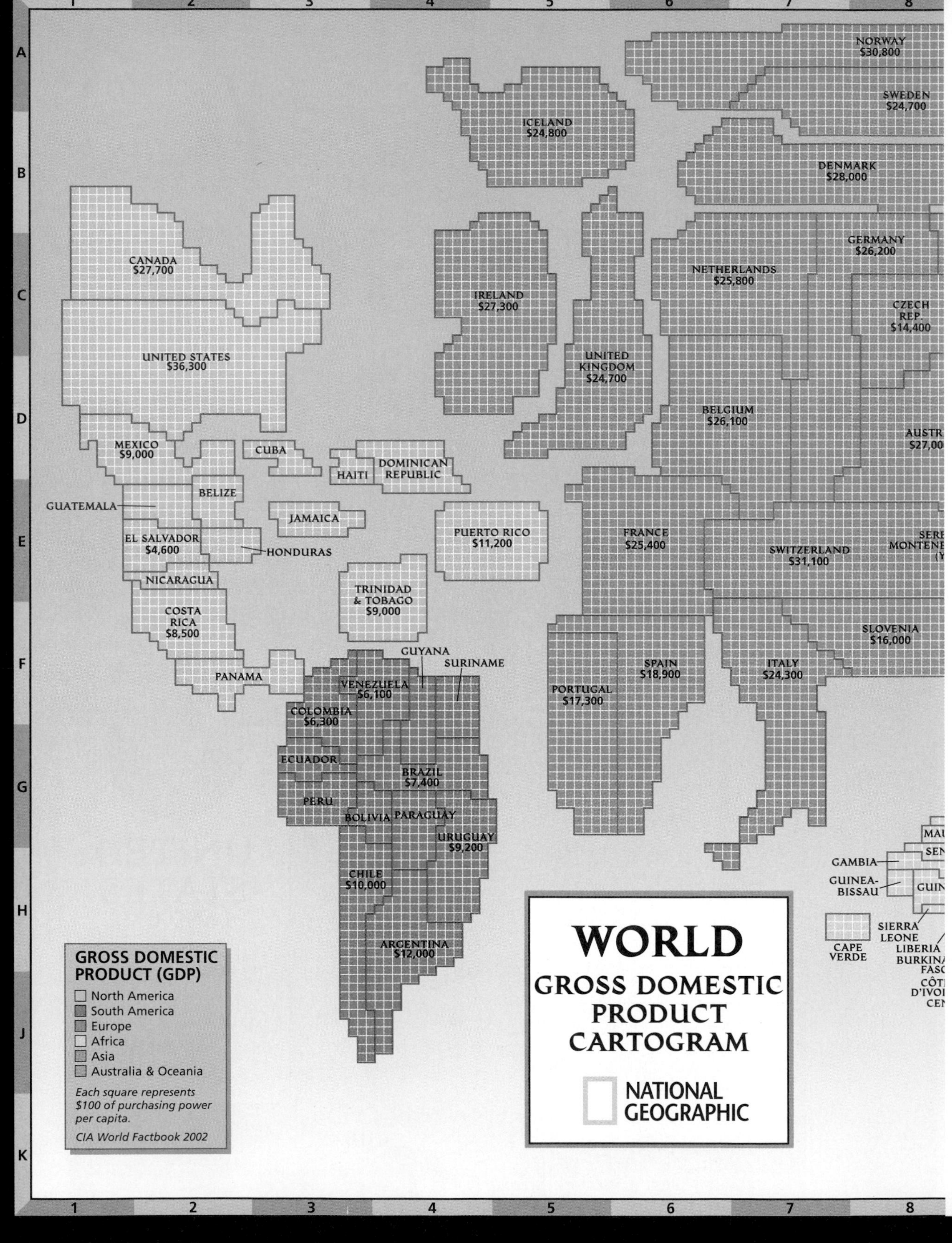

WORLD
GROSS DOMESTIC PRODUCT CARTOGRAM
NATIONAL GEOGRAPHIC
GROSS DOMESTIC PRODUCT (GDP)
North America
South America
Europe
Africa
Asia
Australia & Oceania
Each square represents $100 of purchasing power per capita.
CIA World Factbook 2002
NORWAY $30,800
SWEDEN $24,700
ICELAND $24,800
DENMARK $28,000
GERMANY $26,200
NETHERLANDS $25,800
CZECH REP. $14,400
IRELAND $27,300
UNITED KINGDOM $24,700
BELGIUM $26,100
AUSTR
$27,00
FRANCE $25,400
SWITZERLAND $31,100
SERB
MONTENE
SLOVENIA $16,000
SPAIN $18,900
ITALY $24,300
PORTUGAL $17,300
CANADA $27,700
UNITED STATES $36,300
MEXICO $9,000
CUBA
HAITI
DOMINICAN REPUBLIC
BELIZE
GUATEMALA
JAMAICA
PUERTO RICO $11,200
EL SALVADOR $4,600
HONDURAS
NICARAGUA
TRINIDAD & TOBAGO $9,000
COSTA RICA $8,500
PANAMA
GUYANA
SURINAME
VENEZUELA $6,100
COLOMBIA $6,300
ECUADOR
BRAZIL $7,400
PERU
BOLIVIA
PARAGUAY
URUGUAY $9,200
CHILE $10,000
ARGENTINA $12,000
MAU
SEN
GAMBIA
GUINEA-BISSAU
GUIN
CAPE VERDE
SIERRA LEONE
LIBERIA
BURKINA
FASO
CÔTE
D'IVOI
CEN

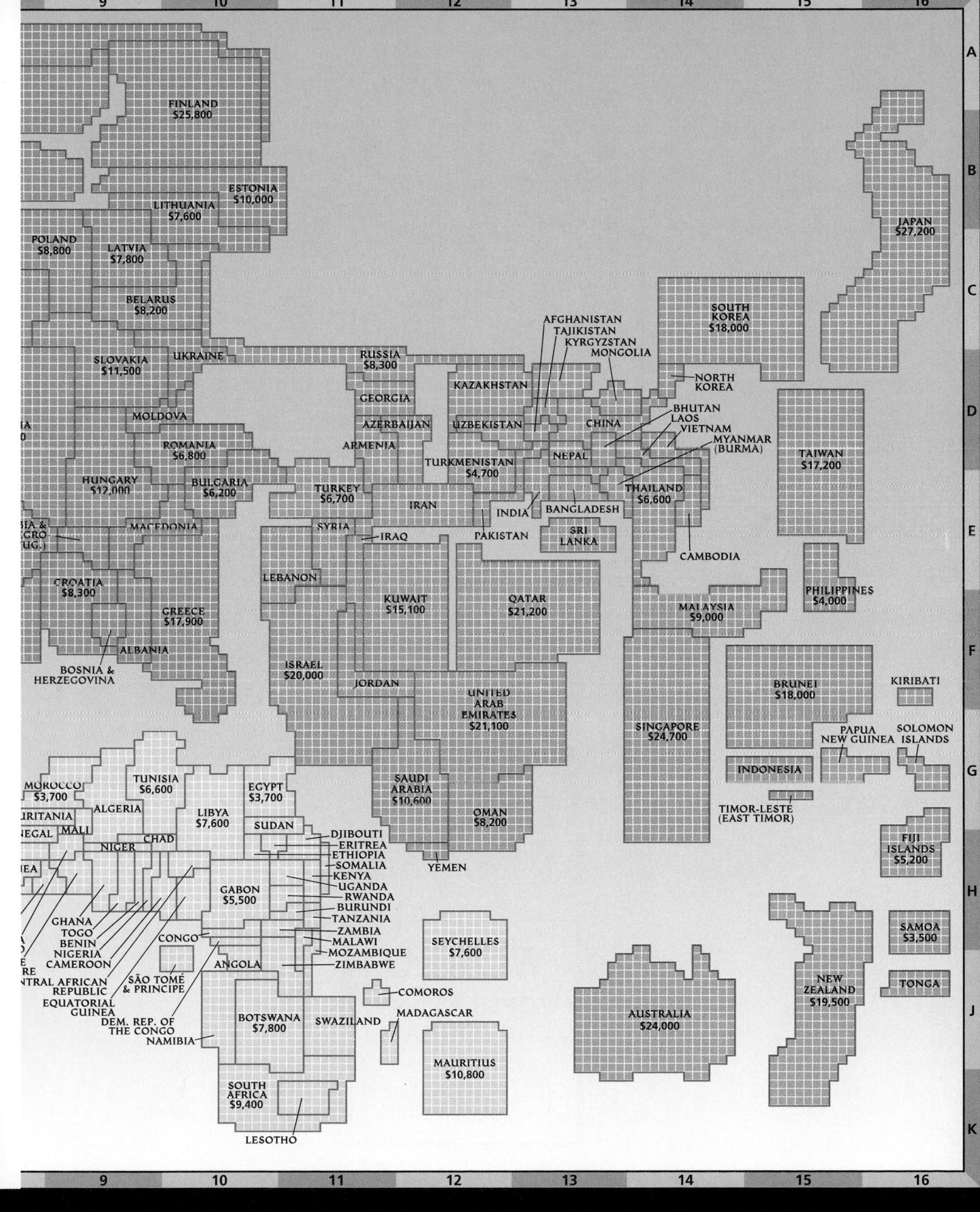

FINLAND
$25,800
ESTONIA
$10,000
LITHUANIA
$7,600
POLAND
$8,800
LATVIA
$7,800
BELARUS
$8,200
SLOVAKIA
$11,500
UKRAINE
RUSSIA
$8,300
MOLDOVA
ROMANIA
$6,800
HUNGARY
$12,000
BULGARIA
$6,200
MACEDONIA
CROATIA
$8,300
GREECE
$17,900
ALBANIA
BOSNIA &
HERZEGOVINA
GEORGIA
AZERBAIJAN
ARMENIA
TURKEY
$6,700
SYRIA
IRAQ
LEBANON
KUWAIT
$15,100
QATAR
$21,200
ISRAEL
$20,000
JORDAN
UNITED
ARAB
EMIRATES
$21,100
SAUDI
ARABIA
$10,600
OMAN
$8,200
YEMEN
IRAN
KAZAKHSTAN
UZBEKISTAN
TURKMENISTAN
$4,700
AFGHANISTAN
TAJIKISTAN
KYRGYZSTAN
MONGOLIA
CHINA
NEPAL
INDIA
PAKISTAN
BANGLADESH
SRI
LANKA
BHUTAN
LAOS
VIETNAM
MYANMAR
(BURMA)
THAILAND
$6,600
CAMBODIA
NORTH
KOREA
SOUTH
KOREA
$18,000
JAPAN
$27,200
TAIWAN
$17,200
PHILIPPINES
$4,000
MALAYSIA
$9,000
SINGAPORE
$24,700
BRUNEI
$18,000
INDONESIA
TIMOR-LESTE
(EAST TIMOR)
PAPUA
NEW GUINEA
SOLOMON
ISLANDS
KIRIBATI
FIJI
ISLANDS
$5,200
SAMOA
$3,500
TONGA
NEW
ZEALAND
$19,500
AUSTRALIA
$24,000
MOROCCO
$3,700
TUNISIA
$6,600
ALGERIA
LIBYA
$7,600
EGYPT
$3,700
SUDAN
MALI
NIGER
CHAD
DJIBOUTI
ERITREA
ETHIOPIA
SOMALIA
KENYA
UGANDA
RWANDA
BURUNDI
TANZANIA
ZAMBIA
MALAWI
MOZAMBIQUE
ZIMBABWE
GABON
$5,500
CONGO
ANGOLA
GHANA
TOGO
BENIN
NIGERIA
CAMEROON
CENTRAL AFRICAN
REPUBLIC
SÃO TOMÉ
& PRINCIPE
EQUATORIAL
GUINEA
DEM. REP. OF
THE CONGO
NAMIBIA
BOTSWANA
$7,800
SWAZILAND
SOUTH
AFRICA
$9,400
LESOTHO
COMOROS
MADAGASCAR
SEYCHELLES
$7,600
MAURITIUS
$10,800
9
10
11
12
13
14
15
16
A
B
C
D
E
F
G
H
J
K

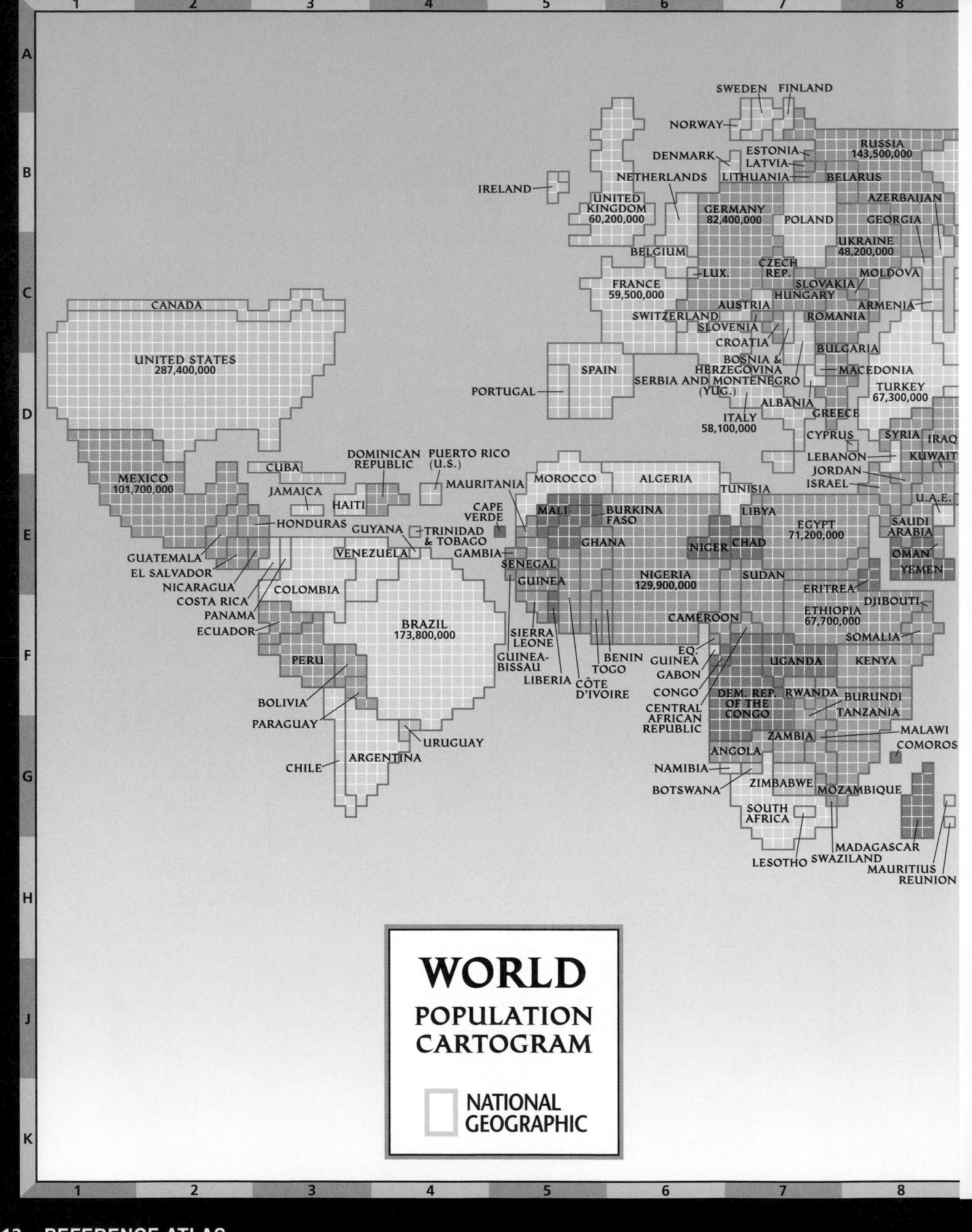

WORLD
POPULATION CARTOGRAM
NATIONAL GEOGRAPHIC
CANADA
UNITED STATES 287,400,000
MEXICO 101,700,000
CUBA
JAMAICA
HAITI
DOMINICAN REPUBLIC
PUERTO RICO (U.S.)
HONDURAS
GUATEMALA
EL SALVADOR
NICARAGUA
COSTA RICA
PANAMA
ECUADOR
COLOMBIA
VENEZUELA
GUYANA
TRINIDAD & TOBAGO
BRAZIL 173,800,000
PERU
BOLIVIA
PARAGUAY
URUGUAY
CHILE
ARGENTINA
IRELAND
UNITED KINGDOM 60,200,000
NETHERLANDS
BELGIUM
LUX.
FRANCE 59,500,000
SWITZERLAND
SPAIN
PORTUGAL
NORWAY
SWEDEN
FINLAND
DENMARK
ESTONIA
LATVIA
LITHUANIA
RUSSIA 143,500,000
BELARUS
GERMANY 82,400,000
POLAND
CZECH REP.
AUSTRIA
SLOVAKIA
HUNGARY
SLOVENIA
CROATIA
BOSNIA & HERZEGOVINA
SERBIA AND MONTENEGRO (YUG.)
ITALY 58,100,000
ALBANIA
MACEDONIA
GREECE
BULGARIA
ROMANIA
MOLDOVA
UKRAINE 48,200,000
AZERBAIJAN
GEORGIA
ARMENIA
TURKEY 67,300,000
CYPRUS
SYRIA
IRAQ
LEBANON
JORDAN
ISRAEL
KUWAIT
U.A.E.
SAUDI ARABIA
OMAN
YEMEN
MOROCCO
ALGERIA
TUNISIA
LIBYA
EGYPT 71,200,000
MAURITANIA
CAPE VERDE
MALI
BURKINA FASO
GAMBIA
SENEGAL
GUINEA
GHANA
NIGER
CHAD
NIGERIA 129,900,000
SUDAN
ERITREA
DJIBOUTI
ETHIOPIA 67,700,000
SOMALIA
SIERRA LEONE
GUINEA-BISSAU
LIBERIA
CÔTE D'IVOIRE
BENIN
TOGO
CAMEROON
EQ. GUINEA
GABON
CONGO
CENTRAL AFRICAN REPUBLIC
DEM. REP. OF THE CONGO
UGANDA
KENYA
RWANDA
BURUNDI
TANZANIA
ZAMBIA
MALAWI
COMOROS
ANGOLA
NAMIBIA
BOTSWANA
ZIMBABWE
MOZAMBIQUE
SOUTH AFRICA
LESOTHO
SWAZILAND
MADAGASCAR
MAURITIUS
REUNION

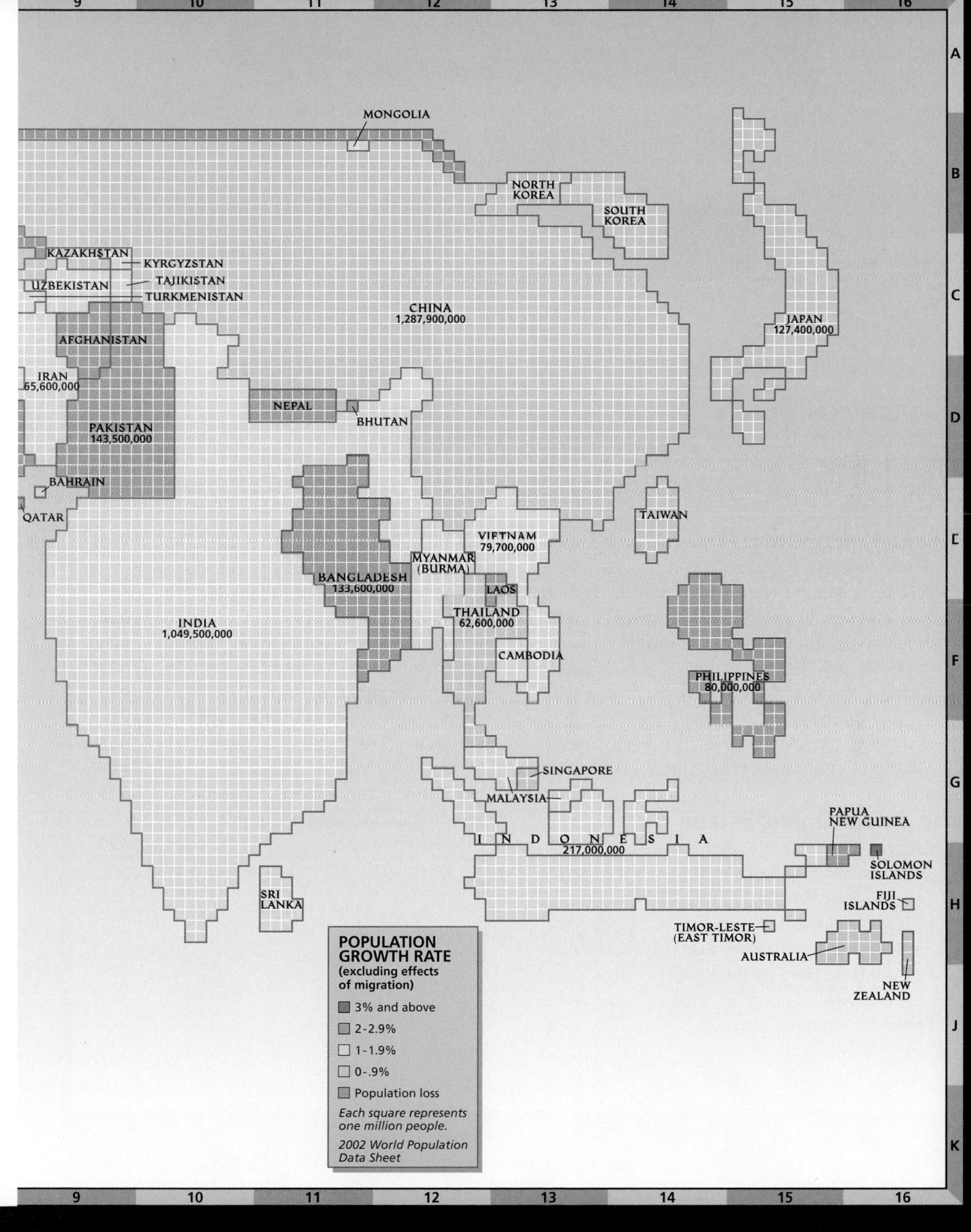
MONGOLIA
NORTH KOREA
SOUTH KOREA
KAZAKHSTAN
KYRGYZSTAN
TAJIKISTAN
UZBEKISTAN
TURKMENISTAN
CHINA
1,287,900,000
JAPAN
127,400,000
AFGHANISTAN
IRAN
65,600,000
NEPAL
BHUTAN
PAKISTAN
143,500,000
BAHRAIN
QATAR
TAIWAN
VIETNAM
79,700,000
MYANMAR
(BURMA)
BANGLADESH
133,600,000
LAOS
THAILAND
62,600,000
INDIA
1,049,500,000
CAMBODIA
PHILIPPINES
80,000,000
SINGAPORE
MALAYSIA
INDONESIA
217,000,000
PAPUA
NEW GUINEA
SOLOMON
ISLANDS
SRI
LANKA
FIJI
ISLANDS
TIMOR-LESTE
(EAST TIMOR)
AUSTRALIA
NEW
ZEALAND
POPULATION GROWTH RATE
(excluding effects of migration)
3% and above
2-2.9%
1-1.9%
0-.9%
Population loss
Each square represents one million people.
2002 World Population Data Sheet

STANDARD & POOR'S DATABANK

The data and forecasts for the graphs, tables, and charts in the Databank are based on information from Standard & Poor's. View the ett.glencoe.com Web site for data updates.

The American People

U.S. Population Projections A15
Civilian Labor Force A15
Hours and Earnings in Private Industries A16

The U.S. Economy

Gross Domestic Product A17
A Look at Market History (S&P 500) A17
Personal Consumption Expenditures . . . A18
Personal Consumption Expenditures, Nondurable Goods A18
Average Prices of Selected Goods A19
Annual Changes in Consumer Price Indexes A20
Inflation in Consumer Prices A20

The Government Sector

Federal Government Expenditures A21
Total Government Expenditures A21
Federal Government Total Receipts and Total Outlays A22
Federal Debt Held by the Public A22
Federal Debt Held by the Public Per Capita A22
Federal Budget Receipts A23

The Financial Sector

Interest Rates A24
Consumer Credit Outstanding A24
Personal Saving A25
Money Stock A25

The Global Economy

Economic Groups: Population, Exports, and GDP A26
Growth Rates in Real GDP Per Capita . . . A26
World Population by Age A27
Countries Ranked by Population A27
Aging Index in Selected Nations of the Americas A28
Median Age, World A28
U.S. Exports and Imports A29
Inflation and Unemployment, Selected Economies A29

The American People

U.S. Population Projections, 2000–2050

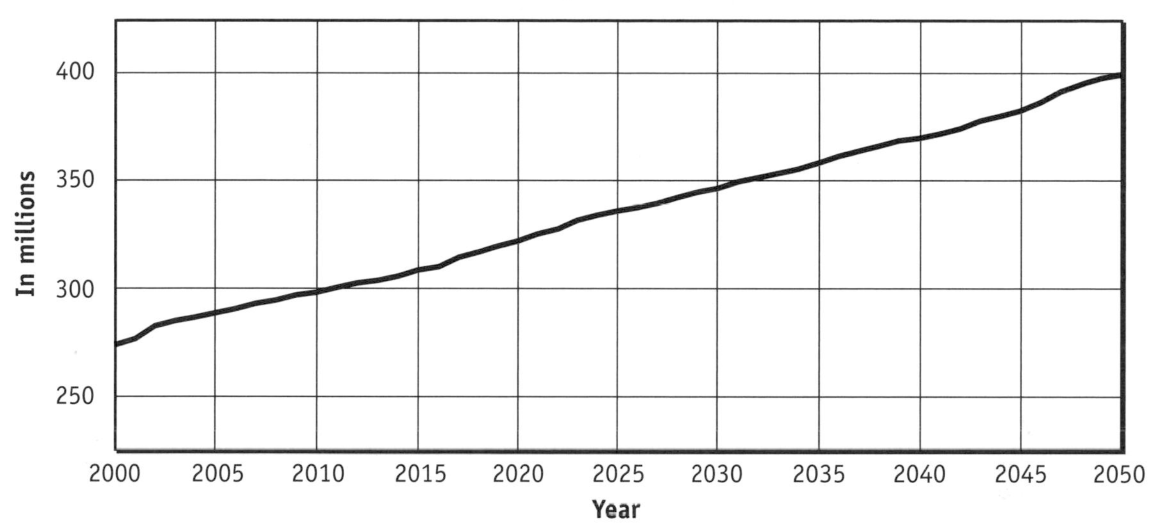

Source: U.S. Bureau of the Census

Civilian Labor Force, 1950–2010

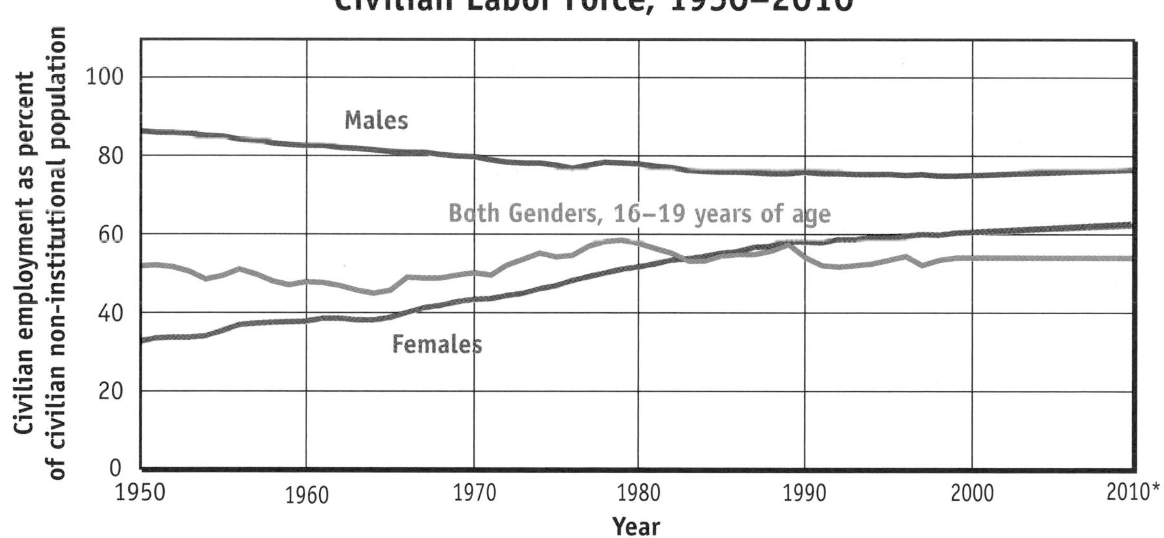

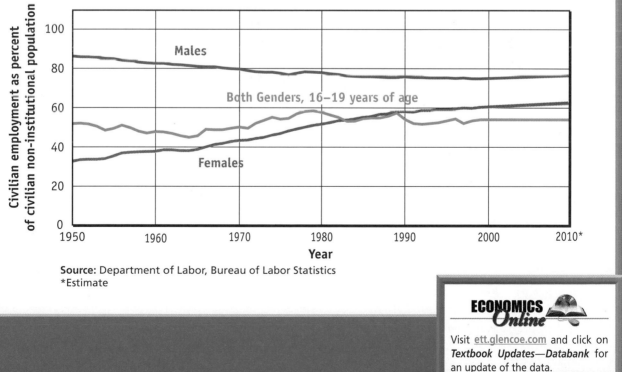

Source: Department of Labor, Bureau of Labor Statistics
*Estimate

ECONOMICS Online

Visit ett.glencoe.com and click on ***Textbook Updates—Databank*** for an update of the data.

The American People

Hours and Earnings in Private Industries, 1960–2003

A Average Weekly Hours of Production Workers

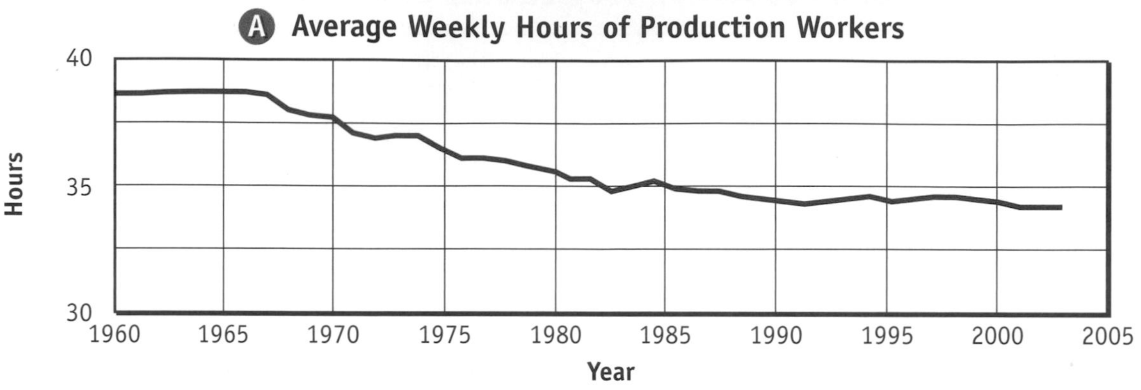

B Average Weekly Earnings of Production Workers, Current Dollars

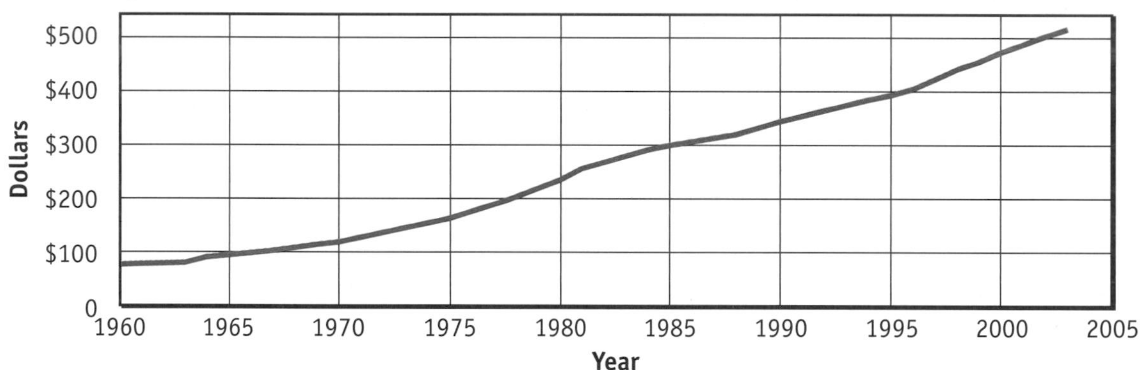

C Average Weekly Earnings, 1982 Dollars

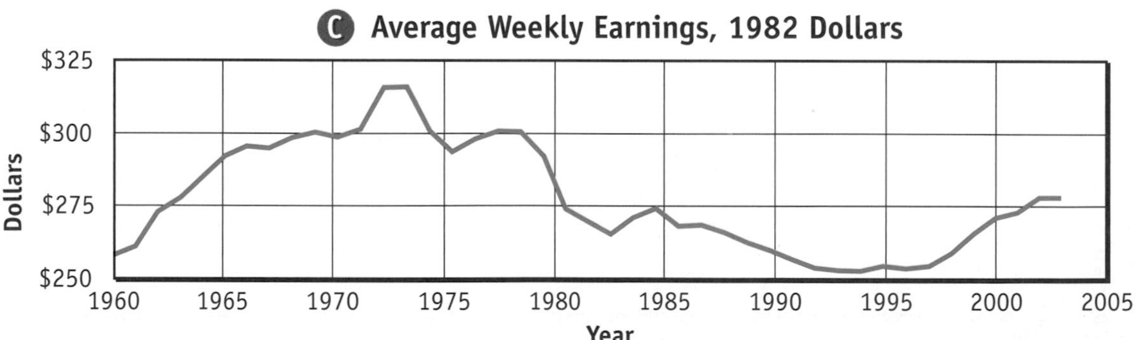

Source: Bureau of Labor Statistics

Visit ett.glencoe.com and click on ***Textbook Updates—Databank*** for an update of the data.

The U.S. Economy

Gross Domestic Product, 1950–2003

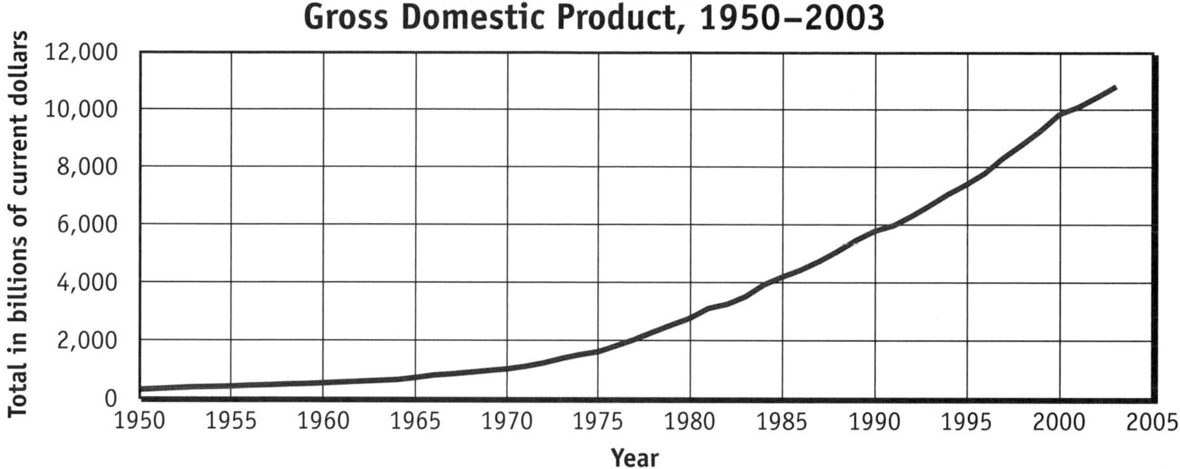

Source: U.S. Department of Commerce

A Look At Market History

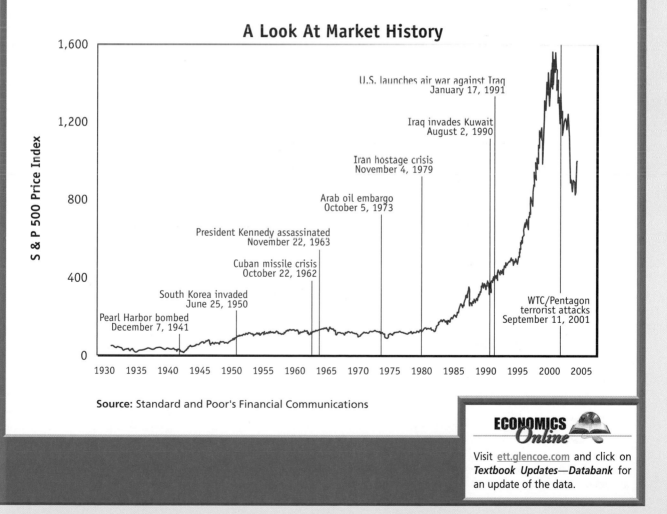

Source: Standard and Poor's Financial Communications

Visit ett.glencoe.com and click on ***Textbook Updates—Databank*** for an update of the data.

The U.S. Economy

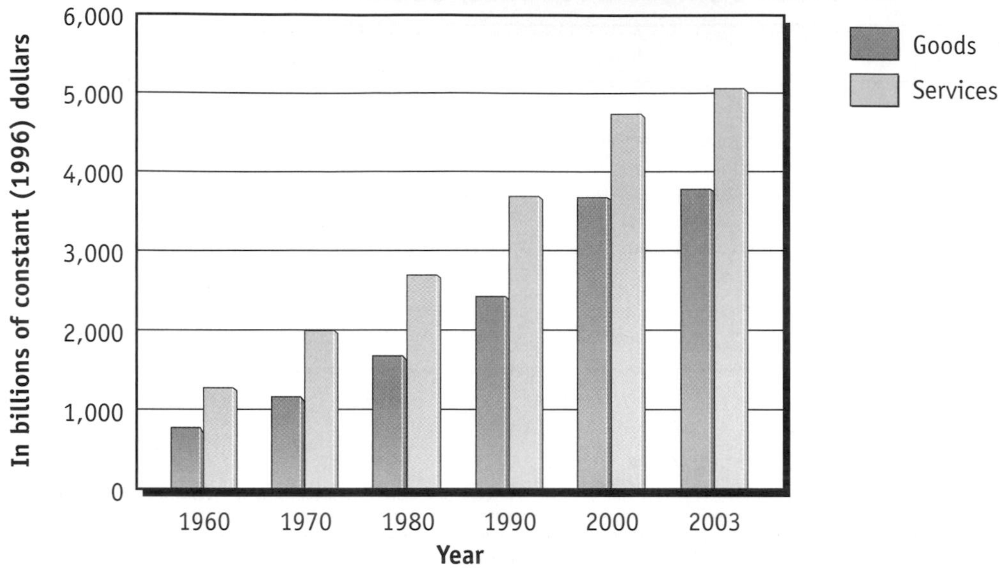

Source: Department of Commerce, Bureau of Economic Analysis

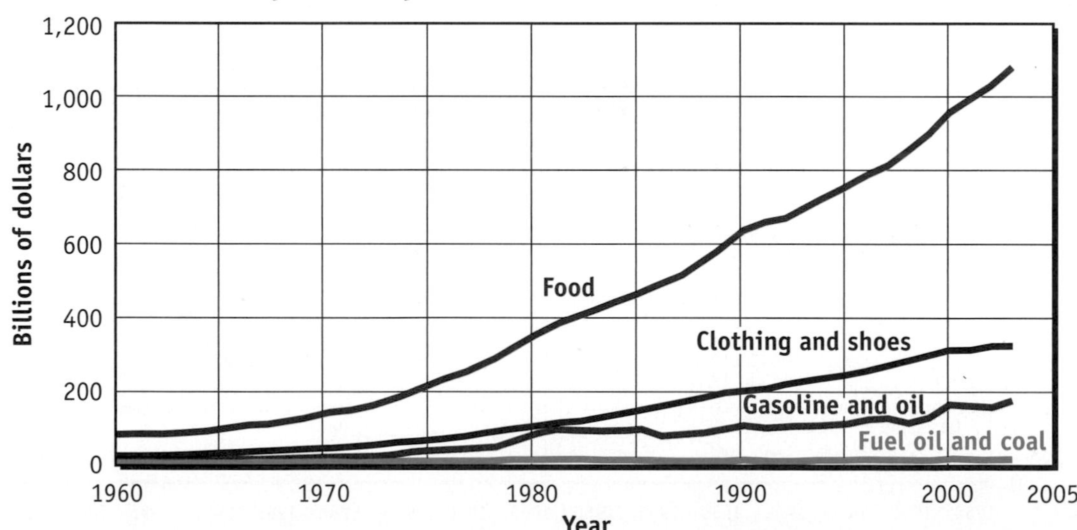

Source: Department of Commerce, Bureau of Economic Analysis

Visit ett.glencoe.com and click on *Textbook Updates—Databank* for an update of the data.

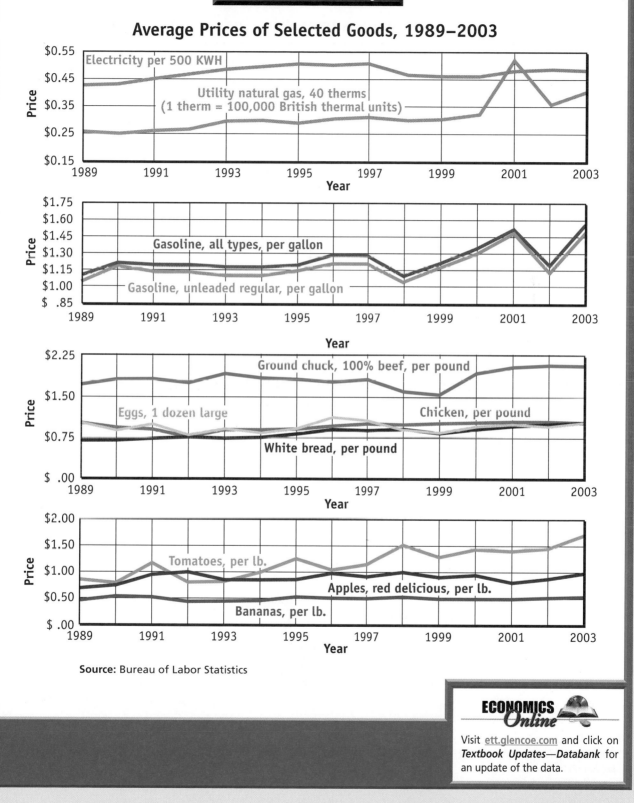

The U.S. Economy

Average Prices of Selected Goods, 1989–2003

$0.55
$0.45
$0.35
$0.25
$0.15

Price

Electricity per 500 KWH

Utility natural gas, 40 therms
(1 therm = 100,000 British thermal units)

1989 1991 1993 1995 1997 1999 2001 2003

Year

$1.75
$1.60
$1.45
$1.30
$1.15
$1.00
$ .85

Price

Gasoline, all types, per gallon

Gasoline, unleaded regular, per gallon

1989 1991 1993 1995 1997 1999 2001 2003

Year

$2.25
$1.50
$0.75
$ .00

Price

Ground chuck, 100% beef, per pound

Eggs, 1 dozen large

Chicken, per pound

White bread, per pound

1989 1991 1993 1995 1997 1999 2001 2003

Year

$2.00
$1.50
$1.00
$0.50
$ .00

Price

Tomatoes, per lb.

Apples, red delicious, per lb.

Bananas, per lb.

1989 1991 1993 1995 1997 1999 2001 2003

Year

Source: Bureau of Labor Statistics

Visit ett.glencoe.com and click on ***Textbook Updates—Databank*** for an update of the data.

STANDARD & POOR'S

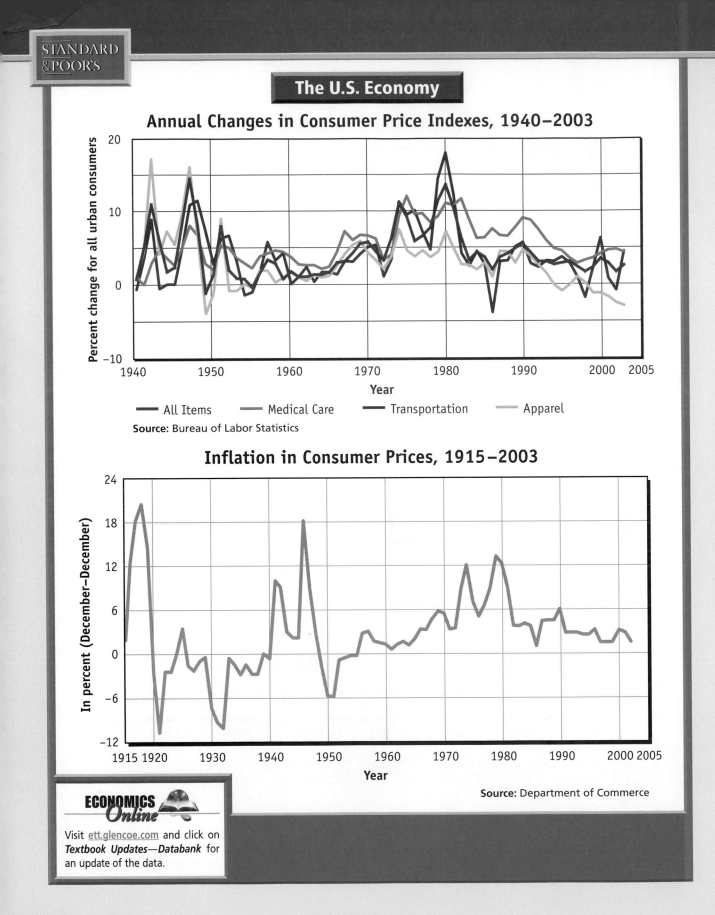

The U.S. Economy

Annual Changes in Consumer Price Indexes, 1940–2003

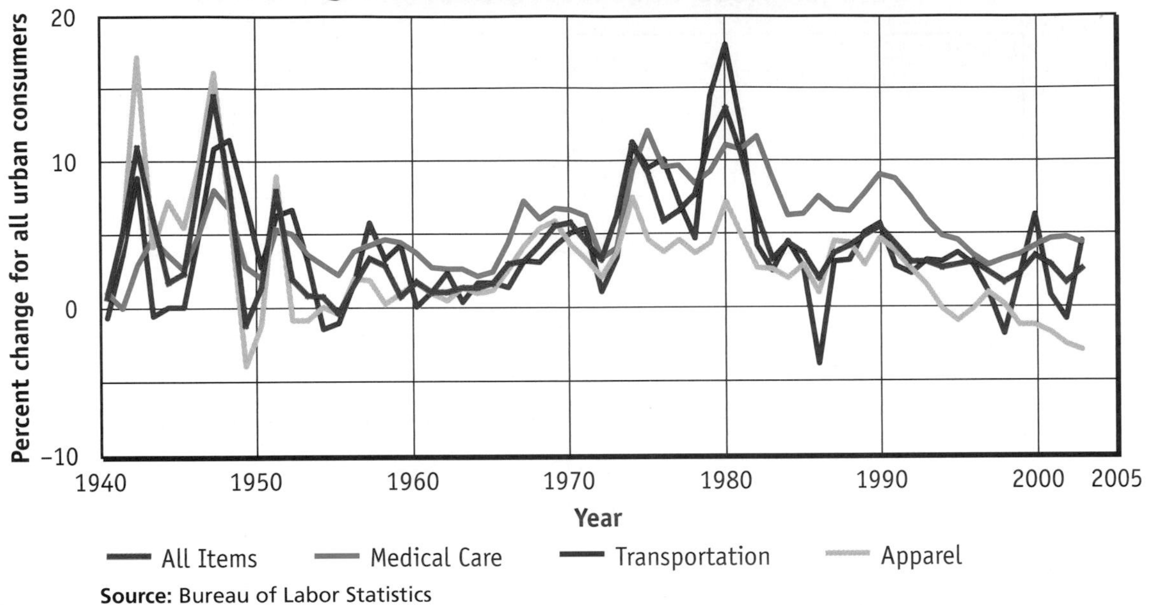

Source: Bureau of Labor Statistics

Inflation in Consumer Prices, 1915–2003

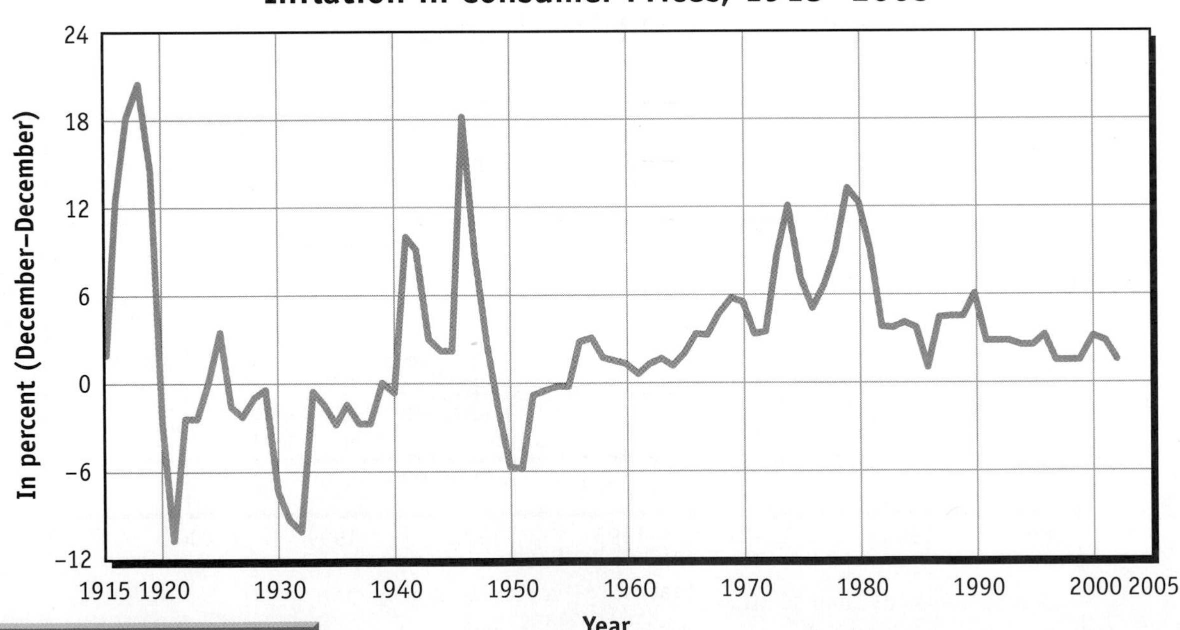

Source: Department of Commerce

Visit ett.glencoe.com and click on ***Textbook Updates—Databank*** for an update of the data.

The Government Sector

Federal Government Expenditures, 1955–2005

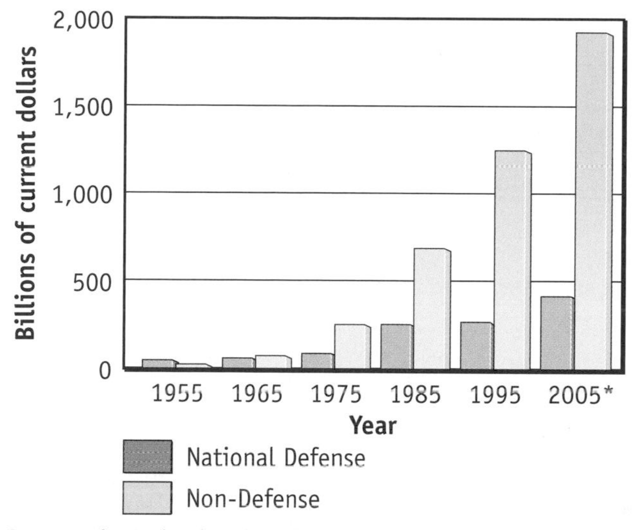

Source: *The Federal Budget for Fiscal Year 2004,* Historical Tables
*Estimate

Total Government Expenditures, 1960–2002

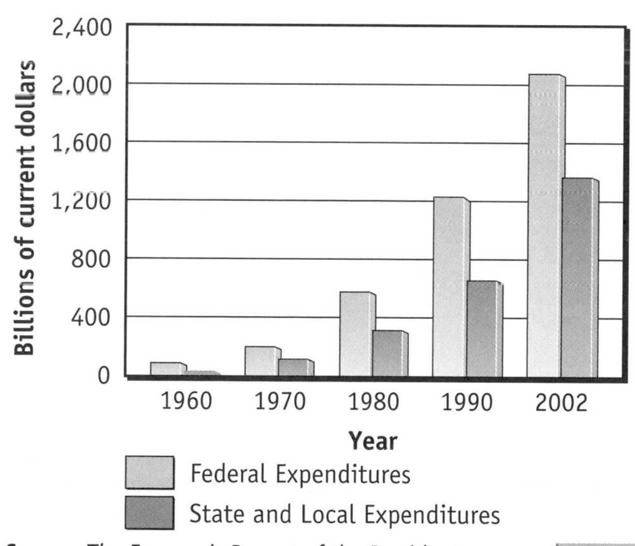

Source: *The Economic Report of the President*

Visit ett.glencoe.com and click on ***Textbook Updates—Databank*** for an update of the data.

STANDARD & POOR'S

The Government Sector

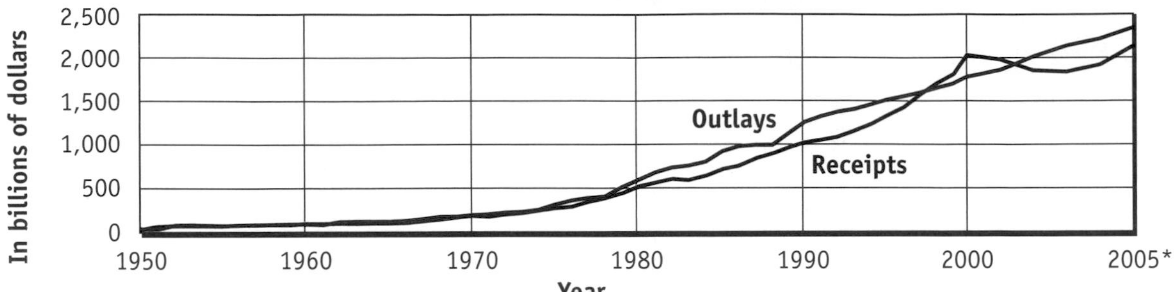

Source: *Budget for Fiscal Year 2004,* Historical Tables
*Estimate

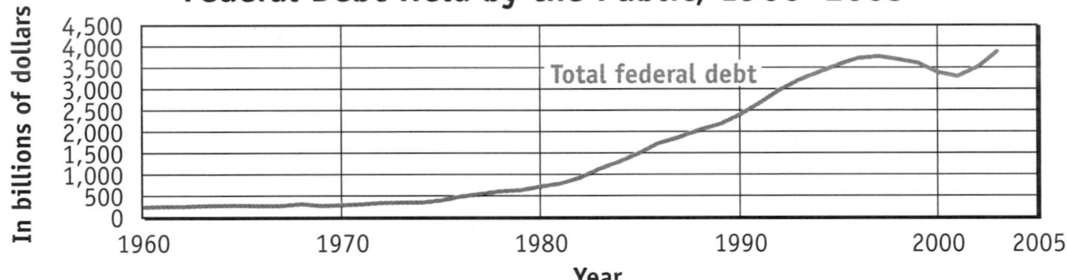

Source: *Budget for Fiscal Year 2004,* Historical Tables

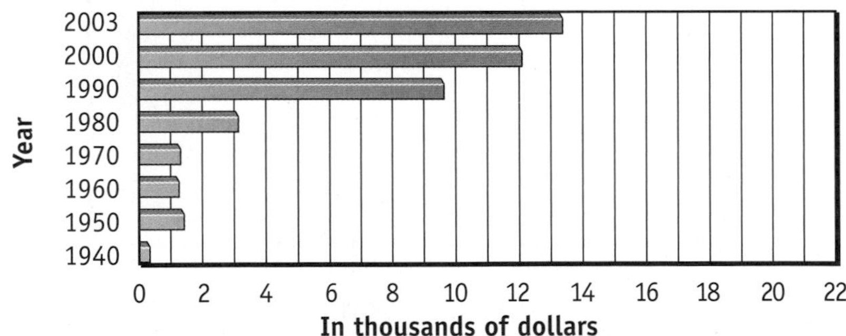

Source: *Budget for Fiscal Year 2004,* Historical Tables

Visit ett.glencoe.com and click on *Textbook Updates—Databank* for an update of the data.

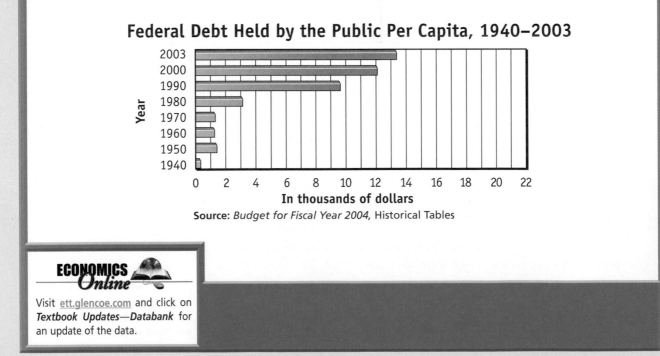

STANDARD
&POOR'S

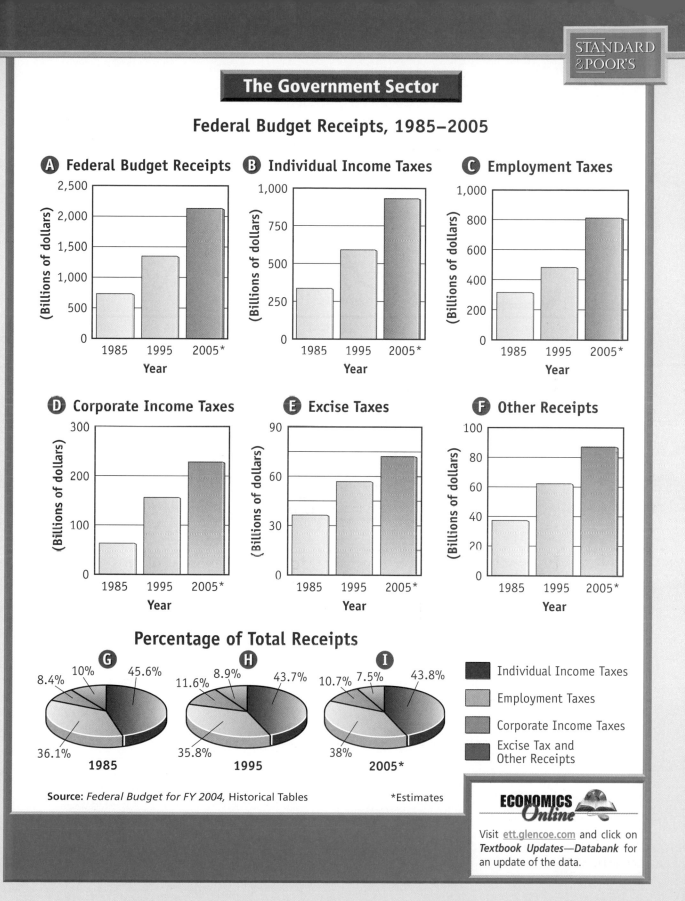

The Government Sector

Federal Budget Receipts, 1985–2005

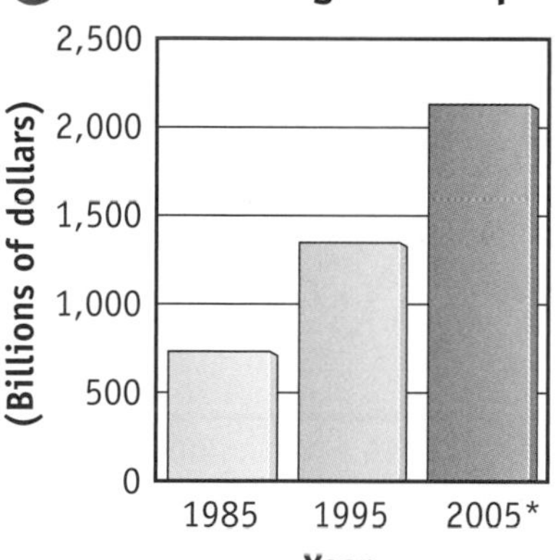

B Individual Income Taxes

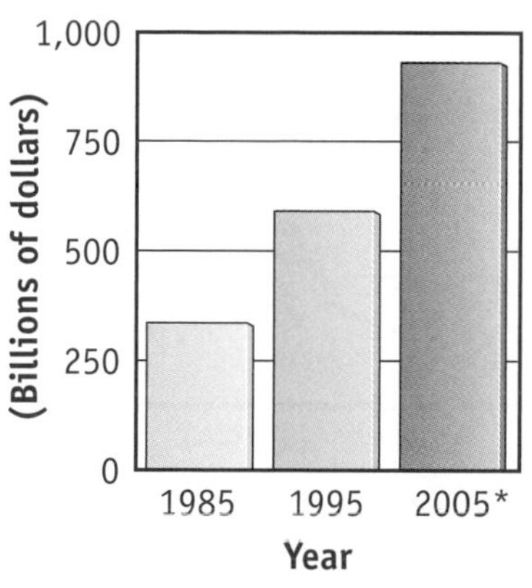

C Employment Taxes

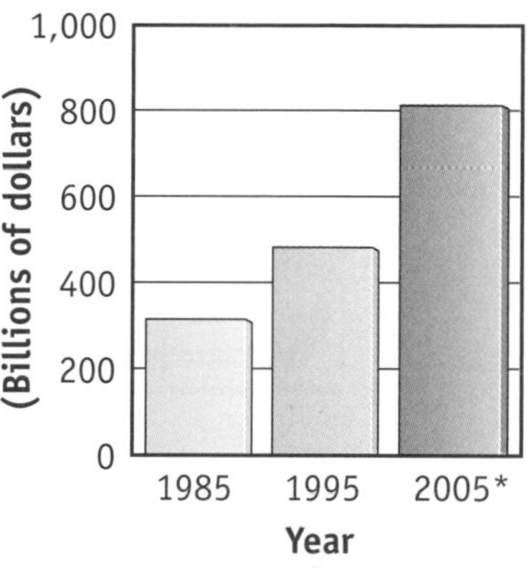

D Corporate Income Taxes

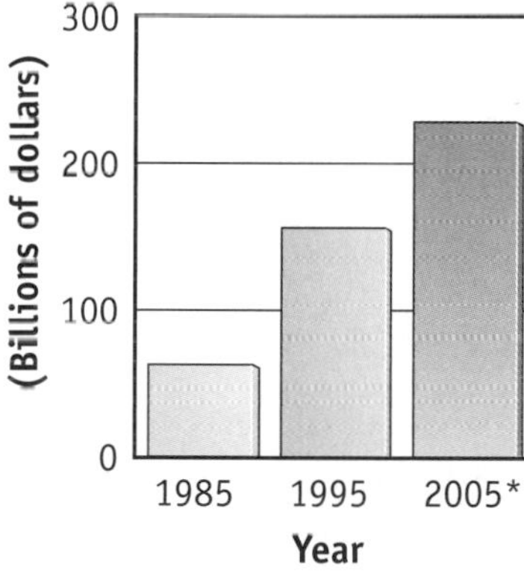

E Excise Taxes

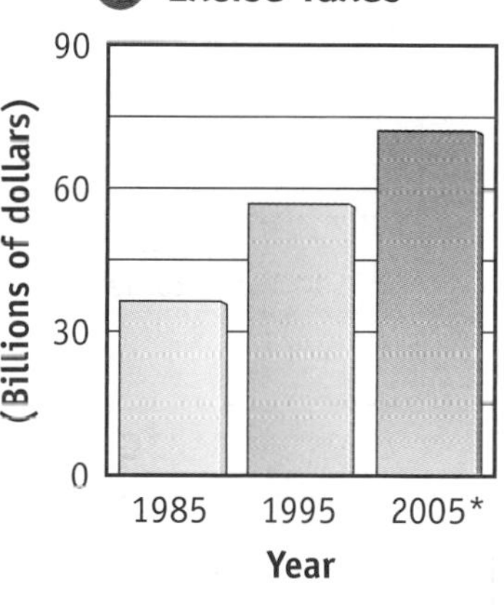

F Other Receipts

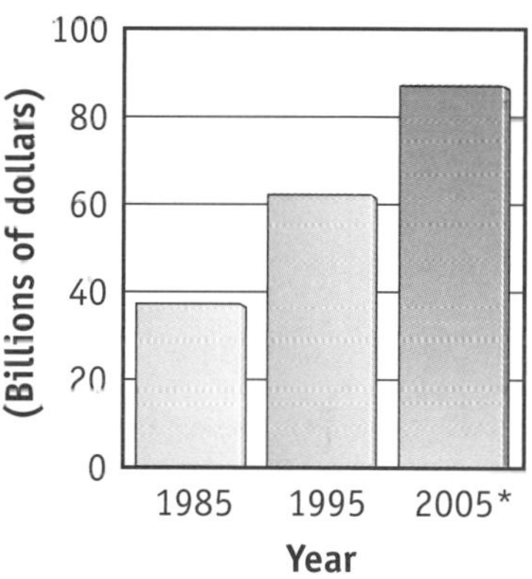

Percentage of Total Receipts

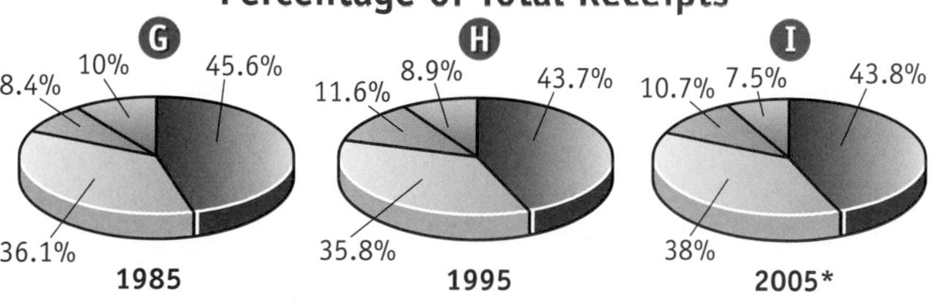

Corporate Income Taxes

Source: *Federal Budget for FY 2004,* Historical Tables

*Estimates

Visit ett.glencoe.com and click on ***Textbook Updates—Databank*** for an update of the data.

STANDARD & POOR'S

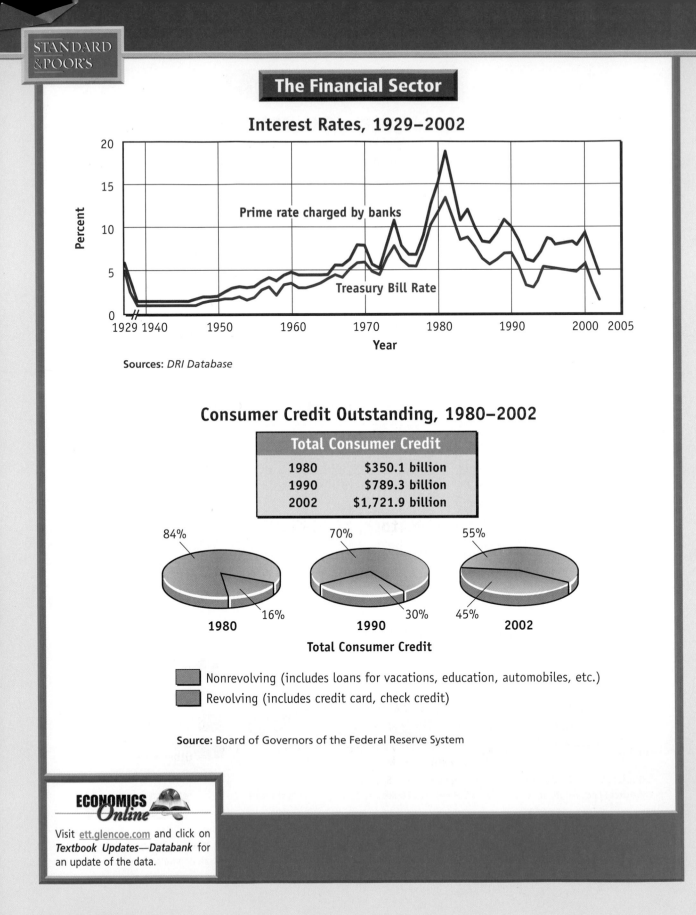

The Financial Sector

Interest Rates, 1929–2002

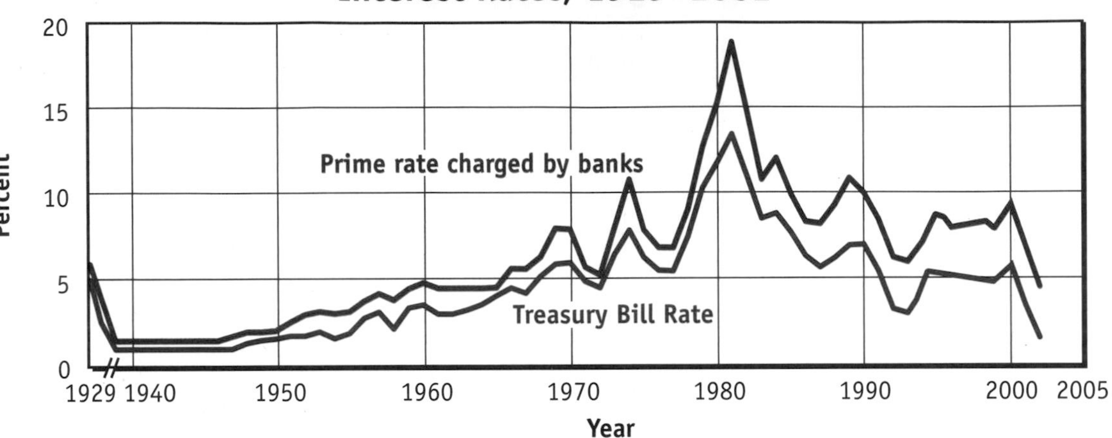

Sources: *DRI Database*

Consumer Credit Outstanding, 1980–2002

Total Consumer Credit	
1980	$350.1 billion
1990	$789.3 billion
2002	$1,721.9 billion

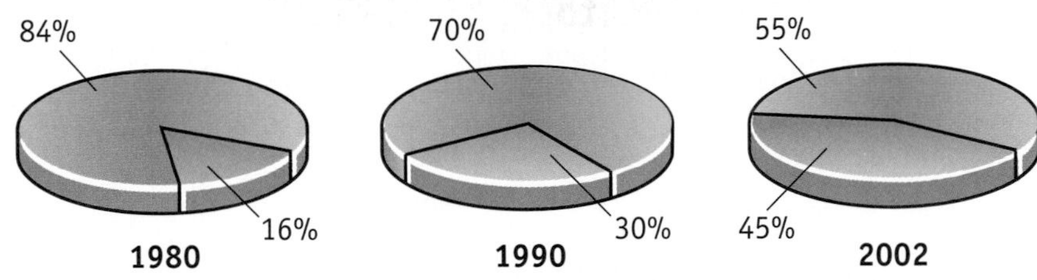

Total Consumer Credit

Nonrevolving (includes loans for vacations, education, automobiles, etc.)

Revolving (includes credit card, check credit)

Source: Board of Governors of the Federal Reserve System

Visit ett.glencoe.com and click on *Textbook Updates—Databank* for an update of the data.

The Financial Sector

Personal Saving, 1960–2003

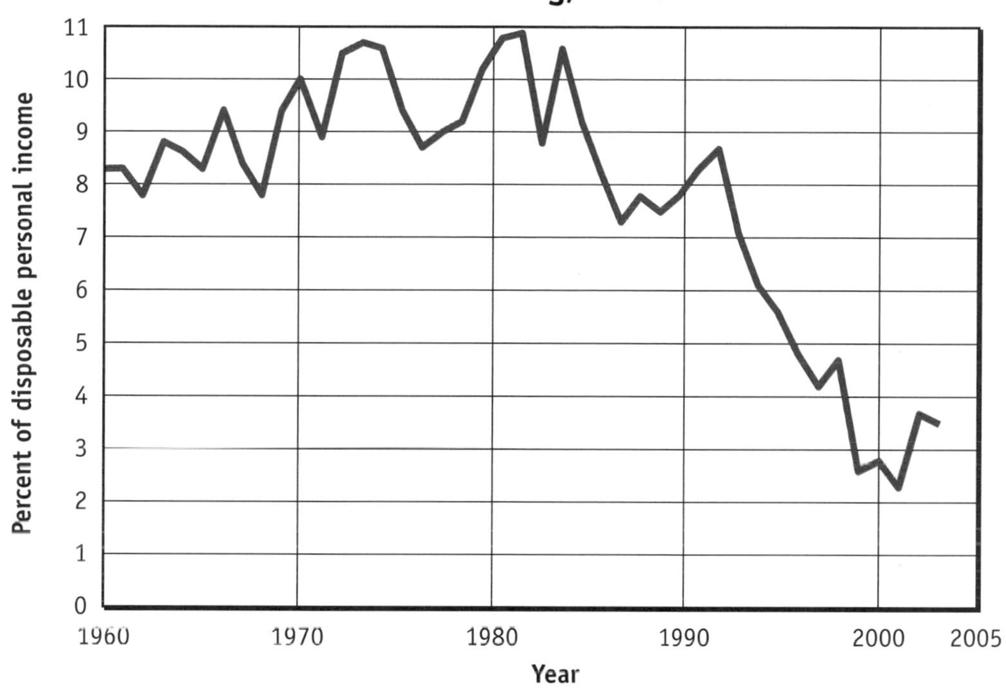

Source: U.S. Department of Commerce, Bureau of Economic Analysis

Money Stock, 1970–2003

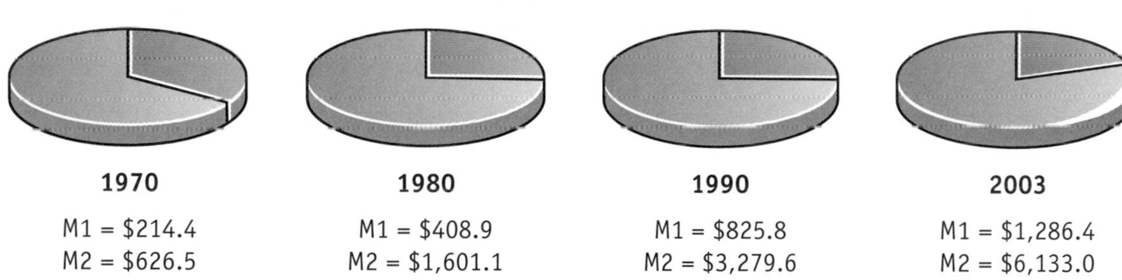

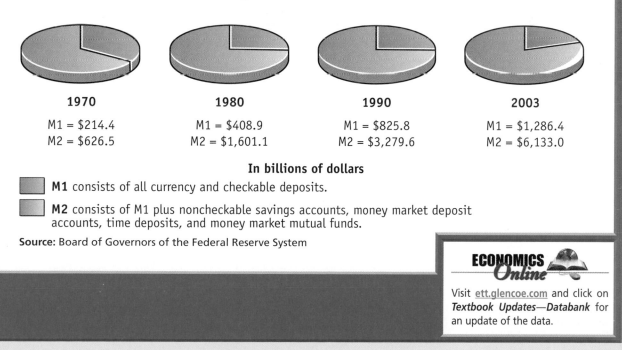

1970	1980	1990	2003
M1 = $214.4	M1 = $408.9	M1 = $825.8	M1 = $1,286.4
M2 = $626.5	M2 = $1,601.1	M2 = $3,279.6	M2 = $6,133.0

In billions of dollars

M1 consists of all currency and checkable deposits.

M2 consists of M1 plus noncheckable savings accounts, money market deposit accounts, time deposits, and money market mutual funds.

Source: Board of Governors of the Federal Reserve System

Visit ett.glencoe.com and click on *Textbook Updates—Databank* for an update of the data.

STANDARD
&POOR'S

The Global Economy

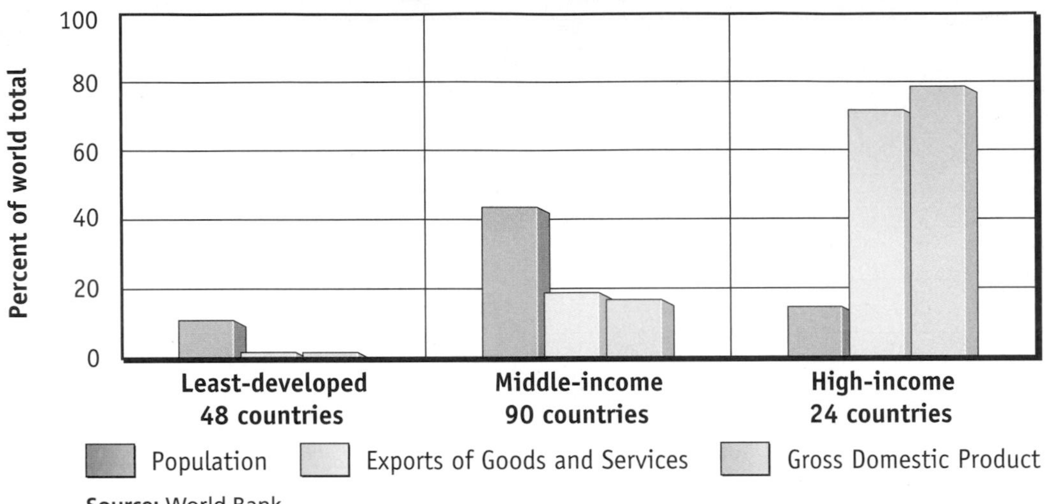

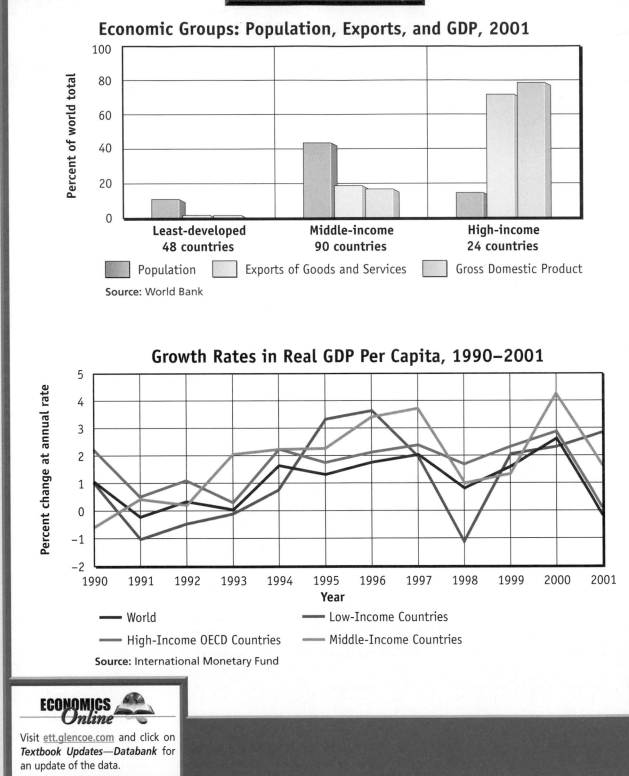

Source: World Bank

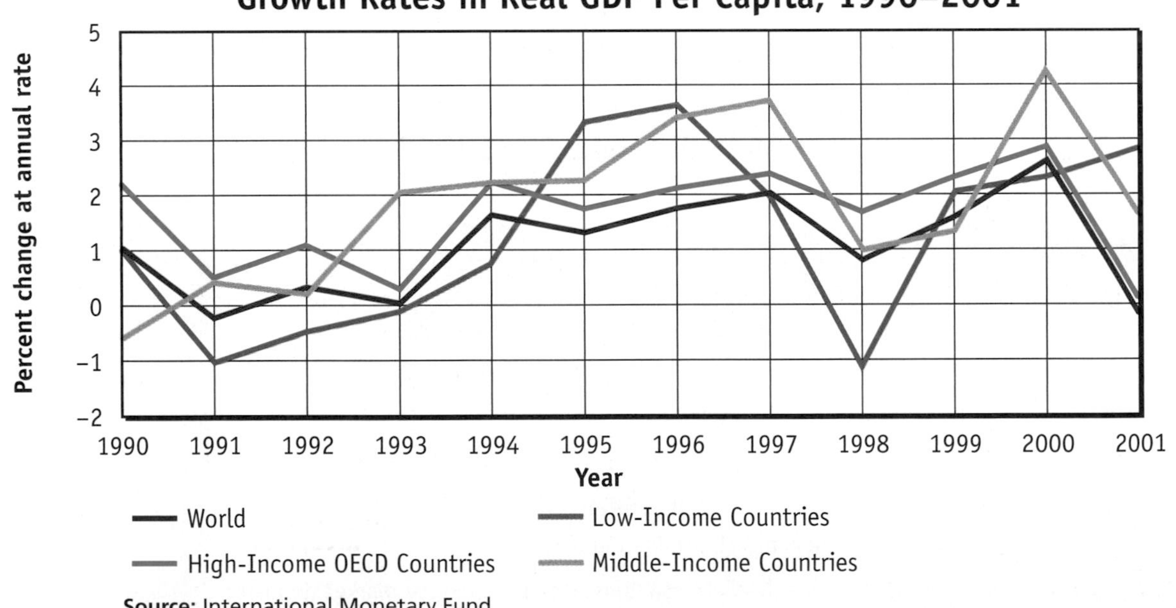

Source: International Monetary Fund

Visit ett.glencoe.com and click on *Textbook Updates—Databank* for an update of the data.

The Global Economy

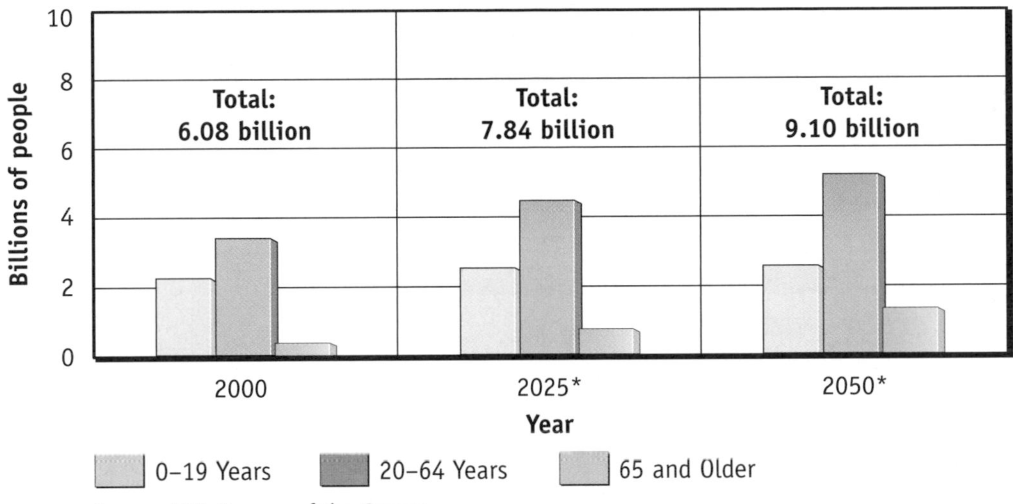

Source: U.S. Bureau of the Census
*Estimate

Countries Ranked by Population, 2000 and 2050

Country	Year 2000 Population (in millions)	Year 2000 Rank	Year 2050* Population (in millions)	Year 2050* Rank
China	1,261	1	1,470	(2)
India	1,014	2	1,620	(1)
United States	276	3	404	(3)
Indonesia	224	4	338	(4)
Brazil	173	5	207	(7)
Russia	146	6	118	(14)
Pakistan	142	7	268	(6)
Bangladesh	129	8	205	(8)
Japan	127	9	101	(16)
Nigeria	123	10	304	(5)
Mexico	100	11	153	(12)

Source: U.S. Bureau of the Census
*Estimate

Visit ett.glencoe.com and click on ***Textbook Updates—Databank*** for an update of the data.

STANDARD & POOR'S

The Global Economy

Aging Index in Selected Nations of the Americas, 2000 and 2025

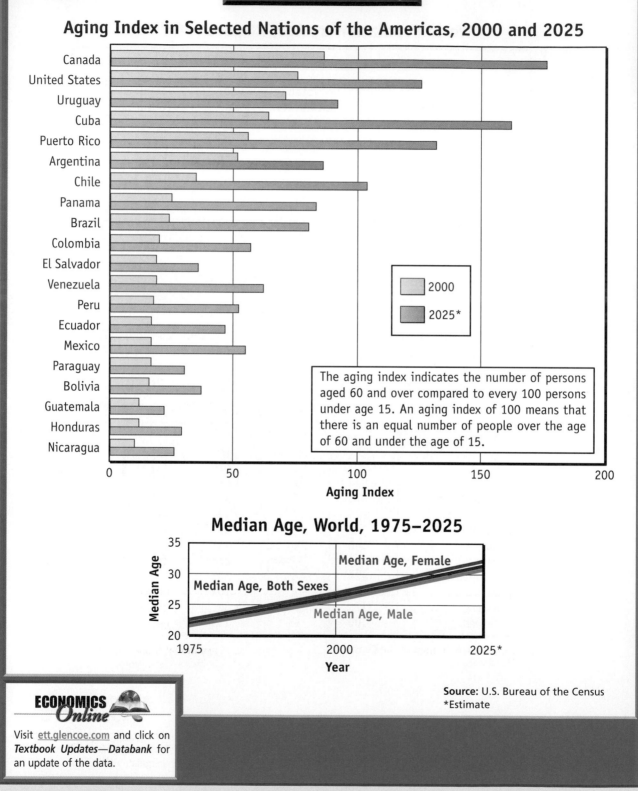

Canada
United States
Uruguay
Cuba
Puerto Rico
Argentina
Chile
Panama
Brazil
Colombia
El Salvador
Venezuela
Peru
Ecuador
Mexico
Paraguay
Bolivia
Guatemala
Honduras
Nicaragua

0 50 100 150 200

Aging Index

2000
2025*

The aging index indicates the number of persons aged 60 and over compared to every 100 persons under age 15. An aging index of 100 means that there is an equal number of people over the age of 60 and under the age of 15.

Median Age, World, 1975–2025

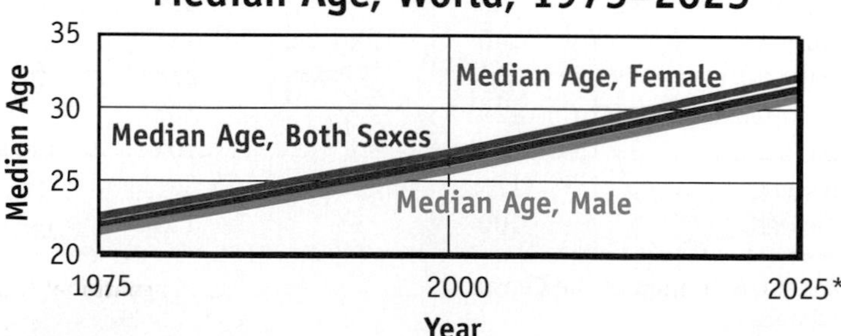

Source: U.S. Bureau of the Census
*Estimate

ECONOMICS Online

Visit ett.glencoe.com and click on ***Textbook Updates—Databank*** for an update of the data.

STANDARD & POOR'S

The Global Economy

U.S. Exports and Imports, 1950–2003

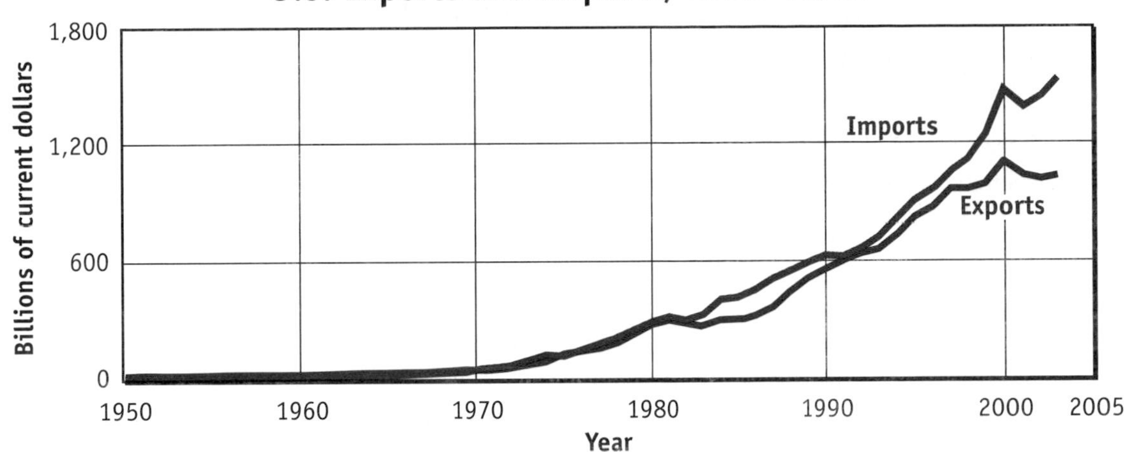

Inflation and Unemployment, Selected Economies 1990–2003

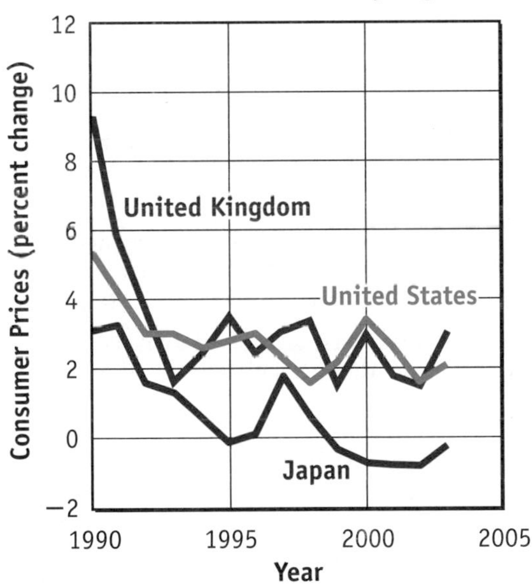

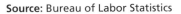

Source: Bureau of Labor Statistics

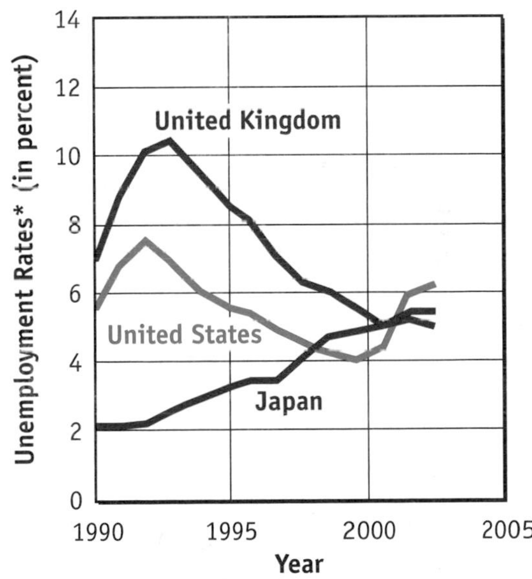

Source: International Monetary Fund
*Based on national definitions

Visit ett.glencoe.com and click on ***Textbook Updates—Databank*** for an update of the data.

A

ability-to-pay principle: principle of taxation in which those with higher incomes pay more taxes than those with lower incomes, regardless of the number of government services they use (p. 442)

absolute advantage: ability of one country to produce a product more efficiently (i.e., with greater output per unit of input) than can another country (p. 475)

agency shop: company in which employees are not required to join the union, but must pay union dues (p. 324)

aggregate demand: total quantity of goods and services in the entire economy that all citizens will demand at any single time (p. 356)

aggregate demand curve: a graphed line showing the relationship between the aggregate quantity demanded and the average of all prices as measured by the implicit GDP price deflator (p. 357)

aggregates: summation of all the individual parts in the economy (p. 356)

aggregate supply: real domestic output of producers based on the rise and fall of the price level (p. 358)

aggregate supply curve: a graphed line showing the relationship between the aggregate quantity supplied and the average of all prices as measured by the implicit GDP price deflator (p. 358)

annual percentage rate (APR): cost of credit expressed as a yearly percentage (p. 92)

antitrust legislation: laws passed by federal and state governments to prevent new monopolies from forming and to break up those that already exist (p. 249)

arbitration: stage of negotiation process in which union and management submit the issues they cannot agree on to a third party for a final decision (p. 329)

articles of incorporation: document listing basic information about a corporation that is filed with the state where the corporation will be headquartered (p. 221)

assembly line: production system in which the good being produced moves on a conveyor belt past workers who perform individual tasks in assembling it (p. 280)

assets: all items to which a business or household holds legal claim (p. 215)

authoritarian socialism: system that supports revolution as a means to overthrow capitalism and bring about socialist goals; the entire economy is controlled by a central government; also called *communism* (p. 500)

automated teller machines (ATMs): units that allow consumers to do their banking without the help of a teller (p. 385)

automation: production process in which machines do the work and people oversee them (p. 280)

B

bait and switch: deceptive advertising practice that attracts consumers with a low-priced product, then tries to sell them a higher-priced product (p. 69)

balance of trade: difference between the value of a nation's exports and its imports (p. 483)

bankruptcy: the inability to pay debts based on the income received (p. 104)

barriers to entry: obstacles to competition that prevent others from entering a market (p. 240)

barter: exchange of goods and services for other goods and services (p. 376)

base year: year used as a point of comparison for other years in a series of statistics (p. 352)

benefits-received principle: system of taxation in which those who use a particular government service support it with taxes in proportion to the benefit they receive; those who do not use a service do not pay taxes for it (p. 440)

black market: "underground" or illegal market in which goods are traded at prices above their legal maximum prices or in which illegal goods are sold (p. 197)

blue-collar workers: category of workers employed in crafts, manufacturing, and nonfarm labor (p. 315)

boom: same as *peak* (p. 360)

boycott: economic pressure exerted by unions urging the public not to purchase the goods or services produced by a company (p. 331)

brand name: word, picture, or logo on a product that helps consumers distinguish it from similar products (p. 70)

broker: person who acts as a go-between for buyers and sellers of stocks and bonds (p. 149)

budget deficit: situation when the amount of government spending exceeds its receipts during the fiscal year (p. 438)

budget surplus: situation when the amount of government receipts is larger than its expenditures during the fiscal year (p. 439)

bureaucracies: offices and agencies of the government that each deal with a specific area (p. 530)

business cycle: irregular changes in the level of total output measured by real GDP (p. 360)

business fluctuations: ups and downs in an economy (p. 360)

C

capital: previously manufactured goods used to make other goods and services (p. 6)

capital flight: the legal or illegal export of currency or money capital from a nation by that nation's leaders (p. 530)

capital gain: increase in value of an asset from the time it was bought to the time it was sold (p. 147)

capitalism: economic system in which private individuals own the factors of production (p. 41)

capital loss: decrease in value of an asset or bond from the time it was bought to the time it was sold (p. 147)

cartel: arrangement among groups of industrial businesses, often in different countries, to reduce international competition by controlling the price, production, and distribution of goods (p. 245)

certificates of deposit: time deposits that state the amount of the deposit, maturity, and rate of interest being paid (p. 143)

channels of distribution: routes by which goods are moved from producers to consumers (p. 302)

charge account: credit extended to a consumer allowing the consumer to buy goods or services from a particular company and to pay for them later (p. 90)

checkable deposits: money deposited in a bank that can be withdrawn at any time by presenting a check (p. 389)

check clearing: method by which a check that has been deposited in one institution is transferred to the issuer's depository institution (p. 405)

checking account: account in which deposited money can be withdrawn at any time by writing a check (p. 389)

circular flow of economic activity: economic model that pictures income as flowing continuously between businesses and consumers (p. 37)

circular flow of income: same as *circular flow of economic activity* (p. 458)

civilian labor force: total number of people 16 years old or older who are either employed or actively seeking work (p. 313)

closed shop: company in which only union members could be hired (p. 324)

closing costs: fees involved in arranging for a mortgage or in transferring ownership of property (p. 123)

club warehouse store: store that carries a limited number of brands and items in large quantities; less expensive than supermarkets (p. 112)

coincident indicators: economic indicators that usually change at the same time as changes in overall business activity (p. 367)

collateral: something of value that a borrower lets the lender claim if a loan is not repaid (p. 98)

collective bargaining: process by which unions and employers negotiate the conditions of employment (p. 328)

command economy: system in which the government controls the factors of production and makes all decisions about their use (p. 34)

commercial bank: bank whose main functions are to accept deposits, lend money, and transfer funds among banks, individuals, and businesses (p. 89)

commodity money: a medium of exchange such as cattle or gems that has value as a commodity or good aside from its value as money (p. 378)

common stock: shares of ownership in a corporation that give stockholders voting rights and a portion of future profits (after holders of preferred stock are paid) (p. 223)

communism: term used by Karl Marx for his ideal society in which no government is necessary (p. 500)

comparative advantage: ability of a country to produce a product at a lower opportunity cost than another country (p. 476)

comparison shopping: getting information on the types and prices of products available from different stores and companies before purchasing a product (p. 69)

competition: rivalry among producers or sellers of similar goods and services to win more business (p. 44)

competitive advertising: advertising that attempts to persuade consumers that a product is different from and superior to any other (p. 68)

complementary good: a product often used with another product; as the price of the second product decreases, the demand for the first product increases (p. 181)

conglomerate: large corporation made up of smaller corporations dealing in unrelated businesses (p. 250)

consumer: any person or group that buys or uses goods and services to satisfy personal needs and wants (p. 59)

consumer-credit laws: laws passed to protect consumers by giving them access to their credit records (p. 578)

consumer goods: goods produced for individuals and sold directly to the public to be used as they are (p. 277)

consumerism: movement to educate buyers about the purchases they make and to demand better and safer products from manufacturers (p. 72)

consumer price index (CPI): measure of the change in price over time of a specific group of goods and services used by the average household (p. 351)

consumer sovereignty: the role of the consumer as ruler of the market when determining the types of goods and services produced (p. 290)

contraction: part of the business cycle during which economic activity is slowing down, leading to a trough (p. 360)

convenience store: store open 16 to 24 hours a day, carrying a limited selection of relatively higher-priced items (p. 113)

copyright: government protection that gives an author or artist the exclusive right to sell, publish, or reproduce their works for a specified number of years (p. 241)

corporate charter: license to operate granted to a corporation by the state where it is established (p. 221)

corporation: type of business organization owned by many people but treated by law as though it were a person; it can own property, pay taxes, make contracts, and so on (p. 220)

cost-benefit analysis: a financial process in which a business estimates the cost of action and compares it with the benefits of that action (p. 265)

cost-of-living adjustment (COLA): union contract or other provision providing for an additional wage increase each year if the general level of prices in the economy rises beyond a certain level (p. 329)

cost-push inflation: theory that the wage demands of labor unions and the excessive profit motive of large corporations push up prices, resulting in stagflation (p. 455)

craft union: union made up of skilled workers in a specific trade or industry (p. 323)

credit: receipt of money either directly or indirectly to buy goods and services in the present with the promise to pay for them in the future (p. 83)

credit bureau: private business that investigates a person to determine the risk involved in lending money to that person (p. 96)

credit card: credit device that allows a person to make purchases at many kinds of stores, restaurants, and other businesses without paying cash (p. 91)

credit check: investigation of a person's income, current debts, personal life, and past history of borrowing and repaying debts (p. 96)

credit rating: rating of the risk involved in lending money to a specific person or business (p. 96)

credit union: depository institution owned and operated by its members to provide savings accounts and low-interest loans only to its members (p. 89)

cybernomics: an economic system driven by Internet commerce (p. 566)

D

day trading: buying and selling securities directly over the Internet (p. 577)

debit card: device used to make cashless purchases; money is electronically withdrawn from the consumer's checkable account and transferred directly to the store's bank account (p. 389)

debt financing: raising money for a business through borrowing (p. 271)

deficit financing: government policy of spending more money than it is able to bring in through revenues (p. 439)

deflation: prolonged decline in the general price level of goods and services (p. 351)

demand: the amount of a good or service that consumers are able and willing to buy at various possible prices during a specified time period (p. 170)

demand curve: downward-sloping line that graphically shows the quantities demanded at each possible price (p. 179)

demand-pull inflation: theory that prices rise as the result of excessive business and consumer demand; demand increases faster than total supply, resulting in shortages that lead to higher prices (p. 454)

demand schedule: table showing quantities demanded at different possible prices (p. 178)

democratic socialism: system that works within the constitutional framework of a nation to elect socialists to office; the government usually controls only some areas of the economy (p. 500)

depreciation: loss of value because of wear and tear to durable goods and capital goods (p. 347); fall in the price of a currency through the action of supply and demand (p. 482)

depression: major slowdown of economic activity during which millions are out of work, many businesses fail, and the economy operates at far below capacity (p. 361)

deregulation: reduction of government regulation and control over business activity (p. 253)

devaluation: lowering a currency's value in relation to other currencies by government order (p. 481)

developed nations: nations with relatively high standards of living and economies based more on industry than on agriculture (p. 518)

developing nations: nations with little industrial development and low standards of living (p. 518)

direct foreign investment (DFI): the purchase by foreigners of real estate and businesses in another country (p. 549)

direct-mail advertising: type of promotion using a mailer that usually includes a letter describing the product or service and an order blank or application form (p. 299)

discount rate: interest rate that the Fed charges on loans to member banks (p. 414)

discretionary income: money income a person has left to spend on extras after necessities have been bought (p. 60)

disposable income: income remaining for a person to spend or save after all taxes have been paid (p. 60)

disposable personal income (DI): same as *disposable income* (p. 348)

distance education: education provided via telecommunications technology (p. 578)

diversification: spreading of investments among several different types of accounts to lower overall risk (p. 158)

dividend: portion of a corporation's profits paid to its stockholders (p. 223)

division of labor: breaking down of a job into small tasks performed by different workers (p. 280)

durability: ability of an item to last a long time (p. 118)

durable goods: manufactured items that have a life span longer than three years (p. 84)

E

e-commerce: conducting business transactions over computer networks, in particular the World Wide Web (pp. 303, 567)

economic assistance: loans and outright grants of money or equipment to other nations to add to their capital resources (p. 525)

economic efficiency: wise use of available resources so that costs do not exceed benefits (p. 47)

economic equity: the attempt to balance an economic policy so that everyone benefits fairly (p. 47)

economic growth: expansion of the economy to produce more goods, jobs, and wealth (p. 48)

economic indicators: statistics that measure variables in the economy (p. 367)

economic model: a theory or simplified representation that helps explain and predict economic behavior in the real world (p. 19)

economics: the study of how individuals and societies make choices about ways to use scarce resources to fulfill their wants (p. 3)

economic system: way in which a nation uses its resources to satisfy its people's needs and wants (p. 31)

economies of scale: decreases in long-run average costs of producing that result from the large size or scale of output (p. 241)

economy: the production and distribution of goods and services in a society (p. 19)

elastic demand: situation in which the rise or fall in a product's price greatly affects the amount that people are willing to buy (p. 184)

elasticity: economic concept dealing with consumers' responsiveness to an increase or decrease in price (p. 181)

electronic funds transfer (EFT): system of putting onto computers all the various banking functions that in the past were handled on paper (p. 384)

embargo: complete restriction on the import or export of a particular good (p. 487)

entrepreneur: person who organizes, manages, and assumes the risks of a business in order to gain profits (p. 208)

entrepreneurship: ability of risk-taking individuals to develop new products and start new businesses in order to make profits (p. 7)

equilibrium price: the price at which the amount producers are willing to supply is equal to the amount consumers are willing to buy (p. 194)

ethical behavior: acting in accordance with moral and ethical convictions about right and wrong (p. 75)

European Union (EU): organization of European nations whose goal is to encourage economic integration as a single market (p. 489)

exchange rate: the price of one nation's currency in terms of another nation's currency (p. 479)

expansion: part of the business cycle in which economic activity slowly increases (p. 361)

exports: goods sold to other countries (p. 474)

externalities: economic side effects or by-products that affect an uninvolved third party; can be negative or positive (p. 432)

F

factors of production: resources of land, labor, capital, and entrepreneurship used to produce goods and services (p. 5)

Fed: the Federal Reserve System created by Congress in 1913 as the nation's central banking organization (p. 399)

federal funds rate: interest rate that banks charge each other on loans (usually overnight) (p. 415)

Federal Open Market Committee (FOMC): 12-member committee in the Federal Reserve System that meets 8 times a year to decide the course of action that the Fed should take to control the money supply (p. 401)

fiat money: money that has value because a government fiat, or order, has established it as acceptable for payment of debts (p. 379)

finance charge: cost of credit expressed monthly in dollars and cents (p. 92)

finance company: company that takes over contracts for installment debts from stores and adds a fee for collecting the debt; consumer finance company makes loans directly to consumers at high rates of interest (p. 90)

financing: obtaining funds or money capital for business expansion (p. 263)

fiscal policy: federal government's use of taxation and spending policies to affect overall business activity (p. 457)

fiscal year: year by which accounts are kept; for the federal government, October 1 to September 30 of the next year (p. 437)

five-year plans: centralized planning system that was the basis for China's economic system; eventually was transformed to a regional planning system leading to limited free enterprise (p. 504)

fixed rate of exchange: system under which a national government sets the value of its currency in relation to a single standard (p. 480)

flexible exchange rates: arrangement in which the forces of supply and demand are allowed to set the price of various currencies (p. 482)

foreign affiliates: branches of multinational firms (p. 554)

foreign aid: money, goods, and services given by governments and private organizations to help other nations and their citizens (p. 525)

foreign exchange markets: markets dealing in buying and selling foreign currency for businesses that want to import goods from other countries (p. 480)

fractional reserve banking: system in which only a fraction of the deposits in a bank is kept on hand, or in reserve; the remainder is available to lend to borrowers or is otherwise invested (p. 408)

franchise: contract in which one business (the franchiser) sells to another business (the franchisee) the right to use the franchiser's name and sell its products (p. 224)

free enterprise system: economic system in which individuals own the factors of production and decide how to use them within legal limits; same as *capitalism* (p. 42)

frequency marketing: marketing directed by stored information about the frequency of a customer's use of a product (p. 568)

full employment: condition of the economy when the unemployment rate is lower than a certain percentage established by economists' studies (p. 453)

G

GDP: see *gross domestic product (GDP)*

GDP price deflator: price index that removes the effect of inflation from GDP so that the overall economy in one year can be compared to another year (p. 353)

General Agreement on Tariffs and Trade (GATT): trade agreement under which countries met periodically to negotiate tariff reductions that were mutually advantageous to all members (p. 488)

generic brand: general name for a product rather than a specific brand name given by the manufacturer (p. 70)

global integration: interdependency among the countries of the world, especially within financial markets and telecommunications (p. 544)

goods: tangible objects that can satisfy people's wants or needs (p. 6)

gross domestic product (GDP): total dollar value of all final goods and services produced in a nation in a single year (p. 344)

H

hypothesis: an assumption involving two or more variables that must be tested for validity (p. 20)

I

import quota: restriction imposed on the value of or on the number of units of a particular good that can be brought into the country (p. 487)

imports: goods bought from other countries for domestic use (p. 473)

income redistribution: government activity that takes income from some people through taxation and uses it to help citizens in need (p. 431)

individual retirement account (IRA): private retirement plan that allows individuals or married couples to save a certain amount of untaxed earnings per year with the interest being tax-deferred (p. 156)

industrial union: union made up of all the workers in an industry regardless of job or skill level (p. 324)

inelastic demand: situation in which a product's price change has little impact on the quantity demanded by consumers (p. 184)

infant mortality rate: death rate of infants who die during the first year of life (p. 520)

inflation: prolonged rise in the general price level of goods and services (p. 350)

Information Age: the period when telecommunications and computer technology gave information significant economic value (p. 571)

informative advertising: advertising that benefits consumers by giving information about a product (p. 68)

injunction: court order preventing some activity (p. 332)

innovation(s): development of new products, systems, or processes that have wide-ranging effects (pp. 365, 573)

installment debt: type of loan repaid with equal payments, or installments, over a specific period of time (p. 84)

intellectual property: creations of a person's intellect that are protected by copyright; for example, written works and music (p. 577)

interest: payment people receive when they lend money or allow someone else to use their money (pp. 84, 142)

interlocking directorate: a board of directors, the majority of whose members also serve as the board of directors of a competing corporation (p. 249)

intermediate-term financing: money borrowed by a business for 1 to 10 years (p. 272)

International Monetary Fund (IMF): agency whose member governments once were obligated to keep their foreign exchange rates more or less fixed; today it offers monetary advice and provides loans to developing nations (p. 481)

Internet: a worldwide system of interconnected computers that store, process, and share information (p. 566)

inventory: extra supply of the items used in a business, such as raw materials or goods for sale (p. 209)

J

joint venture: partnership set up for a specific purpose just for a short period of time (p. 217)

K

Keogh Plan: retirement plan that allows self-employed individuals to save a maximum of 15 percent of their income up to a specified amount each year, and to deduct that amount from their yearly taxable income (p. 156)

knowledge economy: economy in which information is the key to growth (p. 572)

L

labor: human effort directed toward producing goods and services (p. 6)

labor union: association of workers organized to improve wages and working conditions for its members (p. 321)

lagging indicators: indicators that seem to lag behind changes in overall business activity (p. 367)

laissez-faire: economic system in which the government minimizes its interference with the economy (p. 41)

land: natural resources and surface land and water (p. 6)

law of demand: economic rule stating that the quantity demanded and price move in opposite directions (p. 171)

law of diminishing marginal utility: economic rule stating that the additional satisfaction a consumer gets from purchasing one more unit of a product will lessen with each additional unit purchased (p. 174)

law of diminishing returns: economic rule that says as more units of a factor of production (such as labor) are added to other factors of production (such as equipment), total output continues to increase but at a diminishing rate (p. 192)

law of supply: economic rule stating that price and quantity supplied move in the same direction (p. 187)

leading indicators: statistics that point to what will happen in the economy (p. 367)

lease: long-term agreement describing the terms under which property is rented (p. 124)

legal tender: money that by law must be accepted for payment of public and private debts (p. 379)

liability insurance: insurance that pays for bodily injury and property damage (p. 133)

limited liability: requirement in which an owner's responsibility for a company's debts is limited to the size of the owner's investment in the firm (p. 220)

limited partnership: special form of partnership in which one or more partners have limited liability but no voice in management (p. 217)

local union: members of a labor union in a particular factory, company, or geographic area (p. 324)

lockout: situation that occurs when management prevents workers from returning to work until they agree to a new contract (p. 331)

long-term financing: money borrowed by a business for a period of more than 10 years (p. 273)

loose money policy: monetary policy that makes credit inexpensive and abundant, possibly leading to inflation (p. 408)

M

M1: narrowest definition of the money supply; consists of moneys that can be spent immediately and against which checks can be written (p. 391)

M2: broader definition of the money supply; includes all of M1, plus such near moneys as money market mutual fund balances, certificates of deposit, and Eurodollars (p. 391)

macroeconomics: the branch of economic theory dealing with the economy as a whole and decision making by large units such as governments (p. 18)

marginal utility: an additional amount of satisfaction (p. 174)

market: freely chosen activity between buyers and sellers of goods and services (pp. 36, 170)

market basket: representative group of goods and services used to compile the consumer price index (p. 352)

market economy: system in which individuals own the factors of production and make economic decisions through free interaction while looking out for their own and their families' best interests (p. 36)

marketing: all the activities needed to move goods and services from the producer to the consumer (p. 289)

market research: gathering, recording, and analyzing data about the types of goods and services that people want (p. 292)

market structure: the extent to which competition prevails in particular markets (p. 233)

market survey: survey in which researchers gather information about possible users of a product based on such characteristics as age, sex, income, education, and location (p. 293)

maturity: period of time at the end of which time deposits will pay a stated rate of interest (p. 143)

mechanization: combined labor of people and machines (p. 280)

mediation: stage in contract negotiations between union and management in which a neutral person steps in and tries to get both sides to reach an agreement (p. 329)

Medicaid: state and federal public-assistance program that helps pay health care costs for low-income and disabled persons (p. 431)

Medicare: government program that provides health care for the aged (p. 426)

medium of exchange: use of money in exchange for goods or services (p. 376)

merger: a combined company that results when one corporation buys more than half the stock of another corporation and, thus, controls the second corporation (p. 249)

microchip: a tiny electronic circuit that processes and digitally transfers information (p. 565)

microeconomics: the branch of economic theory that deals with behavior and decision making by small units such as individuals and firms (p. 18)

military assistance: economic or technical aid given to a nation's armed forces (p. 525)

minimum wage law: federal law that sets the lowest legal hourly wage rate that may be paid to certain types of workers (p. 319)

mixed economy: system combining characteristics of more than one type of economy (p. 38)

monetarism: theory that deals with the relationship between the amount of money the Fed places in circulation and the level of activity in the economy (p. 462)

monetarists: supporters of the theory of monetarism, often linked with Milton Friedman (p. 462)

monetary policy: policy that involves changing the rate of growth of the supply of money in circulation in order to affect the cost and availability of credit (p. 400)

monetary rule: monetarists' belief that the Fed should allow the money supply to grow at a smooth, consistent rate per year and not use monetary policy to stimulate or slow the economy (p. 463)

money: anything customarily used as a medium of exchange, a unit of accounting, and a store of value (p. 376)

money market deposit account: account that pays relatively high rates of interest, requires a minimum balance, and allows immediate access to money (p. 143)

money market fund: type of mutual fund that uses investors' money to make short-term loans to businesses and banks (p. 152)

monopolistic competition: market situation in which a large number of sellers offer similar but slightly different products and in which each has some control over price (p. 245)

monopoly: market situation in which a single supplier makes up an entire industry for a good or service that has no close substitutes (p. 240)

mortgage: installment debt owed on houses, buildings, or land (p. 85)

multinationals: firms that do business and have offices or factories in many countries (p. 553)

mutual fund: investment company that pools the money of many individuals to buy stocks, bonds, or other investments (p. 151)

N

national debt: total amount of outstanding debt for the federal government (p. 439)

national income (NI): total income earned by everyone in the economy (p. 347)

national income accounting: measurement of the national economy's performance, dealing with the overall economy's output and income (p. 343)

nationalization: placement of railroads, businesses, or other industries under government ownership (p. 525)

near moneys: assets, such as savings accounts, that can be turned into money relatively easily and without the risk of loss of value (p. 390)

net domestic product (NDP): value of the nation's total output (GDP) minus the total value lost through depreciation on machines and equipment (p. 347)

net exports: difference between what the nation sells to other countries and what it buys from other countries (p. 346)

North American Free Trade Agreement (NAFTA): trade agreement designed to reduce and gradually eliminate tariff barriers among Mexico, Canada, and the United States (p. 489)

O

oligopoly: industry dominated by a few suppliers who exercise some control over price (p. 243)

open-market operations: buying and selling of United States securities by the Fed to affect the money supply (p. 416)

opportunity cost: value of the next best alternative given up for the alternative that was chosen (p. 13)

overdraft checking: checking account that allows a customer to write a check for more money than exists in his or her account (p. 384)

over-the-counter market: electronic purchase and sale of stocks and bonds, often of smaller companies, which takes place outside the organized stock exchanges (p. 150)

P

partnership: business that two or more individuals own and operate (p. 215)

passbook savings account: account for which a depositor receives a booklet in which deposits, withdrawals, and interest are recorded (p. 142)

patent: government protection that gives an inventor the exclusive right to make, use, or sell an invention for a specified number of years (p. 241)

peak: period of prosperity in a business cycle in which economic activity is at its highest point (p. 360)

penetration pricing: selling a new product at a low price to attract customers away from an established product (p. 298)

pension plans: company plans that provide retirement income for their workers (p. 155)

perfect competition: market situation in which there are numerous buyers and sellers, and no single buyer or seller can affect price (p. 234)

personal income (PI): total income that individuals receive before personal taxes are paid (p. 348)

picketing: activity in which striking workers walk up and down in front of a workplace carrying signs that state their disagreement with the company (p. 329)

points: fees paid to a lender and computed as percentage points of a loan (p. 123)

preferred stock: shares of ownership in a corporation that give stockholders a portion of future profits (before any profits go to holders of common stock), but no voting rights (p. 223)

price ceiling: a legal maximum price that may be charged for a particular good or service (p. 197)

price elasticity of demand: economic concept that deals with *how much* demand varies according to changes in price (p. 181)

price floor: a legal minimum price below which a good or service may not be sold (p. 198)

price leadership: practice of setting prices close to those charged by other companies selling similar products (p. 298)

prime rate: rate of interest that banks charge on loans to their best business customers (p. 414)

principal: amount of money originally borrowed in a loan (p. 84)

private-labeled products: lower-priced store-brand products carried by some supermarket chains and club warehouse chains (p. 113)

private property: whatever is owned by individuals rather than by government (p. 43)

privatization: change from state ownership of business, land, and buildings to private ownership (p. 509)

producer price index (PPI): measure of the change in price over time that United States producers charge for their goods and services (p. 353)

product differentiation: manufacturers' use of minor differences in quality and features to try to differentiate between similar goods and services (p. 244)

production: process of changing resources into goods that satisfy the needs and wants of individuals and businesses (p. 277)

production possibilities curve: graph showing the maximal combinations of goods and services that can be produced from a fixed amount of resources in a given period of time (p. 14)

productivity: the amount of output (goods and services) that results from a given level of inputs (land, labor, capital) (p. 7)

product life cycle: series of stages that a product goes through from first introduction to complete withdrawal from the market (p. 300)

professionals: highly educated individuals with college degrees and usually additional education or training (p. 316)

profit: money left after all the costs of production—wages, rents, interest, and taxes—have been paid (pp. 43, 265)

profit incentive: desire to make money that motivates people to produce and sell goods and services (p. 43)

progressive tax: tax that takes a larger percentage of higher incomes than lower incomes; justified on the basis of the ability-to-pay principle (p. 443)

proletariat: term used by Karl Marx referring to workers (p. 499)

promotion: use of advertising to inform consumers that a new or improved product or service is available and to persuade them to purchase it (p. 299)

proportional tax: tax that takes the same percentage of all incomes; as income rises, the amount of tax paid also rises (p. 443)

proprietor: owner of a business (p. 215)

protectionists: people who argue for trade restrictions to protect domestic industries (p. 487)

protective tariff: tax on imports used to raise the cost of imported goods and thereby protect domestic producers (p. 487)

public-assistance programs: government programs that make payments to citizens based on need (p. 431)

public goods: goods or services that government supplies to its citizens; can be used by many individuals at the same time without reducing the benefit each person receives (p. 430)

public-works projects: publicly used facilities, such as schools and highways, built by federal, state, or local governments with public money (p. 425)

purchasing power: the real goods and services that money can buy; determines the value of money (p. 351)

Q

quantity demanded: the amount of a good or service that a consumer is willing and able to purchase at a specific price (p. 172)

quantity supplied: the amount of a good or service that a producer is willing and able to supply at a specific price (p. 187)

R

rational choice: choosing the alternative that has the greatest value from among comparable-quality products (p. 62)

rationing: the distribution of goods and services based on something other than price (p. 197)

real GDP: GDP that has been adjusted for inflation by applying the price deflator (p. 353)

real income effect: economic rule stating that individuals cannot keep buying the same quantity of a product if its price rises while their income stays the same (p. 172)

receipts: income received from the sale of goods and/or services; also, slips of paper documenting a purchase (p. 209)

recession: part of the business cycle in which the nation's output (real GDP) does not grow for at least six months (p. 361)

recovery: same as *expansion* (p. 361)

registration fee: licensing fee, usually annual, paid to a state for the right to use a car (p. 130)

regressive tax: tax that takes a larger percentage of lower incomes than higher incomes (p. 443)

representative money: money that is backed by an item of value, such as gold or silver (p. 378)

reserve requirements: regulations set by the Fed requiring banks to keep a certain percentage of their deposits as cash in their own vaults or as deposits in their Federal Reserve district bank (p. 408)

retailers: businesses that sell consumer goods directly to the public (p. 303)

revenues: total income from sales of output (p. 265)

revenue tariff: tax on imports used primarily to raise income without restricting imports (p. 487)

right-to-work laws: state laws forbidding unions from forcing workers to join and pay union dues (p. 325)

robotics: sophisticated computer-controlled machinery that operates an assembly line (p. 281)

Roth IRA: private retirement plan that taxes income before it is saved, but which does not tax interest on that income when funds are used upon retirement (p. 156)

S

saving: setting aside income for a period of time so that it can be used later (p. 141)

savings and loan association (S&L): depository institution that accepts deposits and lends money (p. 89)

savings bank: depository institution originally set up to serve small savers overlooked by commercial banks (p. 89)

savings bonds: bonds issued by the federal government as a way of borrowing money; they are purchased at half the face value and increase every 6 months until full face value is reached (p. 149)

scarcity: condition of not being able to have all of the goods and services one wants, because wants exceed what can be made from all available resources at any given time (p. 5)

secured loan: loan that is backed up by collateral (p. 98)

security deposit: money a renter lets an owner hold in case the rent is not paid or an apartment is damaged (p. 125)

semiskilled workers: people whose jobs require some training, often using modern technology (p. 316)

service flow: amount of use a person gets from an item over time and the value a person places on this use (p. 118)

services: actions that can satisfy people's wants or needs (p. 6)

service workers: people who provide services directly to individuals (p. 315)

shortage: situation in which the quantity demanded is greater than the quantity supplied (p. 196)

short-term financing: money borrowed by a business for any period of time less than a year (p. 271)

skilled workers: people who have learned a trade or craft either through a vocational school or as an apprentice to an experienced worker (p. 316)

small business incubator: private- or government-funded agency that assists new businesses by providing advice or low-rent buildings and supplies (p. 209)

social insurance programs: government programs that pay benefits to retired and disabled workers, their families, and the unemployed; financed by taxes paid into programs by workers and employers (p. 431)

Social Security: federal program that provides monthly payments to people who are retired or unable to work (p. 431)

sole proprietorship: business owned and operated by one person (p. 213)

specialization: concept that a nation should produce and export a limited assortment of goods for which it is particularly suited in order to remain profitable (p. 475)

stabilization policies: attempts by the federal government to keep the economy healthy; includes monetary and fiscal policies (p. 451)

stagflation: combination of inflation and low economic activity (p. 455)

standard of living: the material well-being of an individual, group, or nation measured by how well their necessities and luxuries are satisfied (p. 48)

startup: beginning business enterprise (p. 208)

statement savings account: account similar to a passbook savings account except that instead of a passbook, the depositor receives a monthly statement showing all transactions (p. 142)

stock: share of ownership in a corporation that entitles the buyer to a certain part of the future profits and assets of the corporation (p. 220)

stockholders: people who have invested in a corporation and own some of its stock (p. 147)

store of value: use of money to store purchasing power for later use (p. 377)

strike: deliberate work stoppage by workers to force an employer to give in to their demands (p. 323)

subsistence agriculture: growing of just enough food by a family to take care of its own needs; no crops are available for export or to feed an industrial workforce (p. 519)

substitution effect: economic rule stating that if two items satisfy the same need and the price of one rises, people will buy the other (p. 172)

Supplemental Security Income: federal programs that include food stamps and payments to the aged, blind, and disabled (p. 431)

supply: the amount of a good or service that producers are able and willing to sell at various prices during a specified time period (p. 170)

supply curve: upward-sloping line that graphically shows the quantities supplied at each possible price (p. 189)

supply schedule: table showing quantities supplied at different possible prices (p. 188)

surplus: situation in which quantity supplied is greater than quantity demanded (p. 196)

tariff: tax placed on an imported product (p. 486)

tax-exempt bonds: bonds sold by local and state governments; interest paid on the bond is not taxed by the federal government (p. 148)

technical assistance: aid in the form of professionals such as engineers, teachers, and technicians; supplied by nations to teach skills to individuals in other nations (p. 525)

technology: advance in knowledge leading to new and improved goods and services and better ways of producing them (pp. 7, 190)

telecommunications: long-distance communication, usually electronic, using communications satellites and fiber-optic cables (pp. 544, 571)

Temporary Assistance for Needy Families: state-run public-assistance program that provides assistance and work opportunities to needy families (p. 431)

test-marketing: offering a product for sale in a small area for a limited period of time to see how well it sells before offering it nationally (p. 293)

thrift institutions: mutual savings banks, S&Ls, and credit unions that offer many of the same services as commercial banks (p. 389)

tight money policy: monetary policy that makes credit expensive and in short supply in an effort to slow the economy (p. 408)

time deposits: savings plans that require savers to leave their money on deposit for certain periods of time (p. 143)

time lags: periods between the time fiscal policy is enacted and the time it becomes effective (p. 465)

trade-off: sacrificing one good or service to purchase or produce another (p. 12)

traditional economy: system in which economic decisions are based on customs and beliefs that have been handed down from generation to generation (p. 33)

transfer payments: welfare and other supplementary payments, such as unemployment compensation, Social Security, and Medicaid, that a state or the federal government makes to individuals (p. 348)

Treasury bills: certificates issued by the U.S. Treasury in exchange for a minimum amount of $1,000 and maturing in 3 months to 1 year (p. 149)

Treasury bonds: certificates issued by the U.S. Treasury in exchange for minimum amounts of $1,000 and maturing in 10 or more years (p. 149)

Treasury notes: certificates issued by the U.S. Treasury in exchange for minimum amounts of $1,000 and maturing in 1 to 10 years (p. 149)

trough: lowest part of the business cycle in which the downward spiral of the economy levels off (p. 361)

U

underground economy: transactions by people who do not follow federal and state laws with respect to reporting earnings (p. 453)

unemployment rate: percentage of the civilian labor force that is unemployed but is actively looking for work (p. 452)

union: see *labor union*

union shop: company that requires new employees to join a union after a specific period of time (p. 324)

unit of accounting: use of money as a yardstick for comparing the values of goods and services in relation to one another (p. 376)

unlimited liability: requirement that an owner is personally and fully responsible for all losses and debts of a business (p. 215)

unsecured loan: loan guaranteed only by a promise to repay it (p. 98)

unskilled workers: people whose jobs require no specialized training (p. 316)

usury law: law restricting the amount of interest that can be charged for credit (p. 102)

utility: the ability of any good or service to satisfy consumer wants (p. 173); the amount of satisfaction one gets from a good or service (p. 290)

V

vicious cycle of poverty: situation in which a less-developed country with low per capita incomes cannot save and invest enough to achieve acceptable rates of economic growth and thus is trapped (p. 536)

voluntary exchange: a transaction in which a buyer and a seller exercise their economic freedom by working out their own terms of exchange (p. 170)

W

warranty: promise made by a manufacturer or a seller to repair or replace a product within a certain time period if it is found to be faulty (p. 70)

Web sites: electronic World Wide Web locations that store information to be viewed or downloaded (p. 566)

weightless economy: term coined to identify an economy based on products that are not tangible (p. 572)

welfare: same as *public-assistance programs* (p. 431)

welfare state: country that has a blend of capitalism and socialism, combining private ownership of the means of production and competitive allocation of resources with the goal of social equality for its citizens (p. 510)

white-collar workers: category of workers employed in offices, sales, or professional positions (p. 315)

wholesalers: businesses that purchase large quantities of goods from producers for resale to other businesses (p. 303)

workers' compensation: government program that extends payments for medical care to workers injured on the job (p. 431)

World Trade Organization (WTO): world's largest trade agreement with more than 140 nations (pp. 488, 506)

World Wide Web: part of the Internet, used for communications among consumers, business, governments, and other organizations (p. 566)

A

ability-to-pay principle/principio de la capacidad de pago: principio de tributación que propone que los que tienen más ingresos deben pagar más impuestos que los que tienen menos, sin tomar en cuenta la cantidad de servicios gubernamentales que usan (p. 442)

absolute advantage/ventaja absoluta: capacidad de un país de producir un producto de manera más eficiente (i.e., aumentando producción sin aumentar la cantidad de recursos) que otros países (p. 475)

agency shop/fábrica con cuota por agencia sindical: compañía en que los empleados no tienen que ser miembros del sindicato, pero sí tienen que pagar la misma cuota que los miembros (p. 324)

aggregate demand/demanda agregada: cantidad total de bienes y servicios de una economía entera que todos los habitantes demandan en un momento dado (p. 356)

aggregate demand curve/curva de demanda agregada: línea gráfica que muestra la relación entre la cantidad de demanda agregada y el promedio de todos los precios, medidos por el deflactor de precios del PIB implícito (p. 357)

aggregates/agregado: suma de todas las partes individuales de una economía (p. 356)

aggregate supply/oferta agregada: producción doméstica real, tomando en cuenta los aumentos y rebajas de los precios (p. 358)

aggregate supply curve/curva de oferta agregada: línea gráfica que muestra la relación entre la cantidad de oferta agregada y el promedio de todos los precios, medidos por el deflactor de precios del PIB implícito (p. 358)

annual percentage rate (APR)/tasa de interés anual: costo del crédito expresado como porcentaje anual (p. 92)

antitrust legislation/legislación antimonopolista: leyes aprobadas por los gobiernos federal y estatales para evitar que se formen nuevos monopolios o para deshacer los que ya existen (p. 249)

arbitration/arbitraje: etapa en el proceso de negociar un contrato en que el sindicato y los gerentes entregan los asuntos que no pueden resolver a un tercero para que tome una decisión final (p. 329)

articles of incorporation/escritura de constitución: documento que contiene información básica acerca de una sociedad anónima que se presenta al estado donde tendrá su oficina principal (p. 221)

assembly line/línea de montaje: sistema de producción en que el artículo producido es trasladado por una correa transportadora a distintos obreros que, por turnos, hacen labores particulares para ensamblarlo (p. 280)

assets/activos: todos los bienes que son la propiedad legal de un negocio o persona (p. 215)

authoritarian socialism/socialismo autoritario: sistema que apoya la revolución como modo de derrocar el capitalismo y realizar metas socialistas; la economía entera es controlada por el gobierno central; también se llama *comunismo* (p. 500)

automated teller machines (ATMs)/cajero automático: máquinas que le permiten a los consumidores hacer sus transacciones bancarias sin la ayuda de un cajero (p. 385)

automation/automatización: proceso de producción en que máquinas hacen el trabajo y personas las supervisan (p. 280)

B

bait and switch/engatusar: práctica publicitaria engañosa que atrae a los consumidores con un producto a precio bajo para después tratar de venderles otro producto más caro (p. 69)

balance of trade/balanza comercial: diferencia entre el valor de las exportaciones e importaciones de una nación (p. 483)

bankruptcy/bancarrota: quiebra; no poder pagar las deudas con los ingresos que se reciben (p. 104)

barriers to entry/barreras al mercado: obstáculos que impiden que competidores entren en un mercado (p. 240)

barter/trueque: intercambio de bienes y servicios por otros bienes y servicios (p. 376)

base year/año base: año que se usa como punto de comparación con otros años en una series de estudios estadísticos (p. 352)

benefits-received principle/principio de beneficio obtenido: sistema de tributación en que los que usan un servicio gubernamental pagan impuestos por él en proporción al beneficio que reciben; los que no usan el servicio no pagan impuestos por él (p. 440)

black market/mercado negro: mercado ilegal en que se venden bienes a precios más altos de los que permite la ley o en que se venden productos ilegales (p. 197)

blue-collar workers/obreros: clasificación de trabajadores empleados en artesanías, manufactura y labores no agrícolas (p. 315)

boom/auge: véase *peak/auge* (p. 360)

boycott/boicot: presión económica que ejerce un sindicato, animando al público a que no compre los bienes o servicios producidos por una compañía (p. 331)

brand name/marca de fábrica: palabra, imagen o logotipo que lleva un producto para ayudar a los consumidores a distinguirlo de otros productos similares (p. 70)

broker/corredor de bolsa: persona que sirve de intermediario entre los vendedores y compradores de acciones y bonos (p. 149)

budget deficit/déficit presupuestario: situación en que la cantidad de dinero que el gobierno gasta es mayor que sus ingresos durante el año fiscal (p. 438)

budget surplus/superávit presupuestario: situación en que los ingresos del gobierno son mayores que los gastos durante el año fiscal (p. 439)

bureaucracies/burocracias: oficinas y agencias del gobierno que se ocupan de asuntos particulares (p. 530)

business cycle/ciclo económico: cambios irregulares en el nivel de producción total, medidos por el PIB real (p. 360)

business fluctuations/fluctuaciones comerciales: alzas y bajas en una economía (p. 360)

C

capital/capital: bienes manufacturados que se usan para producir otros bienes y servicios; el dinero es capital financiero (p. 6)

capital flight/fuga de capital al extranjero: exportación legal o ilegal de divisas o del capital financiero de una nación por los líderes del mismo país (p. 530)

capital gain/ganancia de capital: aumento en el valor de un activo en el tiempo que transcurre entre su compra y su venta (p. 147)

capitalism/capitalismo: sistema económico en que individuos son dueños de los factores de producción (p. 41)

capital loss/pérdida de capital: disminución en el valor de un activo o bono entre el momento en que se compra y el momento en que se vende (p. 147)

cartel/cártel: arreglos entre grupos de negocios industriales, a menudo en distintos países, para controlar el precio, producción y distribución de bienes y así reducir la competencia internacional (p. 245)

certificates of deposit/certificados de depósito: depósitos a plazos que especifican la cantidad del depósito, la fecha de vencimiento y el tipo de interés que se paga (p. 143)

channels of distribution/canales de distribución: vías por las cuales se mueven los bienes de los fabricantes a los consumidores (p. 302)

charge account/cuenta de crédito: crédito que se le extiende a un consumidor, que le permite comprar bienes y servicios de una compañía en particular y pagar por ellos más adelante (p. 90)

checkable deposits/depósitos a la vista: dinero depositado en un banco que se puede sacar en cualquier momento con sólo presentar un cheque (p. 389)

check clearing/compensación de cheques: método de pagar y transferir cheques de la institución en que se depositan a la institución depositaria de la persona que los emite (p. 405)

checking account/cuenta corriente: cuenta de la cual se puede sacar dinero depositado por medio de un cheque (p. 389)

circular flow of economic activity/flujo circular de actividad económica: modelo económico que representa a los ingresos circulando continuamente entre negocios y consumidores (p. 37)

circular flow of income/flujo circular de ingresos: modelo económico que representa a los ingresos circulando continuamente entre negocios y consumidores (p. 458)

civilian labor force/fuerza laboral civil: número total de personas mayores de 16 años que tienen empleo o lo están buscando (p. 313)

closed shop/fábrica cerrada: compañía en que sólo se puede dar empleo a miembros del sindicato (p. 324)

closing costs/costos de cierre: cuotas que se pagan para obtener una hipoteca o transferir una propiedad a un dueño nuevo (p. 123)

club warehouse store/club almacén: tienda que tiene un surtido limitado de marcas y artículos que vende en grandes cantidades; es más barato que los supermercados (p. 112)

coincident indicators/indicadores coincidentes: indicadores económicos que cambian a la misma vez que la actividad comercial en general (p. 367)

collateral/garantía: algo de valor que el prestatario se compromete a darle al prestamista si no le devuelve el dinero (p. 98)

collective bargaining/negociación colectiva: proceso mediante el cual los sindicatos y gerentes acuerdan las condiciones de trabajo (p. 328)

command economy/economía dirigida: sistema en que el gobierno controla los factores de producción y toma todas las decisiones sobre su uso (p. 34)

commercial bank/banco comercial: banco cuyas funciones principales son aceptar depósitos, prestar dinero y transferir fondos entre bancos, individuos y negocios (p. 89)

commodity money/dinero material: medios de cambio, como el ganado o las joyas, que tienen valor propio como mercancías además de su valor como dinero (p. 378)

common stock/acciones ordinarias: tipo de participaciones en una sociedad anónima que da a los accionistas el derecho al voto y una porción de las futuras ganancias (después de que se haya pagado a los accionistas con acciones preferentes); también se llaman acciones comunes (p. 223)

communism/comunismo: término usado por Carlos Marx para referirse a la sociedad ideal en que no hace falta gobierno (p. 500)

comparative advantage/ventaja comparativa: capacidad de un país de producir un producto por un costo de oportunidad más bajo que otro país (p. 476)

comparison shopping/comparar antes de comprar: obtener información sobre los tipos de productos y los precios de éstos en distintas tiendas y compañías (p. 69)

competition/competencia: rivalidad entre los productores o vendedores de bienes y servicios semejantes para tener más clientes (p. 44)

competitive advertising/publicidad competitiva: anuncios que tratan de convencer al consumidor que un producto es distinto o mejor que los demás (p. 68)

complementary goods/bienes complementarios: productos que se usan en conjunto; al bajar el precio de uno, la demanda por el otro sube (p. 181)

conglomerate/conglomerado: gran corporación compuesta de empresas más pequeñas cuyos negocios no están relacionados (p. 250)

consumer/consumidor: cualquier persona o grupo que compra o utiliza bienes y servicios para satisfacer sus necesidades o deseos personales (p. 59)

consumer-credit laws/leyes sobre el crédito al consumidor: leyes que protegen al consumidor, dándole acceso a sus expedientes de crédito (p. 578)

consumer goods/bienes de consumo: bienes producidos para individuos y vendidos directamente al público para usarse tal y como son (p. 277)

consumerism/protección al consumidor: movimiento dedicado a informar al consumidor sobre las compras que hace y a exigirles productos mejores y más seguros a los fabricantes (p. 72)

consumer price index (CPI)/índice de precios al consumidor: medida del cambio de precio a través del tiempo de un grupo de bienes y servicios escogidos que se usan en un domicilio típico (p. 351)

consumer sovereignty/soberanía del consumidor: manera en que el consumidor gobierna el mercado cuando determina los tipos de bienes y servicios que se producen (p. 290)

contraction/contracción: parte del ciclo económico en que la actividad económica disminuye hasta llegar al nivel más bajo (p. 360)

convenience store/tiendas de artículos de consumo frecuente: tienda que se mantiene abierta de 16 a 24 horas al día con un surtido limitado de artículos a precios más altos (p. 113)

copyright/copyright: protección que el gobierno le da a un escritor o artista, dándole el derecho exclusivo de vender, publicar o reproducir sus obras por un determinado número de años; también se llama derechos de autor (p. 241)

corporate charter/licencia para negociar: permiso para operar una sociedad anónima que da el estado en que se establece una compañía (p. 221)

corporation/sociedad anónima: tipo de empresa de la cual muchas personas son dueñas, pero la ley la trata como si fuera una persona; puede tener propiedad, pagar impuestos, entrar en contratos, etc.; también se llama corporación (p. 220)

cost-benefit analysis/análisis de coste-beneficios: proceso financiero en que un negocio calcula el costo de emprender una actividad y lo compara con los beneficios de esa actividad (p. 265)

cost-of-living adjustment (COLA)/ajuste por el costo de la vida: contrato sindical u otra provisión que proporciona un aumento de sueldo adicional si el nivel general de los precios en la economía sube por encima de un nivel determinado (p. 329)

cost-push inflation/inflación de costes: teoría que las demandas salariales de los sindicatos y el afán de lucro excesivo de las grandes compañías fuerzan los precios hacia arriba, resultando en estagflación (p. 455)

craft union/sindicato de artesanos: asociación de trabajadores especializados en un oficio o industria en particular (p. 323)

credit/crédito: recibir dinero directa o indirectamente para comprar bienes y servicios en el presente bajo promesa de pagar por ellos en el futuro (p. 83)

credit bureau/oficina de crédito: negocio privado que investiga a individuos para determinar el riesgo de prestarles dinero (p. 96)

credit card/tarjeta de crédito: instrumento de crédito que le permite a una persona hacer compras en muchas clases distintas de tiendas, restaurantes y negocios sin tener que pagar con dinero en efectivo (p. 91)

credit check/investigación de crédito: investigación de los ingresos, deudas actuales, vida privada e historial de préstamos pedidos y deudas pagadas de una persona (p. 96)

credit rating/clasificación de crédito: evaluación del riesgo de prestarle dinero a una persona o negocio en particular (p. 96)

credit union/cooperativa de crédito: institución de depósitos que es propiedad de sus miembros, que es administrada por ellos y que proporciona cuentas de ahorro y préstamos a intereses bajos exclusivamente a sus miembros; también se llama unión crediticia (p. 89)

cybernomics/economía ciberespacial: sistema económico impulsado por el comercio que se lleva a cabo a través de Internet (p. 566)

D

day trading/operar por cuenta propia: comprar y vender valores (acciones y bonos) directamente a través de Internet (p. 577)

debit card/tarjeta de débito: utensilio que se usa para hacer compras sin dinero en efectivo; el dinero se retira electrónicamente de la cuenta de cheques del comprador y se transfiere directamente a la cuenta de banco de la tienda (p. 389)

debt financing/financiamiento mediante deudas: recaudar dinero para un negocio por medio de préstamos (p. 271)

deficit financing/financiamiento del déficit: política gubernamental de gastar más dinero de los ingresos que tiene y obtener préstamos para cubrir los gastos adicionales (p. 439)

deflation/deflación: caída prolongada en el nivel general de los precios de bienes y servicios (p. 351)

demand/demanda: cantidad de un producto o servicio que los consumidores pueden o están dispuestos a comprar a varios precios posibles durante un período de tiempo determinado (p. 170)

demand curve/curva de demanda: línea descendiente en una gráfica cuya inclinación muestra la cantidad de demanda a cada precio posible (p. 179)

demand-pull inflation/inflación de demanda: teoría que los precios suben como consecuencia de la demanda excesiva de los negocios y consumidores; la demanda aumenta más rápido que la oferta total, ocasionando una escasez que conduce a precios más altos (p. 454)

demand schedule/lista de demanda: tabla que muestra la cantidad de demandada a distintos precios (p. 178)

democratic socialism/socialismo democrático: sistema que obra dentro del marco de la constitución de una nación para elegir socialistas a cargos públicos; el gobierno generalmente controla solamente algunos sectores de la economía (p. 500)

depreciation/depreciación: pérdida de valor de los bienes duraderos y bienes capitales por causa del uso constante (p. 347); rebaja en el valor de una moneda a través de la acción de la oferta y la demanda (p. 482)

depression/depresión: disminución tan significativa en la actividad económica que millones de personas pierden el trabajo, muchos negocios quiebran y la economía funciona muy por debajo de su capacidad (p. 361)

deregulation/desregulación: reducción en el número de regulaciones y controles gubernamentales sobre las actividades comerciales (p. 253)

devaluation/devaluación: rebajar el valor de una moneda con relación a otras divisas (monedas extranjeras) por orden gubernamental (p. 481)

developed nations/naciones desarrolladas: naciones con niveles de vida relativamente altos y economías basadas en la industria más que en la agricultura (p. 518)

developing nations/naciones en vías de desarrollo: naciones con poco desarrollo industrial y niveles de vida bajos (p. 518)

direct foreign investment/inversión extranjera directa: compra de bienes inmuebles (terrenos y edificios) y negocios en un país por extranjeros (p. 549)

direct-mail advertising/publicidad por correo directo: tipo de promoción por correo que generalmente incluye una carta describiendo el producto o servicio y un formulario para encargar o solicitarlo (p. 299)

discount rate/tasa de descuento: tipo de interés que el Sistema de Reserva Federal les cobra por préstamos a los bancos que son miembros (p. 414)

discretionary income/ingresos discrecionales: dinero que le queda a una persona de sus ingresos después de cubrir lo imprescindible (p. 60)

disposable income/ingresos disponibles: ingresos que le quedan a una persona para ahorrar o gastar después de pagar los impuestos; también se llama renta disponible (p. 60)

disposal personal income/ingresos personales disponibles: véase *disposable income/ingresos disponibles* (p. 348)

distance education/educación a distancia: enseñanza que se proporciona por medio de la tecnología de la telecomunicación (p. 578)

diversification/diversificación: invertir en varios tipos de cuentas distintas para disminuir el riesgo total (p. 158)

dividend/dividendo: porción de las ganancias de una sociedad anónima que se paga a los accionistas (p. 223)

division of labor/división del trabajo: separar un trabajo en pequeñas tareas desempeñadas por distintos obreros (p. 280)

durability/durabilidad: cualidad de poder aguantar mucho tiempo sin estropearse o romperse (p. 118)

durable goods/bienes duraderos: artículos manufacturados con una vida de más de tres años (p. 84)

E

e-commerce/comercio electrónico: llevar a cabo transacciones de negocio a través de redes de computadoras, en particular World Wide Web (pp. 303, 567)

economic assistance/asistencia económica: préstamos y subsidios de dinero o maquinaria a otras naciones para aumentar sus recursos capitales (p. 525)

economic efficiency/eficiencia económica: buen uso de los recursos disponibles para que los costos no excedan los beneficios (p. 47)

economic equity/equidad económica: una política económica gubernamental que trata de lograr que todos se beneficien de manera justa (p. 47)

economic growth/crecimiento económico: expansión de la economía para producir más bienes, trabajos y riqueza (p. 48)

economic indicators/indicadores económicos: estadísticas que miden muchas variables en la economía (p. 367)

economic model/modelo económico: teoría o representación simplificada que ayuda a explicar y prever la conducta económica en el mundo real (p. 19)

economics/economía: ciencia que trata del estudio de individuos y sociedades y cómo usan recursos limitados para satisfacer sus deseos (p. 3)

economic system/sistema económico: manera en que una nación usa sus recursos para satisfacer las necesidades y deseos de su pueblo (p. 31)

economies of scale/economías de escala: rebaja en el costo promedio de producción a largo plazo que resulta de la producción en gran cantidad o escala (p. 241)

economy/economía: producción y distribución de bienes y servicios en una sociedad (p. 19)

elastic demand/demanda elástica: situación en que el aumento o rebaja del precio de un producto tiene gran efecto en la cantidad de ese producto que los consumidores están dispuestos a comprar (p. 184)

elasticity/elasticidad: concepto económico que se refiere a la reacción de los consumidores a los aumentos o rebajas en los precios (p. 181)

electronic funds transfer (EFT)/transferencia electrónica de fondos: sistema que utiliza computadoras para realizar todas las funciones bancarias que antes se hacían con papel y pluma (p. 384)

embargo/embargo: prohibición total de la importación o exportación de un producto (p. 487)

entrepreneur/empresario: persona que organiza, administra y acepta los riesgos de un negocio para sacarle ganancias (p. 208)

entrepreneurship/espíritu empresarial: capacidad de tomar riesgos al desarrollar nuevos productos y empezar nuevos negocios para sacarles ganancias (p. 7)

equilibrium price/precio de equilibrio: precio al que la cantidad de un producto que los fabricantes están dispuestos a ofrecer es igual a la cantidad que los consumidores están dispuestos a comprar (p. 194)

ethical behavior/comportamiento ético: actuar de acuerdo con convicciones morales y éticas acerca del bien y el mal (p. 75)

European Union/Unión Europea: organización de naciones europeas cuyo objetivo es promover su integración económica para formar un solo mercado (p. 489)

exchange rate/tipo de cambio: valor de la moneda de una nación comparado con la moneda de otra (p. 479)

expansion/expansión: parte del ciclo económico en que la actividad económica aumenta lentamente (p. 361)

exports/exportaciones: bienes que se venden a otros países (p. 474)

externalities/factores externos: consecuencias indirectas de actividades económicas que afectan a terceras personas que no tomaron parte en ellas; pueden ser negativas o positivas (p. 432)

F

factors of production/factores de producción: recursos de tierra, trabajo, capital y espíritu empresarial que se usan para producir bienes y servicios (p. 5)

Fed/Sistema de Reserva Federal: sistema creado por el Congreso en 1913 para servir de organización bancaria central de la nación; conocido como "Fed" (p. 399)

federal funds rate/tasa federal por fondos prestados: tipo de interés que se cobran los bancos unos a otros (generalmente por menos de 1 día) (p. 415)

Federal Open Market Committee/Comité Federal del Mercado Libre: comisión de 12 personas, parte del Sistema de Reserva Federal, que se reúne 8 veces al año para determinar lo que debe hacer la Reserva Federal para controlar la oferta monetaria; también se llama Comité Controlador del Dinero (p. 401)

fiat money/dinero fiduciario: dinero que tiene valor porque un decreto gubernamental ha establecido que se puede aceptar como pago por deudas (p. 379)

finance charge/cargo de financiamiento: costo mensual del crédito expresado en dólares y centavos (p. 92)

finance company/compañía financiera: compañía que asume los contratos de deudas a plazos de tiendas y les añade una cuota por cobrar la deuda; las *compañías de financiamiento directo al consumidor* hacen préstamos directamente a los consumidores a intereses altos (p. 90)

financing/financiamiento: obtener fondos o capital financiero para la expansión de un negocio; también se llama financiación (p. 263)

fiscal policy/política fiscal: uso por el gobierno federal de tributación (impuestos) y gastos para afectar la actividad comercial general (p. 457)

fiscal year/año fiscal: período de un año en que se llevan las cuentas; para el gobierno federal, empieza octubre 1 y termina septiembre 30 del próximo año (p. 437)

five-year plans/planes quinquenales: sistema de planificación central que formaba la base del sistema económico chino; fue transformado en un sistema de planificación regional que ha conducido a la libre empresa limitada (p. 504)

fixed rate of exchange/tipo de cambio fijo: sistema bajo el cual un gobierno nacional establece el valor de su moneda en relación con un patrón único (p. 480)

flexible exchange rates/tipos de cambio flexibles: arreglo bajo el cual la oferta y la demanda determinan el valor de varias monedas (p. 482)

foreign affiliates/sucursales extranjeras: establecimientos que forman parte de empresas multinacionales (p. 554)

foreign aid/ayuda al exterior: dinero, bienes y servicios que gobiernos y organizaciones privadas donan para ayudar a otras naciones y sus ciudadanos (p. 525)

foreign exchange markets/mercados de divisas: mercados donde negocios que desean importar bienes de otros países compran y venden divisas (monedas extranjeras) (p. 480)

fractional reserve banking/reserva bancaria parcial: sistema que permite que los bancos tengan sólo un porcentaje de sus depósitos a mano o en reserva; el resto lo pueden usar para hacer préstamos o inversiones (p. 408)

franchise/franquicia: contrato mediante el cual un negocio vende a otro el derecho de usar su nombre y vender sus productos; también se llama licencia (p. 224)

free enterprise system/sistema de libre empresa: sistema económico en que los individuos son dueños de los factores de producción y deciden cómo los van a usar dentro de los límites legales; lo mismo que *capitalismo* (p. 42)

frequency marketing/promoción según la frecuencia de uso: mercadotecnia dirigida por información almacenada sobre la frecuencia con que el cliente utiliza el producto (p. 568)

full employment/pleno empleo: condición económica en que el índice de desempleo está por debajo de un porcentaje establecido por estudios económicos (p. 453)

G

GDP: véase *gross domestic product (GDP)*

GDP price deflator/deflactor de precios del PIB: índice de precios que sustrae del PIB los efectos de la inflación para poder comparar el estado de la economía en un año con el estado económico en otro (p. 353)

General Agreement on Tariffs and Trade/Acuerdo General sobre Aranceles Aduaneros y Comercio: acuerdo comercial bajo el cual muchos países se reunían periódicamente para negociar rebajas en los aranceles que eran ventajosas para todos los participantes (p. 488)

generic brand/nombre genérico: nombre común de un producto en vez de la marca de fábrica que le da el fabricante (p. 70)

global integration/integración global: dependencia mutua entre los países del mundo, en especial con respecto a los mercados financieros y las telecomunicaciones; también se llama integración mundial (p. 544)

goods/bienes: objetos materiales que pueden satisfacer los deseos o necesidades del público (p. 6)

gross domestic product (GDP)/producto interior bruto (PIB): valor total en dólares de todos los bienes y servicios producidos por una nación en un año (p. 344)

H

hypothesis/hipótesis: suposición que tiene dos o más variables y que se tiene que comprobar para ver si es válida (p. 20)

I

import quota/cuota de importación: restricción en el valor o número de unidades de un producto que se puede traer a un país (p. 487)

imports/importaciones: bienes traídos de otro país para el uso doméstico (p. 473)

income redistribution/redistribución de rentas: actividad gubernamental que toma los ingresos de algunas personas a través de impuestos y los usa para ayudar a otras personas necesitadas (p. 431)

individual retirement account/cuentas de retiro individuales: planes de jubilación privados que permiten que individuos o matrimonios ahorren cierta porción de sus ingresos anuales sin pagar impuestos y que posponen el impuesto sobre los intereses (p. 156)

industrial union/sindicato industrial: asociación de todos los obreros de una industria, que no toma en cuenta el tipo de trabajo ni el nivel de especialización (p. 324)

inelastic demand/demanda inelástica: situación en que el precio de un producto tiene poco efecto en la cantidad demandada por los consumidores (p. 184)

infant mortality rate/índice de mortalidad infantil: porcentaje de muertes de niños en el primer año de vida (p. 520)

inflation/inflación: aumento prolongado en el nivel general de los precios de bienes y servicios (p. 350)

Information Age/Edad de la Información: período en que las telecomunicaciones y la informática dieron a la información valor económico significativo (p. 571)

informative advertising/publicidad informativa: anuncios que benefician a los consumidores al darles información sobre un producto (p. 68)

injunction/prohibición judicial: orden de un juez que impide alguna actividad (p. 332)

innovation(s)/innovación: desarrollo de nuevos productos, sistemas o procesos que tienen efectos de gran alcance (pp. 365, 573)

installment debt/deudas pagadas a plazos: tipo de préstamo que se paga en cantidades iguales durante un período determinado de tiempo (p. 84)

intellectual property/propiedad intelectual: creaciones de la mente de una persona que están protegidas por copyright; por ejemplo, obras escritas y musicales (p. 577)

interest/interés: pago que alguien recibe cuando presta dinero o permite que otra persona use su dinero (pp. 84, 142)

interlocking directorate/directorio entrelazado: junta directiva de una compañía cuya mayoría también sirve en la junta directiva de otra sociedad anónima que compite en el mismo mercado (p. 249)

intermediate-term financing/financiamiento a mediano plazo: dinero prestado que un negocio tiene entre 1 y 10 años para pagar (p. 272)

International Monetary Fund (IMF)/Fondo Monetario Internacional (FMI): agencia que antes obligaba a los gobiernos de países miembros a mantener sus tipos de cambio más o menos fijos; hoy ofrece asesoramiento monetario y proporciona préstamos a países en desarrollo (p. 481)

Internet/Internet: sistema mundial de computadoras interconectadas que almacenan, procesan y comparten información (p. 566)

inventory/inventario: artículos que un negocio tiene almacenados, como materias primas o mercancía para vender (p. 209)

J

joint venture/negocio en participación: sociedad establecida por un corto período de tiempo con un propósito determinado (p. 217)

K

Keogh Plan/Plan Keogh: plan de jubilación que le permite al que trabaja por su cuenta ahorrar un máximo del 15 por ciento de sus ingresos anuales hasta llegar a una cantidad determinada y descontar la cantidad ahorrada de sus ingresos anuales gravables (p. 156)

knowledge economy/economía basada en los conocimientos: economía en la cual la información es la clave del crecimiento (p. 572)

L

labor/trabajo: esfuerzo humano dirigido a la producción de bienes y servicios (p. 6)

labor union/sindicato de obreros: asociación de trabajadores organizados para mejorar los salarios y condiciones de trabajo de sus miembros; también se llama sindicato laboral y gremio de obreros (p. 321)

lagging indicators/indicadores de rezaga: indicadores que ocurren después de los cambios en las actividades comerciales (p. 367)

laissez-faire/dejad hacer: sistema económico en que el gobierno interfiere lo menos posible en la economía (p. 41)

land/tierra: recursos naturales, la superficie terrestre y el agua (p. 6)

law of demand/ley de la demanda: regla económica que dice que al cambiar el precio, la cantidad demandada cambia en sentido contrario (p. 171)

law of diminishing marginal utility/ley de utilidad marginal decreciente: regla económica que dice que el consumidor recibe menos satisfacción adicional cada vez que compra una unidad más de un producto (p. 174)

law of diminishing returns/ley de los rendimientos decrecientes: regla económica que dice que al añadir más unidades de un solo factor económico (como el trabajo) a los otros factores económicos (como máquinas), el aumento en la producción será menos y menos significativo (p. 192)

law of supply/ley de la oferta: regla económica que dice que al cambiar el precio, la cantidad ofrecida cambia en el mismo sentido (p. 187)

leading indicators/indicadores anticipados: estadísticas que pronostican lo que va a suceder en la economía (p. 367)

lease/contrato de alquiler: acuerdo a largo plazo que describe los términos bajo los cuales se alquila o arrienda una propiedad (p. 124)

legal tender/medios de curso legal: moneda que, por ley, se tiene que aceptar en pago de deudas públicas y privadas (p. 379)

liability insurance/seguro de responsabilidad civil: seguro que paga por lesiones corporales y daños a propiedad (p. 133)

limited liability/responsabilidad limitada: requisito que limita la responsabilidad de cada dueño por las deudas de una compañía al tamaño de su inversión en la firma (p. 220)

limited partnership/sociedad limitada: tipo de sociedad en que uno o más socios tienen responsabilidad limitada, pero no pueden participar en la administración del negocio (p. 217)

local union/sección sindical: agrupación de miembros de un sindicato de obreros en una fábrica, compañía o área geográfica en particular (p. 324)

lockout/cierre patronal: situación en que los gerentes impiden que los trabajadores regresen al trabajo hasta que acepten un nuevo contrato; también se llama paro forzoso o paro patronal (p. 331)

long-term financing/financiamiento a largo plazo: préstamo de dinero que un negocio tiene por más de 10 años (p. 273)

loose money policy/política monetaria expansiva: política monetaria que resulta en crédito barato y abundante; puede conducir a la inflación (p. 408)

M

M1/M1: definición más estricta de la oferta monetaria; comprende el dinero que se puede gastar inmediatamente y contra el cual se pueden emitir cheques (p. 391)

M2/M2: definición más general de la oferta monetaria; incluye la M1 más cuasi-dinero como los balances de los fondos de mercado monetario, certificados de depósito y eurodólares (p. 391)

macroeconomics/macroeconomía: rama de la teoría económica que trata de la economía en su totalidad y de los modos en que grandes organismos, como los gobiernos, toman decisiones (p. 18)

marginal utility/utilidad marginal: una cantidad adicional de satisfacción o provecho (p. 174)

market/mercado: actividad libre entre compradores y vendedores de bienes y servicios (pp. 36, 170)

market basket/canasta de compras: grupo representativo de bienes y servicios usado para calcular el índice de precios al consumidor (p. 352)

market economy/economía de mercado: sistema en que particulares son los dueños de los factores de producción y toman decisiones económicas, relacionándose libremente con otros, para el mayor beneficio de sus familias y sí mismos (p. 36)

marketing/mercadotecnia: todas las actividades necesarias para mover bienes y servicios de los productores a los consumidores; también se llama marketing (p. 289)

market research/investigación de mercados: reunir, anotar y analizar datos acerca de los tipos de bienes y servicios que desea el público (p. 292)

market structure/estructura del mercado: punto hasta el cual la competencia predomina en un mercado (p. 233)

market survey/estudio del mercado: encuesta en que los investigadores reúnen información sobre los posibles usuarios de un producto, como su edad, sexo, ingresos, estudios y ubicación (p. 293)

maturity/plazo de vencimiento: período de tiempo al final del cual los depósitos a plazos pagan una tasa de interés establecida (p. 143)

mechanization/mecanización: esfuerzo combinado de personas y máquinas (p. 280)

mediation/mediación: etapa en la negociación de un contrato entre el sindicato y los gerentes en que una persona neutral trata de hacer que ambas partes lleguen a un acuerdo (p. 329)

Medicaid/Medicaid: programa de asistencia público estatal y federal que provee apoyo financiero para los gastos médicos de personas de bajos ingresos y personas incapacitadas (p. 431)

Medicare/Medicare: programa gubernamental que proporciona cuidado de la salud para personas de la tercera edad (p. 426)

medium of exchange/medio de cambio: uso del dinero a cambio de bienes y servicios (p. 376)

merger/corporación: fusión de compañías en una sola que resulta cuando una sociedad anónima compra más de la mitad de las acciones de otra sociedad anónima y así controla la segunda empresa (p. 249)

microchip/chip: circuito electrónico diminuto que procesa y transfiere información digital (p. 565)

microeconomics/microeconomía: rama de la teoría económica que estudia la conducta y modos de tomar decisiones de unidades pequeñas, como individuos y empresas (p. 18)

military assistance/asistencia militar: ayuda económica o técnica dada a las fuerzas armadas de una nación (p. 525)

minimum wage law/ley del salario mínimo: ley federal que establece el sueldo por hora más bajo que se puede pagar legalmente a ciertos tipos de trabajadores (p. 319)

mixed economy/economía mixta: sistema que combina las características de más de un tipo de economía (p. 38)

monetarism/monetarismo: teoría que relaciona la cantidad de dinero que el Sistema de Reserva Federal pone en circulación con el nivel de actividad en la economía (p. 462)

monetarists/monetaristas: partidarios de la teoría del monetarismo, a menudo conectada con Milton Friedman (p. 462)

monetary policy/política monetaria: política que controla el crecimiento de la cantidad de dinero en circulación para afectar el costo y la facilidad de obtener crédito (p. 400)

monetary rule/norma monetaria: creencia de los monetaristas que el Sistema de Reserva Federal debe permitir que la oferta monetaria crezca a un ritmo anual constante y no usar la política monetaria para estimular o reducir la actividad económica (p. 463)

money/moneda: cualquier cosa que se acostumbra usar como medio de cambio, unidad de contabilidad y reserva de valor; también se llama dinero (p. 376)

money market deposit account/cuenta de depósito de mercado monetario: cuentas que pagan intereses relativamente altos, requieren saldos mínimos y mantienen el dinero disponible en cualquier momento (p. 143)

money market fund/fondo de mercado monetario: tipo de fondo mutualista que utiliza el dinero de los inversionistas para hacer préstamos a corto plazo a empresas y bancos (p. 152)

monopolistic competition/competencia monopolística: mercado en que un gran número de vendedores ofrecen productos parecidos aunque algo distintos y en que cada vendedor tiene algún control sobre el precio (p. 245)

monopoly/monopolio: mercado en que hay sólo un proveedor que comprende la industria entera de un producto o servicio sin verdaderos sustitutos (p. 240)

mortgage/hipoteca: tipo de deuda pagada a plazos por casas, edificios o terrenos (p. 85)

multinationals/corporaciones multinacionales: firmas que hacen negocio y tienen oficinas y fábricas en muchos países; también se llaman empresas transnacionales o internacionales (p. 553)

mutual fund/fondo mutualista: compañía inversionista que reúne el dinero de muchos individuos para comprar acciones, bonos y otros tipos de inversiones (p. 151)

N

national debt/deuda pública: cantidad de deuda que tiene el gobierno federal (p. 439)

national income/renta nacional: ingresos totales de todas las personas que forman parte de una economía (p. 347)

national income accounting/cálculo de la renta nacional: medida del rendimiento económico de una nación, tomando en cuenta la producción y los ingresos totales (p. 343)

nationalization/nacionalización: toma de ferrocarriles, negocios y otras industrias por el gobierno como propiedad pública (p. 525)

near moneys/cuasi-dinero: activos, como las cuentas de ahorro, que se pueden convertir en dinero con bastante facilidad sin correr el riesgo de que pierdan valor (p. 390)

net domestic product/producto interior neto: valor de la producción total de un país (PIB) menos el valor total perdido por la depreciación de las máquinas y equipos (p. 347)

net exports/exportaciones netas: diferencia entre lo que una nación le vende a otros países y lo que compra de ellos (p. 346)

North American Free Trade Agreement/Tratado de Libre Comercio Norteamericano: acuerdo comercial diseñado para disminuir y eliminar gradualmente las barreras arancelarias entre México, Canadá y Estados Unidos (p. 489)

O

oligopoly/oligopolio: industria dominada por pocos proveedores que ejercen algún control sobre los precios (p. 243)

open-market operations/operaciones del mercado abierto: compra y venta de valores de los Estados Unidos por el Sistema de Reserva Federal para afectar la oferta monetaria (p. 416)

opportunity cost/costo de oportunidad: valor de la mejor opción a la que se renuncia al escoger otra opción (p. 13)

overdraft checking/cuenta corriente con descubierto: cuenta corriente que le permite al cliente escribir cheques por más dinero del que tiene en la cuenta; también se llama cuenta corriente con sobregiro (p. 384)

over-the-counter market/mercado extrabursátil: compra y venta electrónica de acciones y bonos, a menudo de compañías pequeñas, que se realiza fuera de las bolsas de valores organizadas (p. 150)

P

partnership/sociedad: negocio operado por dos o más individuos que son los dueños (p. 215)

passbook savings account/cuenta de ahorro con libreta bancaria: cuenta para la cual el ahorrador recibe una libreta en que se registran sus depósitos, retiros de fondos e intereses (p. 142)

patent/patente: protección del gobierno que da a un inventor el derecho exclusivo de fabricar, usar o vender su invento por un determinado número de años (p. 241)

peak/auge: período de prosperidad en el ciclo económico en que la actividad económica ha llegado a su nivel más alto (p. 360)

penetration pricing/fijar un precio de penetración: vender un producto nuevo a precio bajo para atraer a los compradores de un producto establecido (p. 298)

pension plans/planes de pensiones: planes que empresas tienen para proporcionar ingresos a sus trabajadores jubilados (p. 155)

perfect competition/competencia perfecta: mercado en que hay muchos vendedores y compradores y ninguno puede afectar el precio independientemente (p. 234)

personal income/ingresos personales: ingresos totales que recibe una persona antes de pagar sus impuestos personales; también se llama renta personal (p. 348)

picketing/piquetear: forma de protesta en que trabajadores en huelga se pasean delante del lugar de trabajo con letreros que declaran sus desacuerdos con la compañía (p. 329)

points/puntos: suma que se le paga a un prestamista y se calcula como puntos porcentuales del préstamo (p. 123)

preferred stock/acciones preferentes: participaciones en una sociedad anónima que dan a los accionistas una porción de las ganancias futuras (antes de pagar a dueños de acciones ordinarias), pero sin el derecho al voto; también se llaman acciones preferidas (p. 223)

price ceiling/precio máximo: precio más alto que la ley permite que se cobre por un producto o servicio en particular (p. 197)

price elasticity of demand/efecto del precio en la elasticidad de la demanda: concepto económico que trata de *cómo* la demanda varía de acuerdo con los cambios en el precio (p. 181)

price floor/precio mínimo: precio más bajo que la ley permite que se cobre por un producto o servicio (p. 198)

price leadership/liderazgo en la fijación de precios: práctica de seguir el ejemplo de una compañía que cambia el precio de un artículo por compañías que cobran aproximadamente el mismo precio por productos semejantes (p. 298)

prime rate/tasa preferencial: tipo de interés que los bancos cobran por préstamos a sus mejores clientes comerciales (p. 414)

principal/principal: cantidad de dinero prestado; también se llama capital (p. 84)

private-labeled products/productos de marca privada: productos a precios más bajos que llevan la marca de la tienda en que se venden y son vendidos por cadenas de supermercados y de clubes almacenes (p. 113)

private property/propiedad privada: todo lo que pertenece a particulares y no al gobierno (p. 43)

privatization/privatización: transferir al sector privado negocios, tierras y edificios que pertenecen al estado (p. 509)

producer price index (PPI)/índice de precios de productores: medida, a través del tiempo, de los cambios en los precios que los productores estadounidenses cobran a los mayoristas por sus bienes y servicios (p. 353)

product differentiation/diferenciación de productos: uso de pequeñas diferencias en calidad y características por parte de los fabricantes para tratar de diferenciar bienes y servicios parecidos (p. 244)

production/producción: proceso de convertir recursos en bienes que satisfacen las necesidades y deseos de individuos y negocios (p. 277)

production possibilities curve/curva de posibilidades de producción: gráfica que muestra la mayor combinación de bienes y servicios que se pueden producir con una cantidad fija de recursos en un período de tiempo determinado (p. 14)

productivity/productividad: producción final (cantidad de bienes y servicios) que rinde una cantidad determinada de insumos (tierra, trabajo y capital) (p. 7)

product life cycle/ciclo de vida de un producto: etapas por las que pasa un producto desde que se introduce hasta que se retira del mercado (p. 300)

professionals/profesionales: personas muy preparadas, que han cursado por lo menos cuatro años al nivel universitario y generalmente tienen educación o preparación adicional (p. 316)

profit/ganancias: dinero que queda después de pagar todos los costos de producción—incluyendo salarios, alquiler, intereses e impuestos; también se llama lucro, beneficios y utilidad (pp. 43, 265)

profit incentive/afán de lucro: deseo de ganar dinero que alienta a las personas a producir y vender bienes y servicios (p. 43)

progressive tax/impuesto progresivo: impuesto que grava un porcentaje mayor a los que tienen más ingresos y menor a los que tienen menos; se justifica con el principio de la capacidad de pago (p. 443)

proletariat/proletariado: término usado por Carlos Marx para referirse a los obreros (p. 499)

promotion/promoción: uso de la publicidad para informar a los consumidores que un producto o servicio nuevo o mejorado está en venta y para convencerlos a que lo compren (p. 299)

proportional tax/impuesto proporcional: impuesto que grava el mismo porcentaje a todos los ingresos; al subir los ingresos, la cantidad de impuestos que hay que pagar también sube (p. 443)

proprietor/propietario: dueño de un negocio (p. 215)

protectionists/proteccionistas: personas que abogan en favor de restricciones comerciales para proteger las industrias domésticas (p. 487)

protective tariff/aranceles proteccionistas: impuestos sobre las importaciones usados para subir el precio de bienes importados y proteger a los productores domésticos (p. 487)

public-assistance programs/programas de asistencia pública: programas gubernamentales que hacen pagos a personas necesitadas (p. 431)

public goods/bienes públicos: bienes y servicios que el gobierno proporciona al público; pueden ser usados por muchas personas a la misma vez sin reducir el beneficio que obtiene cada una (p. 430)

public-works projects/proyectos de obras públicas: edificaciones e instalaciones para el uso público, como escuelas y carreteras, construidas por el gobierno federal, estatal o local con dinero público (p. 425)

purchasing power/poder adquisitivo: cantidad real de bienes y servicios que se pueden comprar con el dinero; determina el valor del dinero (p. 351)

Q

quantity demanded/cantidad demandada: cantidad de un producto o servicio que los consumidores están dispuestos y pueden comprar a un precio dado (p. 172)

quantity supplied/cantidad ofrecida: cantidad de un producto o servicio que un productor está dispuesto y puede ofrecer a un precio dado (p. 187)

R

rational choice/selección racional: escoger la alternativa de mayor valor entre productos de la misma calidad (p. 62)

rationing/racionamiento: basar la distribución de bienes y servicios en razones que no incluyen el precio (p. 197)

real GDP/PIB real: PIB al que se le ha aplicado el deflactor de precios para corregir los efectos de la inflación (p. 353)

real income effect/efecto de ingresos reales: regla económica que dice que los consumidores no pueden continuar comprando la misma cantidad de un producto si el precio de éste sube mientras que sus ingresos se mantienen iguales (p. 172)

receipts/entradas: ingresos recibidos de la venta de bienes o servicios; recibos escritos que comprueban que se han hecho ciertas compras (p. 209)

recession/recesión: parte del ciclo económico en que el rendimiento nacional (PIB real) no aumenta por seis meses al menos (p. 361)

recovery/recuperación: lo mismo que *expansion/ expansión* (p. 361)

registration fee/cuota por la matrícula: suma, generalmente anual, que se paga a un estado por el derecho de usar un automóvil (p. 130)

regressive tax/impuesto regresivo: impuesto que toma un mayor porcentaje de ingresos más bajos que de ingresos más altos (p. 443)

representative money/dinero crediticio: dinero que está respaldado por algo de valor, como el oro o la plata (p. 378)

reserve requirements/reserva obligatoria: regulación establecida por el Sistema de Reserva Federal que requiere que los bancos mantengan un porcentaje de sus depósitos en efectivo en sus propias bóvedas de seguridad o en el banco de la Reserva Federal de su distrito (p. 408)

retailers/tiendas al por menor: negocios que venden bienes directamente al consumidor (p. 303)

revenues/entradas: total de los ingresos provenientes de la venta de la producción de una compañía (p. 265)

revenue tariff/derechos aduaneros: impuesto sobre las importaciones usado principalmente para recaudar ingresos sin restringir las importaciones; también se llaman impuestos aduaneros o derechos arancelarios (p. 487)

right-to-work laws/leyes de derecho al trabajo: leyes estatales que prohiben que los sindicatos fuercen a los trabajadores a afiliarse y a pagar cuotas sindicales (p. 325)

robotics/robótica: maquinaria compleja, controlada por computadoras, que opera una línea de montaje (p. 281)

Roth IRA/cuenta de retiro individual Roth: plan de jubilación privado en que se gravan los ingresos antes de ser ahorrados, pero no se gravan los intereses por los ahorros cuando se usan esos fondos después de jubilarse (p. 156)

S

saving/ahorrar: guardar ingresos por un período de tiempo para poder usarlos más adelante (p. 141)

savings and loan association (S&L)/sociedad de ahorro y préstamos: institución que acepta depósitos y presta dinero (p. 89)

savings bank/banco de ahorro: tipo de institución depositaria establecida originalmente para servir a personas que ahorraban pequeñas cantidades y eran ignorados por los bancos comerciales (p. 89)

savings bonds/bonos de ahorro: bonos emitidos por el gobierno federal para obtener dinero prestado; se compran a la mitad de su valor nominal, y cada 6 meses aumentan en valor hasta llegar al valor nominal completo (p. 149)

scarcity/escasez: condición de no poder tener todos los bienes y servicios que se desean porque los deseos exceden lo que se puede producir con los recursos que hay en un momento dado (p. 5)

secured loan/préstamo garantizado: préstamo que está asegurado por propiedad (p. 98)

security deposit/depósito de garantía: dinero que un inquilino pone en manos del dueño en caso de que no pague el alquiler o deje el apartamento dañado (p. 125)

semiskilled workers/obreros semicalificados: personas cuyos trabajos requieren un poco de preparación, a menudo en el uso de la tecnología moderna; también se llaman obreros semiespecializados (p. 316)

service flow/servicio útil: cantidad de uso que una persona le saca a un artículo a través del tiempo y el valor que le da a su uso (p. 118)

services/servicios: actividades económicas que pueden satisfacer los deseos o necesidades del público (p. 6)

service workers/trabajadores en el área de servicio: personas que proporcionan servicios directamente al público (p. 315)

shortage/escasez: situación en que la cantidad demandada es mayor que la cantidad ofrecida; falta de un producto (p. 196)

short-term financing/financiamiento a corto plazo: préstamo de dinero que un negocio tiene que pagar en menos de un año (p. 271)

skilled workers/obreros calificados: personas que han aprendido un oficio o artesanía en una escuela de artes y oficios o como aprendices de obreros maestros; también se llaman obreros especializados (p. 316)

small business incubator/incubadora de pequeños negocios: agencia privada o financiada por el gobierno que asiste a nuevos negocios, proporcionando asesoramiento, locales con alquileres bajos y artículos de uso diario (p. 209)

social insurance programs/programas de seguridad social: programas gubernamentales que pagan prestaciones a trabajadores retirados o inválidos, a sus familias y a los desempleados; son financiados con impuestos pagados para estos programas por trabajadores y empresas (p. 431)

Social Security/Seguro Social: programa federal que proporciona pagos mensuales a personas que están jubiladas o no pueden trabajar (p. 431)

sole proprietorship/propiedad individual: negocio operado por un solo dueño, el propietario único (p. 213)

specialization/especialización: concepto de que una nación debe limitarse a producir y exportar una selección de aquellos bienes que son más apropiados para ser producidos en ella, para sacar mayores ganancias (p. 475)

stabilization policies/políticas de estabilización: intentos por parte del gobierno federal de mantener sana la economía; incluyen las políticas monetaria y fiscal (p. 451)

stagflation/estagflación: combinación de inflación con poca actividad económica; también se llama estanflación (p. 455)

standard of living/nivel de vida: bienestar material de un individuo, grupo o nación, en forma de cálculo de lo bien que puede satisfacer sus necesidades y obtener lujos (p. 48)

startup/negocio nuevo: empresa nueva (p. 208)

statement savings account/cuenta de ahorro con estado de cuenta: cuenta similar a la cuenta de ahorro con libreta bancaria, pero en vez de tener una libreta, el ahorrador recibe un estado de cuenta mensual que enumera todas sus transacciones (p. 142)

stock/acciones: participaciones en una sociedad anónima que hacen al comprador uno de sus propietarios con derecho a recibir parte de las ganancias y activos de la sociedad (p. 220)

stockholders/accionistas: personas que han invertido en una sociedad anónima y son dueños de un número de acciones (p. 147)

store of value/reserva de valor: uso del dinero como almacén del poder adquisitivo que una persona recibe como pago, a cambio de su trabajo o de un artículo vendido, y que puede usar en el futuro (p. 377)

strike/huelga: paro de trabajo intencional por parte de los trabajadores para forzar a los patronos a que ceden a sus demandas (p. 323)

subsistence agriculture/agricultura de subsistencia: cultivar alimentos suficientes para satisfacer las necesidades de una familia solamente; la cosecha no alcanza para exportar o alimentar a la fuerza laboral industrial (p. 519)

substitution effect/efecto de sustitución: regla económica que dice que si dos artículos satisfacen la misma necesidad y el precio de uno sube, el público comprará el otro (p. 172)

Supplemental Security Income/Ingresos Suplementarios de Seguridad: programa federal que provee beneficios que incluyen cupones de alimentos y apoyo financiero a personas ancianas y personas incapacitadas (p. 431)

supply/oferta: cantidad de un producto o servicio que los productores pueden y están dispuestos a vender a varios precios durante un período de tiempo determinado (p. 170)

supply curve/curva de oferta: línea ascendiente en una gráfica cuya inclinación muestra la cantidad ofrecida a cada precio posible (p. 189)

supply schedule/lista de oferta: tabla que muestra las cantidades que se ofrecen a distintos precios (p. 188)

surplus/superávit: situación en que la cantidad ofrecida es mayor que la cantidad demandada (p. 196)

T

tariff/arancel: impuesto que grava un producto importado (p. 486)

tax-exempt bonds/bonos exentos de impuestos: bonos emitidos por los gobiernos locales y estatales; los intereses que pagan no son gravados por el gobierno federal (p. 148)

technical assistance/asistencia técnica: ayuda que proporcionan profesionales como ingenieros, maestros y técnicos; proporcionada por naciones para enseñar técnicas a personas de otros países (p. 525)

technology/tecnología: avances en los conocimientos científicos que conducen a nuevos y mejorados bienes y servicios y a mejores maneras de producirlos (pp. 7, 190)

telecommunications/telecomunicaciones: comunicaciones a larga distancia, generalmente electrónicas, que usan satélites de comunicación y cables de fibra óptica (pp. 544, 571)

Temporary Assistance for Needy Families/Asistencia Temporal para Familias Necesitadas: programa de asistencia público administrado por los estados que ofrece servicios de apoyo y oportunidades de empleo a familias necesitadas (p. 431)

test-marketing/hacer una prueba de mercado: poner un producto en venta en un área pequeña por un período de tiempo limitado para ver lo bien que se vende antes de ofrecerlo en todo el país (p. 293)

thrift institutions/instituciones de ahorro: bancos de ahorro mutuos, sociedades de ahorro y préstamos y cooperativas de crédito que ofrecen los mismos servicios que los bancos comerciales (p. 389)

tight money policy/política monetaria restrictiva: política monetaria que hace que el crédito sea caro y difícil de obtener para tratar de reducir la actividad económica (p. 408)

time deposits/depósitos a plazos: planes de ahorro que obligan al ahorrador a dejar su dinero en depósito por períodos de tiempo determinados (p. 143)

time lags/demoras: período entre el momento en que se aprueba una política fiscal y el momento en que entra en vigor (p. 465)

trade-off/compensación: renunciar a un producto o servicio para comprar o producir otro (p. 12)

traditional economy/economía tradicional: sistema en que las decisiones económicas se basan en las costumbres y creencias que se han pasado de generación en generación (p. 33)

transfer payments/transferencias: pagos de asistencia social y otros pagos suplementarios como los de seguros de desempleo, Seguro Social y Medicaid que el gobierno estatal o federal le hace a individuos (p. 348)

Treasury bills/letras del Tesoro: certificados emitidos por el Tesoro de los EE.UU. que requieren una inversión mínima de $1,000 y se vencen entre 3 meses y 1 año después (p. 149)

Treasury bonds/bonos del Tesoro: certificados emitidos por el Tesoro de los EE.UU. a cambio de inversiones mínimas de $1,000 con fechas de vencimiento de 10 años o más en el futuro (p. 149)

Treasury notes/pagarés del Tesoro: certificados emitidos por el Tesoro de los EE.UU. a cambio de inversiones mínimas de $1,000 con fechas de vencimiento de 1 a 10 años después (p. 149)

trough/punto bajo: parte del ciclo económico en que la actividad económica en disminución se nivela; también se llama depresión (p. 361)

U

underground economy/economía sumergida: transacciones hechas por personas que no obedecen las leyes federales y estatales que requieren que se de parte al gobierno sobre los ingresos (p. 453)

unemployment rate/índice de desempleo: porcentaje de la fuerza laboral civil que no tiene empleo pero está buscando trabajo (p. 452)

union/sindicato: véase *labor union/sindicato de obreros*

union shop/fábrica sindical: compañía que obliga a nuevos empleados a hacerse miembros del sindicato después de un período de tiempo determinado (p. 324)

unit of accounting/unidad de contabilidad: uso del dinero como medida del valor de distintos bienes y servicios que se puede usar de criterio para compararlos (p. 376)

unlimited liability/responsabilidad sin límite: requisito que hace a un dueño total y personalmente responsable de todas las pérdidas y deudas de su negocio (p. 215)

unsecured loan/préstamo no garantizado: préstamo hecho sin obtener una garantía, sólo la promesa de devolver el dinero (p. 98)

unskilled workers/trabajadores no calificados: personas cuyos trabajos no requieren preparación especial (p. 316)

usury law/ley contra la usura: ley que limita la cantidad de interés que se puede cobrar por el crédito (p. 102)

utility/utilidad: capacidad de un producto o servicio de satisfacer los deseos de los consumidores (p. 173); cantidad de provecho que el consumidor recibe de un producto o servicio (p. 290)

V

vicious cycle of poverty/círculo vicioso de la pobreza: situación en que un país poco desarrollado con ingresos *per capita* bajos no puede ahorrar e invertir dinero suficiente para alcanzar una tasa de crecimiento económico aceptable y queda estancado (p. 536)

voluntary exchange/intercambio voluntario: transacción en que el comprador y el vendedor ejercen su libertad económica al llegar a un acuerdo sobre las condiciones del intercambio (p. 170)

W

warranty/garantía: promesa de un fabricante o vendedor de reparar o reemplazar un producto defectuoso dentro de un plazo de tiempo determinado (p. 70)

Web sites/lugares de Web: sitios en World Wide Web que almacenan información que se puede ver o trasladar a una computadora; también se llaman páginas de Web (p. 566)

weightless economy/economía "sin peso": frase inventada para identificar una economía basada en productos que no son materiales (p. 572)

welfare/bienestar social: lo mismo que *public-assistance programs/programas de asistencia pública* (p. 431)

welfare state/estado de bienestar social: país en que hay una mezcla de capitalismo y socialismo, combinando la propiedad privada de los medios de producción y la distribución competitiva de recursos con la meta de igualdad social para todos los habitantes (p. 510)

white-collar workers/empleados en trabajos no manuales: categoría de trabajadores empleados en oficinas, ventas o puestos profesionales (p. 315)

wholesalers/mayoristas: negocios que compran grandes cantidades de bienes de los fabricantes para vendérselas a otros negocios (p. 303)

workers' compensation/compensación a trabajadores accidentados: programas gubernamentales que hacen pagos para asistencia médica a trabajadores que se lesionan en el trabajo (p. 431)

World Trade Organization/Organización Mundial del Comercio: acuerdo comercial más extenso del mundo entre más que 140 naciones (pp. 488, 506)

World Wide Web/World Wide Web: parte de Internet usada para las comunicaciones entre consumidores, negocios, gobiernos y otras organizaciones (p. 566)

CAPÍTULO  Resumen

SECCIÓN 1 El problema fundamental en la economía

- La **economía** es el estudio de cómo individuos, familias, negocios y sociedades utilizan recursos limitados para satisfacer deseos sin límites.
- Los individuos escogen lo que prefieren para satisfacer sus deseos ilimitados en un mundo cuyos recursos son limitados.
- Es necesario escoger por causa de la **escasez,** el problema fundamental de la economía.
- Los recursos necesarios para producir bienes y servicios se llaman **factores de producción.**
- Los cuatro factores de producción son la **tierra,** o recursos naturales; el **trabajo,** también conocido como recursos humanos; el **capital,** o productos manufacturados que se usan para producir otros bienes y servicios; y el **espíritu empresarial,** o habilidad de empezar nuevos negocios y de introducir nuevos productos y procesos.
- Algunos economistas añaden la **tecnología** a la lista de factores de producción.

SECCIÓN 2 La compensación

- Cada vez que utilizan sus recursos de una manera u otra, las personas aceptan su elección como **compensación** por las opciones que no escogieron.
- El **costo de oportunidad** es el valor de la mejor alternativa a la que se renuncia al escoger una opción en vez de otra.
- Una **curva de posibilidades de producción** es una gráfica que muestra la máxima combinación de bienes y servicios que se pueden producir con una cantidad fija de recursos en un período de tiempo determinado.
- El ejemplo clásico que se usa en la economía para explicar las posibilidades de producción es el modo en que se compensan las armas (defensa militar) y la mantequilla (bienes para los civiles).

SECCIÓN 3 ¿Qué hacen los economistas?

- Los economistas estudian la **economía**—todas las actividades de una nación que afectan la producción, distribución y uso de bienes y servicios.
- Los economistas formulan teorías llamadas **modelos económicos,** que son representaciones simplificadas del mundo real.
- Los economistas ponen a prueba sus modelos de la misma manera que otros científicos comprueban sus **hipótesis** o suposiciones.
- Los economistas se fundan en los hechos, aunque sus opiniones personales pueden influir en sus teorías.
- Los economistas ofrecen soluciones a problemas económicos, pero no evalúan el mérito de las distintas soluciones.

CAPÍTULO 2 Resumen

SECCIÓN 1 Sistemas económicos

- Todo tipo de **sistema económico** tiene que responder a tres preguntas básicas: ¿Qué bienes y servicios se deben producir? ¿Cómo se deben producir? ¿Quién debe disfrutar de lo que se produce?
- Hay cuatro tipos de sistemas económicos: tradicional, dirigido, de mercado y mixto.
- En una **economía tradicional,** las decisiones económicas se basan en las costumbres y creencias que se han pasado de generación en generación.
- En una **economía dirigida,** los líderes del gobierno controlan los factores de producción y, por lo tanto, toman todas las decisiones sobre su uso.
- En una **economía de mercado,** cada cual toma sus propias decisiones económicas para el mayor beneficio de su familia y sí mismo.
- La mayoría de los países del mundo tienen una **economía mixta,** en que individuos tienen propiedad privada y toman sus propias decisiones y a la vez hay regulación gubernamental.

SECCIÓN 2 Características de la economía de los Estados Unidos

- Un sistema de mercado puro tiene seis características principales: poco o ningún control gubernamental, libertad de empresa, libertad de elección, propiedad privada, ánimo de lucro y competencia.
- En Estados Unidos, se practica el **capitalismo** de manera que individuos son dueños de los factores de producción pero los usan dentro de los límites de la ley.
- El **afán de lucro** es el deseo que impulsa al empresario a establecer nuevos negocios, expandir los que ya existen y cambiar el tipo de bienes y productos que se producen.
- Una de las características más importantes del capitalismo es la existencia de la **propiedad privada.**
- La **competencia** conduce al uso eficiente de recursos, a bienes y servicios de mejor calidad y a precios más bajos para el consumidor.

SECCIÓN 3 Las metas de la nación

- Los Estados Unidos tiene un sistema económico de **libre empresa** o capitalista.
- Entre las metas económicas de los estadounidenses están la libertad económica, **eficiencia económica, equidad económica,** seguridad económica, estabilidad económica y **crecimiento económico.**
- Para que un sistema de libre empresa funcione bien, los individuos tienen que aceptar ciertas responsabilidades económicas, entre ellas ser miembros productivos de la sociedad y elegir funcionarios del gobierno que sean responsables.

CAPÍTULO 3 Resumen

SECCIÓN 1 Consumo, ingresos y toma de decisiones

- Un **consumidor** es cualquier persona o grupo que compra o utiliza bienes y servicios para satisfacer sus deseos personales.
- Los ingresos pueden ser **disponibles** y **discrecionales.**
- La educación, ocupación, experiencia y salud influyen en lo que una persona puede ganar y, por lo tanto, en su capacidad para consumir.
- Las decisiones de consumo tienen tres partes: (1) decidir que uno va a gastar dinero; (2) determinar cuál es la mejor compra; (3) decidir cómo usar lo que se compra.
- Cuando uno toma decisiones de consumo basándose en el costo de oportunidad, hace una **selección racional.**

SECCIÓN 2 Principios o estrategias de compra

- Tres principios de compra básicos que ayudan al comprador a obtener la mayor satisfacción de sus ingresos y tiempo limitados son reunir información, usar los anuncios con discreción y comparar antes de comprar.
- El valor del tiempo y el esfuerzo que el comprador emplea en obtener información no debe exceder el valor de la mejor selección.
- La mayoría de los anuncios caen en una de las dos siguientes categorías: **publicidad competitiva** o **publicidad informativa.** Hay que cuidarse de la publicidad engañosa, que incluye la práctica de **engatusar** al comprador.
- Para comparar eficientemente antes de comprar, se deben leer los anuncios de periódicos, hacer llamadas telefónicas, navegar por Internet y visitar distintas tiendas. También se deben considerar la garantía que ofrece el producto y las ventajas de las variedades genéricas y de marca.

SECCIÓN 3 Protección al consumidor

- Existe un movimiento de **protección al consumidor** que tiene como fines informar al comprador acerca de las compras que hace y exigir productos mejores y más seguros de los fabricantes.
- Los defensores de los consumidores reclaman los siguientes derechos para ellos: el derecho a la seguridad, a ser informado, a seleccionar, a ser escuchado y a reparaciones.
- Entre los grupos privados que ayudan al consumidor están las agrupaciones cívicas de acción local y el "Better Business Bureau" (Agencia para el mejoramiento del comercio).
- Muchas agencias federales tienen programas que ayudan al consumidor, incluyendo la "Consumer Product Safety Commission" (Comisión de seguridad de productos) y la "Food and Drug Administration" (Administración de Alimentos y Drogas).
- Las responsabilidades del consumidor incluyen leer contratos y garantías, seguir las instrucciones para el uso correcto del producto, iniciar el proceso de resolver problemas y **comportarse éticamente.**

CAPÍTULO  Resumen

SECCIÓN 1 Los estadounidenses y el crédito

- El **crédito** es la aceptación de fondos directa o indirectamente para comprar bienes y servicios bajo promesa de pagar por ellos en el futuro.
- La cantidad que se debe—la deuda—equivale al **principal** más el **interés.**
- Muchas personas compran **bienes duraderos** y obtienen **hipotecas** en forma de **deudas pagadas a plazos.**
- Las personas asumen deudas porque no quieren esperar para comprar un artículo con dinero en efectivo y quieren extender el tiempo que tienen para hacer los pagos durante la vida útil del artículo.

SECCIÓN 2 Fuentes de préstamos y crédito

- Las instituciones financieras principales que hacen préstamos a consumidores incluyen los **bancos comerciales, sociedades de ahorro y préstamos, cooperativas de crédito** y **compañías financieras.**
- Una **cuenta de crédito** le permite al cliente comprar bienes y servicios de una compañía en particular y pagárselos más adelante.
- Las **tarjetas de crédito** a menudo cobran intereses altos, pero se pueden usar en tiendas, restaurantes u otros negocios.
- Los **cargos de financiamiento** son el costo mensual del crédito en dólares y centavos.
- La **tasa de interés anual** es el costo anual del crédito expresado en porcentajes.

SECCIÓN 3 Solicitar crédito

- Después de que una persona llena un formulario solicitando crédito, una **oficina de crédito** hace una **investigación de crédito** y determina la **clasificación de crédito** del solicitante.
- Antes de dar crédito, el acreedor evalúa la capacidad de pagar del solicitante, su carácter y cualquier **garantía** en forma de propiedad que tenga para asegurar que pagará.
- Las responsabilidades del prestatario incluyen pagar a tiempo, documentar todos los datos sobre la deuda y no gastar más de lo que puede devolver.

SECCIÓN 4 Regulación del crédito por el gobierno

- La ley prohibe que los prestamistas se nieguen a dar crédito por razón de raza, religión, origen nacional, sexo, estado civil o edad del solicitante.
- Una **ley contra la usura** limita la cantidad de interés que se puede cobrar por el crédito, pero también conduce a la escasez de crédito disponible.
- Muchas personas que no pueden pagar sus deudas se tienen que declarar en **bancarrota.**

CAPÍTULO 5 Resumen

SECCIÓN 1 Comprar alimentos

- Para comparar alimentos antes de comprarlos, hay que fijarse en las marcas, los tamaños y las tiendas.
- Un modo de comparar antes de comprar que a la vez ahorra tiempo y dinero es leer los anuncios y recortar los cupones de descuento.
- En general, los supermercados y los **clubes almacenes** tienen los precios más bajos, mientras que las pequeñas **tiendas de artículos de consumo frecuente** pueden ahorrarle tiempo al comprador.
- Los precios de productos por unidad hacen que sea más fácil comparar precios.
- Usando cupones, se puede ahorrar más del 10 por ciento del costo de los alimentos en un período de un año.

SECCIÓN 2 La selección de ropa

- Los estadounidenses gastan unos 400 mil millones de dólares anualmente en ropa y otros productos personales.
- El valor de la ropa depende del precio, estilo, **durabilidad** y costo de mantenerla en buenas condiciones.
- Las prendas de vestir se compran por el **servicio útil** que dan.
- La cantidad de tiempo que hay que trabajar para comprar ropa se ha reducido en los últimos 100 años, pero el consumidor inteligente trata de comprar su ropa en rebaja.

SECCIÓN 3 Alquilar o comprar

- Ambas opciones, alquilar y comprar una casa, tienen ventajas y desventajas económicas y psicológicas.
- Si una persona decide comprar casa, probablemente tendrá que conseguir una hipoteca, por la cual tendrá que pagar un adelanto en efectivo, mensualidades e intereses, además de **los costos de cierre** y **puntos.**
- Los inquilinos generalmente pagan un **depósito de garantía** y firman un **contrato de alquiler** que protege sus derechos y enumera sus responsabilidades.
- Las responsabilidades de los inquilinos incluyen pagar el alquiler a tiempo y cuidar la propiedad adecuadamente.

SECCIÓN 4 Compra y manejo de un vehículo

- Algunas de las decisiones que tiene que tomar el comprador de un automóvil son si comprar un carro pequeño o uno grande, uno nuevo o de uso, con motor poderoso o que consuma poca gasolina.
- Los gastos de operar un automóvil incluyen la **cuota por la matrícula,** el mantenimiento normal, las reparaciones de mayor importancia, la depreciación y el **seguro de responsabilidad civil.**
- Una manera de evitar tener que pagar por reparos costosos es comprando una garantía a largo plazo.

CAPÍTULO 6 Resumen

SECCIÓN 1 ¿Por qué se ahorra?

- Los economistas explican que ***ahorrar*** es dejar de usar los ingresos por un período de tiempo para poder usarlos en el futuro.
- Los ahorros de un individuo son dinero que otros pueden invertir y que permite que los comercios crezcan.
- Los individuos pueden invertir su dinero de muchos modos distintos, como en **cuentas de ahorro** y **depósitos a plazos.**
- El ahorrador que tiene una **cuenta de ahorro con libreta bancaria** recibe una libreta en que se apuntan sus depósitos, retiros de dinero e intereses ganados.
- Una **cuenta de depósito del mercado monetario** paga intereses bastante altos y permite que el depositador tenga libre acceso a su dinero por medio de cheques. Pero estas cuentas requieren que se tenga un saldo mínimo de $1,000 a $2,500.
- Los depósitos a plazos, como los **certificados de depósito (CD),** pagan **intereses** más altos, pero hay que dejar los fondos depositados durante períodos de tiempo más largos.
- La Federal Deposit Insurance Corporation (Corporación Federal de Seguros de Depósitos) o FDIC asegura hasta $100,000 depositados en cuentas de bancos comerciales y bancos de ahorro.

SECCIÓN 2 Las inversiones: correr riesgos con los ahorros

- El comprador de acciones tiene el derecho a recibir parte de las futuras ganancias y activos de la sociedad anónima que vende las acciones.
- Los **accionistas** hacen dinero de sus acciones por medio de dividendos y al vender las acciones por más de lo que pagaron por ellas.
- Muchas empresas y los tres niveles del gobierno emiten bonos para obtener dinero prestado. Los del gobierno incluyen **bonos exentos de impuestos; bonos de ahorro; letras, pagarés** y **bonos del Tesoro.**
- Se pueden comprar acciones por medio de **corredores de la bolsa** o por medio de Internet.
- Las acciones de las grandes sociedades anónimas se compran y venden en las bolsas de valores organizadas, mientras que las acciones de sociedades anónimas pequeñas y nuevas generalmente se venden en el **mercado extrabursátil.**
- Muchas personas invierten en la bolsa de valores por medio de **fondos mutualistas,** compañías inversionistas que reúnen el dinero de muchas personas para comprar acciones, bonos u otras inversiones.

SECCIÓN 3 Metas y planes especiales de ahorro

- Cuando se jubilan, la mayoría de los estadounidenses necesitan ingresos adicionales a sus ahorros para vivir.
- Los **planes de pensiones,** el **Plan Keogh** y las **cuentas de retiro individuales (IRA)** son modos de aumentar la cantidad de dinero que uno tiene cuando se jubila.
- Otra manera de invertir para la jubilación es comprando bienes inmuebles, pero el riesgo es mucho más alto.
- Al decidir cuánto dinero invertir y en qué invertirlo, se debe considerar la **diversificación** para repartir y reducir los riesgos.

CAPÍTULO 7 Resumen

SECCIÓN 1 La demanda

- La **demanda** es la disposición y poder del consumidor para pagar por algo.
- La **ley de la demanda** dice que al subir el precio, la **cantidad demandada** baja. Al bajar el precio, la cantidad que se demanda sube.
- Los factores que explican la relación inversa entre la cantidad que se demanda y el precio incluyen el **efecto de ingresos reales,** el **efecto de sustitución** y la **utilidad marginal** decreciente—es decir, un producto proporciona menos provecho o satisfacción con la compra adicional de cada artículo semejante.

SECCIÓN 2 La curva de demanda y la elasticidad de la demanda

- Una **curva de demanda** descendiente significa que al bajar el precio, la cantidad demandada aumenta.
- Los cambios en la población, ingresos, gustos y preferencias, y la existencia de sustitutos o de **bienes complementarios** afectan la demanda.
- El **efecto del precio en la elasticidad de la demanda** es una medida de cómo los consumidores responden a un cambio de precio.
- Si un cambio pequeño en el precio resulta en un gran cambio en la cantidad demandada, se dice que la demanda por ese producto es **elástica.**
- Si un cambio en el precio no resulta en un cambio importante en la cantidad demandada, la demanda se considera **inelástica.**

SECCIÓN 3 La ley de la oferta y la curva de oferta

- La **ley de la oferta** dice que cuando aumenta el precio de un producto, la **cantidad ofrecida** también aumenta. Cuando el precio baja, la cantidad ofrecida también baja.
- La **curva de oferta** ascendente muestra la correspondencia que existe entre la cantidad ofrecida y el precio.
- Cuatro factores determinan la oferta en una economía de mercado. Estos son el precio de los insumos (bienes usados en la producción), el número de empresas en la industria, los impuestos y la **tecnología.**

SECCIÓN 4 La relación entre la oferta y la demanda

- En un sistema de libre empresa, los precios les sirven de señales a los productores y consumidores.
- El punto en que la cantidad demandada y la cantidad ofrecida son iguales se llama el **precio de equilibrio.**
- La **escasez** o falta de un producto hace que suban los precios, señalando a los productores que deben producir más y a los consumidores que deben comprar menos.
- El **superávit** de bienes hace que bajen los precios, señalando a los productores que deben producir menos y a los consumidores que deben comprar más.
- Los **precios máximos** establecidos por ley no permiten que los precios suban más de una cantidad fija, pero a menudo hacen que escaseen los productos y conducen al **mercado negro.**
- Los **precios mínimos** evitan que ciertos precios, como el salario mínimo, bajen demasiado.

CAPÍTULO 8 Resumen

SECCIÓN 1 Empezar un negocio

- Las personas generalmente deciden empezar un negocio para obtener ganancias, hacer algo por cuenta propia o no tener que responder a un jefe.
- Los **empresarios** tienen que reunir los factores de producción necesarios y decidir qué tipo de organización sería mejor para el negocio que quieren establecer.
- Los que quieren empezar un negocio pequeño pueden obtener ayuda del gobierno o a través de Internet.
- Todo negocio tiene que ocuparse de cuatro elementos básicos: los gastos, la publicidad, la documentación de todas las transacciones (que incluye guardar **recibos**) y el riesgo.

SECCIÓN 2 Propiedades individuales y sociedades

- El tipo de organización empresarial más básico es la **propiedad individual,** un negocio que es propiedad de una sola persona.
- Las mayores ventajas de la propiedad individual son que el propietario único puede sentirse orgulloso de su negocio y recibe todas las ganancias.
- La mayor desventaja es que el propietario único tiene **responsabilidad sin límite** y puede perder todos sus **activos,** incluyendo bienes personales junto con el negocio.
- Una **sociedad** es un tipo de empresa organizada por dos o más dueños.
- Un contrato de sociedad es un acuerdo legal que describe las responsabilidades de cada socio, cómo se dividirán las ganancias y cómo se distribuirán los activos si se disuelve la sociedad.
- En una **sociedad limitada,** un socio general asume responsabilidad por la administración y las deudas, mientras que los otros socios contribuyen dinero pero no tienen responsabilidad.

SECCIÓN 3 Las sociedades anónimas y las franquicias

- Una **sociedad anónima** puede ser dueña de propiedades, pagar impuestos, entrar en contratos y tomar parte en pleitos judiciales.
- Una de las mayores ventajas de las sociedades anónimas es la **responsabilidad limitada.**
- Una desventaja importante es que las sociedades anónimas tienen que pagar impuestos más altos que otros tipos de empresas.
- Para formar una sociedad anónima, los fundadores tienen que inscribirse con el gobierno, vender **acciones** y elegir una junta de directores.
- Una **franquicia** es un contrato en que el franquiciador le vende a otro negocio el derecho de usar su nombre y vender sus productos.

CAPÍTULO 9 Resumen

SECCIÓN 1 La competencia perfecta

- En los Estados Unidos se encuentran cuatro clases de **estructuras de mercado** básicas: **monopolio, oligopolio, competencia monopolística** y **competencia perfecta.**
- La competencia perfecta se caracteriza por un gran número de compradores y vendedores, un producto idéntico, entrada fácil en el mercado, acceso libre a información sobre los precios y ningún control sobre los precios.
- El mercado de productos agrícolas a menudo se usa como ejemplo de la competencia perfecta porque los agricultores no tienen casi ningún control sobre el precio de sus productos en el mercado.
- Cuando existe la competencia perfecta, la sociedad se beneficia de la distribución eficiente de sus recursos productivos.

SECCIÓN 2 Monopolio, oligopolio y competencia monopolística

- En un monopolio, un vendedor único controla la oferta de un producto o servicio y, por lo tanto, determina el precio.
- Los monopolios están protegidos por **barreras al mercado,** que pueden ser regulaciones gubernamentales, una inversión inicial muy grande o propiedad de las materias primas.
- Hay cuatro clases de monopolios: natural, geográfico, tecnológico y estatal.
- Los monopolios naturales a menudo son ventajosos porque les permiten a los fabricantes utilizar la **economía de escala**—es decir, por su gran tamaño, la empresa puede producir grandes cantidades al precio más bajo posible.
- Un oligopolio es una industria dominada por pocos productores que ejercen algún control sobre el precio.
- En los oligopolios y los mercados en que existe la competencia monopolística, los vendedores utilizan la **diferenciación de productos** para aumentar el valor de sus productos en los ojos del consumidor.
- La publicidad de las marcas de fábrica es sumamente importantes en los mercados que tienen competencia monopolística, en que muchos vendedores ofrecen productos muy parecidos con sólo detalles de diferencia.

SECCIÓN 3 Política gubernamental hacia la competencia

- El gobierno ha aprobado **legislación antimonopolista** para impedir que se formen monopolios y deshacer los que ya existían.
- Dos leyes antimonopolistas importantes son la Sherman Antitrust Act (Ley Antimonopolista Sherman) y la Clayton Act (Ley Clayton).
- Se forman corporaciones mediante tres tipos de fusiones: horizontal, vertical y conglomerada.
- Hay agencias reguladoras federales que supervisan varias industrias para asegurar que los precios son razonables y los productos de buena calidad.
- La **desregulación** de algunas industrias en los 1980 y 1990 resultó en más competencia entre negocios.

CAPÍTULO 10 Resumen

SECCIÓN 1 La inversión en el sistema de libre empresa

- El **financiamiento** de las operaciones y del crecimiento de comercios son una parte integral de nuestro sistema de libre empresa. El dinero proviene de los depósitos de personas que ahorran su dinero en instituciones financieras.
- Las instituciones financieras ponen estos depósitos a la disposición de negocios que necesitan fondos para crecer y expandir.
- Los negocios generalmente hacen un **análisis de coste-beneficios** antes de decidir si deben obtener financiamiento para la expansión.
- Un análisis de coste-beneficios comprende estimar los costos, calcular las **entradas** anticipadas, calcular las **ganancias** anticipadas y calcular el costo de obtener los préstamos.

SECCIÓN 2 Tipos de financiamiento para operaciones comerciales

- El **financiamiento mediante deudas,** o reunir dinero para un negocio a través de préstamos, se puede dividir en tres categorías basadas en la cantidad de tiempo que hay para pagarlos.
- Aquellos negocios que necesitan fondos para cubrir las alzas y bajas que ocurren mensualmente o por temporada obtienen **financiamiento a corto plazo.**
- Obtener préstamos por 1 a 10 años para comprar más terreno, edificios y maquinaria o materiales se considera **financiamiento a mediano plazo.**
- El **financiamiento a largo plazo,** como emitir acciones y vender bonos, se usa para la expansión comercial a gran escala.
- Los directores financieros tienen que examinar el tipo de interés que habrá que pagar, el clima comercial y la condición financiera de la compañía y tienen que informar a los dueños de acciones comunes antes de obtener financiación.

SECCIÓN 3 El proceso de producción

- La **producción** es el proceso de convertir recursos en bienes que satisfacen las necesidades y deseos de individuos y otros negocios.
- La producción de **bienes de consumo** y bienes capitales requiere planificación, adquisición de materiales (compras), control de calidad y control del inventario.
- La planificación incluye escoger un local para el negocio y preparar un programa de producción.
- Las personas encargadas de compras tienen que determinar qué bienes comprar, de cuál proveedor obtenerlos y a qué precio comprarlos.
- Cinco avances importantes en la tecnología—la **mecanización,** la **línea de montaje,** la **división del trabajo,** la **automatización** y la **robótica**—han afectado drásticamente los métodos y costos de producción.

CAPÍTULO 11 Resumen

SECCIÓN 1 Los cambios en la mercadotecnia

- La **mercadotecnia** comprende todas las actividades necesarias para mover bienes y servicios del productor al consumidor.
- En la economía de hoy, el único objetivo de la mercadotecnia es convencer a los consumidores que recibirán mayor **utilidad** de un producto o servicio en particular.
- La utilidad es la capacidad de un producto o servicio de satisfacer los deseos de los consumidores. Hay cuatro clases de utilidad: utilidad por la forma que tiene, utilidad por el lugar donde se encuentra, utilidad por el tiempo en que es disponible y utilidad por la facilidad con que se puede transferir la propiedad.
- Por medio de la **investigación de mercados,** las compañías reúnen, anotan y analizan datos sobre los tipos de bienes y servicios que el público quiere.
- El primer paso en la investigación de un mercado es hacer un **estudio del mercado.**
- Antes de ofrecer un producto para distribución nacional, los investigadores del mercado a menudo **hacen una prueba de mercado.**

SECCIÓN 2 Los componentes de la mercadotecnia

- Un plan del mercado tiene cuatro componentes: producto, precio, lugar y promoción.
- "Producto" significa que hay que hay que determinar cuáles servicios ofrecer con el producto, cómo empaquetarlo y qué identidad darle para que sea fácil de reconocer.
- Para establecer el precio de venta, una compañía tiene que tomar en consideración los costos de producción, de publicidad, de venta, de distribución y la cantidad de ganancias que quiere sacar.
- "Lugar" significa dónde se debe vender un producto.
- La **promoción** es el uso de anuncios y otras técnicas para informar a los consumidores que hay un nuevo producto en el mercado y para convencerlos a que lo compren.

SECCIÓN 3 Canales de distribución

- Determinar cuáles **canales de distribución** usar es otra función de la mercadotecnia.
- Los negocios que compran grandes cantidades de productos de los fabricantes para vendérselos a otros negocios se llaman **mayoristas,** o comercios al por mayor.
- Los negocios que venden bienes de consumo directamente al público son **tiendas al por menor.**
- En los últimos 10 a 15 años, los canales de distribución se han aumentado gracias a la expansión de los clubes almacenes, las compras por catálogo y el **comercio electrónico.**

CAPÍTULO 12 Resumen

SECCIÓN 1 Los estadounidenses y el trabajo

- La **fuerza laboral civil** es el número total de personas mayores de 16 años que tienen empleo o lo están buscando.
- Los trabajadores en los Estados Unidos están clasificados de acuerdo con el tipo de trabajo que hacen—**obreros, empleados en trabajos no manuales** y **trabajadores en el área de servicio.**
- Otro modo de clasificar a los trabajadores es de acuerdo con las habilidades especiales que hacen falta para hacer sus trabajos—trabajadores **no calificados, semicalificados, calificados** o **profesionales.**
- Hay tres factores principales—calificación, tipo de empleo y localidad—que afectan como la oferta y la demanda determinan los precios, en este caso los sueldos, en el mercado laboral.
- Dos factores que limitan la influencia de la oferta y la demanda sobre los sueldos son las **leyes de salario mínimo** y los sindicatos laborales.

SECCIÓN 2 Los sindicatos laborales

- Un **sindicato de obreros** es una asociación de trabajadores organizada para mejorar los sueldos y las condiciones de trabajo de sus miembros.
- Los sindicatos se formaron para obligar a los dueños a mejorar las condiciones de trabajo, reducir las horas de trabajo y poner fin al trabajo de menores.
- Durante gran parte de su historia los sindicatos en Estados Unidos han estado divididos en dos grupos: **sindicatos de artesanos** y **sindicatos industriales.**
- Los sindicatos laborales tienen tres niveles de operaciones: la **sección sindical** (local), el sindicato nacional o internacional y la federación.
- Cada sección sindical negocia para crear una **fábrica sindical** o **fábrica con cuota por agencia sindical.**

SECCIÓN 3 Negociación colectiva

- La **negociación colectiva** es el proceso mediante el cual los sindicatos y los gerentes llegan a un acuerdo sobre las condiciones de trabajo.
- Los sindicatos y gerentes pueden negociar las horas de trabajo, los sueldos, beneficios adicionales y **ajustes por el costo de la vida.**
- Si las negociaciones se hacen hostiles o nadie está dispuesto a transigir, los sindicatos y los gerentes pueden probar la **mediación** o el **arbitraje.**
- Los sindicatos en huelga pueden **piquetear** u organizar un **boicot** para ejercer presión económica contra la compañía.
- Para contrarrestar una huelga, los gerentes pueden hacer un **cierre patronal** o pedir una **prohibición judicial** contra la huelga.
- El porcentaje de obreros que se hicieron miembros de sindicatos fue más alto en los 1940 y ha estado en descenso desde entonces.

CAPÍTULO 13 Resumen

SECCIÓN 1 Cálculo de la renta nacional

- El **cálculo de la renta nacional** es una medida de lo que rinde la economía de la nación en su totalidad e incluye cinco estudios estadísticos.
- El **producto interior bruto (PIB)** es el valor total en dólares de todos los bienes y servicios finales producidos en una nación durante un año.
- Cuando se resta la **depreciación** del PIB, se obtiene una estadística llamada **producto interior neto.**
- Tres medidas adicionales—la **renta nacional,** los **ingresos personales** y los **ingresos disponibles**—analizan cuánto dinero tienen para gastar individuos y negocios en todo el país.

SECCIÓN 2 Tomar en cuenta la inflación

- Cuando hay **inflación,** el **poder adquisitivo** del dólar baja.
- La inflación sesga el PIB, haciendo parecer que ha subido la producción cuando, en realidad, sólo han subido los precios de bienes y servicios.
- Para calcular el **PIB real,** el gobierno mide el efecto de la inflación en el PIB actual.
- Tres medidas comunes de la inflación son el **índice de precios al consumidor,** el **índice de precios de productores** y el **deflactor de precios del PIB.**

SECCIÓN 3 La oferta y demanda agregadas

- La **oferta agregada** y la **demanda agregada** relacionan la cantidad total de bienes y servicios en la economía entera con los precios.
- El nivel de producción nacional y el nivel de los precios están en equilibrio donde la **curva de oferta agregada** y la **curva de demanda agregada** se cruzan, indicando que no hay ni inflación ni **deflación.**

SECCIÓN 4 Fluctuaciones comerciales

- La economía sufre alzas y bajas llamadas **fluctuaciones comerciales.**
- El **ciclo económico** comienza con un período de **auge,** entonces se **contrae** hasta llegar a una **recesión** (posiblemente una **depresión**). La actividad comercial disminuye hasta llegar a su **punto bajo** y luego empieza a aumentar de nuevo en una **expansión** o **recuperación.**
- La Gran Depresión fue la peor crisis económica en la historia de los Estados Unidos.

SECCIÓN 5 Causas e indicadores de fluctuaciones comerciales

- Los economistas conectan las fluctuaciones comerciales con cuatro fuerzas principales: las inversiones comerciales, la actividad gubernamental, factores externos y factores psicológicos.
- Para ayudar a los líderes comerciales y gubernamentales a tomar decisiones económicas para el futuro, los economistas crean y revisan **indicadores económicos.**

CAPÍTULO 14 Resumen

SECCIÓN 1 Las funciones y características de la moneda

- La **moneda** tiene tres funciones. Se puede usar como **medio de cambio, unidad de contabilidad** y **reserva de valor.**
- Cualquier objeto que se use como moneda tiene que ser duradero, portátil, divisible, de valor estable, escaso y aceptado como medio de cambio para pagar deudas.
- La moneda que también tiene uso como mercancía—por ejemplo, el ganado, las joyas y el tabaco—se considera **dinero material.**
- La moneda que está respaldada o se puede cambiar por oro o plata se conoce como **dinero crediticio.**
- Hoy en día, toda la moneda de los Estados Unidos es **dinero fiduciario** o **medios de curso legal** cuyo valor lo establece el gobierno.

SECCIÓN 2 Historia de la moneda y banca de Estados Unidos

- En el transcurso de la historia de Estados Unidos, la gente ha usado dinero material, monedas europeas, notas bancarias privadas y muchas otras clases de notas.
- La Constitución de los Estados Unidos le dio al Congreso el poder de imprimir monedas metálicas. No fue hasta la Guerra civil que el gobierno estableció una moneda segura y uniforme.
- Para controlar la cantidad de moneda en circulación, el Congreso estableció el Sistema de Reserva Federal en 1913. Éste sirve de banco central de la nación. En 1914, comenzó a emitir papel moneda llamado notas de la Reserva Federal, que pronto se convirtieron en el tipo de dinero más usado.
- En 1934, la nación cambio del patrón oro al patrón fiduciario (dinero fiduciario).
- La **transferencia electrónica de fondos** ha cambiado totalmente la industria bancaria, con el uso de **cajeros automáticos** y hasta Internet para hacer operaciones bancarias.

SECCIÓN 3 Tipos de moneda en los Estados Unidos

- Hoy en día, la moneda comprende más que el dinero fiduciario emitido por el gobierno. También incluye depósitos en las **cuentas corrientes,** las **tarjetas de débito** y el **cuasi-dinero.**
- Los economistas determinan la cantidad de dinero en la economía calculando la **M1**—dinero fiduciario, **depósitos a la vista** y cheques de viajero. Entonces calculan la **M2**—toda la moneda en la M1 más los depósitos en cuentas de ahorro, depósitos a plazos, certificados de depósito en pequeñas denominaciones y saldos de otros tipos de cuentas.

CAPÍTULO 15 Resumen

SECCIÓN 1 Organización y función del Sistema de Reserva Federal

- El Congreso creó el **Sistema de Reserva Federal** (llamado Fed, en inglés) en 1913 como la organización bancaria central de los Estados Unidos.
- El Sistema de Reserva Federal esta compuesto de una Junta de Gobernadores, asistida por el Consejo Consultivo Federal (Federal Advisory Council), el **Comité Federal del Mercado Libre,** 12 bancos de distritos, 25 sucursales y miles de bancos miembros del sistema.
- Las funciones del Sistema de Reserva Federal incluyen **compensar cheques,** actuar como agente fiscal del gobierno federal, supervisar a los bancos estatales que son miembros, guardar reservas, suministrar papel moneda y llevar a cabo la **política monetaria.**

SECCIÓN 2 La oferta monetaria y la economía

- La función más importante del Sistema de Reserva Federal es realizar la política monetaria, o controlar el aumento en la oferta monetaria.
- Cuando hay una **política monetaria expansiva,** el crédito es abundante y los préstamos son baratos. Cuando hay una **política monetaria restrictiva** el crédito escasea y es caro pedir dinero prestado.
- El sistema bancario está basado en la **reserva bancaria parcial,** en que los bancos mantienen un porcentaje fijo de sus depósitos totales en efectivo en sus propias bóvedas de seguridad o depositado en los bancos del Sistema de Reserva Federal.
- Una vez que los bancos tengan su **reserva obligatoria** separada, pueden prestar el resto del dinero y, de esta manera, crear dinero nuevo.

SECCIÓN 3 Regulación de la oferta monetaria

- El Sistema de Reserva Federal puede controlar la oferta monetaria cambiando la reserva obligatoria que tienen que mantener las instituciones financieras. Al bajar la cantidad que tienen que tener en reserva, los bancos pueden prestar más dinero, así aumentando la oferta monetaria.
- Otra estrategia que puede usar el Sistema de Reserva Federal es cambiar la **tasa de descuento** y la **tasa federal por fondos prestados,** que también afectan la **tasa preferencial.** Al subir el costo del crédito, los bancos y consumidores tienden a gastar menos, lo que frena el crecimiento de la oferta monetaria.
- La estrategia principal que usa el Sistema de Reserva Federal son las **operaciones del mercado abierto**—la compra y venta de valores del gobierno. Cuando deposita dinero en el sistema bancario (al comprar valores), la oferta monetaria crece. Cuando retira dinero del sistema bancario (al vender valores), la oferta monetaria disminuye.

CAPÍTULO 16 Resumen

SECCIÓN 1 El crecimiento en el tamaño del gobierno

- Todos los niveles de gobierno—local, estatal y federal—toman parte en casi todos los aspectos de la economía de los Estados Unidos.
- Juntos, todos los niveles del gobierno emplean unos 20 millones de trabajadores civiles.
- El gobierno paga por carreteras, escuelas y otros **proyectos de obras públicas.** También regula la seguridad de productos y trabajadores.
- Los desembolsos o gastos gubernamentales totales, incluyendo compras actuales y prestaciones sociales (asistencia pública), exceden una tercera parte del PIB.

SECCIÓN 2 Las funciones del gobierno

- Una función del gobierno es proporcionar **bienes públicos,** como parques nacionales y defensa nacional.
- Otra función del gobierno es promover el bienestar público por medio de **programas de seguridad social**—como el **Seguro Social, Medicare** y la **compensación a trabajadores accidentados**—y **programas de asistencia pública**—como los **Ingresos Suplementarios de Seguridad** y **Medicaid.**
- La tercera función del gobierno es regular los **factores externos** negativos del proceso de producción.
- La cuarta función del gobierno es asegurar la estabilidad económica, que significa disminuir las alzas y bajas en la actividad comercial de la nación.

SECCIÓN 3 El presupuesto federal y la deuda pública

- Los gastos principales del gobierno federal son el Seguro Social, Medicare y los ingresos de seguridad; la defensa nacional; los intereses por la deuda pública y la salud.
- Las ramas ejecutiva y legislativa preparan un presupuesto federal para cada **año fiscal.**
- Cuando el gobierno gasta más dinero del que recauda en un año fiscal, el resultado es un **déficit presupuestario.**
- La suma de todos los déficits presupuestarios equivale a la **deuda pública.**

SECCIÓN 4 La tributación

- De acuerdo con el **principio de beneficio obtenido,** las personas que utilizan un servicio gubernamental en particular lo deben apoyar con sus impuestos en proporción al beneficio que reciben.
- De acuerdo con el **principio de la capacidad de pago,** los que tienen más ingresos deben pagar más impuestos y los que tienen menos ingresos deben pagar menos impuestos, sin tenerse en cuenta la cantidad de servicios gubernamentales que usen.
- Los impuestos principales incluyen los que se pagan por ingresos personales, para la seguridad social, por ingresos empresariales, sobre las ventas y sobre los bienes inmuebles.
- Los impuestos se clasifican de acuerdo con el efecto que tienen en las personas que los tienen que pagar. Se consideran **proporcionales, progresivos** o **regresivos.**

CAPÍTULO 17 Resumen

SECCIÓN 1 El desempleo y la inflación

- Dos de las amenazas más importantes para la estabilidad económica de la nación son el desempleo y la inflación.
- El mantenimiento de un **índice de desempleo** bajo es una meta de las **políticas de estabilización.**
- Los cuatro tipos de desempleo son cíclico, estructural, temporal y friccional.
- De acuerdo con la teoría de la **inflación de demanda,** los precios suben cuando la demanda excesiva de los negocios y consumidores sube más rápido que la oferta total.
- La teoría de la **inflación de costes** dice que la demanda por sueldos más altos de los sindicatos y el ánimo de lucro excesivo de las grandes compañías hacen que aumenten los precios.

SECCIÓN 2 La política fiscal y la estabilización

- Algunos economistas creen que la estabilización económica se puede lograr por medio de la **política fiscal**—el uso consciente de los impuestos y gastos por el gobierno federal para afectar la actividad comercial general.
- John Maynard Keynes desarrolló sus teorías acerca de la política fiscal durante la Gran Depresión.
- La teoría keynesiana dice que el retiro e inyección de dinero en el **flujo circular de ingresos** afectan la demanda agregada y que el gobierno debe contrarrestar los efectos por medio de sus políticas de tributación y gastos.
- Para disminuir el desempleo, los economistas keynesianos apoyan la formación de programas de trabajo subvencionados por el gobierno y la rebaja de impuestos federales.

SECCIÓN 3 El monetarismo y la economía

- Los **monetaristas** creen que se debe manipular el ritmo con que crece la oferta monetaria para estabilizar la economía.
- La teoría del **monetarismo** a menudo es relacionada con Milton Friedman.
- Friedman y sus partidarios creen que el Sistema de Reserva Federal debe seguir la **norma monetaria,** es decir, debe aumentar la oferta monetaria por el mismo porcentaje todos los años.
- Los monetaristas critican la política fiscal porque se efectúa en el ruedo político y porque las **demoras** que se producen entre el momento en que se promulga y el momento en que se implementa pueden empeorar la situación.

CAPÍTULO 18 Resumen

SECCIÓN 1 Los beneficios del comercio mundial

- El comercio es importante porque las **importaciones** nos abastecen de muchos bienes y recursos naturales y muchos trabajadores en Estados Unidos están empleados en industrias que **exportan** productos al extranjero.
- La **ventaja absoluta** es la capacidad de un país de producir un producto de manera más eficiente (i.e., aumentando producción sin aumentar la cantidad de recursos) que otro país.
- La **ventaja comparativa** es la capacidad de un país de producir un producto por un costo de oportunidad más bajo que otro país.
- A la larga, las exportaciones pagan por las importaciones.

SECCIÓN 2 El financiamiento del comercio mundial

- Los **mercados de divisas** les permiten a empresas alrededor del mundo cambiar su moneda por la de otros países. Las monedas de otros países se llaman divisas.
- Cuando se usaba el **tipo de cambio fijo,** el valor de la moneda de una nación se establecía de acuerdo con un patrón determinado—generalmente la cantidad de oro que esa nación tenía en reserva.
- Hoy en día se usa el **tipo de cambio flexible,** en que la oferta y la demanda determinan el precio de las divisas.
- La rapidez con que se intercambia la moneda de un país puede afectar su **balanza comercial.**
- Si la moneda de una nación es **depreciada,** esa nación probablemente exportará más. Si la moneda sube en valor, probablemente exporte menos.

SECCIÓN 3 Restricciones al comercio mundial

- Tres barreras importantes al comercio mundial son los **aranceles,** las **cuotas de importación** y los **embargos.**
- Los **proteccionistas** están a favor de las restricciones comerciales para proteger los trabajos, la seguridad nacional y las industrias nacientes de los Estados Unidos.
- Los partidarios del libre comercio creen que la competencia resulta en mejores productos a precios más bajos y que restringir importaciones perjudica a las industrias de exportación.
- Varios acuerdos recientes han tratado de reducir las barreras comerciales, entre ellos la **Organización Mundial del Comercio,** el **Tratado de Libre Comercio Norteamericano** (NAFTA) y la **Unión Europea.**

CAPÍTULO 19 Resumen

SECCIÓN 1 Comparación entre el capitalismo y el socialismo

- El capitalismo puro opera a base de precios, ganancias y propiedad privada.
- El socialismo puro es un sistema económico en que hay poca propiedad privada y el estado es dueño de prácticamente todos los factores de producción.
- Carlos Marx predijo que habría una lucha entre los capitalistas y el **proletariado** que resultaría en un sistema llamado **comunismo.**
- En el **socialismo democrático,** el gobierno generalmente controla sólo algunas áreas de la economía.
- Los **socialistas autoritarios** creen que se debe usar la revolución para derrocar el capitalismo y realizar las metas socialistas.

SECCIÓN 2 Cambios en el socialismo autoritario: el caso de la China

- La República Popular de China es la nación más grande que todavía tiene un tipo de socialismo dirigido.
- Después de la Segunda Guerra Mundial, el gobierno chino comenzó a basar su economía centralizada en **planes quinquenales.**
- Las reformas de los 1970 y 1980 dieron a individuos más poder para tomar decisiones y para vender personalmente parte de los bienes y servicios que producen para sacarles ganancias.
- El derecho incompleto a la propiedad privada, la falta de imperio de la ley y la resultante corrupción son problemas que la China enfrenta hoy.
- El ingreso en la **Organización Mundial del Comercio** ha abierto la economía china al resto del mundo.

SECCIÓN 3 Las naciones adoptan el sistema de mercado

- Cuando Rusia comenzó la **privatización** de la economía, muchos trabajadores perdieron sus trabajos, los precios aumentaron vertiginosamente y la economía rusa se fue en declive.
- El pueblo ruso tiene que enfrentar muchas dificultades durante la transición a la libre empresa.
- Como **estado de bienestar social,** Suecia tiene impuestos muy altos para proporcionar asistencia pública a sus habitantes desde que nacen hasta que mueren.
- Recientemente, Suecia ha iniciado cambios en su sistema económico que combina capitalismo con socialismo.
- Muchos países de América Latina han privatizado sus industrias del transporte y la energía.

CAPÍTULO 20 Resumen

SECCIÓN 1 Características de las naciones en desarrollo

- Las **naciones en vías de desarrollo** tienen poco desarrollo industrial y un nivel de vida relativamente bajo.
- Cinco características de las naciones en vías de desarrollo son un PIB bajo, una economía **agrícola de subsistencia,** malas condiciones de salud (incluyendo un **índice de mortalidad infantil** alto), un nivel bajo de alfabetización y un aumento rápido en la población.
- Muchas naciones en desarrollo no tienen gobiernos que apoyan un sistema sólido que garantice los derechos a la propiedad privada.

SECCIÓN 2 El proceso de desarrollo económico

- Las tres etapas de desarrollo económico son la etapa agrícola, la etapa de manufactura y la etapa del sector de servicios.
- Un problema fundamental de las naciones en desarrollo es cómo financiar la maquinaria y enseñanza necesarias para mejorar su nivel de vida.
- Las naciones en vías de desarrollo reciben financiamiento por medio de inversiones del exterior y de ayuda del exterior.
- La **ayuda al exterior** puede darse en forma de **asistencia económica, asistencia técnica** y **asistencia militar.**
- Agencias internacionales como el Banco Mundial y el Fondo Monetario Internacional dirigen el dinero a las naciones en desarrollo.
- Los países desarrollados proporcionan ayuda al exterior por razones humanitarias, económicas, políticas y militares.

SECCIÓN 3 Obstáculos al crecimiento en las naciones en desarrollo

- Cuatro obstáculos impiden el crecimiento económico en las naciones en desarrollo: creencias y actitudes tradicionales, el crecimiento continuo y rápido de la población, el mal uso de los recursos (incluyendo la **fuga de capital al extranjero**) y restricciones comerciales.
- El fracaso económico de Indonesia demuestra algunos de los problemas asociados con el crecimiento económico rápido: la falta de identidad nacional, un gobierno con **burocracias** enormes y extensa corrupción, dependencia en un producto único y la interferencia del gobierno en el comercio.

SECCIÓN 4 La industrialización y el futuro

- La industrialización rápida presenta cuatro problemas: las malas inversiones, la falta de tiempo para adaptarse a nuevos modos de vida y trabajo, el uso de tecnología inapropiada y la falta de tiempo para atravesar las etapas de desarrollo.
- Los factores que fomentan el crecimiento económico incluyen el comercio con otros países, un sistema apropiado de incentivos (como impuestos relativamente bajos), un sistema político que favorece la libre empresa, recursos naturales y una rebaja en el crecimiento de la población.
- Los países en vías de desarrollo pueden escapar el **círculo vicioso de la pobreza** si sus sistemas políticos permiten que prosperen los empresarios y establecen el derecho a la propiedad privada.

CAPÍTULO 21 Resumen

SECCIÓN 1 Causas y resultados de la integración global

- La **integración global** ha aumentado de manera espectacular durante las últimas décadas, principalmente a causa de los avances en las **telecomunicaciones.**
- El aumento en comunicaciones ha fomentado cambios en las costumbres culturales y los hábitos de compras de personas en otros países, que afectan las exportaciones y el idioma.
- El mundo ha formado un solo mercado financiero, en el cual se compran y venden valores gubernamentales, divisas y acciones 24 horas al día.
- El mercado financiero globalizado hace que se sientan alrededor del mundo los efectos de un pánico financiero.

SECCIÓN 2 La inversión extranjera directa

- Los Estados Unidos tiene una larga historia de inversión extranjera.
- La **inversión extranjera directa** en los Estados Unidos ha aumentado al punto que algunos estadounidenses quieren restringirla.
- Muchas personas están en contra de que extranjeros sean dueños de compañías estadounidenses porque temen el control extranjero de la economía o gobierno de los Estados Unidos.
- Los economistas creen que los extranjeros compran activos en Estados Unidos para maximizar sus ganancias.
- Los inversionistas extranjeros son dueños de un 6 por ciento de las acciones de industrias estadounidenses.
- La participación de los Estados Unidos en la inversión extranjera directa mundial es más del 40 por ciento.

SECCIÓN 3 Las corporaciones multinacionales y la competencia económica

- Gran parte de las inversiones internacionales las llevan a cabo las **corporaciones multinacionales.**
- A fines de los 1990, había unas 63,000 corporaciones multinacionales con unas 690,000 **sucursales extranjeras.**
- Las 100 corporaciones multinacionales principales tienen el 15 por ciento de los activos productivos del mundo.
- La mayoría de las corporaciones multinacionales invierten en regiones cercanas a la oficina central.
- Las corporaciones multinacionales a menudo forman negocios en participación o por licencia.
- Un resultado de la globalización del mundo es el aumento en la inmigración y la diversidad, lo cual significa que la tolerancia e imparcialidad son más necesarias hoy que nunca.

CAPÍTULO 22 Resumen

SECCIÓN 1 El crecimiento del comercio electrónico

- Los números, que también se llaman dígitos, son tan imprescindibles para la vida moderna que nuestra época se ha llamado "la edad digital."
- Los **chips** en una red de computadoras interconectadas están cambiando la manera en que la gente se comunica, produce, consume, aprende y se entretiene.
- Algunos economistas creen que hemos entrado en la edad de la **economía ciberespacial**—una economía impulsada por un enorme aparato digital, **Internet.**
- Los **lugares de Web** conectan a negocios, organizaciones privadas, oficinas gubernamentales e instituciones educacionales y hacen que sea extraordinariamente fácil localizar información y comunicarse con otras partes del mundo. Internet le proporciona a empresas la oportunidad de ponerse en contacto directo con abastecedores y consumidores.
- El **comercio electrónico** se está expandiendo rápidamente, afectando las relaciones entre negocios y con los consumidores.
- En la economía ciberespacial, el consumidor es soberano. Si un vendedor no puede proporcionar un producto superior a un precio competitivo con rapidez, otro vendedor lo hará.
- Los vendedores pueden llevar cuenta de las compras electrónicamente y organizar comunidades ciberespaciales de sus clientes.

SECCIÓN 2 ¿Una nueva economía?

- La **Edad de la Información** puede llegar a tener efectos tan significantes en la vida humana como la Revolución Industrial.
- La **economía basada en los conocimientos** incluye la tecnología de comunicaciones, la propiedad intelectual y los datos almacenados.
- Algunos economistas creen que nuevos conceptos son necesarios para explicar como la economía basada en los conocimientos se diferencia de conceptos y principios económicos anteriores.
- La mayoría de los economistas consideran que la **innovación** afecta los ciclos de crecimiento económicos.

SECCIÓN 3 Cuestiones de la economía ciberespacial

- La economía ciberespacial ha planteado varios asuntos importantes. Las decisiones que hoy toman las personas encargadas de formular la política que la gobierna determinará el futuro económico.
- Entre las cuestiones importantes de hoy están garantizar la seguridad del comercio por Internet, asegurar los derechos a la **propiedad intelectual,** proteger la privacidad del consumidor y ayudar a las naciones en vías de desarrollo a tomar parte en la cambiante economía global.
- La tecnología de comunicación da acceso a los conocimientos y a la **educación a distancia,** pero hay que tomar buenas decisiones para crear un futuro económico mejor.

The following abbreviations are used in the index: *crt* = cartoon; *fig* = figure, chart, graph; *m* = map; *p* = photograph; *q* = quote

A

ability-to-pay principle of taxation, 442, 443

absolute advantage, 475

accountant as career, 417

adjusted balance in compiling finance charges, *fig93*

advertising: analyzing and creating, 310–11, *fig311;* awareness, 289; and bait and switch, 69; checklist for analyzing, *fig68;* competitive, 68, 246, *fig68, p246;* direct-mail, 299; as element of business operation, 211, *p210;* informative, 68, *fig68;* space, 305; wise use of, 68–69; worldwide, *fig286–87. See also* promotion

advertising manager as career, 69

advertising-to-sales ratio, 298

AFL-CIO, 324, 326, 327

African Americans: entrepreneurs, John H. Johnson, 218, *p218, q218;* John W. Rogers, Jr., 154, *p154, q154;* Kenneth Chenault, 106, *p106, q106;* Lloyd Ward, 116, *p116, q116;* Oprah Winfrey, 76, *p76, q76*

agency shop, 324

aggregate demand, 356–58

aggregate demand curve, 357, *fig358*

aggregates, 356

aggregate supply, 358

aggregate supply curve, 358, *fig358*

agriculture: as example of perfect competition, 236, *fig236, fig237;* subsistence, 519

Agriculture, U.S. Department of, *fig74*

Airborne Express, 243

Alcan Aluminum, 553

alliances, 556–57

Amazon.com, 28–29, 186, 568, *p28, p29*

American companies, foreign control of, 549–50, *fig550*

American economy: characteristics of, 40–44, *p41, p42;* credit in, 83–86, *fig84, fig85, fig87;* goals of, 46–49

American Express Company, 106

American Federation of Labor (AFL), 323, 327, 332

American Intl. Group, *fig555*

American Railway Union, 324

Amtrak, 233

annual percentage rates (APRs), 92; computing, *fig94*

antitrust legislation, 248–49, *fig250;* Celler-Kefauver Antimerger Act (1950), *fig250;* Clayton Act (1914), 249, *fig250;* defined, 249; deregulation, 253; Federal Trade Commission Act (1914), *fig250;* Hart-Scott-Rodino Antitrust Improvements Act (1976), *fig250;* Robinson-Patman Act (1936), *fig250;* Sherman Antitrust Act (1890), 249, *fig250*

Apple Computers, 556

arbitrary clauses, *fig126*

arbitration, 329

Ariel Capital Management, Inc., 154

Armstrong, Lance, 448, *p448*

articles of incorporation, 221

assembly line, 280

assets, 215

Australia, 518; economic and social statistics, *fig520;* as foreign investor in U.S., *fig549*

authoritarian socialism, 500, 503–07, *fig504, fig507, p504*

automated teller machines (ATMs), 71, 385, *p71*

automation, 280

automobiles: buying and operating, 129–33, *fig131, p130;* buying new, 562–63, *p562–63;* checklist for buying, 131; computer navigation system, 134, *p134;* depreciation of, 132–33; extended warranty on, 132; insurance on, 132, 133, *fig132;* maintenance of, 130; registration fee for, 130

average daily balance in compiling finance charges, *fig93*

averages, determining mean and median, xx

Aztec, value of cacao beans to, 379

B

bait and switch, 69

balance: past due, in compiling finance charges, *fig93;* previous, in compiling finance charges, *fig93*

balance of payments, 484

balance of trade, and exchange rates, 483–84, *fig483*

Banana Republic, 117

Bangladesh, economic and social statistics for, *fig520;* loans for the poor in, 99

BankAmericard, 92

bank holiday, *fig383*

banking: electronic, 384–85; fees in, 386, *p386;* fractional reserve, 408–09; history of American, 381, 384, *fig382–83;* services, 384

Bank of Amsterdam, 401

bankruptcy, 104; personal, 104–05, *crt105*

banks: commercial, 89, *p89;* federal reserve, 402–03, *m402;* insuring deposits in, 143, *fig144;* member, 403; savings, 89, *p89*

bank teller as career, 389

bar graphs, using, xvi

Barreto, Hector, 392, *p392, q392*

barriers to entry: for monopoly, 240–41, *p241;* for oligopoly, 243

barter, 376; in Russia, 377

Bates, Cooper, 176; *p176*

Beeping Wallet, 207, *p207*

Belgium, as foreign investor in U.S., *fig549*

benefits-received principle, 440, 442

Bezos, Jeff, 28–29, 186, *p28, q29*

bias, recognizing, 552

Big Mac Index, *fig482*

black market, 197, *p199*

Blair, Tony, 433

Blank, Arthur, 258–59, *p258*

blue-collar workers, 315, 333, *p315*

board of directors, 223–24, *fig224–25*

Board of Governors, 400–01

BOC Gases, 277

Bond, John, 219

bond markets, 151

bonds, 147–48, *fig273;* differences between stocks and, *fig148;* savings, 149; tax-exempt, 148; Treasury, 149

boom, 360

INDEX

borrower, responsibilities as, 98–99
boycott, 331
brand-name products, 70, 113, *p113*
Brazil, economic and social statistics, *fig520*
Britain. *See* Great Britain
broad-based index fund, 152
broker, 149
budget. *See* federal budget
Buffett, Warren, 317
bullion, 379
bureaucracies, 530
Bureau of Consumer Protection, 73, *fig74*
Bureau of Engraving and Printing, 388
Bureau of Labor Statistics (BLS), 351
Bureau of the Mint, 388
Burger King, 226
Burgess, Simon, 59
Burke, Richard, 448
business: cycle of, 360–61, *fig361, fig362, p363;* effects of investments in, 146–53; on business fluctuations, 365; elements of, 209, 211, *p210;* elements of operation, 209–11; financing expansion of, *fig264;* financing for, 270–75, *fig271, fig272, fig273, p275;* fluctuations in, 360, 364–66, *p364;* starting, 207–11, 230–31, *p208*
business organizations: corporations, 219–21, 223–24, *fig222, fig224–25;* franchise, 223, 224; joint ventures, 217; partnerships, 215, 217, *fig216;* sole proprietorships as, 213, 215, *fig214*
butter versus guns debate, 14–15, *fig16*
buyer as career, 172
buying decisions, 64, *p64*
buying principles, 66; comparison shopping, 69–70; gathering information, 66–67, *p67;* using advertising wisely, 68, *fig68, p69*

C

Canada: 518; consumers in, *fig62;* as foreign investor in U.S., *fig549;* as member of NAFTA, 489
capacity to pay, 97
capital, 6–7, *fig7*
capital flight, 530
capital gain, 147
capital goods, 277–78
capitalism, 41; benefits of, 500–01; pure market, 498, *fig498. See also* market economy
***Capitalism and Freedom* (Friedman),** 466
capital loss, 147
careers: accountant, 417; advertising manager, 69; bank teller, 389; buyer, 172; city manager, 427; computer programmer, 546; consumer loan officer, 90; customs agent, 487; economist, 19; environmental health inspector, 41; financial manager, 274; foreign correspondent, 504; graphic designer, 245; labor relations specialist, 329; market research analyst, 294; Peace Corps worker, 526; real estate agent, 125; restaurant manager, 215; social worker, 463; statistician, 365; stockbroker, 151; systems analyst, 568
cartels, 245
catalog shopping, 305
categorizing, 9
cause and effect, understanding, 193
celebrity branding, 247
Celler-Kefauver Antimerger Act (1950), *fig250*
central bank, 401
cents-off coupons, 115, 297
certificates of deposit (CDs), 143
change in demand, 180
change in quantity demanded, 180
channels of distribution. *See* distribution channels
character in determining credit rating, 98
charge accounts, 90–91, *p91;* installment, 91; regular, 90; revolving, 90–91
checkable deposits, 389
checkbook, writing checks and balancing, *fig388*
checking, overdraft, 384
checking account, 389
checks: clearing of, 405, *fig403;* writing and balancing checkbook, *fig388*
Chenault, Kenneth, 106, *p106, q106*
Chevron, *fig555*
China, People's Republic of: admission to World Trade Organization (WTO), 506; black market in, 505, *p505;* command economy in, 34; economic system in, 503–07, *p507;* economic and social statistics, *fig520;* per capita GDP in, *fig519*
choice: in economics, 4, 5, *fig4;* freedom of, 42, *p43*
circle graphs, using, xvi
circular flow: of economic activity, 37–38, *fig37;* of income, 458–59, *fig458*
Cisco Systems, 320
city manager as career, 427
Citibank, 88
Citigroup, *fig555*
civilian labor force, 313–14, *fig314*
Clayton Act (1914), 249, 250, *fig250*
closed shop, 324
closing costs, 123
clothes shopping, 117–20; checklist for wants, *fig120;* comparison shopping, 117–19, *p118;* value shopping, 119, *p119*
club warehouse stores, 112, 304–05
Coca-Cola, *fig555*
Coinage Age (1792), *fig382*
coincident indicators, 367, *fig366*
collateral, *fig271;* in determining credit rating, 98
collective bargaining, 328–29, 331–33, *fig330*
college, haggling over costs of, 160
command economy, 34–35, *p35*
commercial banks, 89, 144, *fig144, p89*
commodity money, 378
common stock, 223, *fig273*
communism, 500
Community Reinvestment Act (1977), *fig383*
Compaq Computer, *fig555*
comparative advantage, 475–77
comparisons, making, 39
comparison shopping, 69–70; for clothes, 117–19, *p118;* for food, 111–12; on the Web, 69
competition, 44
competitive advertising, 68, 246, *p68, p246*
complementary goods, 181; change in demand for, 183, *fig183*
Comptroller of the Currency, *fig382*
computer navigation system in vehicles, 134, *fig134*
computer programmer as career, 546

conclusions, drawing, 238

confession-of-judgment clause, *fig126*

conglomerate, 250–51

Congressional Budget Office (CBO), 438

Congress of Industrial Organizations (CIO), 324, 327

consumer-credit laws, 578

consumer finance company, 90

consumer goods, 277–78

Consumer Information Center Program, *fig74*

consumerism: defined, 72; and federal agencies, *fig74*

consumer loan officer as career, 90

consumer price index (CPI), 351, 352–53, *fig352;* compiling, 351; secrets of, 355

Consumer Product Safety Commission, *fig74*

consumers: in Canada, *fig62;* decision making as, 61–64, *fig63;* defined, 59; in developing knowledge base, 67; disclosure of credit card information to, 101; discretionary income of, 60, *p61;* disposable income of, 60; in e-commerce, 568; federal programs for, 73, *fig74;* protecting privacy of, 578; responsibilities of, 73, 75; rights of, 72–73, *p73;* role of Federal Reserve system in protecting, 405; sovereignty of, 290; spending by, 60–61, *fig60, fig61;* testing products, 54–55

consumer sector in computing gross domestic product, 345, *fig346*

consumer utility, meeting, 290–91

Continentals, 384

contraction, 360–61

convenience store, 113

cookies, 576

copyright, 241

copyright laws, 577–78

corporate charter, 221

corporate income tax, *fig441*

corporations: advantages and disadvantages of, *fig222;* chain of command in, *fig224–25;* comparing, *fig221;* defined, 220; reasons for forming, 219–20; registering, 221; structure of, 221, 223–24

cosigning loan, 98

cost-benefit analysis, 266, *fig267–68*

Costco, 112, 305

cost of care, 119

cost-of-living adjustment (COLA), 329, *fig330*

cost-push inflation, 454–55

Council of Economic Advisers, 368

coupons in food shopping, 114, 115

craft union, 323

credit: American use of, 83–86, *fig84, fig85, fig87;* applying for, 96–99, *p97, p98;* checklist for buying on, *fig87;* deciding to use, 86, *fig87;* defined, 83–84; government regulation of, 101–05, *fig103;* and installment debt, 84–85, *fig84, fig85, p85;* and privacy rights, 578, *p579;* reasons for using, 83, 86, *p86;* responsibilities as borrower, 98–99; sources of, 88–92, 94, *fig93, p89, p91;* using, *crt105;* and women, 102, *p104*

credit bureau, 96

credit cards, 91, 389, *p91;* annual percentage rates on, 92, *fig94;* disclosure of information to consumers, 101; finance charges on, 92, *fig93;* first, 92; hard lesson on, 100, *p100;* trade-off, *fig91*

credit check, 96

credit rating, 97–98, *p97*

credit unions, 89–90, 144, 389, *fig144*

creditworthiness, 96–97, *p97*

The Crisis of Vision in Modern Economic Thought **(Heilbroner),** 24

critical thinking skills: distinguishing fact from opinion, 65; drawing inferences and conclusions, 238; evaluating primary and secondary sources, 575; finding main idea, 128; making comparisons, 39; making generalizations, 269; making predictions, 512; recognizing bias, 552; sequencing and categorizing information, 9; summarizing information, 461; synthesizing information, 380; understanding cause and effect, 193

Cross, Harley, 176, *p176, q176*

currency, 388

customs agent as career, 487

customs duties tax, *fig441*

cybercommunities, 569

cybermarket, 48

cybernomics, 566; developing nations in, 578–79; and digital-signal processing chips, 570; and growth of e-commerce, 565–69, *fig567, p566;* innovation in, 573, *p573;* knowledge economy in, 572; protecting consumer privacy in, 578, *p579;* protecting intellectual property in, 577–78

cyclical unemployment, *fig453*

database, using, 95

database management system (DBMS), 95

day trading, 577

debit cards, 94, 389–90

Debs, Eugene V., 324, 500

debt, reasons for going into, 86, *p86*

debt financing, 271

decision making as consumer, 61–64, *fig63*

deficit financing, 438

deficit spending, 435, 438–39

deflation, 351; and purchasing power, 357

Delia's, 169

Dell, Michael, 80–81, *p80, q81*

Dell Computer, 80–81, 569

demand, 169–75; aggregate, 356–58; for American TV shows, 180; creation of, 173; defined, 170; determinants of, 180–81, *fig182–83;* diminishing marginal utility in, 173–75, *p174;* elastic, 181, 184, *fig184;* inelastic, 184, *fig184;* in labor market, 316–19, *fig318;* law of, 171–73; price elasticity of, 181, 184–85; quantity demanded versus, 180; real income effect in, 172; substitution effect in, 172; voluntary exchange in, 170–71

demand curve: defined, 179; graphing, 177–79, *fig178–79*

demand deposits, 389

demand-pull inflation, 454

demand schedule, 178

demerit goods, 430

democratic socialism, 500

Denmark, as supplier of foreign aid, *fig527*

department stores, charge accounts offered by, 90

Depository Institutions Deregulation and Monetary Control Act (1980), *fig383*

depreciation: of automobile, 132–33, 482; defined, 347

depression, 361
deregulation, 253
devaluation, 481, *fig481*
developed nations: cooperation with developing nations, 537; defined, 518; economic and social statistics for selected, *fig520;* foreign aid given by, 526–27, *fig527;* measuring GDP in, *fig519*
developing nations, 517–21, *fig518;* cooperation with developed nations, 537; defined, 518; economic and social statistics for selected, *fig520;* economic characteristics, 519–21; financing economic development in, 524–26, *fig527, p524, p525;* industrialization in, 534–37, *p535, p536;* and the information revolution, 578–79; measuring GDP in, 519, *fig519;* obstacles to growth in, 529–33, *fig532, p533;* trade restrictions in, 531, *p536;* weak property rights, 521
Diaguita Indians, 31, *p31*
digital-rights system, 578
digital-signal processing (DSP), 570
diminishing marginal utility, 173–75, *p174*
diminishing returns, law of, 192
direct-mail advertising, 299
direct marketing, 305
discount rate, changing, 414
discretionary income, 60, 61
disposable income, 60
disposable personal income (DI), 348
distance education, 578
distribution channels, 302–05, *fig303;* defined, 302, *fig303;* storage and transportation in, 304; wholesalers and retailers in, 302–03, *p304*
diversification in investments, 158–59, *p159*
dividend, 223
division of labor, 280
double counting, 345, *p345*
Dow, Charles, 152
Dow Chemical, *fig555*
Dow Jones Industrial Average (DJIA), 151–52
DreamWorks SKG, 580
durability in shopping for clothes, 118
durable goods, 84–85; purchase of, on credit, *fig84*
Dutch East India Company, 265

E

earning power, 60, 61, *fig61*
eBay, Inc., 338–39, *p338, p339*
***Ebony* magazine,** as published by John H. Johnson, 218
e-commerce, 303, 338–39, *p338,* 566–67, *p339*
economic activity, regulating, 432, *fig432*
economic assistance, 525, *p525*
economic competition, role of multinationals in, 553–54, 556–57, *fig555, p556*
economic connection to geography: online learning, 577; world's people, 530
economic connection to history: ancient multinationals, 554; Aztec civilization in, 379; Bank of Amsterdam, 401; Dow-Jones and S&P, 152; first credit card, 92; jobs programs, 460; Socialist Party of America, 500; Soviet Union's quota system, 36
economic connection to literature, 173; muckrakers, 249; Shakespeare, 317
economic connection to math: advertising-to-sales ratio, 298; comparative advantage, 475; compiling consumer price index (CPI), 351; Tax Freedom Day, 442
economic connection to technology: comparison shopping on the Web, 69; computerized refrigerators, 8; robotics, 281
economic development, 523–28, 536–37, *p536;* financing, 524–26, *p524, p525;* stages of, 523, *fig524*
economic efficiency, 47
economic equity, 47, *p47*
economic freedom, 46–47, *p47*
economic goals: conflicts between, 50; trade-offs among, 48
economic growth, 48; in developed nations, 518, *fig520;* in developing nations, 517–21, *fig518, fig519, fig520;* obstacles to, in developing nations, 529–33, *fig532, p533*
economic imperialism, 551
economic indicators, 366–67, *fig366*
economic models, 19–22, *p18;* applying, to real life, 21–22; creating, 20, 165, *fig20;* purpose of, 21, *fig21;* testing, 20–21, *fig21*
economic responsibility, 48–49, *p49*
economics: choices in, 4, 5, *fig4;* defined, 3; factors of production in, 5–6, 17, *fig6–7, p17;* production possibilities curve in, 14–16, *fig15, fig16;* scarcity in, 5; and values, 23; wants versus needs in, 4, *crt4*
economic security, 48
economic stability, 48; ensuring, 432
economic systems: basic questions in, 31–33, *crt33, p32;* in China, 503–07, *p504, p505, p507;* comparing capitalism and socialism, 497–501, *fig498, fig499;* defined, 31; in Latin America, 511; in Russia, 509–10, *p509;* in Sweden, 510–11, *fig510;* types of, 33–38, *fig37, p34. See also* capitalism; socialism
economic thought, schools of, 22–23, *p22*
economies of scale, 241
economist as career, 19
economists, profiles of: Adam Smith, 45, *p45, q45;* Alan Greenspan, 418, *p418, q418;* Alfred Marshall, 200, *p200, q200;* Alice Rivlin, 558, *p558, q558;* James Tobin, 485, *p485, q485;* Janet Yellen, 368, *p368, q368;* John Maynard Keynes, 428, *p428, q428;* Karl Marx, 502, *p502, q502;* Robert L. Heilbroner, 24, *p24, q24;* Thomas Malthus, 522, *p522, q522;* Thomas Sowell, 276, *p276, q276*
economy: circular flow of, 37–38, *fig37;* knowledge, 572; weightless, 572
economy performance: aggregate supply and demand in, 356–59, *fig357, fig358, fig359;* business fluctuations in, 360–62, 364–67, *fig361, fig362, fig363, fig366, p364;* correcting statistics for inflation, 350–54, *fig352, fig354, p353;* national income accounting in measuring, 343–48, *fig344, fig346, fig347, p345, p346;* terrorism effects on, 366, 547
education: distance, 579; effect of, on income, *fig61;* online, 577
elastic demand, 181, 184
elasticity, defined, 181
E.I. du Pont de Nemours, *fig555*
electronic banking, 384–85. *See also* automated teller machines (ATMs)

Electronic Funds Transfer Act (1978), 385, *fig383*

electronic funds transfer (EFT), 384

***Elements of Economics* (Marshall),** 200

E-mail, using, 444

embargoes, 487

employment: full, 453; new styles of, 456, *p456. See also* labor force; unemployment

Endangered Species Act (1973), 50

enterprise, freedom of, 42

entrepreneur, 208, *p208*

entrepreneurs, profiles of: Jeff Bezos, 28–29, *p28, q29;* John H. Johnson, 218, *p218, q218;* John W. Rogers, Jr., 154, *p154, q154;* Kenneth Chenault, 106, *p106, q106;* Lloyd Ward, 116, *p116, q116;* Margaret Whitman, 301, *p301, q301;* Michael Dell, 80–81, *p80, q81;* Harley Cross, 176, *p176, q176;* Oprah Winfrey, 76, *p76, q76;* Steven Spielberg, 580, *p580, q580;* William Gates, 254, *p254, q254*

entrepreneurship, 7, *fig7*

environmental health inspector as career, 41

Equal Credit Opportunity Act (ECOA) (1974), 102, *fig103, fig383, p104*

equilibrium, 459, *crt459*

equilibrium price, 194–95, *fig195;* and quantity, 358–59, *fig359;* shifts in, 195, *fig196*

equity financing, *fig273*

***An Essay on the Principle of Population* (Malthus),** 522

estate tax, *fig441*

ethical behavior, 75

Ethiopia, economic and social statistics for, *fig520*

European Union (EU), 489, *m494–95, p556*

exchange rates, 479; and balance of trade, 483–84, *fig483;* fixed, 480–81; flexible, 482–83

excise tax, *fig441*

expansion, 361

expenses, as element of business operation, 209, *p210*

export industries, 488

exports, 474, *fig476;* net, 346, *fig346*

extended warranty on vehicles, 132

external factors, effect of, on business fluctuations, 365–66, *p365*

externalities, 432

Exxon, *fig555*

fact, distinguishing from opinion, 65

factors of production in economics, 5–6, 17, *fig6–7, p17*

fads, and change in demand, *fig183*

Fair Credit Billing Act (1974), *fig103*

Fair Credit Reporting Act (1970), *fig103*

Fair Debt Collection Practices Act (1977), *fig103*

Farrah, Pat, 258–59

Federal Advisory Council (FAC), 401

federal agencies, 251, *fig252;* and consumerism, *fig74;* Environmental Protection Agency (EPA) (1970), 252, *fig252;* Equal Employment Opportunity Commission (EEOC) (1964), 252, *fig252;* Federal Communications Commission (FCC) (1934), 252, *fig252;* Federal Trade Commission (FTC) (1914), 252, *fig252;* Food and Drug Administration (FDA) (1927), 252, *fig252;* Nuclear Regulatory Commission (NRC) (1974), 252, *fig252;* Occupational Safety and Health Administration (OSHA) (1970), 252, *fig252;* Securities and Exchange Commission (SEC) (1934), 252, *fig252*

Federal Art Project, 460

federal budget, 437–38; deficit in, 435, 438; making, 164–65, 437–38, *fig165, fig437;* and price elasticity of demand, 185; surplus in, 438–39

Federal Communications Commission (FCC) (1934), 253

Federal Deposit Insurance Corporation (FDIC), 143, *fig383*

Federal Express, 243, 543

federal funds rate, 415, *crt415*

federal government. *See* government

Federal Housing Administration (FHA) mortgage, *fig124*

Federal Mediation and Conciliation Service (FMCS), 329

Federal Reserve banks, 402–03, *m402*

Federal Reserve notes, *fig383*

Federal Reserve System, *fig383;* Board of Governors in, 400–01; creation of, 399; Federal Advisory Council in, 401; Federal Open Market Committee in, 401, 411, 414, 416; Federal Reserve banks in, 402–03, *m402;* and foreign investment, 550; functions of, 405, *fig403, fig404;* member banks in, 403; and monetarist theory, 463, *fig464;* and monetary policy, 399, 400, 408, 416–17, *fig464;* organization of, 400–03, *fig400;* and reserve requirements, 412–13, *fig413*

Federal Trade Commission Act (1914), *fig250*

Federal Trade Commission (FTC), 248, *fig74*

Federal Writers Project, 460

fiat monetary standard, *fig383*

fiat money, 379, *fig382*

Fidelity Investments, 389

finance charges, 92; different methods of computing, *fig93*

finance companies, 90, *p89;* consumer, 90

financial condition of company, 274

financial institutions, types of, 88–90, *p89*

Financial Institutions Reform, Recovery, and Enforcement Act (1989), *fig383*

financial manager as career, 274

financial markets, globalization of, 545–46

financial page, reading the, xxiii

financing: for business, 270–75, *fig271, fig272, fig273, p275;* choosing right, 274–75; debt, 271; deficit, 438; defined, 263, *fig264;* economic development in developing nations, 524–26, *fig527, p524, p525;* equity, *fig273;* housing purchase, 123–24, *fig124;* intermediate-term, 272, *fig272;* investment, 266–68; long-term, 273–74, *fig273;* short-term, 271–72, *fig271;* world trade, 479–84

firms, number of, determining supply in an industry, 190, *fig191*

First Bank of the United States, *fig382*

fiscal policy: approach to stabilization, 457–60; defined, 457; and inflation, 459–60; monetarists' criticism of, 464–65; and unemployment, 459

fiscal year, 437

fixed exchange rates, 480–81

fixed incomes, 454

flexible exchange rates, 482–83

flexible rate mortgage, *fig124*

focus groups, 293, *p293*

Food and Drug Administration, *fig74*

food shopping: brand-name products versus private-labeled products, 113, *p113;* checklist for, *fig112;* comparison shopping in, 111–12; coupons in, 114, 115; trade-offs in, 112–15, *fig113, p114;* unit pricing in, 114–15

Ford Motor Company, 280, *fig555*

foreign affiliates, 554

foreign aid, 525–26, *p525;* leading suppliers of, *fig527;* reasons for giving, 527–28; sources of, 526–27

foreign correspondent as career, 504

foreign exchange markets, 480, 545, *fig480*

foreign investment, 525, 549–50, *fig549, fig550;* here and abroad, 550–51, *fig551*

form utility, 290

401(k) plan, 155–56

fractional reserve banking, 408–09

France: as foreign investor in U.S., *fig549;* as supplier of foreign aid, *fig527*

franchises, 223, 224

freedom of choice, 42, *p43*

freedom of enterprise, 42

free enterprise system, 42; goals of, 46–48, *p47;* investing in, 263, 265–68, *fig264, fig266–67*

Free to Choose **(Friedman and Friedman),** 466

free trade: arguments against, 487–88; arguments for, 488

frequency marketing, 568

frictional unemployment, *fig453*

Friedman, Milton, 462, 466, *p466*

Friedman, Rose, 466

fringe benefits, *fig330*

full employment, 453

The Future as History **(Heilbroner),** 24

G

Gap Inc., 117, 246, 490

Gates, William, 254, 317, *p254, q254*

GDP price deflator, 353, 359

Geffen, David, 580

General Agreement on Tariffs and Trade (GATT) (1947), 488–89

General Electric, *fig555*

generalizations, making, 269

General Motors, 220, *fig555*

The General Theory of Employment, Interest, and Money **(Keynes),** 428

generation Y, 295, *p295*

generic brands, 70

generic foods, *p113*

geographic monopolies, 241, *p242*

Germany: as foreign investor in the U.S., *fig549;* per capita GDP in, *fig519;* as supplier of foreign aid, *fig527*

gift tax, *fig441*

Glass-Steagall Banking Act, *fig383*

global economy, 544; and big business, 220; comparing savings rates, *fig143;* cybermarket, 48; day on the town, *fig138–39;* demand for American TV shows, 180; demand for oil, 204–05; Dutch East India Company, 265; history of money, *fig396–97;* housing in Japan, 127; improving working conditions worldwide, 324; leading foreign investors in, *fig549;* learning about capitalism, 510; loans for the poor, 99; pencils in, 10–11; per capita gross domestic product in, 347; rain forest trade-offs, 13; reasons for and results of integration, 543–46, *fig544, p545;* reducing postal monopolies, 243; Russia's barter economy in, 377; unemployment in, *fig454;* Web site challenges in, 572; working in Britain, 433; worldwide advertising, *fig286–87;* worldwide influence, 414

globalization of financial markets, 545–46

global village, 557

gold standard, *fig383*

Gompers, Samuel, 323, *p323*

goods, 6; measuring final, in gross domestic product, 345, *fig345*

government: in computing gross domestic product, 346, 425, *fig346, fig426;* effect of, on business fluctuations, 365; functions of, 429–33, *p430;* growth in size of, 423–27, *fig426, p424–25;* help for small businesses from, 208–09; involvement in economy, 433; limited role of, in pure market economic system, 41–42, *p41;* monetarists on policies of, 463–64, *fig464;* purpose of, 429; regulation of credit, 101–05; regulation of stock market, 153; spending by, 435, 437, *fig436;* stabilization policies of, 451–52

government monopoly, 241, *p242*

government officials, profiles of, Hector Barreto, 392, *p392, q392*

Government Printing Office, *fig74*

graphic designer as career, 245

graphs, using line, circle, and bar graphs, xv, xvi

Great Britain, as foreign investor in U.S., *fig549;* per capita GDP in, *fig519;* as supplier of foreign aid, *fig527;* working in, 433

Great Depression, 362, *fig362, p363, fig383;* and government growth, 424, 425

greenbacks, *fig382*

Greenspan, Alan, 411, 418, *p411, p418, q418*

grievance, *fig330*

grievance procedures, *fig330*

gross domestic product (GDP), *fig426;* categories of, 345–46, 425, *fig346, fig426;* components of, *fig344, fig519;* in current and chained (1996) dollars, *fig354;* defined, 344; impact of deflation on, 351; measuring, 344–47, *p345;* per capita, 347, 519, *fig347, fig519;* real, 353; weaknesses of, 346–47, *p346*

gross domestic product (GDP) price deflator. *See* GDP price deflator

gross investment, *fig426*

guns versus butter debate, 15–16, *fig16*

Gulf and Western Corporation, *p524*

H

haggling over college costs, 160

Haiti, per capita GDP in, *fig519*

HARPO Entertainment Group, 76

Hart-Scott-Rodino Antitrust Improvements Act (1976), *fig250*

Heilbroner, Robert L., 24, *q24*

Hewlett-Packard, *fig555*

Hint Mint, 176, *p176*

Home Depot, 258–59, 569

home ownership: advantages, 122; disadvantages, 122

horizontal merger, 250

House Ways and Means Committee, 465

housing, 121–26; checklist for clauses in leases, 127, *fig126;* financing purchase, 123–24, *fig124;* in Japan, 127; ownership versus renting, *fig122;* renter rights and responsibilities, 124–25, 127, *p125*

housing leases, checklist for clauses, *fig126*

HSBC, 219

humanitarianism, 527, *p528*

hypothesis, 20; using, *fig20*

Iacocca, Lee, 317

IBM, *fig555. See also* International Business Machines (IBM)

imperfect competition, 239–40

imperialism, economic, 551

imports, 473–74, *fig476;* defined, 473; ways to restrict, 486–87

inability-to-sue clause, *fig126*

income: changes in, 180; circular flow of, 458–59, *fig458;* decrease in, and change in demand, *fig182;* discretionary, 60, 61; disposable, 60; effect of education on, *fig61;* fixed, 454; measurements of, 347–48; role of government in redistribution of, 431

index, 151–52

index funds, 151

India, economic and social statistics for, *fig520*

individual pension plans, 156

individual retirement account (IRA), 156; Roth, 156

Indonesia, 531–32, 533, *fig531, p533;* per capita GDP in, *fig519*

industrialization, problems of rapid, 535, *p535*

Industrial Light & Magic (ILM), 584–85, *p584, p585*

industrial union, 324

inelastic demand, 184

infant industries, protection of, 488

infant mortality rate, 520, *fig520*

inferences, drawing, 238

inflation, 454–55; calculating, *fig353;* correcting statistics for, 350–54; cost-push, 454–55; defined, 350; demand-pull, 454; effects of, *crt455;* and fiscal policy, 459–60; measures of, 351–53, *fig352, fig353, fig354;* and purchasing power, 357

information, 537; gathering, 66–67, *p67;* as key to perfect competition, 235; sequencing and categorizing, 9; summarizing, 461; synthesizing, 380

Information Age, 571

information technology workers, 320

informative advertising, 68, *p68*

Ingram Micro, *fig555*

inheritance tax, *fig441*

initial public offering (IPO), 270

injunctions, 332

innovations, 365, 573, *p573*

***An Inquiry into the Nature and Causes of the Wealth of Nations* (Smith),** 41, 45

***An Inquiry Into the Nature and Progress of Rent* (Malthus),** 522

installment charge accounts, 91

installment debt, 84–85, *fig84, fig85;* defined, 84

insurance, automobile, 133, *fig132*

Intel, *fig555,* 556

intellectual property, protecting, 577

interest, 84, 142

interest rates, 274; understanding, xxii

interlocking directorates, 249

intermediate-term financing, 272, *fig272;* defined, 272

International Bank for Reconstruction and Development, 526

International Brotherhood of Teamsters, 326

International Business Machines (IBM), 556, *fig555*

International Development Association (IDA), 527

International Finance Corporation (IFC), 527

International Monetary Fund (IMF), 481, 523, 527

Internet: business help from, 209; business on, 566–67, *fig567;* ensuring safe trade, 576–77; shopping on, 305; using, 212. *See also* Web sites

intersections, 134

inventory, 209

inventory control, 279–80

investment financing: methods of, 268; pursuing, 267–68; reasons for, 266–67

investments, 146–53; and amount of risk, 158, *fig158, p159;* diversification of, 158–59, *p159;* in the free enterprise system, 263, 265–68, *fig264, fig266–67;* real estate as, 156–57, *p157;* regional cross-border, 556; for retirement, 155–57; turning savings into, 265, *fig264;* value in, 159

investment sector in computing gross domestic product, 345, *fig346*

Israel, economic and social statistics for, *fig520*

Italy: economic and social statistics, *fig520;* per capita GDP in, *fig519*

Japan: 518; economic and social statistics, *fig520;* as foreign investor in U.S., *fig549;* housing in, 127; investments in, 556, *p556;* per capita GDP in, *fig519;* as supplier of foreign aid, *fig527*

Jevons, William Stanley, 364

job security, 487, *fig330;* as argument against free trade, 487

jobs programs, 460

Jobs Rated Almanac, 313

Johnson & Johnson, *fig555*

Johnson, John H., 218, *p218, q218*

Johnson Publishing Company, 218

joint ventures, 217

JP Morgan Chase & Co, *fig555*

Katzenberg, Jeffrey, 580

Kennedy, John F., and consumer rights, 73

Keogh Act (1972), 156

Keynes, John Maynard, 428, 457, *p428, q428*

Kmart, 305

knowledge economy, 572

knowledge products, 572

Kopel, David, 207

labor, 6, *fig6*

labor force: categories of workers in, 314–16, *p315;* civilian, 313–14, *fig314;* information technology staff in, 320, *fig320;* jobs categorized by skill level in, 316, *p316*

labor leaders: Eugene V. Debs, 324; Samuel Gompers, 323, *p323;* Walter Reuther, 327, *p327, q327*

labor-management relations: collective bargaining in, 328–29, 332, *fig330, fig331;* injunctions in, 332; legislation in, *fig323;* lockouts in, 331; management in, 321; right-to-work laws in, 325–26, *m325;* strikes in, 329–30, *fig331;* unions in, 321–26, 332–33, *fig332, m322*

labor market, supply and demand in, 316–19, *fig318*

labor relations specialist as career, 329

labor unions: contract issues for, *fig330;* decline of, 332–33, *fig332;* defined, 321; development of, 322–24, *m322;* industrial, 324; local, 324–26; national, 326; organization of, 324–26

lagging indicators, 367, *fig366*

laissez-faire system, 41

land, 6, *fig6*

landlord responsibilities, 127, *fig126*

Landrum-Griffin Act (1959), *p323*

Latin America: economic changes in, 511; property rights in, 521

law of demand, 171–73, 178

law of diminishing marginal utility, 174

law of diminishing returns, 192

law of supply, 186–87

laws: antitrust, 248–49, *fig250;* consumer credit, 102–04; consumer-credit, defined, 578; copyright, 577–78; in labor-management relations, *fig323;* lemon, 72; minimum wage, 319; right-to-work, 325–26, *m325;* state usury, 102, 104

leading indicators, 367, *fig366*

leakage, 458

lease, 124–25

leasing, *fig272*

legal tender, 379

legislation. *See* laws

lemon laws, 72

liability insurance, 133

library resources, 334

life expectancy, *fig520*

limited liability, 220

limited partnerships, 217

line graphs, using, xv

line of credit, *fig271*

literacy rate in developed versus developing nations, 520, *fig520*

literature, economic connection to, 173

Liz Claiborne, 490

loans, *fig272;* cosigning, 98; for the poor, 99; secured, 98; sources of, 88–92, 94, *fig93, p89, p91;* unsecured, 98, *p98*

local governments, spending by, *fig436*

local unions, 324

lockouts, 331

long-term financing, 273–74, *fig273*

loose money policy, 407–08, *fig408*

Lotus, 556

Lucas, George, 584–85, *p584*

Luxembourg, as supplier of foreign aid, *fig527*

luxuries, 18

M1, 391, 416, *fig390*

M2, 391, 416, *fig390*

macroeconomics, 18–19

Madagascar, 518, *fig518, p518*

main idea, finding, 128

Malaysia, per capita GDP in, *fig519*

Malthus, Thomas, 522, *p522, q522*

managed mutual fund, 152

management: in labor-management relations, 321. *See also* labor-management relations

maps, reading, xviii

Marcus, Bernie, 258–59, *p258*

marginal utility, 174

market, 36, 170, *p170–71*

market basket, 352, *fig352;* constructing, 372–73

market climate, 274–75, *fig275, p275*

market economy, 36–38, *p35;* China's transformation to, 507, *p507;* profit incentive in, 187–88, *p187;* pure, 40. *See also* capitalism

market failures, 319

market forces, 197

marketing: cost of, *crt292;* defined, 289; development of, 289–91; four ps in, *p297;* frequency, 568; stages of, *fig290–91*

marketing mix, 296, *p297;* place in, 299; price in, 298, *p297;* product in, 296–98, *p297;* promotion in, 299–300, *crt299*

marketplace, 169–70

market research, 291–94, 296, *crt292;* defined, 292; surveys in, 293, *p293;* test marketing in, 293–94

market research analyst as career, 294

market structure, 233–34; comparing, *fig234;* monopolistic competition, 245–46, *p246;* monopoly, 240–41, 243, *p242;* oligopoly, 243–45, *fig244;* perfect competition, 233–37, *fig236, p235, p237*

market surveys, 293

market system, 36–38

Marshall, Alfred, 200, *p200*

Marshall Plan, 526

Marx, Karl, 499–500, 502, *p502, q502*

Marxian view of socialism, 499–500, *fig499*

maturity, 143

Maytag Corporation, 116

McDonald's, 177

mean averages, determining, xx

mechanization, 280

median averages, determining, xx

mediation, 329

Medicaid, 431

Medicare, 426

medium of exchange, money as, 376

member banks, 403

mergers, 249–51, *fig251;* horizontal, 250; vertical, 250

merit goods, 430, *p430*

Merrill Lynch, 389

Mexico: 518, *fig518, p518;* economic and social statistics, *fig520;* economic changes in, 511; NAFTA in, 490

microchip, 565–66, *p566*

microeconomics, defined, 18

Microsoft, 255, 317, 556. *See also* Gates, William

Midwest Stock Exchange, 150

military assistance, 525–26

minimum wage law, 319

mixed economy, 38; transition toward, 505

Mobil, *fig555*

monetarism, 462; criticism of fiscal policy, 464–65; and Federal Reserve, 463, *fig464;* government policy according to, 463–64, *fig464;* theory of, 462–63

***The Monetary History of the U.S.* (Friedman and Schwartz),** 466

monetary policy, 399, 400, 408; changing, *fig464;* difficulties of, 416–17

monetary rule, 463

money: characteristics of, 377–78, *fig378;* expansion of, 409–10, *fig409;* functions of, 375–77, *p376, p377;* history of, *fig396–97;* items used as, in global economy, 396–97, *p396, p397;* multiple expansion of, 410, 416; purchasing power of, 351; types of, 378–79; in United States, 387–91, *fig390*

money market deposit account (MMDA), 143, 152

money market funds, 152

money policies, loose and tight, 407–08, *fig408*

money supply, 391, *fig390;* expanding, 409–10, *fig409;* regulating, 412–17, *crt415, fig413*

monopolies, 240, *fig234, p240;* barriers to entry, 240–41, *p241;* characteristics of, 240; geographic, 241; government, 241; importance of, 243; natural, 241; reducing postal, 243; types of, 241, *p242*

monopolistic competition, 245, *fig234;* characteristics of, 245–46, *fig246;* defined, 245

mortgages, 85, *p85;* types, 124, *fig124*

Motorola, *fig555*

Mozambique, economic and social statistics for, *fig520*

muckrakers, 249

multinationals, 553; ancient, 554; and regional cross-border investments, 556, *p556;* size and number of, 554, *fig555*

multiple expansion of money, 410, 416

mutual funds, 151–52, *p151*

mutual savings banks, 389

N

National Association for Business Economics (NABE), 547

National Association of Securities Dealers Automated Quotations (NASDAQ), 150–51

national banks, *fig382*

National Council on Economic Education, xxvi–xxvii

national debt, 438–39, *fig439*

national defense, 430

national economic security, as argument against free trade, 487–88, *p488*

National Highway Traffic Safety Administration, *fig74*

national income (NI), 347, *fig344*

national income accounting, 343–44, *fig344;* gross domestic product in, 344–47, *fig344, fig346, p345;* measurements of income in, 347–48; net domestic product in, 347

nationalization, 525, *p524*

National Labor Relations Board (NLRB), *fig323*

national output, *fig359*

national unions, 326

natural monopolies, 241, *p242*

near money, 390–91

needs, 4, *crt4*

net domestic product (NDP), 347

net exports in gross domestic product, 346, *fig346*

Netherlands: as foreign investor in U.S., *fig549;* as supplier of foreign aid, *fig527*

new products, testing, 293–94

New York Stock Exchange (NYSE), 150

Nike, 246, 324

Nixon, Richard: and consumer rights, 73; and the environment, 50

nominal values, understanding, xxi

nonprice competition, 247, *p247*

Norris-LaGuardia Act (1932), *p323*

North American Free Trade Agreement (NAFTA), 489, 490, *p490*

North Korea, command economy in, 34

Norway, as supplier of foreign aid, *fig527*

notes, taking, 349

O

Office of Management and Budget (OMB), 437, 465

oil, demand for, 204–05

Old Navy, 117

oligopoly, 243, *fig234, fig244;* characteristics of, 243–45; defined, 243

Omidyar, Pierre, 338, *p338*

online learning, 577

open market operations, 401, 411, 414, 416

opinion, distinguishing from fact, 65

opportunity cost, 13–14, 62, *fig14, fig63, p64;* and business operation, 209; in shopping for food, 112

organized labor, 321–26

overdraft checking, 384

over-the-counter markets, 150–51

overtime pay, *fig330*

ownership utility, 291

packaging, 297

Pakistan, per capita GDP in, *fig519*

partnerships, 215, 217; advantages and disadvantages of, *fig216;* comparing, *fig221;* limited, 217

passbook savings account, 142

past due balance in compiling finance charges, *fig93*

patent, 241

Peace Corps worker as career, 526

peak, 360

penetration pricing, 298

pension plans, 155–56; individual, 156–57

per capita gross domestic product, 347, *fig347,* 519, *fig519*

percentages, understanding, xix

perfect competition, 233–37, *fig234;* agriculture as example, 236, *fig236, fig237;* benefits to society, 237; conditions of, 234–35

personal bankruptcy, 104–05, *crt105*

personal income (PI), 348; disposable, 348

personal income taxes, *fig441*

Peru, 521

Pfizer, *fig555*

Philip Morris Cos., *fig555*

picketing, 329

place in marketing mix, 299

place utility, 290

planning in production operations, 278, *p278*

points, 123

population, changes in, 180

population growth: and change in demand, *fig182;* in developed versus developing nations, 520–21, 530

poverty: Social Security's impact on, 434, *p434;* vicious cycle of, 536

predictions, making, 512
preferences, changes in, 181
preferred stock, 223, *fig273*
previous balance in compiling finance charges, *fig93*
price: equilibrium, 194–95, *fig194, fig195;* in marketing mix, 298, *p297;* and perfect competition, 235
price ceilings, 197, *fig198*
price controls, 197–99, *fig198, p199*
price elasticity of demand, 181, 184–85; determining, 184–85
price floors, 198–99, *fig198*
price leadership, 298
price of inputs in determining supply, 190, *fig191*
primary sources, evaluating, 575
prime rate, 414
principal, 84
Principles of Economics **(Marshall),** 200
Principles of Political Economy **(Malthus),** 522
privacy, protecting consumer, 578, *p579*
private-labeled products, 113, *p113*
private property, 43
privatization in Russia, 509–10, *p509*
Procter & Gamble, 246, 250–51, *fig555*
producer price index (PPI), 353
product differentiation, 244; role of advertising in, *p246*
product identification, 298
product in marketing mix, 296–98, *p297*
production: basic questions on, 31–32, *p32, p33;* costs of and profit level, 187–88, *p187;* defined, 277; factors of, 5–6, *fig6–7;* and technology, 280–81
production operations: inventory control in, 279–80; planning in, 278, *p278;* purchasing in, 278–79, *p279;* quality control in, 279, *p280*
production possibilities curve, 14–16, *fig15, fig16*
productivity, 7
product life cycle, 300
professionals, 316, *fig316*
profit incentive, 43, 187
profits, 43, 265; incentive of greater, 187–88, *p187*
progressive tax, 443
proletariat, 499
promotion: in marketing mix, 299–300, *crt299. See also* advertising
property rights, 430
property tax, *fig441*
proportional tax, 443
prospectus, 153
protectionists, 487
protective tariff, 487
psychological factors, effects of, on business fluctuations, 366
public-assistance programs, 431
public goods: defined, 430; role of government in providing, 430–31, *p430*
public-works projects, 425
purchasing in production operations, 278–79, *p279*
purchasing power of money, 351
pure market capitalism, 498, *fig498*
pure market economic systems: competition, 44; freedom of choice, 42, *p43;* freedom of enterprise, 42; limited role of government, 41–42; private property, 43; profit incentive, 43; rights and responsibilities, 48–49
pure socialism, 498–500, *fig498*

Q

quality control in production operations, 279, *p280*
quantity demanded, 172; versus demand, 180
quantity supplied, 187; versus supply, 189–90
quotas, 487
quota system in Soviet Union, 36

R

rational choice, 62, 64
rationing, 197, *p197*
real estate agent as career, 125
real estate as investment, 156–57, *p157*
real gross domestic product, 353
real income effect, 172, *p173*
real values, understanding, xxi
receipts, 209, 211
recession, 361
record keeping, as element of business operation, 211, *p210*
recovery, 361
redistribution programs, opponents of, 433
regional cross-border investments, 556, *p556*
registration fee, 130
regressive tax, 443
regular charge accounts, 90
renting: advantages in, *fig122;* disadvantages, *fig122;* rights and responsibilities in, 124–25, 127, *fig126, p125*
representative money, 378
reserve requirements, 408; changing, 412–13, *fig413;* changing discount rate, 414–15
restaurant manager as career, 215
retailers, 303
retirement, investing for, 155–57
Reuther, Walter, 327, *p327, q327*
revenues, 265
revenue tariff, 487
revolving charge accounts, 90–91
Ricardo, David, 475
right-to-work laws, 325–26, *m325*
risk: amount of, and investments, 158, *fig58, p159;* as element of business operation, 211, *p210*
Rivlin, Alice, 558, *p558, q558*
The Road Ahead **(Gates),** 254
Robinson-Patman Act (1936), *fig250*
robotics, 281
Rockefeller, John D., 248
Rogers, John W., Jr., 154, *p154, q154*
Roosevelt, Franklin, and deposit insurance, 143
Roth individual retirement account (Roth IRA), 156
Rule of 72, 149
rule of law, establishing in China, 505
Russia: barter economy in, 377; privatization in, 509–10, *p509. See also* Soviet Union

S

safe drinking water, *fig540*
sales tax, *fig441*
Sam's Club, 305, 387
satellite communications, 544–45, *p545*
savings: comparing rates, 143; decision making on, 141–42; defined, 141; goals in, *p142;* results of, 141; for

retirement, 155–57; taking risks with, 146–53, *fig148, p147, p150, p151;* trade-offs in, 157–58; turning into investments, 265, *fig264*
savings accounts, 142; balances of, 391; passbook, 142; statement, 142
savings and loan association (S&L)/savings bank, 89, 142, 144, 389, *fig144*
savings banks, 89, *p89*
savings bonds, 149
savings institutions, *fig144*
scabs, 331
scarce resources, 62
scarcity in economics, 5
Schumpeter, Joseph, 418, 573–74
Schumpeter cycles, 573, *fig574*
Schwartz, Anna J., 466
seasonal unemployment, *fig453*
secondary sources, evaluating, 575
Second Bank of the United States, *fig382*
secured loans, *fig271;* in determining credit rating, 98
Securities and Exchange Commission (SEC), 153, 577
Securities Exchange Act (1934), 153
security deposit, 125, *fig125*
semiskilled workers, 316, *fig316*
Senate Budget Committee, 465
Senate Finance Committee, 465
seniority, *fig330*
sequencing, 9
service flow, 118
services, 6; measuring final, in gross domestic product, 345, *p345*
service workers, 315, 333, *p315*
7-Eleven, 113
Shakespeare, William, 317
Sherman Antitrust Act (1890), 249
shopping: for clothes, 117–20, *fig120, p118, p119;* for food, 111–15, *p113*
shortages, 5, 196
short-term financing, 271–72, *fig271;* defined, 271
Siemens, 556
signals, prices as, 196–97
Singer, Isaac, 223
skilled worker, 316, *fig316*
Small Business Administration (SBA), 208, 392. *See also* Hector Barreto
small business incubator, 209
Smith, Adam, 41, 42, 45, *p45, q45,* 475
social insurance programs, 431
social insurance taxes, *fig441*
socialism: authoritarian, 500, 503–07, *fig504, fig507, p504;* democratic, 500; Marxian view of, 499–500, *fig499;* pure, 498–500, *fig498*
Socialist Party of America, 500
Social Security, 156, 431, 434, *p434*
social worker as career, 463
society, benefits to, from perfect competition, 237
sole proprietor, 215
sole proprietorships, 213, 215; advantages and disadvantages of, *fig214;* comparing, *fig221*
Soviet Union: quota system in, 36. *See also* Russia
Sowell, Thomas, 276, *p276, q276*
specialization, 475, 488
Spielberg, Steven, 580, *p580, q580*
spreadsheet, using, 145
stabilization, fiscal policy approach to, 457–60
stabilization policies, 451–52
stagflation, 455
standard fixed-rate mortgage, *fig124*
standard of living, 48
Standard Oil Company, 248, 249
Standard & Poor's (S&P), 151, 152
startups, 208
state governments, spending by, *fig436*
statement savings account, 142
state usury laws, 102, 104
statistician as career, 365
statistics, correcting for inflation, 350–54
stockbroker as career, 151
stock certificates, *p147*
stock exchanges, 150, *p150*
stockholders, 147
stock market, 150–51; government regulation of, 153; problems with worldwide, 546
stocks, 146–47, 220, *fig273;* capital gains and losses on, 147; common, 223, *fig273;* differences between bonds and, *fig148;* Internet trade of, 577; preferred, 223, *fig273;* returns on, 147
store of value, money as, 377
strikes, 323, 329, 331, *fig331, m322;* defined, 323
structural unemployment, *fig453*
study and writing skills: applying writing process, 478; library resources, 334; outlining, 406; taking a test, 538; taking notes, 349
subsistence agriculture, 519
substitutes, 181; change in demand for, 183, *fig183*
substitution effect, 172
Suharto, General, 532, *p531*
Sukarno, Achmed, 531, 532, *p531*
Supplemental Security Income, 431
supply: defined, 170; determinants of, 190, *fig191, p192;* impact of agricultural disasters on, 236, *p237;* in labor market, 316–19, *fig318;* law of, 186–87; quantity supplied versus, 189–90
supply curve, 188–89, 189; graphing, *fig188–89*
supply schedule, 188
surpluses, 196
Sweden, economic changes in, 510–11, *fig510;* as foreign investor in U.S., *fig549;* as supplier of foreign aid, *fig527*
Switzerland, as foreign investor in U.S., *fig549*
systems analyst as career, 568

Taft-Hartley Act (1947), 332, *p323*
Tarbell, Ida, 249
tariffs, 486; protective, 487; revenue, 487
tastes, changes in, 181
taxes: in determining supply, 190, *fig191;* forms of, 442–43; major, *fig441;* principles of, 440, 442, *fig441*
tax-exempt bonds, 148
Tax Freedom Day, 442
technical assistance, 525
technological monopoly, 241, *p242*
technology, 7–8; in determining supply, 190, *fig191;* and industrialization, 535, *p535;* and production, 280–81; spread of, 566, *fig567*

INDEX

technology skills: database usage as, 95; E-mail usage as, 444; Internet usage as, 212; multimedia presentations as, 306; spreadsheet usage as, 145

telecommunications, 571; improved, 544–45, *fig544, p545*

television shows, demand for American, 180

Temporary Assistance for Needy Families, 431

tenants: responsibilities of, 125, 127; rights of, 125

terrorism, effect on budget surplus, 439; effects on economy, 366, 547

test-marketing, 293–94

Texaco, *fig555*

thrift institutions, 389

tight money policy, 407–08, *fig408*

time deposits, 143, 391

time lags, 465

time utility, 291, *p292*

Tobin, James, 485, *p485, q485*

Tommy Hilfiger, 296

trade. *See* world trade

trade agreements, 488–89; regional, 489, 490, *m494–95, p490*

trade credit, *fig271*

trade deficit, 484

trade-offs, 12–14, *fig13;* among goals, 48; cost of, 12–13, *fig14;* credit card, *fig91;* in food stores, 112–15, *fig113, p114;* in quality control, *p280;* rain forest, 13; in savings, 157–58

traditional economy, 33–34, *p35*

transfer payments, 348

Treasury bills, 149

Treasury bonds, 149

Treasury Department, 389

Treasury notes, 149

Trek Bicycle Corporation, 448–49, *p448, p449*

trough, 361

Truth in Lending Act (1968), 102, *fig103, fig383*

underground economy, 453

unemployment: and fiscal policy, 459; global comparison of, *fig454;* measuring, 452, *fig452;* rate of, 452; types of, 453, *fig453*

unemployment insurance, 431

unions. *See* labor unions

union shop, 324–25

United Automobile Workers (UAW), 326, 327

United Kingdom. *See* Great Britain

United Nations, 526

United Parcel Service (UPS), 243, 282

United States, economic and social statistics for, *fig520;* per capita GDP, 519, *fig519;* as supplier of foreign aid, 526, *fig527. See also* American economy

United States Note, 389

United Steelworkers of America (USW), 326

unit of accounting, money as, 376

unit pricing, *p114*

unlimited liability, 215

unsecured loans, 98, *fig271, p98*

unskilled workers, 316, *fig316*

U.S. Agency for International Development (USAID), 526

U.S. Postal Service, *fig74*

usury laws, state, 102, 104

utility, 173, 290; form, 290; marginal, 174; place, 290; time, 291, *p292*

V

value, measuring, in gross domestic product, 345

values, 23; and investments, 159

vehicles. *See* automobiles

Venture Capital Online, 263

vertical merger, 250

Veterans Administration (VA) mortgage, *fig124*

vicious cycle of poverty, 536

virtual money, 381

voluntary exchange, 170–71

W

wages, *fig330;* restrictions on, 318–19; supply and demand factors affecting, 316–19, *fig318*

Wagner Act (1933), *p323*

The Wall Street Journal, 152

Wal-Mart, 305, 324, 387, *fig555*

wampum, 376, 381, *p376*

wants, 4, *crt4*

Ward, Lloyd, 116, *p116, q116*

warranties, 70, 297; extended, on vehicles, 132

Web sites, 566, 572; comparison shopping on, 69. *See also* Internet

weightless economy, 572

welfare, 431

welfare state, 510

white-collar workers, 315, 333, *p315*

Whitman, Margaret (Meg), 301, 338, *p301, q301, p338*

wholesalers, 303

Winfrey, Oprah, 76, *p76, q76*

women: and credit, 102, *p104;* economist profiles, Alice Rivlin, 558, *p558, q558;* Janet Yellen, 368, *p368, q368;* entrepreneur profiles, Margaret Whitman, 301, *p301, q301;* Oprah Winfrey, 76, *p76, q76;* median income for, *fig61*

workers' compensation, 431

workforce. *See* labor force

working conditions, *fig330*

working hours, *fig330*

work-time cost, 119

World Bank, 527

***The Worldly Philosophers* (Heilbroner),** 24

world trade: absolute advantage in, 475; benefits of, 473–76, *fig474;* comparative advantage in, 475–77; deficit in, 484; in developing nations, 531, *p536;* exchange rates and balance of, 483–84, *fig483;* exports in, 346, 474, *fig346, fig476;* financing, 479–84; imports in, 473–74; restricting imports in, 486–87; restrictions on, 486–89, *p488*

World Trade Organization (WTO), 488, 506; admission of China to, 506

World War II, 362, *fig362, p363,* 526, 529–30

worldwide advertising, *fig286–87*

World Wide Web, 566

Xerox, *fig555*

Yellen, Janet, 368, *p368, q368*

Yunus, Muhammad, 99

Graphic elements for unit and chapter openers and People & Perspectives pages, icon images for section openers, figure and summary numbers, Case Studies, Global Economy, Careers, Technology Activity and Skills features, and icons for Critical Thinking, Technology, and Study & Writing Skills: PhotoDisc, Inc.

Type design element for Study & Writing Skills pages: Tony Cordoza/Photonica.

Gear design element for Critical Thinking Skills pages: Allen Wallace/Photonica.

Cover i (l)Index Stock Photography, (r)Antonio Rosario/The Image Bank

vi Daniel R. Erickson; **vii** (t)KS Studio, (b)Aaron Haupt; **viii** (tl)Russ Einhorn/Liaison Agency, (tc)CORBIS/Bettmann, (bl) Matt Mendelsohn/CORBIS, (bc)Jonathan Kirn/Liaison Agency, (br)Mark Scott/FPG; **ix** Illustration by Guy Crittendon; **x** (l)Doug Martin, (c)CORBIS, (r)Hulton-Getty Picture Collection/Liaison Agency, **xiv through xxiii** Illustration by Guy Crittendon; **xxiv** StudiOhio; **xxviii–1** Firefly Productions/The Stock Market; **2** Geoff Butler; **3** Jose Caruci/AP/Wide World Photos; **4** (t) Ross Harrison Koty/Tony Stone Images, (b)Charlyn Zlotnik/Woodfin Camp & Assoc.; **6** (l) Mark E. Gibson, (r)Jacques Chemet/Woodfin Camp & Assoc.; **7** (l)Adam Lubroth/Tony Stone Images, (r)Aaron Haupt. Location: Terra Cotta, Columbus OH; **10** Aaron Haupt; **10–11** Tim Flach/Tony Stone Images; **12** Aaron Haupt; **13** Mark Burnett; **14** Aaron Haupt; **14–15** Mark Burnett; **16** Aaron Haupt; **17** Paul L. Ruben; **18** Spencer Grant/PhotoEdit; **19** Aaron Haupt; **22** Mark Burnett; **24** Bernard Gotfryd/Woodfin Camp & Assoc.; **28** (l)Paul Souders/Liaison Agency, (r) Geoff Butler; **28–29** Geoff Butler; **29** Aaron Haupt; **30** Geoff Butler; **31** Jerry Alexander/Tony Stone Images; **32** (t)Richard Laird/FPG, (c)James Westwater, (b)Doug Martin; **34–35** A. Ramey/PhotoEdit; **35** (t)David McIntyre/Black Star, (b)Craig J. Brown/Liaison Agency; **40** Geoff Butler; **41** (l)Roger K. Burnard, (r)Mark Richards/PhotoEdit; **42** Mark Steinmetz; **43** Geoff Butler; **45** CORBIS/Bettmann; **46** Mark Burnett; **47** (t)Spencer Grant/Stock Boston, (b)Michael Newman/PhotoEdit; **49** Rob Gage/FPG; **50** (t)Johnny Johnson, (b)John Cancalosi/Stock Boston; **54** Matt Meadows; **55** (t)Geoff Butler; (others)Matt Meadows; **56–57** **58** Geoff Butler; **59** Stephen Simpson/Getty Images; **61** (t) Tom & DeeAnn McCarthy/The Stock Market, (b)Aaron Haupt; **63** Martucci Studio; **64** Aaron Haupt; **66** Skip Comer; **67** (l) Doug Martin, (r)Chris Mooney/FPG; **68** Mark Steinmetz; **71** (t) Daniel A. Erickson, (b)Ken Frick; **72** IT International Ltd./eStock Photo; **73** Mark Steinmetz; **74** Martucci Studio; **76** Russ Einhorn/Liaison Agency; **80** (l) Pam Francis/Liaison Agency, (r)Mark Steinmetz; **80–81** Diamond; **81** Mark Steinmetz; **82** Geoff Butler; **83** Jessica Wecker/Photo Researchers; **85** (t)David Frazier, (b)Paul Markow/FPG; **86** Bob Daemmrich/Stock Boston; **87 88** Doug Martin; **89** (t)Toby Talbot/AP/Wide World Photos, (others)Mark Burnett; **91** (t) Willie L. Hill, Jr./Stock Boston; (b)Geoff Butler; **93 96 96–97** Doug Martin; **97** (tr)Aaron Haupt, (c)Jeff Greenberg/PhotoEdit, (br)Gianni Dagli Orti/CORBIS; **98** Geoff Butler; **100** (l)Doug Martin, (tr)Geoff Butler, (br)Ron Chapple/FPG; John Maher/Stock Boston/PictureQuest; **103** Doug Martin; **104** Arthur Tilley/FPG; **106** J. Chiasson/Liaison Agency; **109** Geoff Butler; **110** (t)Tina Frissora, (c)StudiOhio, (b)Aaron Haupt; **111** Skip Comer; **112** Doug Martin; **113** Martucci Studio; **114 115** Doug Martin; **116** Courtesy Maytag Corporation; **117** Matt Meadows; **118** (tl)Peter M. Fisher/The Stock Market, (bl) Stewart Cohen/Tony Stone Images, (r)Tom & Deeann McCarthy/The Stock Market; **119** (t)Doug Martin, (b)Jeff Greenberg/Stock Boston; **120 121** Doug Martin; **122** (t) Joseph DiChello, (bl)Aaron Haupt, (br)Tim Courlas; **124** KS Studio; **125** Aaron Haupt; **126** KS Studios; **129** Michael Rosenfeld/Tony Stone Images; **130** (t)Volkswagen of America, (b)courtesy Chrysler Corporation; **131 132** KS Studio; **134** (l)Kazuaki Iwasaki/The Stock Market, (r)Myrleen Ferguson/PhotoEdit; **138** Robert Frerck/Tony Stone Images; **138–139** Tim Flach/Tony Stone Images; **139** Liaison Agency; **140** Llewellyn/Uniphoto; **141** Mark Steinmetz; **142** (t) Aaron Haupt, (b)Doug Martin; **143 144** KS Studio; **146** Aaron Haupt; **147** Mark Steinmetz; **148** Geoff Butler; **149** Aaron Haupt; **150** VCG/FPG; **150–151** Geoff Butler; **154** Courtesy Aerial Capital Management, Inc.; **155** Ken Frick; **157** Eunice Harris/Photo Researchers; **158** Peter Christopher/Masterfile; **159** Martuc3ci Studio; **160** (l)KS Studio, (r)David Young-Wolff/PhotoEdit; **164** (t)KS Studio, (b)Doug Martin; **165** Chuck Keeler/Tony Stone Images; **166–167** Geoff Butler; **168** Ken Reid/FPG; **169** Aaron Haupt; **170** Geoff Butler; **170–171** (t)Geoff Butler, (b)Mark Burnett; **171** (l)Aaron Haupt, (r)Geoff Butler; **173** Aaron Haupt; **174** (t)Bruce Kluckhohn/Liaison Agency, (b)Doug Martin; **176** Courtesy Hint Mint, (t) Matt Meadows; **177** Mark Mellett/Stock Boston/PictureQuest; **181** Mark Steinmetz; **182** Eric Pearle/FPG; **183** (t)Aaron Haupt, (c)Glencoe photo, (b)Mark Burnett; **184** (l) Geoff Butler, (r)Aaron Haupt; **186** Jiang Jin/SuperStock; **186–187** Aaron Haupt; **188–189** KS Studio; **191** (tl, br) Geoff Butler; (tr)Matt Meadows, (bl)Doug Martin; **192** Courtesy Ford Motor Company; **194** Matt Meadows; **196–197** Aaron Haupt; **197** (l)Steven Frame/Stock Boston, (r)Picture Research Consultants; **199** Rat-Rossi/Liaison Agency; **200** Stock Montage; **204** Jim Olive/Uniphoto; **204–205** Tim Flach/Tony Stone Images; **206** Geoff Butler; **207** Susan Van Etten/PhotoEdit; **208** Geoff Butler; **210** (l)Martucci Studios, (tr) Geoff Butler, (others)Mark Burnett; **212** Geoff Butler; **213** Doug Martin; **214 216** Mark Burnett; **218** Jonathan Kirn/Liaison Agency; **219** Uli Degwert/International Stock Photography; **222** Mark Burnett; **225** Mitch Kezar/Tony Stone Images; **226** (t, c)Geoff Butler; (b)Burger King Corporation; **230** Tim Courlas; **231** (tl)courtesy Denny C. Jackson and students, (others) Geoff Butler; **232** Joe Towers/The Stock Market; **233** Don Spiro/Tony Stone Images; **234–235** Roger Ball/The Stock Market; **235** Mark Steinmetz; **236** (t)Aaron Haupt, (b)Hans Wolf/The Image Bank; **237** (t) Steve Proehl/The Image Bank, (b)James Carmichael/The Image Bank; **239** Geoff Butler; **240** M.L. Sinabaldi/The Stock Market; **241** (t)John Olson/The Stock Market, (b)Richard Burda/FPG; **242** (tl)Phil McCarten/PhotoEdit, (tr)Geoff Butler, (bl)Baron Wolman/Tony Stone Images, (br)Tom Bean/The Stock Market; **246** (l)Doug Martin, (r)Geoff Butler; **247** Mario Andretti Petroleum LP; **248** CORBIS/Bettmann; **250** Aaron Haupt; **252** (t)file photo, (bl, r)Geoff Butler; **254** Mitchell Gerber/CORBIS; **258** John Chiasson/Liaison Agency; **258–259** Bob Daemmrich/Stock Boston; **259** Doug Martin; **260–261** **262** Geoff Butler; **263** (currency) Peter Gridley/FPG, (computer) Mark Burnett; **266** Robert Brenner/PhotoEdit; **267** (t) PhotoDisc, Inc., (b)Susan Van Etten; **270** Bill Aron/PhotoEdit;

ACKNOWLEDGMENTS

271 272 273 KS Studio; **275** Mark Scott/FPG; **276** Terry Ashe/Liaison Agency; **277** Ray Soto/The Stock Market; **278 278–279** Geoff Butler; **279** (t)Schneps/The Image Bank, (b)Aaron Haupt; **280** Tony Page/Tony Stone Images; **282** (l)KS Studio, (r)Cindy Charles/PhotoEdit; **286** Paul Stuart: Eye Ubiquitous/CORBIS; **286–287** Tim Flach/Tony Stone Images; **288** Geoff Butler; **290** (l)Doug Martin, (r)CORBIS/Bettmann; **291** (l)Gaslight Advertising Archives, (c)Hulton-Getty Picture Library/Liaison Agency, (r)Geoff Butler; **292** Bob Daemmrich/Tony Stone Images; **293** Spencer Grant/PhotoEdit; **295** (t)Brian Bailey/Tony Stone Images, (bl, r)Aaron Haupt; **296** Doug Martin; **297** (c)Geoff Butler, (others)KS Studio; **301** James D. Wilson/Liaison Agency; **302** Aaron Haupt; **304** (background)Tony Freeman/PhotoEdit, (foreground) Mark E. Gibson; **306 310** Aaron Haupt, **311** (t)Geoff Butler, (b)Doug Martin; **312 313** Geoff Butler; **315** (tl)Doug Martin, (bl)Llewellyn/Uniphoto, (r)Jeff Bates Photography; **316** Lawrence Migdale/Stock Boston; **318** (l)Ted Horowitz/The Stock Market, (r)Richard Drew/AP/Wide World Photos; **320** (t)Geoff Butler, (b)Mark Richards/PhotoEdit; **321** CORBIS; **323** CORBIS/Bettmann; **325** Reuters/CORBIS; **327** CORBIS; **328** PhotoDisc; **330** (t)Geoff Butler, (b)Steve Skjold/PhotoEdit; **331** (l)H. Armstrong Roberts, (r)Viviane Moos/The Stock Market; **334** file photo; **338** (t)KS Studios, (b)James D. Wilson/Liaison Agency; **339** KS Studios; **340–341** Comstock; **342 343** Geoff Butler; **345** Aaron Haupt; **346** Geoff Butler; **346–347** (l) Mark Steinmetz, (r)Fotosmith; **350** Telegraph Colour Library/FPG; **351** Swarthout & Assoc./The Stock Market; **353** Martucci Studio; **355** (l)Aaron Haupt, (r)Geoff Butler; **356** FBM Photography/CORBIS; **358** Rob Lewine/The Stock Market; **360** Aaron Haupt; **363** (l)National Archives, (c)Hulton-Getty Picture Library/Liaison Agency, (r)FPG; **364** NASA/Mark Marten/Photo Researchers; **365** Reuters/CORBIS; **366** Geoff Butler; **368** Mark Reinstein/Uniphoto; **372** file photo; **373** (t)Aaron Haupt, (b)Geoff Butler; **374** Stephen Grohe/The Stock Market; **375** Bridgeman Art Library, London/New York; **376** Martucci Studio; **377 378** Geoff Butler; Dennis Budd Gray/Stock Boston/PictureQuest; **382** Library of Congress; **382–383** Martucci Studio; **386** (l)Aaron Haupt, (r)Geoff Butler; **387** (l)Liaison Agency; (r)Pat Vasquez-Cunningham/Wide World Photos; **391** Department of Treasury, Bureau of Engraving and Printing; **392** AFP/CORBIS; **396–397** Tim Flach/Tony Stone Images; **397** (tl, bl)By courtesy of The Trustees of The British Museum, (tr)Bridgeman Art Library, London, New York, (br)Chris Hellier/CORBIS; **398** Skip Comer; **399** Geoff Butler; **402** Bob Daemmrich; **404** Martucci Studio; **409** Geoff Butler; **411** (l)Peter Beck/Uniphoto, (r)Dennis Brack/Black Star; **418** Matt Mendelsohn/CORBIS; **422** Geoff Butler; **423** Aaron Haupt; **424** (t)Rob Crandall/Stock Boston, (b)Aaron Haupt; **425** (l)Aaron Haupt, (c)Craig Aurness/CORBIS, (r)David Frazier; **428** Hulton-Getty Picture Library/Liaison Agency; **429** Jonathan Selig/Photo 20-20/PictureQuest; **430** (l)Paul Conklin/PhotoEdit, (r)Phyllis Picardi/Stock Boston; **434** (l)Peter L. Chapman/Stock Boston, (tr)Ron Chapple/FPG, (br)Aaron Haupt; **435** Geoff Butler; **440** Painting by Don Troiani, photo courtesy Historic Art Prints, Ltd.; **441** Martucci Studio; **448** Bassignac/Stevens/Liaison Agency; **448–449** Aaron Haupt; **449** Judy Gelles/Stock Boston; **450** Ed Elberfeld/Uniphoto; **451** Aaron Haupt; **453** Geoff Butler; **456** (l)Aaron Haupt, (tr)Mark Joseph/Tony Stone Images, (br)Jon Feingersh/The Stock Market; **457** Geoff Butler; **460** (l)CORBIS, (r)Hulton-Getty Picture Library/Liaison Agency; **462** Geoff Butler; **466** Rose/Liaison Agency; **470–471** Geoff Butler; **472** Uniphoto; **473** Geoff Butler; **474** (t)Geoff Butler, (b)Chad Slattery/Tony Stone Images; **476** Mark Burnett; **477** (t)Mark Burnett, (b)Gilmore J. Dufresne/Uniphoto; **478** Mark Burnett, **479** Llewellyn/Uniphoto; **480** Mark Harwood/Tony Stone Images; **485** Charles Steiner/Corbis Sygma; **486** Photomorgana/The Stock Market; **488** Kent Knudson/Uniphoto; **490** (l)Zigy Kaluzny/Tony Stone Images, (tr)Glencoe photo, (br)Viviane Moos/The Stock Market; **494** Andreas Rudolf/Tony Stone Images; **494–495** Tim Flach/Tony Stone Images; **496** Geoff Butler; **497** Peter Turnley/CORBIS; **498** Geoff Butler; **499** Detail of a painting of Lenin during the October Revolution by Vassilji Chvostenko. Erich Lessing/Art Resource; **502** CORBIS/Archivo Iconografico, SA; **503** Nik Wheeler/CORBIS; **504** Tom Nebbia/CORBIS; **505** Forrest Anderson/Liaison Agency; **507** (l)Forrest Anderson/Liaison Agency, (r)Paul Lau/Liaison Agency; **508** Alexis Duclos/Liaison Agency; **509** Steven Weinberg/Tony Stone Images; **510** (t)PhotoLink/PhotoDisc, Inc., (b)Dave Bartruff/CORBIS; **516** Geoff Butler; **517** Mark Steinmetz; **518** (l)Robert Frerck/Woodfin Camp & Assoc., (r)Thomas Mayer/Black Star; **522** Hulton-Getty Picture Library/Liaison Agency; **523** Jeffrey Markowitz/Corbis Sygma; **524** Paul Conklin/PhotoEdit; **525** Ray Cranbourne/Black Star; **528** Mark Peters/Liaison Agency; **529** Piero Guerrini/Liaison Agency; **531** (t)Tom McHugh/Photo Researchers, (bl)Archive Photos, (br)CORBIS/AFP; **533** (l)Peter Turnley/Black Star, (r)Andres Hernandez/Liaison Agency; **534** AP/Wide World Photos; **535** David Kampfer/Liaison Agency; **536** (t)Mike Yamashita/Woodfin Camp & Assoc., (c)Mike Wilbur/Black Star, (b)Eric Lara Bakke/Black Star; **542** Phil Banko/Tony Stone Images; **543** Toyota Motor Sales, U.S.A., Inc.; **545** Richard Bickel/CORBIS; **547** Stone; **548** International Stock Photography/Getty Images; **551** Geoff Butler; **553** Getty Images; **555** Martucci Studio; **556** Robert Holmes/CORBIS; **558** Jeffrey Markowitz/Corbis Sygma; **562** (l)Geoff Butler, (r)Roger Ball/The Stock Market; **563** Geoff Butler; **564** Salem Krieger/The Image Bank; **565** Geoff Butler; **566** John Madere/The Stock Market; **570** (t)Aaron Haupt, (b) Chuck Savage/The Stock Market; **571** Steve Dunwell/Getty Images; **573** Firefly Productions/The Stock Market; **579** (l)Charles Gupton/The Stock Market; **579** (r)Michael Newman/PhotoEdit; **580** Eric Robert/Corbis Sygma; **584** Frank Trapper/Corbis Sygma; **585** (t)Patrick Aventurier/Liaison Agency, (b)Stan Godlewski/Liaison Agency.

This textbook contains one-stop Internet resources for teachers, students, and parents. Log on to ett.glencoe.com for more information. Online study tools include Chapter Overviews, Self-Check Quizzes, an Interactive Tutor, and E-Flashcards. Online research tools include Student Web Activities, Beyond the Textbook Features, Current Events, Web Resources, and State Resources. The interactive online student edition includes the complete Interactive Student Edition along with textbook updates. Especially for teachers, Glencoe offers an online Teacher Forum, Web Activity Lesson Plans, and Literature Connections.